# 中阿经贸关系发展进程
# 2024年度报告

中国—阿拉伯国家博览会秘书处／编
李绍先／主编

The Development Process of
China-Arab States Economic and Trade
Relations Annual Report

———— 2024 ————

社会科学文献出版社
SOCIAL SCIENCES ACADEMIC PRESS (CHINA)

**图书在版编目(CIP)数据**

中阿经贸关系发展进程2024年度报告/中国—阿拉伯国家博览会秘书处编;李绍先主编.--北京:社会科学文献出版社,2025.6.--ISBN 978-7-5228-5549-3

Ⅰ.F125.537.1

中国国家版本馆CIP数据核字第2025415M8Q号

## 中阿经贸关系发展进程2024年度报告

编　　者 / 中国—阿拉伯国家博览会秘书处
主　　编 / 李绍先

出 版 人 / 冀祥德
责任编辑 / 周志静
责任印制 / 岳　阳

出　　版 / 社会科学文献出版社·人文分社(010)59367215
　　　　　　地址:北京市北三环中路甲29号院华龙大厦　邮编:100029
　　　　　　网址:www.ssap.com.cn

发　　行 / 社会科学文献出版社(010)59367028
印　　装 / 三河市东方印刷有限公司

规　　格 / 开　本:787mm×1092mm　1/16
　　　　　　印　张:38.5　字　数:681千字

版　　次 / 2025年6月第1版　2025年6月第1次印刷
书　　号 / ISBN 978-7-5228-5549-3
定　　价 / 198.00元

读者服务电话:4008918866

版权所有 翻印必究

# 《中阿经贸关系发展进程2024年度报告》编委会

主　　任　戴培吉
副 主 任　庞子杰　聂　丹　李绍先
委　　员　（按姓氏笔画排序）
　　　　　丁　隆　王广大　王林聪　牛新春
　　　　　毛小菁　朱　东　苏　鸿　李　敏
　　　　　李绍先　杨文辉　杨春泉　杨燕萍
　　　　　吴思科　张前进　陆如泉　庞子杰
　　　　　聂　丹　唐志超　崔彦祥　韩志忠
　　　　　戴培吉
主　　编　李绍先
副 主 编　苏　鸿　张前进

# 前　言

2024年是国际格局深刻演变的一年，国际形势依然充满挑战，世界经济增长乏力，全球面临的风险与挑战日益严峻。回首2024年，中东地区多个热点相互交织，使长期处于动荡中的地区形势更加复杂。新一轮巴以冲突仍在持续，造成前所未有的人道主义灾难，其外溢影响持续。黎以冲突、伊以冲突、叙利亚阿萨德政权垮台等热点频发，中东和平进程任重而道远。面对复杂的国际和地区局势，中国与阿拉伯国家始终携手共进，共克时艰，树立了南南合作的典范。

2022年底首届中阿峰会成功举行，习近平主席和阿拉伯各国领导人一致同意构建面向新时代的中阿命运共同体，明确了双方共同努力的方向。两年多来，在习近平主席和阿拉伯国家领导人的指引下，中阿命运共同体建设取得明显进展，中阿关系进入历史最好时期，中阿战略互信越来越深，务实合作越来越实，民众情感越来越亲。2024年，中阿合作论坛第十届部长级会议在北京召开，是首届中阿峰会后举办的部长会，也恰逢论坛成立二十周年，是一次承前启后的重要会议。双方围绕加紧落实首届中阿峰会成果、加快推动中阿命运共同体建设深入探讨，在许多领域达成共识，为中阿关系注入更多新动力。双方同意在中阿务实合作"八大共同行动"的基础上，共同构建中阿"五大合作格局"，为未来中阿务实合作擘画了蓝图，引领新时代中阿合作迈上新台阶，推动中阿命运共同体建设跑出加速度。双方还同意于2026年在中国举办第二届中阿峰会，这将成为中阿关系又一座里程碑。

经贸合作是深化中阿关系的"压舱石"，中阿经贸合作优势互补性强，阿拉伯国家是共建"一带一路"的重要合作伙伴，截至2023年底，中国已同全部22个阿拉伯国家和阿盟签署"一带一路"合作文件，中阿签署共建"一带一路"合作文件实现全覆盖。在双方共同努力下，中阿务实合作持续走深走实。贸易方面，中国继续保持阿拉伯国家最大贸易伙伴国地位，双边贸易额从2013年2388.9亿美元增至2024年4073.94亿美元，商品结构进一步优化。阿拉伯国家已成为中国"新三样"（新能源汽车、锂电池、光伏产品）和中间品出口的重要市场。2024年，中国"新三样"对阿拉伯国家出口总额79.4亿美元，同比增长66.5%；中间品对阿拉伯国家出口总额988.5亿美元，同比增长11.5%，占中国对阿拉伯国家出口总额的比例接近50%。投资方面，中国对阿拉伯国家投资规模持续扩大，阿拉伯国家对华投资也日益活跃。2021年至2023年，中国对阿拉伯国家直接投资流量实现三连增，分别达到23.1亿美元、26.2亿美元和26.9亿美元，增幅分别为13.4%和2.7%。2024年，受地区局势动荡、美国"长臂管辖"政策、阿拉伯国家对华合作意愿以及中国企业出海水土不服等因素影响，中国对阿拉伯国家直接投资流量为23.9亿美元，同比回落11.1%。阿联酋、沙特、伊拉克、阿尔及利亚和埃及依然是中国在阿拉伯国家投资存量最多的前五大投资目的地，占比达79.58%。阿拉伯国家也加大在华投资力度。一方面，阿拉伯国家一些大型公司积极开拓中国市场，拓展石油化工等上下游产业链合作；另一方面，中东主权财富基金看好中国发展前景，纷纷在华设立办事处。阿联酋、沙特仍是对华投资最活跃的阿拉伯国家。2023年，阿拉伯国家新增来华实际投资23亿美元，同比增长120%。基础设施建设方面，2024年中国企业在阿拉伯国家新签合同额654.3亿美元，同比增长38.6%，占新签合同总额的24.5%；完成营业额350.1亿美元，同比增长26.4%，占完成营业额总额的21.1%。沙特是中国在阿拉伯国家最大的承包工程来源国，且呈快速增长趋势。从领域分布来看，建筑类、能源动力类、交通运输类项目是中企承包的主要项目。

鉴于此，宁夏大学中国阿拉伯国家研究院组织相关领域权威专家学者编写《中阿经贸关系发展进程2024年度报告》，梳理了"一带一路"倡议提出以来，中阿经贸合作状况和成果，重点分析了2024年中阿在贸易、投资、金融、科技、农业、数字经济、生态、旅游等领域取得的新进展，描绘了中阿经贸关系发展的进程特征和发展趋势。我们希望本书能够为政府决策部门、学者、企业家、学生等提供有价值的参考。

最后，我们要感谢所有为本书撰写、翻译、编辑、校对等方面做出贡献的人员，感谢广大读者的关注和支持。

李绍先
2025年5月于宁夏

# 目 录

**第1章 中阿经贸合作总体形势** ·········································· 001
  1.1 中阿经贸合作总体情况 ·········································· 001
  1.2 中阿经贸合作领域态势 ·········································· 005
  1.3 中阿经贸合作趋势展望 ·········································· 012

**第2章 中阿贸易合作专题报告** ·········································· 017
  2.1 中国对外贸易发展状况 ·········································· 017
  2.2 阿拉伯国家对外贸易发展状况 ···································· 023
  2.3 中国与阿拉伯国家贸易发展状况 ·································· 029
  2.4 中国与阿拉伯国家贸易合作发展趋势与展望 ······················ 043

**第3章 中阿投资合作专题报告** ·········································· 050
  3.1 中国对阿拉伯国家直接投资状况 ·································· 050
  3.2 阿拉伯国家对华投资状况 ········································ 061
  3.3 中阿投资合作展望 ·············································· 066

**第4章 中阿金融合作专题报告** ·········································· 070
  4.1 阿拉伯国家金融环境概述 ········································ 070

4.2 中阿金融合作稳步推进 ·········································· 074
4.3 中阿金融合作的新趋势 ·········································· 082
4.4 中阿金融合作展望 ·············································· 085

## 第5章 中阿农业合作专题报告 ·········································· 089
5.1 "一带一路"倡议提出以来的中阿农业合作 ······················ 089
5.2 2024年中阿农业合作现状 ········································ 097
5.3 中阿农业合作展望 ·············································· 105

## 第6章 中阿能源合作专题报告 ·········································· 108
6.1 阿拉伯国家能源资源概况 ········································ 108
6.2 中阿传统能源合作现状 ·········································· 116
6.3 中阿新能源合作现状 ············································ 121
6.4 中阿能源合作前景 ·············································· 124

## 第7章 中阿数字经济合作专题报告 ······································ 128
7.1 阿拉伯国家数字经济水平现状 ···································· 128
7.2 中阿数字经济合作现状 ·········································· 139
7.3 中阿数字经济合作展望 ·········································· 146

## 第8章 中阿科技合作专题报告 ·········································· 149
8.1 中阿科技合作的战略基础 ········································ 149
8.2 中阿科技合作的实践进展 ········································ 153
8.3 中阿科技合作前景 ·············································· 164

## 第9章 中阿生态合作专题报告 ·········································· 167
9.1 阿拉伯地区生态环境现状与治理 ·································· 167

9.2　中阿生态环境治理合作 172
9.3　中阿生态环境合作路径展望 178

## 第10章　中阿旅游合作专题报告 183
10.1　2024年度中阿旅游总体情况 183
10.2　中阿旅游合作20年回顾 188
10.3　新时期中阿旅游合作趋势分析 196

## 第11章　中阿博览会专题报告 200
11.1　中阿博览会发展回顾 201
11.2　新形势下中阿博览会面临多重发展机遇 207
11.3　新形势下办好中阿博览会的思路 210
11.4　新形势下办好中阿博览会的路径 212

## 第12章　宁夏对外开放专题报告 216
12.1　宁夏开放型经济稳步推进 216
12.2　宁夏对外通道建设不断加强 228
12.3　宁夏推进高水平对外开放展望 232

**2024年中阿经贸合作大事记** 240

**后　　记** 260

# 第1章 中阿经贸合作总体形势

2024年，国际形势风云变幻，动乱交织，大国博弈持续加剧，各种矛盾与风险积蓄，世界经济增长乏力，全球面临的风险与挑战日益严峻。在阿拉伯地区，巴以冲突外溢扩大，叙利亚阿萨德政权迅速崩塌，苏丹内战走向长期化，地区局势动荡风险加大。与此同时，主要阿拉伯国家寻求和解与发展的意愿强烈，2023年出现的中东和解潮在2024年继续发展，以海湾国家为代表的主要阿拉伯国家积极推进经济发展和多元化转型进程。面对复杂形势，中国与阿拉伯国家始终携手共进，共克时艰，中阿关系处于历史最好时期，中阿经贸合作持续升温，在贸易、投资、承包工程和新兴领域的合作亮点纷呈，成果丰富。

## 1.1 中阿经贸合作总体情况

### 1.1.1 "五大合作格局"推动中阿经贸合作迈上新台阶

2024年5月30日，中国—阿拉伯国家合作论坛第十届部长级会议在北京举行，习近平主席出席会议开幕式并发表主旨讲话。习近平主席在讲话中指出，经过中阿双方的共同努力，在首届中阿峰会期间提出的推进中阿务实合作"八大共同行动"已取得重要早期收获，中阿签署共建"一带一路"合作文件实现全覆盖，科技研发、技术转移取得新进展，经贸、能源合作迈上新台阶①。习近平主席提出，下一阶段，中方愿同阿方构建"五大合作格局"，推动中阿命运共同体建设跑出加速度。"五大合作格局"为进一步提升中阿合作擘画了蓝图，其中更富活力的创新驱动格局、更具规模的投资金融格局、更加立体的能源合作格局、更为平衡的经贸互惠格局将从不同层面推动中阿经贸合作在不同领域的深入合作，促进中阿经贸合作取得更多新成就。

### 1.1.2 贸易额小幅上升

2024年，中阿货物贸易额回升至4073.94亿美元，同比上升2.33%，中国继续保持阿拉伯国家最大贸易伙伴国地位。其中，中国对阿出口2059.86亿美元，同比增长13.63%；中国自阿进口2014.08亿美元，同比下降7.12%，其中自阿进口石油等矿物燃料1771.95亿美元，占比87.98%。沙特、阿联酋、伊拉克、阿曼、卡塔尔依然是中国在阿拉伯国家的前五大贸易伙伴。中国与沙特的进出口贸易额小幅升至1075.34亿美元。中国与阿联酋的贸易额则首次超过1000亿美元，达到1018.38亿美元，同比增长7.2%，其中中国对阿联酋出口655.93亿美元，同比增长17.8%。中国与阿尔及利亚和摩洛哥的贸易增长表现突出，同比涨幅均超过20%，分别达到21.11%和21.61%，贸易额分别为124.82亿美元和90.37亿美元，其中中国对阿尔及利亚的出口增长23.52%，自摩洛哥的进口增长32.66%，对摩洛哥的出口亦增长19.93%。总体来看，新时代以来，中阿贸易往来持续升温，除2015—2016年受原油价格下跌影响、2020年受新冠疫情影响，双边贸易出现较大幅度下跌外，其他年份的贸易额总体稳步增长，尤其是2021年和2022年双边贸易复苏强劲，相继突破3000亿美元和4000亿美元大关，中阿贸易关系日益密切。②

---

① 习近平：《深化合作，继往开来，推动中阿命运共同体建设跑出加速度——在中阿合作论坛第十届部长级会议开幕式上的主旨讲话》，《人民日报》2024年5月31日第2版。
② 中国海关总署相关数据。

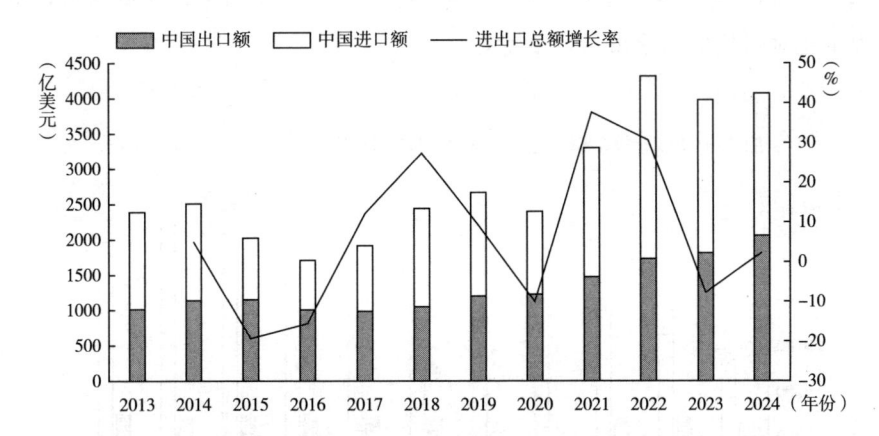

图 1.1　2013—2024 年中国同阿拉伯国家进出口总额
资料来源：中国海关总署。

## 1.1.3　双向投资日益活跃

2024年，中国对阿拉伯国家直接投资流量为23.9亿美元，同比回落11.1%。投资流量前五位的国家分别为阿联酋（15.72亿美元）、沙特（3.67亿美元）、埃及（1.72亿美元）、伊拉克（1.04亿美元）和摩洛哥（0.55亿美元）。① 截至2023年底，中国对阿拉伯国家直接投资存量216.78亿美元，同比下降13.05%（见图1.2）。阿联酋、沙特、伊拉克、阿尔及利亚和埃及依然是中国在阿拉伯国家投资存量最多的前五大投资目的地，占比达到79.58%。② 除直接投资外，中国企业还通过再投资、第三国投资等方式，积极拓展在阿拉伯国家各领域业务，各类投资总量实际超过780亿美元。③ 2013年以来，中国对阿拉伯国家的投资保持稳定，大多数年份的投资流量保持在20亿美元以上，投资存量从2013年的85.65

---

① 中华人民共和国商务部研究院相关报告数据。
② 中华人民共和国商务部、国家统计局、国家外汇管理局：《2023年度中国对外直接投资统计公报》，中国商务出版社，2024年9月。
③ 中华人民共和国商务部国际贸易经济合作研究院：《中国—阿拉伯国家经贸合作回顾与展望2024》。

003

亿美元增长到 2022 年的最高点 249.32 亿美元，10 年间增长了近两倍，中国企业对阿拉伯国家市场持续看好。

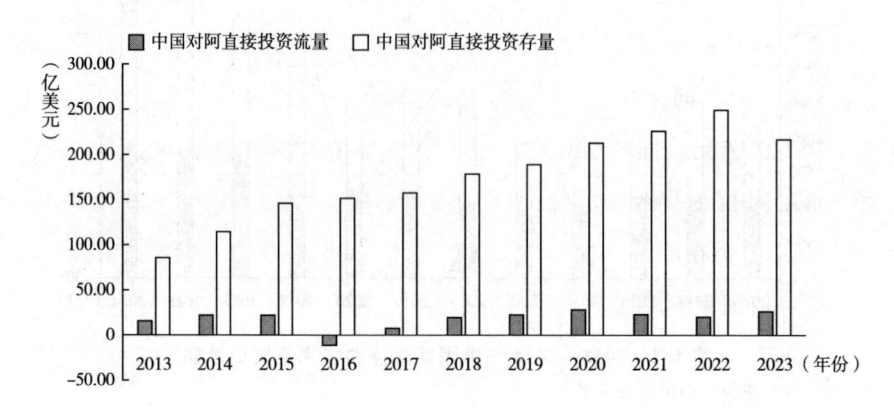

图 1.2　2013—2023 年中国对阿拉伯国家直接投资流量和存量情况
资料来源：2013—2023 年《中国对外直接投资统计公报》。

近年来，阿拉伯国家对华投资日益活跃。2023 年，阿拉伯国家新增来华实际投资 23 亿美元，同比增长 120%。其中阿联酋对华投资增势迅猛，从上年的 9.6 亿美元大幅增至 22 亿美元，成为当年中国第十大投资来源国。[①] 沙特是对华投资第二多的阿拉伯国家。截至 2023 年底，中国实际使用阿联酋和沙特的投资额分别为 45 亿美元和 18.9 亿美元。[②] 究其原因，一方面，阿拉伯国家一些大型公司积极开拓中国市场，拓展石油化工等上下游产业链合作，如沙特国家石油公司（沙特阿美）、沙特基础工业公司等；另一方面，中东主权财富基金看好中国发展前景，纷纷在华设立办事处，扩大在中国市场的布局，扩大对华投资，其中包括沙特公共投资基金、阿联酋阿布扎比投资局、穆巴达拉投资公司、科威特投资局等。

---

① 中华人民共和国商务部：《中国外资统计公报 2024》。
② 中华人民共和国商务部：《中国外资统计公报 2024》。

### 1.1.4 基础设施合作稳步发展

阿拉伯国家是中国对外承包工程的重要市场，基础设施合作也是中阿经贸合作的重要内容。2024年，中国企业在阿拉伯国家新签合同额654.3亿美元，同比增长38.6%，占新签合同总额的24.5%；完成营业额350.1亿美元，同比增长26.4%，占完成营业额总额的21.1%。沙特是中国在阿拉伯国家最大的承包工程来源国，且呈现快速增长趋势。2024年，中企在沙特新签合同额325.5亿美元，同比增长94.3%，占当年在阿拉伯国家新签合同额的49.7%；完成营业额126.3亿美元，同比增长36.2%，占当年在阿拉伯国家完成营业额的36.1%。伊拉克、阿联酋、阿尔及利亚、埃及是中国企业的另四大承包工程市场，2024年在这四个国家的新签合同额占比达到39.2%，完成营业额占比51.5%。从领域分布来看，建筑类、能源动力类、交通运输类项目是中企承包的主要项目。

## 1.2　中阿经贸合作领域态势

### 1.2.1　贸易量稳质增不断优化

2023—2024年，中阿双方着力改善双边贸易结构，促进贸易均衡发展，提升贸易自由化、便利化水平，为双边贸易投资创造更为广阔的发展空间。在双方共同努力下，双边贸易规模在2024年重回4000亿美元以上的历史高位，商品结构进一步优化并日趋合理。油气贸易继续发挥中流砥柱作用。2024年，中国自阿拉伯国家进口原油总量约2.5亿吨，同比下降6.85%，占中国自全球原油进口总量的44.6%。[①] 在前十大原油进口来源国中，阿拉伯国家占据六席，依次是沙特（第2）、伊拉克（第4）、阿曼

---

① 中国海关总署相关数据。

（第5）、阿联酋（第6）、科威特（第9）和卡塔尔（第10）。天然气方面，中国自阿拉伯国家进口液化天然气总量2049万吨，同比增长8%，占中国自全球进口总量的26.7%，共计117.8亿美元。卡塔尔继续保持中国第二大液化天然气进口来源国地位（仅次于澳大利亚），在阿拉伯国家中一枝独秀，液化天然气对华出口量为1836万吨，同比增长10.2%，占中国自全球进口总量的23.9%。油籽油料、饲料、植物油、水产品等大类农产品是中国自阿拉伯国家进口的主要非能源产品，苏丹、阿联酋、埃及、毛里塔尼亚、沙特、摩洛哥是主要进口来源国。除大类农产品外，埃及柑橘和芒果、阿联酋骆驼奶和生蚝、沙特干椰枣、阿曼水产品等特色农产品相继获得输华准入后在中国市场持续热销。

出口方面，阿拉伯国家已成为中国"新三样"（新能源汽车、锂电池、光伏产品）和中间品出口的重要市场。2024年，中国"新三样"对阿拉伯国家出口总额79.4亿美元，同比增长66.5%；中间品对阿拉伯国家出口总额988.5亿美元，同比增长11.5%，占中国对阿拉伯国家出口总额的比例接近50%。从具体产品来看，光伏产品对阿拉伯国家出口总额34.5亿美元，同比增长29.8%。沙特以18.9亿美元成为中国光伏产品海外第五大出口市场。锂电池出口总额共计12.7亿美元，同比增长88.9%。在"新三样"中表现最为亮眼的仍属新能源汽车。随着阿拉伯国家能源转型政策的推进和当地消费者对新能源汽车接受度的提高，中国新能源汽车对阿拉伯国家出口实现快速增长，2024年出口总计17.8万辆，同比增幅高达141.3%。仅对阿联酋一国就出口13.1万辆，阿联酋已成为中国新能源汽车在全球第四大出口市场。以比亚迪、蔚来、小鹏等为代表的中国新能源汽车品牌在电池技术、智能化水平和成本控制方面处于全球领先地位，近年来还针对阿拉伯国家的高温气候和特殊地理环境，不断加强技术创新，通过改进电池的耐高温性能、提升车辆的续航能力和空调系统的效率，推出更适合当地市场的新能源汽车，并凭借丰富的产品线满足阿拉伯国家不同消费群体的需求，不仅在中低端市场具有竞争力，还在高端市场与国际品牌展开竞争。除整车出口外，中国车企正积极考虑通过技术合作、合资建厂等方式深化与阿拉伯国家的合作，布局本地化生产和售后服务网络，这将有助于进一步提升中国新能源汽车在当地的品牌影响力和市场占有率。

### 1.2.2 投资转型升级持续加速

2024年，中国与阿拉伯国家的投资合作升温明显，人员信息交流进一步密切，在谈项目数量、规模、领域、层次显著提升，传统能源、制造业、矿业、新兴产业布局整体推进，呈现出绿色化、融合化的新特点。

能源转型驱动绿色低碳合作。绿色投资成为中阿合作的核心引擎。中国丝路基金与阿联酋新能源巨头马斯达尔签署谅解备忘录，双方计划共同投资"一带一路"共建国家（特别是发展中国家和南半球）的清洁能源项目，总投资额预计达到200亿元人民币（约合28亿美元），标志着两国在绿色能源领域的合作迈上新台阶。[1] 沙特国际电力和水务公司宣布将在上海建立全球创新中心，聚焦光伏、风电、储能、绿色氢能和海水淡化等领域的新技术与新产品研发。[2] 国电电力宣布与阿布扎比未来能源公司及韩国电力公司共同投资位于沙特东部省的2吉瓦光伏项目，总投资额达11.12亿美元（约合人民币81.35亿元）。这些项目不仅体现了中国新能源技术优势，更通过碳足迹追踪系统、绿色金融工具等创新模式，推动沙特加速实现"2030愿景"中的减排目标。

中阿产业双向融合发展持续深入。沙特公共投资基金（PIF）旗下的可再生能源本地化公司（RELC）与远景能源、晶科能源、TCL中环等三家中国新能源企业达成合作协议，旨在推动沙特太阳能和风能所需设备和

---

[1] 《阿联酋能源巨头转型：数十亿美元海外扩张，低碳氢是新征途》，新浪财经网，https://finance.sina.com.cn/cj/2024-11-25/doc-incxhuth8112011.shtml，2024年11月25日。
[2] 《沙特国际电力和水务公司落户浦东》，浦东新区人民政府网站，https://www.shanghai.gov.cn/nw15343/20241016/5f7ea7b1bbdf4687a2c5009fbd30a0b1.html，2024年10月16日。

组件的制造与组装本土化。① 浙江荣盛石化与沙特国家石油公司签署谅解备忘录，交叉持股对方旗下的炼化企业股份，并在此基础上进行产能升级扩建，充分利用中沙两国市场和政策优势，打造一个横跨两国的具有全球竞争优势的大型炼油化工一体化项目，标志着双方向跨国实体项目投资合作迈出了重要的一步。② 中国与摩洛哥围绕新能源汽车产业的投资合作势头强劲，2024年达成的产业投资协议金额达95亿美元，覆盖新能源汽车电池材料（正极、负极、前驱体、隔膜、铜箔、电解液）及汽车零配件等多个领域。通过这些本地化项目的实施，中国企业将先进的技术和管理经验引入阿拉伯国家，促进当地制造业升级，助力其提升在全球产业链供应链上的地位，同时也能更好地满足当地市场需求，实现互利共赢的协同发展。

### 1.2.3 承包工程合作捷报频传

阿拉伯国家是中国企业开展承包工程业务最早和最重要的市场之一。近年来，阿拉伯国家财政状况整体较好，普遍加大基础设施投入，中阿承包工程合作因此实现快速发展。2024年，中国企业在阿拉伯国家新签承包工程合同额占海外新签总额的近四分之一，同比增幅38.6%，远高于1.1%的海外市场整体增速。③ 阿拉伯国家已成为中国企业在全球范围内增长最快的海外承包工程市场板块。从国别来看，中国企业在10个阿拉伯国家的承包工程业务实现了两位数以上的高增长，沙特跃升成为中国企业在海外最大的单一承包工程市场。

重大项目斩获连连。中国化学工程集团有限公司新签伊拉克南方炼油公司的法奥炼化一体化项目，总投资50亿—60亿美元，包含30万桶/

---

① 《总投资百亿级，三家新能源头部民企奔赴沙特》，腾讯网，https://news.qq.com/rain/a/20240717A00Z0Z00，2024年7月17日。
② 《关于与沙特阿美石油有限公司签署谅解备忘录的公告》，荣盛石化股份有限公司网站，http://static.cninfo.com.cn/finalpage/2024-01-03/1218789834.PDF，2024年1月2日。
③ 中华人民共和国商务部。

天炼油厂、300万吨/年石化综合体和配套2000兆瓦发电厂,建成后可推进伊拉克本地成品油跻身欧五标准,实现从原油供应到产品销售的全链条服务。① 中国建筑以20亿美元报价赢得沙特利雅得古城综合区建设项目。② 葛洲坝集团以2.25亿美元中标摩洛哥高铁第9标段土建工程,与此前中标其他标段的中铁四局、山东高速路桥、中铁二十局和中国海外工程集团进一步巩固了中国企业在该项目的主导地位。③ 同时,中国企业越来越多通过与当地公司和国际伙伴组建联营体的方式参与项目投标,互利共赢实现良好发展。中车集团与土耳其两家公司组建的联营体中标迪拜蓝线开发项目,合同额55.8亿美元。④ 中铁六局与阿尔及利亚公司Infrarer联手中标价值4.76亿美元的东部矿区铁路升级合同,帮助其提升铁路运输能力,更好推动矿业和物流产业的发展。中国电建同印度公司Larsen&Toubro组成的联营体中标阿联酋—阿曼铁路连接线项目部分标段合同。

标志性工程稳步推进。中国企业在迪拜实施的光热光伏太阳能电站项目、哈斯彦电站项目、阿联酋联邦铁路二期项目均已进入收尾阶段,整体完成进度分别达到99.9%、99.95%和94%。⑤ 中国建筑承建的埃及新首都中央商务区项目一期分步交付、阿拉曼新城超高综合体项目全面封顶。在伊拉克,中油工程建设的当地首座兆瓦级光伏储能电站正式投产,中国电建新建679所学校项目已完成全部移交,中国建筑承揽的纳西里耶机场项目和川铁国际承建的巴格达市中心尼苏尔立体交通项目,现场施工完成进度分别达到37%和78%。中国能建实施的沙特阿尔舒巴赫光伏电站为全球

---

① 《总投资约200亿美元!中国化学签约1500万吨/年炼化一体化项目协议》,润滑油情报网,http://www.lube-info.com/2024/0603/16124.html,2024年6月3日。
② 《20.8亿美元!中国建筑联合体中标沙特大型公建项目!》,新浪财经网,https://finance.sina.com.cn/roll/2024-11-21/doc-incwvitk4586430.shtml,2024年11月21日。
③ 《葛洲坝2.25亿美元夺摩洛哥高铁最后标段,五家中企主导该项目发展》,搜狐网,https://www.sohu.com/a/831274330_121622815,2024年11月28日。
④ 《中国中车携手土耳其企业中标55.8亿美元迪拜地铁蓝线项目》,腾讯网,https://news.qq.com/rain/a/20241220A02T6W00,2024年12月20日。
⑤ 中华人民共和国商务部。

最大在建单体光伏电站项目，已实现全容量并网发电。此外，中交集团、中国中铁、中国土木等企业还在积极跟进伊拉克"发展之路"、沙特"大陆桥"等大型基建项目进展。

### 1.2.4 新兴领域合作百花齐放

近年来，随着阿拉伯国家经济多元化战略及工业化进程有所加快，中阿双方不断拓展合作空间，在能源、基础设施等传统领域合作的基础上，加强金融、数字经济、交通物流等新兴领域的合作，形成优势互补、协同发展的合作新格局。

在金融合作方面，中国财政部于2024年11月在沙特首都利雅得成功簿记发行20亿美元主权债券，获得来自亚洲、中东、欧洲、美国等地区的国际投资者踊跃认购，总认购金额397.3亿美元，等同于发行金额的19.9倍。[①] 这是中国2021年以来发行的首只境外美元主权债券，发行地点首次选择了沙特，打破了以往20年发行美元计价主权债券均安排在香港的惯例，既彰显中国对沙特致力于成为全球金融投资中心的支持力度，也凸显中沙两国之间日益加深的金融服务合作关系。中国银行通过多边央行数字货币桥平台与阿联酋央行完成首笔"数字迪拉姆"跨境支付交易，金额约1亿元人民币。中国交通银行在迪拜国际金融中心（DIFC）设立地区首家分行，业务范围覆盖整个阿拉伯地区。过去三年来，中资银行在DIFC管理的总资产飙升近33%，截至2024年底已达到653亿美元。DIFC已入驻16家金融类中国公司，其中包括6家代表处、5家商业银行、2家财富管理公司、1家经纪公司、1家顾问公司和1家保险公司。纳斯达克迪拜是迪拜重要证券交易所之一，目前已有来自中国内地和香港的发行人发行22只证券，总价值为123亿美元。首批沙特交易型开放式指数基金（ETF）分别在上海、深圳证券交易所上市，合计筹集金额

---

[①] 《财政部成功发行20亿美元主权债券》，中华人民共和国财政部网站，https://www.mof.gov.cn/zhengwuxinxi/caizhengxinwen/202411/t20241114_3947570.htm，2024年11月14日。

超过12亿元人民币。①阿曼投资局于2024年6月获得中国证监会批准的QFII（境外合格投资机构）牌照，并与中金公司等积极对接，未来或加大在华金融投资力度。

数字经济合作加速推进。2024年2月，中国商务部与阿联酋经济部签署《数字经济投资合作备忘录》。②哈伊马角、阿布扎比两个酋长国分别与腾讯云签署合作文件，阿布扎比的线上政务服务平台（TAMM）由腾讯云定制打造。中国企业继续在阿联酋、沙特、埃及等国建设5G商用网络，阿联酋电信公司（Etisalat）和华为在实验室联合完成6GHz 5G技术的首次实验。TikTok成为阿拉伯国家最受欢迎的社交媒体，在直播市场占据了超过80%的份额。2024年下半年，TikTok宣布将在沙特设立区域总部，进一步拓展阿拉伯国家市场。③阿里巴巴在摩洛哥启动B2B平台，成为其登陆北非阿拉伯国家的首站。华为云在阿联酋为Wio（数字银行）、Dupay（数字货币信息卡）、Neopay（数字银行）等提供云服务，在埃及推出首个公共云服务，为包括埃及、阿尔及利亚在内的28个非洲北部和中部国家提供服务。中国移动与阿联酋公司签署谅解备忘录，双方围绕5G-A解决方案、数字基础设施升级、国际海底光缆等领域加强合作。国内智能驾驶企业文远知行在多个海湾阿拉伯国家启动自动驾驶出租车业务试点。

交通物流合作取得突破。中阿民航往来的网络建设日益完善，中国与沙特在2024年内接连开通五条新航线，北上广深港五大城市均与利雅得之间实现直航直达。中国与摩洛哥之间的直飞航班正式复航。以美团为代表的电商平台企业在阿拉伯国家开发地区市场取得显著成效。美团针对沙特市场开发的外卖平台应用Keeta在沙特下载量高居业内第一；杂货零售

---

① 《境内首批沙特ETF上市首日大涨》，第一财经网，https：//www.yicai.com/news/102192836.html，2024年7月6日。
② 中华人民共和国商务部网站。
③ 《TikTok将在沙特设区域总部，或改变海湾地区电商格局》，搜狐网，https：//www.sohu.com/a/832471330_99936768，2024年12月2日。

部门小象超市实现在沙特业务落地，成为该部门出海阿拉伯国家的首站；美团旗下无人机业务 Drone 获得阿联酋颁发的首个无人机送货商业许可。

## 1.3 中阿经贸合作趋势展望

2025 年是中阿合作承前启后的重要一年，既是落实"五大合作格局"的关键之年，也是筹备 2026 年新一届中阿峰会、中海峰会的启动之年。中阿双方将根据《中国—阿拉伯国家合作论坛 2024 年至 2026 年行动执行计划》的规划设计，进一步深化推进多双边政治、经贸、投资、金融、基础设施、资源环境、人文交流、航空航天、教育卫生等各领域合作，深化产供链融合发展，挖掘双方在数字经济、绿色发展等新兴领域合作的新动能，推动中阿经贸合作提质增效，为高质量共建"一带一路"和中阿战略伙伴关系的发展、中阿命运共同体的建设注入新动力、谱写新篇章。[①]

### 1.3.1 阿拉伯国家政治经济形势

2024 年，阿拉伯国家所在的中东地区成为全球地缘冲突的"风暴眼"。上半年，巴以冲突硝烟未散，黎以边境火光又起，苏丹、也门国内冲突延宕不息；下半年，伊（朗）以（色列）之间的紧张局势不断升级，叙利亚政局突变更是为地区形势增添许多变数。频频发生的冲突引发外界对中东地区局势日益动荡和复杂的担忧。2025 年，阿拉伯国家依旧笼罩在地区形势不确定性的阴影之下。和解与谈判、冲突与重组、灾害与发展，折射出阿拉伯国家面临的希望与困顿交织的复杂图景，也将阿拉伯国家划分成发展形势各异的不同阵营。

海湾阿拉伯国家在国际油价持续低迷的背景下，普遍采取逆周期财政政策，通过维持较高的政府支出刺激经济增长，为经济多元化转型注入动

---

[①] 《中国—阿拉伯国家合作论坛 2024 年至 2026 年行动执行计划》，中阿合作论坛网站，https://www.chinaarabcf.org/chn/lthyjwx/bzjhywj/dshijbzjhy/202406/t20240606_11381295.htm，2024 年 6 月 6 日。

力。虽然低油价对这些产油国的财政收入构成一定压力，但得益于相对稳健的债务管理，财政状况总体保持稳定。根据世界银行的预测，2025年海湾阿拉伯国家的GDP增长率均将位于3%—4%的区间。[①] 同时，这些国家的债务总额预计也将保持稳定。但也要看到，全球经济下行风险仍不可忽视，海湾阿拉伯国家仍需要在确保内外政治环境稳定的情况下，在经济政策上精益求精，确保经济的可持续增长与成功转型。

北非地区的阿拉伯国家有望成为阿拉伯世界中快速发展崛起的另一个重要极。自乌克兰危机爆发以来，摩洛哥、阿尔及利亚、埃及等北非阿拉伯国家对清洁能源的重视程度日渐提升，乌克兰危机、巴以冲突等引发的全球能源供应动荡则进一步坚定了这些国家发展本国清洁能源产业的决心。2025年，北非国家将继续致力于吸引外国投资，以加速可再生能源行业的蓬勃发展，并利用可再生能源服务经济发展的需要，助力本土加工制造业继续保持良好的发展势头。

### 1.3.2 中阿经贸合作面临新的发展机遇

2024年，中国与阿拉伯国家在两大重要合作平台——中阿合作论坛与中非合作论坛——的框架下，展开了密集且富有成效的互动。中阿之间的经贸合作不仅实现了质量的飞跃，还在贸易、投资、承包工程以及新兴领域的合作上稳步前行，展现出了强劲的发展势头。当下，阿拉伯国家"向东看"的趋势越发显著，对于"追求稳定、谋求发展"的渴望比以往任何时候都要强烈。这些国家将经济发展视为首要任务和核心关切，期望通过深化内部改革、扩大对外开放，实现产业发展的"弯道超越"。未来一段时间，阿拉伯国家在基础设施建设、能源结构转型、数字经济领域以及医疗健康行业等方面，依然保持着旺盛的外部需求和内在驱动力。而这些领域，恰好与中国产业具有极高的互补性和契合度，为中阿经贸合作的高质量发展提供了新的发力点和广阔的蓝海市场。

---

① 世界银行：《全球经济展望》。

在2024年5月举行的中阿合作论坛第十届部长级会议开幕式上，习近平主席提出了与阿方共同构建"五大合作新格局"的愿景。这一合作新格局既充分考虑了双方合作的传统优势领域，又进一步挖掘了中阿合作的新潜力，拓展了合作的深度和广度。在创新驱动方面，双方将加强科技创新合作，共同推动产业升级和技术进步；在投资金融领域，将扩大相互投资规模，深化金融合作，为双方经济发展提供有力支撑；在能源合作上，将共同应对能源转型的挑战，推动清洁能源和可再生能源的合作与发展；在经贸互惠方面，将进一步提升贸易便利化水平，促进双边贸易持续健康增长；在人文交流上，将加强教育、文化、旅游等领域的合作，增进双方人民之间的相互理解和友谊。展望2025年，中国与阿拉伯国家的经贸合作将迎来更加广阔的发展前景和新的发展机遇。

### 1.3.3　中阿经贸合作面临的风险与挑战

2025年，中东地区形势复杂多变的基本面并未改变，不确定性、不稳定性仍较为突出，也给中阿经贸合作的深化带来诸多困难和挑战。

一是阿拉伯国家固有的挑战和风险犹在。在地缘格局方面，从2023年10月新一轮巴以冲突爆发至今，黎以冲突、苏丹内战、叙利亚政权更迭此起彼伏，也门、利比亚的国内政治僵局延宕未解，引发外界对中东地区政治安全局势的持续担忧。在国内治理方面，部分阿拉伯国家枪械泛滥，武装冲突、帮派火拼、政治暗杀、汽车炸弹袭击频发，一些国家民众至今仍生活在地雷、榴弹遍布的战争遗留环境中。在营商环境方面，一些阿拉伯国家在世界银行发布的营商环境报告中排名偏后，多项与投资合作相关的指标不尽如人意，行政效率等问题依旧为外界所诟病。一些国家因财政吃紧，预算拨付滞后，贷款还款逾期问题突出，主权违约风险敞口加大。

二是大国博弈等外部干扰风险日益凸显。美国长期干预阿拉伯国家内政外交，通过"长臂管辖"手段钳制部分阿拉伯国家经济发展命脉，借此推行美国利益优先的中东战略，服务其大国博弈的目标。2022年7月，美国总统拜登访问中东，旨在打造中东版北约，推动"印度—中东—欧洲经济走廊（IMEC）"等，谋求在中东构建排华包围圈。特朗普开启第二任期后，有可能进一步通过政治、经济、军事等多种手段，推动阿拉伯国家在高科技、军工军贸、关键基础设施等领域对华脱钩，对中阿经贸合作可能产生不可忽视的影响。

三是中国企业"出海"能力短板亟待补齐。"走出去"的中国企业在风险防控和合规管理的能力方面普遍存在不足，对驻在国政策、法律和文化的研究不够，对应的风险评估和应对机制有待完善。阿拉伯国家国内政治和政策的稳定性不高，法律法规落地不足，以及特殊商业惯例带来的文化冲突等，是中国企业开拓阿拉伯国家市场并在当地站稳脚跟长期面临的主要困难。特别是阿拉伯国家近年来普遍受到经济增速放缓、产业转型升级进展缓慢等因素叠加影响，贸易投资保护主义和经济政策内顾倾向都有所加重，在税赋水平和用工本地化比例方面不断向外国企业转嫁压力，推高包括中国企业在内的商业活动成本。

### 1.3.4　中阿经贸合作的未来重点方向

中国与阿拉伯国家的经贸合作历经多年发展，已形成以能源合作为基石、多元化领域协同推进的格局。展望未来，在全球化格局重塑、绿色经济崛起和数字化转型加速的背景下，中阿经贸合作将超越简单的资源与商品互换，向技术共研、标准共建、价值链共塑的高阶形态演进。这种演进不仅有助于阿拉伯国家实现经济多元化目标，也将推动中阿双方战略互信和务实合作迈向更高水平。

一是绿色能源与低碳产业链深度协同。全球能源转型背景下，中阿合作将从传统油气领域加速向绿色能源全产业链延伸。一方面，中国将继续深化与沙特、阿联酋等国的光伏、风能、氢能合作，推动标志性项目落地。另一方面，双方将共建低碳产业集群，中国的新能源汽车、电池制造企业有望在阿拉伯国家设立区域生产基地，通过技术转移和本地化生产助力阿拉伯国家实现能源密集型产业的低碳转型。

二是数字经济与科技创新联合突破。阿拉伯国家"向东看"战略与中国"数字丝绸之路"倡议高度契合，双方将重点推动5G、人工智能、智慧城市等领域的联合创新。沙特"2030愿景"、阿联酋"人工智能战略2031"等规划，为中国科技企业提供广阔场景。同时，双方可探索设立中阿数字创新联合基金，支持初创企业跨境孵化，并在数据安全、跨境支付等领域建立区域性标准，抢占数字经济发展制高点。

三是基建升级与区域互联互通提质增效。阿拉伯国家经济多元化战略催生大量基建需求，中国"一带一路"倡议与区域发展规划（如埃及"新首都"、沙特"线性城市"）深度融合。未来合作将呈现两大趋势，即从单一工程承包转向"投建营一体化"，通过长期股权合作提升可持续性；聚焦"硬联通"与"软联通"结合，中阿双方可合作推进跨境智慧物流网络、红海—地中海铁路等跨区域通道建设，并加强海关数字化、贸易规则对接等制度性合作，降低区域贸易成本。

四是现代农业与粮食安全协同保障。面对气候变化对阿拉伯国家粮食安全的挑战，中阿农业合作将从农产品贸易向技术协同升级。中国可输出节水灌溉、盐碱地改良、垂直农业等技术，并与绿色发展技术相结合，在部分阿拉伯国家因地制宜试点推广"光伏+农业"项目。同时，双方可共建跨境粮食供应链，利用中国在仓储物流领域的优势，帮助阿拉伯国家构建稳定粮源通道，增强阿拉伯国家应对粮食危机风险的能力。

五是文化交融与民生合作夯实根基。经贸合作深化需以民心相通为纽带。中阿双方应在职业教育、医疗健康、旅游文创等领域进一步加强合作，提高双方在民间合作中的获得感。同时，文旅合作通过签证便利化、直航加密、文化遗产数字化等方式，促进双向人文交流，为经贸合作注入持久动力。

# 第2章 中阿贸易合作专题报告

自"一带一路"倡议提出以来,中阿贸易合作已从"量的积累"迈向"质的飞跃"。贸易规模屡创新高,贸易结构不断优化,从货物贸易拓展到数字贸易等新领域,贸易合作平台和机制不断完善,"中阿合作论坛""中阿博览会""中阿技术转移中心"等发挥了积极的作用。中阿贸易的蓬勃发展,深度拓展了双边投资和经济技术合作,经贸合作取得全方位丰硕成果。中阿贸易合作深刻受益于"一带一路"倡议的战略引领与务实推动。2016年《中国对阿拉伯国家政策文件》首次系统规划双边合作框架,2018年签署《中阿合作共建"一带一路"行动宣言》,2020年中阿合作论坛第九届部长级会议确立"携手打造面向新时代的中阿命运共同体"目标,2022年"三环峰会"更以历史性外交突破,将政治互信推向新高度。中国已同22个阿拉伯国家签署了共建"一带一路"合作文件,彰显了战略对接的深度,标志着中阿共建"一带一路"进入全面深化和高质量发展的新阶段。

## 2.1 中国对外贸易发展状况

自2013年"一带一路"倡议提出以来,中国贸易规模不断扩大,贸易结构不断优化,贸易多元化取得积极成效,产品国际竞争力不断增强,作为世界第二大经济体和第一大货物贸易国,对全球供应链和国际贸易体系具有深远影响,中国庞大的消费市场为各国企业提供了重要机遇。但是，由于全球经济形势、贸易政策以及国内经济结构调整等因素的影响，增长过程中存在波动。

2013—2024年，中国进出口贸易总额呈现波动式增长态势。具体来看：如表2.1所示，进出口贸易总额从2013年的40014亿美元增长至2024年的61623亿美元，年均增长率约为4%。其中，2013年和2014年均呈增长态势，但2015年出现明显下降，降至38096亿美元，同比下降8.35%，这主要是因为汇率波动使得人民币相对美元出现大幅贬值，同时，全球贸易保护主义抬头、贸易壁垒增多、大宗商品价格下跌和主要贸易伙伴经济困难也是重要原因，对我国出口造成较大压力。2016年进出口总额延续下降趋势，降至36855亿美元，同比下降3.26%。2017—2018年开始回升，这主要得益于我国积极推动"一带一路"建设，拓展了国际市场，促进了贸易规模增长。2019—2020年，受到中美经贸摩擦和新冠疫情的影响，中国对外贸易增速放缓，但由于中国经济韧性和"一带一路"倡议的持续推进，进出口规模依然保持了一定的增长。2021年进出口规模大幅增长，达到60467亿美元，同比增长30.14%，这主要得益于中国率先有效控制疫情，稳定产业链供应链，在全球贸易中优势凸显。2022年进出口贸易总额进一步增长。而2023年进出口贸易总额下降，为58322亿美元，同比下降5.73%，这主要是全球经济增长放缓、地缘政治冲突等因素导致国际市场需求减弱，同时国内经济结构调整也对进出口产生一定影响。2024年经济回暖，上升至61623亿美元。

表2.1 2013—2024年中国对外贸易额及增长速度

| 年份 | 进出口贸易 金额（亿美元） | 进出口贸易 同比（%） | 出口贸易 金额（亿美元） | 出口贸易 同比（%） | 进口贸易 金额（亿美元） | 进口贸易 同比（%） | 贸易差额 金额（亿美元） | 贸易差额 同比（%） |
|---|---|---|---|---|---|---|---|---|
| 2013 | 40014 | 7.45 | 22090.07 | 7.82 | 17924.51 | 6.99 | 4165.56 | 11.52 |
| 2014 | 41566 | 3.88 | 23422.93 | 6.03 | 18143.54 | 1.22 | 5279.39 | 26.74 |
| 2015 | 38096 | -8.35 | 22734.68 | -2.94 | 15361.95 | -15.33 | 7372.73 | 39.65 |

续表

| 年份 | 进出口贸易 金额（亿美元） | 同比（%） | 出口贸易 金额（亿美元） | 同比（%） | 进口贸易 金额（亿美元） | 同比（%） | 贸易差额 金额（亿美元） | 同比（%） |
|---|---|---|---|---|---|---|---|---|
| 2016 | 36855 | -3.26 | 20976.37 | -7.73 | 15879.21 | 3.37 | 5097.16 | -30.86 |
| 2017 | 39747 | 7.85 | 22633.71 | 7.90 | 17114.24 | 7.78 | 5519.47 | 8.29 |
| 2018 | 44828 | 12.78 | 24942.30 | 10.20 | 19886.01 | 16.20 | 5056.29 | -8.39 |
| 2019 | 45675 | 1.89 | 24985.78 | 0.17 | 20689.50 | 4.04 | 4296.20 | -15.03 |
| 2020 | 46462 | 1.72 | 25906.01 | 3.68 | 20555.91 | -0.65 | 5350.10 | 24.53 |
| 2021 | 60467 | 30.14 | 33623.02 | 29.79 | 26843.63 | 30.59 | 6779.39 | 26.72 |
| 2022 | 61867 | 2.31 | 35936.01 | 6.88 | 25931.14 | -3.40 | 10004.87 | 47.58 |
| 2023 | 58322 | -5.73 | 33797.48 | -5.95 | 24524.67 | -5.42 | 9272.81 | -7.32 |
| 2024 | 61623 | 5.66 | 35772.22 | 5.84 | 25850.67 | 5.41 | 9921.55 | 7.00 |

注：以中国为报告国。
分类依据：HS2007。
资料来源：2013—2023年数据根据联合国国际贸易数据库整理计算。2024年数据根据中国商务部商务数据中心网站整理计算。

在2015、2021、2023年等关键时间节点，进出口同比增速出现显著拐点。如图2.1所示，从增速变化来看，2013—2015年进出口同比增速整体呈下降趋势，2015年降至-8.35%。2017—2018年增速有所回升，2018年同比增速达到12.78%。2019—2020年增速较为平稳，维持在较低水平。2021年增速大幅提高至30.14%。此后2022—2023年，增速又开始下降，2023年降为-5.73%。2024年增速回升至5.66%。

随着"一带一路"建设的深入，中国推进的贸易多元化战略取得积极成效，贸易格局发生了深刻变化，对美国市场的依赖度不断下降，新兴市场国家贸易地位不断上升，东盟、阿盟以及俄罗斯、印度等地区和国家在中国贸易格局中的重要性日益凸显。

从进口来看，由图2.2可知，2013—2023年，中国前10位进口贸易伙伴格局显著变化，东盟和阿盟地位显著提升。2013年，中国自东盟进口额占中国进口总额的11.13%，位居第二；2023年，这一比重升至

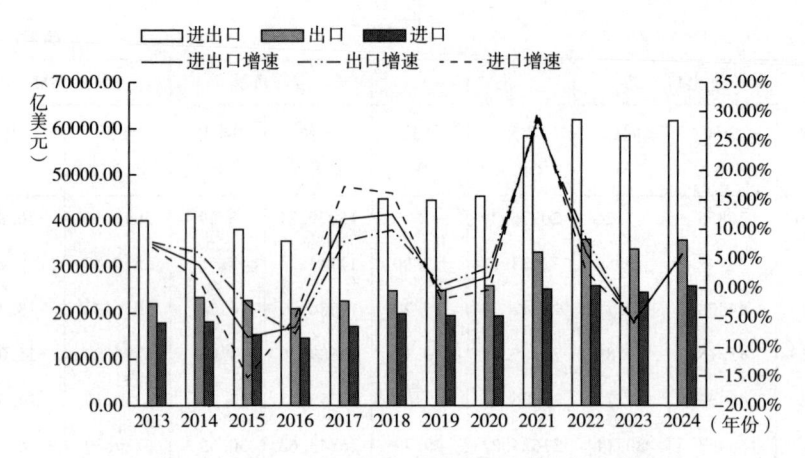

**图 2.1　2013—2024 年中国对外贸易额及增长速度**

注：以中国为报告国。

分类依据：HS2007。

资料来源：2013—2023 年数据根据联合国国际贸易数据库整理计算。本数据已更新至最新版本（更新日志查询网址：https：//wits.worldbank.org/WITS/WITS/Support% 20Materials/TariffDataRefresh.aspx？Page＝TariffDataRefresh）。2024 年数据根据中国商务部商务数据中心网站整理计算。

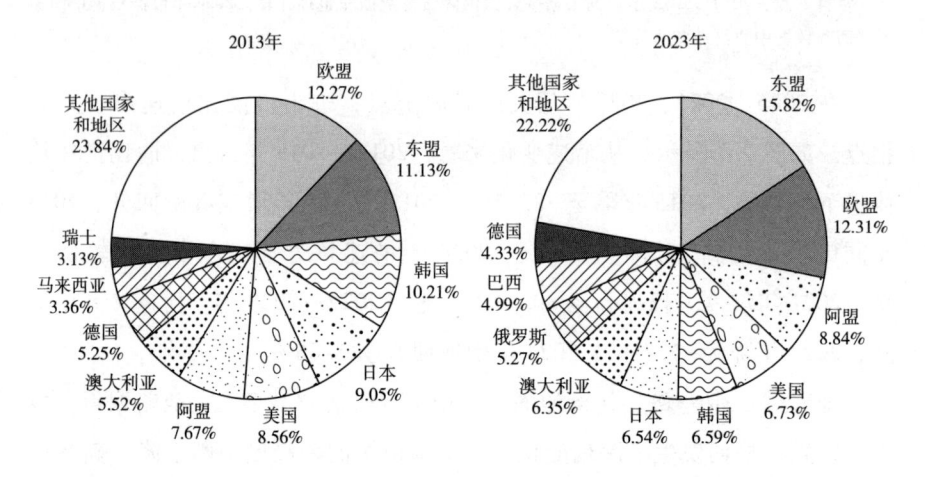

**图 2.2　2013 年与 2023 年中国对前十位进口贸易伙伴进口额占总进口额比重**

注：以中国为报告国。

分类依据：HS2007。

资料来源：根据联合国国际贸易数据库数据整理计算。本数据已更新至最新版本（更新日志查询网址：https：//wits.worldbank.org/WITS/WITS/Support% 20Materials/TariffDataRefresh.aspx？Page＝TariffDataRefresh）。

15.82%，跃居首位。这主要得益于中国—东盟自由贸易区的深化发展以及 RCEP 的生效，区域经济一体化程度不断提高，双方在制造业、农业等领域的贸易往来越发密切。2013 年中国自阿盟进口额占比为 7.67%，排名第六；2023 年，这一比重提升至 8.84%，位列第三。这主要是因为，一是中东地区丰富的石油、天然气等自然资源与中国的能源需求高度契合，双方能源合作不断深化；二是"一带一路"倡议为双方搭建了广阔的合作平台，双方在基础设施建设、贸易投资便利化等方面的合作不断加强，推动了双边贸易规模的扩大；三是中国推动贸易伙伴多元化战略，也为阿盟提升在中国进口贸易中的份额创造了条件。俄罗斯在 2013 年未进入中国前十大进口贸易伙伴行列，2023 年则位列第八，进口额占比 5.27%。巴西同样在 2013 年未进入前十，2023 年位列第九，进口额占比 4.99%。

从出口来看，由图 2.3 可知，2013—2023 年，中国前 10 位出口贸易伙伴中，欧盟、东盟、阿盟地位均有提升。中国对欧盟的出口占比从 2013 年的 15.35% 上升至 2023 年的 17.15%；东盟从 11.05% 大幅增至 15.49%，成为第二大贸易伙伴；阿盟从 4.59% 增至 5.36%。美国份额小幅下降，从 2013 年的第一位 16.71% 降至 2023 年的第三位 14.83%，这反映出中美贸易摩擦及供应链多元化策略的影响，尽管如此，美国仍是中国核心贸易伙伴之一。新兴经济体崛起，越南（4.07%）和印度（3.48%）首次进入前十，取代了荷兰（2013 年占 2.73%）和英国（2013 年占 2.31%）。越南的快速工业化与印度市场潜力释放，推动了中国对两国的出口增长。韩国占比从 4.13% 微升至 4.41%，日本则从 6.80% 降至 4.66%，说明东北亚贸易格局在调整。俄罗斯占比从 2.24% 增至 3.28%。

服务贸易方面，由图 2.4 和表 2.2 可以看出，2013—2024 年，中国对外服务贸易进出口额总体呈现上升趋势，从 2013 年的 5376 亿美元增长至 2024 年的 10565 亿美元，规模扩张明显。与此同时，中国对外服务贸易同比增速波动较大，2014 年增速达到 21.3% 后开始放缓，2020 年受到新冠疫情冲击出现大幅下降，增速下降到 -15.7%，其后两年全球经济复苏，叠加中国疫情防控得力，服务贸易强劲反弹，2023 年全球经济下行、地

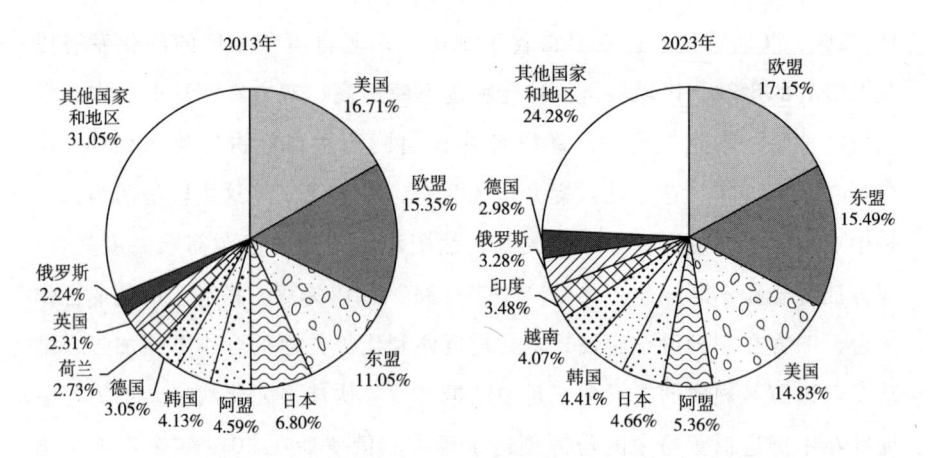

**图 2.3　2013 年与 2023 年中国对前十位出口贸易伙伴出口额占总出口额比重**

注：以中国为报告国。

分类依据：HS2007。

资料来源：根据联合国国际贸易数据库数据整理计算。本数据已更新至最新版本（更新日志查询网址：https://wits.worldbank.org/WITS/WITS/Support%20Materials/TariffDataRefresh.aspx?Page=TariffDataRefresh）。

缘政治冲突、贸易保护主义抬头等因素导致外部需求萎缩，增速再次放缓至 4.9%，2024 年经济回暖，增速上升至 13.2%。贸易逆差持续存在，中国服务贸易长期处于逆差状态，且逆差规模波动较大。2014 年逆差规模达到 -2137 亿美元，此后几年逆差规模有所收窄，2020 年受疫情影响逆差大幅收窄，2021 年以后逆差再次扩大，并在 2023 年达到 -1709 亿美元，2024 年小幅收缩至 -1647 亿美元。

**表 2.2　2013—2024 年中国对外服务贸易额及增长速度**

| 年份 | 进出口贸易 金额（亿美元） | 同比（%） | 出口贸易 金额（亿美元） | 同比（%） | 进口贸易 金额（亿美元） | 同比（%） | 净出口额 金额（亿美元） |
|---|---|---|---|---|---|---|---|
| 2013 | 5376 | 11.3 | 2070 | 2.7 | 3306 | 17.5 | -1236 |
| 2014 | 6520 | 21.3 | 2191 | 5.9 | 4329 | 30.9 | -2137 |
| 2015 | 6542 | 0.3 | 2186 | -0.2 | 4355 | 0.6 | -2169 |
| 2016 | 6616 | 1.1 | 2095 | -4.2 | 4521 | 3.8 | -2426 |

续表

| 年份 | 进出口贸易 金额（亿美元） | 进出口贸易 同比（%） | 出口贸易 金额（亿美元） | 出口贸易 同比（%） | 进口贸易 金额（亿美元） | 进口贸易 同比（%） | 净出口额 金额（亿美元） |
|---|---|---|---|---|---|---|---|
| 2017 | 6957 | 5.1 | 2281 | 8.9 | 4676 | 3.4 | -2395 |
| 2018 | 7965 | 14.5 | 2715 | 19.0 | 5250 | 12.3 | -2536 |
| 2019 | 7850 | -1.4 | 2836 | 4.5 | 5014 | -4.5 | -2178 |
| 2020 | 6617 | -15.7 | 2806 | -1.0 | 3811 | -24.0 | -1005 |
| 2021 | 8212 | 24.1 | 3942 | 40.5 | 4270 | 12.0 | -327 |
| 2022 | 8891 | 8.3 | 4241 | 7.6 | 4650 | 8.9 | -410 |
| 2023 | 9331 | 4.9 | 3811 | -10.1 | 5520 | 18.7 | -1709 |
| 2024 | 10565 | 13.2 | 4459 | 17.0 | 6106 | 10.6 | -1647 |

资料来源：根据中华人民共和国商务部商务数据中心网站整理计算。

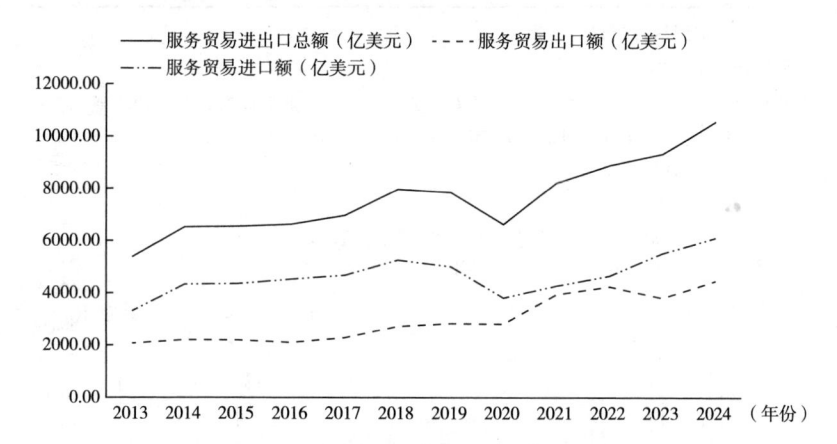

图 2.4　2013—2024 年中国服务贸易趋势

资料来源：根据中华人民共和国商务部商务数据中心网站整理计算。

## 2.2　阿拉伯国家对外贸易发展状况

如表 2.3 和图 2.5 所示，2013—2023 年，阿拉伯国家对外贸易呈现出复杂的动态演变过程，从总体规模上看，阿拉伯国家对外贸易额从 2013 年的 18562.26 亿美元波动上升至 2023 年的 21244.46 亿美元，呈现出明显的周期性波动。

表 2.3 2013—2023 年阿拉伯国家对外贸易额及增长速度

| 年份 | 进出口贸易 金额（亿美元） | 进出口贸易 同比（%） | 出口贸易 金额（亿美元） | 出口贸易 同比（%） | 进口贸易 金额（亿美元） | 进口贸易 同比（%） | 贸易差额 金额（亿美元） | 贸易差额 同比（%） |
|---|---|---|---|---|---|---|---|---|
| 2013 | 18562.26 | 12.51 | 10710.20 | 11.80 | 7852.06 | 13.49 | 2858.14 | 7.43 |
| 2014 | 17659.50 | -4.86 | 9585.43 | -10.50 | 8074.08 | 2.83 | 1511.35 | -47.12 |
| 2015 | 14590.98 | -17.38 | 6409.82 | -33.13 | 8181.16 | 1.33 | -1771.34 | -217.20 |
| 2016 | 13077.09 | -10.38 | 5611.65 | -12.45 | 7465.45 | -8.75 | -1853.80 | 4.66 |
| 2017 | 13901.95 | 6.31 | 6522.73 | 16.24 | 7379.22 | -1.16 | -856.49 | -53.80 |
| 2018 | 14722.13 | 5.90 | 7566.33 | 16.00 | 7155.80 | -3.03 | 410.54 | -147.93 |
| 2019 | 15805.05 | 7.36 | 8156.91 | 7.81 | 7648.15 | 6.88 | 508.76 | 23.93 |
| 2020 | 12763.27 | -19.25 | 6291.84 | -22.86 | 6471.43 | -15.39 | -179.59 | -135.30 |
| 2021 | 17264.86 | 35.27 | 8995.08 | 42.96 | 8269.78 | 27.79 | 725.30 | -503.86 |
| 2022 | 21996.72 | 27.41 | 12042.18 | 33.88 | 9954.55 | 20.37 | 2087.63 | 187.83 |
| 2023 | 21244.46 | -3.42 | 10821.26 | -10.14 | 10423.20 | 4.71 | 398.06 | -80.93 |

注：以阿拉伯国家为报告国。

分类依据：HS2007。

资料来源：根据联合国国际贸易数据库数据整理计算。本数据已更新至最新版本（更新日志查询网址：https://wits.worldbank.org/WITS/WITS/Support%20Materials/TariffDataRefresh.aspx?Page=TariffDataRefresh）。

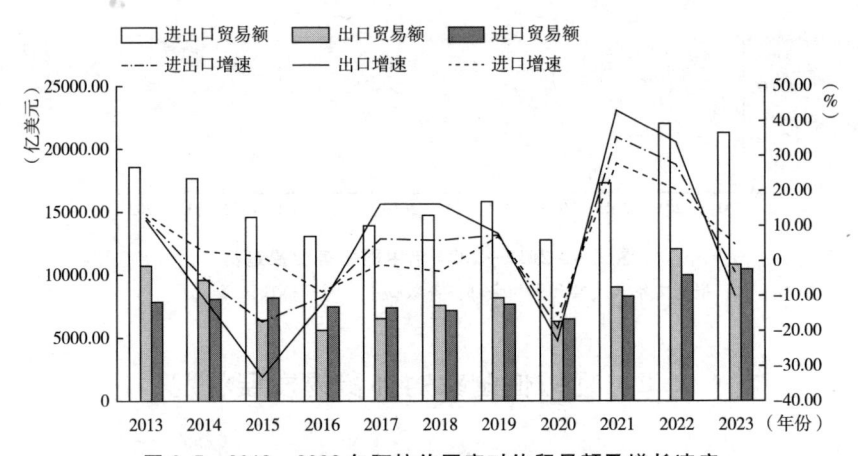

图 2.5 2013—2023 年阿拉伯国家对外贸易额及增长速度

注：以阿拉伯国家为报告国。

分类依据：HS2007。

资料来源：根据联合国国际贸易数据库数据整理计算。本数据已更新至最新版本（更新日志查询网址：https://wits.worldbank.org/WITS/WITS/Support%20Materials/TariffDataRefresh.aspx?Page=TariffDataRefresh）。

2014—2016 年，贸易总额持续下降，2016 年达到谷底 13077.09 亿美元，相对于 2013 年下降幅度达 29.55%。这一阶段出口贸易额降幅显著，从 2013 年的 10710.20 亿美元降至 2016 年的 5611.65 亿美元，降幅高达 47.6%。产生这一现象的主要原因是国际油价下跌显著。此后，随着全球经济逐渐复苏，贸易总额进入恢复增长阶段，并在 2019 年达到 15805.05 亿美元。

2020 年，新冠疫情暴发，全球经济活动陷入停滞状态，需求萎缩，供应链中断，阿拉伯国家对外贸易遭受重创，贸易额大幅下降 19.25% 至 12763.27 亿美元。其中，进出口贸易额均出现明显下降，进口贸易额的降幅相对较小。

2021—2022 年，随着全球经济逐步复苏，特别是能源价格的飙升，阿拉伯国家对外贸易迎来强劲反弹，进出口贸易额分别大幅增长 35.27% 和 27.41%，并在 2022 年达到峰值 21996.72 亿美元。全球经济的复苏以及能源价格的上涨显著提升了阿拉伯国家的出口收入，同时，全球通货膨胀也推高了名义贸易额。然而，受全球经济下行和能源价格回调的影响，2023 年贸易额略下降 3.42% 至 21244.46 亿美元。

综上所述，2013—2023 年，阿拉伯国家对外贸易额经历了显著的波动，并在很大程度上受到国际油价、全球经济形势和突发事件（如新冠疫情）的影响。这种波动显示了阿拉伯国家经济结构的脆弱性和对外部环境的高度依赖性。

如图 2.6 所示，2013—2023 年，阿拉伯国家的出口伙伴关系发生了显著变化。

欧盟一直是阿拉伯国家最重要的出口贸易伙伴，始终占据阿拉伯国家第一大出口贸易伙伴国的位置。2013 年以来，阿拉伯国家对欧盟出口占比显著提升，从 2013 年的 7.84% 增至 2023 年的 10.90%，增加了 3.06 个百分点。随着新兴经济体的崛起和"一带一路"倡议的推动，阿拉伯国家对中国、印度以及东盟等新兴经济体的出口规模逐渐扩大，中国、印度以及东盟成为出口额占比显著增长的贸易伙伴。其中中国的占比增长最为显

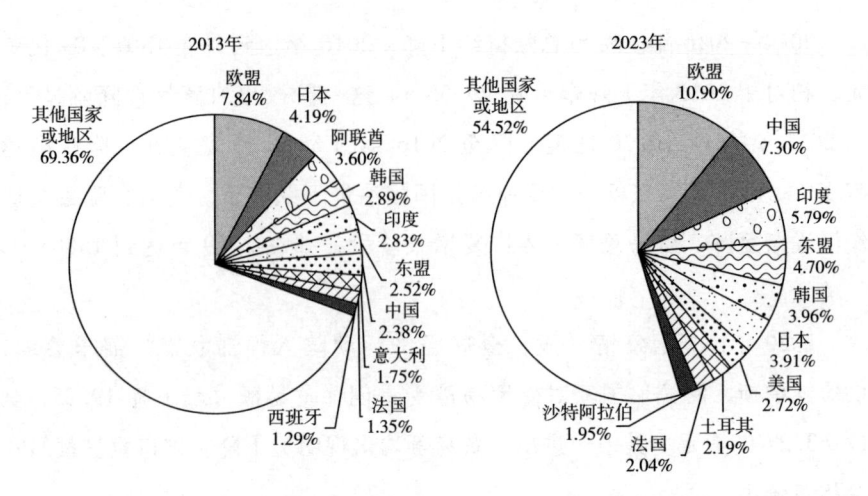

**图 2.6　2013 年与 2023 年阿拉伯国家对前十位出口贸易伙伴出口额占总出口额比重**

注：以阿拉伯国家为报告国。

分类依据：HS2007。

资料来源：根据联合国国际贸易数据库数据整理计算。本数据已更新至最新版本（更新日志查询网址：https：//wits.worldbank.org/WITS/WITS/Support%20Materials/TariffDataRefresh.aspx?Page=TariffDataRefresh）。

著，从 2013 年的 2.38% 增加到 2023 年的 7.30%，从 2013 年的第七大贸易伙伴跃升至 2023 年的第二大贸易伙伴；印度的占比从 2.83% 提升至 5.79%，从 2013 年的第五大贸易伙伴上升至 2023 年的第三大贸易伙伴；东盟的占比从 2.52% 增长至 4.70%，从 2013 年的第六大贸易伙伴上升至 2023 年的第四大贸易伙伴。另外，日本的占比有所下降，从 4.19% 降至 3.91%，从 2013 年的第二大贸易伙伴下降至 2023 年的第六大贸易伙伴，下降了 0.28 个百分点。

阿拉伯国家对前十大贸易伙伴的出口依赖度上升。阿拉伯国家对前十大贸易伙伴的出口占比从 30.64% 上升到 2023 年的 45.48%，与此同时，其他国家或地区的占比从 69.36% 下降到 54.52%，说明出口市场更加集中在前十大贸易伙伴。

2013—2023 年，阿拉伯国家与进口贸易伙伴的关系呈现出如下特点。

阿拉伯国家自中国的进口占比增长显著。从 2013 年的 8.91% 大幅增加到 2023 年的 16.26%，增长了 7.35 个百分点。这主要得益于：中国与阿拉伯国家之间的战略伙伴关系不断深化，政治互信和经济合作水平不断提升；"一带一路"倡议框架下的基础设施建设和互联互通项目降低了贸易成本，促进了中阿贸易便利化；中国制造业的快速发展和产品竞争力的提升，使得中国商品在阿拉伯国家市场更具吸引力，尤其是中低端消费品和工业品领域；阿联酋、沙特、伊拉克等国家开始使用人民币结算，降低了汇率风险，促进了贸易发展。

传统贸易伙伴份额下降。欧盟、德国、日本等传统贸易伙伴市场份额受到挤压，阿拉伯国家从这几个传统贸易伙伴的进口占比下降。这主要是由于：这些国家主要出口汽车、精密仪器等高附加值产品，随着中国、印度等新兴经济体在高技术领域的崛起，阿拉伯国家转向了新兴经济体供应商；欧盟和日本的劳动力成本逐年上升，导致其产品价格竞争力下降等原因。但值得一提的是，欧盟等传统贸易伙伴仍占据重要地位。

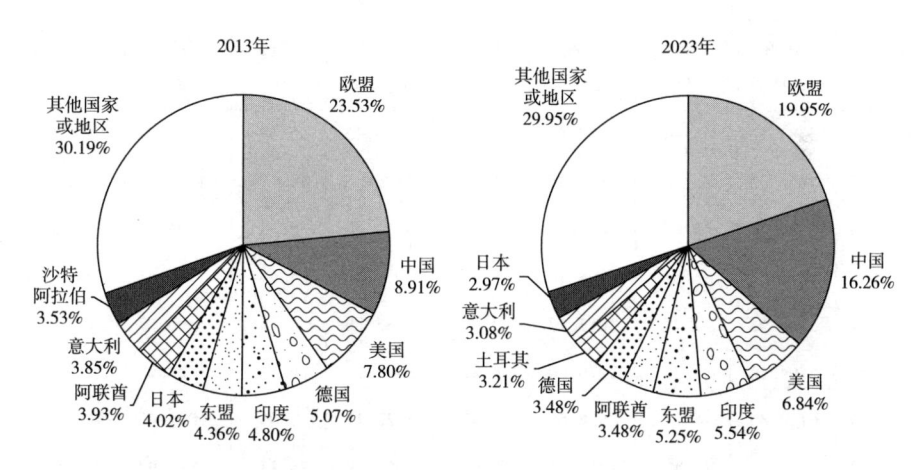

**图 2.7 2013 年与 2023 年阿拉伯国家对前十位进口贸易伙伴进口额占总进口额比重**
注：以阿拉伯国家为报告国。
分类依据：HS2007。
资料来源：根据联合国国际贸易数据库数据整理计算。本数据已更新至最新版本（更新日志查询网址：https：//wits.worldbank.org/WITS/WITS/Support%20Materials/TariffDataRefresh.aspx？Page=TariffDataRefresh）。

由表2.4和图2.8可得，2013—2023年，阿拉伯国家服务贸易进出口总额呈现波动增长态势，从2013年的4382.56亿美元增长至2023年的7985.98亿美元，但是同比增速波动较大，表明其服务贸易发展受到外部环境影响较大。具体来看，2014年，进出口贸易总额和出口额均显著增长，这主要是因为2014年全球经济复苏和阿拉伯旅游业发展等。2015—2016年，服务贸易进出口总额受到地区冲突的影响连续两年下降。2017—2019年均呈现上升趋势。2020年受到新冠疫情全球蔓延的冲击，旅游业、运输业等服务贸易受到重创，导致阿拉伯国家服务贸易总额、出口额和进口额均大幅下降。2021—2022年，服务贸易出现强劲反弹，与全球经济复苏、国际油价上涨和地区旅游业复苏有关。2023年增速相对放缓，但仍呈现增长态势。

表2.4　2013—2023年阿拉伯国家服务贸易进出口额及增长速度

| 年份 | 进出口贸易 金额（亿美元） | 同比（%） | 出口贸易 金额（亿美元） | 同比（%） | 进口贸易 金额（亿美元） | 同比（%） | 净出口额 金额（亿美元） | 同比（%） |
|---|---|---|---|---|---|---|---|---|
| 2013 | 4382.56 | 3.64 | 1373.41 | 0.15 | 3009.15 | 5.31 | -1635.74 | 10.08 |
| 2014 | 5454.52 | 24.46 | 1850.14 | 34.71 | 3604.38 | 19.78 | -1754.24 | 7.24 |
| 2015 | 5244.79 | -3.85 | 1870.39 | 1.09 | 3374.40 | -6.38 | -1504.01 | -14.26 |
| 2016 | 4981.83 | -5.01 | 1898.10 | 1.48 | 3083.73 | -8.61 | -1185.63 | -21.17 |
| 2017 | 5368.93 | 7.77 | 2086.13 | 9.91 | 3282.80 | 6.46 | -1196.67 | 0.93 |
| 2018 | 5764.12 | 7.36 | 2270.00 | 8.81 | 3494.12 | 6.44 | -1224.12 | 2.29 |
| 2019 | 6150.80 | 6.71 | 2528.69 | 11.40 | 3622.11 | 3.66 | -1093.42 | -10.68 |
| 2020 | 4522.85 | -26.47 | 1854.96 | -26.64 | 2667.89 | -26.34 | -812.93 | -25.65 |
| 2021 | 5470.11 | 20.94 | 2299.94 | 23.99 | 3170.17 | 18.83 | -870.23 | 7.05 |
| 2022 | 7294.91 | 33.36 | 3521.42 | 53.11 | 3773.49 | 19.03 | -252.07 | -71.03 |
| 2023 | 7985.98 | 9.47 | 3909.19 | 11.01 | 4076.79 | 8.04 | -167.60 | -33.51 |

资料来源：根据WTO（世界贸易组织）网站数据整理计算。本数据已更新至最新版本（更新日志查询网址：https：//stats.wto.org/inventory/en）。

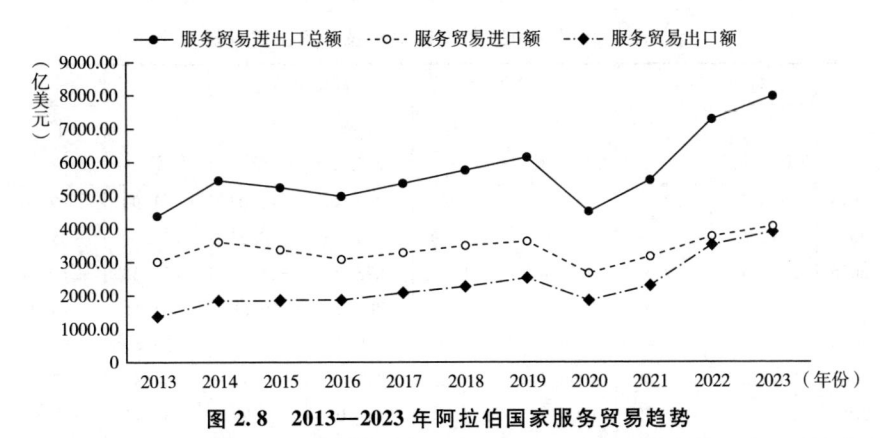

**图 2.8　2013—2023 年阿拉伯国家服务贸易趋势**

资料来源：根据 WTO（世界贸易组织）网站数据整理计算。本数据已更新至最新版本（更新日志查询网址：https://stats.wto.org/inventory/en）。

## 2.3　中国与阿拉伯国家贸易发展状况

双边贸易规模持续扩大，呈现波动上升趋势，见表 2.5。2013 年，中国对阿贸易额为 2388.97 亿美元，2021 年突破 3000 亿美元，2022 年达到 4314.42 亿美元。其间，2015、2016 年贸易额出现了显著下降，分别下降了 19.32% 和 15.56%，这主要是因为全球大宗商品特别是能源价格的下跌造成的。此后，在 2017—2019 年，随着全球经济复苏和中阿在基建和能源领域的合作深化，中阿贸易重回增长轨道。2020 年，新冠疫情导致全球贸易受阻，中阿贸易额亦随之下滑。但随后在 2021 年和 2022 年达到历史峰值，显示出极强的复苏能力。

双边贸易增速较快，引人瞩目。2013—2022 年，中国对阿拉伯国家的平均贸易增速高出中国对外贸易增速 1 个百分点，达到 6.78%，平均增速也高于中国对"一带一路"共建国家的平均增速。2021、2022 年中阿贸易增速尤为突出，分别为 36.29%、31.95%，取得历史性突破，显示出双方贸易增长的强劲势头。然而，2023 年受全球经济下行和中国经济结构性转型的影响，贸易额再次出现回落，呈现负增长。

表 2.5 2013—2023 年中国对阿拉伯国家贸易额

| 年份 | 进出口贸易 金额（亿美元） | 进出口贸易 同比（%） | 出口贸易 金额（亿美元） | 出口贸易 同比（%） | 进口贸易 金额（亿美元） | 进口贸易 同比（%） | 净出口额 金额（亿美元） | 净出口额 同比（%） |
|---|---|---|---|---|---|---|---|---|
| 2013 | 2388.97 | 7.51 | 1013.52 | 4.88 | 1375.45 | 11.03 | -361.93 | -9.20 |
| 2014 | 2510.51 | 5.09 | 1138.21 | 12.30 | 1372.30 | -0.23 | -234.09 | -35.32 |
| 2015 | 2025.41 | -19.32 | 1150.40 | 1.07 | 875.01 | -36.24 | 275.38 | -217.64 |
| 2016 | 1710.29 | -15.56 | 1006.74 | -12.49 | 703.56 | -19.59 | 303.18 | 10.09 |
| 2017 | 1917.57 | 12.12 | 986.73 | -1.99 | 930.84 | 32.30 | 55.89 | -81.57 |
| 2018 | 2442.26 | 27.36 | 1048.70 | 6.28 | 1393.56 | 49.71 | -344.85 | -717.05 |
| 2019 | 2667.00 | 9.20 | 1203.94 | 14.80 | 1463.05 | 4.99 | -259.11 | -24.86 |
| 2020 | 2399.26 | -10.04 | 1228.56 | 2.04 | 1170.70 | -19.98 | 57.85 | -122.33 |
| 2021 | 3269.85 | 36.29 | 1441.05 | 17.30 | 1828.81 | 56.21 | -387.76 | -770.24 |
| 2022 | 4314.42 | 31.95 | 1731.73 | 20.17 | 2582.69 | 41.22 | -850.97 | 119.46 |
| 2023 | 3981.27 | -7.72 | 1812.89 | 4.69 | 2168.38 | -16.04 | -355.49 | -58.23 |

注：以中国为报告国。

分类依据：HS2007。

资料来源：根据联合国国际贸易数据库数据整理计算。本数据已更新至最新版本（更新日志查询网址：https：//wits.worldbank.org/WITS/WITS/Support%20Materials/TariffDataRefresh.aspx?Page=TariffDataRefresh）。

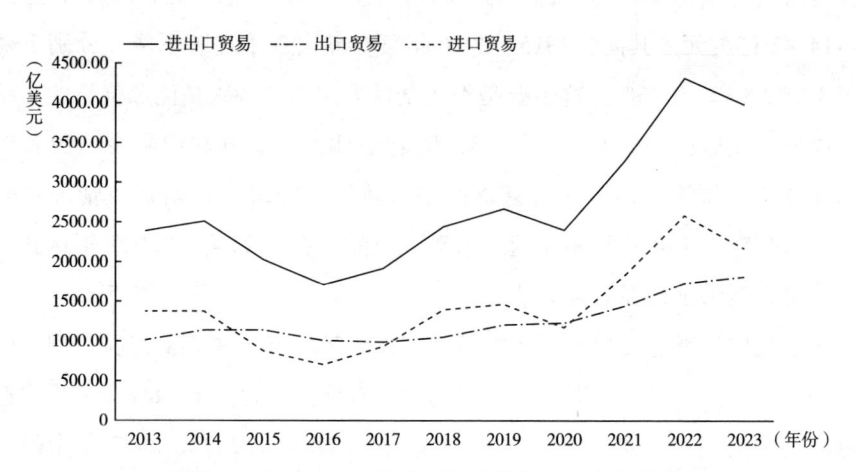

图 2.9 2013—2023 年中国与阿拉伯国家贸易趋势

注：以中国为报告国。

分类依据：HS2007。

资料来源：根据联合国国际贸易数据库数据整理计算。本数据已更新至最新版本（更新日志查询网址：https：//wits.worldbank.org/WITS/WITS/Support%20Materials/TariffDataRefresh.aspx?Page=TariffDataRefresh）。

### 2.3.1 中国对阿拉伯国家出口贸易发展

2013—2023年,中国对阿拉伯国家出口贸易整体呈现明显增长态势,见表2.5。2013年出口额为1013.52亿美元,至2023年已扩张至1812.89亿美元,中国与阿拉伯国家之间的贸易实现了跨越式发展,但出口增速呈现阶段性特征。在2014年增速达到12.30%之后,出现波动下行,2016年降幅达12.49%,自2018年起增速回升,并在2022年达到20.17%增速。这种增速的波动反映出多种因素对贸易的影响,如全球经济周期、地缘政治稳定性和贸易政策等。

2013年,中国在阿拉伯国家的主要出口贸易伙伴分别是阿联酋、沙特、埃及、伊拉克、阿尔及利亚等国家,其中,对阿联酋和沙特出口占比较大,占整个对阿拉伯国家出口的51.46%(见表2.6)。2023年,贸易格局变化不大,而且对出口占比进一步提高。这说明中国对阿拉伯国家的出口市场比较集中。

表2.6 中国在阿拉伯国家的主要出口贸易伙伴

| 排名 | 2013年 国家 | 出口额（亿美元） | 占比（%） | 2023年 国家 | 出口额（亿美元） | 占比（%） |
| --- | --- | --- | --- | --- | --- | --- |
| 1 | 阿联酋 | 334.11 | 32.97 | 阿联酋 | 556.83 | 30.72 |
| 2 | 沙特 | 187.40 | 18.49 | 沙特 | 428.55 | 23.64 |
| 3 | 埃及 | 83.63 | 8.25 | 埃及 | 149.35 | 8.24 |
| 4 | 伊拉克 | 68.94 | 6.80 | 伊拉克 | 142.86 | 7.88 |
| 5 | 阿尔及利亚 | 60.24 | 5.94 | 阿尔及利亚 | 94.58 | 5.22 |
| 6 | 约旦 | 34.35 | 3.39 | 摩洛哥 | 64.54 | 3.56 |
| 7 | 摩洛哥 | 32.72 | 3.23 | 科威特 | 52.25 | 2.88 |
| 8 | 利比亚 | 28.35 | 2.80 | 约旦 | 50.81 | 2.80 |
| 9 | 科威特 | 26.76 | 2.64 | 利比亚 | 39.01 | 2.15 |
| 10 | 黎巴嫩 | 24.91 | 2.46 | 阿曼 | 37.98 | 2.10 |
| 11 | 苏丹 | 23.98 | 2.37 | 卡塔尔 | 36.36 | 2.01 |

注：以中国为报告国。

分类依据：HS2007。

资料来源：根据联合国国际贸易数据库数据整理计算。本数据已更新至最新版本（更新日志查询网址：https://wits.worldbank.org/WITS/WITS/Support%20Materials/TariffDataRefresh.aspx?Page=TariffDataRefresh）。

海合会是中国在阿最重要的出口贸易伙伴。2013 年，中国对海合会的出口额就占中国对阿出口总额的 58.88%，到 2023 年达到 62.19%，这表明海合会国家一直占据中阿出口贸易的主导地位，见表 2.7。

表 2.7　中国对海合会国家出口额占中阿出口总额比重

| 年份 | 中国对海合会国家出口额 金额（亿美元） | 中国对阿拉伯国家出口额 金额（亿美元） | 中国对海合会国家出口额占中阿贸易出口额比重 占比（%） |
| --- | --- | --- | --- |
| 2013 | 596.77 | 1013.52 | 58.88 |
| 2014 | 685.90 | 1138.21 | 60.26 |
| 2015 | 678.10 | 1150.40 | 58.94 |
| 2016 | 561.73 | 1006.74 | 55.80 |
| 2017 | 551.13 | 986.73 | 55.85 |
| 2018 | 568.74 | 1048.70 | 54.23 |
| 2019 | 680.40 | 1203.94 | 56.51 |
| 2020 | 707.80 | 1228.56 | 57.61 |
| 2021 | 852.41 | 1441.05 | 59.15 |
| 2022 | 1067.88 | 1731.73 | 61.67 |
| 2023 | 1127.44 | 1812.89 | 62.19 |

注：以中国为报告国。

分类依据：HS2007。

资料来源：根据联合国国际贸易数据库数据整理计算。本数据已更新至最新版本（更新日志查询网址：https://wits.worldbank.org/WITS/WITS/Support%20Materials/TariffDataRefresh.aspx?Page=TariffDataRefresh）。

中国对阿拉伯国家出口商品结构不断优化，反映出中国制造业结构的升级以及阿拉伯国家需求的多元化，见表 2.8。

中国对阿拉伯国家的出口以制成品为主，占据主导地位，与阿拉伯国家形成高度的贸易互补性。具体来看，机械设备和电气产品（HS 84-85）始终是中国对阿拉伯国家出口的最大宗商品，其出口额从 2013 年的 290.84 亿美元增长至 2023 年的 590.76 亿美元，规模扩张显著，占比也由

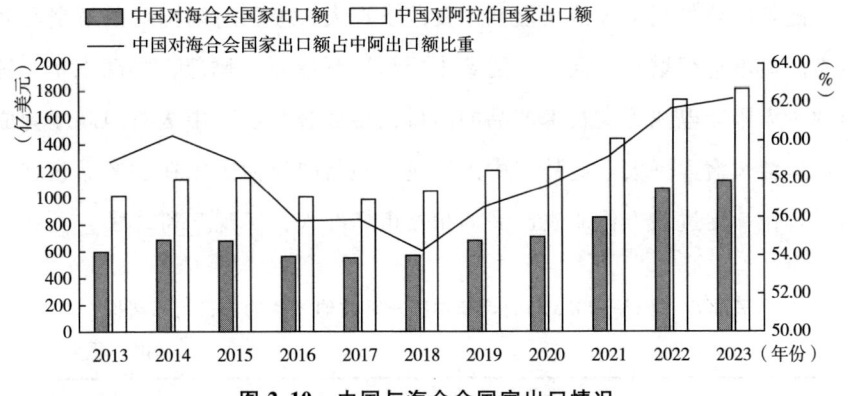

图 2.10　中国与海合会国家出口情况

注：以中国为报告国。
分类依据：HS2007。
资料来源：根据联合国国际贸易数据库数据整理计算。本数据已更新至最新版本（更新日志查询网址：https：//wits.worldbank.org/WITS/WITS/Support% 20Materials/TariffDataRefresh.aspx? Page＝TariffDataRefresh）。

2013 年的 28.70% 提升至 2023 年的 32.59%，表明中国在该领域的技术和产品竞争力日益增强。纺织和服装（HS 50-63）作为传统出口产品，虽然规模相对稳定，但占比持续下降，从 2013 年的 20.20% 降至 2023 年的 11.16%。杂项制品（HS 90-99）、金属产品（HS 72-83）、塑料和橡胶产品（HS 39-40）以及运输设备（HS 86-89）等制成品的出口规模显著扩张，表明中国制造业结构正在朝着多元化和高附加值方向发展。值得注意的是，运输设备在出口总额中的占比从 2013 年的 5.57% 增长至 2023 年的 8.83%，反映出中国汽车、轨道交通等高端制造行业在阿拉伯国家市场取得了显著进展。

另外，出口结构呈现多元化趋势，但部分产品面临挑战。除了上述主要制成品外，中国还向阿拉伯国家出口矿石和玻璃（HS 68-71）、鞋靴类产品（HS 64-67）、木及木制品（HS 44-49）、皮革和毛皮制品（HS 41-43），以及蔬菜（HS 06-15）、食品（HS 16-24）等农产品。然而，矿石和玻璃出口额出现下降，化学制品占比也在降低，表明中国在这些领域的出口面临一定的竞争压力和挑战。

随着阿拉伯国家经济发展和消费需求扩大，中国对阿出口的消费品和资本品需求持续增长。同时，随着中国高端制造业的崛起，电动汽车、锂电池、太阳能电池等高技术产品的出口也将显著增加，中国对阿高端制成品出口增长潜力巨大。此外，中国还应加强与阿拉伯国家在农产品领域的贸易合作，促进双方优质农产品的相互市场准入，实现互利共赢。

表 2.8　2013—2023 年每两年中国对阿拉伯国家的出口商品结构

单位：亿美元

| 产品编码 | 大类产品名称 | 2013年出口额 | 2015年出口额 | 2017年出口额 | 2019年出口额 | 2021年出口额 | 2023年出口额 |
|---|---|---|---|---|---|---|---|
| 84-85 | 机械设备和电气产品 | 290.84 | 340.91 | 319.16 | 368.34 | 438.82 | 590.76 |
| 50-63 | 纺织和服装 | 204.75 | 219.02 | 179.74 | 192.22 | 201.91 | 202.38 |
| 90-99 | 杂项制品 | 97.44 | 109.76 | 95.74 | 127.33 | 180.29 | 196.56 |
| 72-83 | 金属产品 | 113.78 | 138.93 | 117.85 | 145.80 | 169.08 | 245.08 |
| 39-40 | 塑料和橡胶产品 | 64.38 | 64.25 | 59.15 | 76.53 | 96.60 | 121.81 |
| 86-89 | 运输设备 | 56.46 | 54.52 | 36.52 | 72.59 | 94.90 | 160.02 |
| 28-38 | 化学制品 | 28.16 | 33.45 | 33.16 | 41.88 | 85.23 | 80.22 |
| 68-71 | 矿石和玻璃 | 52.85 | 64.14 | 42.06 | 57.01 | 53.54 | 60.89 |
| 64-67 | 鞋靴类产品 | 34.85 | 44.74 | 32.71 | 37.61 | 39.64 | 43.22 |
| 44-49 | 木及木制品 | 23.89 | 29.71 | 25.00 | 29.08 | 29.92 | 40.22 |
| 41-43 | 皮革和毛皮制品 | 16.75 | 19.08 | 15.17 | 18.51 | 15.62 | 20.72 |
| 06-15 | 蔬菜 | 11.15 | 11.42 | 11.56 | 14.34 | 14.98 | 18.03 |
| 27-27 | 矿物燃料和矿物油 | 7.21 | 7.76 | 6.90 | 10.03 | 9.62 | 15.70 |
| 16-24 | 食品 | 8.49 | 8.37 | 8.50 | 9.38 | 8.03 | 14.51 |
| 25-26 | 矿产品 | 0.99 | 2.51 | 1.36 | 1.13 | 1.71 | 1.42 |
| 01-05 | 动物产品 | 1.51 | 1.84 | 2.14 | 2.14 | 1.17 | 1.33 |

注：以中国为报告国。

分类依据：HS2007。

资料来源：根据联合国国际贸易数据库数据整理计算。本数据已更新至最新版本（更新日志查询网址：https://wits.worldbank.org/WITS/WITS/Support%20Materials/TariffDataRefresh.aspx?Page=TariffDataRefresh）。

### 2.3.2 中国对阿拉伯国家进口贸易发展

2013—2023 年,中国对阿拉伯国家进口规模总体呈现波动中不断扩大的态势,增速波动较大(如表 2.5 所示)。一方面,进口额增幅较大。2013 年,中国自阿进口额为 1375.45 亿美元,2023 年达到 2168.38 亿美元,增长了 57.65%,增幅较大,这表明中国对阿拉伯国家商品的进口需求持续增加,这与中国经济的持续发展、国内消费能力的提升以及对能源等大宗商品的需求密切相关。另一方面,进口额增速波动较大。进口额增速在 2013—2019 年呈现明显的波动性。2013 年进口额增速高达 11.03%,2015、2016 年却分别出现 -36.24%、-19.59% 的急剧下滑,2017、2018 年进口额增速则又高达 32.30% 和 49.71%,随后在 2019 年增速下降至 4.99%,波动明显。2022 年进口额达到 2582.69 亿美元的峰值,同比增长 41.22%,2023 年增速下滑至 -16.04%。

中国在阿拉伯国家主要的进口伙伴是沙特、阿联酋、伊拉克、阿曼、卡塔尔和科威特等国家。2013 年排名前 5 位的分别是沙特、阿曼、伊拉克、阿联酋和科威特,2023 年阿联酋的排名上升到第二位,进口比重从 2013 年的 9.32% 上升到 2023 年的 18.13%,上升幅度最大,卡塔尔超过科威特上升到第五位,进口比重有所增大,同时沙特和阿曼的进口额占比有所下降。

表 2.9 中国在阿拉伯国家的主要进口贸易伙伴

单位:亿美元

| 排名 | 2013 年 | | | 2023 年 | | |
|---|---|---|---|---|---|---|
| | 国家 | 进口额 | 占比(%) | 国家 | 进口额 | 占比(%) |
| 1 | 沙特 | 534.51 | 38.86 | 沙特 | 643.61 | 29.68 |
| 2 | 阿曼 | 210.41 | 15.30 | 阿联酋 | 393.09 | 18.13 |
| 3 | 伊拉克 | 179.85 | 13.08 | 伊拉克 | 354.66 | 16.36 |
| 4 | 阿联酋 | 128.24 | 9.32 | 阿曼 | 312.79 | 14.43 |
| 5 | 科威特 | 95.87 | 6.97 | 卡塔尔 | 209.28 | 9.65 |

续表

| 排名 | 2013 年 | | | 2023 年 | | |
|---|---|---|---|---|---|---|
| | 国家 | 进口额 | 占比（%） | 国家 | 进口额 | 占比（%） |
| 6 | 卡塔尔 | 84.63 | 6.15 | 科威特 | 171.65 | 7.92 |
| 7 | 也门 | 30.61 | 2.23 | 利比亚 | 21.99 | 1.01 |
| 8 | 阿尔及利亚 | 21.65 | 1.57 | 毛里塔尼亚 | 11.90 | 0.55 |
| 9 | 苏丹 | 21.00 | 1.53 | 摩洛哥 | 9.80 | 0.45 |
| 10 | 利比亚 | 20.39 | 1.48 | 苏丹 | 8.82 | 0.41 |
| 11 | 埃及 | 18.52 | 1.35 | 埃及 | 8.81 | 0.41 |

注：以中国为报告国。
分类依据：HS2007。
资料来源：根据联合国国际贸易数据库数据整理计算。本数据已更新至最新版本（更新日志查询网址：https：//wits.worldbank.org/WITS/WITS/Support% 20Materials/TariffDataRefresh.aspx?Page＝TariffDataRefresh）。

海合会在中阿进口贸易中占据重要地位，一直是中国自阿拉伯国家进口的主要来源地。2013 年中国自海合会国家的进口额占中国自阿拉伯国家进口总额的 76.83%，之后这一比重不断上升，到 2017 年达到 78.33%。2018 年出现小幅下降，到 2022 年又大幅提高，达到 80.93%。其间，来自海合会国家的进口额始终占据中国自阿进口总额的大部分，占比均超过 75%（见表 2.10 和图 2.11）。

表 2.10　中国自海合会国家进口额占中阿贸易进口额比重

| 年份 | 中国自海合会国家进口额 金额（亿美元） | 中国自阿拉伯国家进口额 金额（亿美元） | 中国自海合会国家进口额在对阿进口总额中的比重 占比（%） |
|---|---|---|---|
| 2013 | 1056.70 | 1375.45 | 76.83 |
| 2014 | 1065.93 | 1372.30 | 77.67 |
| 2015 | 688.05 | 875.01 | 78.63 |
| 2016 | 561.08 | 703.56 | 79.75 |
| 2017 | 729.15 | 930.84 | 78.33 |

续表

| 年份 | 中国自海合会国家进口额 金额（亿美元） | 中国自阿拉伯国家进口额 金额（亿美元） | 中国自海合会国家进口额在对阿进口总额中的比重 占比（%） |
| --- | --- | --- | --- |
| 2018 | 1056.31 | 1393.56 | 75.80 |
| 2019 | 1115.39 | 1463.05 | 76.24 |
| 2020 | 909.70 | 1170.70 | 77.71 |
| 2021 | 1454.93 | 1828.81 | 79.56 |
| 2022 | 2090.12 | 2582.69 | 80.93 |
| 2023 | 1732.33 | 2168.38 | 79.89 |

注：以中国为报告国。

分类依据：HS2007。

资料来源：根据联合国国际贸易数据库数据整理计算。本数据已更新至最新版本（更新日志查询网址：https://wits.worldbank.org/WITS/WITS/Support%20Materials/TariffDataRefresh.aspx?Page=TariffDataRefresh）。

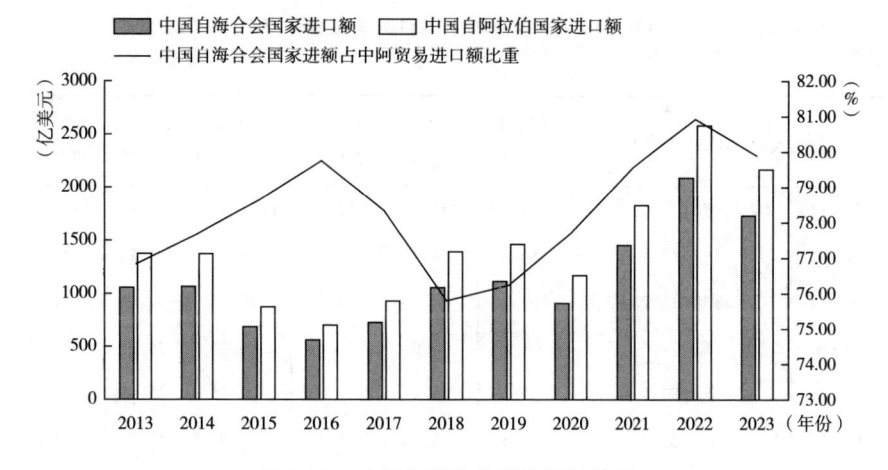

图 2.11 中国自海合会国家进口情况

注：以中国为报告国。

分类依据：HS2007。

资料来源：根据联合国国际贸易数据库数据整理计算。本数据已更新至最新版本（更新日志查询网址：https://wits.worldbank.org/WITS/WITS/Support%20Materials/TariffDataRefresh.aspx?Page=TariffDataRefresh）。

中国对阿拉伯国家的进口商品结构在 2013—2023 年呈现相对稳定的特征。中国对阿进口的主要大类产品是矿物燃料和矿物油、化学产品、塑料和橡胶产品、矿产品、金属产品等商品。其中，矿物燃料和矿物油占据绝对份额，重点商品是原油。矿物燃料和矿物油的进口额从 2013 年的 1173.80 亿美元上升到 2023 年的 1926.25 亿美元，增幅达 64.10%。2013 年自阿拉伯国家进口的矿物燃料和矿物油的进口额占中国自阿拉伯国家进口总额的 85.34%，2023 年这一比重上升到 88.83%，这集中反映了阿拉伯国家的资源禀赋优势，也体现了中国经济快速发展中对能源需求巨大，二者具有极大的互补性。总体来看，机械、纺织等商品的进口额相对较小，这反映了阿拉伯国家制造业相对薄弱。值得注意的是，蔬菜（HS 06-15）、食品（HS 16-24）、机械设备和电器产品（HS 84-85）等商品的进口额呈现出较为明显的增长趋势，反映了中国消费升级和对多元化商品需求的增加。

表 2.11　2013—2023 年每两年中国自阿拉伯国家的进口商品结构

单位：亿美元

| 产品编码 | 大类产品名称 | 2013年进口额 | 2015年进口额 | 2017年进口额 | 2019年进口额 | 2021年进口额 | 2023年进口额 |
| --- | --- | --- | --- | --- | --- | --- | --- |
| 27-27 | 矿物燃料和矿物油 | 1173.80 | 701.00 | 732.10 | 1212.33 | 1524.41 | 1926.25 |
| 28-38 | 化学产品 | 86.67 | 74.42 | 81.27 | 98.88 | 106.91 | 81.32 |
| 39-40 | 塑料和橡胶产品 | 63.24 | 60.33 | 75.40 | 91.24 | 92.74 | 69.14 |
| 25-26 | 矿产品 | 31.07 | 20.96 | 22.11 | 26.85 | 36.33 | 31.83 |
| 72-83 | 金属产品 | 7.83 | 5.41 | 4.82 | 9.76 | 35.69 | 22.10 |
| 06-15 | 蔬菜 | 4.19 | 2.66 | 3.53 | 6.85 | 12.39 | 11.03 |
| 84-85 | 机械设备和电器产品 | 2.54 | 3.16 | 3.92 | 4.38 | 5.91 | 9.17 |
| 68-71 | 矿石和玻璃 | 1.13 | 2.58 | 1.24 | 2.67 | 2.54 | 4.99 |
| 50-63 | 纺织和服装 | 2.84 | 2.93 | 3.48 | 4.18 | 3.76 | 4.74 |
| 16-24 | 食品 | 0.24 | 0.63 | 1.47 | 2.19 | 5.15 | 4.68 |
| 01-05 | 动物产品 | 0.50 | 0.19 | 0.23 | 2.16 | 1.05 | 1.58 |

续表

| 产品编码 | 大类产品名称 | 2013年进口额 | 2015年进口额 | 2017年进口额 | 2019年进口额 | 2021年进口额 | 2023年进口额 |
|---|---|---|---|---|---|---|---|
| 90—99 | 杂项制品 | 0.78 | 0.14 | 0.31 | 0.45 | 0.69 | 0.65 |
| 41—43 | 皮革和毛皮制品 | 0.31 | 0.38 | 0.44 | 0.39 | 0.57 | 0.54 |
| 86—89 | 运输设备 | 0.13 | 0.10 | 0.16 | 0.21 | 0.19 | 0.18 |
| 44—49 | 木及木制品 | 0.15 | 0.07 | 0.32 | 0.48 | 0.44 | 0.15 |
| 64—67 | 鞋靴类产品 | 0.03 | 0.07 | 0.04 | 0.05 | 0.04 | 0.05 |

注：以中国为报告国。

分类依据：HS2007。

资料来源：根据联合国国际贸易数据库数据整理计算。本数据已更新至最新版本（更新日志查询网址：https://wits.worldbank.org/WITS/WITS/Support%20Materials/TariffDataRefresh.aspx?Page=TariffDataRefresh）。

中国与阿拉伯国家的能源进口贸易在双方贸易格局中占据决定性地位，其中原油和天然气是最重要的进口商品。2013年原油进口额为1046.58亿美元，2015—2017年出现较大幅度的下降，主要是原油价格的下降。之后，进口额不断上升，2022年达到历史高点1997.84亿美元，2023年略有下降。从增速来看，2015—2016年出现显著下降，但是2017年后出现增长，2018年增速超过55%，2021年增速达到59.47%，但是2023年又出现负增长。中国主要从卡塔尔进口天然气，历经十余年，中国自阿拉伯国家天然气进口额出现了倍增，2013年仅为105.66亿美元，2022年达到历史峰值248.97亿美元，2023年也超过了200亿美元。天然气进口增速与原油的趋势类似，在2021年达到高点74.81%，同样在2023年出现负增长。

表2.12 2013—2023年中国对阿拉伯国家能源进口贸易额

| 年份 | 原油 金额（亿美元） | 原油 同比（%） | 天然气 金额（亿美元） | 天然气 同比（%） |
|---|---|---|---|---|
| 2013 | 1046.58 | 1.23 | 105.66 | 33.65 |
| 2014 | 1028.31 | −1.75 | 121.87 | 15.34 |
| 2015 | 613.11 | −40.38 | 71.56 | −41.28 |

续表

| 年份 | 原油 | | 天然气 | |
|---|---|---|---|---|
| | 金额（亿美元） | 同比（%） | 金额（亿美元） | 同比（%） |
| 2016 | 473.04 | -22.85 | 63.33 | -11.50 |
| 2017 | 616.11 | 30.24 | 94.85 | 49.77 |
| 2018 | 960.98 | 55.98 | 136.29 | 43.68 |
| 2019 | 1060.58 | 10.36 | 125.52 | -7.90 |
| 2020 | 832.79 | -21.48 | 87.11 | -30.60 |
| 2021 | 1328.07 | 59.47 | 152.29 | 74.81 |
| 2022 | 1997.84 | 50.43 | 248.97 | 63.48 |
| 2023 | 1649.19 | -17.45 | 222.65 | -10.57 |

注：以中国为报告国。
分类依据：HS2007。
资料来源：根据联合国国际贸易数据库数据整理计算。本数据已更新至最新版本（更新日志查询网址：https://wits.worldbank.org/WITS/WITS/Support%20Materials/TariffDataRefresh.aspx?Page=TariffDataRefresh）。

2013—2023 年，中国自阿拉伯国家原油进口的主要贸易伙伴是沙特、伊拉克、阿联酋、阿曼、科威特、卡特尔和利比亚等，贸易格局相对稳定。与 2013 年相比，2023 年中国从阿拉伯国家能源进口贸易的市场结构呈现稳健中略带分化的态势，沙特市场份额有较大幅度下降，由 2013 年的 40.48%下降至 2023 年的 32.67%。与此同时，伊拉克和阿联酋的市场份额则实现了显著增长，分别从 2013 年的 17.10%和 7.99%提升至 2023 年的 21.35%和 16.15%。阿曼的市场份额出现小幅下滑。

表 2.13　中国从阿拉伯国家进口原油情况

单位：亿美元

| | 2013 年 | | 2019 年 | | 2022 年 | | 2023 年 | |
|---|---|---|---|---|---|---|---|---|
| | 金额（亿美元） | 占比（%） | 金额（亿美元） | 占比（%） | 金额（亿美元） | 占比（%） | 金额（亿美元） | 占比（%） |
| 沙特 | 423.68 | 40.48 | 401.75 | 37.88 | 649.72 | 32.52 | 538.78 | 32.67 |
| 阿曼 | 199.32 | 19.05 | 165.79 | 15.63 | 291.58 | 14.59 | 250.39 | 15.18 |

续表

|  | 2013 年 |  | 2019 年 |  | 2022 年 |  | 2023 年 |  |
| --- | --- | --- | --- | --- | --- | --- | --- | --- |
|  | 金额（亿美元） | 占比（%） | 金额（亿美元） | 占比（%） | 金额（亿美元） | 占比（%） | 金额（亿美元） | 占比（%） |
| 伊拉克 | 179.00 | 17.10 | 238.50 | 22.49 | 390.93 | 19.57 | 352.11 | 21.35 |
| 阿联酋 | 83.67 | 7.99 | 75.27 | 7.10 | 322.47 | 16.14 | 266.40 | 16.15 |
| 科威特 | 72.77 | 6.95 | 108.14 | 10.20 | 246.03 | 12.31 | 152.19 | 9.23 |
| 利比亚 | 20.31 | 1.94 | 48.16 | 4.54 | 29.33 | 1.47 | 21.96 | 1.33 |
| 也门 | 20.05 | 1.92 | 8.61 | 0.81 | 6.17 | 0.31 | — | — |
| 苏丹 | 19.00 | 1.82 | 3.16 | 0.30 | 0.61 | 0.03 | 1.05 | 0.06 |
| 阿尔及利亚 | 16.20 | 1.55 | 2.99 | 0.28 | — | — | 0.99 | 0.06 |
| 埃及 | 10.51 | 1.00 | 3.90 | 0.37 | 1.25 | 0.06 | — | — |
| 卡塔尔 | 0.99 | 0.09 | 4.32 | 0.41 | 59.76 | 2.99 | 65.32 | 3.96 |

注：以中国为报告国。
分类依据：HS2007。
资料来源：根据联合国国际贸易数据库数据整理计算。本数据已更新至最新版本（更新日志查询网址：https://wits.worldbank.org/WITS/WITS/Support%20Materials/TariffDataRefresh.aspx?Page=TariffDataRefresh）。

从中国原油进口全局来看，阿拉伯国家一直是中国最大的原油进口来源地，且进口数量占比从 2013 年的 47.65%提升至 2023 年的 48.84%（如图 2.12 所示），表明中国与阿拉伯国家在能源领域的合作进一步加深。从具体国家来看，中国自沙特、伊拉克、阿联酋、阿曼和科威特的进口数量不断上升，2023 年这些国家在中国从世界进口原油排名中分列第二、三、五、六、九位。

表 2.14　中国从世界进口原油前十位国家

| 排名 | 2013 年 |  |  | 2023 年 |  |  |
| --- | --- | --- | --- | --- | --- | --- |
|  | 国家 | 进口数量（万吨） | 占比（%） | 国家 | 进口数量（万吨） | 占比（%） |
| 1 | 沙特 | 4236.81 | 19.29 | 俄罗斯 | 6067.92 | 17.97 |
| 2 | 安哥拉 | 3180.86 | 14.48 | 沙特 | 5387.76 | 15.96 |
| 3 | 阿曼 | 1993.21 | 9.07 | 伊拉克 | 3521.13 | 10.43 |
| 4 | 俄罗斯 | 1974.26 | 8.99 | 马来西亚 | 2861.15 | 8.47 |

续表

| 排名 | 2013 年 |  |  | 2023 年 |  |  |
|---|---|---|---|---|---|---|
|  | 国家 | 进口数量（万吨） | 占比（%） | 国家 | 进口数量（万吨） | 占比（%） |
| 5 | 伊拉克 | 1789.98 | 8.15 | 阿联酋 | 2664.04 | 7.89 |
| 6 | 伊朗 | 1688.76 | 7.69 | 阿曼 | 2503.87 | 7.42 |
| 7 | 委内瑞拉 | 1014.89 | 4.62 | 巴西 | 2295.29 | 6.80 |
| 8 | 哈萨克斯坦 | 937.55 | 4.27 | 安哥拉 | 1854.75 | 5.49 |
| 9 | 阿联酋 | 836.73 | 3.81 | 科威特 | 1521.88 | 4.51 |
| 10 | 科威特 | 727.73 | 3.31 | 美国 | 908.78 | 2.69 |
|  | 阿拉伯国家 | 10465.78 | 47.65 | 阿拉伯国家 | 16491.88 | 48.84 |

注：以中国为报告国。

分类依据：HS2007。

资料来源：根据联合国国际贸易数据库数据整理计算。本数据已更新至最新版本（更新日志查询网址：https：//wits.worldbank.org/WITS/WITS/Support%20Materials/TariffDataRefresh.aspx?Page=TariffDataRefresh）。

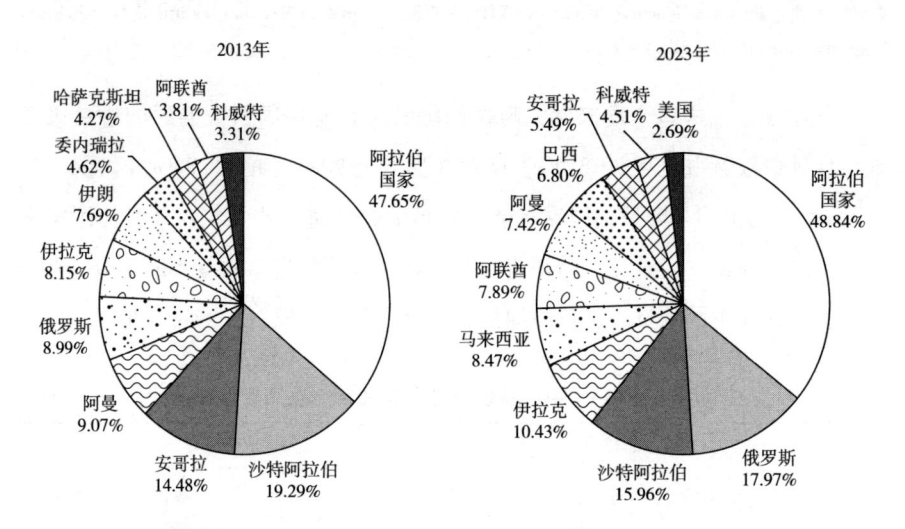

**图 2.12　2013 年与 2023 年中国前十位进口原油贸易伙伴**

注：以中国为报告国。

分类依据：HS2007。

资料来源：根据联合国国际贸易数据库数据整理计算。本数据已更新至最新版本（更新日志查询网址：https：//wits.worldbank.org/WITS/WITS/Support%20Materials/TariffDataRefresh.aspx?Page=TariffDataRefresh）。

## 2.4 中国与阿拉伯国家贸易合作发展趋势与展望

### 2.4.1 经济巨大互补性为中阿贸易持续发展奠定深厚基础

资源禀赋与产业能力双向赋能。中国作为全球第二大经济体，拥有庞大的制造业基础和不断增长的能源需求。而阿拉伯国家，特别是海合会成员，如沙特、阿联酋和卡塔尔等国则拥有丰富的油气资源，是全球重要的能源供应基地。这种资源禀赋与产业结构的巨大互补性，为中阿贸易持续深入发展奠定了基础。

据阿拉伯货币基金组织发布的《2021年阿拉伯经济报告》，早在2021年，阿拉伯国家就拥有全球55.7%的已探明石油储量和26.5%的天然气储量。而中国作为全球最大的能源消费国，《中国油气产业发展分析与展望报告蓝皮书（2022—2023）》显示石油对外依存度长期维持在70%以上，天然气依存度超过40%。2022年中阿能源贸易额高达2246.82亿美元，2023年略有下降，但仍有1872.46亿美元，沙特是中国最大原油供应国。这种能源供需的结构性互补，通过长期供应协议和战略储备合作得到制度性保障。以中沙延布炼厂项目为例，延布炼厂于2016年1月正式投入商业运营，2023年10月23日在第七届沙特未来投资倡议峰会期间，中国石化与沙特阿美签署"延布炼厂+"项目合作谅解备忘录，该项目为液化原料转化成化工产品的大型石化项目。

除了传统的能源贸易，中国与阿拉伯国家在工业制成品领域的互补性也日益凸显。中国拥有完备的工业体系和强大的生产能力，能够以具有竞争力的价格向阿拉伯国家出口各类工业制成品，满足其基础设施建设、工业多元化发展和消费升级的需求。中国对阿拉伯国家的工业制成品出口贸易额持续增长，其中机械和运输设备占比不断提升，中国对阿拉伯国家的工业制成品出口贸易额持续增长，其中机械设备和电气产品占比不断提升，其出口额从2013年的290.84亿美元增长至2023年的

590.76亿美元，规模扩张显著，占比也由2013年的28.70%提升至2023年的32.59%，这说明中国正逐步向价值链上游攀升，满足阿拉伯国家对高端设备的需求。

贸易结构的动态优化和互补性深化。中阿贸易结构从垂直分工向水平分工转变。传统的垂直分工模式是中国进口阿拉伯国家的能源和原材料，出口工业制成品。近年来，随着阿拉伯国家工业多元化战略的推进和中国产业结构的升级，双方贸易模式正逐渐向水平分工转变。越来越多的阿拉伯国家开始出口部分工业制成品到中国，例如化工产品和橡胶制品。中国自阿拉伯国家进口的化学产品、塑料和橡胶产品长期占据主要地位，由表2.11可以看出，2023年进口的化学产品在总进口结构中排名第二，进口额为81.32亿美元；塑料橡胶产品排名第三，进口额为69.14亿美元，表明中国与阿拉伯国家在产业链上下游的合作日益密切。同时，随着中国创新能力的提升，对阿拉伯国家的高科技产品出口呈现出快速增长的趋势，这些高科技产品主要集中在机械设备、电子产品和通信等领域，为阿拉伯国家经济转型和产业升级提供了有力支撑。

### 2.4.2　地缘政治格局重构为中阿贸易合作深化带来新机遇

近年来，全球地缘政治格局的深刻变革为中国与阿拉伯国家经贸合作注入了新动力。美国在中东的战略收缩、能源转型压力以及区域安全架构的调整，促使阿拉伯国家加速推进经济多元化并寻求新的合作伙伴。与此同时，中国通过"一带一路"倡议与中阿命运共同体建设，逐步成为阿拉伯国家在政治、经济和安全领域的重要依托。这一地缘政治格局的演变不仅重构了亚欧非大陆的经济联系网络，也为中阿贸易合作深化提供了新的机遇。

美国在中东的战略重心转移削弱了阿拉伯国家对单一外部力量的依赖。美国从阿富汗撤军和减少对传统盟友的安全承诺，使阿拉伯国家普遍采取"向东看"战略，试图通过深化与中国、俄罗斯等大国的合作实现战略自主性。2023年中国斡旋沙特与伊朗恢复外交关系，标志着中国在中东事务中的政治影响力显著提升，也为中阿经贸合作奠定了更加坚实的互信基础。与此同时，中阿贸易额从2013年的2388.97亿美元增长至2023年的3981.27亿美元，十年间增幅约66.65%（见表2.5），双方经贸往来涵盖能源、基础设施、数字经济等诸多领域。

美国对海上运输通道的潜在干预风险，促使中国加速构建中阿陆路运输替代网络。中欧班列的开行量从2013年的80列增加至2023年的17523列①，部分缓解了"马六甲困局"。而阿塞拜疆等兼具里海与黑海地缘优势的国家，成为"陆上丝绸之路"的关键节点。2024年4月，中国与阿塞拜疆共同发表了中阿两国建立全面战略伙伴关系的联合声明。②同年，沙特宣布启动"中阿大陆桥计划"，旨在通过铁路连通波斯湾和地中海，进一步缩短货物运输的周期，降低对传统海运的依赖。

地缘政治重构不仅体现在经济领域，更延伸至安全治理层面。中国通过上合组织、金砖机制等平台，推动与阿拉伯国家在反恐、网络安全等方面的合作。阿塞拜疆在2024年加入上合组织后，其作为外高加索枢纽的战略价值进一步凸显，有助于稳定中亚—西亚运输走廊。2022年中阿峰会提出构建"面向新时代的命运共同体"，双方在尊重主权、反对外部干涉等原则上达成共识，为跨国投资和贸易提供了更稳定的制度环境。中阿技术转移协作网络的建立以及约旦、迪拜等地技术中心的落地，加速了创新要素的跨境流动。

### 2.4.3 供应链优化为提升中阿贸易商品结构提供新动力

在全球价值链重构和区域经济一体化加速的背景下，供应链优化已经成为推动中国与阿拉伯国家贸易高质量发展的新引擎。2023年，中阿贸

---

① 中欧班列网，https://www.crexpress.cn/#/。
② 《中华人民共和国和阿塞拜疆共和国关于建立战略伙伴关系的联合声明》，中华人民共和国中央人民政府网，https://www.gov.cn/yaowen/liebiao/202407/content_6961034.htm，2024年7月3日。

易结构仍然呈现出"中国向阿拉伯国家出口工业制成品，进口能源资源"的单一特征。但通过系统性优化跨境供应链的物流效率、数字化水平和区域协同能力，中阿贸易正逐步突破传统商品结构的路径依赖，为高附加值产品贸易和技术密集型合作开辟新的空间。

物流网络升级重构贸易时空格局。中阿共建的"海陆空铁"立体物流通道显著压缩了跨境运输周期，中远海运在阿联酋哈利法港建设的自动化集装箱码头的水平运输采用"ARMG+SHC"的方式，是中东地区最先进的集装箱码头，自2018年12月开港以来，哈里发港的阿布扎比码头累计完成集装箱作业量超550万TEU，创造了中阿两国合作共建"一带一路"标志性项目新的里程碑式成果。① 陆路运输方面，中欧班列持续扩展物流运输网络，例如2024年7月10日开通的中欧班列郑州至土耳其线路。② 物流网络的升级，促进了生鲜农产品、精密仪器等对运输时效敏感的商品贸易增长。

跨境电商和物流提速助推小商品供应链优化。早期的贸易模式依赖传统海运，耗时长，商品周转效率低。近年来，随着跨境电商平台的兴起和物流基础设施的改善，商品供应链显著优化。义乌是中国最大的小商品集散地，通过跨境电商渠道出口的商品占比显著提升，《2023年义乌市国民经济和社会发展统计公报》中显示，2023年义乌对阿联酋进出口额同比增长11.1%。菜鸟国际快递等物流企业在阿联酋、迪拜等国家设立海外仓，大幅缩短了配送时间，最快可实现"次日达"。

供应链优化推动高附加值产品出口。沙特正在积极推进多元化战略，通过"2030愿景"减少对原油的过度依赖，并大力发展炼化产业

---

① 《中远海运阿布扎比码头：打造中东枢纽港的辉煌与未来》，中国远洋海运集团有限公司网，https://www.coscoshipping.com/col/col6864/art/2024/art_d209f3afff174bb4a9cb4647b3d06ebd.html，2024年11月15日。

② 翟濯：《中欧班列（郑州）首趟南通道"跨两海"线路开通运行》，中国一带一路网，https://www.yidaiyilu.gov.cn/p/0O3H38DR.html，2024年7月11日。

以提高石油资源的附加值。在此背景下，中国石化工程建设有限公司（SEI）作为中石化炼化工程（集团）股份有限公司（SEG，以下简称"中石化炼化工程集团"）的重要组成部分，参与了沙特多个炼化项目的建设，为其提供技术支持和工程服务。2024年6月，中石化炼化工程集团在沙特签署了贾富拉（Jafurah）气田里亚斯液化天然气分馏装置EPC总承包合同，合同金额达33.5亿美元，这是中石化炼化工程集团在沙特承揽的单体合同额最大的项目。[1] 这些项目提高了沙特高附加值化工产品的生产能力，并为沙特对华出口更多元化的石化产品奠定了基础。

供应链重塑助力产业转移。中国—埃及纺织服装产业合作是供应链优化背景下中阿经贸关系转型的典型案例。为降低生产成本并规避贸易壁垒，中国纺织服装企业逐步将生产基地转移至埃及等阿拉伯国家，构建新的供应链体系，推动双边产业合作。埃及政府出台一系列优惠政策，吸引中国企业赴埃投资建厂，2024年12月，全球最大的染色面料与衬衫生产商鲁泰集团宣布在埃及投资3.85亿美元，涵盖纱线生产、织物制造到成衣加工的全产业链，将引入全球顶尖技术，促进当地纺织服装产业的升级与发展。[2]

### 2.4.4　中阿贸易韧性提高为应对复杂风险提供强动能

在全球经济不确定性日益加剧的背景下，中阿贸易所展现出的韧性已经成为应对复杂风险的关键动能。这种韧性不仅体现在贸易规模的稳步增长，更体现在面对外部冲击时所展示出的强大抗风险能力和迅速恢复

---

[1] 沈满芳：《公司签署沙特市场最大单体合同》，中石化炼化工程（集团）股份有限公司网，http://www.segroup.cn/segroup/news/com_news/20240711/news_20240711_633732224252.shtml，2024年7月11日。

[2] 《The World's Largest Producer of Dyed Fabrics and Shirts Explores Establishing a Factory in Egypt》，埃及投资和自由区总局（GAFI），https://www.gafi.gov.eg/English/MediaCenter/News/Pages/The-World%E2%80%99s-Largest-Producer-of-Dyed-Fabrics-and-Shirts-Explores-Establishing-a-Factory-in-Egypt.aspx，2024年12月16日。

能力。

中阿贸易关系具备较强的内在稳定性和自我修复能力。中阿贸易历经4次重大冲击，包括2008年国际金融危机、2014—2016年地区动荡、2020年新冠疫情和2023年全球经济碎片化。虽然每次冲击都给中阿贸易带来一定的负面影响，但就整体而言，中阿贸易韧性呈现出"阶梯式跃升"的阶段性演进规律。经测算，中阿贸易在恢复调整期内，韧性均值较冲击抵御期平均提升6.9%，展现了较强的抗风险能力与恢复潜力。

中阿贸易有较强的风险抵御能力。中阿贸易能够有效抵御外部冲击，离不开双方长期稳定的能源合作关系。中国作为全球主要能源消费国，与沙特等资源丰富的国家建立了牢固的能源供应关系，这为中阿贸易提供了坚实的基石。同时，中国积极推动与阿拉伯国家在基建、制造等领域的产能合作，促进了双方产业结构的升级和互补。这种多元化的合作战略有效分散了贸易风险，增强了中阿贸易的整体韧性。2008年金融危机期间，尽管中阿贸易韧性均值一度下降至0.119，与多数阿拉伯国家的韧性等级偏低，但是随后通过加强能源合作和推动贸易多元化，例如中海油2008年与卡塔尔石油公司签订了合同量200万吨/年，合同期25年的长期协议等一系列举措①，促进中阿贸易迅速走出低谷，实现了恢复性增长。

中阿展现出显著加速的韧性恢复能力。中阿贸易从2008年金融危机到贸易恢复常态，历时5年；而从应对2020年新冠疫情到贸易基本恢复，中阿贸易仅用了2年。这种恢复周期的缩短，主要得益于以下几个方面：能源合作的加强，能源合作是中阿贸易的压舱石，长期稳定的能源供应关系，为中阿贸易提供了坚实的基础；产能合作的拓展，中国企业积极参加阿拉伯国家的工业化进程，在基础设施建设、制造业等领域展开广泛合

---

① 黄新培：《中国海油与卡塔尔石油公司签署长期LNG购销协议》，新华丝路网，https：//www.imsilkroad.com/news/p/464937.html，2021年9月30日。

作，促进了双方产业结构的升级与互补；疫苗合作的推进，疫情防控期间，中阿积极开展疫苗合作、共克时艰，这些举措进一步深化了双方的互信和友谊；数字规则协同的深化，数字经济时代，加强数字规则的协同，有助于促进跨境电商、数字支付等新型贸易模式的发展，为中阿贸易注入新动力。

# 第3章 中阿投资合作专题报告

近年来，中国与阿拉伯国家之间的经济合作迎来前所未有的"投资热潮"，双向投资合作日益紧密。阿拉伯国家能源和资本富集，经济转型发展诉求强烈。中阿双方在双向投资合作质量方面量质齐升，规模体量、领域范围均不断扩大。中阿双向投资合作的一批重大项目已成为推动新时期中阿经贸合作向高质量发展转型升级的标志性工程。2021年以来，中国对阿拉伯国家直接投资流量实现三连增，除直接投资外，中国企业还通过再投资、第三国投资等方式，积极拓展在阿拉伯国家各领域业务，各类投资总量实际超过780亿美元。[①] 同时，阿拉伯国家积极扩展在中国市场的投资布局，增长迅猛。中阿投资领域日益多元化，不仅涵盖油气、建筑业、制造业等传统领域，还扩展到新能源、数字经济、人工智能、生物医药等众多新兴领域。未来，伴随中阿共建高质量"一带一路"，中阿双向投资仍有很大潜力。

## 3.1 中国对阿拉伯国家直接投资状况

2025年1月，联合国贸易和发展组织发布最新一期《全球投资趋势监测报告》，2024年，全球FDI总额达1.4万亿美元，表面上同比增长

---

[①] 商务部国际贸易经济合作研究院：《中国与阿拉伯国家经贸合作回顾与展望2024》，2024年11月，第2页。

11%。然而，若剔除欧洲通道经济体的金融流动，全球FDI实际下降约8%。① 2024年中国对外非金融类直接投资额10245亿元人民币，比上年增长11.7%，折合1438亿美元，增长10.5%。② 在全球外国直接投资处于低迷、地缘政治冲突加剧的背景下，中国对外投资迈出稳步增长的步伐，为世界经济复苏注入动力。

### 3.1.1 2013年以来中国对外直接投资（ODI）现状和特点

2013年以来，中国对外直接投资（ODI）经历了显著的结构调整和规模扩张，逐步从"高速增长"转向"高质量发展"③，并成为全球经济合作的重要推动力。

中国ODI规模持续扩大，流量与存量跃居全球前列，全球地位显著提升。自2013年"一带一路"倡议提出后，中国ODI规模迅速增长，2023年达到1772.9亿美元，是2013年的1.6倍（见图3.1）；占全球份额的比例从2013年的7.6%上升至2023年的11.4%。中国已连续12年位列全球对外直接投资流量前三，对外投资大国地位日益稳固。党的十八大以来，中国累计对外直接投资达1.68万亿美元，相当于2023年末存量规模的57%，连续8年占全球份额超过一成，在投资所在国家（地区）累计缴纳各种税金5185亿美元，年均解决超过200万个就业岗位，中国投资对世界经济的贡献日益凸显。④ 我国ODI快速发展既是经济发展、产业升级、国际环境变化下的必然，也是战略布局、政策推动与企业发展的共同选择。⑤

---

① UNCTAD, *Global Investment Trends Monitor*, January 2025, p.2.
② 《中华人民共和国2024年国民经济和社会发展统计公报》，国家统计局网站，https://www.stats.gov.cn/sj/zxfb/202502/t20250228_1958817.html，2025年2月28日。
③ 卢进勇、王粉粉、陈虹曦：《党的十八大以来中国对外投资的主要成就与经验》，《国际经济合作》2024年第4期。
④ 中华人民共和国商务部、国家统计局、国家外汇管理局：《2023年度中国对外直接投资统计公报》，中国商务出版社，2024，第6页。
⑤ 董兵兵：《我国对外直接投资这十年：历程、动因与前景》，《中国外汇》2024年第18期。

图3.1  2013—2023年中国对外直接投资流量和投资存量情况

资料来源：中华人民共和国商务部、国家统计局、国家外汇管理局《2023年度中国对外直接投资统计公报》，中国商务出版社，2024，第6页。

中国ODI区域布局优化，"一带一路"成为核心引擎，2013年以来，对"一带一路"共建国家的投资流量增长222.3%，占中国ODI总流量的比重持续攀升。中国对亚洲和非洲投资快速增长，对"一带一路"共建国家直接投资增长三成。行业结构多元化，租赁与商务服务、批发零售、制造业和金融业仍是主要投资领域，合计占比78.1%。[①] 高附加值的新能源、供应链相关产业（如电动汽车、绿色能源）投资增长显著。投资模式从并购转向绿色投资，中国企业战略转型，从"走出去"到"扎下去"。投资主体基本形成国企与民企"双轮驱动"格局，2023年末，在对外非金融类直接投资26315.8亿美元存量中，国有企业占52.2%，非国有企业占47.8%。[②]

2013年以来，中国对外直接投资呈现出"规模扩张、结构优化、区域聚焦、模式创新"的特点，但也面临国际环境复杂化和本土化压力加剧的挑战。未来，随着"一带一路"深化和全球产业链重构，中国ODI将进一步向高附加值、绿色化和数字化领域倾斜，同时需平衡风险防控与开

---

① 中华人民共和国商务部、国家统计局、国家外汇管理局：《2023年度中国对外直接投资统计公报》，中国商务出版社，2024，第12、14页。

② 中华人民共和国商务部、国家统计局、国家外汇管理局：《2023年度中国对外直接投资统计公报》，中国商务出版社，2024，第27页。

放合作，提升全球资源配置能力。

### 3.1.2 阿拉伯国家投资环境日益改善

在当今全球化的经济格局中，中东地区正以惊人的速度崛起，根据 GlobalData 最新发布的报告，中东已成为 2024 年全球第四大最具吸引力的外国直接投资（FDI）地区。这不仅标志着中东经济的转型与发展，也为全球投资者带来了新的机遇和挑战。与此同时，Kearney 的 2024 年外国直接投资信心指数（FDICI）也显示，阿联酋（排名第二）、沙特（排名第三）在全球新兴市场中的 FDI 投资信心指数名列前茅，埃及位列第 15 名，进一步巩固了中东地区作为投资热土的地位。[1] 根据联合国贸易和发展会议 2024 年 6 月发布的报告数据，阿拉伯国家 FDI 流入从 2020 年的 332 亿美元迅速增加到 2021 年的 640 亿美元，此后三年比较稳定。然而，2023 年 10 月开始的新一轮巴以冲突持续延宕，使投资者信心受挫，导致投资流入低于潜在水平。[2] 2023 年流入阿拉伯国家的外国直接投资下降 12.4%，至 677 亿美元，占发展中国家总流入量的 7.8%，占全球总流入量约 1.33 万亿美元的 5.1%（见图 3.2）。流入阿拉伯国家的外国直接投资继续集中在五个国家，份额超过 95%。总流入量最高的是阿联酋，吸引了 307 亿美元，占 45.4%；其次是沙特，吸引了 124 亿美元，占 18.2%；埃及以 98 亿美元排名第三，占流入阿拉伯国家总额的 18.2%；巴林以 68 亿美元排名第四，占总额的 10%，然后是阿曼 47 亿美元，科威特 21 亿美元，分别占总额的 6.9% 和 3.1%。[3]

---

[1] Dhaman, *The Investment Climate in Arab Countries* 2024, July 2024, p. 2.
[2] 绿地投资（Greenfield Investment）又称创建投资或新建投资，是指跨国公司等投资主体在东道国境内依照东道国的法律设置的部分或全部资产所有权归外国投资者所有的企业，创建投资会直接促进东道国生产能力、产出和就业的增长。棕地投资（Brownfield Investment）是指通过并购的方式进入一国市场，即外国投资者通过购买或租赁的方式获得已有的企业或资产，而不是新建厂房或设施。与棕地投资项目相比，绿地投资项目更容易因安全问题而延迟或取消。
[3] UNCTAD, *2024 World Investment Report*, June 2024, p. 156.

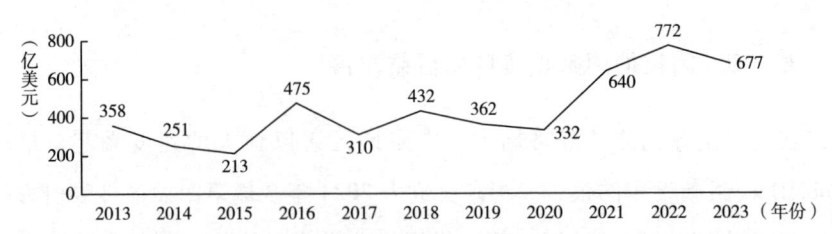

图 3.2 2013—2023 年阿拉伯国家吸引外国直接投资（FDI）流量情况
资料来源：UNCTAD, *2024 World Investment Report*, June 2024, pp.152-156。

### 3.1.3 2013 年以来中国对阿拉伯国家对外直接投资（ODI）发展趋势

中国积极鼓励企业"走出去"，参与阿拉伯国家的经济多元化转型进程。2013 年以来，中国对阿拉伯国家直接投资增长较快，投资领域不断拓宽，投资主体多元化，对阿拉伯国家经济发展起到了重要促进作用。

1. 投资合作机制建设日益完善

中国积极推动与阿拉伯国家商签《双边投资保护协定》与《避免双重征税协定》，为中阿投资合作创造了良好的投资环境。截至 2023 年底，中国与阿尔及利亚、阿联酋等 14 个阿拉伯国家签署了《双边投资保护协定》，与沙特、卡塔尔、摩洛哥等 12 个阿拉伯国家签署了《避免双重征税协定》。目前，中国正就升级《双边投资保护协定》与沙特、阿联酋进行商谈。

2. 发展趋势与规模

自 2013 年"一带一路"倡议提出以来，中国对阿 ODI 流量和存量均快速增长。从投资流量看，中国对阿 ODI 流量从 2013 年的 15.9 亿美元增加至 2023 年的 26.9 亿美元（自 2019 年以来一直保持 20 美元以上的投资流量）。截至 2023 年末，中国对阿 ODI 存量达到 276 亿美元，是 2013 年的 3.2 倍（见图 3.3）。

近年来，中阿投资合作快速发展。2021 年以来，中国对阿拉伯国家

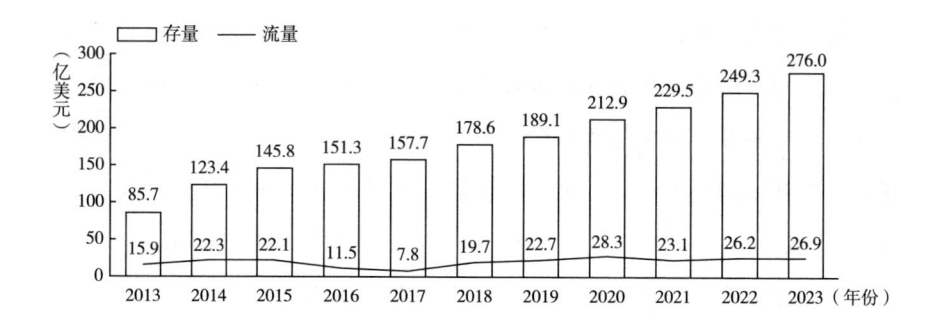

## 图 3.3 2013—2023 年中国对阿拉伯国家直接投资流量和投资存量情况

| 年份 | 存量（亿美元） | 流量（亿美元） |
| --- | --- | --- |
| 2013 | 85.7 | 15.9 |
| 2014 | 123.4 | 22.3 |
| 2015 | 145.8 | 22.1 |
| 2016 | 151.3 | 11.5 |
| 2017 | 157.7 | 7.8 |
| 2018 | 178.6 | 19.7 |
| 2019 | 189.1 | 22.7 |
| 2020 | 212.9 | 28.3 |
| 2021 | 229.5 | 23.1 |
| 2022 | 249.3 | 26.2 |
| 2023 | 276.0 | 26.9 |

资料来源：中华人民共和国商务部、国家统计局、国家外汇管理局《2023年度中国对外直接投资统计公报》，中国商务出版社，2024，第47—54页。

直接投资实现了"三连增"，截至2023年底，中国对阿拉伯国家直接投资存量276亿美元。[①] 除直接投资外，中国企业还通过再投资、第三国投资等方式，积极拓展在阿拉伯国家各领域业务。海湾国家蓬勃发展的资本市场、债券市场、项目融资市场以及财富管理市场，显示了海湾地区强大的投资吸引力，成为中企和中资金融机构"出海"的新兴投资目的地。

3. 中国对阿拉伯国家直接投资集中度比较高，海湾国家和北非国家是主要投资目的地

阿联酋因其发展理念、发展速度、开放包容的社会文化和辐射周边的区位优势，成为中国对阿拉伯国家直接投资的第一大目的地。目前，超过8000家中国企业在阿联酋开拓业务。主要投资项目包括：中阿宣布成立100亿美元的共同投资基金；阿布扎比国家石油公司（ADNOC）和中石油合资成立Al Yasat石油作业公司，中石油占股40%；中石油和振华石油各获得阿布扎比陆上石油区块8%和4%的股份权益；中石油获得阿布扎比海上石油区块中两个区块各10%股份权益；中远海运收购阿布扎比哈利法港2号码头运营权；江苏海投建设中阿（联酋）产能合作示范园。目前，中

---

[①] 中华人民共和国商务部、国家统计局、国家外汇管理局：《2023年度中国对外直接投资统计公报》，中国商务出版社，2024，第47—54页。

资企业在阿联酋油气、新能源、基础设施建设、通信、金融等领域取得良好发展，并积极开拓新兴市场。① 沙特则通过"2030愿景"推动非石油经济转型，中沙两国经贸合作正处在转型升级的重要机遇期。当前，中资企业在沙特主营业务涵盖工程承包、贸易航运、通信服务、工业投资和园区建设，并开始向金融、清洁能源、物流、电子商务等领域延伸。埃及和摩洛哥通过制造业本土化吸引外资流入。中国是对埃及投资最活跃、增长速度最快的国家之一，多家中资企业活跃在埃及制造业、能源、信息技术服务、农业等领域。中埃共建的苏伊士（泰达）经贸合作区已成为促进两国投资合作的重要平台。② 中国企业接连中标埃及新行政首都中央商务区、斋月十日城轻轨等国家级大项目，成为中埃合作的标志性项目。摩洛哥正在加快发展工业化、信息化、农业现代化，特别欢迎出口加工型和技术附加值高的投资项目。摩洛哥是非洲第一大汽车出口国，是欧美航空工业重要的发展伙伴和生产基地。近年来，汽车零部件、新能源汽车电池等一批中国生产企业陆续落户摩洛哥。中信戴卡、南京协众、南京奥特佳、重庆瑞格和中国航空汽车工业控股有限公司控股的耐世特等5家中国汽车零部件制造商均在盖尼特拉保税区投资设厂，并于2019年正式投产，目前运营良好。③ 中国企业在摩洛哥的布局覆盖新能源汽车电池产业链全环节，形成集群效应。核心企业包括国轩高科、中伟股份、贝特瑞等，投资总额超百亿美元。④ 中国在摩洛哥投资建设海外园区——丹吉尔穆罕默德六世科技城项目，目前尚在建设中。2022年，阿尔及利亚政府颁布了新投资法及其实施细则，为外国投资者提供了更多的投资便利和新的经贸合作机

---

① 中华人民共和国商务部：《对外投资合作国别（地区）指南-阿联酋》（2024年版），2024年12月，第4、25页。
② 中华人民共和国商务部：《对外投资合作国别（地区）指南-埃及》（2024年版），2024年8月，第4页。
③ 中华人民共和国商务部：《对外投资合作国别（地区）指南-摩洛哥》（2024年版），2024年9月，第35页。
④ 《开拓海外市场，多家上市企业布局摩洛哥》，《证券日报》，http://qiye.chinadaily.com.cn/a/202502/20/WS67b69726a310510f19ee7f40.html，2025年2月19日。

遇。中国企业在阿尔及利亚整体投资规模不大,主要集中在油气、房地产、建材等行业,主要投资公司有中石化、中建等,主要项目有油气区块勘探开发,目前正积极推进矿业勘探开发投资项目落实。

中国对阿拉伯国家投资主要分布在产油国家。就投资存量来看,2023年,中国对阿联酋直接投资存量为89.1亿美元,占中国对阿拉伯国家直接投资存量总额的比重为41.1%。其次是沙特31.86亿美元、伊拉克21.69亿美元、阿尔及利亚16.99亿美元、埃及12.87亿美元。[①] 就投资流量来看,2023年,阿联酋、沙特和摩洛哥为中国对阿拉伯国家直接投资前三大目的地,其后是阿尔及利亚和埃及。2023年,除了埃及,中国对上述几个阿拉伯国家的投资均实现较大幅度的增长(见图3.4)。阿联酋一直为中国对阿投资第一大投资目的地,占中国对阿直接投资流量总额的67.3%。

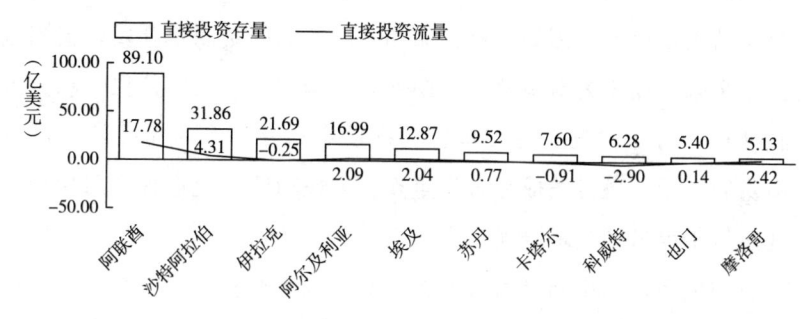

**图3.4 2023年中国对阿拉伯国家直接投资流量和投资存量主要国家**

资料来源:中华人民共和国商务部、国家统计局、国家外汇管理局《2023年度中国对外直接投资统计公报》,中国商务出版社,2024,第47—54页。

### 4. 投资领域各有侧重

中国对阿投资逐步从传统能源向多元化领域扩展,形成以下重点方向。①能源全产业链合作。能源合作以油气行业为主,要集中在沙特、

---

[①] 中华人民共和国商务部、国家统计局、国家外汇管理局:《2023年度中国对外直接投资统计公报》,中国商务出版社,2024,第52—54页。

阿联酋、伊拉克和阿尔及利亚。中国还积极参与阿拉伯国家炼化、储运等下游产业的发展。近年来，中阿双方加速在可再生能源领域的合作，光伏、氢能、储能及碳捕获技术（CCUS）等清洁能源成为新增长点。②基础设施建设与数字化双轮驱动。阿拉伯国家中长期战略推动传统基建与数字基建需求激增。例如，沙特利雅得地铁项目、阿联酋智慧城市计划，促进了中国企业在交通、能源电力、工业互联网等领域与阿拉伯国家的合作。中国企业在阿拉伯国家承建铁路、港口等项目，例如埃及新首都项目、阿联酋铁路二期项目等。③数字经济与科技合作，中阿共建数字经济平台，推动数字货币、人工智能合作。例如商汤科技在阿布扎比设立区域总部，促进技术转移。④制造业与医疗健康，例如制造业园区（如苏伊士运河经贸区）、汽车制造业和医疗合作项目成为重要载体。⑤消费品市场快速扩张。阿拉伯年轻化的人口结构及经济多元化政策，推动智能消费电子、美容护理、跨境电商等领域的投资需求。中国企业通过差异化战略和本地化运营抢占市场，例如有机食品和健康产品的定制化开发，美团进驻沙特。⑥金融合作成为新引擎。中国金融机构加速布局阿拉伯市场，五大行已在沙特、阿联酋设立分支机构，推动本币互换和跨境投资。产融合作、财富管理及金融科技成为合作重点，人民币国际化进程在阿拉伯国家的加速进一步提升了金融合作潜力。

绿色与创新成为中阿经贸合作新趋势。绿色经济是中国与阿拉伯国家经济发展的新驱动力。中阿双方在光伏、风能、水电、氢能、核电等清洁能源领域的合作不断拓展。一方面，大型合作项目不断涌现，例如中国企业承建的阿布扎比风电示范项目、摩洛哥丹吉尔 34 兆瓦光伏项目均已成为当地清洁能源供给的主力。另一方面，贸易投资带动技术转移。中国金龙、宇通、宁德时代等行业龙头企业通过投资建厂、技术转移等方式升级合作模式，积极布局电动汽车全产业链合作，助力阿拉伯国家能源转型和可持续发展。

5. 投资主体日趋多元

中国对阿拉伯国家投资方面，国企民企协同发力。能源、基建等大型项目主要由中石化、中石油、中建等国企推动；生产加工等制造业以浙江巨石、青岛海尔、南京奥特佳等地方民营企业出海埃及、约旦、摩洛哥等国投资建厂；科技和消费领域民营企业，如华为、商汤科技、蔚来汽车、美团等，通过技术合作拓展市场。中阿合作论坛机制、中阿博览会、经贸合作区为企业提供投资平台，据不完全统计，中国在阿拉伯国家建设各类经贸合作区 16 个。① 例如，中埃·泰达苏伊士经贸合作区已形成"港口—园区—城市"三位一体布局，已吸引约 180 家中外企业入驻②，带动埃及本土产业链升级，成为中阿产能合作的新样本。

6. 对阿拉伯国家经济发展的促进作用

中国对阿拉伯国家直接投资有力促进了阿拉伯国家的经济社会发展。①推动经济多元化。中国投资助力阿拉伯国家减少对石油产业的依赖。例如，沙特通过与中国合作发展炼化、新能源产业，支持其"2030 愿景"。②技术转移与产业升级。中国在数字技术、清洁能源等领域的技术输出，帮助阿拉伯国家提升产业水平。中阿技术转移中心在农业、医疗等领域促成多项合作。③就业与民生改善。基建项目创造大量就业岗位，如埃及新行政首都建设带动数万人就业；医疗合作提升当地公共卫生水平。④贸易结构优化。中国扩大进口阿拉伯非石油产品（如埃及柑橘、沙特椰枣），促进阿方出口多元化。⑤区域互联互通。中阿合建港口、物流中心（如吉布提国际自贸区），增强阿拉伯国家作为亚非欧枢纽的地位。

7. 中阿投资合作仍有很大提升空间

除了中国香港地区，2013 年中国 ODI 流量以东盟为第一大投资目的地，占比 14.2%，其次是美国和欧盟。中国对阿拉伯国家 ODI 仅占 1.5%，

---

① 商务部国际贸易经济合作研究院：《中国与阿拉伯国家经贸合作回顾与展望 2024》，2024 年 11 月，第 28 页。
② 商务部国际贸易经济合作研究院：《对外投资合作国别（地区）指南：埃及（2024 年版）》，2024 年 8 月，第 2 页。

投资存量占比不足1%。阿拉伯国家外资主要来源地是欧洲（英、法、德、意）和美国，以及中国、印度、日本和韩国等亚洲新兴经济体。2023年，中国对阿拉伯国家ODI占当年阿拉伯国家吸引直接投资流量的4%（见表3.1）。

表 3.1  2023 年中国对世界主要经济体直接投资情况

| 经济体 | 流量 金额（亿美元） | 同比（%） | 比重（%） | 存量 金额（亿美元） | 比重（%） |
| --- | --- | --- | --- | --- | --- |
| 世界 | 1772.9 | 8.7 | 100 | 29554.0 | 100 |
| 中国香港 | 1087.7 | 11.5 | 61.3 | 17525.2 | 59.3 |
| 东盟 | 251.2 | 34.7 | 14.2 | 1756.2 | 5.9 |
| 欧盟 | 64.8 | -6.1 | 3.7 | 1024.2 | 3.5 |
| 美国 | 69.1 | -5.2 | 3.9 | 836.9 | 2.8 |
| 澳大利亚 | 5.5 | -80.4 | 0.3 | 347.7 | 1.2 |
| 阿拉伯国家 | 26.9 | 13.3 | 1.5 | 276.0 | 0.9 |
| 以上经济体合计 | 1505.2 | 11.3 | 84.9 | 21766.2 | 73.6 |

资料来源：中华人民共和国商务部、国家统计局、国家外汇管理局《2023年度中国对外直接投资统计公报》，中国商务出版社，2024，第30页。

总之，2013年以来，中国对阿拉伯国家投资呈现规模扩张、领域多元、主体协作的特点，不仅深化了双边经贸关系，还通过技术输出、产业合作和基建支持，助力阿拉伯国家经济转型与可持续发展。中阿关系树立了南南合作的典范。中国与阿联酋、沙特、埃及等国在"一带一路"框架下实施了200多个大型合作项目，合作成果惠及约20亿人口，促进了阿拉伯国家经济发展和区域一体化进程。中阿经贸合作的深化，为其他发展中国家提供了宝贵经验，激励了更多发展中国家加强合作，共同推动南南合作的深入发展。展望未来，中国在海外投资方面具有巨大的增长潜力，而沙特、阿联酋等海湾国家，以及北非的埃及和摩洛哥，正因为庞大的经济多元化举措和经济结构性改革，成为海外资本新兴投资目的地，在中国对外投资的指数排名中继续攀升。① 随着"一带一路"倡议与阿拉伯国家发展战略的进一步对接，中阿投资合作有望在绿色经济、数字经济、高端制造、商贸物流等领域释放更大潜力。

## 3.2　阿拉伯国家对华投资状况

近年来，伴随阿拉伯国家"向东看"趋势加强，以及中国市场的强劲韧性和巨大发展潜力，阿拉伯国家资本加大对华投资力度，并在近年来呈现加速发展的势头。

### 3.2.1　2013年以来中国外商投资蓬勃发展

2013年以来，中国坚定实行积极主动的开放战略，大力开展管理和审批制度创新，大幅放宽外资准入限制，充分释放外资潜力，中国利用外资规模、结构与质量提升取得显著成效。中国积极开展制度创新，着力打造全方位开放新格局，各级政府积极优化营商环境，切实为外资企业排忧解难，发挥国家重大发展战略的引领作用。② 2013年，中国吸引外商投资1239.1亿美元，全球占比8.5%。③ 2020—2023年中国吸引外国直接投资整体表现不弱，但高位回落的压力明显，受到全球FDI趋势变化、中国产业结构变化，以及制造业逆全球化等多重因素影响。2023年全年外商直接投资新设立企业53766家，比上年增长39.7%。实际使用外商直接投资额1632.5亿美元，同比下降13.7%，占全球比重为12.3%，稳居世界第

---

① EIU, "China Going Global Investment Index 2025: Key Findings", https://viewpoint-eiu-com-s.ra.cass.cn:8118/analysis/article/822124882?_gl=1*107iduj*_ga*MjAxOTQyNjQzNy4x-NzAwOTIxOTY1*_ga_FQFE2ZLQY2*MTc0MTMxMDg5OC44MC4xLjE3NDEzMTE2MTYu-MC4wLjA.*_ga_7685V0XQ5E*MTc0MTMxMDkwNi43OC4xLjE3NDEzMTE2NDAuMC4wLjA, January 2, 2025.
② 卢进勇、陈虹曦、孙淑彬：《党的十八大以来中国的利用外资事业：成就、经验与未来展望》，《国际贸易》2024年第9期。
③ 中华人民共和国商务部：《中国外资统计公报2024》，2024年9月，第2页。

二（见图3.5）。2024年，中国新设外商投资企业59080家，比上年增长9.9%。实际使用外资8263亿元人民币，比上年下降27.1%，折合1162亿美元，比上年下降28.8%。①

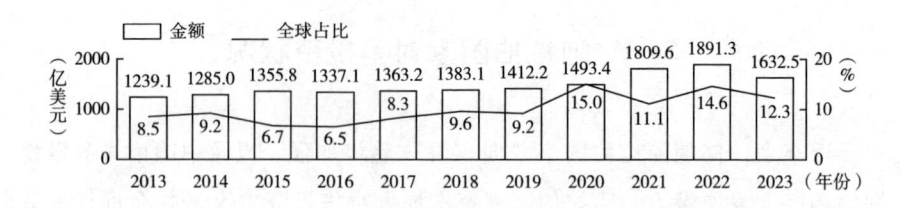

**图3.5 2013—2023年中国实际使用物资金额和全球占比情况**
资料来源：中华人民共和国商务部《中国外资统计公报2024》，2024年9月，第53页。

从行业看，2023年，外商投资主要集中在制造业，科学研究和技术服务业，租赁和商务服务业，信息传输、软件和信息技术服务业，房地产业，批发和零售业，金融业。上述7个行业的新设企业数量占比为86.8%，实际使用外资金额占比为89.5%。其中，高技术产业（高技术制造业和高技术服务业）吸收外资加速，占中国吸收外资总额的37.4%。从投资来源地看，亚洲是中国外资第一大来源地，占比达到81.3%（其中中国香港占比68.1%），其次是欧洲8.9%、拉丁美洲6.4%和北美洲2.4%。就国别（地区）来看，除了中国香港，新加坡、英属维尔京群岛和荷兰占比达到6%、4.2%和3.3%，其次，日本、开曼群岛、韩国、英国、美国占比均超过2%。截至2023年，在华投资前15位国家（地区）累计设立外商投资企业103.4万家，占中国累计设立外商投资企业数的87.6%；累计在华投资金额为2.7万亿美元，占中国累计实际使用外资金额的94.2%。②

---

① 《中华人民共和国2024年国民经济和社会发展统计公报》，国家统计局网站，https：//www.stats.gov.cn/sj/zxfb/202502/t20250228_1958817.html，2025年2月28日。
② 中华人民共和国商务部：《中国外资统计公报2024》，2024年9月，第6—20页。

### 3.2.2 阿拉伯国家对外直接投资状况

一直以来，阿拉伯国家积极利用丰富的石油美元开展对外直接投资。根据 UNCTAD 数据，2023 年阿拉伯国家对外直接投资（ODI）523 亿美元，同比下降 37.1%。对外投资主要集中在阿联酋、沙特、科威特、巴林以及摩洛哥五个国家，占比达到 98.5%，其中，阿联酋占比 42.7%，沙特占比 30.7%，科威特占比 21.4%。从投资存量来看，截至 2023 年，阿拉伯国家对外直接投资总额 6568.2 亿美元，同比增长 7.7%，集中在阿联酋（39.9%）、沙特（31%）、科威特（7.6%）和卡塔尔（7.6%）以及巴林（3.4%）等五国，占比高达 89.5%。[①] 对华投资仍以海湾合作委员会国家（GCC）为主，2023 年海湾国家对外投资流量 506.7 亿美元，投资存量 5943.8 亿美元。[②]

### 3.2.3 阿拉伯国家对华直接投资激增

长期以来，阿拉伯国家对外直接投资主要流向欧美及本地区，对华直接投资每年约为 0.5 亿美元。近年来，伴随中国市场潜力扩大，阿拉伯国家"向东看"趋势明显，对华直接投资增长迅速。2021—2023 年，阿拉伯国家对华直接投资额分别为 1.1 亿美元、10.5 亿美元和 23 亿美元，接近中国对阿投资规模。截至 2023 年底，阿拉伯国家对华直接投资累计达到 72.9 亿美元。[③]

海湾国家是对华投资主力军。近三年阿拉伯国家对华新增投资中几乎全部来自海湾国家，尤以阿联酋和沙特两国最活跃且力度最大。其中，阿联酋是中国外商投资第十大来源地，2023 年在华新设企业数 72 家，全球占比 0.1%，实际投资金额 22 亿美元，全球占比 1.3%，占阿拉伯国家对华投资流量的 95.6%。其次是沙特，2023 年对华直接投资 0.8 亿美元。从

---

[①] Dhaman, *The Investment Climate in Arab Countries* 2024, July 2024, pp.82-83.
[②] Dhaman, *The Investment Climate in Arab Countries* 2024, July 2024, pp.82-83.
[③] 中华人民共和国商务部：《中国外资统计公报 2024》，2024 年 9 月，第 27—30 页。

投资存量看，阿联酋、沙特和科威特是对华投资最多的阿拉伯国家，分别为45亿美元、18.9亿美元和3.3亿美元，共占阿拉伯国家对华投资存量的92.1%（见图3.6）。但需要指出的是，阿拉伯国家对华直接投资仍处于起步阶段。2023年，阿拉伯对华直接投资流量占当年阿拉伯国家对外直接投资总额的比重为4.4%，占当年中国实际利用外资总额的比重仅为1.4%。①

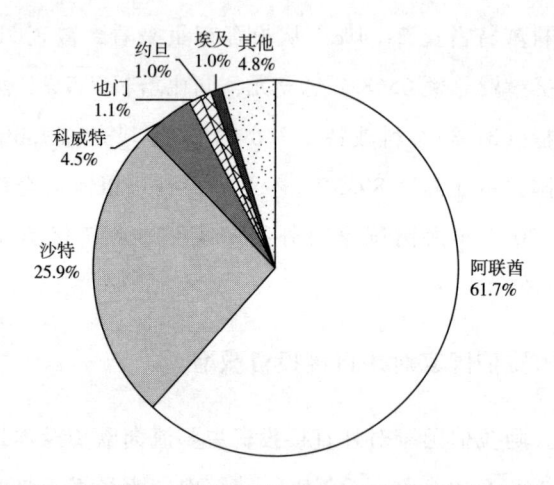

**图3.6 2023年主要阿拉伯国家对华直接投资占比情况**

资料来源：中华人民共和国商务部《中国外资统计公报2024》，2024年9月，第27—30页。

在投资领域方面，阿拉伯国家对华直接投资仍聚焦石油石化"主业"。以沙特国家石油公司（沙特阿美）、沙特基础工业公司（SABIC）为代表的大型能源及化工企业担纲主力，前者在华累计投资已超千亿元人民币，成为目前在华累计投资最多的外企之一。② 此外，沙特国际电力和水务公司在上海设立全球创新中心，推动光伏、储能等领域研发。

---

① 中华人民共和国商务部：《中国外资统计公报2024》，2024年9月，第27—30页。
② 商务部国际贸易经济合作研究院：《中国与阿拉伯国家经贸合作回顾与展望2024》，2024年11月，第22页。

### 3.2.4　海湾主权财富基金加大对华投资布局

海湾国家被认为是全球主权财富基金的发源地和聚集地，市场地位举足轻重，投资动向引人瞩目。近年来，重仓中国，投资中国市场，已经成为海湾资本布局的重点之一。作为"国家级"机构投资者，多家海湾主权财富基金在华设立办公室，活跃在中国的一、二级市场，通过股权投资、基金合作等方式布局中国产业链，如阿布扎比投资局、沙特公共投资基金PIF、穆巴达拉投资公司、阿布扎比投资局是主要投资主体等。科威特投资局和卡塔尔投资局也是中国A股市场的传统投资者。例如，沙特公共投资基金已与中国六大顶尖金融机构签署了一系列谅解备忘录，总价值高达500亿美元，其旗下公司埃耐特（Alat）提供20亿美元投资联想；阿布扎比投资局投资中芯国际；阿布扎比投资机构CYVN Holdings对蔚来汽车累计投资33亿美元；穆巴达拉投资公司投资大连新达盟；科威特投资局投资中国仿生机器人企业三花智控；卡塔尔投资局参与小鹏汽车融资；等等。[①] 根据Global SWF数据，海湾主权财富基金在2023年6月到2024年6月已在中国投资70亿美元，投资额是以前12个月的5倍，同比增幅高达400%。[②] 据彭博社消息，2024年海湾主权财富基金继续加大海外投资力度，前9个月对华投资已达到95亿美元。[③]

海湾主权财富基金对华投资呈现以下特点。第一，海湾主权财富基金投资将战略导向与本地化结合，投资不仅追求财务回报，更注重技术合作与产业链整合。第二，海湾主权财富基金对华投资领域实现多元化发展，

---

[①]《4.9万亿中东主权基金，入华投了谁？》，新浪财经网，https://finance.sina.com.cn/roll/2025-03-10/doc-inepetxa0414237.shtml，2025年3月10日。

[②]《中东主权财富基金为何持续扩大对华投资》，北大汇丰智库微信公众号，https://mp.weixin.qq.com/s?__biz=MjM5MDc1OTU2MA==&mid=2650250128&idx=1&sn=1221450d188f193e398c406879c1d494&chksm=bf3aa854f3df05e609ca02c3e765590bb97b7c3a-b06b09636d7b734427c2d69527befb0fba1&scene=27，2025年2月5日。

[③]《继续大撒钱！中东主权财富基金今年前9月投资交易额高达550亿美元》，财联社网站，https://www.cls.cn/detail/1839322，2024年10月28日。

从传统能源、基建扩展到新能源（光伏、风电）、高科技（半导体、人工智能）、生物医药、消费互联网等领域。第三，聚焦高增长行业，新能源、数字经济、高端制造成为核心方向。第四，政策驱动与长期布局。沙特等国家发展愿景与中国"一带一路"倡议深度对接，推动投资从传统能源向绿色经济和创新经济转型。第五，双向合作与第三市场开发。海湾资本与中国企业合作开发"一带一路"国家市场。阿拉伯国家对华投资正从"资源驱动"转向"技术和战略协同"，未来双方合作将更注重绿色转型与创新生态共建。

## 3.3 中阿投资合作展望

当今世界正经历百年未有之大变局，国际政治经济碎片化发展，全球经济复苏缓慢，地缘政治割裂加剧，逆全球化和保护主义兴起。与此同时，国际政治经济格局"东升西降"趋势明显，全球南方集体崛起。中国与阿拉伯国家同为全球南方重要成员国，国内面临发展复兴的重任，国际上对改善全球治理体系有着相似的诉求。

### 3.3.1 未来重点投资合作领域

展望未来，中阿将持续加大双向投资，拥抱发展机遇。中阿投资合作将在保持传统领域（能源、基建）的基础上，聚焦多个新兴领域。

1. 新能源与绿色科技

阿拉伯国家正加速推进能源转型升级，推动太阳能、风能、氢能及碳捕获技术（CCUS）等领域的发展。沙特等油气资源丰富的国家也在推动可再生能源项目，中国企业在技术输出和项目投资上具有显著优势。

2. 传统能源与下游产业

为确保石油消费市场稳定，海湾国家通过投资炼化、化工项目深度绑定中国市场。例如，沙特阿美近年来在中国辽宁、浙江等地投资超百亿美元的石化项目，要求配套采购其原油，以巩固市场地位。2023年，沙特阿美收购荣盛石化、盛虹石化等企业股份，进一步深入中国能源产业链下游。与此同时，伊拉克等产油国仍是中国传统能源企业出海合作重要目的地。

3. 数字经济与人工智能

海湾资本瞄准中国在人工智能、半导体、云计算等领域的领先技术。双方在智慧城市、跨境电商业态优化、金融科技等领域合作潜力巨大。阿布扎比已设立中东首个人工智能大学，并计划整合 AI 技术到医疗、农业等领域。中国科技企业（如商汤科技）正与阿方合作推动技术落地，未来可能进一步深化数据共享和智能化管理合作。

4. 建筑业和基础设施建设

建筑业和基础设施建设包括传统基建（交通、能源电力），数字基建（通信、数据中心、智慧城市）和房地产。阿拉伯国家基建需求旺盛，中企与阿拉伯国家在港口建设、智能物流等领域已有合作基础，未来可拓展至 5G 网络和数字基建项目。

5. 医疗健康与高端制造

海湾国家推动医疗健康产业升级，中国生物医药技术成为其关键合作方向。中国在生物医药领域的技术优势与阿拉伯国家的需求形成互补。在高端制造领域，沙特资本对汽车制造（如吉利与雷诺合资公司）、半导体设备等行业的投资额显著增加。

6. 金融服务与资本合作

海湾资本通过设立人民币基金、与中国金融机构合作等方式深化金融联动。例如，沙特 PIF 与中国六家金融机构①签署 500 亿美元合作备忘录，推动双向资本流动；阿联酋与中国深圳合作成立私募基金，探索人民币投资路径。阿联酋主权财富基金（如穆巴达拉投资公司）计划加码中国新能源和高端制造业，而中资金融机构也在拓展中东市场布局。

---

① 中国建设银行、中国农业银行、中国出口信用保险公司、中国银行、中国进出口银行以及中国工商银行。

双方通过共建金融自由区（如阿布扎比 ADGM、易达资本中沙经济区）推动资本双向流动。

### 3.3.2 中阿投资合作面临的主要挑战

中阿投资合作前景广阔，同时面临一系列地缘政治、文化和市场挑战。

1. 地缘政治风险与政策波动

中美博弈背景下，海湾资本面临平衡战略压力的挑战。尽管阿拉伯国家试图减少对美国的依赖，但部分投资可能因国际政治环境变化（如技术出口管制、制裁风险）受阻。阿拉伯国家内部政治环境复杂，部分国家存在地区冲突风险，可能影响项目稳定性。例如，不同国家对"一带一路"项目的接受度差异较大，需加强相关风险评估。

2. 监管与合规差异

中国与海湾国家的税收、外资准入等政策存在显著差异。例如，沙特企业需适应中国的劳动法、数据安全法等法规，而中企在阿拉伯国家也面临本地化比例要求（如沙特"2030 愿景"中的劳动力本地化政策），中企需加强跨文化培训并制定本地化策略。

3. 文化与认知障碍

宗教文化和商业习惯差异可能影响管理效率。例如，阿拉伯投资者更重视面对面沟通与长期信任的建立，而中国企业的快速决策模式可能与之冲突；部分中国企业对阿拉伯市场缺乏深入了解，导致合作效率低下。语言障碍（如阿拉伯语的专业术语翻译问题）也增加了沟通成本。

4. 技术与产业对接难题

尽管技术合作是核心，但双方在标准制定、知识产权保护等方面存在分歧。例如，阿联酋在人工智能领域倾向于自主技术研发，可能对中国企业的技术输出形成竞争。此外，中国新能源产业链的本地化需求与海湾国家"技术引进"目标需进一步协调。中企需探索合作模式以平衡技术输出与本地化创新。

5. 市场竞争与资本回报压力

欧美企业、印度在阿拉伯国家布局较早，中国对阿直接投资需在技术、成本或服务上形成差异化优势。同时，部分投资（如早期科技项目）回报周期长，可能面临资本退出压力。例如，中国初创企业在阿拉伯市场的拓展需适应本地消费习惯（如对有机食品和高端电子产品的偏好），否则难以实现预期收益。

总之，基于良好的宏观经济前景和经济多元化转型驱动，阿拉伯国家正成为包括中国在内国际资本的新兴投资目的地。海湾国家"向东看"趋势逐渐加强，对华投资持续加码。因此，尽管中阿投资合作仍处于起步阶段，但合作潜力巨大。中阿之间的"投资热"不仅是全球经济格局变化的结果，也是双方经济互补性和科技创新推动的成果。无论是FDI还是ODI，双向投资正在推动中阿合作进入一个新的高度。中阿合作不仅是一场资本的流动，更是一场全球经济格局的转型。展望未来，中阿投资合作将更多依赖技术协同与长期战略互信，在政治、技术、文化层面持续磨合，通过中阿合作论坛、中阿博览会等机制化平台，共建高质量"一带一路"，为中阿命运共同体跑出加速度做出贡献。

# 第4章　中阿金融合作专题报告

在中阿合作论坛、"一带一路"倡议和金砖合作机制的总体战略性规划下，中国与阿拉伯国家的金融合作有力推动了双边在经贸、基础设施和产能合作等领域的发展。阿拉伯国家出于拓展对外投资、摆脱对能源经济的过度依赖、补充财政资金等实际发展需求的考虑，同中国开展金融合作的步伐日益走深走实；中阿双方加快资本市场互联互通，人民币国际化进程不断取得突破。双边优势互补，务实创新，合作持续深化，取得了丰硕成果，在全球投融资体系中共同提升了发展中国家的国际影响力和话语权。展望未来，中阿金融合作将在新时代中阿关系发展中迎来更广阔的发展空间。

## 4.1　阿拉伯国家金融环境概述

### 4.1.1　阿拉伯国家经济结构决定金融发展水平不一

2024年，国际金融环境复杂多变，全球经济复苏情况不等，各主要经济体货币政策调整、地缘政治风险及金融市场波动的不确定性是发展中国家面临的主要挑战。2024年9月，美联储在时隔四年之后重启降息，深刻影响了国际金融市场的跨境资本流动，全球资产定价，以及各国央行货币政策的制定与调整；阿拉伯地区的地缘政治事件仍在持续，金融稳定性面临极大考验。

世界银行发布的《国际债务报告》显示，2023年，发展中国家偿还外债支出总额达 1.4 万亿美元，创历史新高。国际货币基金组织在《财政监测报告》中预测，2024 年各国公共债务总量将超过 100 万亿美元，占全球国内生产总值（GDP）之比升至 93%，债务可持续风险加剧。随着外债负担加重和偿债成本上升，不但政府的财政空间和央行政策空间受到制约，发展中国家在国际金融市场的融资渠道也将日益收窄。当长期经济滞后和财政基础薄弱的国家过度依赖外部融资，债务规模超过经济承受能力时，就极有可能陷入主权债务困境。

用外债存量和偿债情况反映一国的债务水平和偿债压力，用总储备和经常账户余额相关指标衡量各国金融稳定性，在整体上对比各国为抵御全球经济不确定冲击的金融韧性可以看出，在阿拉伯国家当中，金融稳定性整体较好的国家主要包括高收入经济体（海合会六国），以及中等收入偏上经济体（利比亚等三国）。这些国家主要依赖能源出口，积累了大量资本并实现了财政盈余。其余阿拉伯国家的金融发展整体滞后，金融体系开放程度也普遍偏低，面临外部冲击时的风险抵御能力脆弱（见表 4.1）。

表 4.1　2023 年阿拉伯国家债务水平及金融稳定指标

| 国别 | 外债存量总额（百万美元） | 外债存量总额占GDP比重（%） | 总储备（百万美元） | 总储备占GDP比重（%） | 偿债额占出口比重（%） | 经常账户余额（百万美元） |
|---|---|---|---|---|---|---|
| 高收入经济体 | | | | | | |
| 巴林 | / | / | 5117.6 | 11.1 | / | 2699.5 |
| 科威特 | / | / | 52619.4 | 32.1 | / | 51396.2 |
| 阿曼 | / | / | 17298.2 | 15.9 | / | 2637.6 |
| 卡塔尔 | / | / | 51538.7 | 24.2 | / | 36452.6 |
| 沙特 | / | / | 457948.6 | 42.9 | / | 34070.5 |
| 阿联酋 | / | / | 189490.9 | 36.9 | / | / |
| 中等偏上收入经济体 | | | | | | |
| 利比亚 | / | / | 92427.3 | 205.0 | / | 5675.3# |
| 阿尔及利亚 | 7315.3 | 3.0 | 81216.7 | 32.8 | 0.8 | 5423.6 |
| 伊拉克 | 20331.4 | 8.1 | 112232.9 | 44.7 | 4.0 | 28374.6 |

续表

| 国别 | 外债存量总额（百万美元） | 外债存量总额占GDP比重（%） | 总储备（百万美元） | 总储备占GDP比重（%） | 偿债额占出口比重（%） | 经常账户余额（百万美元） |
|---|---|---|---|---|---|---|
| 中等偏下收入经济体 | | | | | | |
| 科摩罗 | 409.3 | 30.3 | 324.6 | 24.0 | 11.6 | -24.6 |
| 吉布提 | 3428.7 | 83.7 | 502.0 | 12.2 | 1.7 | 718.6 |
| 埃及 | 168062.0 | 42.4 | 33070.2 | 8.4 | 30.4 | -12564.3 |
| 约旦 | 44629.8 | 87.6 | / | / | 16.1 | -1910.4 |
| 黎巴嫩 | 66296.5 | 315.8* | 32512.9 | 154.9* | 34.5 | -5642.8 |
| 突尼斯 | 41278.7 | 85.1 | 9239.7 | 19.0 | 23.2 | -1110.5 |
| 毛里塔尼亚 | 4603.6 | 48.2# | 2038.6# | 21.3# | 10.2 | -966.5 |
| 摩洛哥 | 69267.3 | 48.0 | 36327.7 | 25.2 | 9.2 | -891.2 |
| 低收入经济体 | | | | | | |
| 索马里 | 3022.8 | 27.6 | / | / | 16.9 | / |
| 苏丹 | 22580.6 | 20.7 | / | / | 3.0* | -4442.8* |
| 叙利亚 | 4875.5 | 20.6* | / | / | / | / |
| 也门 | 7283.0 | / | 1250.8* | / | / | / |

注：各国数据以2023年数据进行计算和比较，当年如无报告，则选择近期的数值替代，以"*"标记2022年数据，以"#"标记2021年数据，三年内无数据的视为缺失。总储备包括持有的货币黄金、特别提款权、IMF持有的IMF成员国的储备以及在货币当局控制下的外汇资产。

资料来源：世界银行国际债务统计（IDS）数据库，世界发展指标（WDI）数据库。数据库访问日期为2025年3月。

在阿拉伯国家中，高收入和中等偏上收入经济体外债水平较低，同时总储备较为充裕。从总量来看，沙特（4579.5亿美元）、阿联酋（1895.0亿美元）和伊拉克（1122.3亿美元）的总储备充足，在阿拉伯国家中位列前三，从总储备占GDP比重来看，又以利比亚（205.0%）居于首位，显示了较强的国际支付能力和金融稳定性。这些国家在国际贸易中获得了较突出的贸易顺差额，实现了经常账户盈余，具备保持金融稳定的良好基础。海合会国家因其相对稳定的政局和多元化的经济策略，在国际金融环境中表现出较为稳健的状态；相比之下，伊拉克和利比亚由于长期的地缘政治动荡，金融体系和经济发展受外部不确定性冲击的可能性较大。

高收入国家普遍经常账户盈余，而中低收入国家经常账户多为赤字，这反映了经济结构的差异。中等偏下收入经济体中，埃及、黎巴嫩和约旦存在较高风险：埃及外债存量极高（1680.6亿美元，占GDP的42.4%），总储备仅占GDP的8.4%，偿债额占出口30.4%，叠加经常账户赤字（12.6亿美元），面临严重偿债压力；黎巴嫩外债占GDP的比重高达315.8%，经常账户赤字，政治腐败和银行系统崩溃加剧了金融风险；约旦外债依赖度过高，占GDP的87.6%。

四个低收入国家国际支付能力不足，苏丹、也门和索马里长期战乱，叙利亚受十年内战与制裁影响，其国内金融市场受到严重冲击，尚未建立起完善高效的现代金融体系，未来发展前景不明。

### 4.1.2 阿拉伯国家多个国际金融中心地位稳中有升

阿拉伯国家拥有多个重要的国际金融枢纽，在全球金融版图中的作用日益突出。迪拜国际金融中心以及阿布扎比全球市场国际化的法律框架和监管体为其金融市场的稳定和创新提供了有力保障；沙特政府通过一系列改革措施，推动金融市场的开放和创新，吸引了大量国际金融机构入驻，不断提升利雅得金融市场的影响力。阿拉伯国家通过多元化经济战略，逐步将资源优势转化为金融竞争力，雄厚的主权财富基金在全球投资领域具有重要地位，其多元化的投资组合涵盖了能源、基础设施、科技等多个领域，进一步提高了在全球金融市场中的话语权。

根据2024年9月的全球金融中心指数（Global Financial Centres Index，GFCI）报告，在综合测评营商环境、人力资本、基础设施、税收和声誉等相关金融业发展水平的竞争力排名中，阿拉伯国家在全球前121个金融中心占有7个席位（见表4.2）。阿联酋和沙特保持着阿拉伯地区的金融领导地位，迪拜、阿布扎比和利雅得已成为阿拉伯国家中最具影响力的金融中心，以完善的金融基础设施和开放的国际化程度闻名，在全球金融中心排名靠前。从得分看，阿拉伯国家七大金融中心评分均有所提高，整体平均得分相比2023年9月提高了1.4%。迪拜是阿拉伯国家中最为领先和最具代表性的金融中心，在"基础设施"和"声誉及综合"两个分领域中进入全球前15，分别为第14位和第12位；在竞争力次级指标的排名中，迪拜在"专业服务"领域排名全球第11位，在"金融科技"领域位列全球第6位，表现亮眼。

表4.2 阿拉伯国家地区金融中心排名情况

| 金融中心 | GFCI 36 地区排名 | GFCI 36 全球排名 | GFCI 36 得分 | 去年同期排名变化 | 去年同期得分变化 |
| --- | --- | --- | --- | --- | --- |
| 迪拜 | 1 | 15 | 723 | ↑6 | ↑4 |
| 阿布扎比 | 2 | 35 | 704 | 0 | ↑2 |
| 卡萨布兰卡 | 3 | 57 | 682 | ↓3 | 0 |
| 利雅得 | 5 | 63 | 676 | ↑8 | ↑17 |
| 多哈 | 6 | 64 | 675 | ↑14 | ↑19 |
| 科威特城 | 7 | 69 | 670 | ↑13 | ↑24 |
| 巴林 | 4 | 80 | 659 | ↓6 | ↓1 |

资料来源：第36期全球金融中心指数。

阿拉伯国家的金融中心有望成为连接东西方金融市场的关键纽带，为全球投资者带来丰富的投资选择和多样化的金融服务。展望未来，通过加速金融科技的应用和推进数字化转型，这些金融中心将进一步增强在全球金融市场中的竞争力和影响力。

## 4.2 中阿金融合作稳步推进

中阿双方依托中阿合作论坛、"一带一路"倡议和金砖合作机制，持续深化资金融通合作，金融合作平台与机制不断完善。双方在央行合作、人民币国际化进程以及吸引阿拉伯主权财富基金参与对华融资、对阿发展项目融资等领域均取得了显著进展，合作形式日益多样化，范围逐步扩大。

### 4.2.1 机制与平台建设

资金融通是共建"一带一路"的重要内容，亚洲基础设施投资银行（以下简称"亚投行"）是不可或缺的金融支持力量，为共建国家和地区的经济发展提供了重要的资金保障。亚投行积极支持阿拉伯国家的大型基础设施建设项目。2017年1月，亚投行与阿曼杜库姆经济特区管委会签署贷款协议，向阿曼杜库姆港商用码头终端建设项目提供2.65亿美元贷款，是亚投行首次向阿拉伯半岛国家提供贷款。2023年4月，亚投行在阿布扎比开设首个海外办事处，亚投行与阿联酋签署了《东道国协议》，该办事处的设立有助于拉近银行与客户及其一线业务的距离，提升亚投行影响力。2024年10月，亚投行与沙特发展基金签署谅解备忘录，旨在深化合作，推动亚洲及其他地区实现可持续、具有韧性和包容性的发展目标，是双方在扩大合作、助力发展中国家取得实质性进展方面的关键一步。

金砖合作机制为中国与阿拉伯国家提供了更多元的合作平台。2024年1月1日起，沙特、埃及、阿联酋、伊朗、埃塞俄比亚成为金砖国家正式成员。阿拉伯国家加入金砖国家合作机制后，可在新开发银行框架下开展多样化的金融合作，推动建立更加多极化的国际金融体系，通过金砖国家间的政策对话和协商，就金融合作达成更多共识，共同应对金融风险和挑战。1月4日，阿联酋经济部部长阿卜杜拉表示，阿联酋有意增资新开发银行，助力该行更好支持新兴市场国家、发展中国家的开发建设。8月31日，阿尔及利亚正式获准成为新开发银行成员。11月11日，新开发银行独立评价局与阿联酋财政部在迪拜联合举办专题研讨会，旨在加强新开发银行与阿拉伯国家的合作，聚焦可持续发展项目的全球经验分享。金砖合作机制建立了一种新的货币互换机制，即金砖国家应急储备安排，当成员国出现国际收支困难或面临偿债压力时，其他成员国将向其提供流动性资金支持，从而稳定成员国金融状况、缓解国际收支危机。

2024年5月30日，中阿合作论坛第十届部长级会议在北京召开，中阿双方在金融领域的互信得到进一步增强，为未来的金融合作奠定了坚实的基础。会议通过了《中阿合作论坛2024年至2026年行动执行计划》（以下简称《行动执行计划2024—2026》），中方欢迎更多阿拉伯国家加强中阿银联体机制建设，并将加快实施中东工业化专项贷款、中阿金融合作专项贷款合作项目。中阿双方通过完善金融合作机制、深化金融领域务实合作、拓展金融合作新领域、促进经济共同发展和提升中阿关系水平等多方面的共识，为未来合作提供重要的动力和支持，金融领域的积极影响也将为中阿关系的全面发展注入新的活力。

### 4.2.2 推广人民币使用

中国与阿拉伯国家的经贸往来日益紧密，中国与阿拉伯国家中央银行间进一步加强双边本币互换和人民币清算合作，促进本币直接兑换结算，有效减轻投资和贸易融资负担，妥善应对短期流动性波动，为人民币的区域化提供了有力支撑。

双边本币互换。截至2024年8月末，中国人民银行共与42个国家和地区的中央银行或货币当局签署了双边本币互换协议，扩大了本币使用并促进双方贸易和投资便利化，其中阿拉伯国家包括阿联酋、卡塔尔、摩洛哥、埃及和沙特（见表4.3）。本币互换安排旨在便利中阿贸易和投资，为合作国家提供流动性支持。

表4.3 "一带一路"倡议提出以来中国人民银行与阿拉伯国家
签署的双边本币互换协议情况

| 国别 | 互换规模 | 签署时间 | 备注 |
| --- | --- | --- | --- |
| 阿联酋 | 350亿元人民币/200亿阿联酋迪拉姆 | 2015年12月14日 | 续签 |
|  | 350亿元人民币/180亿阿联酋迪拉姆 | 2023年11月28日 | 续签 |
| 卡塔尔 | 350亿元人民币/208亿里亚尔 | 2014年11月3日 |  |
|  | 350亿元人民币/208亿里亚尔 | 2017年11月2日 | 续签 |
|  | 350亿元人民币/208亿里亚尔 | 2021年1月6日 | 续签 |
| 摩洛哥 | 100亿元人民币/150亿摩洛哥迪拉姆 | 2016年5月11日 |  |

续表

| 国别 | 互换规模 | 签署时间 | 备注 |
|---|---|---|---|
| 埃及 | 180亿元人民币/470亿埃及镑 | 2016年12月6日 | |
| | 180亿元人民币/410亿埃及镑 | 2020年2月10日 | 续签 |
| | 180亿元人民币/807亿埃及镑 | 2023年2月20日 | 续签 |
| 沙特 | 500亿元人民币/260亿沙特里亚尔 | 2023年11月20日 | |

资料来源：中国人民银行《人民币国际化报告》。

双边本币结算。阿联酋、沙特是与中国经贸往来密切的重要"一带一路"合作国家，且货币具备银行间外汇市场挂牌条件，经中国人民银行授权，2016年9月26日，人民币对阿联酋迪拉姆和沙特里亚尔在银行间外汇市场开展直接交易。根据公开数据，在起始交易阶段的2018年，两种货币交易量分别达到86亿元人民币和74亿元人民币，自2019年起规模明显减少，但走势较为平稳，近五年内平均交易量分别达到7.6亿元人民币和27.4亿元人民币。

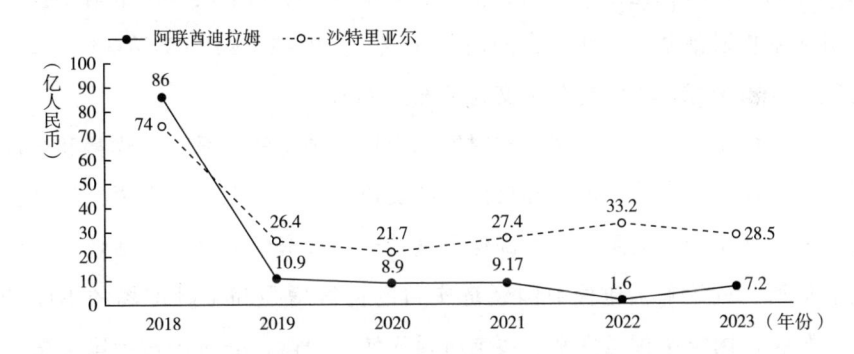

图4.1　2018—2023年银行间外汇即期市场人民币对沙特和阿联酋货币交易量
资料来源：中国人民银行《人民币国际化报告》。

人民币清算与支付。阿拉伯国家的人民币清算和支付网络持续优化。2014年11月4日，中国人民银行授权中国工商银行多哈分行担任多哈人民币业务清算行，2016年12月9日授权中国农业银行迪拜分行担任阿联酋人民币业务清算行。截至2025年1月，人民币跨境支付系统（CIPS）

共有169家直接参与者，在阿拉伯国家中有中国银行（吉布提）有限公司、中国银行股份有限公司迪拜分行、中国银行股份有限公司阿布扎比分行、中国银行卡塔尔金融中心分行、中国银行利雅得分行、中国工商银行股份有限公司多哈分行、中国工商银行股份有限公司利雅得分行、中国工商银行股份有限公司迪拜国际金融中心分行、中国工商银行股份有限公司科威特分行、中国工商银行股份有限公司阿布扎比分行、中国农业银行迪拜分行，以及中国农业银行股份有限公司迪拜国际金融中心分行等12家机构成为CIPS直参行。

### 4.2.3 阿主权财富基金在华投资

国家主权财富基金作为国际金融市场的重要新兴力量，近年来在全球资本流动和投资活动中扮演着越发关键的角色。根据全球主权财富基金组织（Global SWF）发布的2024年前三季度研究报告，以阿联酋和沙特为代表的主权财富基金表现尤为突出。阿联酋的阿布扎比投资局、穆巴达拉投资公司、阿布扎比控股公司、沙特公共投资基金和卡塔尔的卡塔尔投资局五大主权财富基金，在报告期内共完成了126项交易，投资总额达550亿美元，占全球主权财富基金交易总额的40%。

长期以来，阿拉伯国家主权财富基金以其独特的地缘政治优势和全球投资布局而著称，传统上主要聚焦于欧美市场，并与东西方主要经济体保持稳固的战略合作关系，从而确保了其在全球投资中的高度灵活性和影响力。然而，近年来，随着中国经济实力的持续增强和金融市场的不断开放，阿拉伯国家主权财富基金逐渐将目光转向中国，表现出对中国金融市场的高度关注以及对中国经济长期增长前景的积极评价。在中国市场，阿拉伯国家主权财富基金通过一、二级市场的多元化投资，展现出对中国资产的长期信心和战略布局。其中，阿布扎比投资局（ADIA）和穆巴达拉投资公司（Mubadala）是中国一级市场中比较活跃的阿拉伯国家主权财富基金，其投资偏好主要集中在金融与互联网、半导体、生物医药等高增长行业。截至2024年6月底，沙特公共投资基金（PIF）在中国的投资总额已达到 220 亿美元，重点布局科技、汽车及卫生保健等领域。例如，2024年 5 月，联想集团获得沙特公共投资基金子公司 20 亿美元的战略投资，进一步凸显阿拉伯资本对于中国科技企业的青睐。此外，穆巴达拉投资公司在中国已完成 100 多个投资项目，总投资额超过 150 亿美元；阿布扎比投资局旗下 CYVN 对蔚来汽车的投资累计超过 30 亿美元，显示出其对中国新能源汽车行业的高度关注。在二级市场方面，阿拉伯国家主权财富基金的表现同样引人注目。截至 2024 年三季度末，阿布扎比投资局（ADIA）和科威特投资局（KIA）分别现身 24 只和 17 只 A 股个股的前十大流通股东名单中，持仓市值分别达到 89 亿元人民币和 43.8 亿元人民币，投资领域广泛分布于新能源、医药、化工和半导体等高技术行业，充分反映了其对中国新经济领域发展潜力的认可。

阿拉伯国家主权财富基金参与中国境内金融市场的目的日益明确，其诉求也呈现出更加积极主动的态势。这一趋势不仅是阿拉伯国家政府加快产业布局、推动经济多元化战略的重要渠道，也是其深化与中国经济合作的关键举措。在这一背景下，易达资本作为首家专注于沙特与中国跨境投资的投资机构，成为少数获得沙特公共投资基金（PIF）、阿曼投资局（OIA）等多家主权基金支持的中国背景基金之一。易达资本成功支持了极兔中东、联晟智达等企业在沙特落地，推动了中国企业在阿拉伯地区的业务扩展，也为当地的经济发展和产业升级提供了重要支持。2024 年 10 月，阿曼主权基金宣布出资 1.5 亿美元参与易达资本二期美元基金，旨在引入中国成熟市场的行业领先企业，将其产品、技术和服务能力推动阿曼本地经济发展。同期，沙特交通和物流服务部宣布，萨勒曼国王国际机场将与易达资本合作开发沙特—中国特别经济区。该国家级经济区规划总面积 4 平方千米，旨在打造覆盖物流与供应链解决方案的综合服务体系，降低中国企业进入沙特市场的门槛，进一步促进双边经济合作。

阿拉伯国家主权财富基金通过投资人工智能、新能源、先进制造、生物医药等新兴产业，致力于推动当地产业的转型与升级。这一战略不仅为阿拉伯国家的经济多元化注入了新动能，也为中国企业出海提供了巨大的发展机遇。通过与中国企业的深度合作，阿拉伯国家正在逐步实现从传统能源依赖型经济向创新驱动型经济的转变，而中国企业则借助这一契机，进一步拓展其在阿拉伯市场的业务版图，形成了互利共赢的合作格局。

### 4.2.4 中国对阿发展项目融资

"一带一路"倡议提出以来，以中国国家开发银行和中国进出口银行为代表的金融机构积极向阿拉伯国家基础设施项目和产能合作项目提供贷款融资，契合了阿拉伯国家经济和社会发展的迫切需要。中国已成为全球最大的双边开发性融资来源国，全球发展融资为发展中国家提供了重要的资金支持。除海合会成员国，大部分阿拉伯国家经济和社会发展所需的资金和金融服务相对不足，中国对阿发展项目融资有力地促进了当地基础设施建设和产业升级。

从资金流向的国别分布来看，中国对阿拉伯国家的发展融资项目主要集中在埃及（见表4.4），其中埃及新首都中央商务区项目是2013年以来中国在阿拉伯国家融资金额最高的单个项目，项目一期和二期投资金额分别为30亿美元和35亿美元，2019年由中国进出口银行、中国工商银行、中国银行、民生银行、中信银行、中国建设银行、科威特国民银行、汇丰银行等8家银行组建银团提供融资。项目建成后将提供175万个长期工作岗位，带动苏伊士运河经济带和红海经济带开发，助推埃及国民经济长期发展。

表4.4 "一带一路"倡议提出以来中国国家开发银行和中国进出口银行向阿拉伯国家发展融资项目情况

| 国别 | 融资金额（百万美元） | 项目数量 |
| --- | --- | --- |
| 吉布提 | 1178 | 4 |
| 埃及 | 7340 | 11 |
| 科摩罗 | 82 | 1 |

续表

| 国别 | 融资金额（百万美元） | 项目数量 |
| --- | --- | --- |
| 摩洛哥 | 300 | 1 |
| 毛里塔尼亚 | 226 | 2 |
| 阿曼 | 3200 | 1 |
| 总计 | 12326 | 20 |

资料来源：中国海外发展融资数据库（China's Overseas Development Finance，CODF），数据库更新至2023年。

由政府信用保证的公共管理（委托代理）项目开始在国际发展融资中占有重要位置，在该类项目中，中国向阿拉伯国家的融资金额占总额的近一半（见图4.2）。公共管理领域当中最大的一笔发展融资项目，是2017年8月阿曼政府从中国多家银行获得35.5亿美元的五年期贷款，该财政赤字融资计划旨在为阿曼政府填补财政赤字提供充足支持，同时支持阿曼的经济发展和基础设施建设。

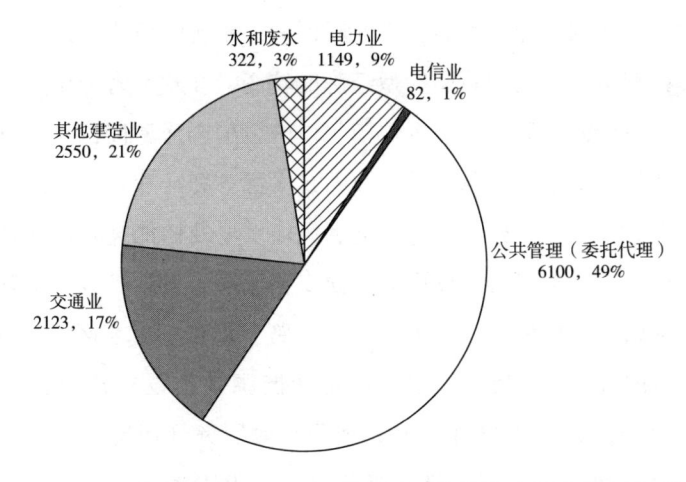

图4.2 "一带一路"倡议提出以来中国国家开发银行和中国进出口银行向阿拉伯国家发展融资项目的行业分布（单位：百万美元）

## 4.3 中阿金融合作的新趋势

中阿金融合作近年来呈现出多元化、创新化和深度化的新趋势。双方在传统金融领域的基础上，逐步拓展至新能源经济和数字货币等新兴领域。中国与阿拉伯国家在数字货币领域的合作取得突破，通过数字货币桥（mBridge）等项目推动跨境支付效率提升和人民币国际化进程。中国资本市场双向开放机制不断完善，深交所、港交所与阿拉伯资本市场的对接日益紧密，促进了资本流动与资源配置优化。中阿金融合作正朝着更加高效、创新和可持续的方向发展，为全球金融体系注入新动能。

中阿新能源合作共筑经济多元化的可持续发展桥梁。自2016年4月沙特发布"2030愿景"以来，阿拉伯国家逐步确立了以经济多元化为核心的长期发展战略。随后，科威特的"2035国家愿景"和卡塔尔的"2030国家愿景"也相继出台，进一步强调了经济结构转型的重要性，特别是在新能源和数字化领域的开放与合作。当前，阿拉伯国家正积极推进能源转型，并在制造业、科技、"互联网+"等领域加速布局，以实现从传统能源依赖型经济向创新驱动型经济的转变。在这一背景下，中国与阿拉伯国家在新能源、数字经济等创新领域的金融合作不断深化，展现出广阔的发展前景。中国在绿色能源领域的技术优势和产业实力为全球能源转型提供了重要支持。中国在光伏发电、风能发电及储能技术等领域均处于世界领先地位，这不仅为全球应对气候变化做出了贡献，也为中阿合作奠定了坚实基础。阿拉伯地区作为"一带一路"倡议的重要区域，与中国在新能源领域的合作潜力巨大。双方围绕新能源基础设施建设，已开展了多项金融合作项目。2024年9月，迪拜金融服务管理局与香港金融管理局签署协议，旨在加强可持续金融发展，并联合举办了气候融资会议，进一步推动绿色金融合作。2024年11月，阿联酋新能源巨头马斯达尔与中国丝路基金签署谅解备忘录，计划共同投资"一带一路"共建国家，特别是发展中国家和南半球地区的清洁能源项目，预计总投资额达

200亿元人民币（约合28亿美元）。这一合作标志着中阿两国在绿色能源领域的合作迈上新台阶，双方将共同推动全球能源转型和可持续发展。此外，2024年6月，沙特国际电力水务公司ACWA Power宣布，丝路基金将收购其旗下可再生能源公司49%的股份。这一合作不仅深化了中沙两国在可再生能源领域的伙伴关系，也为"一带一路"倡议下的绿色能源项目注入了新动力。

中资金融机构在区域金融中心的发展势头强劲。纳斯达克迪拜作为迪拜重要的金融交易平台之一，已成为中国与国际资本市场互联互通的重要桥梁。截至目前，已有来自中国香港和内地的发行人在纳斯达克迪拜发行了约22只证券，总价值达123亿美元。2024年11月13日，中国财政部在纳斯达克迪拜成功上市两只总额为20亿美元的债券，这一举措不仅是中国金融市场高水平双向开放的又一重要例证，也充分体现了国际资本市场对中国经济发展的高度信任与信心。通过发行美元主权债券，中国进一步拓宽了融资渠道，优化了债务结构。与此同时，中资金融机构在阿拉伯地区快速扩展。根据迪拜金融服务管理局的数据，截至2024年底，中资银行在迪拜国际金融中心（DIFC）管理的总资产达到653亿美元，已有16家中资公司入驻DIFC，涵盖6家代表处、5家商业银行、2家财富管理公司、1家经纪公司、1家顾问公司和1家保险公司。中资金融公司在联通境内外金融与产业合作中发挥着重要作用。2024年6月11日，中金公司作为唯一在海湾地区配备当地专家的中资投行，成功协助沙特政府和沙特阿美完成了股票减持二次发售，进一步巩固了其在跨境金融服务领域的领先地位。

深交所和港交所与海湾地区资本市场联系更加紧密。中国境内与境外主要资本市场已建立起高效的双向开放机制，显著促进了资本流动与资源配置的优化。2024年8月14日，深圳证券交易所（深交所）与迪拜金融市场在迪拜联合举办"中国阿联酋（迪拜）资本市场合作研讨会"，并签署合作谅解备忘录，明确将建立高层定期会晤机制，进一步深化双方多层次的交流与合作。这一举措不仅加强了中阿资本市场的互联互通，也为双方在金融产品创新、市场规则对接等领域的合作奠定了坚实基础。香港作为国际金融中心，在阿拉伯地区与内地的资金融通中发挥着关键作用。得益于香港特区政府在推动经济、贸易和金融等领域合作的持续努力，中国香港与阿拉伯地区的经贸往来日益深化，合作成果显著。2023年9月，香港交易所宣布将沙特证券交易所纳入认可证券交易所名单，允许在沙特市场主要上市的公司来港申请第二上市。2024年7月，香港交易所进一步将阿布扎比证券交易所和迪拜金融市场纳入认可证券交易所名单，进一步拓宽了双方资本市场的合作渠道。2024年10月30日，沙特投资中国香港市场的交易所买卖基金（ETF）——Albilad南方东英MSCI香港中国股票ETF（Albilad CSOP MSCI Hong Kong China Equity ETF）在沙特证券交易所上市，首募规模达百亿港元，是投资中国市场的ETF首次登陆沙特市场，具有里程碑意义，标志着中国香港与阿拉伯地区之间的投资流动进一步打通。此外，中金香港证券已正式获得迪拜金融服务管理局（DFSA）颁发的运营资质，进一步巩固了中资机构在阿拉伯市场的布局。香港正积极争取大型主权基金合作，共同出资成立基金，并持续拓展和深化与阿拉伯地区的金融合作网络。这些举措不仅提升了中国香港作为国际金融枢纽的地位，也为中国与阿拉伯地区的资本流动和金融合作注入了新的动力。

  数字货币领域合作推动全球金融体系的创新与变革。《行动执行计划2024—2026》明确提出，中国愿根据阿拉伯国家在建设本地央行数字货币系统及区域性基础设施方面的需求，提供相关技术支持与合作。这一倡议旨在推动数字货币领域的创新与应用，进一步深化中阿金融合作。在数字货币桥（mBridge）项目中，中国与阿拉伯国家的合作已取得显著进展。自2022年参与数字货币桥试点以来，中国工商银行阿布扎比分行通过该平台拓展了人民币国际化的实际应用场景，为中资企业的海外发展提供了更加便捷的金融服务。2024年1月29日，阿联酋中央银行通过mBridge平台与中国银行成功完成了价值5000万阿联酋迪拉姆（约合9800万元人民币）的首笔数字迪拉姆跨境支付交易；中国银行阿联酋机构也利用该平台完成了阿联酋境内首笔数字人民币跨境汇款交易。mBridge借助区块链技术，显著提升了跨境支付效率，降低了交易成本，同时增强了金融体系的透明度和监管能力，成为多边央行跨境支付合作的典范，相对自主国际网络也为人民币国际化进程提供了重要支持。2024年6月7日，瑞士国际清算银行（BIS）宣布沙特央行全面加入mBridge项目。沙特的参与不仅进一步扩大了mBridge的覆盖范围，有望成为全球石油交易迈向非美元结算的重要一步，也为石油人民币结算在技术层面的可行性提供了重要支持。

## 4.4 中阿金融合作展望

中阿金融合作展现出巨大的发展潜力和广阔前景。展望未来，双方在绿色能源转型、资本市场互联互通、人民币国际化及国际债务治理等领域的合作不断深化，将为全球金融治理和经济可持续发展注入新动力。

海湾地区对绿色能源转型的需求日益迫切，这一趋势与中国提出的"3060双碳目标"（即2030年前碳达峰、2060年前碳中和）高度契合。中国作为世界第二大经济体，对全球能源行业的影响至关重要；中国政府在立法、政策导向和产业支持等方面对新能源的高度重视，为国际能源企业提供了良好的投资环境。国际原油价格波动和地缘政治的不确定性，促使海湾依赖能源出口的阿拉伯国家通过战略调整，加强同中国市场的合作，实现风险的有效管理。随着全球能源市场格局的持续变化，沙特阿美积极调整其战略布局，高度重视中国市场。与中国市场的深入合作，不仅有助于沙特阿美减少对其他市场的依赖，还能通过技术共享和经验交流，推动其在新能源转型过程中实现更加稳健的发展。作为全球新能源技术和装备制造的领先国家，中国可充分发挥其技术和产业优势，与阿拉伯国家在新能源领域展开深度合作，共同推动绿色能源的布局与发展。此外，中阿双方还可通过绿色债券等金融工具，为经济低碳转型提供资金支持，不仅符合双方的战略利益，也为全球能源转型和可持续发展提供了重要范例。

中阿双方头部金融机构在资本市场互联互通进程中发挥更大引领作用。《行动执行计划2024—2026》提出，"积极支持双方主权财富基金、私募投资基金、商业银行等金融机构及有关监管部门加强交流合作，互设分支机构，为双方提供优质金融服务，将推动双方资本市场互联互通"。一方面，以主权财富基金为代表的阿拉伯资本在中国境内金融市场中的作用日益凸显。获得阿拉伯资本支持的创新型企业，能够利用其广泛的网络和资源优势，创造显著的协同效应，不仅有助于推动阿拉伯国家的经济转型和技术发展，也为双方实现互利共赢提供了重要契机。另一方面，中资金融机构在阿拉伯国家金融中心的业务布局稳步推进，这不仅是中国金融机构国际化进程中的重要举措，也为跨境投资与金融创新注入新动力。2024年4月24日，中国投资有限责任公司（中投公司）与巴林投资机构Investcorp成立初始规模为10亿美元的"中海基金Investcorp Golden Horizon"，计划投资中国、海湾合作委员会成员国的高成长企业。这是中投公司设立的第七只创新型双边基金，进一步强化了中国与海湾国家在金融和产业领域的联结。

中阿能源合作助推人民币国际化进程，借助央行货币数字化进程和金砖成员国新开发银行机制建设，未来能源合作有望实现人民币结算。全球货币体系的数字化进程可能引发各国货币支付体系的重大调整。2023年起，中国与阿联酋在金融技术创新和央行数字货币领域的合作不断推进，在多边货币桥框架下推动跨境支付互联互通，以减少对当前美元支付体系的依赖。在大宗商品交易领域，人民币的结算货币功能不断深化。2024年，人民币已成为全球第四大支付货币，初步具备了国际通用的网络效应。中阿双方以深厚的能源合作为基础，为人民币在国际结算和交易中的扩大使用创造了有利条件。随着大宗商品结算和定价机制的重构，人民币作为国际货币的角色将持续加强。金砖国家于2015年成立的新开发银行，旨在减少对美元的依赖，推动建立更加多极化的国际金融体系，阿拉伯国家加入金砖之后，依托能源贸易，统一的金砖国家结算体系有望逐步形成。沙特、阿联酋等阿拉伯国家表现出对使用人民币结算石油的开放态度，标志着"去美元化"趋势的加速。考虑到地缘政治因素，沙特等石油输出国在跨境原油交易中使用人民币结算的过程仍然面临美元霸权的挑战，这一转变将是一个循序渐进的长期过程，需要通过逐步的改革与开放实现。

中国与阿拉伯国家在国际债务问题上的合作具有重要的战略意义和实际价值。随着"一带一路"倡议的深入推进，中国与阿拉伯国家在经济、金融等领域的合作不断深化，双方在债务问题上的合作也展现出新的机遇。首先，中国与阿拉伯国家在基础设施建设、能源开发等领域的合作日益密切，这些项目往往需要大量资金支持，容易产生债务问题。中国在债务管理方面积累了丰富经验，特别是在"债务可持续性"框架下，能够为阿拉伯国家提供有效的债务解决方案。通过合作，中阿双方可以共同探索更加灵活和可持续的融资模式，例如通过公私合营（PPP）或混合融资等方式，减轻债务压力。其次，中国与阿拉伯国家在国际多边金融机构中具有重要影响力。双方可以在世界银行、国际货币基金组织（IMF）等平台上加强协调，推动国际债务治理体系的改革，特别是为发展中国家争取更多话语权和资源支持。中国倡导的"共商共建共享"理念与阿拉伯国家的发展需求高度契合，双方可以共同推动建立更加公平合理的国际债务规则。此外，中国与阿拉伯国家在绿色金融和可持续发展领域的合作，也为债务问题提供了新的解决思路。随着全球对气候变化和可持续发展的关注，绿色债券、气候融资等新型金融工具逐渐成为国际债务管理的重要方向。中国在绿色金融领域处于全球领先地位，可以为阿拉伯国家提供技术支持和经验分享，帮助其实现经济转型和债务的可持续性。中阿双方长期保持友好关系，在重大国际问题上相互支持，在债务问题上形成共识，避免因债务问题引发政治或经济摩擦。中国可以通过加强政策协调、创新融资模式、推动多边合作等方式，协助有需要的阿拉伯国家应对债务挑战，为全球债务治理提供新的合作范例。

中阿金融合作展现出巨大的发展潜力和广阔前景。双方合作的持续深化，不仅体现了彼此间的高度信任以及对加强经济贸易与投资合作的共同意愿，还推动了金融及其他领域的务实合作迈向新高度。这种合作模式为双边关系注入了持久而强劲的动力，同时有助于提升发展中国家在全球金融治理中的话语权，推动国际金融体系朝着更加平衡和多元化的方向演进。

# 第5章　中阿农业合作专题报告

农业是当前中阿合作较为活跃的领域之一。中国和阿拉伯国家在农业领域的合作历史悠久，近年来，随着中阿关系的持续深化，中阿农业合作取得了显著成果。

## 5.1 "一带一路"倡议提出以来的中阿农业合作

### 5.1.1 加强顶层设计，农业重视程度高

农业合作是中阿合作的重点内容。中阿合作论坛和中阿博览会作为中阿合作重要的机制性平台，都将农业合作列为中阿合作的重要议题。"一带一路"倡议的提出与实施，为中阿农业合作创造了历史机遇，双方通过政策对接和务实合作，合作水平不断提升。与此同时，首届中阿峰会、中阿合作论坛第十届部长级会议以及中非合作论坛都强调了中国与阿拉伯国家和非洲国家加强农业合作的重要性。[1] 这些顶层设计，为中阿农业合作

---

[1] 首届中阿峰会提出的"粮食安全共同行动"和"绿色创新共同行动"。"粮食安全共同行动"：中方愿帮助阿方提升粮食安全水平，提升农业综合生产能力；同阿方共建5个现代农业联合实验室，开展50个农业技术合作示范项目，向阿方派遣500名农业技术专家，帮助阿方增加粮食产量、提高收储减损能力、提升农业生产效率；为阿方优质农食产品建立输华准入"绿色通道"。"绿色创新共同行动"：中方愿同阿方设立中阿干旱、荒漠化和土地退化国际研究中心，实施5个应对气候变化南南合作项目。中阿合作论坛第十届部长级会议提出的"更富活力的创新驱动格局"。"更富活力的创新驱动格局"：中方将同阿方在生命健康、人工智能、绿色低碳、现代农业、空间信息等领域共建10家联合实验室；愿同阿方加强人工智能领域合作，共同促进人工智能赋能实体经济，（转下页注）

指明了方向，描绘了蓝图。

表 5.1 罗列了历届中阿合作论坛部长级会议有关农业合作的内容，从表中可看出，中阿农业合作更加强调农业领域的机制化建设、农产品贸易的扩大以及在现代农业、农业科技等方面的合作，执行计划更加具体，针对性更强。

表 5.1　历届中阿合作论坛部长级会议有关农业合作内容

| 部长级会议 | 相关内容 |
| --- | --- |
| 第一届 | 行动计划：在农业与环保领域，特别是新技术、遗传工程、农机具、现代化灌溉系统、防治荒漠化等领域开展合作，交流经验 |
| 第二届 | 2006—2008 年行动执行计划：鼓励双方质检、海关、税收和工、农业等部门开展多种形式的交流与技术合作 |
| 第三届 | 2008—2010 年行动执行计划：第六条　农业合作<br>（一）双方愿加强在农业领域的交流与合作，密切农业高层互访，增加信息沟通，加强在种植业、养殖业等专业领域的专业人员交流，鼓励双方有意愿、有实力的农业企业开展经贸合作<br>（二）促进双方农产品贸易，为双方优质农产品进入对方市场提供便利 |
| 第四届 | 2010—2012 年行动执行计划：第七条　农业合作<br>（一）双方愿加强在农业和粮食安全领域的合作，鼓励双方农业科技人员和管理人员加强交流，增加信息沟通<br>（二）鼓励双方有意愿、有实力的农业企业开展经贸合作，促进双方农产品贸易发展，为双方农产品进入对方市场提供便利 |
| 第五届 | 2012—2014 年行动执行计划：第七条 农业合作<br>（一）双方愿加强农业、粮食安全领域的合作，鼓励双方技术管理人员的交流，增加信息沟通。鉴于农业领域越发重要，特别是当前世界粮食价格高企，并对粮食安全造成影响，探讨建立中国—阿拉伯国家农业合作机制 |

---

(接上页注①) 推动形成具有广泛共识的全球人工智能治理体系；愿同阿方共建空间碎片联合观测中心、北斗应用合作发展中心，加强载人航天、民用客机等合作。中非合作论坛北京峰会提出的"兴农惠民伙伴行动"：中方将向非洲提供 10 亿元人民币紧急粮食援助，建设 10 万亩农业标准化示范区，派遣 500 名农业专家，建设中非农业科技创新联盟。实施 500 个公益项目。鼓励中非企业"双向奔赴"投资创业，把产业附加值留在非洲，为非洲创造不少于 100 万个就业岗位。

续表

| 部长级会议 | 相关内容 |
| --- | --- |
| 第五届 | （二）举办两次或两次以上农业经贸与投资合作研讨会，其中一次在中国举行，另一次在某个阿拉伯国家举行。鼓励双方农业企业开展经贸合作，促进双方农产品贸易发展，为双方农产品进入对方市场提供便利<br>（三）中阿研究机构开展农业研究、农业生产和粮食安全领域的合作与协调 |
| 第六届 | 中国—阿拉伯国家合作论坛 2014 年至 2024 年发展规划：<br>实施在农业、粮食安全、动物和渔业资源、食品工业、荒漠化防治、环境技术等领域的共同项目，建立中阿荒漠化防治技术培训中心<br>2014—2016 年行动执行计划：第七条 农业合作<br>（一）致力于巩固和加强农业领域的双多边机制，在农业、生物农业、粮食安全、动物资源和兽医服务领域加强合作，交换在卫生监管领域的相关法律法规，借鉴中国在基因改良方面的经验，鼓励双方农业科技和管理人员加强交流，增加信息沟通<br>（二）举办中国—阿拉伯国家农业贸易与投资洽谈活动，鼓励双方有意愿有实力的农业企业开展经贸合作，促进双方农产品贸易发展，为双方农畜产品进入对方市场提供便利<br>（三）加强水务技术、水资源利用和节约领域的合作 |
| 第七届 | 《多哈宣言》<br>加强防治荒漠化领域合作，欢迎在摩洛哥王国建立中阿防治荒漠化中心，同时欢迎中华人民共和国环境保护部与阿拉伯国家联盟签署环境合作谅解备忘录。欢迎双方专业人员参加 2016 年在苏丹召开的荒漠化和干旱治理研讨会。积极建立机制，促进农业领域合作<br>2016—2018 年行动执行计划：第七条 农业合作<br>（一）致力于巩固和加强农业领域的双多边机制，在农业、有机农业/生物农业、粮食安全、动物资源和兽医服务领域加强合作，交换在卫生监管领域的相关法律法规，借鉴中国在基因改良方面的经验，鼓励双方农业科技和管理人员加强交流，增加信息沟通<br>（二）积极建立中国与阿拉伯国家农业合作机制，继续加强双方农业领域的合作，包括通过双多边机制加强节水旱作农业、有机农业/生物农业、粮食安全、动物和渔业资源及食品工业等领域合作，积极开展农业领域经验交流，借鉴中国的经验<br>（三）举办中阿农业贸易与农业投资洽谈会，鼓励双方有意愿、有实力的农业企业开展经贸合作，促进双方农产品贸易发展，为双方农牧产品进入对方市场提供便利。双方呼吁为对方企业在本国投资营造良好的投资环境，出台相关优惠政策，提供便利措施和服务<br>（四）加强在水务技术、水资源利用和节约领域的合作<br>（五）鼓励在农业领域建立联合企业，包括化肥生产、农业机械装备制造、提高各类农业活动生产率 |

续表

| 部长级会议 | 相关内容 |
| --- | --- |
| 第八届 | 《北京宣言》<br>积极建立加强农业领域务实合作的机制。推动在阿联酋建立农牧渔业批发市场，欢迎中国农业农村部和阿联酋气候变化和环境保护部签署关于加强农业合作的谅解备忘录，以及中国原农业部和苏丹农业和林业部在 2016 年签署的农业领域合作备忘录，欢迎中国农业农村部和埃及农业和农垦部签署农业合作行动计划（2018—2020）<br>加强林业经贸与防治荒漠化领域的合作与交流。鼓励双方开展荒漠化和土地退化治理方面的专业探讨，欢迎双方专业人员参加对方举办的荒漠化、干旱与土地退化防治座谈与研讨活动，继续探讨在摩洛哥建立中阿荒漠化防治中心<br>2018—2020 行动执行计划：第六条　农业合作<br>（一）致力于巩固和加强农业领域的双多边机制，在农业、有机农业/生物农业、粮食安全领域加强合作，交换在卫生监管领域的相关法律法规，借鉴中国在基因改良方面的经验，鼓励双方农业科技和管理人员加强交流，增加信息沟通<br>（二）积极建立中国与阿拉伯国家农业合作机制，继续加强双方农业领域的合作，包括通过双多边机制加强节水农业、有机农业/生物农业、粮食安全、农产品市场体系建设、动物和渔业资源及食品工业和兽医服务等领域合作，积极开展农业领域经验交流，借鉴中国的经验<br>（三）充分发挥中阿博览会平台作用，在中阿博览会期间举办中阿农业贸易与农业投资洽谈会。双方呼吁为对方企业在本国投资营造良好的投资环境，出台相关优惠政策，提供便利措施和服务<br>（四）加强在水务技术、水资源利用和节约、雨水收集、废水处理再利用和干旱地区水资源管理等领域的合作，加强双方水资源研究中心的合作关系<br>（五）鼓励在农业领域建立联合企业，包括化肥生产、农业机械装备制造，以提高各类农业活动生产率<br>（六）推动在阿联酋建立农牧渔业批发市场，欢迎中国农业农村部和阿联酋气候变化和环境保护部签署关于加强农业合作的谅解备忘录，以及中国原农业部和苏丹农业和林业部在 2016 年签署的农业领域合作备忘录，欢迎中国农业农村部和埃及农业和农垦部签署农业合作行动计划（2018—2020） |
| 第九届 | 《安曼宣言》<br>双方强调应进一步加强经济、社会、发展与新闻合作，特别是贸易、投资、金融、工业与交通运输、能源、自然资源与环境、农业、旅游、人力资源开发、知识产权、文化与文明对话、图书馆与信息、教育与科研、科学与技术、卫生与社会发展、新闻、民间合作、妇女、青体、可持续发展与人口政策领域的合作 |

续表

| 部长级会议 | 相关内容 |
|---|---|
| 第九届 | 2020—2022年行动执行计划：第六条　农业合作<br>（一）致力于巩固和加强农业领域的双多边机制，在农业、有机农业/生物农业、粮食安全领域加强合作，交换在卫生监管领域的相关法律法规，借鉴中国在基因改良方面的经验，鼓励双方农业科技和管理人员加强交流，增加信息沟通<br>（二）积极建立中国与阿拉伯国家农业合作机制，继续加强双方农业领域的合作，包括通过双多边机制加强节水农业、有机农业/生物农业、粮食安全、农产品市场体系建设、动物和渔业资源及食品工业和兽医服务等领域合作，积极开展农业领域经验交流，借鉴中国的经验。继续深化中阿农业领域务实合作和经验交流<br>（三）充分发挥中阿博览会平台作用，在中阿博览会期间举办中阿农业贸易与农业投资洽谈会。双方呼吁为对方企业在本国投资营造良好的投资环境，出台相关优惠政策，提供便利措施和服务<br>（四）加强在水务技术、水资源利用和节约、雨水收集、废水处理再利用和干旱地区水资源管理等领域的合作，加强双方水资源研究中心的合作关系<br>（五）鼓励在农业领域建立联合企业，包括化肥生产、农业机械装备制造，以提高各类农业活动生产率 |
| 第十届 | 2024—2026年行动执行计划：第七条　农业合作<br>（一）加强农业、渔业和畜牧业合作，推动现代种植技术、中小农户适用技术使用、土壤健康、农业机械化与绿色发展等重点领域合作，扩大可持续农业投资。加强粮食安全、水培农业、无土栽培、农用无人机使用领域合作，开展粮食仓储、减损、科技合作。中方愿与阿方共享技术发展成果，并将其本土化，帮助阿方改进现有农田灌溉系统，加强农业节水能力，使其谷物和战略性农产品等达到自给自足的安全线<br>（二）共同培育区域性特色优势产业，重点围绕旱作农业、盐碱地综合利用、动物疫病防控等领域开展农业科技交流 |

资料来源：根据中阿合作论坛网站内容整理所得。

中阿博览会作为中阿经贸合作的重要机制性平台，历届都设有农业板块。2013年以来，农业农村部和宁夏回族自治区人民政府成功举办了五届中阿博览会农业板块活动，通过十余年的合作交流，活动规模不断扩大，取得丰硕成果，展现出强劲韧性和旺盛活力，已成为中阿博览会的重要组成部分和中外农业国际合作交流的重要平台。先后有100多个国家和地区的重要嘉宾、国内外60多家大型商协会以及600多家重点企业参会参展，举办了一系列经贸洽谈、投资推介等活动，签署合作协议近100项，培训发展中国家农业官员、技术人员400多名，与"一带一路"共建国家广泛开展农业技术、贸易投资、人才交流等领域的合作交流，共同促进现代农业高质量发展，为共建"一带一路"发挥了积极作用。[①]

### 5.1.2 农产品贸易呈增长态势

近年来，随着中阿农业贸易的推进，中阿农产品贸易额不断扩大，阿拉伯国家的非油类商品在中国的市场不断扩大，尤其是农产品。例如，埃及的鲜橙、葡萄，沙特的椰枣等在中国市场受到欢迎，中国的茶叶等农产品在阿拉伯国家市场占有一席之地。从表5.2和图5.1可看出，2013—2024年，中阿农产品贸易整体呈上升趋势，2013年进出口总额为272050.4万美元，2024年为583172.7万美元，涨幅达114.36%。即使在新冠疫情期间，中阿农产品贸易合作仍呈上升态势。尽管贸易规模在中国农业贸易进口总量中占比不高，但逐年上升的份额占比表明，阿拉伯国家在中国农产品进口中发挥着越来越重要的作用。

表5.2 2013—2024年中国与阿拉伯国家进出口农产品额

单位：万美元

| 年份 | 出口额 | 进口额 | 进出口总额 |
| --- | --- | --- | --- |
| 2013 | 214528.3 | 57522.1 | 272050.4 |
| 2014 | 214581.2 | 42548.3 | 257129.5 |
| 2015 | 222586.8 | 38294.8 | 260881.6 |
| 2016 | 217965.1 | 30789.9 | 248755.0 |
| 2017 | 223868.0 | 57281.6 | 281149.6 |
| 2018 | 223107.4 | 74907.0 | 298014.4 |
| 2019 | 259872.0 | 122824.5 | 382696.5 |

---

[①] 《这十年，中阿农业合作硕果累累》，《宁夏日报》2023年9月22日第6版。

续表

| 年份 | 出口额 | 进口额 | 进出口总额 |
| --- | --- | --- | --- |
| 2020 | 246672.5 | 159135.5 | 405808.0 |
| 2021 | 245548.3 | 194445.6 | 439993.9 |
| 2022 | 309218.2 | 198117.9 | 507336.1 |
| 2023 | 375847.9 | 197428.4 | 573276.3 |
| 2024 | 427325.4 | 155847.3 | 583172.7 |

资料来源：根据中华人民共和国商务部《中国进出口月度统计报告·农产品（2013年—2024年）》统计数据计算所得。

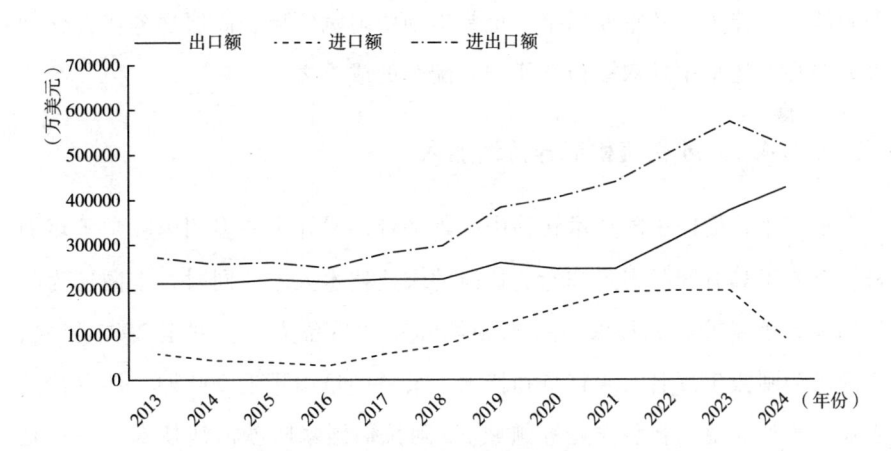

图 5.1　2013—2024 年中国与阿拉伯国家农产品贸易额

资料来源：根据中华人民共和国商务部《中国进出口月度统计报告·农产品（2023年—2024年）》统计数据计算所得。

### 5.1.3　农业技术转移与合作持续深化

随着科学技术的发展，在农产品贸易持续增长的同时，中阿农业科技合作和技术交流也日益密切。中阿技术转移中心、中阿农业技术转移中心等双边合作机构的成立将进一步推动中国现代农业技术进入阿拉伯国家。中阿农业技术转移中心在毛里塔尼亚、摩洛哥等多个阿拉伯国家示范运营，取得丰硕成果。例如，智能灌溉系统、荒漠苜蓿种植技术、智能 LED 植物工厂技术等在阿拉伯国家得到成功应用和推广。此外，双方还在盐碱地治理利用、旱作农业等领域开展了深度合作。中国加大了在阿拉伯国家推广技术和培训专业人员的努力，包括在毛里塔尼亚推广奶牛胚胎移植技术，在约旦建立蔬菜种植示范区，在阿联酋沙漠中种植水稻，以及在埃及推广智能灌溉和节水技术。由宁夏大学孙兆军团队研发的风光互补高效节水灌溉系统，在中国—阿拉伯国家技术转移中心的支持下，在阿曼、阿联酋、埃及、卡塔尔等国家成功进行了试验示范和技术转移，使宁夏农业节水技术走出国门，服务了共建"一带一路"。在新技术成果的助力下，卡塔尔构建了绿色农产品产业链和场地绿化产业链。中阿农业合作既是深化中阿战略伙伴关系的重要抓手，也是推动中阿宽领域、高层次务实合作的重要路径，还是中阿双多边合作相互配合的成果之一。

### 5.1.4 人才交流和培养持续加大

多年来，借助中阿技术转移中心等平台，累计举办多期国际学术培训班，培养了具有国际视野和专业技能的农业技术人才。同时，中国还为阿拉伯国家培养了一大批农业技术领域领军和后备人才。截至2022年底，中国已为阿盟1万名农业官员和技术人员举办培训班近500期，涉及沙漠农业、水产养殖、智慧农业等领域。[①] 阿拉伯国家防沙治沙技术培训班是中国面向阿拉伯国家举办的无偿技术多边培训班，由商务部主办，宁夏农林科学院林业与草地生态研究所承办，已连续举办13期，吸引多个阿拉伯国家的国际学员，相互交流学习、互通有无、共谋发展。

### 5.1.5 国际交流合作不断加强

农业议题作为中阿合作的重要议题，近年来，中国和阿拉伯国家通过举办线上线下研讨会、实地调研等活动，加强中阿双方农业合作交流。农业农村部、阿拉伯国家驻华使馆以及农业技术部、地方政府、科研院所、高校等

---

① Pramod Kumar, "China and Arab States Sign $471m Worth of Agri Deals", September 25, 2023, https://www.agbi.com/agriculture/2023/09/china-and-arab-states-sign-471m-worth-of-agri-deals/.

举办多场农业研讨会，围绕农业技术、贸易投资、粮食安全等领域展开讨论。在中阿博览会框架下，围绕中阿农业合作，举办了主旨演讲、高端对话、"一带一路"粮食安全及农业合作圆桌会、发展中国家高级官员研修及现代农业考察交流等系列活动，进一步促进了中国和阿拉伯国家国际交流合作。

## 5.2 2024年中阿农业合作现状

2024年，中阿农业合作保持良好发展势头，主要表现在农产品贸易、协议签署、项目合作、人才交流与培训等方面。

### 5.2.1 中阿农产品贸易往来

#### 5.2.1.1 中阿农产品贸易规模

根据商务部2024年12月发布的农产品统计报告，2024年，中国农产品进出口额为3181.60亿美元，同比下降4.5%，其中出口额为1030.00亿美元，同比增长4.1%；进口额为2151.60亿美元，同比下降8.1%。中阿农产品贸易额为51.89亿美元，同比增长12.8%，其中出口额为42.73亿美元，同比增长21.4%；进口额为9.16亿美元，同比下降0.3%。一些阿拉伯国家也成为中国农产品进出口的重要来源国和目的地。2024年，摩洛哥成为中国茶叶出口的第一大市场，出口额为24231.20万美元，同比增长27.5%。伊拉克是中国番茄酱罐头出口的第一大市场，出口额为15840.00万美元，同比下降21.4%。阿联酋成为中国烟草第二大出口市场，出口额为7862.70万美元，同比增长10.3%。阿联酋还是中国菜籽油第二大进口市场，进口额为31787.30万美元，同比下降0.4%。①

---

① 中华人民共和国商务部对外贸易司：《中国进出口月度统计报告·农产品（2024年12月）》，2025年2月21日，http：//wms.mofcom.gov.cn/cms_files/filemanager/271034535/attach/20252/08b1bab98c774d78b54d8edea96af766.pdf?fileName=%E4%B8%AD%E5%9B%BD%E5%86%9C%E4%BA%A7%E5%93%81%E8%BF%9B%E5%87%BA%E5%8F%A3%E6%9C%88%E5%BA%A6%E7%BB%9F%E8%AE%A1%E6%8A%A5%E5%91%8A2024%E5%B9%B412%E6%9C%88.pdf。

### 5.2.1.2 中阿农产品贸易结构

从表5.3可以看出,2024年,中国从阿拉伯国家进口的主要农产品依次为:"(12)含油子仁及果实;杂项子仁及果实;工业用或药用植物;稻草、秸秆及饲料""(15)动、植物油、脂及其分解产品;精制的食用油脂;动、植物蜡""(23)食品工业的残渣及废料;配制的动物饲料",进口额均在3亿美元以上;"(03)鱼、甲壳动物、软体动物及其他水生无脊椎动物"进口额超1亿美元。此外,有4类农产品中国未从阿拉伯国家进口。与2023年相比,2024年进口涨幅最大的农产品为"(06)活树及其他活植物;鳞茎、根及类似品;插花及装饰用簇叶",涨幅达18217.5%,降幅最大的农产品为"(16)肉、鱼、甲壳动物、软体动物及其他水生无脊椎动物、昆虫的制品",降幅为99.39%。

表5.3 2024年中国与阿拉伯国家进出口农产品情况

单位:万美元

| (代码)产品名称 | 进口 金额(万美元) | 进口 同比(%) | 出口 金额(万美元) | 出口 同比(%) |
|---|---|---|---|---|
| 第一类 活动物;动物产品 | | | | |
| (01)活动物 | 0 | 0 | 15.54 | 70.21 |
| (02)肉及食用杂碎 | 0 | 0 | 5814.91 | 145.00 |
| (03)鱼、甲壳动物、软体动物及其他水生无脊椎动物 | 13510.35 | -15.24 | 11241.38 | 33.00 |
| (04)乳品;蛋品;天然蜂蜜;其他食用动物产品 | 485.99 | 309.05 | 3160.86 | 64.43 |
| (05)其他动物产品 | 388.78 | 71.37 | 1057.54 | 25.84 |
| 第二类 植物产品 | | | | |
| (06)活树及其他活植物;鳞茎、根及类似品;插花及装饰用簇叶 | 135.55 | 18217.57 | 2884.65 | 28.58 |
| (07)食用蔬菜、根及块茎 | 13.61 | 158.25 | 42697.98 | 45.85 |
| (08)食用水果及坚果;甜瓜或柑橘属水果的果皮 | 9204.06 | -20.87 | 39039.24 | 50.66 |
| (09)咖啡、茶、马黛茶及调味香料 | 132.38 | -12.14 | 64321.91 | 1.47 |
| (10)谷物 | 0 | 0 | 6782.68 | -50.24 |
| (11)制粉工业产品;麦芽;淀粉;菊粉;面筋 | 0 | 0 | 1350.91 | -29.05 |

续表

| （代码）产品名称 | 进口 金额（万美元） | 进口 同比（%） | 出口 金额（万美元） | 出口 同比（%） |
| --- | --- | --- | --- | --- |
| （12）含油子仁及果实；杂项子仁及果实；工业用或药用植物；稻草、秸秆及饲料 | 49824.24 | -18.32 | 43090.14 | 10.48 |
| （13）虫胶；树胶、树脂及其他植物液、汁 | 778.24 | 20.27 | 2309.15 | -1.69 |
| （14）编结用植物材料；其他植物产品 | 15.91 | 13.48 | 340.17 | -0.10 |
| 第三类 动、植物油、脂及其分解产品；精制的食用油脂；动、植物蜡 | | | | |
| （15）动、植物油、脂及其分解产品；精制的食用油脂；动、植物蜡 | 33093.14 | -10.17 | 2857.68 | 26.47 |
| 第四类 食品；饮料、酒及醋；烟草及烟草代用品的制品 | | | | |
| （16）肉、鱼、甲壳动物、软体动物及其他水生无脊椎动物、昆虫的制品 | 0.05 | -99.39 | 20941.93 | 65.14 |
| （17）糖及糖食 | 240.85 | -59.90 | 14280.54 | -7.30 |
| （18）可可及可可制品 | 778.63 | -28.84 | 4757.7 | 47.19 |
| （19）谷物、粮食粉、淀粉或乳的制品；糕饼点心 | 228.91 | -21.96 | 5300.34 | -0.90 |
| （20）蔬菜、水果、坚果或植物其他部分的制品 | 85.78 | -61.44 | 66753.9 | -4.61 |
| （21）杂项食品 | 139.39 | 51.02 | 22495.6 | 27.67 |
| （22）饮料、酒及醋 | 861.07 | 20.98 | 5297.88 | 3.05 |
| （23）食品工业的残渣及废料；配制的动物饲料 | 30178.67 | -28.72 | 4650.74 | 43.11 |
| （24）烟草、烟草及烟草代用品的制品；非经燃烧吸用的产品，不论是否含有尼古丁；其他人体供摄入尼古丁的含尼古丁的产品 | 1192.19 | 19.38 | 51216 | 13.48 |

资料来源：根据中国海关总署数据整理计算。

2024年，中国向阿拉伯国家出口的前五类农产品依次为"（20）蔬菜、水果、坚果或植物其他部分的制品""（09）咖啡、茶、马黛茶及调味香料""（24）烟草、烟草及烟草代用品的制品；非经燃烧吸用的产品，不论是否含有尼古丁；其他人体供摄入尼古丁的含尼古丁的产品""（12）含油子仁及果实；杂项子仁及果实；工业用或药用植物；稻草、秸秆及饲料""（07）食用蔬菜、根及块茎"，出口额均在4亿美元以上；出口最少的农产品为"（01）活动物"，出口额仅为15.54万美元。与2023年相比，

2024年涨幅最大的农产品为"（02）肉及食用杂碎"，增幅为145%；降幅最大的农产品为"（10）谷物"，降幅为50.24%。

#### 5.2.1.3 中国与阿拉伯国家农产品贸易来源国和目的国

从表5.4可看出，2024年，中国主要的农产品进口来源国为阿联酋、苏丹、毛里塔尼亚、埃及、沙特等国家。中国从上述五国进口农产品金额占从阿拉伯国家进口农产品的96.45%。从表5.5可看出，从主要农产品进口国来说，"（03）鱼、甲壳动物、软体动物及其他水生无脊椎动物"的主要进口国为沙特（8092.0274万美元）、毛里塔尼亚（4507.1908万美元）和阿曼（680.1876万美元）；"（08）食用水果及坚果；甜瓜或柑橘属水果的果皮"的主要进口国为埃及（7858.4725万美元）、沙特（449.0842万美元）和伊拉克（446.8554万美元）；"（12）含油子仁及果实；杂项子仁及果实；工业用或药用植物；稻草、秸秆及饲料"主要进口国为苏丹（49650.8937万美元）和摩洛哥（112.8869万美元）；"（15）动、植物油、脂及其分解产品；精制的食用油脂；动、植物蜡"主要进口国为阿联酋（31787.3419万美元）、摩洛哥（938.2705万美元）和毛里塔尼亚（319.0681万美元）；"（18）可可及可可制品"的主要进口国为黎巴嫩（543.0967万美元）和阿联酋（235.4760万美元）；"（23）食品工业的残渣及废料；配制的动物饲料"的主要进口国为阿联酋（18042.2847万美元）、毛里塔尼亚（9163.8859万美元）和苏丹（1828.2351万美元）。

表5.4 2024年中国从阿拉伯国家进口农产品来源国

单位：万美元

| 排名 | 国家 | 进口额 | 排名 | 国家 | 进口额 |
| --- | --- | --- | --- | --- | --- |
| 1 | 阿联酋 | 53394.57 | 6 | 摩洛哥 | 2034.53 |
| 2 | 苏丹 | 52024.52 | 7 | 约旦 | 929.91 |
| 3 | 毛里塔尼亚 | 14065.34 | 8 | 阿曼 | 680.84 |
| 4 | 埃及 | 8930.82 | 9 | 黎巴嫩 | 585.47 |
| 5 | 沙特 | 8721.05 | 10 | 伊拉克 | 448.88 |

续表

| 排名 | 国家 | 进口额 | 排名 | 国家 | 进口额 |
|---|---|---|---|---|---|
| 11 | 索马里 | 210.68 | 17 | 巴林 | 0.64 |
| 12 | 突尼斯 | 89.40 | 18 | 科威特 | 0.15 |
| 13 | 叙利亚 | 34.20 | 19 | 卡塔尔 | 0.11 |
| 14 | 也门 | 30.76 | 20 | 巴勒斯坦 | — |
| 15 | 科摩罗 | 1.85 | 21 | 吉布提 | — |
| 16 | 阿尔及利亚 | 1.68 | 22 | 利比亚 | — |

资料来源：根据中国海关总署数据计算所得。

**表 5.5 2024 年中国在阿拉伯地区主要农产品进口来源国**

单位：万美元

| 商品名称 | 贸易伙伴名称 | 进口额 |
|---|---|---|
| （03）鱼、甲壳动物、软体动物及其他水生无脊椎动物 | 沙特 | 8092.0274 |
| | 毛里塔尼亚 | 4507.1908 |
| | 阿曼 | 680.1876 |
| （08）食用水果及坚果；甜瓜或柑橘属水果的果皮 | 埃及 | 7858.4725 |
| | 沙特 | 449.0842 |
| | 伊拉克 | 446.8554 |
| （12）含油子仁及果实；杂项子仁及果实；工业用或药用植物；稻草、秸秆及饲料 | 苏丹 | 49650.8937 |
| | 摩洛哥 | 112.8869 |
| | 埃及 | 57.8120 |
| （15）动、植物油、脂及其分解产品；精制的食用油脂；动、植物蜡 | 阿联酋 | 31787.3419 |
| | 摩洛哥 | 938.2705 |
| | 毛里塔尼亚 | 319.0681 |
| （18）可可及可可制品 | 黎巴嫩 | 543.0967 |
| | 阿联酋 | 235.4760 |
| | 沙特 | 0.0443 |
| （23）食品工业的残渣及废料；配制的动物饲料 | 阿联酋 | 18042.2847 |
| | 毛里塔尼亚 | 9163.8859 |
| | 苏丹 | 1828.2351 |

资料来源：根据中国海关总署数据计算所得。

从表5.6可以看出，2024年，中国向阿拉伯国家出口的十大主要目的地为阿联酋、沙特、伊拉克、摩洛哥、阿尔及利亚、埃及、约旦、科威特、利比亚、黎巴嫩，出口额占总出口额的88.05%。阿联酋连续多年是中国对阿拉伯国家农产品出口的首要目的地，2024年出口额为126887.22万美元，同比增长22.8%，占中国对阿拉伯国家出口总额的32.39%。

表5.6 2024年中国对阿农产品贸易出口目的地国

单位：万美元

| 序号 | 国家 | 出口 | 序号 | 国家 | 出口 |
| --- | --- | --- | --- | --- | --- |
| 1 | 阿联酋 | 126887.22 | 12 | 阿曼 | 8341.21 |
| 2 | 沙特 | 55218.84 | 13 | 毛里塔尼亚 | 8149.45 |
| 3 | 伊拉克 | 50717.00 | 14 | 巴林 | 7122.36 |
| 4 | 摩洛哥 | 41511.46 | 15 | 卡塔尔 | 5495.71 |
| 5 | 阿尔及利亚 | 29421.38 | 16 | 苏丹 | 4435.75 |
| 6 | 埃及 | 21497.95 | 17 | 突尼斯 | 3497.76 |
| 7 | 约旦 | 13945.43 | 18 | 叙利亚 | 1623.46 |
| 8 | 科威特 | 13013.83 | 19 | 索马里 | 1392.87 |
| 9 | 利比亚 | 10043.72 | 20 | 吉布提 | 672.20 |
| 10 | 黎巴嫩 | 9909.24 | 21 | 巴勒斯坦 | 571.23 |
| 11 | 也门 | 8984.97 | 22 | 科摩罗 | 206.36 |

资料来源：根据中国海关总署数据计算所得。

从主要农产品出口上，2024年，阿联酋是"（07）食用蔬菜、根及块茎"（20640.2900万美元）、"（08）食用水果及坚果；甜瓜或柑橘属水果的果皮"（22500.6991万美元）、"（24）烟草、烟草及烟草代用品的制品；非经燃烧吸用的产品，不论是否含有尼古丁；其他供人体摄入尼古丁的含尼古丁的产品"（31337.8175万美元）的最主要目的地。"（09）咖啡、茶、马黛茶及调味香料"最主要目的地是摩洛哥（25491.3999万美元)、"(20)蔬菜、水果、坚果或植物其他部分的制品"的主要出口目的地为伊拉克(19969.4469万美元)和沙特(14988.7701万美元),见表5.7。

表5.7 2024年中国在阿拉伯地区主要农产品出口目的地国

单位:万美元

| 商品名称 | 贸易伙伴名称 | 美元 |
| --- | --- | --- |
| (07)食用蔬菜、根及块茎 | 阿联酋 | 20640.2900 |
|  | 沙特 | 9477.1053 |
|  | 卡塔尔 | 2132.0469 |
| (08)食用水果及坚果;甜瓜或柑橘属水果的果皮 | 阿联酋 | 22500.6991 |
|  | 摩洛哥 | 4381.4015 |
|  | 伊拉克 | 4329.7293 |
| (09)咖啡、茶、马黛茶及调味香料 | 摩洛哥 | 25491.3999 |
|  | 阿联酋 | 10253.2228 |
|  | 毛里塔尼亚 | 6595.5123 |
| (20)蔬菜、水果、坚果或植物其他部分的制品 | 伊拉克 | 19969.4469 |
|  | 沙特 | 14988.7701 |
|  | 阿联酋 | 8026.9008 |
| (24)烟草、烟草及烟草代用品的制品;非经燃烧吸用的产品,不论是否含有尼古丁;其他供人体摄入尼古丁的含尼古丁的产品 | 阿联酋 | 31337.8175 |
|  | 科威特 | 6695.6845 |
|  | 沙特 | 6350.9083 |

资料来源:根据中国海关总署数据计算所得。

### 5.2.2 中阿农业合作进展

中阿农业合作不仅体现在农产品贸易方面,在协议签署、项目合作、交流互访、产品展览展示等方面也取得了新进展。

协议签署方面,4月19日,中国铁建国际集团北非区域公司与阿尔及利亚农业物流集团、中国浙江金华供销社在阿尔及利亚首都阿尔及尔签署合作框架协议。此次合作框架协议内容包括农业建设、农业深加工等诸多领域。这是落实 2023 年 7 月中阿两国元首重要共识,实现共建"一带一路"和"新阿尔及利亚"愿景的又一双边经济合作成果。① 5 月 30 日,中阿合作论坛第十届部长级会议在北京举行。会议期间,农业农村部与阿拉伯国家联盟共同签署《中华人民共和国农业农村部与阿拉伯国家联盟关于农业合作的谅解备忘录》,旨在进一步深化双方在作物种植、动植物疫病防控、畜禽水产养殖、农产品经贸等领域合作,践行中阿务实合作"八大共同行动",为中阿构建"五大合作格局"做出积极贡献。

项目合作方面,椰枣是阿联酋的重要传统产业,也是中国与阿联酋及阿拉伯国家深化合作与交流的重要桥梁。12 月 6 日,在三亚举办的全球热带农业创新大会上,阿联酋赠送中国第二批椰枣苗交接仪式举行。第二批椰枣苗共计 23500 株,将定植于文昌,进一步加强两国在热带农业领域的合作与交流。② 阿联酋向中国捐赠 10 万株椰枣树苗的倡议是 2019 年两国领导人达成的重要共识。

交流互访方面,5 月 23 日,阿曼农业科技代表团莅临瑞和科技,进行访问与交流。此次到访的阿曼农业科技代表团成员包括多位阿曼国家部委级的农业高级官员及专家学者,双方积极探讨国际农业科技发展经验及农业可持续发展方向。此外,还就阿曼与中国农业科技研发、农业产业化以及农产品贸易等领域的合作机会进行了深入的讨论。7 月,"2024 中国农业国际经贸合作会议"在北京举办。会议邀请了包括部分国家驻华使节、专家学者、国际组织、地方贸促会和企业嘉宾代表等约 300 人出席会议。约旦驻华大使胡萨姆·侯赛尼表示,自 2015 年建立战略伙伴关系以来,约中两国的经贸合作不断加深,希望两国未来在农业重点领域开展更多合作。③ 11 月 6—26 日,由商务部主办、甘肃省治沙研究所承办的阿拉伯国

---

① 《中企签约阿尔及利亚农业合作框架协议》,人民网-国际频道,https://world.people.com.cn/n1/2024/0421/c1002-40220261.html,2024 年 4 月 21 日。
② 陈婧:《阿联酋向中国赠送第二批椰枣苗 深化热带农业合作》,今日头条,https://www.toutiao.com/article/7445321599533761033/,2024 年 12 月 6 日。
③ 姚雯祎:《2024 中国农业国际经贸合作会议举办》,《农民日报》2024 年 7 月 3 日,http://xm.shandong.gov.cn/art/2024/7/3/art_24617_10337484.html。

家荒漠化和风沙灾害防治技术培训班在甘肃举行，来自突尼斯、阿曼、巴勒斯坦、沙特及埃及的24名学员参加了培训班。①

产品展览展示方面，11月16—23日，中国农产品中东地区供采对接活动分别在阿联酋和沙特两国举办。该活动由农业农村部农业贸易促进中心主办，中阿农业技术转移中心阿联酋分中心（宁夏中阿产业投资基金管理有限公司承建）、迪拜龙城总商会等协办，中国驻阿联酋使馆、驻迪拜总领馆给予指导支持。其间，举办了国际农产品流通研讨、中国农产品品鉴推介、中东农食市场经贸对接等分项活动，中阿两国200余名代表积极参与，包括宁夏在内十个省区的近30家中国农业企业向中东伙伴推介了水果、蔬菜、茶叶等优质特色农产品，宁夏10家企业展览展示的枸杞、中草药、蜂蜜、果蔬、小杂粮、调味品等30类农产品现场广受阿拉伯客商好评。②

## 5.3 中阿农业合作展望

展望未来，中阿农业合作大有可为，双方将对标"八大共同行动"、"五大发展格局"以及"十大伙伴行动"，持续深化农业合作，推动农业高质量发展，为构建面向新时代的中阿命运共同体做出更大贡献。

第一，加强战略对接。中阿农业合作是建立在充分尊重阿拉伯国家需求和合作意愿的基础上，寻求合作利益契合点。从阿拉伯国家农业发展基础看，由于农业基础设施不足，农业生产技术水平不高，土地沙化、盐碱化等问题严重，农业生产效率有待提升，普遍面临提升粮食安全保障能力、提高农业生产技术、稳定农产品价格、增加农业投入等重要任务。如

---

① 《全球连线｜阿拉伯国家学员在甘肃研学"治沙术"》，国际在线，https://www.163.com/dy/article/JHOL5V0K051497H3.html，2024年11月24日。
② 丁逸菲：《中阿农业技术转移中心阿联酋分中心助力宁夏特色农产品走进中东市场》，自治区农业国际合作项目服务中心，https://nynct.nx.gov.cn/xwzx/zwdt/202412/t20241216_4760273.html，2024年12月16日。

何保障本国粮食安全，成为阿拉伯国家重要的利益交汇点。中国和阿拉伯国家都相继出台了国家战略或农业发展战略。2017年，中国农业农村部联合有关部门发布《共同推进"一带一路"建设农业合作的愿景与行动》，这与阿拉伯国家的农业发展愿景形成了政策对接。2024年，农业农村部与阿盟共同签署《中华人民共和国农业农村部与阿拉伯国家联盟关于农业合作的谅解备忘录》，进一步推动了中阿双方在农业领域的战略对接。中阿双方应借助中阿合作论坛、中阿博览会、中非经贸论坛等平台，进一步加强战略对接，完善中阿农业合作机制，共同应对全球粮食危机，携手维护粮食安全。

第二，加强农业技术研发和技术转移合作，拓宽农业合作领域。一方面，经过多年积累与发展，我国在旱作农业、畜牧养殖、经济作物种植、现代农产品加工、土地荒漠化及盐碱地治理等领域具备了世界领先的技术水平，积累了丰富的实践经验，与阿拉伯国家农业发展现实需求形成较强的互补性。近年来，中阿在耐盐碱水稻种植、沙漠化防治等方面成果丰硕。展望未来，中阿双方可通过建立联合现代农业实验室，加快实施创新驱动发展战略，充分发挥科技在现代种业发展中的支撑引领作用，推动农业转型升级，保障粮食安全。双方将进一步加强在旱作节水、荒漠治理等领域的科技研发和技术转移合作，提升粮食生产和供应能力，推动中阿双方农业合作向更深层次发展，让更多合作成果惠及人民。另一方面，数字农业是农业新质生产力的典型代表，是全球农业发展的重要趋势和新增长点，在改变传统农业生产模式、应对气候变化方面发挥着重要作用。未来主动对接阿拉伯国家数字农业战略，积极推动中国优势数字化农业设备，如农业无人机、自动导航农机、精准牲畜饲养设备等，在阿拉伯国家农业生产中推广场景应用，并通过技能培训、知识分享等多种途径，加强与阿拉伯国家农业数字化合作。

第三，加强农产品贸易和投资合作，推动农产品产业升级和附加值提升。自"一带一路"倡议提出以来，中阿农产品贸易规模持续扩大，重点项目有序推进。随着中阿农业贸易的推进，阿拉伯国家的非油类商品在中国的市场不断扩大，尤其是农产品，未来，持续推动阿拉伯国家农产品出现在中国市场，缩小贸易差额。

第四，继续加强人才交流与培养，为农业合作提供坚实的人才支撑。一是结合阿拉伯国家发展需求，组织本土优秀人才线上线下开展智慧节水农业、荒漠化治理、盐碱地治理、畜牧养殖等技术培训，培养一批复合型人才，主动承担国家对外农业技术援助任务，积极参与"一带一路"共建国家的农业援外活动。二是积极开展农业培训，除开展线下学习交流以及实地调研，还可依托国内高校、科研院所，积极推进农业技术推广示范培训课程的创新，采用视频录制、直播课程、云参观等多种方式，打造一批精品课程，满足阿拉伯国家对农业技术的需求。三是建立面向阿拉伯国家的储备人才库，在农业投资规划、企业经营管理、投资风险分析等领域储备一批人才梯队，为深化我国与阿拉伯国家农业合作提供坚实的人才保障。

# 第6章 中阿能源合作专题报告

能源合作是中国和阿拉伯国家务实合作的重要领域，是中国同阿拉伯国家战略伙伴关系的核心内容。中阿双方在能源领域具有高度互补性，双方能源合作经过多年发展已建立了涵盖传统能源、新能源等各领域，相互紧密依赖的关系，合作规模持续扩大，合作水平不断提升，未来仍有广阔的合作前景。

## 6.1 阿拉伯国家能源资源概况

### 6.1.1 阿拉伯国家石油资源储量与生产情况

主要阿拉伯国家目前已探明的石油储量占全球已探明石油储量的37.80%，原油产量占全球原油总产量的26.43%（见表6.1、表6.2）。在可探明储量方面，近年来，阿拉伯国家可探明石油储量规模小幅增加。在原油产量方面，乌克兰危机后主要阿拉伯国家石油产量在短暂增加后回落，叠加OPEC+多次延长自愿减产协议，石油产量在2024年降低至119422万吨，较上年减少4.02%。

阿拉伯国家石油资源总量丰富，但分布不均衡，集中于沙特、伊拉克、科威特、阿联酋等国家，2024年末，上述4国可探明储量总计占主要阿拉伯国家原油可探明储量的94.33%，占全球原油可探明储量的35.66%。在产量方面，2024年，上述4国原油总产量为98658万吨/年，占主要阿拉伯国家原油总产量的82.61%，占全球原油总产量的21.84%（见表6.1、表6.2）。

### 表6.1 2021—2024年阿拉伯国家可探明石油储量

单位：亿吨，%

| 国家 | 2021年 | 2022年 | 2023年 | 2024年 | 2024年占比 |
|---|---|---|---|---|---|
| 阿尔及利亚 | 15.37 | 15.37 | 15.37 | 15.37 | 0.62 |
| 埃及 | 4.13 | 4.13 | 4.13 | 4.13 | 0.17 |
| 伊拉克 | 195.71 | 195.71 | 195.71 | 195.71 | 7.88 |
| 科威特 | 139.81 | 139.81 | 139.81 | 139.81 | 5.63 |
| 阿曼 | 7.29 | 7.29 | 7.29 | 7.29 | 0.29 |
| 卡塔尔 | 26.46 | 26.46 | 26.46 | 26.46 | 1.07 |
| 沙特 | 408.69 | 408.69 | 411.96 | 411.96 | 16.59 |
| 阿联酋 | 134.56 | 136.98 | 138.21 | 138.21 | 5.56 |
| 主要阿拉伯国家总计 | 932.02 | 934.44 | 938.94 | 938.94 | 37.80 |
| 世界 | 2461.55 | 2467.00 | 2477.07 | 2483.76 | 100 |

注：包括原油和凝析油。

资料来源：中国石油集团经济技术研究院。

### 表6.2 2021—2024年阿拉伯国家原油产量

单位：万吨，%

| 国家 | 2021年 | 2022年 | 2023年 | 2024年 | 2024年占比 |
|---|---|---|---|---|---|
| 阿尔及利亚 | 5820 | 6360 | 6038 | 5810 | 1.29 |
| 埃及 | 2960 | 2990 | 2982 | 3000 | 0.66 |
| 伊拉克 | 20061 | 22230 | 22213 | 21928 | 4.85 |
| 科威特 | 13000 | 13505 | 13500 | 12636 | 2.80 |
| 阿曼 | 4212 | 4350 | 4307 | 4028 | 0.89 |
| 卡塔尔 | 7850 | 7753 | 7884 | 7926 | 1.75 |
| 沙特 | 51750 | 52530 | 49378 | 46069 | 10.20 |
| 阿联酋 | 16649 | 18129 | 18123 | 18025 | 3.99 |
| 主要阿拉伯国家总计 | 122302 | 127847 | 124425 | 119422 | 26.43 |
| 世界 | 425929 | 439116 | 447749 | 451832 | 100 |

注：包括原油和凝析油。

资料来源：中国石油集团经济技术研究院。

### 6.1.2 阿拉伯国家天然气资源储量与生产情况

阿拉伯国家天然气资源丰富,但储量和产量在全球占比中都显著低于石油资源。2024年,主要阿拉伯国家可探明天然气储量为50.18万亿立方米,占全球可探明天然气总储量的24.99%。主要阿拉伯国家天然气总产量为6022亿立方米,占全球天然气总产量的13.72%(见表6.3、表6.4)。

表6.3　2021—2024年阿拉伯国家可探明天然气储量

单位:万亿立方米,%

| 国家 | 2021年 | 2022年 | 2023年 | 2024年 | 2024年占比 |
| --- | --- | --- | --- | --- | --- |
| 阿尔及利亚 | 4.50 | 4.50 | 4.50 | 4.50 | 2.24 |
| 埃及 | 2.14 | 2.14 | 2.14 | 2.14 | 1.07 |
| 伊拉克 | 3.53 | 3.53 | 3.53 | 3.53 | 1.76 |
| 科威特 | 1.70 | 1.70 | 1.70 | 1.70 | 0.85 |
| 阿曼 | 0.67 | 0.67 | 0.67 | 0.67 | 0.33 |
| 卡塔尔 | 24.67 | 24.67 | 24.67 | 24.67 | 12.28 |
| 沙特 | 6.02 | 6.50 | 6.66 | 6.66 | 3.32 |
| 阿联酋 | 6.30 | 6.31 | 6.31 | 6.31 | 3.14 |
| 主要阿拉伯国家总计 | 49.53 | 50.02 | 50.18 | 50.18 | 24.99 |
| 世界 | 193.45 | 199.51 | 200.47 | 200.83 | 100 |

资料来源:ETRI。

表6.4　2021—2024年阿拉伯国家天然气产量

单位:亿立方米,%

| 国家 | 2021年 | 2022年 | 2023年 | 2024年 | 2024年占比 |
| --- | --- | --- | --- | --- | --- |
| 阿尔及利亚 | 1050 | 1005 | 1043 | 1001 | 2.28 |
| 埃及 | 678 | 645 | 571 | 548 | 1.25 |
| 伊拉克 | 122 | 124 | 100 | 115 | 0.26 |
| 科威特 | 181 | 191 | 157 | 160 | 0.36 |
| 阿曼 | 389 | 406 | 430 | 446 | 1.02 |
| 卡塔尔 | 1780 | 1833 | 1810 | 1820 | 4.15 |

续表

| 国家 | 2021年 | 2022年 | 2023年 | 2024年 | 2024年占比 |
|---|---|---|---|---|---|
| 沙特 | 1105 | 1228 | 1252 | 1360 | 3.10 |
| 阿联酋 | 557 | 574 | 561 | 572 | 1.30 |
| 主要阿拉伯国家总计 | 5862 | 6006 | 5924 | 6022 | 13.72 |
| 世界 | 42255 | 42480 | 42684 | 43886 | 100 |

资料来源：中国石油集团经济技术研究院。

在阿拉伯国家中，卡塔尔的天然气可探明储量和产量均最大。2024年，卡塔尔可探明天然气储量占主要阿拉伯国家的比例为49.16%，产量占主要阿拉伯国家的比例为30.22%。除卡塔尔外，沙特、阿联酋、阿尔及利亚、伊拉克等国家也拥有较丰富的天然气资源，2024年沙特的天然气产量占主要阿拉伯国家的比例为22.58%，产量在主要阿拉伯国家中排名第二。

### 6.1.3 阿拉伯国家其他能源开发利用情况

除传统能源外，随着全球应对气候变化压力的增加，阿拉伯国家积极推进可再生能源发展，大多以能源发展战略、能源发展愿景等设定清洁能源发展目标，并持续加大对清洁能源产业的政策支持和财政支持力度。阿联酋启动《2050能源战略》，计划到2050年，向可再生能源领域投资约1637亿美元，清洁、可再生能源发电量占国内总发电量的比例从25%提高至50%，并于2023年批准了《国家能源战略2050更新》，拟到2030年将清洁能源在总能源结构中的比例提高到30%。阿曼提出《阿曼2040愿景》，设定了在2030年前至少约20%的电能来自可再生能源，且该比例在2040年前提升至35%—39%的目标。卡塔尔提出《国家可再生能源战略》，计划到2030年将太阳能光伏发电装机总量提升至4吉瓦，太阳能发电装机总量占总电力生产能力的比例提升至30%。沙特启动"绿色沙特倡议"和"绿色中东倡议"，致力于发展光伏发电和绿氢蓝氢项目，到2030年可再生能源项目提供超过50%的电力供应。科威特《2030—2050可再生能源战略》提出，要在2030年实现22100兆瓦的可再生能源生产。在政策推动下，阿拉伯国家可再生能源快速发展，2020—2024年，阿拉伯国家可再生能源发电能力由21093兆瓦增加至37311兆瓦，年均增长17.90%，高于全球12.36%的年均增速（见表6.5）。

表6.5 2020—2024年阿拉伯国家可再生能源发电能力

单位：兆瓦

| 国家 | 2020年 | 2021年 | 2022年 | 2023年 | 2024年 |
| --- | --- | --- | --- | --- | --- |
| 阿尔及利亚 | 585 | 505 | 590 | 601 | 601 |
| 巴林 | 11 | 22 | 48 | 59 | 69 |
| 埃及 | 5934 | 6258 | 6322 | 6709 | 7752 |
| 伊拉克 | 1594 | 1594 | 1599 | 1599 | 1599 |
| 约旦 | 2088 | 2460 | 2615 | 2638 | 2725 |
| 科威特 | 97 | 97 | 114 | 114 | 114 |
| 黎巴嫩 | 382 | 482 | 1167 | 1297 | 1297 |
| 毛里塔尼亚 | 122 | 122 | 123 | 260 | 294 |
| 利比亚 | 5 | 6 | 6 | 8 | 8 |
| 摩洛哥 | 3522 | 3638 | 3725 | 4105 | 4375 |
| 阿曼 | 179 | 205 | 705 | 722 | 722 |
| 巴勒斯坦 | 118 | 178 | 192 | 192 | 198 |
| 卡塔尔 | 24 | 24 | 824 | 824 | 1699 |
| 沙特阿拉伯 | 113 | 443 | 843 | 2988 | 4743 |
| 索马里 | 14 | 22 | 46 | 49 | 49 |
| 苏丹 | 1798 | 1817 | 1871 | 1871 | 1871 |
| 叙利亚 | 1509 | 1530 | 1557 | 1557 | 1557 |
| 突尼斯 | 406 | 406 | 508 | 817 | 1084 |
| 阿联酋 | 2334 | 3003 | 3606 | 6075 | 6144 |
| 也门 | 258 | 258 | 264 | 290 | 410 |
| 阿拉伯国家总计 | 21093 | 23070 | 26725 | 32775 | 37311 |
| 世界 | 2812981 | 3075931 | 3378790 | 3862881 | 4448051 |

资料来源：国际可再生能源署。

## 第6章 中阿能源合作专题报告

在可再生能源中，由于阿拉伯国家地处西亚北非地区，气候炎热干燥，水资源短缺，水电发展潜力有限。除埃及、苏丹尼罗河流域，伊拉克底格里斯河流域和叙利亚等建有水力发电设施外，其他阿拉伯国家水能资源匮乏。2024年，阿拉伯国家水力发电能力为10202兆瓦，占世界水力发电能力的比例仅为0.72%（见表6.6）。

表 6.6　2020—2024 年阿拉伯国家水力发电能力

单位：兆瓦

| 国家 | 2020年 | 2021年 | 2022年 | 2023年 | 2024年 |
| --- | --- | --- | --- | --- | --- |
| 阿尔及利亚 | 209 | 129 | 129 | 129 | 129 |
| 埃及 | 2832 | 2832 | 2832 | 2832 | 2832 |
| 伊拉克 | 1797 | 1797 | 1797 | 1797 | 1797 |
| 约旦 | 6 | 4 | 4 | 4 | 4 |
| 黎巴嫩 | 282 | 282 | 282 | 282 | 282 |
| 摩洛哥 | 1770 | 1770 | 1770 | 1770 | 2120 |
| 苏丹 | 1482 | 1482 | 1482 | 1482 | 1482 |
| 叙利亚 | 1490 | 1490 | 1490 | 1490 | 1490 |
| 突尼斯 | 66 | 66 | 66 | 66 | 66 |
| 阿拉伯国家总计 | 9934 | 9852 | 9852 | 9852 | 10202 |
| 世界 | 1332363 | 1359536 | 1393299 | 1409865 | 1425374 |

资料来源：国际可再生能源署。

阿拉伯国家充分挖掘太阳能和风能资源，近年来，建立了一定规模的光伏和风电产业集群，推动"风光"产业发展。在光伏发电方面，西亚北非地区是全球光热资源较丰富的地区之一，太阳能开发在阿拉伯国家可再生能源资源开发中占据重要地位。2024年，阿拉伯国家光伏发电能力占可再生能源发电能力总量的58.49%，2020—2024年，阿拉伯国家光伏发电能力由7824兆瓦增加至21822兆瓦，年均增长率处于44.73%的高位，高于全球39.45%的年均增速。阿拉伯国家的太阳能资源开发呈显著的不均衡趋势，2024年，光伏发电以阿联酋、沙特、约旦、埃及和黎巴嫩等国家为主，上述五国的光伏发电能力占阿拉伯国家光伏发电能力总量的比例为73.43%（见表6.7）。在风力发电方面，阿拉伯国家风力发电能力目前还较低，2024年风力发电能力为5925兆瓦，仅占全球风力发电能力的0.52%（见表6.8）。但部分国家风力发电发展潜力较大，未来风力发电比重将继续增加。例如，根据阿曼国家能源战略，2027年阿曼将有20%的电力来自可再生能源，其中21%来自风能。

表6.7 2020—2024年阿拉伯国家光伏发电能力

单位：兆瓦

| 国家 | 2020年 | 2021年 | 2022年 | 2023年 | 2024年 |
| --- | --- | --- | --- | --- | --- |
| 阿尔及利亚 | 366 | 366 | 451 | 462 | 462 |
| 巴林 | 10 | 21 | 46 | 57 | 66 |
| 埃及 | 1643 | 1663 | 1724 | 1856 | 2590 |
| 伊拉克 | 37 | 37 | 42 | 42 | 42 |
| 约旦 | 1541 | 1811 | 1966 | 1990 | 2077 |
| 科威特 | 84 | 84 | 102 | 102 | 102 |
| 黎巴嫩 | 90 | 190 | 875 | 1005 | 1005 |
| 毛里塔尼亚 | 88 | 88 | 89 | 123 | 157 |
| 利比亚 | 5 | 6 | 6 | 8 | 8 |
| 摩洛哥 | 774 | 854 | 854 | 934 | 934 |
| 阿曼 | 129 | 155 | 655 | 672 | 672 |
| 巴勒斯坦 | 117 | 178 | 192 | 192 | 197 |
| 卡塔尔 | 5 | 5 | 805 | 805 | 1680 |
| 沙特 | 109 | 439 | 440 | 2585 | 4340 |
| 索马里 | 11 | 19 | 42 | 46 | 46 |
| 苏丹 | 117 | 136 | 190 | 190 | 190 |
| 叙利亚 | 12 | 33 | 60 | 60 | 60 |
| 突尼斯 | 95 | 95 | 197 | 506 | 773 |
| 阿联酋 | 2333 | 3002 | 3596 | 5942 | 6011 |
| 也门 | 258 | 258 | 264 | 290 | 410 |
| 阿拉伯国家总计 | 7824 | 9440 | 12596 | 17867 | 21822 |
| 世界 | 723638 | 866830 | 1060522 | 1413548 | 1865490 |

资料来源：国际可再生能源署。

表 6.8　2020—2024 年阿拉伯国家风能发电能力

单位：兆瓦

| 国家 | 2020 年 | 2021 年 | 2022 年 | 2023 年 | 2024 年 |
| --- | --- | --- | --- | --- | --- |
| 阿尔及利亚 | 10 | 10 | 10 | 10 | 10 |
| 巴林 | 1 | 1 | 3 | 3 | 3 |
| 埃及 | 1380 | 1640 | 1643 | 1890 | 2199 |
| 约旦 | 529 | 632 | 632 | 631 | 631 |
| 科威特 | 12 | 12 | 12 | 12 | 12 |
| 黎巴嫩 | 3 | 3 | 3 | 3 | 3 |
| 毛里塔尼亚 | 34 | 34 | 34 | 137 | 137 |
| 摩洛哥 | 1435 | 1471 | 1558 | 1858 | 2128 |
| 阿曼 | 50 | 50 | 50 | 50 | 50 |
| 沙特 | 3 | 3 | 403 | 403 | 403 |
| 索马里 | 4 | 4 | 4 | 4 | 4 |
| 叙利亚 | 1 | 1 | 1 | 1 | 1 |
| 突尼斯 | 245 | 245 | 245 | 245 | 245 |
| 阿联酋 | 0 | 0 | 0 | 99 | 99 |
| 阿拉伯国家总计 | 3707 | 4106 | 4598 | 5346 | 5925 |
| 世界 | 733780 | 824380 | 903171 | 1019603 | 1132837 |

资料来源：国际可再生能源署。

氢能也是阿拉伯国家可再生能源发展的重要方向，海湾国家纷纷出台氢能发展规划，提出氢能发展目标。沙特的《绿色沙特倡议》提出，致力光伏发电和绿氢蓝氢项目，成为全球氢能源重要供应商。埃及的《国家低碳氢战略》提出，到 2040 年绿氢年产量达到 620 万吨，占全球氢市场 5%—8% 的份额。阿联酋也批准了《国家氢能战略》，加速氢经济的增长，并增强阿联酋作为世界最大低碳氢生产国之一的地位。同时，阿拉伯多国全方位加速布局大型氢能项目，并建立国家氢能联盟。阿曼、沙特都在建造世界级的绿氢工厂，阿曼近年来大力发展氢能，截至 2024 年 6 月共签署了8个绿氢领域的合作协议，总投资490亿美元，预计到2030年可年产绿氢138万吨。阿联酋致力于成为中东乃至世界的绿氢集散中心，投资价值达1400亿美元，预计到2050年可年产绿氢近800万吨。阿联酋和阿曼已成立了本国的氢能联盟。

## 6.2　中阿传统能源合作现状

### 6.2.1　中阿油气贸易情况

油气贸易是中国与阿拉伯国家贸易合作的顶梁柱。阿拉伯国家是中国油气进口的重要贸易伙伴。2024年，中国累计进口原油55349万吨，排名前10的进口来源国分别是俄罗斯、沙特、马来西亚、伊拉克、阿曼、巴西、阿联酋、安哥拉、科威特和卡塔尔。其中，阿拉伯国家有6个（沙特、伊拉克、阿曼、阿联酋、科威特和卡塔尔），占进口总量的44.25%。

表6.9　中国自阿拉伯国家进口原油情况

单位：万吨

| 国家 | 2020年 | 2021年 | 2022年 | 2023年 | 2024年 |
| --- | --- | --- | --- | --- | --- |
| 沙特 | 8492.20 | 8755.72 | 8748.89 | 8954.40 | 7863.63 |
| 伊拉克 | 6011.62 | 5406.92 | 5548.83 | 5925.50 | 6382.93 |
| 阿联酋 | 3117.51 | 3193.68 | 4276.64 | 4181.72 | 3554.51 |
| 阿曼 | 3784.38 | 4481.46 | 3936.70 | 3914.67 | 4077.34 |
| 科威特 | 2749.58 | 3016.26 | 3328.16 | 2453.32 | 1596.95 |
| 卡塔尔 | 619.89 | 784.99 | 770.41 | 1046.11 | 1017.99 |
| 利比亚 | 169.67 | 613.76 | 374.30 | 333.83 | 175.62 |
| 阿尔及利亚 | 40.44 | 3.98 | 0.00 | 14.66 | 0.00 |
| 也门 | 182.57 | 94.34 | 84.04 | 0.00 | 0.00 |

续表

| 国家 | 2020年 | 2021年 | 2022年 | 2023年 | 2024年 |
| --- | --- | --- | --- | --- | --- |
| 埃及 | 132.41 | 49.00 | 18.94 | 0.00 | 0.00 |
| 苏丹 | 16.00 | 0.00 | 7.87 | 16.01 | 0.00 |
| 世界 | 54240.00 | 51292.00 | 50823.00 | 56394.00 | 55349.00 |

资料来源：GTT。

天然气进口贸易方面，中国从阿拉伯国家进口天然气以液化天然气为主，2024年，中国累计进口液化天然气7737.82万吨，同比增长8.69%，从阿拉伯国家进口液化天然气2059.92万吨，同比增长8.65%，占中国液化天然气进口总量的26.62%。液化天然气进口排名前10的国家分别是澳大利亚、卡塔尔、俄罗斯、马来西亚、美国、印尼、巴布亚新几内亚、尼日利亚、阿曼和阿联酋，其中阿拉伯国家3个（卡塔尔、阿曼、阿联酋）。中国从阿拉伯国家进口天然气主要集中于卡塔尔，2024年从卡塔尔进口液化天然气占中国从阿拉伯国家进口液化天然气的89.54%，占进口总量的23.84%。

表6.10　中国自阿拉伯国家进口液化天然气（LNG）情况

单位：万吨

| 国家 | 2020年 | 2021年 | 2022年 | 2023年 | 2024年 |
| --- | --- | --- | --- | --- | --- |
| 卡塔尔 | 816.75 | 897.78 | 1568.02 | 1664.88 | 1844.37 |
| 阿曼 | 106.95 | 162.27 | 95.71 | 102.20 | 113.40 |
| 阿联酋 | 30.09 | 70.80 | 11.92 | 66.82 | 85.87 |
| 阿尔及利亚 | 12.24 | 24.38 | 6.83 | 33.83 | 3.60 |
| 埃及 | 6.43 | 131.20 | 34.85 | 28.21 | 12.68 |
| 世界 | 6730.65 | 7878.95 | 6336.29 | 7119.07 | 7737.82 |

资料来源：GTT。

### 6.2.2　中阿油气全产业链投资合作

2024年，中国与阿拉伯国家在油气全产业链合作方面取得显著进展，涵盖勘探开发、工程技术服务、炼化加工等多个领域。

在勘探开发和产能提升领域，中国不断深化与阿联酋、伊拉克、沙特、阿尔及利亚等国家的合作。在伊拉克，2024年5月，振华石油、中海油、安东石油、中曼等中国石油企业在伊拉克第5轮+（即第5轮招标活动中流标的15个区块）和第6轮油气招标中获得多个区块，其中振华石油中标Abu Khema、Qurnain两个区块，中海油中标Block 7区块，安东石油中标Dbufriyah区块，中曼中标Middle Furat（Euphrates）和Northern Extension of East Baghdad区块，中国民营石油公司抓住机遇与伊拉克深化合作。6月，由中国石油（伊拉克）哈法亚公司投资、中国石油工程建设公司（CPECC）负责项目的EPCC和两年运行维护总承包工作的伊拉克哈法亚天然气处理厂（GPP）投产，天然气设计处理能力为30亿立方米/年，凝析液处理能力为95万吨/年。在沙特，2024年，中国石化（占股40%）和西班牙Tecnicas Reunidas公司（占股60%）组成的合资企业与沙特阿美石油公司签署了一份合作意向书（LoI），内容包括在沙特最大的非常规气田Jafurah建设三座天然气压缩厂，在气田变电站安装230千伏的电源连接并升级水泵系统，合同价值22.4亿美元。沙特还从中国购入一座重量达17200吨的大型海洋油气集输平台——马赞油气集输平台，投入使用后，预计马赞油田的日产量大幅提升，甚至有望成为全球最大的海上油气处理油田之一。在阿联酋，2024年3月，中国石油阿布扎比陆海项目二期贝尔巴泽姆油田实现首油投产，项目达到日产原油5万桶的规模。7月，阿联酋工业和先进技术部部长兼阿布扎比国家石油公司（ADNOC）首席执行官Sultan Al Jaber率阿联酋代表团访问中国，与中国签署了多项合作协议和谅解备忘录。其中，在油气领域，ADNOC与中国石油签署战略合作协议，合作范围包括油气勘探开发、LNG、低碳解决方案、先进技术、炼化及贸易。ADNOC与中国海油签署合作协议，双方将深化在油气勘探开发、上游服务及工程建设、LNG、原油贸易、新能源及低碳发展等领域的合作。①

---

① 资料来自新华网、BEDigest、新华社、Arabian Business、国资委官网、中国对外承包工程商会等网站。

在油气下游炼化加工领域，2024年9月，国务院总理李强访问沙特期间，沙特阿美石油公司宣布，分别与中国荣盛石化、恒力集团签订开发框架协议、战略合作协议，涉及沙特阿美朱拜勒炼化公司（SASREF）设施扩建的潜在联合开发、收购恒力石化有限公司10%股份的谈判。① 同月，荣盛石化全资子公司宁波中金石化有限公司收购SASREF的50%股权进入该项目，拟联合扩建该项目，计划建造大型蒸汽裂解装置，并将相关的下游衍生产品整合到现有炼厂生产流程中。② 11月，中国荣盛石化股份有限公司与沙特阿美石油公司签署炼化项目框架协议，共同推进沙特SASREF扩建工作。根据协议，双方约定了SASREF炼化项目扩建联合指导委员会的设立、指导方针的制定及未来联合工作的开展等事宜，旨在为SASREF扩建项目后续工作提供高效协作机制及有力组织保障。同时，中国与阿拉伯国家积极开展在中国的炼化合作。7月，阿联酋ADNOC、奥地利北欧化工（Borealis）、博禄化学（Borouge）以及万华化学集团控股子公司万融新材料签署合作协议，启动位于福建省福州市的年产能160万吨的特种聚烯烃一体化设施的可行性研究。11月，中沙合作的福建古雷炼化一体化工程二期项目开工，项目由中国石化、福建炼化和沙特阿美石油公司合资建设，总投资711亿元人民币，包括1600万吨/年炼油、150万吨/年乙烯、200万吨/年对二甲苯和下游衍生物装置，以及30万吨级原油码头等配套工程，是福建省迄今投资规模最大的产业项目，也是中国石化迄今最大的一次性投资炼化产业项目。③

在工程技术和建设服务领域，2024年初，中国石化（占股40%）和

---

① 《沙特阿美与荣盛石化签署框架协议 共同推动SASREF扩建工作》，沙特阿美中国官网，https://china.aramco.com/zh-cn/news-media/china-news/2024/aramco-and-rongsheng-petrochemical-sign-a-framework-agreement-to-advance-sasref-expansion，2024年11月19日。

② 《阿联酋能源巨头携手万华化学建设特种聚烯烃项目》，财联社，https://www.cls.cn/detail/1742532，2024年7月24日。

③ 《福建古雷炼化一体化工程二期项目开工活动举行》，福建省人民政府网站，https://www.fujian.gov.cn/zwgk/ztzl/gjcjgxgg/dt/202411/t20241118_6568200.htm，2024年11月18日。

西班牙 Tecnicas Reunidas 公司（占股60%）组成的合资企业被沙特阿美选为沙特 Jafurah 气田 Riyas NGL 分馏设施的 EPC 承包商，合同价值33亿美元。① 11月，阿布扎比国家石油公司（ADNOC）与中石油东方物探公司签署全球最大的单体陆地地震勘探合同，价值4.9亿美元，② 东方物探将扩大在阿布扎比的三维地震采集范围。阿布扎比国家石油公司陆上公司（ADNOC ONSHORE）与中国杰瑞集团签署井场数字化改造 EPC 合同，价值9.2亿美元，杰瑞集团将在阿布扎比 Bab、Bu Hasa、South East 等油田进行全面数字化升级。阿尔及利亚国家石油公司与 CPECC 签署 ALRAR 气田天然气增压三期 EPC 总承包项目合同，价值2.1亿美元，对 CPECC 公司拓展阿尔及利亚乃至西亚北非地区业务、形成规模化市场具有重要意义。

在油气船运领域，2024年4月，卡塔尔能源公司与中国船舶集团有限公司签署协议，将建造18艘超大型液化天然气（LNG）运输船，用于满足卡塔尔北方气田扩产后的运输需求。③ 卡塔尔能源公司与招商轮船等3家中资船东签署9艘超大型 LNG 船舶的长期运输租约。7月，阿联酋 AW 船运公司与江南造船厂、中船工贸（CSTC）签署大型乙烷运输船采购协议，共计购买9条运输船只、合同总额约14亿美元，购买4艘大型液氨运输船、合同金额2.5亿—5亿美元。

### 6.2.3 其他能源相关领域合作

除油气外，中国也积极扩展与阿拉伯国家在可再生能源领域的合作。2024年11月，中国石油在伊拉克首座兆瓦级光伏储能电站投产，实施装机容量1兆瓦/4兆瓦时电池储能系统，年发电量约160万千瓦时。投产后不仅能满足高峰期800人营地的生活和办公用电，还能满足夜晚及施工现

---

① 《中石化炼化工程与西班牙企业合资获沙特超大气田33亿美元合同》，经济观察网，https://www.eeo.com.cn/2024/0125/631389.shtml，2024年1月25日。
② 《东方物探公司（BGP）成功中标全球最大单体陆地地震勘探合同》，腾讯网，https://news.qq.com/rain/a/20241108A01W8600，2024年11月8日。
③ 《中国船舶今与卡塔尔能源签约，建造18艘全球最大 LNG 船》，中国新闻网，https://www.chinanews.com.cn/cj/2024/04-29/10208698.shtml，2024年4月29日。

场部分设施设备的用电需求。同时，中国也与阿拉伯国家积极开展能源金融合作。第29届联合国气候变化大会（COP29）会议期间，阿联酋阿布扎比未来能源公司（Masdar）与中国丝路基金（SRF）签署了一份谅解备忘录，双方将在"一带一路"共建国家投资28亿美元支持可再生能源项目，对Masdar在中东、中亚、东南亚和非洲等地区开发、投资或运营的可再生能源项目进行共同投资。

## 6.3 中阿新能源合作现状

### 6.3.1 中阿新能源合作的驱动力

气候变化议题持续引发全球普遍关注。目前，全球已有150余个国家提出了碳中和发展目标，覆盖全球约88%的温室气体排放、92%的经济体量和89%的人口，新能源逐渐成为推动全球能源转型和可持续发展的重要力量。中国和阿拉伯国家都高度重视绿色转型发展，加强在新能源领域合作已成为双方重要共识。2024年5月，在中阿合作论坛第十届部长级会议开幕式上，中方宣布，同阿方构建"五大合作格局"，其中之一便是构建更加立体的能源合作格局，支持中国能源企业和金融机构在阿拉伯国家参与可再生能源项目，推动中阿新能源合作跑出加速度。

中国与阿拉伯国家在发展新能源方面有相同的政策导向。近年来，多个阿拉伯国家将发展可再生能源视为国家发展战略，纷纷制订本国的转型计划，减少对石油等资源的依赖。其中，沙特在"2030愿景"框架下，全力推进经济多元化和能源转型，计划到2030年实现可再生能源装机容量130吉瓦的目标。阿联酋提出《国家能源战略2050更新》计划，明确到2030年可再生能源装机容量增加两倍以上达14.2吉瓦。此外，阿联酋政府2024年还发布了《国家氢能战略》，计划到2031年使阿联酋成为十大绿色氢能生产国之一，年产量达到140万吨，并到2050年实现每年氢气产量达到1500万吨。阿曼提出"2040愿景"，加速可再生能源和绿氢等项目的投资和推广。埃及计划到2040年可再生能源发电占比达到40%。中国方面，中国要实现碳达峰以及2030年非化石能源消费占比达到25%，还需要继续推动风电光伏大规模高质量发展。2024年5月，在中阿合作论坛第十届部长级会议开幕式上，中方宣布将以首届中阿峰会"八大共同行动"为基础，同阿方构建"五大合作格局"，构建更加立体的能源合作格局，中方愿同阿方联合开展新能源技术研发和装备生产，支持中国能源企业和金融机构在阿拉伯国家参与总装机容量超过300万千瓦的可再生能源项目。

中国与阿拉伯国家在新能源发展技术和资源方面互补。技术方面，中国正在形成新质生产力，拥有全球领先的新能源产业体系，在光伏、风能、储能等行业具有领先的技术优势和丰富的项目建设经验，可以为阿拉伯国家提供先进的技术支持和管理支持，帮助其快速发展新能源产业。资源方面，阿拉伯国家拥有丰富的太阳能资源，且分布均匀，日照强度普遍高于2000千瓦时/平方米，在沙特、埃及、也门等部分地区可高于2600千瓦时/平方米。此外，阿拉伯国家坐拥优质的风能资源，沙特等国家的陆上风力发电潜能全球排名靠前，沙特中部和北部、阿曼南部和科威特西北部的大片地区拥有良好的风力发电资源，为大规模新能源项目开发提供了理想条件。中阿双方新能源合作，一方面有助于阿盟国家实现能源结构多样化的目标，提高能源利用效率，完善基础设施建设，同时带动当地就业，从而加速经济复苏和繁荣；另一方面将助力中国可再生能源领域企业国际化发展，拓展阿拉伯市场，进一步增强国际竞争力，同时带动相关产业链企业出口。

### 6.3.2 中阿新能源合作的新进展

2024年，中国与阿拉伯国家在新能源合作领域继续提质升级，主要是在光伏、氢能、新能源汽车等领域，体现了双方在经济多样化、技术创新、政策支持和环境保护等方面的共同努力。

光伏领域，多家中国公司签署大型合作项目，参与阿拉伯国家光伏产业链各个环节。其中，2024年7月，中国晶科能源公司全资子公司晶科中东与沙特公共投资基金（PIF）全资子公司 Renewable Energy Localization Company，以及 Vision Industries Company 签订《股东协议》，在沙特成立合资公司建设 10 吉瓦高效电池及组件项目，项目总投资约合 9.85 亿美元；同月，TCL 中环与 Ⅵ、PIF 子公司 Renewable Energy Localization Company 签署《股东协议》，设立合资公司，共同在沙特建设年产 20 吉瓦光伏晶体晶片项目，总投资额预计约为 20.8 亿美元；同月，中国光伏企业阳光电源与沙特 ALGIHAZ 签约全球最大的 ALGIHAZ 储能项目，容量高达 7.8 吉瓦时；同月，中国电建公司阿布扎比分公司与公司下属子企业华东院中东有限责任公司（HDEC）组成联合体，与阿吉班光伏项目控股有限公司签订阿布扎比 PV3 阿吉班 1.5 吉瓦光伏项目 EPC 合同，项目位于阿联酋阿布扎比阿吉班地区，合同金额约为 7.55 亿美元。2024 年 8 月，中国能建所属的多家子公司组成的联营体成功与沙特国际电力和水务公司、沙特公共投资基金及沙特阿美电力公司旗下的项目公司布瑞克可再生能源公司签署了沙特 PIF 四期 Haden 2 吉瓦光伏项目 EPC 合同，合同总金额高达 9.72 亿美元；同月，中国能建国际集团与法国道达尔能源签署伊拉克拉塔维 1 吉瓦光伏项目 EPC 合同，该项目是伊拉克政府光伏建设规划中的首个大型项目。

氢能领域，中国公司与阿拉伯国家签署氢能领域合作协议。2024 年 6 月，沙特国际电力和水务公司（ACWA Power）与中石化广州工程有限公司签署合作备忘录，在绿色氢氨领域将开展务实合作，主要包括共同探索、开发、建设、管理和运营绿色氢能、绿色合成氨等项目，区域将覆盖 ACWA Power 目前已拥有开发合作项目的中东、北非、中亚、东南亚，以及包括中国在内的全球其他国家和地区。同时，双方也将加强在绿色氢能技术开发和应用等领域的合作，同月，海默科技与河南中科清能就阿曼氢能产业项目签订战略合作协议，有效期为 1 年，根据协议，双方将基于各自的专业优势，在阿曼开展绿电制氢、氢气液化技术产业化应用合作，形成从氢气供应到液氢制取、氢气加注、液氢运营以及氢能冷链物流车的一体化氢能源产业链。此外，2024 年 10 月，阿布扎比国家石油公司（ADNOC）旗下的 ADNOC 供应与服务有限公司与中国万华化学集团的战略合资企业"AW 航运公司"中国江南造船厂签署价值 2.5 亿美元的合同，订购两艘超大型氨运输船，将成为全球大规模氨运输船之一。

新能源汽车领域，中国新能源汽车成为中国汽车在阿拉伯国家的一张新名片。2024 年 3 月，比亚迪在阿联酋迪拜举行产品发布会，宣布旗下海豹、宋 PLUS 及秦 PLUS 三款车型正式投放阿联酋市场；6 月，小鹏汽车宣布面向埃及市场发售小鹏 G9、小鹏 P7 两款产品；8 月，长安汽车品牌中东非洲发布会在沙特利雅得举行，推出了长安、深蓝、阿维塔三大品牌，并介绍了未来产品的投放计划；10 月，蔚来汽车与战略投资者 CYVN 签署战略合作协议，宣布将在阿联酋阿布扎比建立先进技术研发中心，并将与 CYVN 联合研发一款针对当地市场的全新车型，还将与 CYVN 合资成立蔚来中东北非公司；12 月，宇通与卡塔尔国家运输公司 Mowasalat 合作的新能源商用车工厂在卡塔尔乌姆阿尔霍尔自由区开工建设，成为卡塔尔第一家电动商用车组装厂，也是共建"一带一路"下中卡两国深化合作的重要实践。①

此外，2024 年 11 月，阿联酋清洁能源巨头马斯达尔公司与中国丝路基金签署谅解备忘录，计划在"一带一路"共建国家共同投资可再生能源项目，总金额达 200 亿元人民币，合作范围覆盖中东、中亚、东南亚等地区，重点支持太阳能、风能、水电等清洁能源项目。②

## 6.4 中阿能源合作前景

当前，世界百年未有之大变局加速演进，能源格局深刻重构。全球能

---

① 《中国汽车品牌踏上中东新热土》，腾讯网，https://news.qq.com/rain/a/20240913A01Z5B00，2024 年 9 月 13 日。
② 《海湾资本加力布局中国新能源》，腾讯网，https://news.qq.com/rain/a/20250227A01G2U00，2025 年 2 月 27 日。

源需求持续增长，在较长时期内，油气仍将扮演重要的主体能源角色，天然气将成为能源绿色发展的关键支撑。能源转型是大势所趋，是应对气候变化的关键行动。作为全球能源市场的重要力量，中国和阿拉伯国家比以往任何时候都更需要加强合作、携手前行，共担能源发展使命，携手推动绿色转型，构建中阿立体能源合作格局。

### 6.4.1 进一步推动和深化传统能源合作，特别是油气全产业链合作

未来一段时间，世界油气需求仍将长期维持较高水平，预计2040年前油气占比将维持在50%左右，2045年前将处于115亿吨标煤以上年需求量的峰值平台期，能源主体地位稳固。[1] 近年来，沙特、阿联酋、科威特、伊拉克、阿曼等阿拉伯国家是中国前十大原油进口来源国。未来一段时间，中国将继续从阿拉伯国家进口原油和天然气，传统油气贸易合作仍将是中阿能源合作的主轴。此外，中阿双方在油气全产业链合作领域仍然具有巨大合作空间，包括加强在阿联酋、阿曼等国的优质油气资产投资，力争扩大卡塔尔天然气上游投资，积极引进沙特、科威特等国能源企业特别是中东主权基金的对华投资合作等。[2]

### 6.4.2 推动建立清洁能源合作伙伴关系，加大在传统能源清洁化利用、风光发电等领域合作

近年来，沙特、阿联酋等阿拉伯国家提出"2030愿景""2050净零排放"等低碳转型规划，并将其作为多元化发展的重要抓手，与中国提出的"双碳"目标相契合，优势高度互补。中国与阿拉伯国家在新能源合作方面具有广阔的合作前景，如与沙特、阿联酋、阿曼等国的新能源发展全面合作，推动建立清洁能源合作伙伴关系，在传统能源清洁化利用、风光发电、绿电制氢、先进核电、海水淡化等阿拉伯国家技术需求较大的领域

---

[1] 《2060年世界与中国能源展望报告》，搜狐网，https://news.sohu.com/a/841343738_121856153。

[2] 中国石油集团经济技术研究院。

开展合作，加快布局建设一批"小而美"的清洁能源项目，使中国能源企业成为阿拉伯国家落实能源多元化战略、实施能源转型发展的重要参与者。中国与阿拉伯国家在全面履行《联合国气候变化框架公约》及《巴黎协定》的基础上，共同推动建立全球气候治理体系。

### 6.4.3 加强中阿之间的能源金融合作，积极创造条件开展油气贸易人民币结算

在当前全球百年未有之大变局下，中阿双方可积极创造条件，多措并举扩大人民币在中阿能源合作中的使用，完善人民币跨境使用基础设施建设，推动中资银行、证券、保险等金融机构在阿拉伯国家设立更多分支机构，并与当地金融机构加强在支付结算、资金拆借、风险评估方面的合作，使人民币能用、好用。此外，中阿双方可加快推进能源金融一体化合作，打通融资途径，为中阿能源贸易和投资提供更有力支持。

### 6.4.4 构建中阿立体能源合作机制，携手维护全球能源安全

中国是当今世界上最大的能源消费国和进口国，是全球能源治理的重要力量。阿拉伯世界或中东产油国油气资源富集，对全球能源供应和价格稳定具有重大影响，也是全球能源治理的重要力量。展望未来，贯彻落实中阿能源立体合作新格局的战略构想，构建能源安全合作机制，携手应对能源危机，维护全球能源安全，可成为"构建能源立体合作新格局"的重要内容。中阿双方可加强能源政策协调，在保障供应与需求安全、合理与公平能源价格、运输与通道安全、危机预警与处理以及全球和地区能源治理等方面，探索构建能源安全合作机制的路径和框架，共同畅通供应链，建立保障能源稳定供需的长效机制，维护双方、地区和全球能源安全。

### 6.4.5 中阿能源合作需防范地缘政治和政策等方面的风险

一是地缘政治风险高企。当前，世界百年未有之大变局加速演进，新兴经济体和发展中国家兴起，国际力量对比深刻调整；经济全球化遭遇逆

流,"脱钩断链""阵营对抗"风险上升,全球"治理赤字""发展赤字""安全赤字"累积,单边制裁、合作歧视、市场壁垒深度影响能源国际合作。阿拉伯国家政局整体趋向稳定,外交自主性日益增强。但当前中东乱局异常复杂,"巴以冲突"持续外溢,叙利亚局势风云突变,地区局势持续紧张,尽管阿拉伯国家无意卷入冲突,但存在发生"擦枪走火"、冲突参与方在阿拉伯国家制造恐怖袭击的可能,能源合作安全风险值得关注。此外,近年来,大国在阿拉伯国家的博弈不断升级,西方国家对中国的遏制和打压力度不断加大,如在5G、人工智能等高科技领域,向与中国合作的阿拉伯国家施压,使之放弃与中国的合作,使用西方国家的替代产品。上述破坏行为恐将对一些阿拉伯国家与中国的合作造成一定的影响。

二是阿拉伯国家继续收紧本地化和财税政策。本地化方面,沙特、阿曼、卡塔尔、科威特等海合会国家再次收紧本地化政策,促进经济多元化发展,为本国公民提供更多的就业机会。其中,沙特推出"Nuwatin"计划,推动能源产业的本地化发展,减少对进口的依赖,提升国内生产能力和技术水平;卡塔尔宣布启动强化版提升国内价值计划,优化国内价值的计算公式,设置奖励制度,以奖励本地化成绩优异的公司;阿曼启动提高能源行业本地化的项目,强调油气、新能源、绿氢等项目的物资采购和用工本地化;科威特石油公司提出要消除用工障碍,增加石油行业本国雇员数量,推动石油行业用工全面本地化。财税方面,阿联酋、阿曼、科威特等国家从2025年1月1日起对在本国运营的大型跨国公司征收15%的最低补充税,一方面通过统一税率和现代化的管理机制提升税收透明度,另一方面实现经济多元化和减少对石油收入依赖。该税收改革将对在上述国家运营的跨国企业盈利能力产生影响,企业需提前布局,调整运营策略以应对新规。

三是国际油价变化给中阿"碳减排"合作带来不确定性。阿拉伯油气资源国实施"碳减排"项目的资金主要来自国家财政投入,国际油价下滑对财政平衡的冲击可能导致阿拉伯油气资源国"碳减排"项目建设延期甚至取消,进而对中国与阿拉伯国家在"碳减排"领域的合作带来不确定性和不利影响。

# 第7章　中阿数字经济合作专题报告

在全球数字化转型加速推进的背景下，数字经济正成为推动经济增长和提升产业竞争力的关键驱动力。随着新一轮科技革命和产业变革，阿拉伯国家积极布局数字经济，加速数字基础设施建设，深化数字技术在政务、贸易等领域的应用，并积极寻求与全球领先国家的合作机遇。同时，作为全球数字经济发展的重要引领者，中国持续推动技术创新和产业升级，为中阿数字经济合作提供广阔空间和坚实基础，共同推动数字经济成为中阿经贸合作的新增长极。面对国际环境的不确定性和科技竞争加剧的挑战，中阿在数字经济领域的互信与协作不断增强，2024年双方数字经济合作进一步深化，为全球数字治理和科技创新注入新的活力。

## 7.1　阿拉伯国家数字经济水平现状

### 7.1.1　数字经济发展硬实力：以ICT基础设施为例

信息与通信技术（ICT）基础设施是数字经济发展的底座，也是推动产业数字化和智能化升级的关键要素。一国的ICT建设水平不仅决定了数字技术的普及程度，还直接影响数字经济的发展速度和增长格局。因此，ICT基础设施的完善程度成为衡量数字经济竞争力的重要标尺。面对全球数字化浪潮，各国正加速推进先进通信网络和基础设施建设，以夯实数字经济基础，提升在全球数字生态体系中的影响力。

1. 地区层面

根据国际电信联盟（ITU）2024 年更新的 ICT 统计数据[①]，近年来，阿拉伯地区 ICT 各项指标整体呈增长趋势，但大部分指标仍低于全球平均水平（见表 7.1）。2024 年，阿拉伯地区的互联网渗透率已达到 69.6%，略高于全球平均水平 67.6%，但在其他关键指标上，阿拉伯地区与全球平均水平仍存在一定差距。具体而言，固定电话普及率为 9.1%，低于全球平均水平 10.3%；固定宽带渗透率为 12.5%，低于全球平均水平 19.6%；移动蜂窝电话普及率为 103.7%，低于全球平均水平 112.1%；活跃移动宽带渗透率为 85.2%，低于全球平均水平 94.6%；移动蜂窝网络渗透率为 97.4%，略低于全球平均水平 97.9%。进一步细分移动蜂窝网络类型可见，阿拉伯地区 3G 及以上移动网络渗透率为 94.9%，略低于全球平均水平 95.6%；4G 及以上移动网络渗透率为 86.9%，低于全球平均水平 91.8%；5G 及以上移动网络渗透率为 12.7%，远低于全球平均水平 51.2%。

表 7.1　2021—2024 年阿拉伯地区 ICT 基本情况汇总

| | | 2021 年 | 2022 年 | 2023 年 | 2024 年 |
|---|---|---|---|---|---|
| 互联网渗透率（%） | | 64.7 | 67.4 | 68.6 | 69.6 |
| 城乡 | 城市 | 77.9 | 80.5 | 81.6 | 82.9 |
| | 乡村 | 46.4 | 49.3 | 49.5 | 50.1 |
| 性别 | 女性 | 59.8 | 61.8 | 63 | 64.4 |
| | 男性 | 69.3 | 72.6 | 73.8 | 75.1 |
| 年龄 | 青年（15—24 岁）人口 | 80 | 82.5 | 84.1 | 86.1 |
| | 青年之外人口 | 62 | 64.7 | 65.8 | 66.7 |

---

[①] 数据来源于国际电联 ICT 统计数据库更新至 2024 年的数据，官方网址请见 ITU，ICT statistics database，https://www.itu.int/cn/ITU-D/Statistics/Pages/stat/default.aspx。其中，由于部分指标数据起始于 2021 年，所以统计范围为 2021—2024 年数据。另外，值得说明的一点是，对于部分相同年度指标数据，2024 年最新统计结果与 2023 年统计结果存在出入，本章内容以 2024 年最新统计结果为准。

续表

|  | 2021 年 | 2022 年 | 2023 年 | 2024 年 |
| --- | --- | --- | --- | --- |
| 固定电话普及率（%） | 8.8 | 8.9 | 8.9 | 9.1 |
| 固定宽带渗透率（%） | 9.6 | 10.6 | 11.4 | 12.5 |
| 移动蜂窝电话普及率（%） | 96.5 | 99.3 | 101.2 | 103.7 |
| 活跃移动宽带渗透率（%） | 66.9 | 70.4 | 76.8 | 85.2 |
| 移动蜂窝网络渗透率（%） | 96.8 | 97.1 | 97.2 | 97.4 |
| 3G 及以上移动网络渗透率（%） | 91.3 | 92.8 | 94.7 | 94.9 |
| 4G 及以上移动网络渗透率（%） | 74 | 80.6 | 85.7 | 86.9 |
| 5G 及以上移动网络渗透率（%） | 8.5 | 9.7 | 10.9 | 12.7 |
| 手机普及率（%） | 82.1 | 82.7 | 82.8 | 83.1 |

注：在表中，固定电话普及率（Fixed Telephone Subscriptions per 100 inhabitants，%）指每 100 人中拥有固定电话线路的比例，反映固定电话网络的普及情况。移动蜂窝电话普及率（Mobile Cellular Subscriptions per 100 inhabitants，%）表示每 100 人拥有的移动电话 SIM 卡数量，可能超过 100%（由于多 SIM 卡现象），用于衡量移动通信服务的渗透程度。固定宽带渗透率（Fixed-broadband Subscriptions per 100 inhabitants，%）指每 100 人中订阅固定宽带服务的比例，反映固定互联网基础设施的覆盖情况。活跃移动宽带渗透率（Active Mobile-broadband Subscriptions per 100 inhabitants，%）衡量实际使用移动数据服务的用户比例，反映移动互联网的普及程度。移动蜂窝网络渗透率（Percentage of Population Covered by a Mobile-cellular Network per 100 inhabitants，%）则表示覆盖 2G/3G/4G/5G 网络的人口比例，反映移动通信基础设施的覆盖水平。随着 5G 建设的推进，该指标持续提升。

资料来源：根据 ITU 统计数据库 2024 年最新数据整理。

与此同时，阿拉伯地区的数字鸿沟依然明显，主要体现在城乡差距和性别差异两个方面。在城乡方面，城市互联网渗透率为 82.9%，与全球平均水平相当，而乡村互联网渗透率为 50.1%，高于全球平均水平 47.5%。在性别方面，女性互联网渗透率为 64.4%，低于全球平均水平 65.3%，而男性互联网渗透率为 75.1%，高于全球平均水平 69.5%。综上所述，阿拉伯地区在数字鸿沟的多个维度上仍面临较大挑战，特别是在高端网络技术的普及和性别差异方面，与全球平均水平存在一定差距。此外，阿拉伯地区的互联网用户结构以年轻群体为主。2024 年，青年互联网渗透率达到 86.1%，显著高于其他年龄群体的 66.7%，且这两项指标均超过全球平均水平（分别为78.5%和65.6%），侧面反映出阿拉伯地区年轻群体在数字化转型中的主导作用。

为进一步衡量ICT发展水平，宽带服务的可负担性①也是一个重要参考指标。根据国际电联《衡量数字发展：事实与数据2024》② 报告，2024年阿拉伯地区的移动宽带（2GB）价格占人均国民总收入的0.8%，低于全球平均水平1.1%，且较上一年有所下降。而固定宽带（5GB）价格占人均国民总收入的3.2%，高于全球平均水平2.5%，且与上一年水平持平。这一对比反映出，阿拉伯地区在移动宽带普及方面取得进展，但固定宽带的成本仍然较高，制约了更广泛的数字接入和应用。

2. 国别层面

根据国际电联《衡量数字发展：信通技术发展指数2024》③，阿拉伯各国的ICT发展水平存在显著差异（见表7.2）。在互联网渗透率方面，吉布提、毛里塔尼亚、索马里和也门，均低于世界平均水平69.3%，再加上突尼斯、埃及和阿尔及利亚，均低于中国水平75.6%。在家庭互联网普及率方面，吉布提、突尼斯和索马里，均低于世界平均水平70.1%，再加上阿尔及利亚和埃及，均低于中国水平81.2%。在移动宽带渗透率方面，毛里塔尼亚、约旦、埃及、伊拉克、吉布提、也门、叙利亚、巴勒斯坦和索马里，均低于世界平均水平84.3%，再加上阿尔及利亚、摩洛哥、突尼斯，均低于中国水平107.8%。在3G及以上移动网络渗透率方面，吉布提、也门、索马里、巴勒斯坦和毛里塔尼亚均低于世界平均水平90.5%，阿联酋、巴林、科威特、卡塔尔、沙特和阿曼6个海合会国家均高于中国水平99.9%。在4G及以上移动网络渗透率方面，吉布提、叙利亚、也门、毛里塔尼亚、索马里和巴勒斯坦，均低于世界平均水平81.1%，巴林、科

---

① 联合国宽带委员会（Broadband Commission）设定的目标是将基础宽带服务的价格降低到不超过人均国民总收入（GNI per capita）的2%，以确保互联网接入的经济可负担性。
② ITU, "Measuring Digital Development Facts and Figures 2024", https://www.itu.int/en/ITU-D/Statistics/Pages/facts/default.aspx.
③ ITU, "Measuring Digital Development the ICT Development Index 2024", https://www.itu.int/en/ITU-D/Statistics/Pages/facts/default.aspx.

威特和沙特均高于中国水平99.9%。在手机普及率方面，巴勒斯坦、吉布提、伊拉克、毛里塔尼亚、也门和索马里低于全球平均水平79.7%和中国水平83%。

表7.2  2024年中国和阿拉伯国家的ICT基本情况

| 国别 | 互联网渗透率（%） | 家庭互联网普及率（%） | 移动宽带渗透率（%） | 3G及以上移动网络渗透率（%） | 4G及以上移动网络渗透率（%） | 手机普及率（%） |
|---|---|---|---|---|---|---|
| 阿尔及利亚 | 71.2† | 80.6† | 99.7 | 98.1 | 85.9 | 85.9† |
| 巴林 | 100.0 | 100.0 | 157.6 | 100.0 | 100.0 | 100.0 |
| 吉布提 | 65.0† | 68.4† | 35.6 | 90.0 | 76.0 | 74.4† |
| 埃及 | 72.2 | 73.2 | 64.8 | 99.7 | 98.0 | 97.4 |
| 伊拉克 | 78.7 | 88.7 | 46.2 | 98.2 | 96.6 | 65.7 |
| 约旦 | 90.5 | 92.2 | 67.6 | 100.0 | 99.8 | 91.1† |
| 科威特 | 99.7 | 99.4 | 151.5 | 100.0 | 100.0 | 99.2 |
| 利比亚 | 88.4† | n.a. | 125.6 | 93.5 | 90.0 | 89.1† |
| 毛里塔尼亚 | 44.4† | n.a. | 73.4 | 43.9 | 34.7‡ | 61.3† |
| 摩洛哥 | 89.9 | 87.4 | 88.6 | 99.5 | 99.4 | 96.5 |
| 阿曼 | 97.8† | 97.1† | 115.9 | 100.0 | 99.0 | 97.8† |
| 巴勒斯坦 | 88.6 | 92.3 | 21.9 | 58.3 | 0.0 | 79.2 |
| 卡塔尔 | 99.7‡ | 95.0‡ | 144.0 | 100.0 | 99.8 | 99.6‡ |
| 沙特 | 100.0 | 100.0 | 126.0 | 100.0 | 100.0 | 100.0 |
| 索马里 | 19.9† | 11.9‡ | 2.6 | 70.0 | 30.0 | 18.9† |
| 叙利亚 | n.a. | n.a. | 21.9 | 98.9 | 75.7 | n.a. |
| 突尼斯 | 73.8† | 57.0† | 85.8 | 99.0 | 95.0 | 87.9† |
| 阿联酋 | 100.0 | 100.0 | 234.9 | 100.0 | 99.8 | 100.0 |
| 也门 | 17.7† | n.a. | 29.2 | 73.7 | 45.0 | 34.6† |
| 中国 | 75.6 | 81.2† | 107.8 | 99.9 | 99.9 | 83† |

注："†"表示ITU估计值；"‡"表示2021年的滞后值；"n.a."表示缺失值。
资料来源：根据《衡量数字发展：信通技术发展指数2024》整理。

## 第7章 中阿数字经济合作专题报告

另外，根据Speedtest于2024年12月更新的Speedtest全球指数（Speedtest Global Index）[①]，全球110个国家和地区参与移动网速测评，154个国家和地区参与固定宽带网速测评。从移动网络和固定宽带下载速度来看（见表7.3），阿拉伯地区仅阿联酋进入全球前10名，卡塔尔、科威特和沙特进入全球前50名。进一步分析单项指标可以发现，阿联酋、卡塔尔、科威特、巴林、沙特和阿曼6个海合会国家的移动网络下载速度超过世界平均水平62.79Mbps，其中的阿联酋、卡塔尔、科威特的速度更是高于中国平均水平147.14Mbps；阿联酋、卡塔尔、科威特、沙特和约旦的固定宽带网络下载速度超过世界平均水平96.45Mbps，仅阿联酋的速度超越中国平均水平230.11Mbps。总体而言，海合会国家在移动网络方面整体领先，固定宽带建设也表现较好，但除阿联酋外，其整体水平仍与中国存在一定差距。

表7.3 2024年中国和阿拉伯国家的互联网速度及排名情况

| 国别 | 移动网络 下载速度（Mbps） | 世界排名 | 固定宽带 下载速度（Mbps） | 世界排名 | 国别 | 移动网络 下载速度（Mbps） | 世界排名 | 固定宽带 下载速度（Mbps） | 世界排名 |
|---|---|---|---|---|---|---|---|---|---|
| 阿联酋 | 453.87 | 1 | 304.24 | 3 | 埃及 | 24.2 | 92 | 77.89 | 80 |
| 卡塔尔 | 383.5 | 2 | 185.08 | 26 | 阿尔及利亚 | 23.09 | 95 | 15.65 | 140 |
| 科威特 | 257.3 | 3 | 192.99 | 23 | 利比亚 | 16.83 | 104 | 10.44 | 147 |
| 巴林 | 130.74 | 12 | 86.61 | 69 | 叙利亚 | 13.23 | 107 | 3.38 | 153 |
| 沙特 | 129.16 | 14 | 120.41 | 44 | 毛里塔尼亚 | n.a. | n.a. | 23.16 | 129 |
| 阿曼 | 94.46 | 28 | 80.36 | 75 | 索马里 | n.a. | n.a. | 18.53 | 134 |
| 摩洛哥 | 45.67 | 64 | 35.57 | 116 | 吉布提 | n.a. | n.a. | 18.15 | 135 |

---

① Speedtest Global Index 由 Ookla 公司提供，是一项用于评估和排名全球各国家和地区固定宽带及移动网络速度的月度指数。该指数基于用户在 Speedtest 平台上进行的数十亿次测试数据，呈现全球互联网速度的最新概况。用户可通过该指数查看各国的下载速度、上传速度及延迟等关键指标的排名与趋势。2024年官方数据请见 Speedtest, Speedtest Global Index (Median Country Speeds Updated December 2024), https://www.speedtest.net/global-index。

续表

| 国别 | 移动网络 下载速度（Mbps） | 世界排名 | 固定宽带 下载速度（Mbps） | 世界排名 | 国别 | 移动网络 下载速度（Mbps） | 世界排名 | 固定宽带 下载速度（Mbps） | 世界排名 |
|---|---|---|---|---|---|---|---|---|---|
| 伊拉克 | 38.04 | 71 | 33.58 | 118 | 也门 | n.a. | n.a. | 10.12 | 148 |
| 黎巴嫩 | 31.81 | 83 | 13.11 | 145 | 巴勒斯坦 | n.a. | n.a. | 65.17 | 92 |
| 约旦 | 30.57 | 84 | 162.74 | 34 | 中国 | 147.14 | 8 | 230.11 | 14 |
| 突尼斯 | 27.12 | 90 | 11.72 | 146 | | | | | |

注："n.a."表示缺失值。
资料来源：根据Speedtest整理。

### 7.1.2 数字经济发展软实力：以创新潜力、人力资本与科研能力为例

创新潜力是推动数字经济可持续发展的核心驱动力，决定了数字技术的应用深度与广度。持续的技术创新不仅能够提升产业数字化水平，还能塑造国家在全球数字经济格局中的竞争优势。同时，人力资本作为创新的关键载体，在数字经济时代发挥着至关重要的作用，高素质人才的储备与培养已成为决定国家技术创新能力和国际竞争力的重要因素。因此，本章将从创新潜力和人力资本两个维度评估阿拉伯国家数字经济发展的软实力水平。

全球创新指数（Global Innovation Index，GII）由世界知识产权组织（WIPO）发布，旨在评估各国创新能力和表现。《全球创新指数2024》[1]对全球133个经济体进行了排名，并划分为四个梯队：第1—33名为第一梯队，第34—66名为第二梯队，第67—99名为第三梯队，第100—133名为第四梯队。调查数据显示（见表7.4），阿联酋是阿拉伯国家中唯一

---

[1] WIPO, "Global Innovation Index 2024", https://www.wipo.int/web-publications/global-innovation-index-2024/assets/67729/2000%20Global%20Innovation%20Index%202024_WEB3lite.pdf.

进入第一梯队的经济体，全球排名第32位，但与排名第11位的中国仍存在较大差距。此外，沙特、卡塔尔和摩洛哥位列第二梯队，其他阿拉伯国家大多排名靠后。科研与创新是推动数字经济发展的核心支撑。近年来，位于第一和第二梯队的阿拉伯国家持续加大研发投入，以增强技术创新能力，缩小与领先经济体的差距。

表7.4 2024年部分阿拉伯国家与中国的创新能力世界排名情况
（基于全球创新指数和人力资本与科研指数）

| 国别 | 全球创新指数 | 人力资本与科研指数 | 国别 | 全球创新指数 | 人力资本与科研指数 |
|---|---|---|---|---|---|
| 阿联酋 | 32 | 17 | 阿曼 | 74 | 66 |
| 沙特 | 47 | 33 | 突尼斯 | 81 | 47 |
| 卡塔尔 | 49 | 48 | 埃及 | 86 | 96 |
| 摩洛哥 | 66 | 81 | 黎巴嫩 | 94 | 59 |
| 科威特 | 71 | 53 | 阿尔及利亚 | 115 | 76 |
| 巴林 | 72 | 75 | 毛里塔尼亚 | 126 | 120 |
| 约旦 | 73 | 85 | 中国 | 11 | 22 |

资料来源：根据《全球创新指数2024》整理。

全球创新指数中的人力资本与科研指数综合衡量基础教育、高等教育及研发能力三个维度。从最新评估结果来看，阿拉伯国家整体人力资本水平仍处于较低水平，与上一年水平一致。在2024年全球排名中，阿联酋是阿拉伯地区唯一超越中国的国家。

### 7.1.3 数字经济应用场景：以电子政务为例

数字经济的广泛应用为政务服务数字化提供了重要机遇，电子政务的推进也进一步促进了数字经济的发展。随着数字技术的进步，政府治理模式正在向数字政府转型，阿拉伯国家纷纷加强电子政务基础设施建设，以提升行政效率和公共服务能力。

为评估全球电子政务发展水平,联合国经济和社会事务部(UNDESA)自2001年起,每两年发布电子政务发展指数(EGDI),覆盖联合国193个成员国。该指数综合衡量电子政务基础设施、在线服务水平和公众参与度,已成为衡量政府数字化能力的重要参考指标。EGDI采用0至1的评分体系,并将国家划分为四个等级:得分0.75及以上的国家归为极高分组(VH),表示其电子政务发展水平全球领先;得分在0.50至0.75的国家为高分组(H),表明其电子政务体系较为成熟;得分0.25至0.50的国家列为中等组(M),说明其电子政务处于过渡阶段;得分低于0.25的国家为低分组(L),反映其电子政务建设仍处于起步阶段。

随着全球电子政府的持续推进,世界平均电子政务发展指数不断上升。根据《联合国电子政务调查报告2024》[①],该指数从2022年的0.610升至2024年的0.638,这一趋势反映了各国对数字化治理的重视不断加深,电子政务基础设施和服务水平也在不断优化。阿拉伯国家整体电子政务水平也呈上升趋势(见表7.5)。其中,13个国家的电子政务发展水平跻身高分组及以上,10个国家的得分超过全球平均水平。然而,仅沙特、阿联酋和巴林的电子政务发展指数超过中国的0.872。进一步分析2022—2024年阿拉伯国家电子政务水平变化发现,15个阿拉伯国家的全球排名有所上升,其中利比亚、巴林、沙特和卡塔尔的进步最为显著,分别上升了44、36、25和25名。与此同时,7个国家的排名有所下降,表明部分国家在电子政务发展过程中仍面临挑战。从电子政务分组来看,卡塔尔和科威特从高分组提升至极高分组,利比亚从中等组跃升高分组,而也门则从中等组跌落至低分组。这一变化凸显了阿拉伯国家在电子政务发展上的分化趋势,不同国家的发展进程和政策实施效果存在显著差异。

---

① 联合国经济和社会事务部:《联合国电子政务调查报告2024》,UN E-Goverment Knowledgebase,https://publicadminis-tration.un.org/egovkb/en-us/Reports/UN-E-Government-Survey-2024。

表 7.5　2024年中国和阿拉伯国家的电子政务发展指数水平及变化情况

| 国家 | 电子政务指数 | 等级 | 等级变动 | 世界排名 | 排名变动 |
| --- | --- | --- | --- | --- | --- |
| 沙特 | 0.960 | 极高 | — | 6 | ↑25 |
| 阿联酋 | 0.953 | 极高 | — | 11 | ↑2 |
| 巴林 | 0.920 | 极高 | — | 18 | ↑36 |
| 阿曼 | 0.858 | 极高 | — | 41 | ↑9 |
| 卡塔尔 | 0.824 | 极高 | ↑ | 53 | ↑25 |
| 科威特 | 0.781 | 极高 | ↑ | 66 | ↓5 |
| 突尼斯 | 0.694 | 高 | — | 87 | ↑1 |
| 约旦 | 0.685 | 高 | — | 89 | ↑11 |
| 摩洛哥 | 0.684 | 高 | — | 90 | ↑11 |
| 埃及 | 0.670 | 高 | — | 95 | ↑8 |
| 阿尔及利亚 | 0.596 | 高 | — | 116 | ↓4 |
| 利比亚 | 0.547 | 高 | ↑ | 125 | ↑44 |
| 黎巴嫩 | 0.545 | 高 | — | 126 | ↓4 |
| 伊拉克 | 0.457 | 中等 | — | 148 | ↓2 |
| 叙利亚 | 0.389 | 中等 | — | 162 | ↓6 |
| 毛里塔尼亚 | 0.349 | 中等 | — | 165 | ↑7 |
| 吉布提 | 0.291 | 中等 | — | 174 | ↑7 |
| 苏丹 | 0.276 | 中等 | — | 178 | ↓2 |
| 科摩罗 | 0.259 | 中等 | — | 180 | ↑2 |
| 也门 | 0.232 | 低 | ↓ | 185 | ↓7 |
| 索马里 | 0.147 | 低 | — | 191 | ↑1 |
| 中国 | 0.872 | 极高 | — | 35 | ↑8 |

注："↑"表述上升，"↓"表示下降，"—"表示无变化。
资料来源：根据《联合国电子政务调查报告2024》整理。

### 7.1.4　数字经济发展市场支撑：以数字产业与高科技制造业为例

数字经济的硬实力和软实力主要衡量一国内部的发展水平，而数字产业的进出口贸易,特别是高科技产业和ICT产业的国际流动,则是推动数字经济全球化和可持续增长的重要支撑。这不仅促进了国内外市场的联动,还直接影响数字经济的技术积累与产业升级。从进口角度看,引进先进的高科技产品和ICT服务不仅能增强本国数字产业的竞争力,还能推动数字技术与传统产业的深度融合,提升整体产业升级水平。而从出口角度看,拓展国际市场布局不仅有助于提升一国在全球数字经济体系中的影响力,还加速了数字经济的国际化进程。根据《全球创新指数2024》数据,阿拉伯国家在高科技产品和ICT服务的进出口方面存在显著差异(见表7.6)。高科技产品进口占贸易比重排名前五的国家分别为阿联酋、阿尔及利亚、突尼斯、黎巴嫩和沙特,但这些国家均低于中国。高科技产品出口占贸易比重排名前五的国家分别为阿联酋、突尼斯、摩洛哥、黎巴嫩和阿曼,同样落后于中国。在ICT服务进口方面,卡塔尔、巴林、阿联酋、阿曼和埃及排名地区前五,其中前三名领先于中国。ICT服务出口方面,科威特、巴林、摩洛哥、埃及和阿联酋排名前五,前三名也领先于中国。

表7.6 2024年中国和阿拉伯国家的数字产业贸易及高科技制造业占比情况

| 国别 | 高科技进口占贸易总额 占比(%) | 排名 | 高科技出口占贸易总额 占比(%) | 排名 | ICT服务进口占贸易总额 占比(%) | 排名 | ICT服务出口占贸易总额 占比(%) | 排名 | 高科技制造占制造业总额 占比(%) | 排名 |
|---|---|---|---|---|---|---|---|---|---|---|
| 阿联酋 | 12.8 | 20 | 9.4 | 21 | 1.1 | 70 | 1.7 | 63 | 20 | 62 |
| 沙特 | 8.2 | 68 | 0.8 | 83 | 0.7 | 99 | 0.5 | 100 | 26.3 | 47 |
| 卡塔尔 | 4.2 | 118 | 0.3 | 101 | 1.6 | 45 | 1 | 82 | 40.9 | 25 |
| 科威特 | 4.7 | 111 | 0.2 | 111 | 0.1 | 131 | 5.6 | 18 | 20.9 | 59 |
| 巴林 | 3.2 | 128 | 1 | 79 | 1.5 | 54 | 3.9 | 28 | 9.8 | 88 |
| 阿曼 | 4.1 | 120 | 1.9 | 66 | 1 | 80 | 0.4 | 104 | 16.5 | 71 |
| 摩洛哥 | 7.2 | 86 | 2.1 | 57 | 0.9 | 88 | 3.2 | 36 | 39.9 | 27 |
| 约旦 | 1.2 | 71 | 7.2 | 82 | 0.1 | 125 | 0.2 | 125 | 17.7 | 67 |

续表

| 国别 | 高科技进口占贸易总额 || 高科技出口占贸易总额 || ICT服务进口占贸易总额 || ICT服务出口占贸易总额 || 高科技制造占制造业总额 ||
|---|---|---|---|---|---|---|---|---|---|---|
| | 占比(%) | 排名 | 占比(%) | 排名 | 占比(%) | 排名 | 占比(%) | 排名 | 占比(%) | 排名 |
| 突尼斯 | 8.4 | 63 | 4.2 | 42 | 0.6 | 106 | 1.7 | 64 | 21.9 | 55 |
| 埃及 | 4.8 | 110 | 0.7 | 85 | 0.9 | 83 | 2 | 57 | 18.5 | 63 |
| 黎巴嫩 | 8.3 | 65 | 2 | 59 | 0.3 | 123 | 1.3 | 74 | 14.6 | 76 |
| 阿尔及利亚 | 10.4 | 35 | 0 | 131 | 0.3 | 119 | 0.2 | 126 | 4.1 | 101 |
| 毛里塔尼亚 | 1.9 | 131 | 0 | 130 | 0.5 | 107 | 0.2 | 122 | n/a | n/a |
| 中国 | 19.9 | 8 | 26.3 | 1 | 1.1 | 72 | 2.4 | 52 | 48.4 | 11 |

注："n/a"表示缺失值。

资料来源：根据《全球创新指数2024》整理。

此外，从高科技制造业在制造业总额中的占比来看，阿拉伯国家中排名前五的分别是卡塔尔、摩洛哥、沙特、突尼斯和科威特。尽管这些国家进入全球前60名，但整体水平仍低于中国，说明高科技制造业的生产能力相对薄弱，是制约阿拉伯国家数字产业贸易竞争力的重要因素。从数字经济视角来看，高科技制造业的发展滞后不仅影响数字产品和服务的全球竞争力，还制约了数字基础设施、数字化转型和智能产业的进步，进而影响整体数字经济的发展质量。因此，加强高科技产业研发投入、提升制造业数字化水平，成为阿拉伯国家提升数字经济竞争力的关键路径。

## 7.2 中阿数字经济合作现状

自2016年"网上丝绸之路"倡议提出以来，中阿数字经济合作不断深化，合作领域逐步扩展，涵盖了数字基础设施、电子商务、数字治理、人才培养等多个领域，形成了广泛的合作网络。

### 7.2.1 政策与机制建设

随着中阿数字经济合作机制的不断完善，中阿合作从政策倡议阶段逐步向机制化建设迈进，为中阿长期合作奠定了制度性保障。

**1. 政策倡议阶段：强化合作指引**

2017年，中国与阿联酋、沙特等国在第四届世界互联网大会上共同发起《"一带一路"数字经济国际合作倡议》，为中阿数字经济合作提供政策指引。[①] 2018年，中阿合作论坛第八届部长级会议提出加快网上丝绸之路建设，推动网络基础设施、大数据、云计算、电子商务等领域的合作。[②] 2020年，中阿合作论坛第九届部长级会议发布《中国—阿拉伯国家论坛2020年至2022年行动执行计划》，明确加强数字经济和科技人文交流合作。[③] 2021年，中阿共同发布《中阿数据安全合作倡议》，推动双方在数字治理规则制定方面的合作，强化数据安全合作，共同构建网络空间命运共同体，彰显双方在数字治理领域的高度共识以及共同担当数字时代的全球责任。[④]

**2. 机制化建设阶段：深化合作体系**

自2022年起，中阿合作进入更高水平发展阶段。中国分别与阿拉伯国家、海合会国家召开了首届中国—阿拉伯国家峰会及首届中国—海合会国家峰会，推动双边经济合作迈向系统化、机制化。首届中阿峰会强调开拓数字经济、航空航天等新兴领域合作，并在务实合作"八大共同行动"中明确，推动人工智能、信息通信、空间信息等领域的联合实验室或研发中心建设，深化《中阿数据安全合作倡议》的落实，增强网络安全、数据治理等领域

---

[①] 《多国共同发起"一带一路"数字经济国际合作倡议》，新华网，http://www.xinhuanet.com/zgjx/2017-12/04/c_136798586.htm，2017年12月4日。

[②] 习近平：《携手推进新时代中阿战略伙伴关系》，《人民日报》2018年7月11日第2版。

[③] 《中国—阿拉伯国家合作论坛2020年至2022年行动执行计划》，中阿改革发展研究中心网站，http://infadm.shisu.edu.cn/_s114/07/09/c7779a132873/page.psp，2018年8月19日。

[④] 《中阿数据安全合作倡议》，中华人民共和国外交部网站，https://www.mfa.gov.cn/web/ziliao_674904/1179_674909/202103/t20210329_9180823.shtml，2021年3月29日。

的合作与对话。① 首届中海峰会则着重于数字经济、绿色发展领域的投资合作，推动双边投资和经济合作机制建设，深化数字货币合作，推动 5G 技术、6G 技术、跨境电商及通信网络建设等项目。② 与此同时，中国与沙特签署了全面战略伙伴关系协议，明确提出深化数字经济投资合作及电子商务合作。③

2024 年是中阿合作论坛成立 20 周年，亦是双方数字经济合作深化的重要节点。5 月 30 日，中阿合作论坛第十届部长级会议在北京召开，会议提出构建中阿"五大合作格局"，进一步夯实双方在数字经济领域的伙伴关系，特别是在人工智能、电子商务等领域的合作。④

### 7.2.2 数字基础设施建设

阿拉伯国家庞大的数字人口红利为数字基础设施合作提供了广阔市场空间，成为推动中阿合作加速的重要动力。双方在 5G 通信、云计算、智慧城市等领域的合作不断深化，为阿拉伯国家数字经济的发展提供了有力支撑。

5G 通信网络建设。中国企业在阿拉伯国家 5G 网络建设中发挥了关键作用，特别是在海湾国家。例如，华为与沙特签署了多项 5G 合作协议，并完成了首个 5GLAN 项目⑤；与阿联酋电信运营商 du 合作推进"5G-A 智慧家庭"项目，助力智慧城市和 5G 技术应用的落地。⑥ 与

---

① 《习近平在首届中国—阿拉伯国家峰会上提出中阿务实合作"八大共同行动"》，中华人民共和国中央人民政府网站，https：//www.gov.cn/xinwen/2022-12/10/content_5731138.htm，2022 年 12 月 10 日。
② 《习近平出席首届中国—海湾阿拉伯国家合作委员会峰会并发表主旨讲话》，《人民日报》2022 年 12 月 10 日第 1 版。
③ 《中华人民共和国和沙特阿拉伯王国联合声明》，中华人民共和国中央人民政府网站，https：//www.gov.cn/xinwen/2022-12/10/content_5731174.htm，2022 年 12 月 10 日。
④ 《习近平出席中阿合作论坛第十届部长级会议开幕式并发表主旨讲话》，中华人民共和国中央人民政府网站，https：//www.gov.cn/yaowen/liebiao/202405/content_6954536.htm，2024 年 5 月 30 日。
⑤ 《华为助力沙特 Zain 完成中东北非地区首个 5GLAN 项目》，华为网站，https：//www.huawei.com/cn/news/2022/3/first-5g-lan-in-mena，2022 年 3 月 7 日。
⑥ 《du 联合华为发布全球首个"5G-A 智慧家庭"》，华为网站，https：//www.huawei.com/cn/news/2023/10/mbbf2023-5gafamily，2023 年 10 月 9 日。

此同时，中国企业作为全球数字经济的领先者，正积极拓展在中东的数字化商业模式，在5.5G领域深化合作，共同打造支撑中阿经贸往来的"信息桥"。

云计算中心与大数据中心建设。随着数字化转型的加速，云计算中心和大数据中心已成为阿拉伯国家数字经济的重要支柱。近年来，中国企业积极布局中东地区的云服务基础设施，为当地数字经济发展提供强劲支撑。例如，腾讯云在巴林设立数据中心，助力其打造中东云服务枢纽，以满足当地企业的数字化升级需求[1]；阿里云联合当地企业成立云计算公司，计划在沙特建设多个数据中心，并推动利雅得成为区域管理与培训中心。[2] 华为则持续扩展云服务网络，在沙特设立数据中心，支持政府数字化转型，并推动阿拉伯语人工智能应用。[3] 此外，华为还与阿联酋电信公司合作，建立本地云基础设施，为当地企业提供定制化云服务和尖端技术，助力中小企业利用大数据、人工智能和物联网技术，降低创新门槛。[4] 在中国企业的助力下，北非地区的云计算发展取得重要进展。埃及正式上线北非首个公有云服务，这不仅提升了该地区的云计算能力，也为北非国家的数字经济发展注入了新的动力。[5]

### 7.2.3 智慧城市建设

智慧城市作为新型基础设施建设的重要组成部分，在推动城市数字化

---

[1] 《腾讯云宣布将在巴林设立数据中心，海外业务布局提速》，中国日报网，https：//cnews.chinadaily.com.cn/a/202103/01/WS603c85f6a3101e7ce974177c.html，2021年3月1日。
[2] 《阿里云在沙特创立云计算合资公司》，中华人民共和国商务部网站，http：//sa.mofcom.gov.cn/article/sqfb/202206/20220603319867.shtml，2022年6月18日。
[3] 《华为在沙特阿拉伯推出云数据中心，未来5年为该地区20万名新开发者提供支持》，新浪网，https：//k.sina.com.cn/article_1878726905_6ffb18f902001bkzg.html？from=finance，2023年9月5日。
[4] 《华为与阿联酋综合电信公司DU合作，建立本地云基础设施》，搜狐网，https：//www.sohu.com/a/732003550_99900524，2023年10月28日。
[5] 《华为云埃及正式开服，成为北部非洲第一朵公有云》，华为网站，https：//www.huaweicloud.com/news/2024/20240522173651457.html，2024年5月22日。

转型和信息互联方面发挥着关键作用。① 中国企业积极参与阿拉伯国家的智慧城市建设，涵盖智慧能源、智能治理和数字政府服务等多个领域。例如，华为与沙特智慧城市解决方案公司（SC2）签署协议，共同推动沙特智慧城市项目的实施。② 华为还助力阿联酋在智能交通、电网、住房等领域的智慧化升级，并率先在中东推广窄带物联网（NB-IoT）技术，推动城市管理智能化，促进医疗、教育、金融等行业的智慧应用落地，加速阿拉伯国家智慧城市建设进程。③

此外，中阿在智慧城市建设领域的合作也得到了重要国际平台的支持。2023 年，首届数字经济赋能城市高质量发展高端论坛在北京召开，会议围绕智慧城市建设与数字经济发展展开讨论。中国的智慧城市建设经验为阿拉伯国家提供了宝贵的借鉴。④ 2024 年 10 月，阿拉伯数字经济联盟在西安举行的数字经济产业发展论坛上，与西安市政府签署谅解备忘录，明确在数字技能建设、智慧城市等领域的合作框架。⑤ 11 月，迪拜举办"数字经济赋能高质量发展与城市现代化"圆桌会议，进一步推动中阿在智能电网、人工智能等领域的深度合作，为区域智慧城市建设注入新动能。⑥

### 7.2.4　跨境电商合作

近年来，中阿跨境电商合作日益深化，中国电商平台在阿拉伯市场的

---

① 周记顺、宋颜希：《新型基础设施建设对地区出口的影响——来自国家智慧城市试点的证据》，《产业经济研究》2022 年第 5 期，第 117 页。
② 《华为与 SC2 公司达成合作 为沙特打造智慧城市》，环球网，https：//baijiahao.baidu.com/s？id=1670917657561774548&wfr=spider&for=pc，2020 年 6 月 30 日。
③ 《华为与迪拜等阿联酋国家合作 共建未来智慧城市》，环球网，https：//tech.huanqiu.com/article/9CaKrnJVvYy，2016 年 5 月 17 日。
④ 《数字经济赋能城市高质量发展高端论坛举办》，人民网，http：//www.people.com.cn/n1/2023/0104/c363567-32599820.html，2023 年 1 月 4 日。
⑤ 《阿拉伯数字经济联盟参与中国西安市数字经济产业发展论坛》，阿联酋数字经济网站，https：//arab-digital-economy.org/10581，2024 年 10 月 31 日。
⑥ 《"数字经济赋能高质量发展与城市现代化"圆桌会议在迪拜举行》，中阿合作论坛网站，https：//www.chinaarabcf.org/zagx/wshz/202411/t20241120_11529771.htm，2024 年 11 月 20 日。

影响力持续提升。阿里巴巴旗下的速卖通（AliExpress）、希音（Shein）、跨境版拼多多（Temu）和TikTok Shop等平台加快布局中东市场，推动当地数字消费模式升级。其中，TikTok Shop在阿联酋和沙特市场已占据重要份额，直播电商迅速兴起，带动社交电商和内容电商的发展，成为区域数字零售的重要增长点，进一步促进了数字经济生态的完善。与此同时，中国物流企业加速拓展中东市场，为跨境电商提供高效的物流支持。极兔速递（J&T Express）和艾麦（iMile）等物流企业积极布局本地化仓储和配送网络，提升物流效率，优化跨境电商供应链体系，助力中阿跨境电商的高质量发展。

此外，中阿在数字支付领域的合作持续深化，阿联酋、沙特等国的电子支付体系逐步完善，中国金融科技企业与当地银行及支付平台展开深度合作。2022年，义乌与沙特完成首单跨境人民币支付，推动中阿本币结算合作进程。[①] 2023年，"义乌付"在阿联酋落地，进一步加速数字支付体系的融合，提升跨境支付效率。[②]在此背景下，中阿跨境电商合作不断拓展。2024年，第三届全球数字贸易博览会在杭州举办，数字经济国际合作对接会吸引了埃及等20多个国家以及阿盟、联合国等国际组织参与，进一步促进了中阿在数字贸易领域的合作，增强双方在全球数字经济治理中的影响力。[③]随着跨境电商的快速发展，中阿在支付体系优化和贸易便利化方面的合作将持续深化，为双方数字经济合作提供坚实的支撑。

### 7.2.5 数字经验交流与人才培养

近年来，中阿在数字治理领域的合作持续深化，涵盖数字基础设施、

---

[①] 《义乌和沙特完成首单跨境人民币支付业务，外交部：中阿经贸合作不断迈上新台阶》，中国日报网，https://cn.chinadaily.com.cn/a/202212/09/WS6393057ba3102ada8b226067.html，2022年12月9日。

[②] 《义支付首单迪拜跨境人民币业务落地》，中华人民共和国商务部网站，http://ae.mofcom.gov.cn/article/ztdy/202403/20240303486777.shtml，2024年3月28日。

[③] 《2024年数字经济国际合作对接会在杭举办：共享数字发展新红利》，《浙江日报》2024年9月26日第6版。

智慧城市、数据安全等多个关键领域。中国企业积极助力阿拉伯国家的数字化转型，推动智能政务和技术标准建设，而阿拉伯国家也借鉴中国经验，加快本国数字治理进程。双方合作逐步从政策对话拓展至技术应用、产业对接和人才培养，合作层次不断提升。在此背景下，2024年，阿拉伯大学协会等机构主办的首届"一带一路"政策沟通研讨会暨"中阿数字治理工作坊"在线举行，40余位中阿专家围绕数字治理、数据安全和技术应用展开深入讨论，促进公共政策的信息共享与经验传递。[①] 5月，在阿联酋举办的全球数字经济大会中东分会场吸引了中阿政府、企业及专家参与，共同探讨数字经济发展趋势，推动国际合作与政策协调，进一步夯实双方在数字治理和技术创新领域的合作基础。[②]

在数字人才培养方面，华为自2008年发起的"未来种子"计划，已成为阿拉伯国家培养ICT人才的重要平台。[③] 该计划在多个国家落地，助力提升当地ICT人才储备，推动数字经济发展。在突尼斯，华为自2015年以来已与72所大学签署ICT学院合作协议，惠及超过6800名学生。[④] 在埃及，华为设立华为信息与通信技术学院，并发起"未来种子"计划和ICT技能大赛，同时积极参与"数字埃及建设者"倡议，为当地培养了大批信息与通信技术专业人才。[⑤] 此外，2022年，华为与沙特数字学院签署

---

[①]《全球院举办首届"一带一路"政策沟通研讨会暨"中阿数字治理工作坊"》，复旦大学全球公共政策研究院网站，https://igpp.fudan.edu.cn/37/40/c18211a669504/page.htm，2024年4月23日。

[②]《聚焦数字经济发展 助力中阿友好合作——2024全球数字经济大会中东分会场论坛成功举办》，北京市经济和信息化局网站，https://jxj.beijing.gov.cn/jxdt/gzdt/202405/t20240529_3698061.html，2024年5月29日。

[③]《未来种子2.0，助力培养ICT人才，激发创新》，华为官网，https://www.huawei.com/cn/sustainability/the-latest/stories/seeds-cultivating-ict-talent-to-stimulate-innovation，2024年4月12日。

[④]《张建国大使出席华为突尼斯2022"未来种子"计划结业式》，中国驻突尼斯大使馆网站，http://tn.china-embassy.gov.cn/sgxw/202211/t20221115_10974957.htm，2022年11月14日。

[⑤] 管克江：《中东地区国家大力发展数字经济（国际视点）》，《人民日报》2023年11月22日第14版。

了合作协议，计划培养 8000 名沙特数字人才。[①] 2024 年，华为进一步深化在沙特的 ICT 和 AI 人才培养合作，与沙特数据与人工智能管理局（SDAIA）签署谅解备忘录，推出系列培训项目，并推动人工智能知识普及，为沙特数字经济的长期发展提供人才支撑。[②] 为进一步促进区域 ICT 人才成长，华为连续多年举办"中东 ICT 竞赛"，推动本地人才培养和 ICT 产业链建设。[③]

与此同时，中阿青年在数字经济和科技创新领域的交流也日益活跃。世界青年发展论坛[④]、中阿青年发展论坛[⑤]等活动为双方在数字人才培养和科技创新合作方面提供了重要平台。2024 年 11 月，中阿青年发展论坛在海南海口举办，该论坛以"数字赋能与创新发展"为主题，推动了中阿青年在数字经济领域的进一步互动交流。[⑥]

## 7.3 中阿数字经济合作展望

中阿携手推进数字经济合作，不仅将促进双方经济的可持续发展，还将推动全球数字经济的开放、包容与共赢，为构建人类命运共同体的数字化未来贡献中阿智慧与实践。

第一，深化政策对接与合作机制建设是推进数字经济合作的基础。中

---

[①] "Saudi Digital Academy signs deal with Huawei to develop local talents"，http://www.china.org.cn/business/2022-02/04/content_78027315.htm，2022-2-4。

[②] 《沙特与华为携手推进 ICT 与 AI 人才培养》，阿中产业研究院网站，https://www.aciep.net/blog/archives/3471，2024 年 9 月 20 日。

[③] 《中东 ICT 人才培养与教育峰会暨华为 2018 中东 ICT 大赛决赛圆满落幕》，华为官网，https://www.huawei.com/cn/news/2018/11/huawei-middle-east-ict-talent-competition-2018，2018 年 11 月 28 日。

[④] 《2023 年世界青年发展论坛 青年数字发展主题论坛在北京举办》，中国青年网，https://news.youth.cn/gj/202311/t20231101_14881126.htm，2023 年 11 月 1 日。

[⑤] 《赋能青年发展 共创美好未来——中阿青年发展论坛扫描》，新华网，https://www.xinhuanet.com/2023-12/07/c_1130013186.htm，2023 年 12 月 7 日。

[⑥] 《2024 中阿青年发展论坛聚焦数字赋能与创新发展》，新华网，https://www.news.cn/world/20241111/54f938d0140d47cfa7148a372ccb264d/c.html，2024 年 11 月 11 日。

阿在数字经济领域的合作机制不断完善，涵盖政策倡议、机制化建设及多层次合作框架，尤其是在数据治理、数字贸易和技术标准等领域，双方已建立起稳定的沟通机制。中阿峰会在推动数字经济战略对接和促成多个合作项目落地方面发挥了积极作用。未来，双方应进一步提升政策协调的制度化水平，优化现有合作机制，可依托中阿合作论坛，推动《数字经济合作行动计划》的制订，深化数字经济治理和贸易规则的对接与合作。此外，双方将积极探索成立中阿数字经济联合委员会，推动跨境数据流动、隐私保护、数字金融等关键领域的标准互认，进一步加强数字经济治理议题在全球多边框架下的协调合作。

第二，加强数字基础设施合作，夯实数字经济发展基石。数字基础设施是数字经济高质量发展的关键支柱。尽管阿拉伯国家在5G、云计算和人工智能等领域加大了投入，但区域内部发展不均衡，部分国家的数字化建设仍显滞后。未来，中阿双方可在多个领域深化合作，共同推动区域数字经济体系的完善。在5G和云计算领域，中国企业已在沙特、阿联酋等国推进基站和云计算中心建设，推动智能城市与工业互联网发展。双方可进一步扩展5G网络的覆盖范围，特别是在埃及、摩洛哥、约旦等新兴市场，提升区域数字基础设施的普及率。在人工智能、大数据和智慧城市等领域，双方可联合建立研究中心和实验室，推动新兴技术的应用，助力阿拉伯国家产业智能化升级，特别是在沙特未来城（NEOM新城）和阿联酋智慧迪拜等标志性项目中深化合作。

第三，推动跨境电商合作向高质量发展迈进，提升贸易数字化水平。跨境电商是中阿数字经济合作的重要领域，但未来仍需优化市场结构，提升物流与支付体系，并增强本地化运营能力。中阿应通过自贸区、海外仓等资源提高商品流通效率，探索建立中阿电子商务自由贸易区，降低物流和关税成本，提升贸易便利化水平。随着阿拉伯国家对数字支付需求的持续增长，跨境支付渠道仍较为有限。2023年，数字支付系统如"义乌付"已在阿联酋落地，未来双方可推动数字人民币与"数字迪拉姆"的跨境支付对接，提升数字金融合作的便利性，优化支付结算体系。此外，随着社交电商和直播带货模式在阿拉伯地区的快速崛起，双方可借此契机深化短视频电商和社交直播合作，推动跨境电商向智能化、个性化方向发展，拓展数字贸易新模式。

第四，加强数字人才培养，构建科技交流长效机制。数字人才培养是中阿数字经济合作的基础保障，也是推动区域数字化转型的重要支撑。中阿可在高校联合办学、跨境电商人才培养、企业与高校合作等方面深化合作，打造更加完善的数字人才培养体系。双方可以鼓励高校共建"数字经济学院"，围绕人工智能、区块链、大数据等前沿技术领域，联合培养复合型数字经济人才。针对中东跨境电商市场的快速增长，双方可设立跨境电商实训基地，培养能够适应市场趋势、精通物流与支付体系的本土化人才。此外，双方还可以推动中国企业在阿拉伯国家设立数字技术实验室，共同开展创新研发，提升当地高端技术人才储备，推动科技与产业的深度融合，促进数字经济合作的高质量发展。

第五，加强数字治理合作，推动全球数字经济治理框架升级。随着数字经济的迅猛发展，数据安全、数字主权和人工智能伦理等问题已成为全球关注的焦点。中阿应携手推动全球数字治理规则的制定，增强发展中国家在国际数字经济体系中的话语权。双方可在数据安全、跨境数据流动、隐私保护和人工智能伦理等方面深化合作，共同构建更加开放、安全、互信的数字治理体系。2021年，中阿共同发布的《中阿数据安全合作倡议》成为发展中国家数据安全合作的典范，未来应进一步推动相关议题的标准化建设。在金融科技领域，双方还可探索区块链跨境结算等合作机会，共同推动数字金融体系的创新与变革，为全球数字经济治理提供"中阿方案"。

# 第8章 中阿科技合作专题报告

自"一带一路"倡议提出以来,在理念相通、政策融通、平台联通的有利条件下,中阿科技合作提质升级,已发展成为中阿双边合作的重要支柱。目前,中阿科技合作的发展势头总体向好,整体呈现互补、务实、全面的特征。未来,在构建中阿"五大合作格局"的机遇背景下,科技合作既是中阿合作的"新"方向和"新"重点,也将是中阿双边的"新"挑战与"新"突破。

## 8.1 中阿科技合作的战略基础

自"一带一路"倡议提出以来,中阿交往不断深入。目前,中阿关系进入了历史最好时期。[①] 在共同追求高质量发展的背景下,科技合作成为中阿共建"一带一路"的重要支撑。以共建"一带一路"为契机,中阿科技合作不断走深走实,形成了全方位、多层次、多领域的科技合作体系,有效回应了"一带一路"倡议的"五通"目标指数。目前来看,"一带一路"倡议从战略层面为中阿双方搭建了交流平台与合作载体,切实助推和巩固中阿科技合作。"数字丝绸之路"已成为中阿互联互通的重要支撑。随着科技赋能效应的不断凸显,科技合作将成为中阿共建"一带一路"的潜力场域及新型增长点。

---

① 《命运与共 携手同行——首届中阿峰会两周年回望》,中华人民共和国中央人民政府网站,https://www.gov.cn/yaowen/liebiao/202412/content_6994024.htm,2024年12月22日。

### 8.1.1 理念支撑

中阿"共商、共享、共建"的理念基础不断夯实。"一带一路"倡议作为联结中阿合作的战略机制，有力助推中阿理念互通，夯实了双边科技合作的认同基础。2013年，习近平主席提出共建"一带一路"倡议，得到了阿拉伯国家的积极响应和广泛支持。2016年，习近平主席在访问阿盟总部期间，正式提出中阿合作共建"一带一路"倡议。双方共同认为，共建"一带一路"是中阿深化合作、互利共赢、实现共同发展的良好契机。2018年，中国同阿盟签署《中国和阿拉伯国家合作共建"一带一路"行动宣言》，开创了地区组织签署此类文件的先河。截至目前，中国已与22个阿拉伯国家及阿盟签署共建"一带一路"合作文件，在众多领域实施200多个大型合作项目，合作成果惠及双方近20亿人民。[①] 在中阿共同把握数字化发展机遇，全面推动技术创新、数字基础设施建设、绿色能源开发应用、数字通信建设等多领域合作过程中，中阿科技合作已经成为阿拉伯国家实现经济发展、产业转型、技术升级的优先选项。通过共建"一带一路"，中阿双方已在发展理念和指导思想层面，实现了发展战略的"软对接"。

中阿"追求科技自主"的理念共识越发契合。目前，"实现科技自主、推动科技多极化"已成为中阿科技创新的共同目标。双方一致认可，科技自主是实现经济可持续发展、应对全球性挑战、摆脱外部依赖的根本途径。进入新时代，中国坚持推动高水平科技自立自强战略，成功走出了一条从人才强、科技强，到产业强、经济强、国家强的中国特色自主创新道路。[②] 与此同时，埃及、沙特、阿联酋、科威特等阿拉伯国家也纷纷将"科技兴国"融入国家整体战略规划。区域层面，阿盟也围绕科技创新为

---

[①] 《新时代的中阿合作报告》，中华人民共和国外交部网站，https://www.mfa.gov.cn/web/ziliao_674904/zcwj_674915/202212/t20221201_10983991.shtml，2022年12月1日。

[②] 《中国式现代化关键在科技现代化》，人民网，http://politics.people.com.cn/n1/2024/0623/c1001-40262087.html，2024年6月23日。

地区提供行动指南。在全球孤立主义抬头、科技门罗主义上升的背景下，通过构架中阿科技命运共同体，以实现国家的自主自强和全球多极化的科技格局，是中阿共同的发展夙愿。在共建"一带一路"过程中，中阿双方围绕科研开发、科技交流、技术转移等形式，实现了平等互利的"科技共赢"。从《国际科技合作倡议》到《全球人工智能治理倡议》，阿方一直是赞赏中方理念、回应中方呼吁、践行中方主张的坚定支持者。[①] 在"一带一路"倡议的支撑下、在"科技兴国"的战略主张下、在"科技共赢"的合作理念下，中阿双方以科技合作为重要载体，逐步迈向中阿科技共同体。

### 8.1.2 政策支撑

在"一带一路"倡议的助推下，中阿经贸合作有序开展，中国已连续多年稳居阿拉伯国家第一大贸易伙伴国地位。2004—2023年，中阿贸易额从367亿美元攀升至超3980亿美元，年均增长13%，实现了中阿经贸关系的跨越式发展。[②] 同时，中阿科技领域的投资占比稳步提升，中阿科技合作的重要性不断凸显。

"一带一路"倡议有力推动了中国与共建国家围绕科技人文交流、科技成果落地、科技创新转移等领域开展广泛合作。在此背景下，中阿科技合作实现了机制化发展。2014年6月，习近平主席在中阿合作论坛第六届部长级会议上指出，中阿共建"一带一路"，构建以能源合作为主轴，以基础设施建设、贸易和投资便利化为两翼，以核能、航天卫星、新能源三大高新领域为突破口的"1+2+3"合作格局。[③] 科技合作首次成为中阿合作的主要支撑。2016年1月，中国首次发布的《中国对阿拉伯国家政策

---

[①] 孙德刚：《以科技共同体助推中阿命运共同体建设跑出加速度》，《当代世界》2024年第10期，第59页。

[②] 《中阿合作行稳致远惠及各方》，《光明日报》，https://news.gmw.cn/2024-05/31/content_37354903.htm，2024年5月31日。

[③] 《习近平：做好顶层设计，构建"1+2+3"中阿合作格局》，新华网，https://jhsjk.people.cn/article/25109122，2014年6月5日。

文件》指出，务实推动双边在可再生能源、航天、民用核领域合作，以及加快政府间科技创新合作机制建设。① 2018年7月，中阿共同签署《中国和阿拉伯国家合作共建"一带一路"行动宣言》，其中明确指出，双方重点开展"空中丝绸之路""网上丝绸之路"和建设"一带一路"空间信息走廊合作。通过在数字经济、信息技术、卫星通信等领域的互惠合作，推进构建中阿科技伙伴关系。② 2023年12月，中国国家主席习近平在首届中国—阿拉伯国家峰会上提出中阿务实合作"八大共同行动"，其中重点涵盖了科技创新、技术交流与联合开发等科技合作内容。③ 在此基础上，2024年中阿合作论坛第十届部长级会议首次提出，加快构建中阿命运共同体，构建中阿"五大合作格局"。④ 至此，从重要组成到主要支撑，再到核心引领，中阿科技合作已进阶成为中阿共建"一带一路"、构建中阿命运共同体的主力军。中阿合作"向新而行"也将成为中阿关系未来发展的主旋律。

### 8.1.3 平台支撑

"一带一路"倡议提出后，中阿科技合作的平台不断扩充。除中阿合作论坛外，中国—阿拉伯国家博览会、中阿技术转移中心等，也有力支撑了双边科技合作走深走实。

自成立以来，中阿博览会始终高度重视中阿科技创新领域的展示与交流，实践形成了"政府搭台、企业唱戏"的中阿科技合作模式。围绕农业科技、核电技术、人工智能等主题，六届中阿博览会先后举办了中阿技术转

---

① 《中国对阿拉伯国家政策文件（全文）》，中华人民共和国中央人民政府网站，https：//www.gov.cn/xinwen/2016-01/13/content_5032647.htm，2016年1月13日。
② 《中国和阿拉伯国家合作共建"一带一路"行动宣言》，中阿合作论坛网站，https：//www.chinaarabcf.org/chn/lthyjwx/bzjhywj/dbjbzjhy/201807/t20180713_6836934.htm，2018年7月10日。
③ 《习近平在首届中国—阿拉伯国家峰会上提出中阿务实合作"八大共同行动"》，中华人民共和国中央人民政府网站，https：//www.gov.cn/xinwen/2022-12/10/content_5731138.htm，2022年12月10日。
④ 《习近平：中方愿同阿方构建"五大合作格局"》，中华人民共和国中央人民政府网站，https：//www.gov.cn/yaowen/liebiao/202405/content_6954500.htm，2024年5月30日。

移暨创新合作大会、高新技术及装备展暨技术成果推介对接会等科创交流活动,有效助力中阿深化科技合作。此外,围绕云计算、大数据、数字治理、"互联网+"、5G应用等数字经济领域,中阿博览会专设了"网上丝绸之路大会"等系列活动,实质推动中阿数字技术合作的纵深发展,实现了数字赋能中阿科技合作。以中阿共建"一带一路"为时代契机、以中阿博览会为平台依托,中阿科技合作逐渐形成了互动密切、交流深入、实效显著的积极趋势。

此外,中阿技术转移中心也为中阿科技合作搭建了重要平台。2015年,中华人民共和国科技部、宁夏回族自治区人民政府共同创立中国—阿拉伯国家技术转移中心。多年来,该中心主要围绕拓展中阿技术转移协作网络、搭建中阿技术转移信息服务系统、培养国际技术转移人才、联通"一带一路"共建国家学术信息平台等业务范畴,通过助推中阿科技交流促进双边科技合作。截至目前,中心已开设国际人才培训班30余期,培养1400余名具有"种子"效应的国际技术转移人才,成功共建8个双边国家技术转移中心,搭建了链接近5000家中外成员的技术转移协作网络,有效促进了中阿科技合作的技术交流、成果转换和项目落地。[①]

## 8.2 中阿科技合作的实践进展

2024年,中阿科技合作保持了平稳发展势头。针对阿拉伯国家的技术发展诉求,中阿在数字信息、农业科技、能源技术、医疗卫生、高新基础设施及人才技术培养等领域开展了密切合作。

### 8.2.1 总体合作环境

2024年,海湾阿拉伯国家科创发展仍保持强劲势头。据美国高德纳(Gartner)公司预测(见表8.1),2024年中东地区的IT支出总额将达

---

① 《中心业务》,中阿技术转移中心网站,https://www.casttc.org/node/business.html,2024年5月18日。

1937亿美元，同比增长5.2%。有分析认为，IT软件和IT服务支出大幅增长表明，中东国家正在为云迁移、人工智能和物联网等高新技术开发做业务筹备。目前，海湾阿拉伯国家是中东地区科创投资的主力军，沙特、阿联酋、卡塔尔和巴林，都企图通过科技创新驱动经济转型。据普华永道预测，到2030年人工智能将通过产品创新和提高生产率，可为该地区生产总值提升320亿美元。① 为此，海湾阿拉伯国家充分发挥经济优势，抢占世界科技领域的领导者地位。

表8.1　2023—2024年中东地区IT支出统计

| 项目 | 2023年支出（百万美元） | 2023年增长（%） | 2024年支出（百万美元） | 2024年增长（%） |
| --- | --- | --- | --- | --- |
| 数据中心系统 | 4826 | 5.5 | 4809 | -0.3 |
| 设备 | 28379 | -1.8 | 27092 | -4.5 |
| 软件 | 13555 | 8.0 | 15229 | 12.3 |
| IT服务 | 17338 | 4.6 | 19016 | 9.6 |
| 通信服务 | 120026 | 9.0 | 127584 | 6.3 |
| 整体信息技术 | 184124 | 6.6 | 193730 | 5.0 |

资料来源：根据Cartner数据统计整理。

近五年来，海湾阿拉伯国家在人工智能领域加大投资。据沙特数据和人工智能管理局（SDAIA）最新报告：2019年以来，沙特政府在该领域支出的复合年增长率高达59%。2024年9月，沙特支持数字合作组织（DCO）建立全球首个生成式人工智能卓越中心（CoE），并投资一项价值1000亿美元的人工智能"超越计划"（Project Transcendence），力争将沙特打造为世界级科技中心。② 除项目投资外，阿联酋在国家创新体系培育

---

① Vivek Adatia, "Emerging Tech Trends in the Middle East: Opportunities for Businesses in 2024", https://www.wdcstechnology.ae/emerging-tech-trends-in-the-middle-east-opportunities-for-businesses-in-2024, 2024-07-04.

② Telcom Review, "Project Transcendence: Saudi Arabia's Upcoming Multi-Billion Investment", https://www.telecomreview.com/articles/reports-and-coverage/8565-project-transcendence-saudi-arabia-s-upcoming-multi-billion-investment, 2024-11-08.

方面也表现抢眼。阿联酋通过实施一揽子政策，计划通过政府机构、基金、教育计划、平台建设等激励措施，扶持中小型科创企业，以推进国家整体创新体系构建。计划至2030年，阿联酋将中小科创企业数量从2022年的55.8万家增加至100万家。据《阿拉伯国家可持续发展报告2024》数据，阿联酋的"创业政策与文化""营商政策""风险投资"指标分别位居全球第1位、全球第5位及全球第18位，呈现出积极的科技创新活力。[①] 根据《2024年全球创新指数》统计（见图8.1），沙特、卡塔尔两国与巴西、毛里求斯、印度尼西亚共同成为近五年全球创新指数排名涨幅最快的国家。

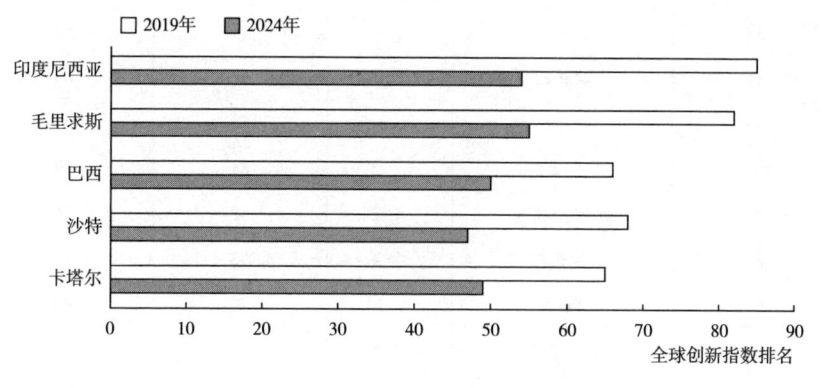

**图8.1 近五年全球创新指数排名涨幅最快国家**

资料来源：根据世界知识产权组织（WIPO）《2024年全球创新指数》数据汇总整理。

在阿拉伯国家共同科技进步的背景下，多数阿拉伯国家科技创新水平呈稳步递增的趋势，但地区整体水平仍存在较大提升空间。虽然，近年来海湾阿拉伯国家科创发展表现抢眼，但地区内部一些发展滞后、稳定失序的国家，科技发展仍明显落后于地区领先国家和全球发展进程。以能源转型为例，据阿拉伯投资担保公司（Dhaman）统计，2023年阿拉伯国家能源转型平均排名位居第82位，在120个被统计国家中处于中后位次。如表8.2所

---

① ESCWA, Arab Sustainable Development Report 2024, 2024, p. 144.

155

示,卡塔尔(第53位)、约旦(第56位)、摩洛哥(第64位)、沙特(第60位)位居中列,处地区领先地位。但以巴林(第103位)、科威特(第107位)、黎巴嫩(第115位)、也门(第120位)为代表的阿拉伯国家仍存在极大的能源转型需求。[①] 作为阿拉伯国家发展转型的核心事项,能源转型既是推动阿拉伯国家科技创新的原动力,也是具体展现阿拉伯国家科技创新发展的立体指标。这充分体现了阿拉伯国家科技创新需求及必要性仍然较大。

表8.2 2022—2023年阿拉伯国家全球能源转型指数排名

| 阿拉伯排名 | 国家 | 变化 | 全球排名2023 | 全球排名2022 |
| --- | --- | --- | --- | --- |
| 1 | 摩洛哥 | ↑8 | 64 | 56 |
| 2 | 沙特 | ↑3 | 60 | 57 |
| 3 | 卡塔尔 | ↓6 | 53 | 59 |
| 4 | 阿联酋 | ↓13 | 50 | 63 |
| 5 | 约旦 | ↓15 | 56 | 71 |
| 6 | 埃及 | ↑2 | 81 | 79 |
| 7 | 阿尔及利亚 | ↑2 | 88 | 86 |
| 8 | 突尼斯 | ↑4 | 93 | 89 |
| 9 | 阿曼 | ↓14 | 76 | 90 |
| 10 | 科威特 | ↑5 | 107 | 102 |
| 11 | 巴林 | ↓7 | 103 | 110 |
| 12 | 黎巴嫩 | ↑3 | 115 | 112 |
| 13 | 也门 | — | 120 | 120 |
| 阿拉伯国家平均排名 |  | ↓2 | 82 | 84 |
| 国家总数 |  |  | 120 | 120 |

资料来源:根据全球经济论坛(WEF)《2024促进有效能源转型报告》(*Fostering Effective Energy Transition 2024 Report*)数据整理。

另外,海湾阿拉伯国家人力资源开发仍有上升空间。联合国开发计划署发布的《人类发展报告2023/2024》指出,地区发展不均衡是阻碍全球

---

① Dhaman, The Investment Climate in Arab Countries 2024, 2024, p. 28.

合作、加深世界分化的主要因素。① 阿拉伯国家普遍存在人才缺口，自身在技术开发、科技革新领域的能力仍然有限。如表 8.3 所示，阿拉伯国家技术人才资源总体落后，地区平均全球排名（第 70 位），位于 133 个统计国家排名的后位次。另外，阿拉伯国家的人才培育能力也相对较弱。虽然以阿联酋（第 1 位）、科威特（第 3 位）为代表的个别国家在职业技术教育领域处于世界领先水平，但阿拉伯国家整体高等教育水平（第 86 位）、职业技术教育水平（第 59 位）缺乏比较优势。特别是，阿拉伯国家高等教育水平与世界平均水平差距较大，卡塔尔作为地区领先国家仅排名全球第 28 位。在列入统计的 12 个阿拉伯国家中，有 10 个国家排名在 70 位及以后。这将直接影响到阿拉伯国家科技自主创新能力。

表 8.3　2023 年阿拉伯国家全球知识指数及其子指标全球排名

| 国家 | 政策支撑 | 经济水平 | 信息通信技术 | 研发与创新 | 高等教育 | 职业技术教育 | 全球排名 | 年度变化 |
| --- | --- | --- | --- | --- | --- | --- | --- | --- |
| 阿联酋 | 45 | 13 | 14 | 28 | 47 | 1 | 26 | ↓ 1 |
| 卡塔尔 | 44 | 25 | 58 | 47 | 28 | 62 | 39 | ↑ 2 |
| 沙特 | 73 | 39 | 19 | 28 | 70 | 40 | 40 | ↑ 3 |
| 科威特 | 71 | 25 | 26 | 88 | 70 | 3 | 44 | ↑ 3 |
| 巴林 | 75 | 40 | 33 | 101 | 102 | 21 | 56 | ↓ 1 |
| 阿曼 | 90 | 54 | 48 | 92 | 86 | 50 | 66 | ↓ 12 |
| 突尼斯 | 86 | 86 | 81 | 72 | 87 | 76 | 81 | ↑ 1 |
| 巴勒斯坦 | 101 | 97 | 100 | 58 | 100 | 87 | 89 | ↑ 4 |
| 埃及 | 114 | 85 | 85 | 89 | 94 | 46 | 90 | ↑ 5 |
| 摩洛哥 | 83 | 87 | 72 | 72 | 114 | 79 | 92 | ↓ 7 |
| 约旦 | 82 | 69 | 92 | 82 | 105 | 109 | 97 | ↓ 1 |
| 毛里塔尼亚 | 126 | 119 | 116 | 102 | 132 | 129 | 125 | ↑ 2 |
| 地区平均排名 | 83 | 62 | 62 | 72 | 86 | 59 | 70 | 0 |

资料来源：根据《阿拉伯可持续发展报告2024》（Arab Sustainable Development Report 2024）数据整理。

---

① UNDP，《人类发展报告2023/2024》（Human Development Report 2023/2024），2024，p.7.

总体来看，阿拉伯国家长期存在发展转型需要与科技创新需求，这为中阿科技合作奠定了坚实的市场基础。从现实条件看，阿拉伯国家在科技水平、人才储备等发展条件方面还存在较大缺口，这也为中阿持续深化科技合作、务实开展技术转移提供了持久动力。

### 8.2.2 具体合作实践

2024年，中阿科技合作有序推进。双方在数字经济与通信技术、农业科技与粮食安全、新能源与清洁能源、高新技术基础设施、医疗健康与卫生合作、专业技术与人才培养等领域展开了广泛合作。

一是中企出海赋活中阿数字通信合作。华为云、商汤科技等大批中企，依靠稳定的网络环境、可靠的数据保护和完善的线下服务，成功进军阿拉伯市场。通过大数据、人工智能、云计算技术供应和创新经验分享，助力阿拉伯国家迈向更智能发展阶段。2024年，华为云海外增速超50%，有效推动了中阿在运营商、政府、金融、媒体娱乐等领域数智升级合作。目前，华为云在中东地区有超过6000家全球合作伙伴，超过300家当地合作伙伴。2024年5月，华为云在埃及正式开服，成为全球首家在埃及建立公有云的公司，这同时也是北非地区首个公有云节点。[①] 作为非洲大陆数字化的新枢纽，埃及节点不仅进一步增强了华为云在北非和阿拉伯地区的数字使能策略，还突破性地推动了当地行业的数字化进程。2024年5月，联想集团与沙特公共投资基金（PIF）旗下的阿拉特集团（Alat）签署战略合作协议，内容包括：阿拉特集团向联想集团提供20亿美元无息可换股债券投资；联想集团在利雅得设立中东和非洲市场地区总部，并新建计算机与服务器制造基地。[②] 在技术交流合作外，中企通过"文化+技术"的合作形式，深入阿拉伯市场。2024年春节期间，商汤科技在阿联

---

[①] 《华为云埃及正式开服，成为北部非洲第一朵公有云》，华为云网站，https://www.huaweicloud.com/intl/zh-cn/news/20240522173651457.html，2024年5月22日。

[②] 《联想将在沙特设立中东非洲地区总部》，人民网，http://world.people.com.cn/n1/2024/0529/c1002-40246085.html，2024年5月29日。

酋亚斯岛（Yas Island）举行了一系列中国春节庆祝活动，利用 AIGC 技术赋能阿拉伯国家智能文旅项目。目前，该公司已推动包括阿联酋亚斯岛、沙特利雅得季、吉达季等多个智慧文旅项目落地阿拉伯国家，有效利用科技合作推动民心相通。①

二是农业科技合作推动中阿打破资源束缚、提升农业生产、共同回应粮食安全挑战。近年来，中阿双方在土壤治理、旱作农业、畜牧兽医、种业科技等技术层面开展了深度合作。2022 年，习近平主席在中阿峰会期间提出中阿务实合作"八大共同行动"，其中在"粮食安全共同行动"中承诺同阿方共建 5 个现代农业联合实验室，开展 50 个农业技术合作示范项目，向阿方派遣 500 名农业技术专家。② 作为回应，在中阿博览会推动下，2024 年 8 月，宁夏沃之源科技有限公司与沙特海湾龙贸易控股公司签订合作协议，包括风光互补智能控制、复合渗灌产品加工、土壤快速改良、特种光伏农业装备建造等数十项，多项具有自主知识产权的技术装备将落地沙特，助力沙特农业技术革新和土壤环境改良。③ 2024 年 11 月，山东寿光蔬菜产业集团与阿布扎比农业食品技术公司 Silal 签署战略协议，双方合作包括启动育种开发计划和温室示范园建设。利用中企在种苗培育、嫁接栽培、反季种植等领域的技术优势，疏通阿联酋种苗链条堵点、提升农业产业的丰富性与可及性。同月，中国与埃及共同计划在埃及河谷省开发投资高达 70 亿美元的农业综合体，通过采用高效节水技术，推动包括玉米、大豆、小麦等战略作物的可持续化种植。此外，该项目还将通过中埃共同研发温室、苗圃技术，提升高价值的药用植物及芳香植物的育种种植。除项目合作外，中阿农业技术交流也日

---

① 《中国"年味儿"远飘海外，商汤 AIGC 助力阿布扎比新年庆典活动》，商汤科技网站，https://www.sensetime.com/cn/news-detail/51167501?categoryId=72，2024 年 2 月 22 日。
② 《中阿粮食安全共同行动为世界树立典范》，中国日报，https://cn.chinadaily.com.cn/a/202212/20/WS63a192d3a3102ada8b2278db.htm，2022 年 12 月 30 日。
③ 《抢抓"一带一路"机遇 共建"一园一屋"项目——宁夏技术出海逐浪沙特》，宁夏新闻网，https://www.nxnews.net/zt/24n/esjszqh/mdxdhgg/202408/t20240809_9623460.html，2024 年 8 月 9 日。

益紧密。① 例如在2024年，中国水稻研究所、山东农科院湿地农业与生态所分别与埃及水稻研究所、埃及农业研究中心，围绕水稻种植、耐盐、育种等技术开展了交流互鉴。面对共性需求和挑战，科技合作已成为中阿农业合作的重点项目，确保粮食安全、实现种业自主、保障农业可持续发展，将为中阿农业科技合作提供不竭动力。

　　三是可再生能源合作跃然成为中阿科技合作的新增量。中国作为全球清洁能源供应链的主导者，占据了能源技术合作的市场优势。由于高度契合阿拉伯国家能源转型的现实需求，新能源汽车、光伏产品、锂电池等"新三样"在中阿科技合作中的占比显著增加。2024年6月，中国协鑫科技宣布与阿联酋主权财富基金穆巴达拉投资公司（Mubadala）旗下企业合作，在阿联酋建设多晶硅生产基地，助力中阿光伏领域合作。在氢能领域，以阿曼、沙特为代表的阿拉伯国家，致力成为氢能开发领域的全球领导者。目前，沙特已制定"国家氢能战略（2020）"、阿曼也提出"要在2030年，成为中东最大及世界第六大氢能出口国"。② 对此，中国电力建设集团、双良节能集团和阳光氢能集团等众多中国企业，纷纷同约旦签订绿氢合作项目；远景能源集团、仁洁智能集团和海德氢能集团等企业也深度参与沙特未来城（NEOM新城）氢能开发项目，以把握阿拉伯国家氢能开发的市场机遇。在新能源应用方面，新能源汽车成为2024年中阿科技合作的新亮点。据中国海关总署数据，截至2024年上半年，中国对中东出口乘用车数量高达42万辆，同比增长46.2%。中东地区一跃成为中国汽车最大的出口市场。其中，新能源汽车占比19.6%，成为2024年中阿科技合作进展最为显著的模块。2024年，比亚迪成功进军沙特市场，并完成在阿联酋市场的第

---

① Emirates News Agency, "Silal Partners with China's Shouguang to Boost UAE Agriculture and Food Security", https://www.freshplaza.com/north-america/article/9682503/silal-partners-with-china-s-shouguang-to-boost-uae-agriculture-and-food-security/, 2024-11-27.
② Hydrogen Council, "The Middle East Has the Chance to Lead on Hydrogen", https://hydrogen-council.com/en/the-middle-east-has-the-chance-to-lead-on-hydrogen/, 2024-10-24.

1000次交付；小鹏、长安、埃安成功进入埃及、沙特和卡塔尔市场。同年10月，蔚来与阿联酋政府旗下的CYVN战略投资公司（CYVN Holdings）签署协议，宣布在阿布扎比建立研发中心并开展针对本土市场的中阿联合开发。①

四是高新技术基础设施建设，推动中阿"数字丝绸之路"互联互通。在"一带一路"倡议的基础上，中国推出"数字丝绸之路"整体发展方案，着重强调同共建国家共同建设包括光缆、5G网络、数据中心、智慧城市、云计算和人工智能应用在内的数字基础设施合作。近年来，阿拉伯国家也高度重视高新基础设施建设在可持续创新发展中的基础作用，有效推进了中阿共建"数字丝绸之路"。据麦肯锡公司（McKinsey Company）研究推测，云服务开发是中东市场的潜在领域，预计到2030年，云服务将为中东国家创造高达1830亿美元的市场价值，相当于目前地区生产总值的6%。② 面对市场机遇，阿里巴巴、腾讯、华为等中企，凭借价廉物优的市场优势成功进入阿拉伯市场。2024年3月，阿里巴巴同沙特人力资源部、沙特电信公司（STC）签署数字化转型合作协议，共同探索人工智能、数字信息及网络安全等方面的能力建设。同年4月，华为公司在迪拜建设了阿联酋首个5G智能仓库。该项目通过利用5G技术、云计算、大数据和人工智能技术的深度融合，成功为传统仓储物流行业融入智能元素，树立了行业智能新标杆。此外，在2024年巴塞罗那世界移动大会期间，华为同沙特电信公司签署了深化推进5.5G战略合作协议，通过开发SuperLink多频段无线传输通信技术，为沙特偏远地区提供了高效的5G连接。SuperLink技术将有效减少67%的天线需求，通过降低部署复杂性克服沙特地理条件对5G信

---

① 《中国车企涌入中东》，人民网，http://paper.people.com.cn/zgjjzk/pc/content/202411/15/content_30046097.html，2024年11月15日。

② McKinsey Digital, "The Middle East Public Cloud: A Multibillion-dollar Prize Waiting to Be Captured", https://www.mckinsey.com/capabilities/mckinsey-digital/our-insights/the-middle-east-public-cloud-a-multibillion-dollar-prize-waiting-to-be-captured, 2024-01-30.

号传播的限制。这不仅在市场应用层面直接推动了沙特网络业务的用户增长，而且间接扩展了沙特在医疗、教育和电子商务等领域的数字化应用，为沙特数字化转型提供了可持续发展方案。

五是医疗卫生技术合作，不断深化中阿"科技为民"的发展共识。2024年5月，习近平主席指出，中方愿同阿方构建"五大合作格局"。其中，在创新驱动格局中"生命健康"被排在首位，成为中阿科技合作的新重点。此前，为应对阿拉伯国家医疗技术、人才的短缺问题，中国长期对阿开展医疗援助和医疗技术培训。通过开展医护培训班、讲座等方式，对摩洛哥、吉布提、阿尔及利亚、突尼斯等受援国开展技术支持。中阿医疗合作模式，已逐步从"输血式"向"造血式"转型，为中阿共同推动人类卫生健康共同体提供不竭动力。[①] 在新时期，中阿医疗卫生科技合作成果丰硕。2024年5月，国药集团研制的四价流感疫苗中标阿联酋采购订单，成功进入阿拉伯市场。同年11月，上海复宏汉霖生物技术公司与沙特医疗企业SVAX达成战略合作，以合资形式在中东市场开展创新生物药研发与生产。[②] 此外，中国沃森生物也在2024年12月宣布，与埃及两家本土医药企业Vacsera和VBC开展疫苗研发和在地生产，致力带动埃及疫苗产业的技术自主。在智能化医疗领域，2024年3月，上海健麾信息公司与沙特阿吉兰兄弟控股集团合作，在沙特Dallah医院试点建立医药物流自动化应用方案。通过向沙特提供智能化医疗技术支持，相关中企已凭借技术优势加速推动阿拉伯国家医疗数字化转型。在科技制药领域，中国多家知名药企纷纷进军阿拉伯市场，旨在依靠科技创新合作，拓展海外市场。截至2024年，东北制药、科兴制药、汇宇制药、康希诺生物、康泰生物等企业，已成功同沙特、阿曼、埃及等阿拉伯国家本土企业开展研发与生产合作。

---

[①] 徐丽莉、张可心、宋欣阳：《中国与非洲阿拉伯国家的卫生发展合作研究》，《阿拉伯世界研究》2024年第2期，第36页。

[②] 《复宏汉霖战略携手SVAX，开启全球布局新篇章》，Henlius，https://www.henlius.com/NewsDetails-4743-26.html，2024年11月7日。

六是中阿技术转移合作，夯实中阿科技人才基础，为双边科技合作的可持续发展提供不竭动力。自"一带一路"倡议提出以来，中国高度重视对共建国家的技术援助及人才培养。截至2024年，中国已同81个共建国家签署了政府层面的科技合作协定、同50余个共建国家形成了知识产权合作关系，支持千余项中外科技人才联合培养项目。[①] 在此背景下，中阿技术转移有序推进并取得显著成果。目前，在中阿科技伙伴计划的带动和引领下，中阿技术转移会议联动机制不断完善。2024年9月，中阿技术转移中心同全球能源互联网发展合作组织西亚北非办公室，围绕技术转移、技术培训、协作网络共建等领域，达成合作共识。除坚持开展联合援外培训、培育创新平台外，双方还将建立"1+2+N"[②] 的多层次会议联动机制，通过中阿共同宣介，鼓励和吸纳更多国内创新主体参与中阿技术转移。2024年5月，中阿技术转移中心和河北省科学技术厅联合主办了"中国（河北）—沙特（吉达）国际科技合作会议"，中沙围绕沙漠种植、地质勘探、海洋经济等领域，共同签署《科技人才合作备忘录》。同月，中阿技术转移中心联合上海科学技术交流中心共同举办了"2024共建'一带一路'国家新能源技术线上培训班"，课程从阿拉伯国家实际的技术需求出发，邀请国内新能源领域专家授课，吸引了来自埃及、苏丹、摩洛哥、阿尔及利亚等国的50余名科技人员参加。除政府推动外，中企也为中阿科技转移添砖加瓦。华为与沙特数据与人工智能管理局旗下的国家人工智能中心合作，联合培训当地的人工智能工程师，以支持沙特向数据驱动型经济转型。阿里云在沙特本土启动"AI赋能计划"，通过与沙特电信学院（STC Academy）和图瓦伊克学院（Tuwaiq Academy）联合培养本土技术人才，以推动阿

---

① 《深入推进"一带一路"国际科技合作》，中国社会科学报网，https://www.cssn.cn/skgz/bwyc/202401/t20240126_5730932.shtml，2024年1月26日。

② "1+2+N"联动机制主要指："1"是定期举办双边工作推进会；"2"是依托中国—阿拉伯国家技术转移与创新合作大会和全球能源互联网大会，整合资源协同推进更深层次的中阿科技转移合作；"N"是利用阿拉伯国家举办的能源、科技领域的系列国际会议，全面做好有关技术转移、人才交流的推介、宣传工作。

拉伯国家的人才资源培育。据统计，自2023年4月起，阿里云通过提供300余门线上线下课程、250余类动手实验，培训赋能超过60000名科技人才。[1]总体来看，在政府和企业的共同推动下，中阿科技转移合作正朝着机制化、规模化的趋势有序发展。

## 8.3　中阿科技合作前景

在高质量共建"一带一路"、推进建设"五大合作格局"背景下，中阿科技合作已迎来战略机遇期，亟须可持续整体推进。当前来看，中阿技术合作机遇多于挑战，总体形势向好。面向未来，助力阿拉伯国家实现科技自主、进一步推动中阿科技成果转换是现实之需。

从机遇维度看，高度的需求互补、完善的机制保障，为中阿科技合作提供了有力的基础支持。除了带来从数字化到智能化的技术革新外，第四次工业革命也通过科技多极化为广大发展中国家提供了难得的发展机遇。对此，阿拉伯国家集中投入大量资本和政策支持以推动本国的科技发展。相对发展期待，阿拉伯国家在技术水平、人才支撑和基础硬件层面仍存在现实短板。一方面，阿拉伯国家科技创新能力总体薄弱，核心技术长期依赖进口。除个别海湾阿拉伯国家外，多数阿拉伯国家研发经费投入普遍低于GDP的1%，远低于全球平均水平，存在科技发展内生动力不足和区域发展不平衡的情况。另一方面，阿拉伯国家在创新人才培养和高新基础设施建设等配套条件上仍较薄弱，技术人才断层并阻碍了科技成果的应用转化。因此，阿拉伯国家仍面临更多现实挑战亟须外部支持。一直以来，中国对外科技合作秉持着共商共享的合作理念、包容开放的合作政策以及协同高效的合作模式，为众多科技后发国家提供科技支持和发展援助。因此，面对阿拉伯国家发展需求，预计中阿科

---

[1] Jon Truby, "Sino-Arab Free Trade Agreement, AI Diplomacy, and the Realisation of AI and Sustainability Goals in the Middle East", *Asian Journal of Law and Society*, 2025, p. 11.

技合作将持续保持旺盛的合作潜力。此外，完善的机制建设也为稳固中阿科技合作提供制度保障。从地区总体行动到国家自主发展，从科技的整体提升到技术单领域突破，众多阿拉伯国家已制订完备详细的科技发展计划。目前，在科技创新机制建设中，阿拉伯国家初步形成了以政策驱动为核心、国际合作为补充、平台建设为支撑的系统性模式，展现了良好的发展潜力，为中阿携手迈入知识型经济时代提供了合作动力。与此同时，中阿科技合作伴随中阿关系走深走实，中国也围绕数字经济、科技转移、数字安全等领域，为中阿科技合作制订了丰富详尽的行动计划。阿拉伯国家已逐渐成为中国对外科技合作的主要对象和潜力市场。总体来看，在条件互补、理念契合、机制完善的有利背景下，中阿科技合作前景广阔。

  从挑战层面看，在大国竞争的外部环境下，阿拉伯国家科技水平滞后的现状，或将对中阿科技合作设置一定障碍。目前，中阿科技合作效能仍需提升。从合作形式看，中阿科技合作呈现较明显的"非对称性"，以中方的技术援助、技术转移为主要模式，尚未充分发挥双边协同效应；从落地效果看，阿拉伯各国的科技水平发展不均衡，缺乏区域联动的基础条件，尚未形成"以点带面"的区域升级效能。[1] 因此，如何在现有合作体量下，充分发挥实践效能、提升成果效应，是中阿科技合作有待突破的核心挑战。此外，在中阿科技发展水平差异化的背景下，大国竞争或将深度干预中阿科技合作。中阿科技合作秉持共同繁荣的发展愿景，主张通过科技进步推动经济发展和政治治理，在科技多极化发展过程中逐渐挑战西方中心主义的科技地缘政治版图。[2] 随着中阿科技合作的加速发展，一些大国将科技合作泛安全化，通过间接施压和直接阻挠，干扰和破坏中阿科技合作。在零和博弈的舆论渲染和以"去风险"为由的"长臂管辖"下，众多阿拉伯国家将不得不面临

---

[1] 郝诗羽：《新时期中阿科技合作前瞻》，《中国投资》2025年第Z1期，第51页。
[2] 孙德刚：《以科技共同体助推中阿命运共同体跑出加速度》，《当代世界》2024年第10期，第58页。

"选边站"的长期挑战。①从美国逼迫阿联酋人工智能公司G42从中国撤资事件来看，阿拉伯国家战略自主和外部抗压能力相对有限，中阿科技合作将长期面临被政治化、武器化的外部干扰。在大国结构性竞争背景下，如何坚持理念互信、推进合作共赢、共同抵御外部挑战，是中阿双边亟须思考和应对的关切事项。

面向未来，中阿双边需坚持深化理念认同、突出互补优势、重视人才培养，形成中阿科技合作的可持续发展。着眼于中阿共同关切的和平与发展，坚持树立中阿命运共同体理念、倡导开放包容的多边主义、完善中阿科技的互惠合作，将是回应外部舆论阻挠、打破大国科技竞争范式的有效途径。

---

① 丁隆：《阻挠中阿科技合作不得人心》，环球时报网站，https://opinion.huanqiu.com/article/4Ge0txqlKdf，2024年2月19日。

# 第9章　中阿生态合作专题报告

中国与阿拉伯国家同属发展中国家，双方国土面积之和占世界陆地面积 1/6，人口之和占世界总人口近 1/4，经济总量占世界经济总量 1/8。中阿双方资源禀赋各异，发展水平不一，但双方合作潜力巨大。中国和阿拉伯国家之间的关系源远流长，和平合作、开放包容、互学互鉴、互利共赢始终是中阿历史交往的主旋律。

长期以来，中国致力于生物多样性保护和绿色发展，积极开展国际交流与合作，其中也包括开展与阿拉伯国家生态环境领域的交流。中国与阿拉伯国家在生态环境领域的合作是近些年乃至未来中阿经贸合作凸显的一个新领域，双方合作潜力巨大，合作领域广泛，合作意义深远。[①] 十年来，在共建"一带一路"过程中，中国始终注重将绿色发展理念贯穿其中，在努力实现自身绿色发展的同时，与阿拉伯国家围绕绿色发展开展了领域广泛、内容丰富、形式多样的交流与合作，推动共建绿色"一带一路"取得积极进展和显著成效。

## 9.1　阿拉伯地区生态环境现状与治理

阿拉伯国家主要分布在西亚和北非地区，地理范围从大西洋沿岸的摩洛哥到波斯湾沿岸的沙特。这些国家总面积约为 1313 万平方千米，其中

---

① 王林伶：《中国与阿拉伯国家生态环境领域合作研究——兼论防沙治沙合作与技术输出》，《宁夏党校学报》2013 年第 6 期，第 90 页。

非洲部分占72%，亚洲部分占28%。阿拉伯国家的气候以热带沙漠气候为主，常年受副热带高压和信风带的影响，大部分地区干燥少雨，生态环境极其脆弱。近年来，生态环境恶化带来的严重后果正在很多阿拉伯国家显现，环境恶化可能带来粮食产量下降、人口流离失所、资源争夺和社会冲突，甚至导致社会秩序的崩溃和战争。[①]

### 9.1.1 水资源短缺与治理举措

阿拉伯世界主要位于北回归线附近，受副热带高压和信风带的影响，形成了大面积的热带沙漠气候。这种气候特点导致降水稀少且分布不均衡，许多地区年降水量不足200毫米。阿拉伯地区大部分是沙漠，伸入陆地的红海和波斯湾面积小，对气候的调节作用微弱。这种地理特征进一步加剧了水资源的稀缺。近年来，随着人口的增长，对水资源的需求不断增加，水资源压力增大。同时，工业和农业的发展，城镇化的推进，都增加了对水资源的需求，使得本已紧张的水资源更加匮乏。此外，阿拉伯地区跨国水资源争端激烈，尼罗河、幼发拉底河、约旦河等跨境河流的分配矛盾长期存在，埃及与埃塞俄比亚因"复兴大坝"争议持续紧张，该坝威胁埃及90%的淡水供应；以色列通过军事控制约旦河西岸水源，占据该地区2/3的天然地下水池，加剧与阿拉伯国家的冲突。

近年来，阿拉伯国家的水资源治理取得了积极成效。2024年11月27日，第六届阿拉伯水事会议在约旦死海地区开幕，会议以"实现水资源可持续发展治理"为主题，旨在推动阿拉伯国家共同应对水资源相关挑战。约旦水利和灌溉大臣拉伊德·阿布·萨乌德在会议开幕式指出：受全球气候变暖、水资源枯竭、地区冲突及其带来的难民潮等影响，阿拉伯国家缺水问题日益严重。同时，他呼吁阿拉伯国家共同努力寻求解决方案，提高民众节约用水意识，发挥科研机构作用，实现粮食、水和环境安全一体

---

① 邹志强：《2030年可持续发展议程与阿拉伯国家转型》，《阿拉伯世界研究》2020年第3期，第121页。

化，并制定确保阿拉伯国家水安全的联合战略。为了应对严重的水资源短缺问题，阿拉伯国家普遍采取海水淡化技术。沙特是全球最大海水淡化国，反渗透技术占比达 90%，沙特立法强制节水，推广滴灌技术使农业用水效率提高 40%。阿尔及利亚政府投资 24 亿美元新建 5 座海水淡化厂，计划 2030 年前再建 6 座，淡化水占比将从 18% 提升至 42%。①

### 9.1.2 清洁能源与技术创新

阿拉伯地区长期以来一直处于全球能源世界的中心。阿拉伯投资和出口信贷担保公司发布最新报告显示，阿拉伯国家石油储量达 7040 亿桶，占全球石油储量比重为 41.3%。阿拉伯地区石油储量主要集中在沙特、伊拉克、阿联酋、科威特和利比亚 5 国，5 国石油储量合计 6500 亿桶，占阿拉伯国家石油储量的 92%。② 尽管在可预见的未来，该地区无疑将继续在传统石油和天然气领域占据主导地位，但一些关键国家及其石油公司正在战略性定位自己，成为新兴能源市场的关键枢纽和全球引领者。例如，沙特 2023 年非石油经济占比首次超过 50%，但其能源出口仍严重依赖石油，天然气发电计划在 2030 年覆盖全国电网的 50% 以上。

阿拉伯地区除了丰富的传统石油和天然气资源外，还具有独特的可再生能源潜力，特别是太阳能和风能，再加上其资金实力、人才和战略位置，使其在传统石油和燃气以及新能源市场处于领先地位。阿拉伯地区可再生能源资源丰富，具有发展以太阳能和风能为代表的可再生能源的良好条件，可再生能源的分布相对于传统化石能源更为均衡，各国都具有发展可再生能源的基础，这为平衡区域经济发展提供了重要基础。③ 随着全球

---

① 《阿尔及利亚推进海水淡化以应对水资源短缺》，央视网，https：//news.cctv.com/2025/02/10/ARTIbndxytpD9PRC2P2fnIi4250210.shtml，2025 年 2 月 10 日。
② 中华人民共和国商务部西亚非洲司：《阿拉伯国家石油储量占全球石油储量达 41.3%》，中华人民共和国商务部网站，http：//xyf.mofcom.gov.cn/xxzb/art/2024/art_e235ffb106dd47e-4a19cb3a3981538c5.html，2024 年 9 月 13 日。
③ 邹志强：《2030 年可持续发展议程与阿拉伯国家转型》，《阿拉伯世界研究》2020 年第 3 期，第 121 页。

能源转型加速，海湾国家正面临减少石油依赖的迫切需求。沙特"2030愿景"提出，将可再生能源装机容量提升至130吉瓦，并计划出口绿色电力和氢能。根据阿联酋《国家能源战略2050更新》，阿联酋计划到2030年将可再生能源装机容量增加两倍以上，达到14.2吉瓦，使清洁能源在总能源结构中的份额提高到30%。目前，阿联酋可再生能源装机容量6吉瓦，核能装机容量5.6吉瓦。① 阿曼的经济规模相对较小，石油和天然气储量也较为有限，因此采取了更为传统的招标方式吸引新能源领域的合作伙伴和投资者。阿曼寻求开发其巨大的太阳能和风电潜力，以实现国内能源结构的多样化，并计划从2030年开始逐步成为绿色氢气出口中心。

2024年4月16—18日，第16届世界未来能源峰会（WFES）在阿联酋首都阿布扎比国家展览中心举行。此次峰会由阿布扎比未来能源公司马斯达尔（Masdar）主办。作为西亚北非地区规模最大、最有影响力的可再生能源展览和会议，本届峰会吸引了来自世界各地的3万多名参观者和400多家企业参展，350多名行业领袖和专家就太阳能与清洁能源、生态垃圾、水、能源转型、智慧城市、气候与环境等专题展开讨论。

值得一提的是，本届峰会吸引的中国企业有100多家，尤其是在太阳能领域，140家参展企业中有90多家来自中国，优势十分明显。隆基绿能公司西亚北非区域总裁金剑介绍，中东地区发展光伏的自然禀赋好，像沙特、阿联酋、阿曼等国家都有非常明确的国家能源转型战略，虽然起步相对较晚，但这几年发展速度很快。通过与顶尖企业的竞争与合作，中国企业提升了在中东市场的竞争力，包括技术、品牌影响力和价格优势。核能作为清洁能源的重要组成部分，也是本届展会的一个重点。中核集团中国中原对外工程有限公司副总经理乔刚介绍说，核能作为清洁能源已经成为共识。可再生能源有很多优点，但也存在波动较大、需要储能、能源密度较小等缺点。而核电能源密度高，电力输出稳定，能够独自承担基本负荷

---

① 《阿联酋拟投资5000亿迪拉姆推动经济脱碳》，中国经济网，http://m.ce.cn/ttt/202501/02/t20250102_39254588.shtml，2025年1月2日。

的责任，可以解决大范围的能源安全，是实现脱碳和零碳的重要选择之一，从长远来看也会是大规模制造氢气的能源之一。[①]

### 9.1.3 荒漠化与生态环境保护

荒漠化、土地退化和干旱是当今世界最紧迫的环境挑战之一。阿拉伯地区的荒漠化现状非常严峻，主要表现为土地退化和沙漠扩张。近年来，由于气候变化和人为活动的影响，阿拉伯地区的荒漠化问题日益严重，具体表现为沙漠面积扩大、绿地减少、水资源短缺等。

2024年6月5日，沙特举办一年一度的2024年世界环境日庆祝活动，关注的重点是荒漠化、土地退化和抗旱能力。沙特已将防治荒漠化作为优先事项。沙特绿色倡议于2021年3月启动，旨在将沙特30%的土地转变为自然保护区，种植100亿棵树，恢复4000万公顷退化土地。沙特的短期目标是到2030年种植4亿棵树。通过签署中东绿色倡议，沙特正带头在该地区种植400亿棵树，旨在减少水土流失、保护生物多样性并减轻气候变化的影响。沙特还与二十国集团和《联合国防治荒漠化公约》（UNCCD）合作发起了G20全球土地倡议，旨在到2040年将土地退化减少50%。[②] 近年来，阿联酋采取多项政策措施，努力防治荒漠化，推动实现联合国2030年可持续发展议程。2022年，阿联酋政府发布了《防治荒漠化国家战略（2022—2030）》，提出到2030年将农业系统生产率在2022年基础上提高40%，至少恢复80%的已退化土地，把灌溉用处理水的使用率提高60%等。

阿拉伯国家积极利用创新技术防治荒漠化。阿联酋建立了多个研究中心和实验站，致力于防治荒漠化和监测气候变化方面的研究与开发活动，包括成立专门的技术合作中心，开展耐盐植物研究和推广种植。阿联酋还

---

[①] 《沙特绿色倡议：种100亿棵树，恢复4000万公顷退化土地》，中国绿发会网站，https：//www.cgdg.com/index.html，2024年5月9日。

[②] 《沙特绿色倡议：种100亿棵树，恢复4000万公顷退化土地》，中国绿发会网站，https：//www.cgdg.com/index.html，2024年5月9日。

使用无人机对全国农业区进行调查和测绘，在境内25个选定地点播种树木等，以改善这些地区的荒漠化状况。阿联酋还发起《穆罕默德·本·扎耶德水倡议》，希望促进相关创新技术的应用以应对水资源短缺等挑战。

## 9.2 中阿生态环境治理合作

《中国对阿拉伯国家政策文件》指出，大力推动中阿在《联合国气候变化框架公约》《生物多样性公约》《联合国防治荒漠化公约》等机制下的沟通协调，通过双多边渠道积极开展在环境政策对话与信息交流，环境立法，水、空气、土壤污染防治，提高公众环境保护意识，环境影响评估，环境监测，环保产业与技术，保护生物多样性，防治荒漠化，干旱地区造林，森林经营，环保人员培训和举办研讨会等方面的交流与合作，共同提高应对气候变化和环境保护能力。[①] 十年来，中国积极同阿拉伯国家携手打造绿色"一带一路"。随着绿色顶层制度设计不断完善、绿色务实合作持续拓展深化、绿色发展理念成为广泛共识，绿色"一带一路"建设稳步推进，并取得了丰硕成果。

### 9.2.1 中阿节水灌溉与合作

《中国对阿拉伯国家政策文件》指出，加强中阿在旱作农业、节水灌溉、粮食安全、畜牧与兽医等农业领域的双多边合作，鼓励双方农业科技人员加强交流。继续在阿拉伯国家建设农业技术示范项目，扩大农业管理和技术培训的规模，加强项目跟踪和评估。习近平主席指出，共建"一带一路"就是要建设一条开放发展之路，同时也必须是一条绿色发展之路。[②] 农业技

---

[①] 《中国对阿拉伯国家政策文件》，中华人民共和国中央人民政府网站，https://www.gov.cn/xinwen/2016-01/13/content_5032647.htm，2016年1月13日。

[②] 《生态兴 文明兴——"一带一路"中的人与自然和谐共生理念》，中华人民共和国中央人民政府网站，https://www.gov.cn/yaowen/liebao/202310/content_6909198.htm，2025年6月5日。

术是中阿技术交流和转移的一个缩影。中阿技术转移中心自 2015 年成立以来，相继在沙特、约旦等国共建了 8 个双边技术转移中心，推动一批契合阿拉伯国家可持续发展需求和关切的先进适用技术与装备在阿拉伯地区应用。在第五届中阿技术转移与创新合作大会上，中国面向阿拉伯国家发布了 300 项先进适用技术，涉及生态环境保护、资源能源利用、污染控制等领域。

2023 年，在第六届中阿博览会水资源论坛上，16 项在"一带一路"共建国家推广并取得成效的水利合作成果发布。这些成果涉及交流合作、科研平台、关键技术、技术推广等多种类型。有些成果不仅使国内受益，还走出国门，为他国贡献了中国治水智慧。

2024 年 9 月 16—18 日，第六届阿拉伯水论坛在阿联酋阿布扎比举行，应阿拉伯水理事会主席阿布扎伊德邀请，水利部副部长朱程清出席论坛并在部长级全体大会发言。论坛期间，朱程清与阿联酋能源与基础设施部部长苏海勒、阿拉伯水理事会主席阿布扎伊德、埃及水资源和灌溉部部长赛维拉姆举行会谈，就加强在非常规水源利用、水旱灾害防御等领域的务实合作交换了意见。代表团还调研了迪拜哈斯彦海水淡化厂、马克图姆光伏产业园。

2025 年 1 月 7 日，中国水利部副部长李良生在北京会见沙特驻华大使阿卜杜拉赫曼·哈勒比，双方就深化中沙水利合作进行了深入交流。李良生表示，中沙在水利领域长期保持友好合作，双方自 2016 年签署水利合作谅解备忘录以来，在高层互访、技术交流、国际水事活动协调配合等方面取得了良好的合作成果。中国水利部深入践行习近平总书记"节水优先、空间均衡、系统治理、两手发力"治水思路，统筹解决水灾害、水资源、水生态、水环境问题，不断提升国家水安全保障能力。中国水利部愿同沙方深化友好交流合作，围绕非常规水利用、地下水保护、节水、抗旱、水土保持等双方共同关心的议题开展政策对话、技术交流和务实项目合作，为丰富两国全面战略伙伴关系内涵、夯实"一带一路"建设水利合作做出更大贡献。[①] 同

---

① 《水利部召开节约用水工作会议》，中华人民共和国中央人民政府网站，https：//www.gov.cn/lianbo/bumen/202502/content_7003581.htm，2025 年 6 月 6 日。

时，双方将加强在国际水事活动中的互相支持与配合，为推动联合国2030年可持续发展议程涉水目标在全球范围内的早日实现贡献力量。阿卜杜拉赫曼·哈勒比表示，沙方高度重视与中方开展水利合作。中国拥有引领全球的治水经验，期待双方继续在中沙全面战略伙伴关系下深化水利合作，造福于两国人民；同时也期待双方不断巩固拓展多边合作，为全球水治理贡献中沙两国的智慧和力量。①

### 9.2.2 中阿清洁能源领域的合作

在中阿合作论坛第十届部长级会议开幕式上，中国国家主席习近平发表主旨讲话并指出，将以首届中阿峰会"八大共同行动"为基础，同阿方构建"五大合作格局"，推动中阿命运共同体建设跑出加速度。"五大合作格局"之一是构建更加立体的能源合作格局，支持中国能源企业和金融机构在阿拉伯国家参与可再生能源项目。

随着中国在新能源产业技术领域的厚积薄发，中阿新能源合作方兴未艾，成为双边合作的重要增长极。近年来，阿拉伯国家加速出台改革措施，大力发展可再生能源，沙特提出2030年可再生能源在能源结构中占比达50%，阿联酋计划到2050年将清洁能源占比提高至50%。这些中东国家的能源转型战略，与中国实现"双碳"目标，实现建设人与自然和谐共生的现代化愿景高度契合，为双方携手合作共创未来创造了广阔前景。根据国际能源署报告，目前阿拉伯国家公布的能源转型计划，到2030年，阿拉伯地区可再生能源（不含水力发电）总发电能力将超过192吉瓦，为当前水平的17倍，其中太阳能发电所占比例将达42%以上、风能约占35%。② 在"一带一路"倡议推动下，中国与阿拉伯多国在清洁能源领域的合作将面临广阔发展空间。

---

① 《李良生会见沙特阿拉伯驻华大使阿卜杜拉赫曼·哈勒比》，中华人民共和国水利部网站，http://www.mwr.gov.cn/xw/slyw/202501/t20250108_1726026.html，2025年1月8日。
② 《中国—中东能源合作向"新"逐"绿"》，网易，https://www.163.com/dy/article/JMOJEP9L0550TYQ0.html，2025年1月25日。

随着中国与中东国家大力推进在清洁能源领域的双多边合作，一批由中企承建的基础设施项目在中东多国落地。在沙特，中企正在红海新城建设全球最大离网储能项目，该储能电站与光伏发电系统相结合，将使占地2.8万平方千米的红海新城全部使用绿色电力。与此同时，作为中国外贸"新三样"之一的新能源汽车，成为许多中东国家街头的一道风景。比亚迪、小鹏、长安、蔚来、广汽等多个中国汽车品牌积极开拓中东市场，面向当地推出新能源汽车产品。中国海关总署数据显示，2024年上半年，中国对中东地区的乘用车出口量达到42.0万辆，同比增长46.2%，中东成为中国汽车最大的出口目的地。其中，新能源汽车占比达19.6%。[①]

阿拉伯地区的核能发展潜力巨大，尤其是在电力需求不断增长、能源转型加速的背景下，核能作为清洁、高效的能源形式具有广阔的应用前景。中国核工业集团有限公司与阿联酋核能公司在阿联酋首都阿布扎比联合举办"中核集团—阿联酋核能公司第二届核电供应商研讨会"。随着中阿两国全面战略伙伴关系走深走实，近年来，中核集团与阿联酋核能公司的合作稳步推进，反映了两国在和平利用核能领域合作的共同愿景。2024年5月，中阿两国签署了和平利用核能的双边合作文件，在双方发表的联合声明中强调，中国与阿联酋决心探讨实施核电建设等示范性联合项目，加强和平利用核能领域研发合作和经验交流，以支持和平核能的发展。

总的来看，中国与阿拉伯国家在清洁能源领域的合作展现出强大的生命力和广阔前景。从规模宏大的光伏电站到街头巷尾的新能源汽车，中国技术、中国经验正在为阿拉伯国家的能源转型和可持续发展注入强大动力。这种合作不仅体现了双方在技术、资源和市场方面的优势互补，更彰显了"一带一路"倡议下互利共赢的理念。随着阿拉伯国家能源转型计划的加速推进，中国与阿拉伯在清洁能源领域的合作将迎来更加广阔的发展空间。这不仅将促进双方经济的共同发展，也将为全球能

---

[①] 《中国—中东能源合作向"新"逐"绿"》，网易，https://www.163.com/dy/article/JMOJEP9L0550TYQ0.html，2025年1月25日。

源的绿色转型做出重要贡献。展望未来，中阿双方必将继续深化合作，共同推动清洁能源技术的创新与应用，为构建一个更加清洁、绿色的世界贡献力量。

### 9.2.3 土地荒漠化综合治理

经过 40 多年不懈努力，中国成功走出了一条具有中国特色的防沙治沙道路，保护生态与改善民生步入良性循环，成为防沙治沙国际典范。中国政府高度重视与阿拉伯国家的战略合作与伙伴关系。2022 年 12 月 9 日，中国国家主席习近平在首届中阿峰会上提出中阿务实合作"八大共同行动"。同阿方共同设立中阿中心，是推动"绿色创新共同行动"的重要内容之一。中方积极联络中阿双方涉及干旱、荒漠化和土地退化防治领域的政府机构、科研院所和高校、私营部门、社会组织、国际组织和金融机构等利益相关方，筹建中阿荒漠化治理网络。举办"绿色长城"建设专题研修班，研讨共同推进中国、非盟和阿盟荒漠化和土地退化防治三方合作的机会。开展中阿合作政策与技术体系框架研究，与中国科学院大数据中心合作开发适合阿盟成员国的土地退化数据工具和产品，为中阿深化可持续发展合作提供数据支撑。

2023 年 8 月，中国国家林业和草原局与阿拉伯国家联盟秘书处签署备忘录，宣布正式成立中阿干旱、荒漠化和土地退化国际研究中心。中阿中心的目标宗旨是为中阿抵御干旱影响、防治荒漠化和土地退化提供科技支撑、决策支持和智库服务，聚焦关键技术创新、成果转化和经验分享，推动区域及全球绿色发展和民生改善，帮助实现全球土地退化零增长目标。中国林业科学研究院作为中阿中心的执行机构，成立了专门的管理和专家团队提供支撑保障。

2024 年 11 月，阿拉伯国家荒漠化和风沙灾害防治技术培训班在甘肃省兰州市开班，来自突尼斯、阿曼、埃及等阿拉伯国家的 24 名学员参加培训。此次培训由中国商务部主办，甘肃省治沙研究所承办，为期 21 天。培训开设了课堂教学、专业实习等课程，内容涉及荒漠化防治、风沙灾害治理、绿洲生态系统保护、工程治沙、退化生态恢复等。2024年12月，《联合国防治荒漠化公约》第十六次缔约方大会在利雅得召开，大会通过公约2025—2026年预算、应对沙尘暴、应对干旱、强化科研创新等39项决议文件。会议期间，中国代表团积极与各方沟通协调，切实履行缔约国义务，举办中国馆系列活动，累计举办10余场边会，为携手推动全球荒漠化防治、共同迈向更加清洁美丽的世界贡献中国智慧和力量。会议期间，东道国沙特发起的"利雅得全球抗旱伙伴关系"倡议吸引了121.5亿美元资金，用于支持世界上最脆弱的80个国家抗旱能力建设。此外，沙特还宣布了五个新项目，价值6000万美元，以加强气候和环境工作，作为沙特绿色倡议的一部分。

2024年是中国签署《联合国防治荒漠化公约》30周年。中国开拓"一带一路"防治荒漠化合作机制，与同样面临荒漠化问题的中亚、西亚和非洲国家分享治沙技术和经验，提供技能培训，为全球南方共谋绿色发展注入动力。一批批外国治沙专家来到中国学习治沙经验和技术，并应用于本国的治沙实践。中国以诚意和善意"授人以渔"，让越来越多的国家和地区获益。[1]

总之，中国和阿拉伯国家生态治理与绿色产业合作前景广阔。中国和阿拉伯国家积极推进太阳能、风能等可再生能源合作，努力探索能源科技创新、产业结构转型升级合作，不断拓展互联网、大数据、人工智能、5G等新型技术与绿色低碳产业深度融合。作为重要合作成果，中国在应对气候变化南南合作项目下为埃及提供援助，中国与埃及签署农业绿色发展联合实验室合作备忘录。中国公司承建的中东地区首个清洁燃煤电站迪拜哈斯彦清洁燃煤电站、全球在建最大海水淡化工程阿联酋塔维勒海水淡化项目、世界单机容量最大的塔式光热电站项目摩洛哥努奥太阳能聚热电站三期等，为破解地区国家能源结构调整和经济社会发展瓶颈带来重要机遇。

---

[1] 《沙漠里的绿色故事 值得世界聆听》，一带一路网，https://www.yidaiyilu.gov.cn/p/0IGKBVG6.html，2024年12月13日。

## 9.3 中阿生态环境合作路径展望

分享治国理政经验是中阿合作论坛机制下中国对阿拉伯外交的重要着力点之一。2024年，第十届中阿合作论坛在北京召开，中阿双方所达成的共识性文件均强调开展治国理政理念和经验交流互鉴。中国和阿拉伯国家绿色发展理念高度契合。作为世界上最大的发展中国家，中国坚持不懈推动绿色低碳发展，努力建设人与自然和谐共生的现代化。而作为全球最大石化能源生产和出口地区，阿拉伯国家普遍面临优化能源消费结构、促进绿色转型发展、实现多元增长等紧迫挑战。中国和阿拉伯国家均为此做出重要顶层设计，中国提出实现"双碳"目标，加快构建"1+N"政策体系，组织实施"碳达峰十大行动"，积极推进低碳发展和绿色转型。沙特提出"绿色沙特""绿色中东"倡议，阿联酋提出《2050年零排放战略倡议》，埃及启动《2050年国家气候变化战略》，其他地区与国家也纷纷提出降碳减排战略。高度契合的顶层设计和战略认知，为双方应对气候变化合作提供了根本遵循，指明了前进方向。

### 9.3.1 中阿应加强生态环境领域的政策协调，构建"政策对接—平台共建—多边协同"的全链条机制

一是中阿积极构建多层次政策对接框架，签署联合公报与战略文件。早在2006年《中华人民共和国政府和阿拉伯国家联盟环境保护合作联合公报》中，双方就明确在环境政策立法、生物多样性保护等领域的合作方向，并设立执行计划推动具体项目落地。[①] 2016年《中国对阿拉伯国家政策文件》进一步提出绿色发展合作目标，推动中阿环保技术标准互认与政策协同。为了全面落实双方战略文件，中阿围绕荒漠化防

---

[①] 《中华人民共和国政府和阿拉伯国家联盟环境保护合作联合公报》，中阿合作论坛网，http：//www.chinaarabcf.org/zagx/rwjl/201110/t20111012_6842688.htm，2011年10月12日。

治、气候变化等议题制订专项计划，例如中国与沙特联合推动的"绿色中东倡议"，以及中埃低碳城市发展合作框架，强化政策衔接与目标对齐。中阿同属发展中国家，在加强气候环境治理、推进可持续发展方面有着相近立场和相同意愿。双方可以此为基础，通过加强绿色基建、绿色能源、绿色金融等领域合作，共同参与完善"一带一路"绿色发展国际联盟、"一带一路"绿色投资原则等多边合作平台，建设更紧密的绿色发展伙伴关系，以绿色筑底中阿合作，推动中阿各自经济社会可持续发展。[①]

二是搭建常态化对话与协作平台。设立部长级对话与专业论坛，中国生物多样性保护与绿色发展基金会（简称"中国绿发会"）与阿联酋、埃及等国建立定期部长级环境对话机制，聚焦碳排放核算、生态修复技术共享等议题，推动政策经验互鉴。[②] 通过"中国—阿拉伯国家环境合作论坛"和"欧亚经济论坛生态环保分会"，深化区域绿色经济转型共识，促进政策沟通与项目对接，深入推进绿色"一带一路"建设。同时，加强智库与民间合作网络。中阿智库联合发布绿色转型合作白皮书，推动环保政策创新与标准协同；中国绿发会与阿拉伯民间组织合作建立生物多样性监测网络，促进基层治理经验共享。

三是强化多边机制协同与全球治理参与。中阿共同参与《联合国防治荒漠化公约》《巴黎协定》等国际公约，在第二十八届联合国气候变化大会（COP28）等平台协同发声，推动建立"南南合作治沙基金"，维护发展中国家环境权益。联合推动设立"中阿干旱、荒漠化和土地退化国际研究中心"，整合区域生态治理资源。通过"一带一路"绿色发展国际联盟，中阿合作规划跨国生态走廊（如红海—波斯湾生态走廊），制订跨境水资源管理、荒漠化防治等联合行动计划。

---

① 《以绿色筑底，共谋中阿可持续发展》，中阿合作论坛网，http：//www.chinaarabcf.org/zagx/sssb/202104/t20210425_9156375.htm，2021年4月25日。

② 《中国倡议将中国与阿拉伯国家环境合作推向多样化》，中国新闻网，https：//www.chinanews.com.cn/news/2006/2006-02-09/8/687733.shtml，2006年2月9日。

### 9.3.2 中阿搭建"荒漠化防治—清洁能源—数字生态"三位一体的合作框架，推动技术转移向纵深和智能化发展

一是荒漠化防治技术转移与示范。近年来，中国积极推动核心技术输出，在第六届中阿博览会发布生物降解沙障、地下根际灌溉技术及水分平衡造林固沙技术，助力阿拉伯国家退化土地修复。沙特引进中国亿利资源集团的智能机器人植树、光伏治沙技术及区块链碳链技术，提升"绿色沙特"计划实施效率。中阿合作建立"干旱、荒漠化和土地退化国际研究中心"，联合开展跨境荒漠化防治技术研发与资金申请，推动区域退化土地修复率提升至15%。[①] 随着新能源技术的发展与成熟，中国在沙特、阿联酋等国推广"光伏+治沙"模式，通过光伏板遮阴减少水分蒸发，同步发展清洁能源与植被恢复，形成"双向碳中和"效应。

二是清洁能源技术转移与协同应用。近年来，中国积极拓展同阿拉伯国家在绿色科技方面的合作，以清洁能源领域最具代表性，双方先后建立了中阿清洁能源培训中心、中埃（及）可再生能源联合实验室，实施了卡塔尔哈尔萨光伏项目、186兆瓦埃及本班光伏产业园光伏发电项目、165兆瓦（直流）埃及光伏电站EPC项目等大批合作项目。中国可再生能源装备向阿拉伯国家的出口不断增加。中国为沙特比沙储能项目（2000兆瓦时）、埃及本班光伏产业园（1.8吉瓦）提供光伏组件与储能设备，推动阿拉伯国家可再生能源装机量增长5倍。中国在埃及新行政首都建设中引入绿色建筑技术，阿尔及利亚水利设施改造项目应用智能水循环系统，实现城市水资源利用率提升30%。[②]

三是数字化生态治理技术合作。中国向沙特输出卫星遥感监测数据分析平台，结合无人机播种技术精准定位植被恢复区域，提升沙漠化治理效

---

① 《中阿共商荒漠化防治合作新路径》，宁夏回族自治区林业和草原局网站，http://lcj.nx.gov.cn/xwzx/mtgz/202309/t20230925_4285177.html，2023年9月25日。
② 王佳、艾哈迈德·哈ま：《阿拉伯国家绿色经济：发展、困境与中国角色》，《阿拉伯世界研究》2024年第3期，第54页。

率。中阿联合开发生态数据库，实时监测红海—波斯湾生态走廊的植被覆盖率与水资源分布，优化跨国生态修复方案。随着人工智能技术的迅猛发展，智能装备与机器人技术得到了广泛应用。沙特引进中国智能植树机器人技术，单机日种植效率达2000株，较传统人工效率提升15倍，并减少90%的淡水消耗。未来需强化技术本地化适配（如耐盐碱植物联合培育）、跨境生态补偿机制及绿色金融支持体系，构建更具韧性的区域生态治理网络。

未来"一带一路"的绿色发展仍需深化绿色清洁能源合作，推动能源国际合作低碳转型。中国应积极承担相应产品的"提供者"责任，依托自身优势，助力绿色"一带一路"新发展。一方面，中国应积极鼓励太阳能发电、风电等企业"走出去"，推动建成一批绿色能源最佳实践项目；另一方面，中国应深化能源技术装备领域合作，重点围绕高效低成本可再生能源发电、先进核电、智能电网、氢能、储能、二氧化碳捕集利用与封存等开展联合研究及交流培训。

### 9.3.3　中阿在生态环境领域加强多边机制协作，强化全球环境治理

一是多边机制协作强化全球环境治理。中国积极为发展中国家提供技术援助与资金支持。中国是世界上遭受荒漠化危害严重的国家之一。中国通过展示"三北"工程治沙技术与荒漠化防治成果，为全球南方国家提供可复制的生态治理经验。中国政府高度重视、持续推进荒漠化综合防治和"三北"等重点生态工程建设，推动53%的可治理沙化土地得到有效治理，实现了生态保护与民生改善的良性循环，荒漠化区域经济社会发展和生态面貌发生翻天覆地的变化，成为全球增绿贡献最大的国家和防沙治沙国际典范，为全球防沙治沙进程做出了贡献。

此外，重视区域治理平台共建。依托"一带一路"绿色发展国际联盟，中阿发起"欧亚经济论坛生态环保分会"和"中国—阿拉伯国家环境合作论坛"，聚焦绿色经济转型、跨境生态修复等议题，促进政策沟通与项目对接。双方通过中阿合作论坛机制，发布绿色转型合作白皮书，推

动区域环境标准互认与联合行动计划制订。

二是建设跨国生态走廊与区域联动项目。积极推进红海—波斯湾生态走廊建设。中阿联合规划覆盖沙特、阿曼等6国的生态走廊，通过跨境电力网络、海水淡化工程和卫星遥感监测技术，实现水资源调配、荒漠化防治与生物多样性保护一体化管理，该项目集成中国智能水循环系统与光伏治沙技术，提升区域生态韧性，同时加快绿色基建与能源协同发展。

三是联合科研与能力建设。在生态环境治理方面，中阿成立"干旱、荒漠化和土地退化国际研究中心"，整合双方科研资源开展跨境生态治理技术研发，推动生物降解沙障、无人机播种等技术的本地化应用。中国通过商务部环保研修班，为阿拉伯国家培训超500名技术人员，覆盖环境政策制定、污染治理技术等领域，强化区域生态治理能力。双方智库联合开展"中阿节水农业示范基地"等示范项目，推广滴灌技术并降低农业用水量40%。

习近平总书记提出"绿水青山就是金山银山"，这是中国生态文明建设的核心理念，也为全球可持续发展提供了中国智慧。新时代绿色发展既是发展观的深刻革命，也是国际潮流所向、大势所趋。中国将继续秉持绿色发展理念，不断深化同中东国家在应对气候变化领域的合作，携手应对挑战，共同打造绿色"一带一路"，构建地球生命共同体，开启全球应对生态危机新征程。在"一带一路"倡议下，中国与阿拉伯国家积极应对全球生态环境危机，持续深化生态环境领域合作，为推动阿拉伯国家经济发展、生态治理和发展转型，构建中阿命运共同体贡献了坚实力量。

# 第10章 中阿旅游合作专题报告

## 10.1 2024年度中阿旅游总体情况

2024年，中国文旅产业呈现蓬勃发展态势，悠久灿烂的东方文明、充满活力的现代街区、良好的产品及服务品质、融入先进科技元素的文旅活动异彩纷呈，不但拉动入境旅游人数大幅提升，同时也极大提高了中国旅游的国际形象，增强了中国文旅产业的国际竞争力。根据2025年1月中国国家移民管理局发布的最新数据，2024年，全国累计检验出入境人员6.1亿人次，同比上升43.9%，其中，外国人出入境6488.2万人次，同比上升82.9%；签发外国人签证证件259.7万本，同比上升52.3%；全国各口岸免签入境外国人2011.5万人次，同比上升112.3%，过境免签政策适用人数同比上升113.5%，特别是全面放宽优化过境免签政策后，适用该政策来华人数环比上升29.5%。[①]

在友好的国际关系与中阿双方积极推动下，2024年，中阿旅游合作取得显著进展。摩洛哥官方派遣赴华代表团，开展宣介活动积极开拓中国市场，增强对中国游客的吸引力[②]，前往摩洛哥旅游的中国游客数量增长明显，旅游人次突破10万人次，增长约78%。埃及接待的中国游客数量

---

[①] 《2024年移民管理工作主要数据》，国家移民管理局网站，https：//www.nia.gov.cn/n897453/c1693437/content.html，2025年1月14日。

[②] 《摩洛哥媒体：摩洛哥旅游业将迎"中国时刻"》，中阿合作论坛网站，http：//www.chinaarabcf.org/zagx/rwjl/202501/t20250120_11538833.htm，2025年1月20日。

超过30万人次，同比增长近65%。① 2024年1—6月，阿联酋沙迦接待的中国游客数量较2023年同期增长5倍，占远东地区游客总数的56%。② 阿联酋经济和旅游部数据显示，2024年，中国游客在阿布扎比的旅游订单同比增长超75%，阿布扎比游客来中国旅游订单同比增长近4倍。③ 1—8月，迪拜共接待54.7万名来自中国的过夜游客，同比增长39%。中阿旅游呈现出强劲的发展势头。

### 10.1.1　不断完善的合作机制为中阿旅游合作提供了长效保障

2024年5月30日，中国—阿拉伯国家合作论坛第十届部长级会议通过《中国—阿拉伯国家合作论坛2024年至2026年行动执行计划》，明确提出在旅游等多个领域加大合作力度，为未来中阿旅游合作指明方向。稳定的合作平台、不断完善的合作机制、不断细化的合作计划，为未来中阿之间旅游领域的深度合作提供坚实保障。

### 10.1.2　中国加快推动与阿拉伯国家的旅游合作

2024年，中国不断优化过境免签、区域性入境免签、口岸签证等政策，进一步扩大单方面免签、互免签证范围，持续提升外籍人员来华、在华便利度。④ 持续推动包括阿拉伯国家在内的外国游客入境中国旅游便利化，过境免签政策不断优化，包括240小时过境免签、外国旅游团乘坐邮轮入境免签、扩大59国人员免签入境海南事由、9个枢纽机场实施24小时直接过境免办查验手续等18项便利外国人来

---

① 《更多中国游客"打卡"埃及感受古国魅力》，中阿合作论坛网站，http：//www.chinaarabcf.org/zagx/rwjl/202501/t20250107_11528271.htm，2025年1月7日。
② 《2024年上半年沙迦接待中国游客数量较去年同期增长5倍》，中国新闻网，https：//baijiahao.baidu.com/s?id=1808366744666560138&wfr=spider&for=pc，2024年8月25日。
③ 《去阿联酋过春节》，中国经济网，http：//www.ce.cn/xwzx/gnsz/gdxw/202502/02/t20250202_39281531.shtml，2025年2月2日。
④ 《免签政策红利充分释放》，经济日报网站，http：//paper.ce.cn/pc/content/202501/11/content_307352.html，2025年1月11日。

华政策。① 同时，中国不断推动旅游景区、演出场所、餐厅酒店等场景支付便利化，加密中阿空中航线，丰富入境旅游产品和服务供给等，充分展示出中国对中阿之间旅游合作的积极态度。

### 10.1.3 阿拉伯国家高度重视拓展中国旅游市场

自 2024 年 7 月 1 日起，沙特在中国展开了一系列营销活动，推出多项便利中国游客的举措，中国已成为沙特签发快速电子签证的对象国之一。沙特旅游局官方微信小程序为中国游客量身定制了多样化的旅行辅助服务功能，包括普通话导游服务、沙特旅游产品介绍和预订、沙特当地重要节庆活动和演艺信息、沙特景点介绍等②，官方网站则专门开设中文服务热线，在沙特首都利雅得机场增设中文指示牌，并在沙特境内开通银联支付渠道等。沙特正式成为中国公民出境团队游目的地国家③，预计到 2030 年底，实现吸引中国游客人数从 15 万人增加至 300 万—500 万人④的目标。阿联酋等国家高度期待与中国文化中心和中国旅游业界开展合作，将中国作为重要目标市场。阿联酋航空明确展示出利用阿联酋航空全球航空网络协助推介中国充满活力的城市和独特的美景，推动中国与中东旅游业共同合作与发展的愿望。摩洛哥、阿联酋、卡塔尔、突尼斯等国陆续对中国公民实施免签入境政策，为中国游客赴阿旅游消除签证阻碍。

### 10.1.4 航线数量的增加为中阿旅游往来提供了必要支撑

根据 2025 年 1 月中国国家移民管理局发布的最新数据，2024 年全年

---

① 《"China Travel" 同比上升 112.3%！来过，就会爱上》，新华网，https://www.news.cn/world/20250114/71ec65d8e0c4450c8e878960a2503f13/c.html，2025 年 1 月 14 日。
② 《沙特将持续为中国游客提供便利》，中国旅游新闻网，https://www.ctnews.com.cn/huanqiu/content/2024-11-26/content_167470.html，2024 年 11 月 28 日。
③ 《7 月 1 日起，沙特将成为中国公民出境团队游目的地国家》，新京报网站，https://www.bjnews.com.cn/detail/1719357418129747.html，2024 年 6 月 26 日。
④ 《沙媒体回顾沙特 2024 年成就：愿景焕新，前景广阔》，中华人民共和国驻沙特阿拉伯王国大使馆经济商务处网站，http://sa.mofcom.gov.cn/jmxw/art/2025/art_2eb28d96a0a343-d484b394c9b882d7f2.html，2025 年 1 月 1 日。

累计查验出入境交通运输工具 3256.6 万架（列、艘、辆）次，同比上升 38.8%；其中飞机 87.9 万架次，同比上升 62.6%①。2024 年 1—6 月，中国陆续开通北京至利雅得、上海至利雅得、深圳至利雅得以及厦门至多哈等直飞新航线，加密了双方空中交通网络。这些新航线的开通，确保了利雅得、吉达、多哈等城市与中国主要城市之间航班的全面覆盖。

2024 年，由于赴阿拉伯国家旅游的中国游客数量大幅增加，许多阿拉伯国家航空公司纷纷增设直航线路或提高航班运力。沙特航空开通吉达—达曼—北京航线，每周 9 个航班从利雅得和吉达往返中国主要城市，大大缩短了中阿之间的时空距离，不但为中阿游客往来提供了极大便利，降低了出行成本，也极大地推动了中阿旅游合作的发展。埃及航空将开罗至上海航班增加至每周 4 班，并计划在现有北京、上海、杭州和广州航线基础上，将厦门列为直航目的地。2024 年 5 月，海湾航空 GF124 航班从巴林首都麦纳麦飞抵上海浦东国际机场，中国往返巴林的首条国际直飞航线正式开通。②摩洛哥航空公司则宣布将于 2025 年 1 月 20 日起恢复卡萨布兰卡直飞北京航线。此外，迪拜经济和旅游部数据显示，迪拜国际机场在 2024 年上半年共接待中国旅客超过 100 万人次，同比增长 80%。③

### 10.1.5 中阿文化旅游交流互动频繁

2024 年，中阿文化旅游交流互动频繁。5 月，第 31 届阿拉伯旅游展在迪拜举办，中国文化和旅游部国际交流与合作局、阿联酋中国文化中心组织中国 9 个省（市）的文化和旅游主管部门、航空公司、旅游企业的代表近百人参展，并设面积 135 平方米的"你好！中国"展区，面向全球旅行商和观众展示中国文化和旅游产品，这是中国展团在 2019 年后首次集

---

① 《2024 年 6.1 亿人次出入境 同比上升 43.9%》，国家移民管理局网站，https://www.nia.gov.cn/n741440/n741567/c1693512/content.html，2025 年 1 月 14 日。

② 《国际识局：从丝绸之路走来，中阿这样缔造"南南合作"典范》，中国新闻网，http://www.chinanews.com.cn/gj/2024/06-01/10226960.shtml，2024 年 6 月 1 日。

③ 《去阿联酋过春节》，中国经济网，http://www.ce.cn/xwzx/gnsz/gdxw/202502/02/t20250202_39281531.shtml，2025 年 2 月 2 日。

体亮相阿拉伯旅游展。① 10月，中国和沙特签署了《中华人民共和国文化和旅游部与沙特王国文化部关于举办2025中国—沙特文化年的执行计划》，两国将于2025年举办文化年，通过举办一系列文化活动，展示各自丰富的文化和旅游资源，进一步推动中阿文化交流与互鉴。②

2024年，中阿人文交流活动也呈现积极发展态势。埃及788件珍贵文物首次走出国门在上海博物馆亮相，极大吸引了中国观众的观展热情。"埃尔奥拉：阿拉伯半岛的奇迹绿洲展""金字塔之巅：古埃及文明大展"等展会相继在北京、上海举办。为庆祝中国—阿联酋建交40周年，东方演艺集团和中国交响乐团在阿联酋首都阿布扎比举办"千年一声唱"国风音乐会和专场音乐会，中央芭蕾舞团在阿联酋上演中国贺岁芭蕾舞剧《过年》，让当地观众领略中外艺术结合的魅力。中国武术和中国象棋在黎巴嫩广受欢迎，众多优质中国影视作品和新媒体平台产品在黎巴嫩掀起"中国热"。《山海情》《当法老遇见三星堆》等优质影视作品在阿拉伯国家总点击量超过5亿次。③

阿拉伯国家数百所学校开设中文课程，"汉语热"在黎巴嫩等阿拉伯国家持续升温。④ 阿联酋、沙特、埃及、突尼斯、阿尔及利亚、摩洛哥、约旦、伊拉克等阿拉伯国家中文学习者踊跃参加第23届"汉语桥"世界大学生中文比赛。埃及举办了"学成语，识中华"第一届成语大会，吸引200余名大学中文系学生和中文爱好者参赛。北京故宫成功举办中阿诗会，多名阿拉伯国家诗人与中国诗人以诗会友，通过诗歌吟诵，表达对和

---

① 《"你好！中国"展区亮相2024年ATM阿拉伯旅游展》，中华人民共和国文化和旅游部网站，https://www.mct.gov.cn/preview/whzx/bnsj/dwwhllj/202405/t20240508_952749.html，2024年5月8日。

② 《沙特将持续为中国游客提供便利》，中国旅游新闻网，https://www.ctnews.com.cn/huanqiu/content/2024-11/26/content_167470.html，2024年11月28日。

③ 《中阿合作二十载，潮平岸阔再扬帆》，中东瞭望，https://www.chinaarabcf.org/zagx/sssb/202406/t20240617_11436908.htm，2024年6月17日。

④ 《驻黎巴嫩大使钱敏坚在〈消息报〉发表署名文章〈推动中阿命运共同体建设跑出加速度〉》，中华人民共和国外交部网站，https://www.mfa.gov.cn/web/wjdt_674879/zwbd_674895/202406/t20240604_11376473.shtml，2024年6月3日。

平、友谊等共同美好价值的追求。尽管苏丹武装冲突不断，但阿特巴拉市的汉语培训中心依旧吸引了大量学员，其中约60%是来自战乱地区的避难者，充分反映了中国在阿拉伯世界的影响力不断提升。此外，埃及的中文教育也取得了显著进展，开罗大学等高校的中文专业注册学生数量大幅增加，显示出中阿人文领域的交流不断深化。①

2024年，中阿旅游领域的诸多合作成果为中阿双方实现2029年1000万游客互访的目标奠定了坚实基础，未来双方的旅游合作必将迎来更加辉煌的发展。

## 10.2　中阿旅游合作20年回顾

2004年1月30日，时任中国国家主席胡锦涛访问埃及时在开罗会见了阿盟秘书长穆萨和阿盟22个成员国代表，提出建立中阿新型伙伴关系的四项原则，即：以相互尊重为基础，增进政治关系；以共同发展为目标，密切经贸往来；以相互借鉴为内容，扩大文化交流；以维护世界和平、促进共同发展为宗旨，加强在国际事务中的合作。② 当日，"中国—阿拉伯国家合作论坛"成立。中阿合作论坛的成立，为中国和阿拉伯国家在平等互利基础上进行对话与合作提供了一个新的平台，使中阿关系的内涵进一步丰富，巩固和拓展双方在政治、经贸、科技、文化、教育、卫生等诸多领域内的互利合作，全面提升合作水平。至2023年12月，中国同全部22个阿拉伯国家及阿盟组织签署了共建"一带一路"合作协议，绘制出中阿广泛合作的宏伟蓝图。③

---

① 《"中文热"推动2024年中阿人文交流跑出加速度》，中华人民共和国国务院新闻办公室网站，http://www.scio.gov.cn/gxzl/ydyl_26587/rwjl/rwjl_26595/202412/t20241230_879310.html，2024年12月28日。

② 《胡锦涛会见阿盟秘书长穆萨和阿盟22个成员国代表》，中华人民共和国外交部网站，https://www.fmprc.gov.cn/gjhdq_676201/gjhdqzz_681964/lhg_682830/xgxw_682836/200401/t20040131_9638906.shtml，2004年1月31日。

③ 《中阿共建"一带一路"成绩亮眼》，中华人民共和国国务院新闻办公室网站，http://www.scio.gov.cn/gxzl/ydyl_26587/zxtj_26590/zxtj_26591/202312/t20231219_822728.html，2023年12月19日。

2024年，是中国—阿拉伯国家合作论坛成立20周年。20年来，中阿之间不断深化战略互信，拓展务实合作，扩大人文交流，彰显了"守望相助、平等互利、包容互鉴"的中阿友好精神，实现了跨越式发展；20年来，中国与阿拉伯国家之间包含旅游服务贸易在内的贸易额已超过4000亿美元，中国成为阿拉伯国家最大的贸易伙伴，阿拉伯国家也成为中国最主要的海外原油供应国，阿拉伯地区已成为同中国建立战略合作伙伴关系密度最高的地区之一[①]；20年来，中阿文化旅游交流呈现蓬勃发展态势，阿拉伯地区的独特魅力吸引了越来越多的中国游客前往旅游观光，高水平开放的中国更是以不断提升的国际旅游影响力和竞争力，在中阿旅游合作中取得斐然成绩。

### 10.2.1　20年来中阿合作机制与平台建设不断完善丰富了中阿旅游合作成果

#### 10.2.1.1　"一带一路"建设为中阿旅游合作带来新的发展机遇

2013年9月和10月，中国国家主席习近平先后提出建设"丝绸之路经济带"和"21世纪海上丝绸之路"的重大倡议，得到国际社会高度关注。2014年6月5日，习近平主席出席中阿合作论坛第六届部长级会议开幕式并发表题为《弘扬丝路精神，深化中阿合作》的重要讲话，首次提出打造中阿命运共同体倡议。[②] 中阿共建"一带一路"，构建以能源合作为主轴，以基础设施建设、贸易和投资便利化为两翼，以核能、航天卫星、新能源三大高新领域为突破口的"1+2+3"合作格局。中阿双方在共建"一带一路"框架内，实施了200多个大型项目，中方为阿方培训3400多名各领域专业人才，中国连续多年稳居阿拉伯国家第一大贸易伙伴国地位，中阿贸易额从2004年的367亿美元增至2023年的3980亿美元，增长

---

[①]《中国与阿拉伯国家的投资合作及展望》，新浪网，https：//cj.sina.com.cn/articles/view/1686546714/6486a91a02002kvhu，2025年1月23日。

[②]《弘扬丝路精神，深化中阿合作》，人民网－中国共产党新闻网，http：//cpc.people.com.cn/n/2014/0606/c64094-25110795.html，2014年6月5日。

约11倍，合作成果惠及双方近20亿人民。[①]

"一带一路"倡议的提出对中阿旅游发展产生了显著影响，中阿旅游合作迎来了新的发展机遇。在"一带一路"倡议提出之前，中阿旅游合作虽然已经形成一定基础，但整体发展较为缓慢。部分阿拉伯国家政局不稳定、双边旅游合作机制不完善、中阿旅游相关产业基础薄弱等成为制约中阿旅游合作进一步发展的重要因素。"一带一路"倡议促进了中阿之间的文化交流，增进了双方的相互了解，旅游成为文化交流的重要载体。倡议推动了签证便利化、加强了人才培养和旅游信息技术的发展，很大程度上提升了中阿旅游合作的效率和质量。

2017年，中国公民赴阿拉伯国家共133.8万人次，阿拉伯国家公民来华共33.6万人次，同比分别增长9.9%和2.5%；2018年，"一带一路"倡议提出五周年，中阿全方位合作进入新阶段。中阿旅游往来规模不断扩大，中国公民自费组团出境旅游目的地国家名单中，阿拉伯国家已达10个[②]。总体来说，2016—2019年，入境中国大陆的阿拉伯国家公民人数保持稳步上升，中国公民首站出境阿拉伯国家的人数保持了平均10%的增速，并在2019年达到历史峰值[③]。新冠疫情结束之后，中阿旅游合作迅速恢复。摩洛哥、阿联酋、卡塔尔、埃及、突尼斯等国实施对中国游客的免签入境政策，不断开通新航线，吸引越来越多中国游客赴阿拉伯国家旅游，有力促进了中阿之间的民间交流。巴林等诸多阿拉伯国家明确将中国列为重点开拓的旅游市场之一[④]。旅游在中阿命运共同体建构中发挥着日益重要的作用。

---

[①] 《春华秋实二十载 中阿合作再扬帆》，中华人民共和国中央人民政府网，https：//www.gov.cn/yaowen/liebiao/202405/content_6954155.htm，2024年5月29日。

[②] 《牵手"一带一路" 中阿共谋文化和旅游融合发展》，中华人民共和国中央人民政府网，https：//www.gov.cn/xinwen/2018-10/25/content_5334496.htm？use_xbridge3=true&loader_name=forest&need_sec_link=1&sec_link_scene=im，2018年10月25日。

[③] 《中阿旅游市场潜力大，专家建议推动签证便利化、加强人才培养》，澎湃新闻网，https：//www.thepaper.cn/newsDetail_forward_24677749，2023年9月20日。

[④] 《中阿合作20载硕果累累，经贸人文双向奔赴》，荆楚网，https：//news.china.com/socialgd/10000169/20240530/46618377.html，2024年5月30日。

旅游合作同时促进了贸易的发展。中阿旅游合作不仅是游客的流动，还能带动相关产业的发展，如航空运输、餐饮住宿、旅游商品销售等。中国游客在阿拉伯国家旅游期间的消费，推动了当地商业发展；而阿拉伯国家游客来华旅游，也为中国相关产业带来新机遇，促进了双方贸易的活跃。为提升旅游体验，阿拉伯国家借助"一带一路"建设契机，吸引中国资金改善旅游基础设施建设。中国企业参与阿拉伯国家旅游项目投资，建设酒店、景区设施等，双方在旅游领域的资金互动，为旅游合作注入活力。中阿旅游合作借助旅游业"溢出效应"，增进了双方人文关系和文化交流。通过旅游，中国游客深入了解阿拉伯国家的历史文化、风俗习惯，阿拉伯国家游客也对中国文化有了更直观的感受，促进了不同文明间的对话与理解，加深了双方民众之间的友谊和信任。显然，旅游在促进中阿之间的政策沟通、设施联通、贸易畅通、资金融通、民心相通等方面发挥了重要作用。

#### 10.2.1.2　中国—阿拉伯国家合作论坛

中阿合作论坛是中国同阿拉伯国家联盟加强对话与合作、促进和平与发展的重要平台。截至 2024 年 7 月，中国—阿拉伯国家合作论坛已举办 10 届部长级会议、19 次高官会议，并召开了 8 次中阿高官级战略政治对话。2024 年 5 月，中国—阿拉伯国家合作论坛第十届部长级会议在北京举行，会议通过了《中国—阿拉伯国家合作论坛 2024 年至 2026 年行动执行计划》，明确提出中阿将在经贸、投资、旅游、人文交流和文化文明、教育、科技等多个领域加大合作力度，共谋长远发展。随着合作机制的不断成熟与未来发展路径的有序铺展，中阿文化和旅游合作逐渐步入机制健全、互信加深、成果频出的新时代。

旅游合作是推动人文交流合作的重要载体、促进民心相通的重要方式、加强多领域合作的重要推动力。中国—阿拉伯国家合作论坛成立 20 年来，中阿文化和旅游合作更加迅速，丰富多彩的文化艺术交流活动和务实落地的旅游合作计划，切实推动了中阿文化关系发展，增进了中阿人民的相互了解和友好往来，更为共建"一带一路"和构建中阿命运共同体夯实了社会根基和民意基础。探索以旅游合作促进中阿人文交流的道路，为中阿关系的世代友好奠定强大的文化根基，具有重要的理论和现实意义。中国同阿拉伯国家共同设立"全球文明倡议中国—阿拉伯中心"，加快智库联盟、青年发展论坛、大学联盟、文化和旅游合作研究中心等平台建设，实现中国每年邀请阿拉伯国家200名政党领导人访华，未来5年将同阿方力争实现1000万游客互访的合作目标。

#### 10.2.1.3 中国—阿拉伯国家峰会为中阿旅游合作提供有力政策支持

以中国—阿拉伯国家合作论坛为平台，2022年12月，首届中国—阿拉伯国家峰会在沙特首都利雅得举行。此次峰会是中阿关系史上的一座里程碑，双方全力构建面向新时代的中阿命运共同体，标志着中阿关系迈进全面深化发展的新时代。自首届中阿峰会举办以来，双方不断扩大共识、增进互信，中阿关系进入历史最好时期。2022—2024年，中国与巴林、突尼斯、巴勒斯坦等多个阿拉伯国家的双边关系得到提升。目前，中国已同20个阿拉伯国家和阿盟建立了全面战略伙伴关系或战略伙伴关系，阿拉伯地区成为中国战略伙伴最密集的地区之一。① 随着中阿传统友好关系深入发展、政治互信不断加深，中阿各领域合作取得务实成果。

自2022年首届中国—阿拉伯国家峰会以来，中阿基于"八大共同行动"框架，中阿双方积极构建合作机制，为旅游合作提供有力政策支持。力促500家文化和旅游企业开展合作，致力于为阿拉伯国家培养千名文化和旅游人才。近5年，中阿围绕文化和旅游的深度融合，更是连续举办了一系列专业培训，培训近200名阿拉伯旅游界专业人士。

#### 10.2.1.4 中国—阿拉伯国家博览会为中阿旅游务实合作发挥了重要平台作用

中国—阿拉伯国家博览会是经国务院批准，由中国商务部、中国国际贸易促进委员会、宁夏回族自治区人民政府共同主办的国家级、国际性综

---

① 《命运与共 携手同行——首届中阿峰会两周年回望》，新华社，https://www.gov.cn/yaowen/liebiao/202412/content_6994024.htm，2024年12月22日。

合博览会。2013—2023年，以"传承友谊 深化合作 互利共赢 促进发展"为宗旨，宁夏银川已连续成功举办六届中阿博览会，共有112个国家和地区、29位中外政要、383位中外部长级嘉宾以及7500多家国内外企业参会参展，累计签订各类合作项目1616项[1]，合作项目覆盖基础设施、先进农业、生态治理、绿色能源、医疗健康、数字技术、智能制造等多个领域。中国—阿拉伯国家博览会为中阿双方企业相互交流合作搭建了桥梁、创造了条件，有力地促进了中国与包括阿拉伯国家在内的"一带一路"共建国家和地区的经贸投资交流合作，成为中阿共建"一带一路"的重要平台。

2023年9月，第六届中阿博览会中阿旅行商大会在宁夏银川市召开。会议以"共享发展机遇·共促旅游合作·共建'一带一路'"为主题，包括中阿旅游合作论坛、"一带一路"文旅合作推介会等内容，为中外旅游业界务实合作搭建有效平台。中阿双方在旅游政策对接、产业合作、人才培养、市场推广等方面深化合作，签署了多项战略合作协议。[2] 会议推进了中阿在旅游领域共享共赢的发展机遇，增强了国内国际两个市场文旅资源的有效联动，为增进中外旅游业界务实合作发挥了重要的平台作用，充分发挥了推动中阿游客互访、以旅游推动中阿文明交流互鉴、促进中阿民心相通的重要作用。

### 10.2.2　20年来中阿人文交流活动更加频繁

2006年，第一届"阿拉伯艺术节"在北京和南京举行，这是中国与阿盟所有成员国首次在华联合举办的阿拉伯艺术节，也是中国和阿拉伯世界之间第一次大规模的包括阿拉伯艺术展、中阿文化部长圆桌会

---

[1]《2023年第六届中国-阿拉伯国家博览会》，中国—阿拉伯国家博览会网站，https://www.cas-expo.org.cn/zh/preExposite.html，2025年2月8日。

[2]《第六届中阿博览会中阿旅行商大会开幕》，中华人民共和国文化和旅游部网站，https://www.mct.gov.cn/preview/whzx/qgwhxxlb/nx/202309/t20230920_947360.htm，2023年9月20日。

议、阿拉伯艺术演出、阿拉伯服饰和美食展会的文化交流活动，16个阿拉伯国家政府文化代表团和阿盟高级文化代表团共51人及250名阿拉伯艺术家参加艺术节相关活动。2010年，第二届"阿拉伯艺术节"在北京和上海两地举办，艺术节的主题是"艺术交流、文明对话"，主要包括中阿文化论坛、阿拉伯艺术团联合演出和阿拉伯艺术展。参加论坛的阿拉伯国家政府文化代表团还赴宁夏参观访问、考察调研，内容涵盖文化、旅游、艺术等诸多领域。2014年，第三届"阿拉伯艺术节"在北京国家大剧院举行，艺术节以"扩大交流，增进友谊"为宗旨，以"丝路精神 再谱新篇"为主题，开展了论坛、文艺汇演、艺术工作室等多项活动。2018年，第四届"阿拉伯艺术节"中阿城市文化和旅游论坛在成都举行，中国文化和旅游部部长、阿拉伯城市组织秘书长等出席论坛并致辞，中阿业界代表100余人参加论坛。中阿双方代表围绕"文化和旅游：让世界更加和平美好"主题，针对文化和旅游领域多个议题积极分享发展经验，共同探讨伙伴关系，成功开展了中阿城市之间直接而友好的对话。出席论坛的中方14个城市、阿方9个城市代表一致通过《中阿城市文化和旅游合作成都倡议》。[①] 中阿城市文化和旅游论坛的举办是双方积极推动"一带一路"倡议下深入合作的体现，具有重要意义，不但有效推动了中阿城市之间的互相学习和共同发展，扩大了文化和旅游交流合作，而且在建设中阿城际交流机制、打造中阿城市文化和旅游交流品牌、开展城市旅游目的地推广合作等方面达成务实合作，通过积极发挥文化和旅游的桥梁和纽带作用，进一步推进了相关领域的交流合作。第五届阿拉伯艺术节·中阿文化产业论坛在景德镇市举办。中国文化和旅游部部长、江西省省长、阿联酋文化和青年部部长等来自中国和阿拉伯国家政府机构及学界、企业等170名代表以线上线下结合的方式参加论坛。中阿双方代表围绕"融合共进 赋能未来——开创

---

① 《中阿城市文化和旅游论坛举行》，中华人民共和国文化和旅游部网站，https：//www.mct.gov.cn/preview/special/8672/8676/201810/t20181026_835601.htm，2018年10月26日。

中阿文化产业合作新局面"主题，针对数字文化产业、手工艺创新、文创园区开发等特色领域进行交流，对接合作意向，并发布论坛成果《2022中阿文化产业景德镇倡议》①，促进了中阿双方在文化产业领域的深入合作。

2008年，第一届中国艺术节在叙利亚举行，这是在中阿合作论坛框架下举办的重要文化活动之一，标志着中阿互办艺术节机制的正式启动。②2012年，中阿合作论坛第二届中国艺术节在巴林举办。第二届中国艺术节为巴林人民和其他阿拉伯国家的观众了解中国传统与现代的文化和风貌提供良好的平台，进一步加强了中国与巴林两国间的文化交流，促进了中阿文化发展，成为中阿文化关系史上的盛事。③ 2016年，突尼斯举办中阿合作论坛第三届中国艺术节，艺术节开幕式上的口技、杂技、魔术、变脸等中国艺术表演，为突尼斯民众提供了一个领略中国文化魅力的重要机会，也成为包括突尼斯在内的阿拉伯国家的民众了解中国古老文化和现代风貌的新平台。突尼斯斯法克斯举办的中国艺术节，对中突文化交流和中阿文化交流都具有重要的意义，将为中突两国文化交流与互鉴增添新的动力。④

截至2024年6月，中阿共合作举办了5届阿拉伯艺术节、10届中阿关系暨中阿文明对话研讨会等重大文化交流活动，着力打造了"欢乐春节""中阿丝绸之路文化之旅""艺汇丝路"等文旅品牌项目。"汉语热"蔚然成风。中国已同13个阿拉伯国家合作建设21所孔子学院和2所孔子课堂，15个阿拉伯国家在高校开设中文课程，阿联酋、沙特、巴勒斯坦、

---

① 《中阿文化产业论坛成功举办》，中华人民共和国文化和旅游部网站，https://www.mct.gov.cn/whzx/whyw/202212/t20221220_938184.htm，2022年12月20日。
② 《首届中国艺术节在叙利亚举行》，中阿合作论坛网站，http://www.chinaarabcf.org/ltjz/ysj/sjzgysj/200902/t20090220_6914529.htm，2009年2月20日。
③ 《中阿合作论坛第二届中国艺术节在巴林举办》，中阿合作论坛网站，http://www.chinaarabcf.org/zagx/rwjl/201203/t20120329_6842725.htm，2012年3月29日。
④ 《中阿合作论坛第三届中国艺术节在突尼斯开幕》，中华人民共和国文化和旅游部网站，https://www.mct.gov.cn/whzx/bnsj/dwwhllj/201608/t20160829_773179.htm，2016年8月5日。

埃及、突尼斯、吉布提6个阿拉伯国家先后将中文纳入国民教育体系。中阿共同搭建的"中阿典籍互译工程"截至目前已翻译出版50种中阿典籍图书。①

## 10.3 新时期中阿旅游合作趋势分析

中国与阿拉伯国家在旅游领域的合作具有深厚的历史文化基础和广阔的发展前景，结合当前国际旅游趋势及中阿双方发展战略，未来中阿双方可能在以下方面展开深度合作。

### 10.3.1 绿色可持续发展将成为中阿旅游合作的重要内容

近年来，随着荒漠化加剧、极端气候频发、生物多样性丧失等问题逐渐加重，人类生存和发展面临越发严峻的挑战，共谋绿色发展已经受到包括中国和阿拉伯国家在内的国际社会的高度关注。

2020年9月，习近平主席在第七十五届联合国大会上指出，中国将提高国家自主贡献力度，采取更加有力的政策和措施，二氧化碳排放量力争于2030年前达到峰值，努力争取2060年前实现碳中和。② 这充分表明了中国对于保护世界生态环境，应对气候变暖的大国态度与担当。中国通过加速调整产业结构，广泛推广风能和太阳能等清洁能源的研发，致力于低碳技术和应用，通过技术创新减少温室气体排放，促进绿色低碳产业的发展。2023年，迪拜经济和旅游局推出可持续旅游印章认证，在能源和用水效率、废弃物管理以及员工教育等19个方面提出可持续发展标准，目前已有70家酒店获得认证。2024年，阿布扎比文旅局推出碳计算器，强制要求所有阿布扎比的酒店在相关平台提交在油、气、水、电等方面的消

---

① 《深化务实旅游合作，促进中阿人文交流》，中国旅游新闻网，https：//www.ctnews.com.cn/guandian/content/2024-07/12/content_162461.html，2024年7月12日。
② 《减碳，中国设定硬指标》，人民日报网站，https：//www.gov.cn/xinwen/2020-09/30/content_5548478.htm，2020年9月30日。

耗量，并转化成碳排放数据。① 摩洛哥等国已开始借鉴中国沙漠化防治经验。卡塔尔已与中国签署了"美丽多哈"项目合作协议，全面推广中国绿色智能节水灌溉技术与装备。

由此可见，中阿双方均对旅游的可持续发展和创新贡献力量，绿色能源与低碳旅游将是未来双方合作共享的重点领域之一。可以预测，未来中阿双方将秉承可持续发展理念，持续加强旅游方面的深度合作。共同建设生态景区、酒店和景区的可持续电力支持系统、开发沙漠生态旅游线路、在沙漠旅游项目应用太阳能供电技术、推广低碳住宿、发展绿色交通、鼓励游客参与环保活动等。通过推动绿色旅游发展和创新，确保文旅产业发展与环境保护和谐共生，实现长远的旅游可持续发展目标。

### 10.3.2　人工智能技术将在中阿旅游合作中发挥越来越重要的作用

人工智能技术的发展与应用，为旅游产业的发展提供了科技保障。一是人工智能技术在平台建设方面的应用。中阿共同搭建了功能先进的综合服务平台，可向中阿游客提供文旅大数据、人工智能推荐、多语言翻译、无接触支付等服务，游客可以通过平台获取个性化行程规划，享受便捷的服务预订，平台支持多语言交流，使用无接触支付功能保障游客的交易安全。二是人工智能技术在深度挖掘中阿历史文化资源、中阿世界遗产和历史文化名城的数字化复原、中阿文化旅游的数字化展示等方面展示出极大的技术优势。这对于保护世界历史文化资源，增强文化和旅游深度融合发挥了重要作用。三是人工智能技术利用虚拟现实技术（VR）、增强现实技术（AR）、扩展现实技术（XR）等前沿科技开发虚拟游览项目，能够让游客身临其境地感受中国的悠久历史和阿拉伯的古老文明，极大提升了游客的体验感。四是中国科技企业以科技赋能智慧旅游，助力阿拉伯国家建

---

① 《合作推动旅游业创新发展》，人民网-国际频道，http://world.people.com.cn/n1/2024/0511/c1002-40233741.html，2024年5月11日。

设智能旅游基础设施，包括高速网络覆盖、移动支付系统、AI 导游服务等，极大提升了中阿游客的体验感和满意度。

2024 年 5 月，国家主席习近平在出席中阿合作论坛第十届部长级会议开幕式时发表主旨讲话，表达了中国同阿方构建"五大合作格局"的愿望，强调双方应该加强人工智能领域合作，共同促进人工智能赋能实体经济，推动形成具有广泛共识的全球人工智能治理体系。[①] 中国同阿拉伯国家在 5G、人工智能、大数据、云计算等高新领域的合作快速发展，未来将成为中阿旅游合作新的增长点。

### 10.3.3　中阿文化旅游合作领域将更加多元

中国和阿拉伯国家都拥有悠久的历史和灿烂的文化，处于社会经济发展重要阶段，在文化旅游领域有共同的发展目标和巨大的合作潜力。阿曼、沙特等阿拉伯国家都曾是古代海上丝绸之路的重要枢纽，古代丝绸之路为中阿各国留下丰富的历史遗存。展望未来，双方可以围绕丝路遗产展开文化旅游合作，通过联合考古、文化遗产保护等项目，开发"丝路主题"的旅游线路；开发阿拉伯香料文化体验项目；围绕中阿传统节日、非物质文化遗产技艺等设计互动体验活动；利用影视、游戏等数字媒介推广文化旅游 IP；可结合阿拉伯国家独特的自然景观开发温泉疗养、沙漠瑜伽等旅游项目；在中国可与阿拉伯国家共建国际医疗旅游试点，提供高端诊疗服务，吸引阿拉伯游客赴华进行医养康养旅游。相信中阿双方在文化旅游深度合作方面定会迎来更好发展。

### 10.3.4　中阿旅游合作将更加注重旅游专业人才培养

2024 年 5 月，国家主席习近平在出席中阿合作论坛第十届部长级会议时发表的主旨讲话指出，中国愿同阿拉伯国家设立"全球文明倡议中国—

---

[①] 《习近平出席中阿合作论坛第十届部长级会议开幕式并发表主旨讲话》，新华社，https：//www.gov.cn/yaowen/liebiao/202405/content_6954536.htm，2024 年 5 月 30 日。

阿拉伯中心",加快智库联盟、青年发展论坛、大学联盟、文化和旅游合作研究中心等平台建设①,充分显示了未来中阿将在中阿人才培养和科研方面加强合作。

可以预测,中阿双方将依托平台优势,加快构建产学研用合作机制,充分发挥其指导作用和旅游企业的协同育人功能,培养一批既熟悉中阿国情文化,又掌握现代旅游管理与服务技能的复合型人才。② 目前,中阿旅游人才培养的成果大多集中在培养阿语导游、中阿合作办学等方面。今后,可以通过优化旅游教育合作,促进中阿旅游人才共育成长。应增设更多涉及科技、环保、艺术等多领域的交流项目,鼓励中阿旅游相关专业学生参与国际竞赛、志愿服务和创新创业合作,开发更多研学旅游项目,促进中阿各个专业人才加强沟通和相互学习交流,培养并会聚起一批具有国际视野、前瞻视角的多领域技能的旅游专业人才,为中阿旅游合作提供智力支持,发挥人才在中阿旅游合作中的关键作用。展望未来,共同探索数字化时代旅游人才的核心能力,建设高素质的旅游规划、策划、经营和管理人才队伍,提升旅游从业者水平,培养更多国际化复合型旅游专业人才,一定会成为中国与阿拉伯国家加强人才培养合作的重要方面。

---

① 《习近平出席中阿合作论坛第十届部长级会议开幕式并发表主旨讲话》,新华社,https://www.gov.cn/yaowen/liebiao/202405/content_6954536.htm,2024年5月30日。
② 《深化务实旅游合作,促进中阿人文交流》,中国旅游新闻网,https://www.ctnews.com.cn/guandian/content/2024-07/12/content_162461.html,2024年7月12日。

# 第11章　中阿博览会专题报告

2024年5月30日，国家主席习近平在北京出席中阿合作论坛第十届部长级会议开幕式并发表题为《深化合作，继往开来　推动中阿命运共同体建设跑出加速度》的主旨讲话，为中阿团结合作注入力量，推动新时代中阿关系迈上新台阶。这是习近平主席第三次出席中阿合作论坛部长级会议开幕式，也是第五次面向阿拉伯世界进行重要政策宣示。习近平主席强调，中方愿同阿方守望相助，平等互利，包容互鉴，紧密协作，把中阿关系建设成维护世界和平稳定的标杆、高质量共建"一带一路"的样板、不同文明和谐共生的典范、探索全球治理正确路径的表率。[①] 中阿关系处于历史最高水平，中阿全方位合作迎来重大战略机遇。2024年6月10—20日，习近平总书记在宁夏考察时指出："坚持对内对外开放相结合，积极参与共建'一带一路'和西部陆海新通道建设，深化与阿拉伯国家经贸合作，提高内陆开放水平。"[②] 这是新时期宁夏深化高水平对内对外开放、高质量办好中阿博览会的根本遵循和行动指南，中阿博览会理应顺势而为、加速作为，力争在新时代的中阿合作大局中发挥更加重要的作用，力争在新时代推进西部大开发形成新格局中做出新的贡献。

---

[①] 习近平：《深化合作，继往开来　推动中阿命运共同体建设跑出加速度——在中阿合作论坛第十届部长级会议开幕式上的主旨讲话》，《人民日报》2024年5月31日第2版。

[②] 《习近平在宁夏考察时强调 建设黄河流域生态保护和高质量发展先行区 在中国式现代化建设中谱写好宁夏篇章》，《人民日报》2024年6月22日第1版。

## 11.1　中阿博览会发展回顾

中国—阿拉伯国家博览会（以下简称中阿博览会）是中华人民共和国商务部、中国国际贸易促进委员会和宁夏回族自治区人民政府共同主办的国家级、国际性综合博览会，其前身是2010—2012年举办的中国·阿拉伯国家经贸论坛（以下简称中阿经贸论坛）。2013年以来，习近平主席连续5次向中阿博览会致贺信，多次指出中阿博览会为深化中阿务实合作、推动共建"一带一路"高质量发展发挥了积极作用，充分体现出中国政府对办好中阿博览会的重视和支持。随着中阿关系的深入发展和宁夏实践的不断积累，中阿博览会的功能定位从"高度集成中阿多领域合作"向"深化经贸合作"逐步聚焦，服务范围从促进中阿合作到"一带一路"国际合作不断拓展。机制建设方面，科技板块活动从地方经验上升为国家认可的中阿科技交流合作机制，中阿博览会成为中阿共建"一带一路"框架下重要的国际经贸合作机制。

### 11.1.1　聚焦经贸合作：中阿博览会的功能特征

进入21世纪以来，经党中央、国务院批准同意，中国部分地方政府开始举办区域性涉外会展活动，承担在经贸合作领域服务国家总体外交的职能，办会特色和成效十分突出。但从国家和地方层面来看，始终缺少一个主要面向阿拉伯国家开放合作的国家级经贸会展平台。2004年，中阿合作论坛首次举办，中阿双方本着"加强对话与合作、促进和平与发展"的宗旨，广泛开展了政治、经贸、文化、环境等领域的交流与合作，很好地发挥了促进中阿经贸合作的平台效应。但从总体来看，仍缺少一个能够充分发挥非官方力量，进而将政府和民间力量整合起来的中阿经贸合作平台。从阿方视角看，国际、地区和国内政治经济形势的变化，为中阿进一步合作提供了发展机遇和空间。其中，国际层面，中国发展模式得到阿拉伯国家的认可，阿拉伯国家普遍出现了"向东看"趋势，2008年国际金融危机后阿拉伯国家对与中国的经贸合作乃至政治合作有了更多期待；地区层面，2010年底，西亚北非地区陷入动荡，阿拉伯世界总体处于在变革中求稳定、谋发展、惠民生的历史阶段，中国经济的转型升级给中阿合作提供了更大空间，在探索符合各自国情发展道路的过程中，发展与中国的互利合作符合阿拉伯各国的战略利益；国内层面，阿拉伯各国正面临大力加强基础设施建设、实施产业多元化发展战略、加快实现经济转型和改善民生的艰巨任务，深化中阿经贸合作已成为双方实现自身经济发展的战略选择。在此背景下，探索建立深化中阿关系、构建经贸合作平台的现实需要呼之欲出。基于宁夏区位特点、对阿交往实践和经贸合作基础，这一重要使命历史性地落在了宁夏身上。

中阿经贸论坛的功能呈现高度集成性特征。在中阿经贸论坛机制下，其功能模块（活动内容）包含经贸政策沟通、投资贸易、基础设施建设和能源、金融、农业、科技、教育、广电、生态环保合作等，主要服务于三大功能。一是配合国家对阿战略及政策。主要是邀请党和国家领导人出席中阿经贸论坛开幕式并发表主旨讲话，积极承接中阿合作论坛框架下机制性活动，以体现其规格高、有权威性的特色。二是广泛推进中阿多领域合作。中阿经贸论坛以"传承友谊、深化合作、共同发展"为主题，为中阿政府、企业和民间搭建共商经贸交流的高层对话平台，致力于建设中阿经贸合作的国际性新机制。三是推动宁夏内陆开放型经济发展。

中阿博览会的功能呈现出由"高度集成多领域合作"向"聚焦经贸合作"逐步集中的特征。其功能模块以聚焦经贸合作为导向进行优化调整，包括推进中阿共建"一带一路"框架下的经贸促进、产能合作、技术合作等，主要服务于四大功能。一是着力服务国家经贸合作机制和平台建设。积极发挥政府间经贸联委会、中国与阿拉伯国家联合商会等双多边机制作用，充分发挥中阿博览会平台功能，促进中阿双方政府和企业间的互访和交流。二是着力落实中国对阿拉伯国家投资贸易合作政策文件。坚持企业主体、市场主导、政府推动、商业运作的原则，对接中国产能优势和阿拉伯国家需求，与阿拉伯国家开展先进、适用、有效、有利于就业、绿色环保的产能合作，支持阿拉伯国家工业化进程。三是着力构建中阿政府间科技创新合作平台。构建覆盖中国和阿拉伯国家的一体化技术转移协作网络，实施中阿科技伙伴计划，积极推进双方科技成果和先进适用技术在彼此之间的应用和推广。四是着力促进各地方与阿经贸合作。创新活动组织形式，服务全国各省（区、市）"走进阿拉伯国家"开拓市场，服务阿方在中国各地投资合作，扩大双向经贸实效。

### 11.1.2 服务国家战略：中阿博览会的机制建设

2013—2023年，中阿博览会已连续举办6届。为实现好各项功能及作用，中阿博览会主动落实习近平主席在历届中阿合作论坛部长级会议上的重要讲话精神，积极配合实施中国对阿政策文件，形成了促进中阿经贸合作的一系列重要机制。一是围绕国家经贸合作机制和平台建设，充分发挥中阿博览会的经贸政策沟通和项目对接洽谈作用，举办国家级、国际性、机制化的中阿工商峰会，由中国贸促会、阿拉伯农工商会总联盟组织政府部门、重要商协会和各类企业参会参展，密切中阿双方政府和企业间的互访和交流，积极推进贸易投资便利化，形成政策沟通促共识、经贸合作惠民生的良好态势。二是围绕落实中国对阿投资贸易合作政策文件，充分发挥中阿博览会促成企业与境外产业园区招商和政策协调等作用，盘活部分阿拉伯国家的投资优势与中国的产能优势，推进中阿产业和市场双循环，带动中阿双向投资和经贸可持续发展。三是围绕构建中阿政府间科技创新合作平台，率先落实习近平主席在中阿合作论坛第六届部长级会议开幕式上提出的"探讨设立中阿技术转移中心"重要倡议，宁夏回族自治区人民政府与科学技术部于2015年9月共同创办了"中国—阿拉伯国家技术转移与创新合作大会"，共同组建了中国—阿拉伯国家技术转移中心，成为推进中阿科技创新合作的重要机制和务实平台。四是围绕提升服务地方对阿经贸合作能力，创新办会机制，设立"双主宾国""双主题省"，征集全国对阿经贸合作优质案例，全面展示地方经济特色与实力，汇集阿方经贸合作需求，服务全国各省（区、市）开拓阿拉伯国家市场，服务阿方在中国各地的投资合作。2016年1月，习近平主席在访问阿盟总部时指出，中阿博览会成为服务中阿共建"一带一路"的重要平台。

### 11.1.3 共建"一带一路"：中阿博览会的举办成效

中国与阿拉伯国家的合作是全方位、多层次、跨领域的合作，中阿博览会始终坚持"服务国家战略、聚焦经贸合作"的目标导向，已逐渐发展成为以中国和阿拉伯国家为主体，集高层对话、经贸促进、会展洽谈等功能于一体，向全世界开放的国际性博览会，成为推进和落实中阿务实合作的重要平台，在国际社会产生广泛而深远的影响。2019年9月，阿拉伯农工商会总联盟秘书长哈立德·哈纳菲在接受新华社专访时表示，中阿博览会是推进中阿经贸合作的好平台，中国对包括阿拉伯国家在内的世界各国保持开放姿态，将惠及中阿双方。① 中阿博览会为赓续中阿友谊、深化中阿友好合作关系、推动中阿共建"一带一路"合作共识不断凝聚、促进中阿经贸合作高质量发展，深化各省（区、市）对阿多领域合作，助力宁夏对外开放和经济全面发展提速做出了积极贡献，取得了丰硕成果。

一是产能合作取得积极进展。产能合作是中国与阿拉伯国家共建"一带一路"的重点合作领域，也是中阿博览会的重要议题。中国在埃及、沙特、阿曼等阿拉伯国家设立的产业园区则是推进中阿产能合作的重要支点，担负着将中阿发展战略对接落实落地的使命。中阿博览会推动中阿产能合作的主要途径是促成企业与境外产业园区签约并在后续招商和政策协调等方面给予支持。在中阿博览会框架下，中国与埃及、沙特、阿曼产能合作取得初步进展。

其一，2016年5月，宁夏与商务部、中国贸促会在开罗成功举办了中阿博览会走进埃及系列活动，这是宁夏落实习近平主席访埃成果、参与中埃建交60周年庆祝活动的重要举措，第三届中阿博览会邀请埃及担任主

---

① 《中阿务实合作向新领域扬帆起航——访阿拉伯农工商联合会秘书长哈立德》，新华网，http://www.xinhuanet.com/world/2019-09/06/c_1124968827.htm，2019年9月6日。

宾国，推动中埃曼凯纺织产业园落地埃及萨达特市工业城，受到埃及总统塞西的高度赞赏。其二，中国—沙特（吉赞）产业园成为深化中沙产能合作的大型投资项目，在沟通协调机制、园区基础设施建设和招商方面取得进展，首个入园项目广州泛亚聚酯有限公司沙特石油化工化纤一体化项目开工建设。其三，签订了印尼奇拉塔漂浮光伏项目、沙特红海综合智慧能源投资类项目两个，凸显了"聚焦经贸合作·共建一带一路"的平台支撑作用，丰富完善了我国与"一带一路"共建国家经贸、技术、能源合作机制与成果。其四，2024年10月1—7日，宁夏贸促会组织宁夏5家企业参加第26届中东迪拜电力能源、环保、水处理展览会，并带领企业拜访阿联酋、沙特重点经贸部门和机构，就新能源、新材料及相关产业领域等达成多个合作意向，为进一步拓展中东市场奠定了基础。①

二是技术合作不断迈上新台阶。科技、农业合作是中国对阿拉伯国家整体合作的重要组成部分，对于阿拉伯国家发展和改善民生具有战略意义。在中阿博览会框架下创办的中阿技术转移暨创新合作大会、中阿技术转移中心、中阿农业技术转移中心，是集中展示中阿科技合作成果、推进常态化技术转移的主渠道。

其一，中阿技术转移中心促进了中阿在高科技领域的全方位合作，既有利于双方的科技进步和社会发展，也有利于技术相对落后的发展中国家跟上第四次工业革命的时代步伐。在中阿科技合作框架下，中阿技术转移中心推动华为与沙特国王科技城共建联合创新"4G-LTE"实验室，中国与沙特开展卫星导航领域合作，中阿绿色智能控制节水技术平台建设、中阿（约旦）马铃薯科技试验示范基地建设等项目顺利开展。宁夏大学孙兆军团队的绿色智能节水灌溉技术与装备实质性进入阿曼和卡塔尔。2018年10月，宁夏大学与阿曼马斯喀特苏瓦迪（Suwadi）农场签订了节水设备技术转移合作协议和价值1.1亿元人民币的节水灌溉技术转移合同；

---

① 《陆海丝路携手 共创合作商机 宁夏贸促会组织企业走进阿联酋、沙特》，宁夏新闻网，https：//www.nxnews.net/yc/ztyx/202410/t20241015_9855360.html，2024年10月15日。

2020年8月,宁夏大学、卡塔尔纳阿斯(NAAAS)集团、华新国联(北京)企业管理有限公司三方举行"美丽多哈"项目线上签约仪式,项目投资额约12.64亿美元。2021年第五届中阿博览会期间,签署了中阿技术转移协作网络尼日利亚工作基地谅解备忘录、中国—阿拉伯国家(约旦、迪拜)技术转移中心框架合作协议3个;2023年9月举办的第五届中阿技术转移与创新合作大会上,中国面向阿拉伯国家发布了300项先进适用技术,涉及生态环境保护、资源能源利用、污染控制等领域。其二,中阿农业技术转移中心立足宁夏,发挥海外分中心支点作用助力阿拉伯国家农业科技升级。①例如,宁夏在毛里塔尼亚海外分中心开展奶牛胚胎移植、优质牧草、热带水果引进及试种实验;在约旦海外分中心开展了宁夏蔬菜种子栽培示范推广等农业合作,宁夏的蔬菜种子进入中东、非洲12个国家和地区;在摩洛哥海外分中心重点开展鱼粉加工生产、水产品加工贸易领域的试验示范。

三是有力促进了宁夏对外开放。2013年以来,宁夏充分利用中阿博览会积极融入和服务"一带一路"建设,搭建合作平台,深挖贸易潜力,优化投资环境,完善政策支撑,建设开放载体,畅通对外通道,坚持整体推进与重点突破相结合,机制创新与政策引领相结合,在更大范围、更高层次上实现高水平对外开放,推动建设向西开放战略高地,参与"一带一路"建设取得阶段性成果。开放通道功能逐步增强。截至2023年底,银川河东国际机场已开通96个通航城市的140条航线,其中国内航点85个,省会城市直飞率达到100%;国际航点11个,已开通中国香港、迪拜等12条国际(地区)航线。宁夏加强与沿海港口合作,强化与西部陆海新通道省区市交流,初步构建了通边达海、连南接北的陆上开放通道格局,搭建起集国际铁路、铁海联运等多种运输方式于一体的国际货物体系,形成了西北向出境、东南向出海的口岸通道网络,为建设区域性国际

---

① 张帅:《中阿合作论坛框架下的农业合作:特征、动因与挑战》,《西亚非洲》2020年第6期,第98页。

物流中心提供了重要支撑。开放型经济发展水平稳步提升。2013—2023年，宁夏累计利用外资27.1亿美元，年均增速8.2%，在全球36个国家和地区设立对外直接投资企业152家，对外投资总额43.9亿美元，其中在6个阿拉伯国家投资设立了23家境外投资企业，总投资额4.35亿美元。2023年，宁夏与阿拉伯国家进出口额3.2亿元人民币；2024年进口额4.6亿元人民币，同比增长43.7%。①

## 11.2 新形势下中阿博览会面临多重发展机遇

### 11.2.1 高质量共建"一带一路"新机遇

中方持续深化"一带一路"倡议同阿拉伯国家自身发展战略相互对接，中阿高质量共建"一带一路"合作，全面带动中阿关系发展。中国已同所有阿拉伯国家及阿盟秘书处签署了共建"一带一路"合作倡议，实现"全覆盖"。在共建"一带一路"框架下，中阿双方实施了200多个大型合作项目，打造了埃及新行政首都中央商务区、中国沙特延布炼厂、阿布扎比哈利法港二期集装箱码头、阿尔及利亚东西高速公路、摩洛哥穆罕默德六世大桥等一批"旗舰项目"，合作成果惠及双方近20亿人民，有效促进了各国商品、资金、技术、人员的大流通。

### 11.2.2 阿拉伯国家现代化转型带来的新机遇

阿拉伯国家现代化转型是指海湾及中东地区国家为突破传统经济结构依赖（如石油出口）、应对国际竞争压力、提升国家竞争力而实施的系统性改革。其核心是通过经济多元化、社会文化开放、数字化升级和治理模式创新，推动国家从资源驱动型向创新驱动型、从封闭保守型向开放包容

---

① 《政协委员梁万荣：支持宁夏企业与阿拉伯国家开展经贸往来 助力宁夏特产"走出去"》，人民网，http://nx.people.com.cn/n2/2025/0121/c192493-41116040.html，2025年1月21日。

型转变。阿拉伯国家现代化转型为新时期中阿经贸合作带来以下新机遇。

一是能源转型与绿色经济合作。阿拉伯国家普遍将能源多元化作为战略核心，而中国在光伏、风电等清洁能源领域的技术优势与阿拉伯国家的资源禀赋高度互补。双方已合作实施全球最大单体光伏电站（阿联酋宰夫拉太阳能电站）、红海新城储能项目等标志性工程，未来在氢能、核能及智能电网领域的合作潜力巨大。二是数字化转型与新兴产业发展。阿拉伯国家加速推进数字化升级，沙特、阿联酋等国将5G、人工智能、智慧城市列为优先领域。中国企业在云计算、数据中心、工业互联网等数字基建领域具备竞争力，例如华为云通过优化网络延迟和成本助力卡塔尔电商平台发展，富士康与沙特合作布局电动车产业。中阿合作正从传统基建向"数字基建+产业升级"转型，涵盖跨境电商、金融科技、电竞等新兴业态，契合阿拉伯国家年轻人口红利与消费习惯变化。三是基础设施互联互通升级。阿拉伯国家在电力、交通、住房等领域存在大规模基建需求，中国企业在传统基建（如铁路、港口）和新兴领域（如海水淡化、光伏产业园）的综合优势持续凸显。例如，中国电建承建的沙特红海公用基础设施项目融合多能源互补技术，成为绿色基建典范。中阿基建合作正从"工程承包"向"建设—投资—运营"一体化模式转型，推动"中国建造"品牌在阿拉伯市场深化。四是金融合作与人民币国际化。中阿金融合作从贸易结算向多层次资本联动扩展，中国与阿拉伯国家签署本币互换协议，人民币在阿盟支付体系中的占比提升。中阿银行联合体、丝路基金等平台为能源、基建项目提供融资支持，同时，沙特、阿联酋等国金融机构加速进入中国市场。此外，阿拉伯金融市场开放为中资机构拓展海外业务提供契机，例如参与当地证券交易所和绿色债券发行。五是消费品市场与多元化投资。阿拉伯国家人口年轻化（平均年龄30岁）及"她经济""健康消费"等趋势推动消费品市场扩张。中国在家电、纺织、数字经济产品等领域具有价格与技术优势，可通过本土化策略（如定制化产品、节日营销）抢占市场份额。同时，阿拉伯国家经济多元化政策减少对石油出口的依赖，中企在制造业、农业科技、医疗健康等领域的投资空间扩大，例如埃及的可再生能源合作园区和约旦的医疗项目。

### 11.2.3 西部地区对内对外开放新机遇

2024年4月23日下午，习近平总书记在重庆主持召开新时代推动西部大开发座谈会并发表重要讲话。习近平总书记强调："要坚持以大开放促进大开发，提高西部地区对内对外开放水平。大力推进西部陆海新通道建设，推动沿线地区开发开放，深度融入共建'一带一路'。完善沿边地区各类产业园区、边境经济合作区、跨境经济合作区布局，推动自贸试验区高质量发展。稳步扩大制度型开放，打造市场化法治化国际化营商环境。更加主动服务对接区域重大战略，积极融入全国统一大市场建设，创新东中西部开放平台对接机制，深化与东中部、东北地区务实合作。"[1]为一以贯之抓好党中央推动西部大开发政策举措的贯彻落实，进一步形成大保护、大开放、高质量发展新格局，西部各省（区、市）以共建"一带一路"为引领，加强东、中、西部协同合作，因地制宜发挥各自特色优势，加大西部开放力度。

### 11.2.4 可持续发展与绿色合作新机遇

中阿双方坚持可持续发展，持续推进绿色创新。中国同阿拉伯国家一道践行全球发展倡议，共同迈向创新、协调、绿色、开放、共享的发展新阶段。中阿技术转移、清洁能源、北斗卫星、干旱、荒漠化和土地退化国际研究等中心的陆续成立，在阿联酋等国家建立了8个技术转移双边中心，形成了连接数千家中阿科研机构和创新企业的技术转移协作网络。中阿双方应进一步挖掘绿色低碳、信息通信、航空航天、数字经济、人工智能等新兴和高技术领域合作潜力，促进数字技术和实体经济融合，为双方可持续发展注入不竭动力。

---

[1] 《习近平主持召开新时代推动西部大开发座谈会强调 进一步形成大保护大开放高质量发展新格局 奋力谱写西部大开发新篇章 李强蔡奇丁薛祥出席》，《人民日报》2024年4月24日第1版。

## 11.3 新形势下办好中阿博览会的思路

### 11.3.1 指导思想

以习近平新时代中国特色社会主义思想为指导，全面贯彻落实党的二十大和党的二十届二中、三中全会精神，认真贯彻落实习近平总书记考察宁夏时的重要讲话精神，坚持对内对外开放相结合，积极参与共建"一带一路"和西部陆海新通道建设，培育开放型经济主体，营造开放型经济环境，提高内陆开放水平，深化与阿拉伯国家经贸合作，将中国式现代化在产能、技术、高科技等领域的优秀成果，与阿拉伯国家现代化的具体需求高效衔接起来，形成央地高质量协作推进中阿合作总体格局，为推动构建面向新时代的中阿命运共同体、奋力谱写中国式现代化宁夏篇章做出新的贡献。

### 11.3.2 总体思路

随着中阿关系的深入发展和宁夏实践的不断积累，中阿博览会的功能定位从"高度集成中阿多领域合作"向"深化经贸合作"逐步聚焦，服务范围从促进宁阿合作、中阿合作到"一带一路"国际合作不断拓展，成为推动中阿共建"一带一路"的重要平台。未来十年，中阿博览会将高举人类命运共同体旗帜，传承和弘扬丝路精神，坚持目标导向、行动导向，以落实中阿务实合作"八大共同行动"和"五大合作格局"为指引，积极构建功能定位更趋完善、办会机制务实创新、服务水平显著提升、合作基础更加坚实、经贸实效更为突出的升级版中阿博览会，扎实推进中阿高质量共建"一带一路"不断取得新的更大成效，为宁夏高水平开放和高质量发展做出更大贡献。

在习近平主席同阿方领导人战略引领下，当前中阿关系处于历史最好时期，中阿全方位、多层次、宽领域合作格局不断充实和深化。中国共产党宁夏回族自治区第十三届委员会第十次全体会议指出："主动融入和服务高质量共建'一带一路',稳步扩大制度型开放,积极参与西部陆海新通道建设,进一步深化区域战略合作,为经济社会发展增添新动力、拓展新空间。"[1] 在此背景下,中阿博览会迎来重大战略机遇,应顺势而为、练好内功、加速作为,力争在新时代的中阿合作大局中发挥更加重要的作用,注重做好"五个统筹"。

一是统筹继承和创新。维护好中阿博览会朋友圈,夯实高质量发展根基,做精做实存量活动;着力提升创新发展能力,聚焦新时代中阿合作格局,打造特色增量活动。二是统筹政府和市场。坚持"政府引导、市场运作、企业主体、合作共赢"的协调推进原则,充分激发各方参与中阿博览会的积极性。三是统筹双边和多边。秉持"多边谈合作、双边促落实"工作思路,与阿方共同推动落实中阿峰会和中阿合作论坛部长级会议议定事项,着力提升中阿博览会框架下活动与双边经贸合作议程有效对接、协同增效,以双边促多边,通过双边合作、三方合作、多边合作等各种形式,增强经贸合作的有效性。四是统筹规模和效益。稳步提升中阿博览会的规模和效益,将"小而美"项目作为合作优先事项,多搞投资小、见效快、经济社会环境效益好的项目,形成更多接地气、聚人心合作成果。五是统筹发展和安全。牢固树立和践行总体国家安全观,完善风险防控制度机制,强化统筹协调,压实各方责任,做好要素保障,不断提高应对风险、迎接挑战、化险为夷的能力水平。

### 11.3.3 功能定位

一是服务中阿经贸合作的主要机制。加强国家层面中阿经贸合作机制统筹,明确中阿博览会作为对内对外集中统一的对阿经贸合作机制和综合服务平台功能定位;加强省区层面中阿经贸合作机制协同,通过建立互利合作关系、轮流举办机制,优化配置会议论坛等经贸合作资源,着力提升

---

[1] 《自治区党委十三届十次全会暨党委经济工作会议在银川召开全会由自治区党委常委会主持 李邑飞作报告并讲话 张雨浦安排明年经济工作》,《宁夏日报》2024年12月26日第1版。

中阿博览会平台功能。

二是推进中阿高质量共建"一带一路"的重要平台。以推动构建面向新时代的中阿命运共同体为战略目标，聚焦中阿高质量共建"一带一路"重点合作领域，盘活中国对阿经贸合作总体资源，适配阿拉伯国家发展需求，协同落实新时代中阿合作的战略、规划、政策和项目，将中阿博览会打造成中阿高质量共建"一带一路"的重要平台。

三是助推宁夏高水平开放的重要引擎。深入贯彻落实习近平总书记历次考察宁夏时的重要讲话精神，巩固宁夏对阿合作基础，充分发挥对阿合作特色和优势，完善与其他省份开放平台对接机制，抢抓东部地区资金、技术、产业向中西部转移的重大机遇，因地制宜构建特色化、差异化的现代化产业体系，形成高水平开放工作任务与中阿博览会开放平台功能有效融合的发展态势。

## 11.4 新形势下办好中阿博览会的路径

按照总体思路、功能定位和发展目标，重点完成深度融入和服务中阿高质量共建"一带一路"、提升投资贸易创新发展水平、统筹构建数字经济合作新机制、助推宁夏高水平对内对外开放等工作任务。

### 11.4.1 深度融入和服务中阿高质量共建"一带一路"

加强战略及政策研究。全面梳理习近平主席五次对阿拉伯世界政策宣示和中阿多双边合作政策文件内容，结合中阿博览会功能定位及其机制性活动特点，研究制订中阿博览会落实中阿高质量共建"一带一路"的行动计划和工作方案，推动中阿博览会框架下活动常办常新。系统研究"一带一路"国际经贸合作机制和国内国际机制性论坛博览会先进经验，以推进中阿经贸合作为出发点，商建立体多维、务实管用的战略合作关系，加快补齐中阿博览会筹办工作短板，全面提升对阿经贸合作资源整合能力。

增强对接协调有效性。更大力度协同商务部和中国贸促会支持，推动商务部、中国贸促会与宁夏签署深化对阿经贸合作的框架协议，积极发挥中阿政府间经贸联委会、中国与阿拉伯国家联合商会等双多边机制作用，充分发挥中阿博览会平台功能，促进中阿双方政府和企业间的互访和交流。积极争取外交部支持，协调中阿合作论坛框架下机制性经贸促进活动在宁夏举办，继续保持中阿博览会规格和影响力。

### 11.4.2 提升投资贸易创新发展水平

持续提升贸易投资促进平台能级。争取国家发展改革委、商务部、丝路基金、亚投行及相关央企支持，高水平、高质量办好"一带一路"贸易投资促进大会，凸显和强化大会作为中阿共建"一带一路"框架下引领投资贸易创新发展方向的平台、政策机制探索平台、合作项目发布平台、国际交流合作平台的定位功能，在保持国内各类专业元素集聚的基础上，持续邀请国内外国际组织、行业协会、企业家等出席并发表主旨演讲，根据大会主题组织策划高质量对接活动，提高大会举办实效，推动中阿构建更具规模的投资金融格局、更为平衡的经贸互惠格局。

探索建立中国—海合会经贸中心。研究组建中国—海合会经贸中心的必要性和可行性，总体思路是将其打造成为中国—海合会经贸合作"一站式"服务平台，依托海关特殊监管区域，吸引中国与海合会国家商协会、知名企业以及国际机构等入驻，提供商贸投资、法务服务、金融、物流、数字信息、农业经济合作、文旅合作、专业人才等服务。

研究推行线上线下融合办展新模式。大力推动展会项目数字化转型，在中阿博览会会期举办"云展览"，提升展示、宣传、洽谈等效果。设立展览交易服务平台，配套建设海关监管保税仓库，运用"前店后仓"模式，直接对接展商和创新交易模式，会前在展览交易服务平台先行展销，会中在展馆内展出，会后实行延期展览销售，探索线上线下同步互动、有机融合的办展新模式。

建立市场化办会办展机制和非会期常态化办展机制。坚持市场主导和政府引导的基本原则，系统改革中阿博览会会展工作体制机制，积极探索专业化、市场化、国际化、数字化路径，建立市场化办会办展机制和非会期常态化办会办展机制。招展方面，组建专业招展队伍，用好战略性合作伙伴资源拓宽招展渠道，引入先进产品技术；紧紧围绕服务国家战略和民生需要设立展览专区；成立参展商联盟，组建相关领域专业委员会；展位施行市场化的定价机制。招商方面，利用市场化机制组建行业和联合交易团，通过路演招商、对接会招商等措施增强采购商主动性，以绩效考核、佣金激励等手段推进合作单位协助招商。中阿博览会开幕式及"一带一路"贸易投资促进大会，稳步推进市场化的"会员制+注册制"，加大国际知名专家邀请力度，提升国际化水平。现场服务方面，全面实现市场化运作，通过市场化采购方式，引入专业服务商。

### 11.4.3 统筹构建数字经济合作新机制

筹办中国—阿拉伯国家数字经济合作论坛。着眼于推动中国式现代化与阿拉伯国家现代化良性互动，在中阿博览会框架下，高规格、高水平策划举办中阿数字经济合作论坛及配套活动，推动数字经济发展战略对接，为阿拉伯国家政府和企业提供云计算、人工智能算力算法等服务，推动数字基础设施、电子商务、移动支付、数字文化产业、智慧城市、远程教育和数字人才培养等领域务实合作。

深度参与"丝路电商"交流合作。对接上海市"丝路电商"合作先行区建设，在中阿博览会框架下开展"丝路电商"本土化、合规化运营交流、"丝路电商"智库研修交流，推动更多阿拉伯国家与中国建立电子商务合作机制，畅通中阿电子商务交流合作，促进中国"跨境电商+产业带"融合发展，带动中国跨境电商企业、数字技术、数字商业模式、先进物流系统落地阿拉伯国家，提高中国产业链供应链的国际竞争力。

### 11.4.4 高质量促进中阿科技创新与技术转移

支持中阿技术转移与创新合作大会越办越好。探索科技合作新机制新模式，连接科技创新高端资源，推动中阿在生命健康、人工智能、绿色低碳、现代农业、空间信息等领域共建联合实验室，共建空间碎片联合观测中心、北斗应用合作发展中心，加强载人航天、民用客机等合作，提升区域创新能力水平，打造更富活力的创新驱动格局。

支持中阿技术转移中心高水平常态化运行。持续拓展中阿技术转移协作网络，力争用10年时间达到技术转移海外双边中心在阿拉伯国家全覆盖；对接中阿干旱、荒漠化和土地退化国际研究中心，联合举办论坛研讨会，推动技术成果转移；加强与中阿农业技术转移中心协同，推动同阿方共建现代农业联合实验室，开展农业技术合作示范项目，向阿方派遣农业技术专家，帮助阿方增加粮食产量、提高收储减损能力、提升农业生产效率；加强中阿技术转移中心能力建设，争取科技部和宁夏回族自治区政府专项资金支持，加大专业技术人才培训及储备力度，做实做深技术转移工作。

### 11.4.5 助推宁夏高水平对内对外开放

策划举办中国内陆地区高水平开放专题论坛。邀请甘肃、青海、新疆、陕西、内蒙古、贵州等内陆地区省份，东部地区自贸试验区管理委员会，以及国家发展改革委、商务部等国家部委，共同研究落实《进一步推动西部大开发形成新格局的若干政策措施》《中共中央 国务院关于新时代推进西部大开发形成新格局的指导意见》的具体措施，发挥各自特色优势，以共建"一带一路"为引领，加大内陆地区开放力度，加强东、中、西部协作，积极参与西部陆海新通道建设，构建内陆多层次开放平台，建立东、中、西部开放平台对接机制，推动西部地区对外开放由商品和要素流动型逐步向规则制度型转变。

# 第12章 宁夏对外开放专题报告

2013年以来，宁夏积极融入共建"一带一路"，聚焦大项目、大平台、大通道、大数据建设，发挥内陆开放型经济试验区及中阿博览会国家级平台作用，坚持对内对外、平台通道、硬件软件、外贸外资一起抓，构建内陆开放型经济新格局，有力促进了宁夏更宽领域、更深层次、更高水平对外开放。

## 12.1 宁夏开放型经济稳步推进

### 12.1.1 经济质效全面提升

2024年，宁夏地区生产总值为5502.8亿元人民币，同比增长5.4%，居全国第14位，连续10个季度超过全国平均水平。第一产业增加值增长6.2%、居全国第四，第二产业增加值增长7%、居全国第五。规上工业增加值增长9.6%、居全国第三，固定资产投资增长7.9%、居全国第三，社会消费品零售总额增长5%、居全国第六，地方一般公共预算收入517亿元人民币、增长2.8%，其中地方税收增速居全国第八。以上指标均高于全国平均水平。第三产业增加值、建筑业增加值、进出口总额等稳步回升，商品房销售面积等止跌企稳。与此同时，居民人均可支配收入增长5.5%、居全国第六，超过经济增速；城镇化率达68.2%，高于全国平均水平。由图12.1、图12.2、图12.3可以看出，宁夏地区生产总值从2013年的2328亿元人民币增长到2024年的5503亿元人民币，

## 第12章 宁夏对外开放专题报告

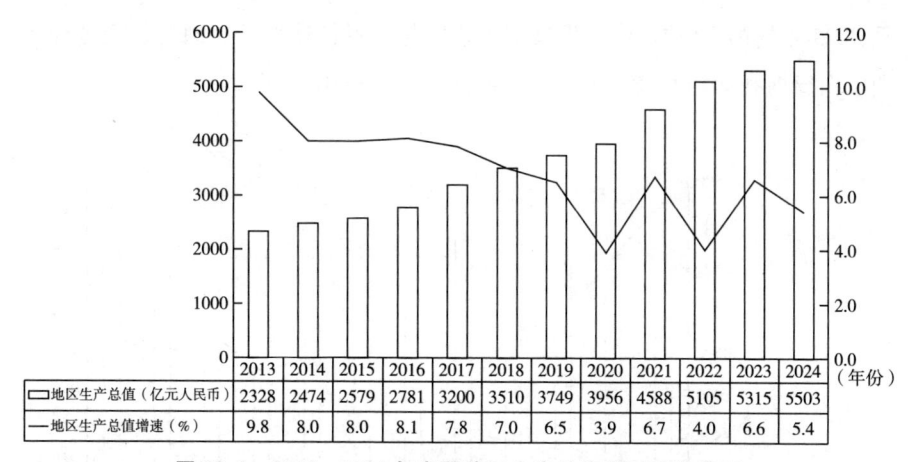

| 年份 | 2013 | 2014 | 2015 | 2016 | 2017 | 2018 | 2019 | 2020 | 2021 | 2022 | 2023 | 2024 |
|---|---|---|---|---|---|---|---|---|---|---|---|---|
| 地区生产总值（亿元人民币） | 2328 | 2474 | 2579 | 2781 | 3200 | 3510 | 3749 | 3956 | 4588 | 5105 | 5315 | 5503 |
| 地区生产总值增速（%） | 9.8 | 8.0 | 8.0 | 8.1 | 7.8 | 7.0 | 6.5 | 3.9 | 6.7 | 4.0 | 6.6 | 5.4 |

**图 12.1　2013—2024 年宁夏地区生产总值发展变化情况**

资料来源：根据国家统计局官方数据库、中国与宁夏统计年鉴数据计算所得。其中 2004、2005、2006、2010、2011、2020 年人均地区生产总值增速为估算值。

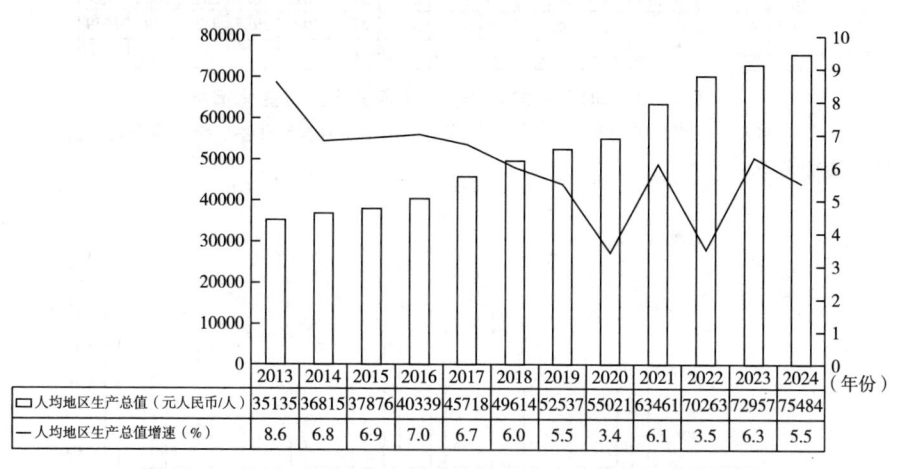

| 年份 | 2013 | 2014 | 2015 | 2016 | 2017 | 2018 | 2019 | 2020 | 2021 | 2022 | 2023 | 2024 |
|---|---|---|---|---|---|---|---|---|---|---|---|---|
| 人均地区生产总值（元人民币/人） | 35135 | 36815 | 37876 | 40339 | 45718 | 49614 | 52537 | 55021 | 63461 | 70263 | 72957 | 75484 |
| 人均地区生产总值增速（%） | 8.6 | 6.8 | 6.9 | 7.0 | 6.7 | 6.0 | 5.5 | 3.4 | 6.1 | 3.5 | 6.3 | 5.5 |

**图 12.2　2013—2024 年宁夏人均地区生产总值发展变化情况**

资料来源：根据国家统计局官方数据库、中国与宁夏统计年鉴、统计局及统计公报数据计算所得。

绝对值扩大到 2.36 倍，年均增长 8.98%；人均地区生产总值从 2013 年的 35135 元人民币增长至 2024 年的 75484 元人民币，绝对值扩大到 2.15 倍，平均增长 7.95%；固定资产投资额由 2013 年的 2681 亿元人民币增长到 2024 年的 3659 亿元人民币，投资额总量为 2013 年的 1.36 倍，经济发展取得了显著成就。横向看，宁夏人均地区生产总值排名由 2013 年的全国第 21 位上升

217

至2024年的第20位，经济发展实现速度与总量快速增长，同时，全区经济向实向绿向智向新步伐明显加快，质效与格局全面提升。

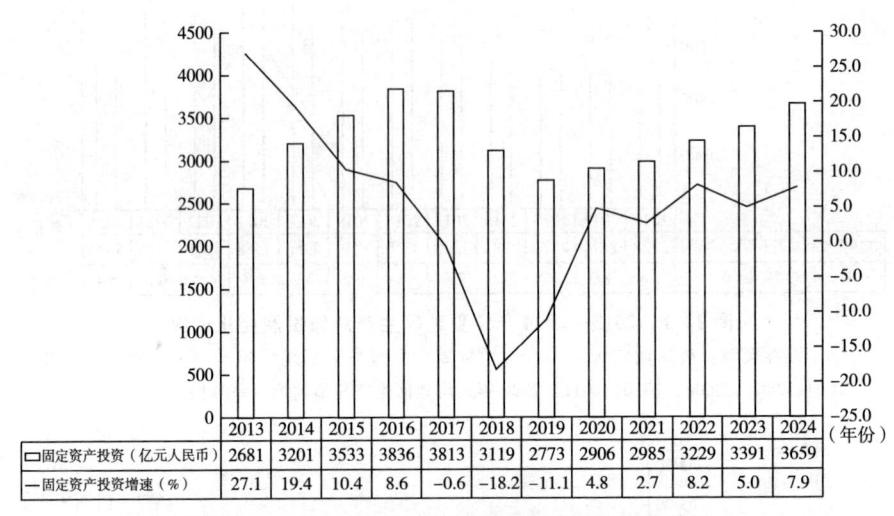

图 12.3　2013—2024 年宁夏固定资产投资变化情况

| 年份 | 2013 | 2014 | 2015 | 2016 | 2017 | 2018 | 2019 | 2020 | 2021 | 2022 | 2023 | 2024 |
|---|---|---|---|---|---|---|---|---|---|---|---|---|
| 固定资产投资（亿元人民币） | 2681 | 3201 | 3533 | 3836 | 3813 | 3119 | 2773 | 2906 | 2985 | 3229 | 3391 | 3659 |
| 固定资产投资增速（%） | 27.1 | 19.4 | 10.4 | 8.6 | -0.6 | -18.2 | -11.1 | 4.8 | 2.7 | 8.2 | 5.0 | 7.9 |

资料来源：根据国家统计局官方数据库、中国与宁夏统计年鉴、统计局及统计公报数据计算所得。

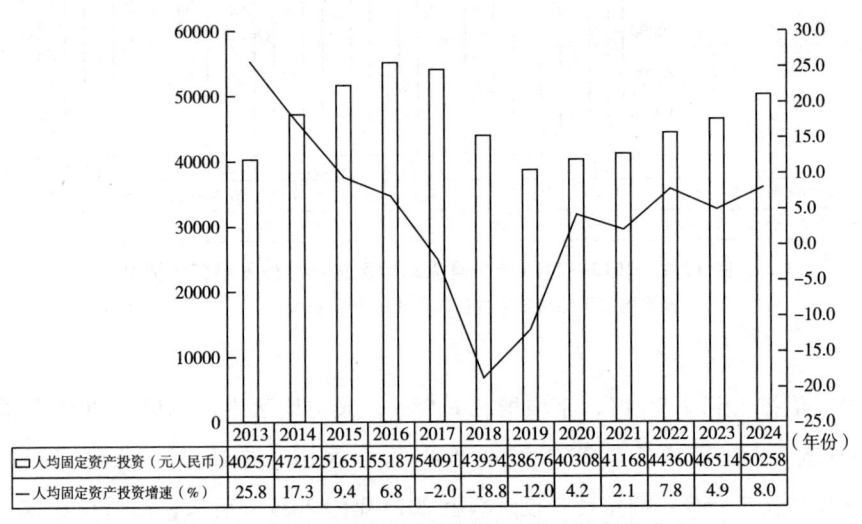

图 12.4　2013—2024 年宁夏固定资产投资变化情况

| 年份 | 2013 | 2014 | 2015 | 2016 | 2017 | 2018 | 2019 | 2020 | 2021 | 2022 | 2023 | 2024 |
|---|---|---|---|---|---|---|---|---|---|---|---|---|
| 人均固定资产投资（元人民币） | 40257 | 47212 | 51651 | 55187 | 54091 | 43934 | 38676 | 40308 | 41168 | 44360 | 46514 | 50258 |
| 人均固定资产投资增速（%） | 25.8 | 17.3 | 9.4 | 6.8 | -2.0 | -18.4 | -12.0 | 4.2 | 2.1 | 7.8 | 4.9 | 8.0 |

资料来源：根据国家统计局官方数据库、中国与宁夏统计年鉴、统计局及统计公报数据计算所得。

## 12.1.2 产业结构不断优化

投资结构不断优化，综合竞争力不断增强。持续加强现代煤化工基地建设，宁东基地成为西部首个产值超过2000亿元的化工园区，综合竞争力位列全国第三，入选国家先进制造业集群。高端装备制造业不断壮大，吴忠仪表等3家企业入选全国首批卓越级智能工厂，制造业质量竞争力指数排名西北第二，创历史最高水平。"六特"产业稳步发展，特色农牧业产值占农业总产值超过88%，酒庄酒、枸杞深加工产品产量保持全国首位，蒙牛宁夏全数智化工厂获评全球首个乳业"灯塔工厂"。资源能源开发利用力度不断加大，煤炭产量首次突破1亿吨、居全国第八；新增新能源发电超530万千瓦，绿电装机占比提高到55%。大唐源网荷储一体化等11个绿电园区加快推进，宁夏首个万吨级绿氢一体化、异质结太阳能电池等高新技术项目开工建设，域内投资700亿元的"宁电入湘"工程宁夏段全线贯通。这些标志性工程项目，为产业结构不断优化积蓄了强大后劲，由图12.5可以看出，2013—2024年宁夏三次产业结构比例逐渐得到优化。三次产业结构由2013年的9.1∶45.5∶45.4变为2024年的8.2∶42.4∶49.4，实现了产业结构从"二三一"向"三二一"转变，"三二一"格局比较稳定，走出了一条具有当地特色的产业发展道路，工业和服务业双轮支撑格局基本形成。总体来看，宁夏产业结构处在由初级向高级演变的过渡阶段，经济发展处在工业化中期发力阶段。

## 12.1.3 外贸外资较快发展

**1. 外贸发展**

2024年，据银川海关统计，宁夏实现进出口206.1亿元人民币，同比增长0.3%，增速排名全国第26位、西部省区市第11位，实现止跌回稳，其中54家企业的外贸值超1亿元人民币，比2023年增加12家。招商引资到位资金1854亿元人民币。银川综合保税区完成进出口贸易额25.8亿元人民币，同比增长20.6%；规上产值2.89亿元人民币，同比增长28.3%。宁夏21家企

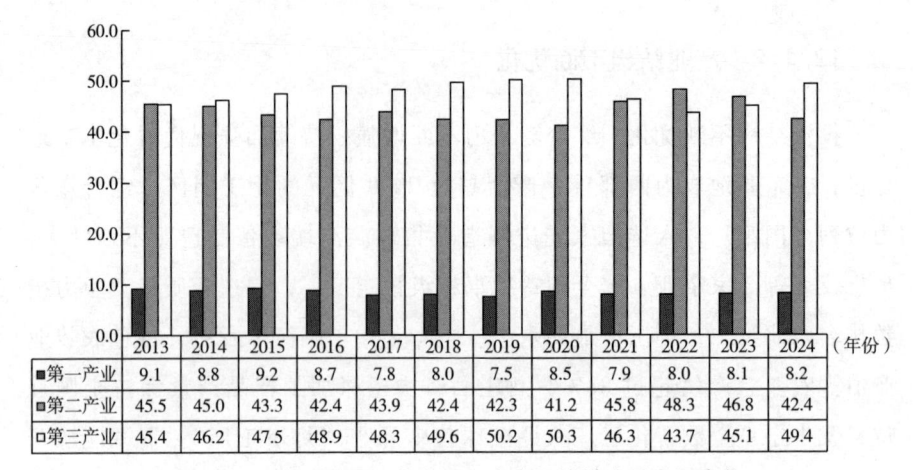

图 12.5  2013—2024 年宁夏三次产业结构比重发展变化

| 年份 | 2013 | 2014 | 2015 | 2016 | 2017 | 2018 | 2019 | 2020 | 2021 | 2022 | 2023 | 2024 |
|---|---|---|---|---|---|---|---|---|---|---|---|---|
| 第一产业 | 9.1 | 8.8 | 9.2 | 8.7 | 7.8 | 8.0 | 7.5 | 8.5 | 7.9 | 8.0 | 8.1 | 8.2 |
| 第二产业 | 45.5 | 45.0 | 43.3 | 42.4 | 43.9 | 42.4 | 42.3 | 41.2 | 45.8 | 48.3 | 46.8 | 42.4 |
| 第三产业 | 45.4 | 46.2 | 47.5 | 48.9 | 48.3 | 49.6 | 50.2 | 50.3 | 46.3 | 43.7 | 45.1 | 49.4 |

资料来源：根据国家统计局官方数据库、中国与宁夏统计年鉴、统计局及统计公报数据计算所得。

业上榜《出口商品品牌认证名录（2024）》数量居全国第四，西部第一。由图 12.6 可以看出，2013—2024 年，宁夏外贸总额在新冠疫情之后总体呈恢复增长趋势，但进出口贸易比例结构还不尽合理，出口总额为 150.8 亿元人民币，进口总额仅为 55.3 亿元人民币；对外贸易依存度也较低，仅有 3.8%。

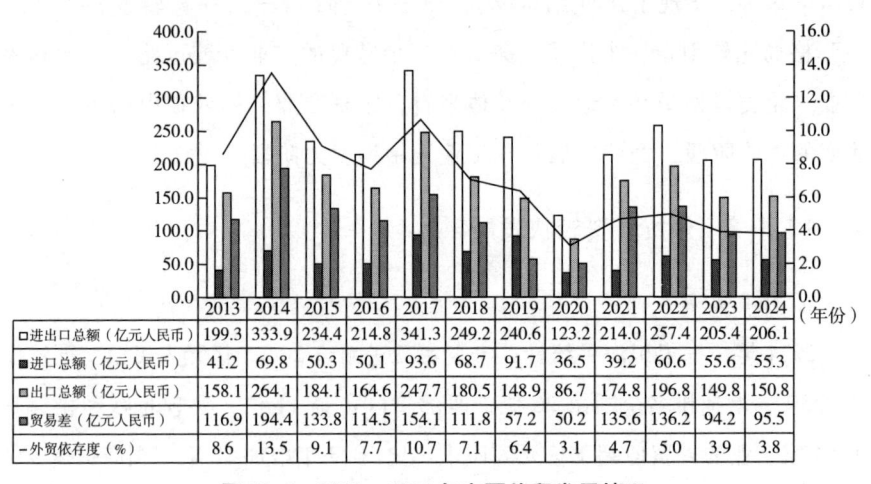

图 12.6  2013—2024 年宁夏外贸发展情况

| 年份 | 2013 | 2014 | 2015 | 2016 | 2017 | 2018 | 2019 | 2020 | 2021 | 2022 | 2023 | 2024 |
|---|---|---|---|---|---|---|---|---|---|---|---|---|
| 进出口总额（亿元人民币） | 199.3 | 333.9 | 234.4 | 214.8 | 341.3 | 249.2 | 240.6 | 123.2 | 214.0 | 257.4 | 205.4 | 206.1 |
| 进口总额（亿元人民币） | 41.2 | 69.8 | 50.3 | 50.1 | 93.6 | 68.7 | 91.7 | 36.5 | 39.2 | 60.6 | 55.6 | 55.3 |
| 出口总额（亿元人民币） | 158.1 | 264.1 | 184.1 | 164.6 | 247.7 | 180.5 | 148.9 | 86.7 | 174.8 | 196.8 | 149.8 | 150.8 |
| 贸易差（亿元人民币） | 116.9 | 194.4 | 133.8 | 114.5 | 154.1 | 111.8 | 57.2 | 50.2 | 135.6 | 136.2 | 94.2 | 95.5 |
| 外贸依存度（%） | 8.6 | 13.5 | 9.1 | 7.7 | 10.7 | 7.1 | 6.4 | 3.1 | 4.7 | 5.0 | 3.9 | 3.8 |

资料来源：根据国家统计局官方数据库、中国与宁夏统计年鉴、统计公报及海关数据计算所得。

从外贸结构看，民营企业占据市场主体，结构不断优化，外贸基本盘稳固，活力不断增强。全区有进出口实绩的企业713家，增长21.3%。其中民营企业659家，较上年增加131家，增长24.8%。2024年，民营企业进出口161.9亿元人民币，增长10.9%，高于全区增速10.6个百分点，占宁夏进出口总值（下同）的78.6%，较上年提升7.5个百分点。外资、国有企业进出口分别为28.2亿元人民币、16亿元人民币，分别占13.6%、7.8%。

从贸易伙伴看，外贸广度不断拓展，形成多元发展。2024年，宁夏有贸易往来的国家和地区超过150个，对东盟进出口34.8亿元人民币，增长0.4%，占16.9%；对欧盟进出口31.6亿元人民币，占15.3%；对中国香港地区进出口14.4亿元人民币，增长304%，占7%。对中东、非洲、南美洲等新兴市场贸易增长强劲，进出口增速分别为32.3%、27.5%和5.1%，增速远高于传统市场。此外，对"一带一路"共建国家合作扩大，进出口增速高于整体，占比达45.5%，形成良好的外贸支撑。

从产品结构看，优势特色产业进出口持续扩增。进口方面，金属矿砂增长14.3%，占2024年宁夏进口总值（下同）的20.2%，其中锰矿砂和铌、钽或钒矿砂分别增长22.4%和20.0%，分别位列全国同类商品进口值的第二、第三；石英增长22.7%，占14.1%；农产品增长3.9%，占11.5%。出口方面，基本有机化学品增长28.8%，占2024年宁夏出口总值的21.9%；农产品出口增长23.3%，占11.7%，其中蔬菜及食用菌增长24.1%，占5.7%。枸杞、冷冻马铃薯、葡萄酒分别位列全国同类商品出口值的第一位、第四位、第四位，为宁夏优势特色产业发展打下了良好基础。

2. 利用外资

启动"外资三年外贸五年倍增计划"。2024年，宁夏新设外商直接投资企业23家，实际利用外商投资额3亿美元。由图12.7、图12.8、图12.9、图12.10、图12.11可知，2013年以来宁夏累计实际利用外资

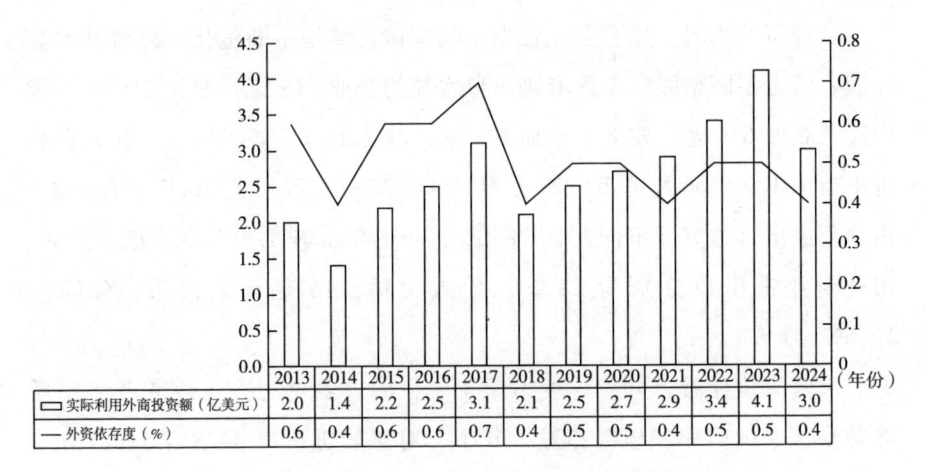

| 年份 | 2013 | 2014 | 2015 | 2016 | 2017 | 2018 | 2019 | 2020 | 2021 | 2022 | 2023 | 2024 |
|---|---|---|---|---|---|---|---|---|---|---|---|---|
| 实际利用外商投资额（亿美元） | 2.0 | 1.4 | 2.2 | 2.5 | 3.1 | 2.1 | 2.5 | 2.7 | 2.9 | 3.4 | 4.1 | 3.0 |
| 外资依存度（%） | 0.6 | 0.4 | 0.6 | 0.6 | 0.7 | 0.4 | 0.5 | 0.5 | 0.4 | 0.5 | 0.5 | 0.4 |

**图 12.7　2013—2024 年宁夏实际利用外资投资额变化情况**

资料来源：根据国家统计局官方数据库、中国与宁夏统计年鉴、统计公报数据计算所得。

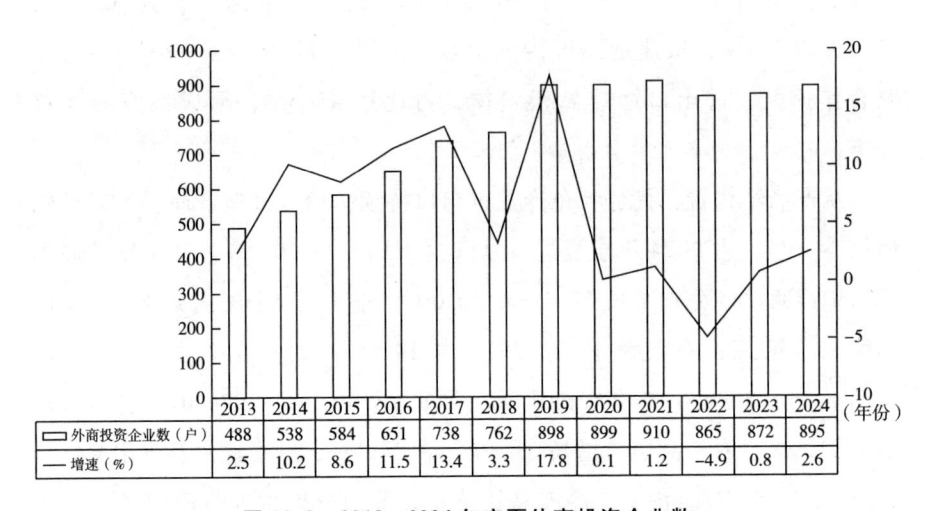

| 年份 | 2013 | 2014 | 2015 | 2016 | 2017 | 2018 | 2019 | 2020 | 2021 | 2022 | 2023 | 2024 |
|---|---|---|---|---|---|---|---|---|---|---|---|---|
| 外商投资企业数（户） | 488 | 538 | 584 | 651 | 738 | 762 | 898 | 899 | 910 | 865 | 872 | 895 |
| 增速（%） | 2.5 | 10.2 | 8.6 | 11.5 | 13.4 | 3.3 | 17.8 | 0.1 | 1.2 | -4.9 | 0.8 | 2.6 |

**图 12.8　2013—2024 年宁夏外商投资企业数**

资料来源：根据国家统计局官方数据库、中国与宁夏统计年鉴、统计公报数据计算所得。

达到 33.7 亿美元，年均增速约为 4.1%；宁夏外商投资企业数为 895 家，年均增速约为 6.3%。宁夏外商投资企业投资总额为 286 亿美元，年均增速约为 23.3%；外商投资企业注册资本为 135 亿美元，年均增速

第12章 宁夏对外开放专题报告

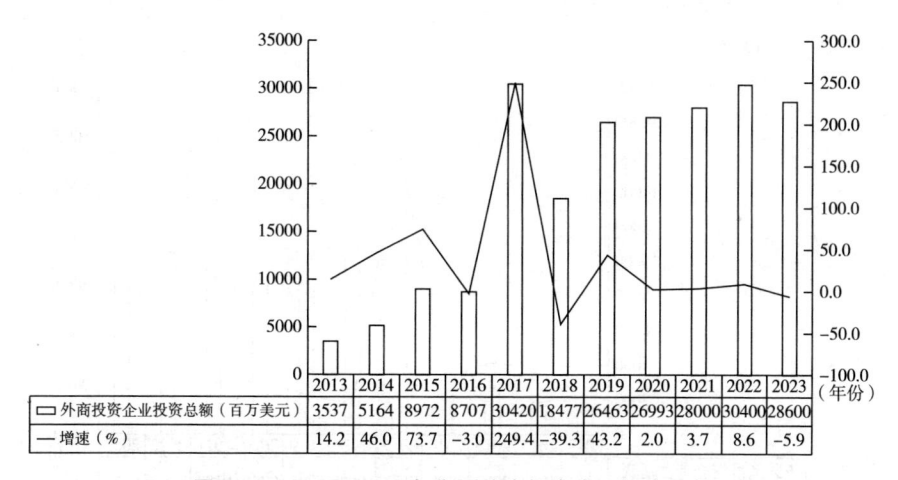

图12.9 2013—2023年宁夏外商投资企业投资总额

| 年份 | 2013 | 2014 | 2015 | 2016 | 2017 | 2018 | 2019 | 2020 | 2021 | 2022 | 2023 |
|---|---|---|---|---|---|---|---|---|---|---|---|
| 外商投资企业投资总额（百万美元） | 3537 | 5164 | 8972 | 8707 | 30420 | 18477 | 26463 | 26993 | 28000 | 30400 | 28600 |
| 增速（%） | 14.2 | 46.0 | 73.7 | -3.0 | 249.4 | -39.3 | 43.2 | 2.0 | 3.7 | 8.6 | -5.9 |

资料来源：根据国家统计局官方数据库、中国与宁夏统计年鉴、统计公报数据计算所得。

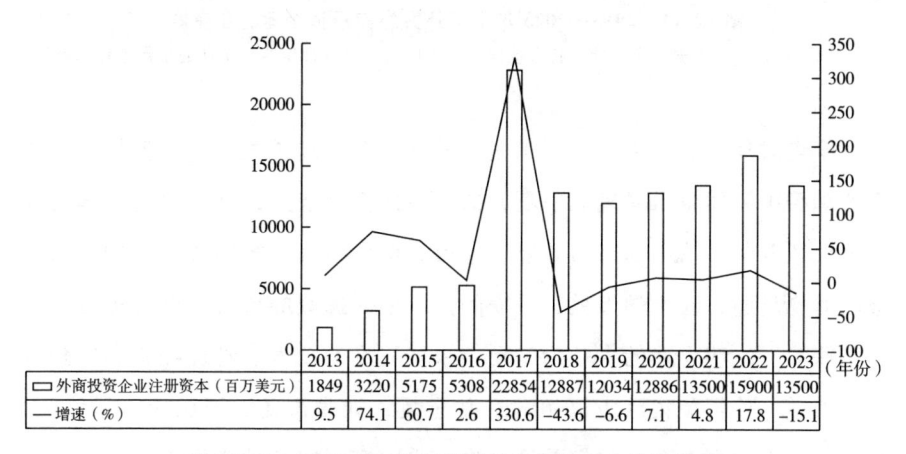

图12.10 2013—2023年宁夏外商投资企业注册资本

| 年份 | 2013 | 2014 | 2015 | 2016 | 2017 | 2018 | 2019 | 2020 | 2021 | 2022 | 2023 |
|---|---|---|---|---|---|---|---|---|---|---|---|
| 外商投资企业注册资本（百万美元） | 1849 | 3220 | 5175 | 5308 | 22854 | 12887 | 12034 | 12886 | 13500 | 15900 | 13500 |
| 增速（%） | 9.5 | 74.1 | 60.7 | 2.6 | 330.6 | -43.6 | -6.6 | 7.1 | 4.8 | 17.8 | -15.1 |

资料来源：根据国家统计局官方数据库、中国与宁夏统计年鉴、统计公报数据计算所得。

约为22.0%；外商投资企业注册资本为90亿美元，年均增速约为20.8%。2024年，宁夏与美国莱卡、意大利世科姆、以色列耐特菲姆、澳大利亚富邑等全球知名企业合作实现突破。成功争取在宁夏设立国际葡萄酒组织实体机构，宁夏葡萄酒走向世界迈出重要步伐。科技、教育、卫生等领域对外交流不断深化，对阿拉伯国家文化服务贸易出口进入全国前列。①

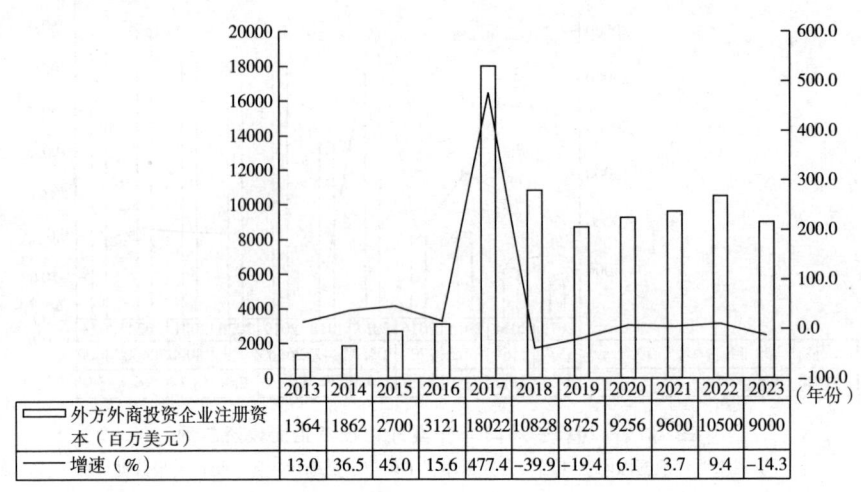

| 年份 | 2013 | 2014 | 2015 | 2016 | 2017 | 2018 | 2019 | 2020 | 2021 | 2022 | 2023 |
|---|---|---|---|---|---|---|---|---|---|---|---|
| 外方外商投资企业注册资本（百万美元） | 1364 | 1862 | 2700 | 3121 | 18022 | 10828 | 8725 | 9256 | 9600 | 10500 | 9000 |
| 增速（%） | 13.0 | 36.5 | 45.0 | 15.6 | 477.4 | -39.9 | -19.4 | 6.1 | 3.7 | 9.4 | -14.3 |

**图 12.11　2013—2023 年宁夏外方外商投资企业注册资本**

资料来源：根据国家统计局官方数据库、中国与宁夏统计年鉴、统计公报数据计算所得。

宁夏对外开放政策的不断深化，外资企业逐步扩大，众多世界 500 强企业和跨国公司将目光投向宁夏，选择在此投资建厂，其中包括美国的亚马逊、辛普劳，法国的路易威登轩尼诗、保乐力加，德国的舍弗勒，新加坡的斯伦贝谢，瑞士的雀巢，丹麦的嘉士伯，挪威的埃肯，以及奥地利的奥钢联等，这些企业的入驻为宁夏带来了先进的技术、管理经验和广阔的市场渠道。外资零售巨头也相继进驻宁夏，如麦德龙、屈臣氏、星巴克、优衣库、无印良品等，它们的到来进一步丰富了宁夏的市场格局，提升了消费品质，为宁夏人民带来了更多的消费选择。

但总体上看，宁夏实际利用外资规模较小，对经济增长影响能力有限。从企业数量来看，每年有实际到位资金的外资企业和有实际境外投资的企业数量均是个位数，反映出宁夏在吸引外资企业入驻和推动本土企业国际化方面存在不足。

---

① 《宁夏开行铁海联运图定班列 184 列　居西北第二》，中国服务贸易指南网，http：//tradein-services. mofcom. gov. cn/article/yanjiu/hangyezk/202501/172151. html，2025 年 1 月 20 日。

## 12.1.4 科技创新不断进步

宁夏充分发挥东西部科技合作引领区作用，出台《宁夏回族自治区知识产权保护条例》（2024年9月26日宁夏回族自治区第十三届人民代表大会常务委员会第十二次会议通过），强化政策保障机制。由图12.12可以看出，近5年来，宁夏科研经费投入强度逐年提高，由2019年的1.45%增至2023年的1.57%，2021—2023年宁夏社会研发经费投入年均增长12.8%，企业研发经费占比超过80%，均高于全国平均水平。国家高新技术企业、科技型中小企业和专精特新"小巨人"企业增长82.0%。宁夏连续两年荣获国家测绘工程金奖，首次获得全国科学实验展演汇演一等奖。部区合建的宁夏高等研究院完成首批硕博招生。由自治区人民政府设立的新型科研机构六盘山和贺兰山两个实验室，围绕宁夏高端装备制造业布局创新链。新材料产业关键技术研发与创新，吸引集聚了国内外优势科研力量，组织开展跨领域跨学科协同攻关，建成集基础研究与应用基础研究、关键技术开发、人才培养、产业孵化、公共服务等于一体的综合性、开放性创新高地。上海和深圳的两个宁夏科创中心、香港标准及检定中心宁夏实验室相继投入使用，其中上海宁夏科创中心是宁夏在全国设立的首个科技研发飞地。这些飞地实验室主要围绕宁夏"六新六特六优+N"产业高质量发展，通过"技术研发在外地、成果应用在本地"的飞地研发模式，破解长期困扰宁夏企业高端人才引用难题。[1] 此外，宁夏首个生物安全三级实验室启动运行，宁东煤化工中试基地相关中试项目行业领先。科技创新不断进步，成果显著，攻克了高性能铌钨抗氧化涂层、耐盐碱春小麦新品种选育等关键技术，研制出国内最大智能化反井钻机、特大型风电轴承热处理装备等多项首台套产品。全球最快高铁用上了"宁夏造"联系枕梁，长征火箭用上了宁夏煤制油，科技创新成为高质

---

[1] 《宁夏上海科创中心构建引才"强磁场"》，《宁夏日报》2024年11月16日第4版。

量发展的强大引擎。①

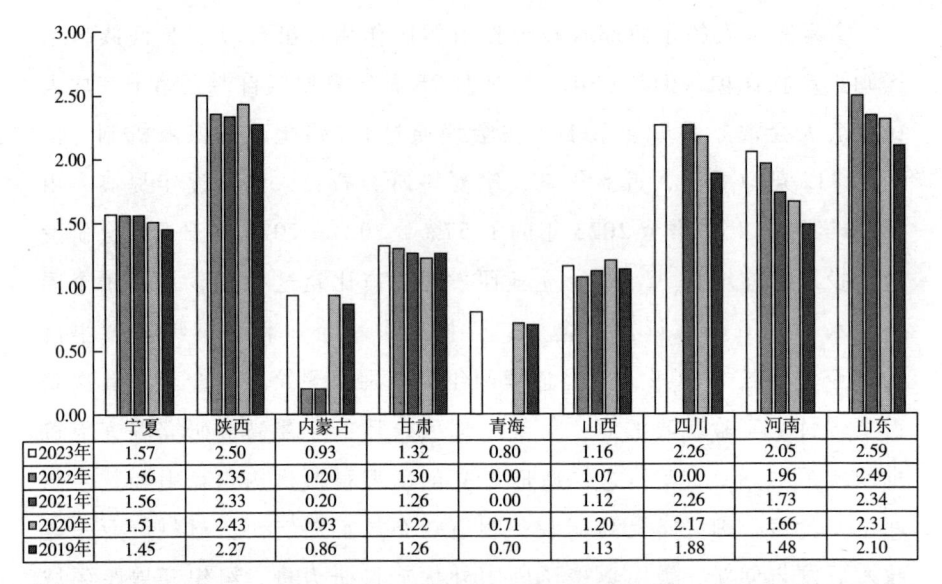

| | 宁夏 | 陕西 | 内蒙古 | 甘肃 | 青海 | 山西 | 四川 | 河南 | 山东 |
|---|---|---|---|---|---|---|---|---|---|
| 2023年 | 1.57 | 2.50 | 0.93 | 1.32 | 0.80 | 1.16 | 2.26 | 2.05 | 2.59 |
| 2022年 | 1.56 | 2.35 | 0.20 | 1.30 | 0.00 | 1.07 | 0.00 | 1.96 | 2.49 |
| 2021年 | 1.56 | 2.33 | 0.20 | 1.26 | 0.00 | 1.12 | 2.26 | 1.73 | 2.34 |
| 2020年 | 1.51 | 2.43 | 0.93 | 1.22 | 0.71 | 1.20 | 2.17 | 1.66 | 2.31 |
| 2019年 | 1.45 | 2.27 | 0.86 | 1.26 | 0.70 | 1.13 | 1.88 | 1.48 | 2.10 |

**图 12.12  2019—2023 年宁夏与沿黄八省区 R&D 经费支出占地区生产总值比重对比（%）**
资料来源：根据国家统计局官方数据库、中国与宁夏统计年鉴、统计公报数据计算所得。

### 12.1.5  营商环境持续优化

一是多措并举提升外向型经济发展水平。2024 年，宁夏新出台《推动民营经济高质量发展三年行动计划（2024—2026 年）》，提出"三项重点"，打造"硬支撑"，强力推进市场环境提升、企业梯次培育、政务服务提效、诚信政府建设、公正法治保障、企业精神弘扬等"六大行动"，实施"八项支持政策"，以促进民营经济做强做优做大。新出台《宁夏回族自治区加快内外贸一体化发展行动方案》（宁政办发〔2024〕37 号）②，

---

① 《2025 年宁夏回族自治区人民政府工作报告》，《宁夏日报》2025 年 1 月 26 日第 1 版。
② 宁夏回族自治区人民政府办公厅关于印发《宁夏回族自治区加快内外贸一体化发展行动方案》的通知，宁夏回族自治区人民政府网，http://yjs.nx.gov.cn/xxgk/zfxxgkml/zzqwj/202409/t20240912_4656382.html，2024 年 8 月 6 日。

提出建设力目标，争取到2027年：自治区内外贸政策规则衔接更加有效，融合发展基础不断夯实，内外联通物流网络更加畅通；推进内陆开放型经济试验区建设取得新成效，成为融入国内国际双循环的重要区域、黄河流域生态保护和高质量发展先行区开放新高地；全区外贸产业基础更加稳固，经营主体不断壮大，每年新增有进出口实绩的企业30家，机电和高新技术产品出口占比在40%左右。[1]银川市成立市营商环境促进局，审批局+营商局双模式领跑全国，获评"2024营商环境十佳城市"，连续三年荣获"中国投资热点城市"。[2]

二是不断提升对标国际水平的服务保障能力。宁夏持续聚焦和优化口岸营商环境，银川国际公铁物流港海关监管作业场所、银川综保区跨境电商综合监管中心通过验收，石嘴山保税物流中心（B型）封关运营，天津港、京唐港来宁建设"内陆无水港"。在全区全面实施"提前申报""两步申报"等便利化措施。高水平推广应用国际贸易"单一窗口"，开通"单一窗口"宁夏95198服务热线，落地"网购保税（1210）"等跨境电商全业务监管模式、RCEP海关原产地证书和贸促会原产地证书申领功能，布局建设17个"关银一KEY通"[3]合作制卡代理点，实现出口退税申报身份验证"一卡通"、进出口环节监管证件"一窗受理"、海关原产地证书"秒过秒签"，电子口岸卡"就近办、多点办、一站办"，有效提升通关效率。探索建立宁夏涉企服务专家咨询服务库，免费为企业提供专业法律咨询、产业发展指导、技术改造指引等。同时，健全政务守信践诺机制，常态化开展清理拖欠企业账款工作，全面梳理归集涉企政策，并构建利企政策库，推动各项惠企政策统一发布、精准推送、一键直达、免申

---

[1] 《宁夏回族自治区人民政府办公厅关于印发〈宁夏回族自治区加快内外贸一体化发展行动方案〉的通知》（宁政办发〔2024〕37号），宁夏回族自治区人民政府网，https://www.nx.gov.cn/zwgk/qzfwj/202408/t20240805_4614245.html，2024年8月5日。

[2] 《宁夏银川：厚植营商沃土 打造"宜商银川"品牌》，中国日报网，https://cn.chinadaily.com.cn/a/202503/03/WS67c5757ea31051of19ee9837.html，2025年3月3日。

[3] 《宁夏"关银一KEY通"业务正式落地实施》，宁夏回族自治区商务厅网站，https://dofcom.nx.gov.cn/swdt_42675/kdkf/202102/t20210201_2588657.html，2021年2月1日。

即享。

三是不断提升区域经济合作及重点招商水平。宁夏紧盯国内外大企业、大集团投资动向和产业转移趋势，围绕重点企业、优势产业和重点园区，赴京津冀、长三角、粤港澳大湾区、黄河流域重点省区，组织实施了一系列招商引资活动。与长三角共建"飞地园区"，新能源装备制造在技术嫁接中迭代升级；同京津冀深化数字经济战略合作，"东数西算"枢纽节点建设让"塞上云谷"算力持续赋能。国际物流通道建设成效显著，构建起"陆港+空港+口岸"三位一体的开放通道体系，逐步实现通道带物流、物流带经贸、经贸带产业的联动效应。全面加强与周边省区、高校、央企合作，圆满举办中国—中亚合作论坛、中国产业转移发展对接会、央企深化产业合作座谈会等系列活动，签约项目投资 3200 多亿元。引进世界 500 强和中国 500 强企业 100 余家，招商引资项目形成的固定资产投资占全社会固定资产投资比例连续多年保持在 45% 左右，有力推动了全区经济结构调整和经济增长动能转换。宁夏的海外"朋友圈"越扩越大，获得"国际友好城市杰出贡献奖"。宁夏所创建的中国首个"纯绿电小镇"、葡萄酒产品碳足迹研究、防沙治沙新技术等多项成果分别在联合国气候变化大会、防治荒漠化大会等国际性会议上亮相交流，向世界生动展示了美丽宁夏建设的最新成果。

## 12.2　宁夏对外通道建设不断加强

### 12.2.1　公路通畅显著提升

2024 年，银川加强向东出发，与天津港、青岛港开展战略合作，共建银川—天津港、银川—青岛港陆海联运通道，实现进出口货物"一次申报、全域通关"，跨境物流时效提升 30% 以上。随着银川至布达佩斯国际货运班列实现首发，银川将西向班列境外目的地拓展至欧洲。西部陆海新通道的重要组成部分银昆高速宁夏段正式建成通车，让宁夏高速公路通车里程数突破 2300 千米。首条宁东至蒙古国扎门乌德国际货物运输线路顺利开通，成功打通宁东能源化工基地经二连浩特口岸至蒙古国扎门乌德口岸的国际货物运输线路，标志着宁夏企业和车辆国际道路货物运输业务实现"零"的突破。目前，宁夏已建成"三环四纵六横"高速公路网，省际出口达到 13 个，是西部第 2 个县县通高速的省区，综合立体交通网加速成型。公路网密度 56.59 千米/百平方千米，高于全国平均水平，在中国 31 个省区市中排名第 25 位。宁夏高速公路网已实现向西通达阿拉山口、霍尔果斯等口岸，向东顺畅连接天津港、上海港等港口；与周边的兰州、西安、包头、太原等经济中心城市均实现高速公路连通。特别是银昆高速宁夏段全线通车，将与福银、青兰、泾华等数条高速公路实现互联互通，有效改善宁夏中南部地区交通路网条件，将成为一条连接宁、甘、陕三省区的南北大通道，带动沿线地区资源开发和产业发展，助力宁夏群众共同富裕。

### 12.2.2 铁路联通扎实推进

2024 年，宁夏全年铁路旅客发送量增长 8.7%，包银高铁银川至惠农段通车，银昆高速全线通车，宝中铁路宁夏段扩能改造工程开工，群众出行明显改善。宁夏重点推进银川国际公铁物流港供应链基础设施建设项目，建成国家商贸服务型物流枢纽核心载体，银川市成为国家综合货运枢纽补链强链支持城市。目前，宁夏有 9 条铁路纳入国家铁路网中长期规划，国家规划的"八纵八横"高速铁路网中有"两横一纵"经过宁夏，为宁夏铁路项目的建设奠定了良好基础。其中，银川至西安高铁、中卫至兰州高铁、包头至银川高铁建成后，将实现银川至北京、西安、川渝、兰州等重点城市 2~5 小时到达，使宁夏真正融入全国高速铁路网，宁夏融入"一带一路"、服务全国的路网能力将大幅提升。在国际铁路通道方面，宁夏开行铁海联运图定班列 184 列、居西北第二。东向出海，宁夏开通银川—天津港铁海联运"一箱到底"亚麻籽进口货运班列、银川—天津港—迪拜"一单制"铁海联运出口班列，以及银川

（惠农、平罗）—天津港、银川—青岛港、银川（平罗）—京唐港"一单制""一箱制"铁海联运图定班列等常态化班列，为宁夏进出口企业提供了更多出海选择。除了东向出海，宁夏持续深化与沿边沿海口岸以及铁路、海关等部门合作，强化与西部陆海新通道省份交流，构建东南西北四向通道。

### 12.2.3 航空枢纽不断夯实

目前，宁夏境内有银西高铁和银兰高铁，有福银、京藏、银昆等多条国家高速公路，但是宁夏距离东部沿海以及华东、华南等人口密集地区直线距离均超过1000千米，相比于铁路和公路，民航具有得天独厚的优势。加快空中通道的构建，是宁夏加速融入国内国际双循环的关键。2024年，宁夏三地机场（包括银川河东国际机场、固原六盘山机场和中卫香山机场）共计保障航班起降7.3万架次，实现旅客吞吐量935.4万人次，货邮吞吐量4.7万吨，同比增长分别为8.4%、16.4%和14.3%。其中，银川机场的运输起降达到6.94万架次，旅客吞吐量更是攀升至898.3万人次，货邮吞吐量为4.59万吨，同比分别增长8.0%、16.5%和13.7%。值得一提的是，银川机场的航班量和旅客吞吐量增长幅度均超过全国平均水平，分别高出0.1个百分点和0.6个百分点，同时在西北地区也以3个百分点和4.5个百分点的优势位居榜首。宁夏进一步加密银川至各大中心城市的航班，成功打造了包括北京、上海、广州、成都、杭州、乌鲁木齐等在内的19条骨干航线，这些航线的日均航班频次均超过5班，从而确保关键航线的畅通无阻。同时，新开通的伊宁、阿克苏、吐鲁番、阿勒泰等航线，以及对乌鲁木齐航线的加密，不仅加强了宁夏与新疆的联系，更凸显了银川的区位优势，为进出新疆中转提供了便捷通道。另外，宁夏复飞香港、迪拜航线，开通了银川至曼谷、银川至芽庄等10余条国际航线，这不仅契合了宁夏回族自治区向西开放的战略布局，同时也满足了区内人民群众对东南亚旅游的迫切需求。未来宁夏将围绕打造银川河东国际机场为面向丝绸之路经济带共建国家的门户枢纽机场目标，全力增开加密国内外航线航班，实现除兰州外所有省会城市和 28 个区域枢纽城市直飞的目标。

### 12.2.4 数字通道加快建设

宁夏坚持把数字经济作为发展第一增长极，已经建成中国西部唯一的算力和互联网交换"双中心"。2024 年，宁夏建立"双中心"，制定出台宁夏数字经济高质量发展三年行动和"东数西算"工程宁夏枢纽建设两个方案。北京百度智能云数据产业基地、福建算力服务器生产线、中交云数据中心等集中落地，大语言模型、微医大模型、量子技术应用等取得突破。算力投资、标准机架、高端算卡、算力规模较 2023 年实现"四个翻番"，服务器上架率、智算占比、综合算力指数、电能利用效率、5G 用户渗透率 5 个指标全国领先。建成大型、超大型数据中心 9 个，在建数据中心项目 25 个，标准机架 11.6 万架，智算算卡 9.3 万张，算力规模约 4 万P。中卫云数据中心机柜上架率超过 85%，为自治区政务云、互联网交换中心、金山云、联想等政府部门和企业客户提供算网一体化服务。其中，"闽宁云"建设项目实现了东部数据毫米级"西算"，加快推进闽宁数字经济协作。宁夏获批全国一体化算力网监测调度试点，银川市入选全国首批 5G-A 网络商用城市，石嘴山市建成 IPv6 综合试点城市，吴忠市获评国家级中小企业数字化转型城市，固原市跻身国家"双千兆"城市，中卫市获得"绿色算力发展先锋"称号，宁东基地建成西北首个国家级智慧化工园区。宁夏亚马逊、中国移动、美团、西云等 100 多家企业在宁夏建立了数据中心或者应用数据中心进行数据储备。银川市聚焦"智算""智能""智产"，致力打造"算力之都"，已形成智能算力 3000P 以上，政务数据资源 5 亿余条，数据规模 8000 余 TB，居宁夏首位。同时，围绕数据生产、流通交易、创新应用、安全治理等产业链关键环节，首批引入中国电子云、宁夏希望信息、银川智慧城市、启迪控股等数据服务商等第三方专业服务机构参与"银川数据港"建设。

加快建设国家级银川跨境电子商务综合试验区，在用好中阿博览会和中国（银川）跨境电商综试区金字招牌的基础上，聚焦自治区"六新六特六优"产业布局，以"两平台六体系"为建设目标，打造企业主体集聚、服务体系完备、监管模式创新的跨境电商产业生态。目前，银川跨境电商综试区共建成银川综保区、宁浙电商创业园等6个产业聚集区，引育跨境电商卖家、服务平台、供应商、仓储物流等跨境电商企业475家，较跨境电商综试区获批前增加424家，增幅超过9倍，先后在德国、哈萨克斯坦、马来西亚等6个国家租用海外仓19座。2024年，银川跨境电商综试区实现跨境电商交易额7.75亿元人民币。[①] 银川跨境电商综试区已成为宁夏推动外贸转型升级、培育外贸新业态的新型对外开放平台。

## 12.3 宁夏推进高水平对外开放展望

宁夏处于新时代西部大开发、黄河流域生态保护和高质量发展等重大国家战略的叠加区，自治区党委、政府提出要打造黄河流域生态保护和高质量发展的先行区，具有打通与北向、西向、南向和东部地区之间的流通循环，发展更高层次开放型经济的地理和经济发展优势。2025年是"十四五"规划圆满收官和"十五五"规划谋篇布局的承启之年，面临的挑战、机遇和不确定性前所未有。宁夏要以党的二十大精神和习近平总书记历次考察宁夏时的重要讲话精神为根本遵循，扎实推进高质量共建"一带一路"行稳致远，促进内陆高水平开放。

### 12.3.1 推动"通道经济"提质升级

加强"一带一路"通道顶层设计。放大中阿峰会效应，加强与"一带一路"高峰合作论坛、博鳌亚洲论坛等全球性国际组织以及东盟、上海

---

[①] 《银川跨境电商综试区闪耀第五届跨交会　彰显外贸新动力》，宁夏新闻网，https://www.nxnews.net/yc/jrww/202503/t20250319_10402600.html，2025年3月19日。

合作组织等区域性国际组织的联系和对话，在这些国际组织的业务范围框架下，探索建立合作平台的可能性与可行性，力争在国际交通设施互联互通、国际运输协定签署、跨境直达通关便利化等方面取得新突破。着力构建陆海新通道、铁海联运、国际公铁物流3条国际通道，打通更多南向衔接西部陆海新通道的出宁通道，推动宁夏班列运营企业利用"中（国）—吉（尔吉斯斯坦）—乌（兹别克斯坦）"国际物流通道，打造自宁夏—新疆伊尔克什坦口岸至中亚、西亚、欧洲的"中阿快线"，开辟面向中亚五国、阿富汗、伊朗等的国际物流"第二通道"。着力推动"通道经济"提质升级，持续增开、加密更多直飞国外重要枢纽城市航线航班，构建面向"一带一路"共建国家、辐射国内中西部省份的航线网络，进一步提升空、铁、海通达能力，助力宁夏对外开放高质量发展。强化区域性合作和省区协作联动，按照补断点、强内联、疏堵点的基本思路，推动通道基础设施建设，共享通道建设发展成果。建立跨区域协同机制，打破行政区划限制，支持发展"飞地经济"及产业园区共建共享，努力走出一条差异化、特色化、协同化发展的新路子。启动新一轮"铁公机"建设三年计划，加快宝中铁路宁夏段扩能改造和银巴铁路建设，开工建设包兰铁路扩能改造银川至中卫段。实现包银高铁全线通车，银川经包头至北京时间由18小时缩短到5小时。积极推进现有机场改扩建等重点项目，国道629线中卫段全面开工，实现乌玛高速宁夏段全线贯通，着力构建"七位一体"现代交通体系。

加快推进"数字丝绸之路"。不断夯实数字经济发展基础，对标《数字经济伙伴关系协定》（DEPA）、《全面与进步跨太平洋伙伴关系协定》（CPTPP）等国际规则，构建具有竞争力的数字经济发展体系，建设西部数字经济示范区，扩大宁夏在世界数字经济发展中的话语权。全面实施新一轮数字经济高质量发展三年行动，建设算力枢纽"十项工程"，设立数字经济引导基金，数字经济规模超过2200亿元人民币。实施数字基础设施提升行动，启动5G规模化应用"扬帆"行动和设立万兆光网试点，推动5G网络行政村、千兆光纤县域全覆盖。加快建设亚马逊、腾讯、中国电信、中国移动、航天云等25个数据中心和智算项目,积极争取一批重大项目和灾备中心落地,力争新建数据中心100%使用绿电,争创算电协同示范区。①

创新数字合作机制,建设国家数字经济创新发展试验区,加快发展新模式新业态,大力发展智慧物流、数字金融、数字经济总部基地等金融数字经济产业,打造"数字丝绸之路"的产业多态。强化中阿峰会在数字经济合作中全局性牵引作用,挖掘阿盟各国在数字贸易竞争中优势和合作利益共同点,延展宁夏在数字贸易发展中的价值链和产业链。实施数字产业化能级提升行动,办好第三届"西部数谷"算力产业大会,推动数字经济"聚储通算用"全产业链发展,建设数据要素综合服务平台,提升数据安全发展能力。实施产业数字化赋能提升行动,推动三次产业与数字技术深度融合,力争规上企业数字化转型比例达到60%。全域全方位推进"人工智能+""量子技术+""数据要素×"等系统工程,为宁夏发展插上智慧的翅膀。

### 12.3.2 奋力构筑对外开放新高地

提升中阿博览会平台功能。连续举办6届中阿博览会,112个国家和地区的6000多家中外企业,超过40万客商参加,成为中阿共建"一带一路"的重要平台。未来要以"世界眼光、中国平台"重新审视和定位中阿博览会,着力建设中国与阿拉伯国家、经贸合作、商事调节、法律服务的总平台、总枢纽、总通道。务实创新办好第七届中阿博览会,加强与外交部、商务部协调对接,将中阿合作论坛经贸投资类活动整合在中阿博览会期间举办,并形成机制性运行,提升中阿博览会经贸合作能级,助力中阿经贸合作走深走实,推动宁夏对阿经贸合作实现新突破。加快研究并依托银川综合保税区,吸引中国与海合会国家商协会、

---

① 《2025年自治区政府工作报告全文》,宁夏回族自治区人民政府网,https://www.nx.gov.cn/wxb/wxlzsl/202501/t20250126_4807319.html,2025年1月26日。

知名企业以及国际机构等入驻,提供商贸投资、法务服务、金融、物流、数字信息、农业经济合作、文旅合作、专业人才等服务。探索在中阿博览会下成立中阿企业家经贸促进会,加快促进中阿企业精英的交流与协作,让政策、资源、资本实现有效对接。以中阿博览会为牵引、加快构建国际会展经济新发展格局,形成促进宁夏产业联动发展的长效机制。

提升中国(宁夏)国际葡萄酒文化旅游博览会平台影响力。推进葡萄酒与文化深度融合,打造具有宁夏风格、中国特色、世界水平的国际知名葡萄酒业专业展会,成为推动宁夏社会经济发展及对外开放的重要平台。加强内涵发展,制定展会高质量发展目标,办好第五届国际葡萄酒博览会、第32届布鲁塞尔国际葡萄酒大奖赛。通过国际展览业协会认证和中国质量认证中心质量管理体系认证,成为国内经过双认证的国际酒类高质量专业展会。扩大展会影响力。力争每届国际国内葡萄酒行业商(协)会、重要生产、营销企业负责人和国际国内酒类采购商、经销商等重要客商出席会议,成为国内外酒行业的重要盛会。加强同世界主要葡萄酒国家及国内葡萄酒产区与销区的交流合作,不断提升博览会影响力。探索与法国、德国等国家合作举办中国(宁夏)国际葡萄酒博览会,让国内外更多消费者了解和关注宁夏贺兰山东麓葡萄酒产区,中国葡萄酒的未来在宁夏,引领中国葡萄酒更好地融入世界。

提升"西部数谷"算力产业大会驱动未来内涵。宁夏作为全国唯一的"交换中心+枢纽节点"双中心省区,其地位在数字经济领域显得尤为突出。西部算力产业联盟在宁夏成立后,宁夏将与京津冀、长三角、粤港澳大湾区和成渝等四大核心区域紧密合作,共同聚焦"数据中心算力提升工程"、"数字制造壮大工程"以及"网络联通加速工程"等八大关键任务,合力推动算力产业的繁荣与发展,进而为宁夏数字经济的腾飞提供坚实支撑。同时,推动"算力+产业"理论研究,依托高端平台汇聚多方资源,共同商讨算力领域的重大战略和标准规范。此外,还应深入研判"算力+产业"的整体态势、演进路径以及关键问题,为产业发展提供有力的理论支撑，拓宽"连接+算力+价值"的资源要素共享通道。通过深化数据的带动作用，以数据流引领技术流、资金流、人才流和物资流的联动发展，进一步打通数字经济大动脉，构建经济大循环，吸引更多行业头部企业入驻宁夏。以"全球视野、算力合作、价值创新、驱动未来"作为办会理念，推动算力行业深度融合、增强科技创新能力。加强与"一带一路"共建国家交流，拓展合作领域、丰富合作项目，共享算力创新发展的成果。

加强综合保税区建设。综合保税区具有承接国际产业转移、联结国内国际两个市场的特殊功能和政策。深入实施"外资三年外贸五年倍增计划"，推动银川综合保税区和石嘴山保税物流中心（B型）设施互联互通、产业优势互补、通关高效对接，重点发展口岸通关、保税加工、保税物流等外向型产业，打造贸易投资便利、功能特色突出、公共服务高效的海关特殊监管区域。银川保税区继续坚持目标导向和问题导向，围绕"进位晋级双高发展"主题，"服务型园区、产业型园区"两大定位，"服务立区、项目兴区、创新强区"三大理念，"保税加工、保税物流、保税服务、口岸作业"四大功能，"产业培育提质、招商引资提效、项目建设提速、营商环境提优、绩效评估提升"五大行动，积极培育电子信息、食品加工、跨境电商等主导产业及配套产业，广泛吸引与主导产业关联度高的外资外贸项目，构建集生产、贸易、结算、物流于一体的跨境电商产业链和生态圈。跨境电子商务逐渐成为宁夏发展速度最快、潜力最大、带动作用最强的外贸业态之一，要加大政策支持力度，引进跨境电商龙头企业、物流龙头企业，引导企业用好跨境电商零售出口增值税、消费税免税政策和所得税核定征收办法。鼓励外贸企业和物流企业在欧美市场、"一带一路"共建国家、《区域全面经济伙伴关系协定》（RCEP）成员国市场布局海外仓。加大枸杞、羊绒等优势特色外向型产业培育力度，引导更多内贸主体开展外贸，激发市场活力。全力将银川综合保税区和石嘴山保税物流中心打造成为对外开放新高地、产业转型升级新引擎，为中国扩大高水平对外开放、为宁夏打造高水平对外开放门户枢纽做出贡献。

### 12.3.3 加强同国家重大战略区域合作

加强与京津冀、长江经济带、长三角一体化、粤港澳大湾区、海南自贸港、西部陆海新通道等国家重大战略对接交流合作，更好融入和支撑新发展格局。把宁夏未来的发展放在全国区域发展大局中考量，进一步提高站位，以前瞻眼光想问题、谋对策。遵循经济发展规律，发挥各地比较优势，融入增长极，培育新增长极，加快形成方向明晰、活力强劲的区域战略新架构，为落实重大战略、服务全国大局做出宁夏贡献。全面深化供给侧结构性改革，推动重点领域和关键环节改革取得新突破，实施制度型开放战略，释放改革红利，促进各类要素合理流动和高效集聚。围绕迈入国内大循环和国内国际双循环的中高端、关键环，大力推进跨区域产业分工协作，创新产业协同合作机制，协同建设现代化产业体系。聚焦主导产业生态体系构建、产业集群和新兴产业链培育等，把项目建设作为根本抓手，强化区域共赢发展项目支撑。充分激发各类市场主体融入国家重大战略的主动性、创造性，增强合作活力。统筹推进重大基础设施建设，提升互联互通和现代化水平，构建跨区域综合交通运输走廊，引导产业优化布局和分工协作。全面落实全国统一大市场建设指引和规范招商引资规定，深入推进东西协作、西部合作、央地合作等，开展宁港澳合作提升年活动，在充分利用两个市场、两种资源上迈出新步伐。打破地区分割和隐性壁垒，推动形成统一开放、竞争有序的市场体系。

### 12.3.4 着力提升产业核心竞争力

突出科技创新引领，奋力打好特色优势产业升级攻坚战。统筹推进"六新六特六优+N"产业，协调推进传统产业提升、新兴产业壮大、未来产业培育，进一步推动现代煤化工、新型材料、清洁能源、数字信息、特色农牧业、文化旅游等产业集群发展，加快构建体现宁夏优势、具有较强竞争力的现代化产业体系。启动特色优势产业高质量发展三年行动计划和制造业重点产业链高质量发展行动，深入实施产业链、产业基地、产业园区、产业集群"四大升级工程"，着力打造"世界葡萄酒之都""中国算力之都""中国枸杞之乡""中国氨纶谷""中国绿氢谷"等全国重要产业基地，积极争取国家战略腹地和关键产业备份基地建设。出台发展新质生产力实施方案，加快培育智能算力、人工智能、新型储能、绿色氢能、绿色环保、生物制造、量子科技、低空经济、生命健康等新兴和未来产业，大力支持新技术新产业新业态新模式新赛道发展。全面强化科技创新，启动实施"八大行动"，全社会研发经费投入增长10%以上。办好用好高等研究院、科创中心、中试基地和各类实验室。着力强化人才支撑，提高人才培养资金额度，赋予科研机构、科研人员更大自主权，培育引进一批科技领军人才、卓越工程师、大国工匠和高技能人才。充分发挥企业主体作用，进一步加强技术、标准、品牌、质量建设，不断提升国家高新技术企业和重要技术攻关、引进转化科技成果项目数量，让科技创新"关键变量"转化为高质量发展的"最大增量"。

### 12.3.5 持续打造一流营商环境

坚定不移落实"两个毫不动摇"，持续打造市场化、法治化、国际化一流营商环境。持续举办全区民营经济高质量发展暨营商环境全方位提升推进大会及全国优强民营企业塞上行等活动。深入实施企业培育三年计划，加大支持力度，设立民营经济发展专项资金，大力培育雏鹰、瞪羚、独角兽企业，不断增加"专精特新"科技型企业数量。加力落实"十项机制"，全方位加大对企业的扶持力度。着力解决"预期弱"问题，全面落实更加积极的财政政策和适度宽松的货币政策，切实增强经济政策与非经济政策一致性，做到支持企业的政策、资金一律"免申即享""直达直享"。着力解决"门槛高"问题，严格实行"非禁即入"，强化公平竞争审查，为民营企业公平参与重大项目建设、重大科技攻关等提供更多机会，进一步提高民营经济和民间投资比重。着力解决"经营难""融资难"问题，加大"一题一解""一企一策"帮扶企业的力度。开展"千企万户"大走访、"中小企业融资促进行动"等活动，落实"无还本续贷"等政策，创新特色金融产品，有效降低企业融资成本。力推"高效办成一件事"，完善政企沟通、办事指引、需求收集、投诉受理、结果反馈等机制，最大限度为企业提供便利。开展规范涉企行政检查和行政执法专项行动，严格执行"五个严禁""八个不得"，坚持不具备法定资格的组织不得实施行政检查，没有法定依据的行政检查坚决清理，对违法违规行为企业有权投诉、有权说不，切实做到有事快办、无事不扰，让所有企业家在宁夏投资放心、办事顺心、生活舒心。

# 2024年中阿经贸合作大事记

1月1日,沙特、埃及、阿联酋、伊朗等国成为金砖国家正式成员。

1月7日,驻巴林大使倪汝池拜会巴林副首相哈立德,双方就深化两国务实合作深入交换意见。

1月10日,国家主席习近平同突尼斯总统赛义德互致贺电,庆祝两国建交60周年。

1月12日,驻突尼斯大使万黎会见突尼斯总理哈沙尼,就中突关系和两国各领域合作等交换意见。

1月13—18日,中共中央政治局委员、外交部部长王毅应邀访问埃及、突尼斯、多哥、科特迪瓦,这也是中国外长连续34年年初首访非洲。

1月14日,埃及总统塞西在开罗会见到访的中共中央政治局委员、外交部部长王毅。

1月14日,中共中央政治局委员、外交部部长王毅在开罗同埃及外长舒克里举行会谈。

1月14日,中共中央政治局委员、外交部部长王毅在开罗会见阿盟秘书长盖特。

1月15日,突尼斯总统赛义德在首都突尼斯市会见到访的中共中央政治局委员、外交部部长王毅。

1月15日,中共中央政治局委员、外交部部长王毅在突尼斯市同突尼斯外长阿马尔举行会谈。

1月15—17日,中共中央政治局委员、国务院副总理刘国中率中国政府代表团应邀访问阿尔及利亚。访问期间，阿总统特本、总理阿尔巴维分别会见刘国中，双方就中阿关系和各领域合作深入交换意见。

1月16日，驻毛里塔尼亚大使李柏军会见毛石油、能源矿业部部长兼政府发言人舒鲁克，就推动中毛务实合作和双方共同关心的问题深入交换意见。

1月18日，在黎巴嫩看守内阁总理米卡提的见证下，驻黎巴嫩大使钱敏坚和黎重建委主席纳比勒·吉斯尔分别代表本国政府签署中国援黎巴嫩太阳能发电设备项目换文。

1月19日，驻毛里塔尼亚大使李柏军出席毛里塔尼亚中资企业商会成立大会并致辞。

1月23日，驻摩洛哥大使李昌林出席艾郎摩洛哥兆瓦级风电叶片工厂建设项目开工仪式并致辞。

1月23日，驻毛里塔尼亚大使李柏军会见毛雇主协会主席艾哈迈德，双方就加强中毛两国企业间交流与合作，促进双边经贸发展交换了意见。

1月24日，驻叙利亚大使史宏微会见叙财政部部长基南·亚基，双方就双边务实合作深入交换意见。

1月28日，国家主席习近平致电阿扎利·阿苏马尼，祝贺他当选连任科摩罗联盟总统。

1月29日，阿联酋中央银行通过mBridge平台与中国银行成功完成了价值5000万阿联酋迪拉姆（约合9800万元人民币）的首笔数字迪拉姆跨境支付交易；同日，中国银行阿联酋机构也利用该平台完成了阿联酋境内首笔数字人民币跨境汇款交易。

1月30日，商务部部长王文涛在北京与阿尔及利亚住房、城市规划和城市部部长贝勒阿里比共同主持召开中阿第八届经贸联委会，就深化中阿双边经贸合作深入交换意见。

1月30日，驻卡塔尔大使曹小林到任拜会卡塔尔交通大臣苏莱提，双方就中卡交通领域合作交换意见。

2月1日，驻卡塔尔大使曹小林会见卡塔尔国家旅游委员会主席萨德，就中卡旅游交流合作交换看法。

2月1日，驻摩洛哥大使李昌林赴卡萨布兰卡出席中远海运集运（摩洛哥）有限公司揭牌仪式并致辞。

2月1日，驻毛里塔尼亚大使李柏军会见毛装备与运输部部长穆罕默德，双方就进一步加强两国基础设施建设领域务实合作深入交换意见。

2月1日，中国援助毛里塔尼亚医疗物资交接仪式在中国援毛医疗队驻地举行。在李柏军大使的见证下，我馆负责经济事务的席威参赞分别与毛首都医院院长韦迪赫、国家公共卫生研究院副院长宰伊娜和友谊医院副院长赫特里签署医疗物资交接证书。

2月5日，驻约旦大使陈传东访问亚喀巴经济特区，会见特区特首纳伊夫·法耶兹。

2月6日，驻卡塔尔大使曹小林到任拜会卡塔尔国务大臣兼自由区管理委员会主席艾哈迈德，双方就深化中卡投资合作交换意见。

2月6日，驻毛里塔尼亚大使李柏军会见毛经济与可持续发展部部长萨利赫，双方就进一步加强两国经贸务实合作深入交换意见。

2月7日，驻卡塔尔大使曹小林会见卡塔尔环境与气候变化大臣苏拜伊，双方就环境保护与气候变化议题交换意见。

2月18日，驻阿尔及利亚大使李健会见来阿工作访问的中国进出口银行主权客户部工作组，双方就推动中阿金融合作及项目融资交换意见。

2月23日，驻科摩罗大使郭志军会见科摩罗海关总署署长穆斯塔法，双方就进一步推动中科海关合作交换意见。

2月25日，驻卡塔尔大使曹小林会见卡塔尔能源集团液化天然气公司首席执行官哈立德，就中卡能源合作交换意见。

2月25日，驻卡塔尔大使曹小林会见中国船级社范强副总裁，双方就服务和拓展中卡海洋运输合作进行了交流。

2月26日，驻卡塔尔大使曹小林会见中国国际金融股份有限公司总裁吴波一行，双方就促进中卡金融投资合作进行了交流。

2月27日，商务部部长王文涛与阿联酋经济部部长玛尔伊在阿联酋阿布扎比共同主持召开中国—阿联酋经贸联委会第八次会议。双方就加快落实两国元首达成的重要共识，共同推动中阿高质量共建"一带一路"深入交换意见。

2月27日，中国商务部与阿联酋经济部签署加强《数字经济投资合作备忘录》。

2月27日，商务部部长王文涛在阿联酋阿布扎比会见沙特商务大臣卡斯比。双方就落实两国领导人达成的重要共识，推动中沙经贸合作向更高水平发展深入交换意见。

2月27日，驻科摩罗大使郭志军会见科领土整治、城市化、不动产事务及陆路运输部部长阿夫雷坦·优素法，双方就进一步推动中科基础设施合作交换意见。

2月28日，商务部部长王文涛在埃及新行政首都应约拜会埃及总理马德布利。

2月28日，商务部部长王文涛在埃及新行政首都同埃及贸易与工业部部长萨利赫举行会谈。双方就落实两国领导人达成的重要共识，推动中埃经贸合作高质量发展深入交换意见。

2月29日，商务部部长王文涛在埃及开罗主持召开埃及中资企业圆桌会。会议围绕企业经营发展现状、推动中埃经贸关系高质量发展、深化中非和中阿务实合作等进行深入交流。

2月29日，驻阿联酋大使张益明应邀出席渣打银行"中国与中东经贸走廊"主题晚宴并致辞。

3月1日，商务部部长王文涛在摩洛哥拉巴特主持召开摩洛哥中资企业圆桌会。会议围绕企业经营发展现状、推动中摩经贸关系高质量发展、深化中非和中阿务实合作等进行深入交流。

3月1日，商务部部长王文涛在摩洛哥拉巴特同摩洛哥工业与贸易大臣梅祖尔举行会谈。双方就落实两国元首达成的重要共识，促进中摩经贸合作持续健康发展深入交换意见。

3月1日，中国移动通信集团有限公司与阿联酋电信集团公司在2024

年世界移动通信大会期间签署战略合作谅解备忘录。

3月5日,驻阿尔及利亚大使李健出席中阿经济论坛塞提夫省专场活动。

3月7日,驻巴林大使倪汝池会见巴林铝业总裁鲁迈希,双方就中巴合作和共同关心的问题交换了意见。

3月10日,驻卡塔尔大使曹小林会见卡塔尔能源事务国务大臣、卡塔尔能源集团副主席兼首席执行官卡阿比,就加强两国能源合作交换意见。

3月11日,驻叙利亚大使史宏微会见叙利亚工业部部长阿卜杜勒·卡迪尔·朱赫达尔,双方就加强双边合作深入交换意见。

3月16日,沙特航空一架B777全货机由深圳机场起飞前往利雅得,这是深圳机场今年加密的第三条货运航线,也是沙特航空首次在深圳机场开通定期国际货运航线。

3月20日,驻埃及使馆赵刘庆公参与苏伊士运河经济区管理总局主席瓦利德共同签署援埃及苏伊士运河经济区职业培训中心项目实施协议。

3月21日,驻卡塔尔大使曹小林会见卡塔尔商工大臣兼卡塔尔自由区管理委员会主席穆罕默德,双方就深化双边经贸合作交换意见。

3月24日,国家发展改革委主任郑栅洁在钓鱼台国宾馆会见来华参加中国发展高层论坛年会的沙特国家石油公司总裁兼首席执行官纳瑟尔一行,双方就深化中沙能源合作等议题进行了交流。

3月24日,驻巴林大使倪汝池会见巴林王宫大臣哈立德,双方就进一步推动中巴友好合作关系进行了友好交谈。

3月25日,驻吉布提大使胡斌会见吉布提通讯、邮政与电信部部长巴赫敦,双方就深化中吉互利合作深入交换意见。

3月26日,驻阿尔及利亚大使李健,阿知识经济、初创企业和微型企业部部长瓦利德,高教和科研部秘书长本特利斯出席华为2024年度"初创企业扶持"计划闭幕式并致辞。

3月29日,驻摩洛哥大使李昌林在拉巴特参加贝特瑞公司与摩政府投资协议签署仪式。

4月1日，中国政府向吉布提派遣医疗队合作议定书（2024—2028年度）续签仪式在吉外交与国际合作部举行。驻吉大使胡斌和吉外长优素福代表两国政府签署议定书。

4月8日，驻巴林大使倪汝池拜会巴林财政与国民经济大臣萨勒曼，双方就加强两国经贸与投资合作深入交换了意见。

4月17日，驻索马里使馆临时代办陈文玓拜会索外长菲基，双方就共同落实中索两国元首共识，进一步密切双方传统友谊、深化各领域合作交换了意见。

4月18日，驻卡塔尔大使曹小林会见卡塔尔通讯与信息技术大臣马奈伊，双方就中卡通讯与信息技术合作交换意见。

4月18日，驻科摩罗大使郭志军会见科卫生、团结、社会保障及促进性别平等部部长扎伊杜，双方就进一步加强两国卫生领域合作交换意见。

4月20日，阿尔及利亚国家数字政务中心项目签约仪式在阿尔及尔举行，驻阿尔及利亚大使李健、阿数字化部长级高级专员玛丽亚姆·本米璐德，及阿外交部、财政部、国防部等多部委代表共同出席见证，华为阿尔及利亚公司负责人易翔、阿数字化部秘书长亚辛·贝拉尔比代表双方签字。

4月20日，第四届中国—海湾论坛在纽约大学阿布扎比分校举行。驻阿联酋大使张益明应邀出席开幕式并作主旨演讲。

4月20日，首届"一带一路"政策沟通研讨会暨"中阿数字治理工作坊"在线举行，40余位中阿专家围绕数字治理、数据安全和技术应用展开深入交流，促进公共政策的信息共享与经验传递。

4月24日，中国投资有限责任公司（中投公司）与巴林投资机构Investcorp成立初始规模为10亿美元的"中海基金Investcorp Golden Horizon"，计划投资于中国、沙特及海湾合作委员会国家的高成长企业。这是全球最大的主权财富基金之一的中投公司设立的第七只创新型双边基金，进一步强化了中国与海湾国家在金融和产业领域的联结。

4月25日，巴林国家航空公司海湾航空宣布，自今年5月28日起开通飞往中国的直航航班，每周4班飞往上海，每周3班飞往广州。

4月25日，驻巴林大使倪汝池会见巴林工商大臣法赫鲁，双方就加强两国经贸投资产业合作深入交换意见。

4月27日起，东航新开"上海—利雅得"往返直飞航线。

4月29日，驻阿尔及利亚大使李健出席阿尔及利亚中资企业协会2024年度第一次全体大会并发表讲话。

5月5日，驻巴林大使倪汝池会见巴交通与通讯大臣穆罕默德·本·塔梅尔·卡阿比，双方就加强交通领域合作深入交换意见。

5月9日，驻毛里塔尼亚大使李柏军会见毛渔业与海洋经济部部长拉姆，双方就进一步加强渔业领域务实合作深入交换意见。

5月14日，驻毛里塔尼亚大使李柏军出席中国驻毛里塔尼亚使馆向毛阿塔尔市捐赠太阳能水泵等物资仪式，阿塔尔市长贝德巴出席捐赠仪式并同李大使共同签署交接证书。

5月15日，"2024中阿企业家峰会"隆重开幕，200余名来自中阿政商各界的代表共聚阿联酋阿布扎比。中国原外经贸部副部长、中国入世谈判原首席代表、中外企业家联合会联席主席龙永图先生，中国驻阿联酋大使张益明阁下，阿联酋对外贸易部部长萨尼·阿尔·泽尤迪阁下应邀在开幕式上致辞。

5月16日，国家主席习近平向阿拉伯国家联盟首脑理事会会议轮值主席巴林国王哈马德致贺信，祝贺第33届阿拉伯国家联盟首脑理事会会议在麦纳麦召开。

5月16日，驻约旦大使陈传东会见约旦卫生大臣菲拉斯·哈瓦里，双方就促进中约卫生合作等交换意见。

5月21日，驻摩洛哥大使李昌林拜会摩数字转型与行政改革大臣级代表梅祖尔，双方就中摩关系与合作进行了交流。

5月23日，中共中央政治局常委、国务院副总理丁薛祥在厦门出席中国—海合会国家产业与投资合作论坛，宣读习近平主席贺信并致辞。

5月23日，驻叙利亚大使史宏微同叙高教部部长巴萨姆、大马士革大学校长乌萨玛、阿萨德医院院长尼扎尔共同出席使馆捐赠的医疗设备交接仪式。

5月27日，中国援建的约旦萨尔特公路升级改造项目主体工程举行完工仪式。约旦首相哈萨瓦纳、公共工程与住房大臣兼交通大臣萨曼、驻约旦大使陈传东、项目参建单位代表等出席。

5月27日，习近平主席特使、全国政协副主席何报翔与科摩罗总统阿扎利共同考察由中国沈阳国际经济技术合作有限公司承建的埃尔-马鲁夫国立中心医院项目并出席中资企业、机构座谈会。

5月29日，中国—阿拉伯国家合作论坛第十九次高官会和第八次高官级战略政治对话在北京举行。

5月29日，中共中央政治局委员、外交部部长王毅在北京会见来华出席中阿合作论坛第十届部长级会议的利比亚民族统一政府总理兼外长德拜巴。

5月29日，中共中央政治局委员、外交部部长王毅在北京会见来华出席中阿合作论坛第十届部长级会议的伊拉克副总理兼外长侯赛因。

5月29日，国家主席习近平在北京人民大会堂同来华出席中国—阿拉伯国家合作论坛第十届部长级会议开幕式并进行国事访问的埃及总统塞西举行会谈。

5月29日，巴林国家航空公司海湾航空上海至巴林直飞航线首航航班顺利落地巴林国际机场。

5月29日，联想集团获沙特主权财富基金20亿美金战略投资。

5月30日，中国—阿拉伯国家合作论坛第十届部长级会议在北京举行。中共中央政治局委员、外交部部长王毅同阿方主席、毛里塔尼亚外长马尔祖克共同主持。

5月30日，国家主席习近平在北京人民大会堂同来华国事访问并出席中国—阿拉伯国家合作论坛第十届部长级会议开幕式的阿联酋总统穆罕默德举行会谈。

5月30日，商务部部长王文涛会见阿联酋外贸国务部部长宰尤迪。双方就推动中阿双边贸易投资合作高水平发展深入交换意见。

5月30日，驻约旦大使陈传东会见约旦参议院能源矿产委员会主席马利克·卡巴莱提，双方就深化中约能源合作交换意见。

5月30日，中阿合作论坛第十届部长级会议在北京举行。会议期间，农业农村部与阿拉伯国家联盟共同签署《中华人民共和国农业农村部与阿拉伯国家联盟关于农业合作的谅解备忘录》。

5月30日，在国家主席习近平与阿联酋总统穆罕默德共同见证下，科技部部长阴和俊代表中国政府同阿联酋政府代表、工业与先进技术部部长苏尔坦共同签署《中华人民共和国政府和阿拉伯联合酋长国政府科学技术合作协定》。

5月31日，国家主席习近平在北京人民大会堂同来华国事访问并出席中阿合作论坛第十届部长级会议开幕式的巴林国王哈马德举行会谈。

5月31日，中共中央政治局委员、外交部部长王毅在京会见来华出席中阿合作论坛第十届部长级会议的沙特外交大臣费萨尔。

6月2日，驻沙特大使常华到任拜会沙特外交事务国务大臣兼气候事务特使朱贝尔，双方就中沙双边关系、应对气候变化领域合作等共同关心的议题交换意见。

6月3日，驻阿尔及利亚大使李健会见阿工业和制药部部长阿里·奥恩，双方就中阿工业领域合作交换意见。

6月3日，驻毛里塔尼亚大使李柏军会见毛装备与运输部部长穆罕默德，双方就进一步加强两国基础设施建设领域务实合作深入交换意见。

6月6日，中国联通沙特公司在利雅得正式开业。

6月7日，中国援助科摩罗莫埃利岛公路项目在科摩罗莫埃利岛尼欧马希瓦市正式竣工。

6月9日，中共中央政治局委员、国务院副总理何立峰在钓鱼台国宾馆会见沙特对华经济合作事务负责人、沙特公共投资基金总裁、沙特国家石油公司董事长鲁梅延。

6月11日，中金公司作为唯一在海湾地区配备当地专家的中资投行，成功协助沙特政府和沙特阿拉伯国家石油公司完成了股票减持二次发售。

6月12日，驻沙特大使常华会见数字合作组织秘书长叶海亚。

6月12日，驻也门使馆临时代办邵峥与也门规划和国际合作部部长瓦伊德进行视频会见，双方围绕中也关系、中阿合作论坛等进行交流。

6月13日，驻吉布提大使胡斌会见吉布提数字经济与创新部长级代表阿里。

6月20日，驻索马里大使馆临时代办陈文玓会见索外长菲基，双方就两国共建"一带一路"、落实全球发展倡议、深化各领域合作交换了意见。

6月25日，驻沙特大使常华到任拜会沙特交通和物流服务大臣萨利赫。

6月26日，驻约旦大使陈传东会见约旦工业、贸易与供给大臣优素福·沙麦利，双方就促进两国贸易进行深入交流。

7月3日，驻沙特大使常华会见沙特国家电竞协会主席费萨尔·班达尔亲王。

7月10日，中共中央对外联络部部长刘建超在北京会见沙特对华经济合作事务负责人、沙特公共投资基金总裁鲁梅延。

7月10日，郭志军大使会见科新任卫生部部长纳叙哈·乌塞纳·萨利姆，双方就两国医疗卫生合作及对口医院机制建设深入交流。

7月11日，驻沙特大使常华到任拜会沙特工业与矿业资源大臣班达尔·胡莱夫。

7月11日，商务部部长王文涛同来访的沙特对华经济合作事务负责人、沙特公共投资基金总裁、沙特国家石油公司董事长鲁梅延举行会谈。双方就中沙经贸合作深入交换意见。

7月16日，驻约旦大使陈传东会见约旦旅游和文物大臣马克拉姆·卡伊西，双方就促进中约旅游合作交换意见。

7月17日，驻阿尔及利亚大使李健赴布尔吉·布阿雷里吉省工业区参访阿Condor集团家电工厂、生产线和工地，拜会该集团创始人、董事长阿卜杜拉赫曼·本哈马迪和总经理穆罕默德·达斯。

249

7月18日，驻巴林大使倪汝池会见巴水电大臣亚希尔，双方就加强水电领域方面的合作深入交换意见。

7月19日，香港交易及结算所有限公司（港交所）全资附属公司香港联合交易所有限公司（联交所）宣布，已将阿布扎比证券交易所及迪拜金融市场纳入其认可证券交易所名单。

7月19日，驻科摩罗大使郭志军会见科新任经济、工业、投资及经济一体化部部长穆斯塔法·哈萨尼·穆罕默德。

7月22日，驻约旦大使陈传东会见约旦卫生部秘书长拉伊德·舍布勒，双方就促进两国传统医学等领域合作交换了意见。

7月23日，驻科摩罗大使郭志军会见科新任政府秘书长努尔·埃尔·法特·阿扎利，双方就双边关系和各领域合作交换意见。

7月25日，驻科摩罗大使郭志军会见科新任农业、渔业及手工业部部长丹尼尔·阿利·邦达尔。

7月28日，驻沙特大使常华应邀参访沙特国家石油公司（沙特阿美）总部，并会见公司总裁兼首席执行官阿明·纳赛尔。

8月14日，深圳证券交易所（深交所）与迪拜金融市场在迪拜联合举办"中国阿联酋（迪拜）资本市场合作研讨会"，并签署合作谅解备忘录，明确将建立高层定期会晤机制，进一步深化双方在多层次的交流与合作。

8月15日，驻阿尔及利亚使馆陈忠参赞出席中国有关公司与阿国家石油公司天然气增压项目合同签字仪式。

8月15日，驻毛里塔尼亚大使李柏军会见毛新任能源与石油部部长穆罕默德·哈立德，双方就进一步推动中毛油气能源开发合作深入交换意见。

8月16日，中国—阿拉伯国家博览会顾问委员会换届及咨询工作会议在宁夏银川召开。商务部外贸发展事务局、中国贸促会产业促进部、自治区相关部门负责同志及中外顾问委员参加了会议。

8月18日，驻沙特大使常华应邀出席由深圳证券交易所在沙特利雅得举办的"投资中国新视野"A股上市公司推介活动。

8月18日，驻沙特大使常华会见沙特对华经济合作事务负责人、沙特公共投资基金总裁、沙特国家石油公司（沙特阿美）董事长鲁梅延。

8月19日，驻毛里塔尼亚大使李柏军会见毛新任渔业、海事与港口基础设施部部长法迪勒·西达提，双方就深化两国渔业、海事与港口基础设施领域务实合作深入交换意见。

8月20日，驻毛里塔尼亚大使李柏军会见毛新任卫生部部长阿卜杜拉希·韦迪赫，双方就进一步深化中毛医疗卫生领域合作深入交换意见。

8月20日，驻毛里塔尼亚大使李柏军会见毛新任经济与财政部部长西德·艾哈迈德·埃布赫，双方就进一步深化中毛经贸领域务实合作深入交换意见。

8月20日，驻突尼斯大使万黎会见突新任总理马杜里，双方就双边关系和中非合作论坛峰会交换意见。

8月21日，驻毛里塔尼亚大使李柏军会见毛雇主协会主席艾哈迈德，双方就加强中毛两国企业间交流与合作，促进双边经贸发展交换意见。

8月22日，商务部国际贸易谈判代表（正部长级）兼副部长王受文在沙特利雅得出席中国—海合会自贸协定谈判会议期间，视频会见沙特商务大臣卡斯比，沙特外贸总局局长贾巴尔和海合会自贸谈判总协调人马尔祖基线下参加会见。同日，王受文与海合会助理秘书长欧维什格、海合会自贸谈判总协调人马尔祖基分别举行会见。双方就加快推动中海自贸协定谈判及深化中沙、中海双边经贸合作等议题深入交换意见。

8月26日，驻索马里大使王昱会见索灾害管理局局长莫林，双方就巩固深化中索传统友谊，加强两国防灾减灾合作交换意见。

8月28日，驻科摩罗大使馆举办中科医疗卫生合作招待会，胡冰临时代办、广西卫健委副主任李勇强、科卫生部行财司司长哈希姆、中国援科第二期抗疟技术援助项目专家组组长陈银环主任致辞。

8月30日，2024中国—中东商事法律合作论坛暨京师律所庆祝中国和阿联酋建交40周年特别活动在北京朝阳区东四环中路37号的京师律师大厦举办。

9月3日，中非合作论坛第九届部长级会议在北京举行。

9月4日，驻阿联酋大使张益明应邀与沙迦酋长国执行委员会成员、政府关系部主席谢赫法希姆一道出席由阿联酋外交部和沙迦政府关系部共同主办的"沙迦外交日"中国专场活动。

9月5日，驻沙特大使常华拜会沙特商务大臣卡斯比。

9月8日，驻沙特大使常华会见沙特旅游部次大臣苏尔坦。

9月9—10日，以连接全球旅游市场而闻名的中国游客峰会（CVS）首次在沙特利雅得举办活动，这是中国游客峰会首次在沙特举办。

9月11日，国务院总理李强在利雅得王宫同沙特王储兼首相穆罕默德举行会谈并共同主持召开中国—沙特高级别联合委员会第四次会议。

9月11日，国务院总理李强在利雅得同沙特工商界代表座谈交流。

9月11日，驻突尼斯大使万黎会见突装备和住房部部长扎赫夫拉尼，双方就落实中非合作论坛北京峰会成果和推进双边合作交换意见。

9月12日，国务院总理李强在迪拜出席中国—阿联酋工商论坛并致辞。

9月12日，沙特数据和人工智能管理局（SDAIA）与华为在利雅德签署谅解备忘录，启动培养信息与通信技术（ICT）和人工智能人才的项目。

9月16日，迪拜金融服务管理局与香港金融管理局签署协议，旨在加强可持续金融发展，并联合举办了气候融资会议，进一步推动绿色金融合作。

9月19日，驻索马里大使王昱馆内会见索通讯部部长穆罕默德，双方就深化中索传统友谊及加强双边务实合作交换意见。

9月20日，驻毛里塔尼亚大使李柏军会见毛装备与运输部部长艾勒费勒凯，双方就推进重大项目建设、进一步拓宽中毛基础设施领域合作范围交换意见。

9月25日，驻突尼斯大使万黎会见突海关总署署长梅杰里。双方就两国海关部门在人员培训、经验交流等方面加强合作交换意见。

9月27日，中国—阿拉伯国家智库联盟首次会议在上海举办。外交部副部长邓励出席会议开幕式并致辞。

9月27日，中共中央政治局委员、外交部部长王毅在纽约出席第79届联大期间集体会见海湾阿拉伯国家合作委员会外长。

9月28日，驻摩洛哥大使李昌林出席在拉巴特中国文化中心举办的中摩电竞交流活动。

9月30日，驻毛里塔尼亚大使李柏军会见毛经济与财政部部长埃布赫，双方就落实中非合作论坛北京峰会有关精神、深化双边经贸合作交换意见。

10月初，阿曼主权基金宣布出资1.5亿美元参与易达资本二期美元基金。

10月8日，驻科摩罗大使郭志军会见科电信部部长乌姆里，双方就两国电信与数字经济领域的交流与合作深入交换意见。

10月8日，驻科摩罗大使郭志军会见科环境及旅游部部长阿布巴卡尔·本·马哈穆德，双方就落实中非合作论坛峰会成果、加强两国环境、旅游交流合作等交换意见。

10月9日，国家主席习近平致电凯斯·赛义德，祝贺他当选连任突尼斯共和国总统。

10月10日，驻约旦大使陈传东拜会约旦新任工业、贸易与供给大臣雅鲁布·古达，双方就中约经贸合作交换意见。

10月10日，驻毛里塔尼亚大使李柏军会见毛全国渔业协会主席哈马迪。双方就推动中毛友好关系发展、加强两国渔业合作交换了意见。

10月13日，沙特交通和物流服务大臣萨利赫在利雅得宣布，将在萨勒曼国王国际机场内建设一个面积为4平方千米的沙特—中国特别经济区。

10月14日，驻约旦大使陈传东会见约旦公共工程与住房大臣马希尔·哈姆迪·艾布萨曼，双方就进一步深化基础设施领域合作交换意见。

10月15日，驻毛里塔尼亚大使李柏军会见毛职业培训、手工业与工艺部部长埃伊赫，双方就深化中毛人力资源培训领域合作交换意见。

10月15—18日，中国—海合会自贸协定第十一轮谈判在广州举行。商务部国际贸易谈判代表兼副部长王受文与海合会自贸谈判总协调人马尔祖基分别率代表团出席。双方认真落实中海双方领导人共识，加快推进谈判进程，取得积极进展，确保2024年底前结束谈判。

10月16日，驻索马里大使王昱会见索渔业和蓝色经济部部长阿丹。双方就加强两国渔业等领域合作交换意见。

10月17日，驻科摩罗大使郭志军出席埃尔-马鲁夫国立中心医院大楼项目协调会，科执政党总书记兼总统办公厅主任优素福、马鲁夫医院院长、业主代表等科方官员、技术专家以及承建企业中沈国际代表出席会议。

10月17日，中国和沙特阿拉伯签署了《中华人民共和国文化和旅游部与沙特阿拉伯王国文化部关于举办2025中国—沙特文化年的执行计划》。

10月18日，驻科摩罗大使郭志军会见科商业、工业、手工业联合会主席查姆西丁。

10月18日，驻毛里塔尼亚大使李柏军拜会毛总理艾贾伊，双方就推动中毛友好关系发展和加强务实合作交换意见。

10月18—26日，沙特旅游节在北京天坛公园举办。

10月20日，中国援科摩罗紧急抗疟药运抵科首都莫罗尼，郭志军大使与科卫生部部长萨利姆共同出席药品交接仪式。

10月22日，驻卡塔尔大使曹小林会见卡塔尔环境与气候变化大臣苏拜伊，双方就两国有关领域合作交换意见。

10月22日，广州中医药大学在科摩罗举办第四届中非青蒿素复方控制疟疾研讨会，郭志军大使、科卫生部部长萨利姆、大科摩罗岛行政长官易卜拉欣出席并致辞。

10月22日，驻索马里大使王昱会见索交通部部长法杜萨，双方就加强交通领域合作交换意见。

10月23日，驻叙利亚大使史宏微拜会叙新任副总统费萨尔·米格达德，双方就双边关系和共同关心的问题交换意见。

10月23日，驻叙利亚大使史宏微拜会叙利亚新任总理穆罕默德·加齐·贾拉利，双方就双边关系和各领域务实合作交换意见。

10月28日，香港特区政府财政司司长陈茂波带领由香港金融及创科界代表组成的商务代表团，前往沙特利雅得进行三天访问，探讨合作和双向投资。

10月28日，驻叙利亚大使史宏微拜会叙新任地方管理和环境部部长卢埃·哈里塔，就加强双边合作等议题交换意见。

10月29日，深圳航空公司在卡塔尔多哈哈马德机场举行深圳—多哈航线首航仪式，驻卡塔尔大使曹小林出席活动并致辞。

10月29日，在利雅得举行的第八届未来投资倡议大会上，TikTok首席执行官周受资宣布将在沙特阿拉伯的首都利雅得设立区域总部。

10月30日，驻巴林大使倪汝池会见巴旅游大臣法蒂玛。双方就加强旅游合作深入交换意见。

10月30日，沙特阿拉伯投资中国香港市场的交易所买卖基金（ETF）——Albilad南方东英MSCI香港中国股票ETF在沙特证券交易所上市，首募规模达百亿港元，成为中东地区规模最大的ETF产品。这是投资中国市场的ETF首次登陆沙特市场，具有里程碑意义，标志着中国香港与中东地区之间的投资流动进一步打通。

10月31日，香港交易所宣布，计划于2025年在沙特首都利雅得开设办事处。

11月1日，国家主席习近平同阿联酋总统穆罕默德互致贺电，庆祝两国建交40周年。

11月1日，商务部国际贸易谈判代表兼副部长王受文与海合会自贸谈判总协调人马尔祖基，以视频方式举行中国—海合会自贸协定首席谈判代表会议。国家发展改革委、工业和信息化部、财政部、农业农村部、海关总署等相关部门代表参加。

11月4日，驻毛里塔尼亚大使李柏军会见毛装备与运输部部长阿里·艾勒费勒凯，双方就加强两国基础设施领域合作深入交换意见。

11月5日，驻毛里塔尼亚大使李柏军会见毛卫生部部长韦迪赫，双方就深化中毛卫生健康领域合作深入交换意见。

11月6日，阿拉伯国家荒漠化和风沙灾害防治技术培训班在甘肃省兰州市开班，来自突尼斯、阿曼、埃及等阿拉伯国家的24名学员参加培训。此次培训由我国商务部主办，甘肃省治沙研究所承办，为期21天。

11月6日，驻叙利亚大使史宏微拜会叙新任经济和外贸部部长穆罕默德·卡拉吉，双方就加强两国经贸合作深入交换意见。

11月10日，驻约旦大使陈传东拜会约旦新任财政大臣阿卜杜勒哈基姆·舍布利，双方就加强两国金融、经贸领域合作交换意见。

11月12日，驻卡塔尔大使曹小林会见卡中央银行行长兼卡塔尔投资局董事会主席班达尔，双方就中卡开展金融和投资领域合作进行友好交谈。

11月13日，中国财政部代表中国政府在沙特阿拉伯首都利雅得成功簿记发行20亿美元主权债券，总认购金额397.3亿美元，等同于发行金额的19.9倍。

11月14日，驻吉布提大使胡斌出席新能源泵水设备慈善捐赠项目启动仪式并致辞。

11月15日，由阿联酋中华工商总会主办，明日世界冠名的"世界华商周（迪拜）暨第二届双湾论坛"活动在迪拜盛大举行。

11月16日，驻阿尔及利亚使馆临时代办赵平盛出席由华为阿尔及利亚公司组织举办的数字化人才专场招聘会。

11月17日，驻叙利亚大使史宏微拜会叙新任水资源部部长莫阿塔兹·卡塔尼，就加强两国务实合作深入交换意见。

11月20日，驻约旦大使陈传东会见约旦战略论坛首席执行官巴尔卡特，双方就促进中约智库合作和经贸关系等进行交流。

11月21日晚，国家主席习近平结束对巴西国事访问乘专机回国途中在卡萨布兰卡作技术经停。受摩洛哥国王穆罕默德六世指派，摩洛哥王储哈桑、首相阿赫努什专程赴机场迎接习近平，并在机场举行欢迎仪式。

11月11—22日，第29届气候大会期间，阿联酋新能源巨头马斯达尔与中国丝路基金（SRF）签署谅解备忘录，计划共同投资"一带一路"共建国家，特别是发展中国家和南半球地区的清洁能源项目，预计总投资额达200亿元人民币（约合28亿美元）。

11月26日，驻阿尔及利亚使馆临时代办赵平盛参观第二十届阿国际公共工程展览会，并参观部分中方参展企业。

11月27日，驻科摩罗大使郭志军出席由山东外贸职业学院承办的工艺服装生产科摩罗培训班的开班仪式。

11月27日，驻叙利亚大使史宏微拜会叙新任卫生部部长艾哈迈德·达米里亚，双方就加强两国卫生领域合作深入交换意见。

11月27日，商务部西亚非洲司、中国贸促会产业促进部和中阿博览会秘书处（宁夏商务厅）在北京共同举办了中国—阿拉伯国家博览会阿拉伯国家驻华使节座谈会。

11月28日，驻叙利亚大使史宏微拜会叙新任农业与农业改革部部长法耶兹·米格达德，双方就加强两国农业合作深入交换意见。

12月4日，驻索马里大使王昱在索卫生部出席中方援索医疗包交接仪式。

12月5日，驻科摩罗大使郭志军会见科外交部部长姆巴埃、财政部部长易卜拉欣，双方就进一步深化双边各领域务实合作交换意见。

12月8日，商务部副部长兼国际贸易谈判副代表凌激在沙特首都利雅得与沙特投资部助理大臣阿卜杜拉、次大臣莎拉共同主持召开中沙投资和经济合作工作组第一次会议，并会见沙特投资大臣法利赫。

12月8日，卡塔尔达尔维什控股公司举办海信卡塔尔新专卖店开业仪式，驻卡塔尔大使曹小林出席剪彩仪式并参观海信展厅。

12月9日，驻科威特大使张建卫拜会科首相艾哈迈德亲王。

12月10日，驻阿联酋大使张益明应邀出席由汇丰集团在2024阿布扎比金融周（ADFW）期间举办的"中国—阿联酋投资峰会"并致辞。

12月11日，商务部在阿联酋首都阿布扎比举办"投资中国"中东专场推介暨中国与中东产业资本对接活动。商务部副部长兼国际贸易谈判副代表凌激、中国驻阿联酋大使张益明出席活动并致辞。

12月12日，商务部副部长兼国际贸易谈判副代表凌激在迪拜与阿联酋经济部次长萨利赫共同主持召开中阿投资和经济合作工作组第一次会议。双方就落实两国元首达成的重要共识，推动中阿投资合作高质量发展深入交换意见。

12月15日，宇通客车和卡塔尔"交通公司"合资设立的电动巴士组装厂开工奠基仪式在卡塔尔自由区举办，驻卡塔尔大使曹小林、卡交通大臣穆罕默德、商工大臣费萨尔、环境和气候变化大臣阿卜杜拉、卡投资局首席执行官穆罕默德、"交通公司"董事会主席萨阿德等出席仪式。

12月15日，中国电工与巴林迪亚地产合作的3D打印建造技术样板房项目奠基仪式在迪亚地产穆哈拉格销售中心举行。中国驻巴林大使倪汝池、迪亚地产董事会主席阿卜杜哈基姆·阿尔哈亚（Abdulhakeem Alkhayyat）、执行总裁艾哈迈德·阿姆迪（Ahmed Al Ammadi）及中国电工副总经理葛健等出席活动。

12月15日，驻吉布提大使胡斌陪同吉总统盖莱出席我援建的塔朱拉医院项目揭幕仪式。

12月19日，中共中央政治局委员、外交部部长王毅在北京集体会见阿拉伯各国驻华使节。

12月19日，阿里巴巴在摩洛哥启动B2B平台，成为其登陆北非阿拉伯国家的首站。

12月22日，驻巴林倪汝池大使会见巴水电大臣亚希尔，双方就深化"一带一路"能源合作交换意见。

12月25日，驻科威特大使张建卫拜会科首相艾哈迈德亲王。

12月26日，驻巴林大使倪汝池会见巴新任巴林交通与通讯大臣谢赫·阿卜杜拉，双方就深化交通与通信领域合作交换意见。

12月31日，驻吉布提大使胡斌同吉外交与国际合作部部长优素福分别代表两国政府签署经济技术合作协定。

# 后 记

《中阿经贸关系发展进程年度报告》已成为中阿经贸合作的重要文献和中阿博览会的重要成果之一。《中阿经贸关系发展进程2024年度报告》(中英文版)是在中国—阿拉伯国家博览会秘书处和宁夏回族自治区商务厅指导下,由宁夏大学中国阿拉伯国家研究院组织国内外专家编写完成的。本课题系统梳理了"一带一路"倡议提出以来,中阿经贸合作状况和成果,重点分析了2024年中阿在贸易、投资、科技、农业、数字经济、生态、旅游等领域取得的新进展,描绘了中阿经贸关系发展的进程特征和发展趋势。

本课题组包括中文撰写团队和英文翻译团队。中文由李绍先、张前进、丁丽萍担任全书统稿工作,英文由宁夏大学外国语学院杨春泉带领的翻译团队完成。衷心感谢课题组每一位成员,他们不计名利,勤恳工作,以良好的学术素养,克服困难,顺利完成报告的撰写和翻译工作。感谢社会科学文献出版社、宁夏商务厅和宁夏大学对本报告给予的支持和帮助。如没有以上团队成员、机构的大力支持,本书不可能顺利出版。

本报告具体分工如下:

**统稿**

李绍先　宁夏大学中国阿拉伯国家研究院

张前进　宁夏大学中国阿拉伯国家研究院

丁丽萍　阳光出版社

**中文章节撰写**

前　言　李绍先　宁夏大学中国阿拉伯国家研究院

第一章　王　诚　毛小菁　商务部国际贸易经济合作研究院西亚非洲所

第二章　杨韶艳　宁夏大学经济管理学院

中国-阿拉伯国家博览会
معرض الصين والدول العربية
CHINA-ARAB STATES EXPO

# The Development Process of China-Arab States Economic and Trade Relations Annual Report

## 2024

The Secretariat of China-Arab States Expo /Edit
Li Shaoxian /Editor in Chief

# 中阿经贸关系发展进程
# 2024年度报告

社会科学文献出版社
SOCIAL SCIENCES ACADEMIC PRESS (CHINA)

# Editorial Committee for *The Development Process of China-Arab States Economic and Trade Relations Annual Report 2024*

**Director**

Dai Peiji

**Deputy director**

Pang Zijie, Nie Dan, Li Shaoxian

**Members (Arranged by the number of strokes in the Chinese characters of each surname)**

Ding Long, Wang Guangda, Wang Lincong, Niu Xinchun, Mao Xiaojing, Zhu Dong, Su Hong, Li Min, Li Shaoxian, Yang Wenhui, Yang Chunquan, Yang Yanping, Wu Sike, Zhang Qianjin, Lu Ruquan, Pang Zijie, Nie Dan, Tang Zhichao, Cui Yanxiang, Han Zhizhong, Dai Peiji

**Editor-in-chief**

Li Shaoxian

**Deputy editor-in-chief**

Su Hong, Zhang Qianjin

# Preface

The year 2024 witnessed profound transformations in the global landscape, as persistent challenges and escalating risks unfolded amid sluggish economic growth worldwide. Looking back on 2024, multiple flashpoints in the Middle East intertwined, further complicating the already volatile regional situation. A new round of the Palestinian-Israeli conflict continues, causing unprecedented humanitarian catastrophe with ongoing spillover effects. Frequent flare-ups—such as the Lebanon-Israel clashes, Iran-Israel tensions, and the collapse of the Assad regime in Syria—highlight the long and arduous path ahead for Middle East peace. Facing complex international and regional dynamics, China and Arab countries have stood together in solidarity, overcoming difficulties and setting a model for South-South cooperation.

At the end of 2022, the first China-Arab States Summit was successfully held. President Xi Jinping and the leaders of Arab countries unanimously agreed to build a China-Arab states community with a shared future for the new era, defining the direction of joint efforts between the two sides. Over the past two-plus years, under the guidance of President Xi Jinping and the leaders of Arab countries, notable progress has been made in the construction of the China-Arab states community with a shared future. China-Arab states relations have entered the best period in history, with deeper strategic mutual-trust, more practical cooperation, and closer emotional bonds between the people. In 2024, the 10th Ministerial Meeting of the China-Arab States Cooperation Forum was held in Beijing. It was the first ministerial meeting after the first China-Arab States Summit, and it also coincided with the 20th anniversary of the forum. It was an important meeting that connected the past and the future. The two sides had in-depth discussions on stepping up the implementation of the outcomes of the first China-Arab States Summit and accelerating the construction of the China -Arab community with a shared future, reaching a consensus in many areas

and adding fresh momentum to China-Arab states ties. The two sides agreed to jointly build the "Five-Major Cooperation Patterns" between China and Arab states on the basis of the "Eight Major Common Actions" for China-Arab states practical cooperation, which mapped out a blueprint for future China-Arab states practical cooperation, leading China-Arab states cooperation in the new era to a new level, and promoted the construction of the China-Arab states community with a shared future at an accelerated pace. The two sides also agreed to hold the second China-Arab States Summit in China in 2026, which will become another milestone in China-Arab states relations.

Economic and trade cooperation serves as the anchor for deepening China-Arab states relations. The two sides enjoy strong complementary advantages in economic and trade collaboration, and Arab countries are key partners in the joint construction of the Belt and Road Initiative (BRI). By the end of 2023, China had signed BRI cooperation documents with all 22 Arab countries and the Arab League, achieving full coverage. Through joint efforts, practical cooperation between China and Arab states has continued to deepen and solidify. In trade, China remains the largest trading partner of Arab countries. Bilateral trade surged from USD238.89 billion in 2013 to USD407.394 billion in 2024, with further optimization in the structure of traded goods. Arab nations have become a crucial market for China's new three products referring to new energy vehicles, lithium batteries, and photovoltaic products and intermediate goods. In 2024, China's exports of the new three exports to Arab countries reached USD7.94 billion, a year-on-year increase of 66.5%, while intermediate goods exports totaled USD98.85 billion, up 11.5% year-on-year, accounting for nearly 50% of China's total exports to the region. In investment, China's outbound investment in Arab countries has continued to expand, while Arab investment in China has also grown more active. From 2021 to 2023, China's direct investment flows to Arab states recorded three consecutive years of growth, reaching USD2.31 billion, USD2.62 billion, and USD2.69 billion, with growth rates of 103.3%, 13.3%, and 2.7%, respectively. However, in 2024, due to regional instability, the impact of U.S. long-arm jurisdiction on Arab countries' willingness to cooperate with China, and Chinese companies' challenges in adapting to local conditions, China's direct investment flows to the region declined by 11.1% year-on-year to USD2.39 billion. The UAE, Saudi Arabia, Iraq, Algeria, and Egypt remained the top five destinations for China's investment stock in Arab countries, accounting

# Preface

for 79.58% of the total. Meanwhile, Arab countries have ramped up investment in China. On one hand, major Arab corporations are actively exploring the Chinese market and expanding cooperation in upstream and downstream industrial chains, particularly in petrochemicals. On the other hand, Middle Eastern sovereign wealth funds, optimistic about China's development prospects, have been setting up offices in China. The UAE and Saudi Arabia remain the most active Arab investors in China. In 2023, newly realized Arab investment in China reached USD2.3 billion, a 120% year-on-year increase. In infrastructure construction, Chinese companies secured new project contracts worth USD65.43 billion in Arab countries in 2024, a 38.6% year-on-year rise, accounting for 24.5% of China's total overseas contract value. Completed turnover reached USD35.01 billion, up 26.4% year-on-year, making up 21.1% of China's global project completion value. Saudi Arabia remains the largest source of contracted projects for China in the Arab world, with rapid growth momentum. Key sectors include construction, energy and power, and transportation projects.

In view of this, the China-Arab States Research Institute at Ningxia University has organized leading experts and scholars in relevant fields to compile the 2024 Report on the Development of China-Arab States Economic and Trade Relations. This report systematically reviews the progress and achievements in China-Arab states economic cooperation since the launch of the Belt and Road Initiative, with a focus on analyzing new developments in 2024 across key areas such as trade, investment, technology, agriculture, the digital economy, ecology, and tourism. It outlines the evolving characteristics and future trends in China-Arab states economic and trade relations. We hope this publication will serve as a valuable reference for government policymakers, academics, entrepreneurs and students.

Finally, we would like to express our sincere gratitude to all those who contributed to the writing, translation, editing, and proofreading of this book, and we deeply appreciate the attention and support from our readers.

Professor Li Shaoxian
May of 2025, Ningxia

# CONTENTS

**Chapter 1   Overall Situation of China-Arab States Economic and Trade Cooperation**   **/ 001**

1.1   General Status of China-Arab States Economic and Trade Cooperation   / 001

1.2   Current Trends of China-Arab States Economic and Trade Cooperation   / 006

1.3   Prospects for China-Arab States Economic and Trade Cooperation   / 014

**Chapter 2   Special Report on China-Arab States Trade Cooperation**   **/ 022**

2.1   Overview of China's Foreign Trade Development   / 023

2.2   Development of Foreign Trade in Arab Countries   / 029

2.3   Development of Trade Relations Between China and Arab Countries   / 035

2.4   Trends and Prospects of China-Arab States Trade Cooperation   / 050

**Chapter 3   Special Report on China-Arab States Investment Cooperation**   **/ 058**

3.1   Chinese Direct Investment in the Arab States   / 059

| | | |
|---|---|---|
| 3.2 | Arab States' Investment in China | / 071 |
| 3.3 | Prospect of China-Arab States Investment Cooperation | / 077 |

**Chapter 4  Special Report on China-Arab States Financial Cooperation** / 082

| | | |
|---|---|---|
| 4.1 | Overview of the Financial Situation in Arab States | / 082 |
| 4.2 | Steady Progress in China-Arab States Financial Cooperation | / 087 |
| 4.3 | New Trends in China-Arab States Financial Cooperation | / 096 |
| 4.4 | Prospects for China-Arab States Financial Cooperation | / 100 |

**Chapter 5  Special Report on China-Arab States Agricultural Cooperation** / 104

| | | |
|---|---|---|
| 5.1 | China-Arab States Agricultural Cooperation since the Proposal of the Belt and Road Initiative (BRI) | / 104 |
| 5.2 | Current Situation of China-Arab States Agricultural Cooperation in 2024 | / 115 |
| 5.3 | Prospects for China-Arab States Agricultural Cooperation | / 125 |

**Chapter 6  Special Report on China-Arab States Energy Cooperation** / 128

| | | |
|---|---|---|
| 6.1 | Overview of Arab States' Energy Resources | / 128 |
| 6.2 | Status of China-Arab States Cooperation in Conventional Energy | / 136 |
| 6.3 | Status of China-Arab States Cooperation in New Energy | / 141 |
| 6.4 | Prospects for China-Arab States Energy Cooperation | / 146 |

**Chapter 7  Special Report on China-Arab States Digital Economy Cooperation** / 151

| | | |
|---|---|---|
| 7.1 | The Digital Economy Development in Arab States | / 151 |
| 7.2 | China-Arab States Cooperation in the Digital Economy | / 163 |
| 7.3 | The Future of China-Arab States Cooperation in the Digital Economy | / 172 |

CONTENTS

**Chapter 8 Special Report on China-Arab States Science and Technology Cooperation** / 176

8.1 Strategic Foundations of China-ArabStates Science and Technology Cooperation / 176

8.2 Practical Progress in China-Arab States Science and Technology Cooperation / 182

8.3 Future Prospects of China-Arab States Science and Technology Cooperation / 195

**Chapter 9 Special Report on China-Arab States Ecological Cooperation** / 199

9.1 The Status Quo and Governance of the Ecological Environment in the Arab Region / 200

9.2 China-Arab States Cooperation in Ecological and Environmental Governance / 205

9.3 Outlook on China-Arab States Cooperation in Ecological and Environmental Protection / 213

**Chapter 10 Special Report on China-Arab States Cooperation in Tourism** / 221

10.1 Overview of China-Arab States Tourism in 2024 / 221

10.2 A 20-Year Review of China-Arab States Cooperation in Tourism / 228

10.3 Analysis of Tourism Cooperation Trends Between China and Arab States in the New Era / 238

**Chapter 11 Special Report on China-Arab States Expo** / 244

11.1 Review of the Development of the China-Arab States Expo / 245

11.2 Multiple Development Opportunities Faced by the China-Arab States Expo Under the New Situation / 255

11.3 Ideas on Successfully Holding the China-Arab States Expo Under the New Situation / 259

003

The Development Process of China-Arab States Economic and Trade Relations
Annual Report 2024

11.4 Approaches to Successfully Holding the China-Arab
States Expo Under the New Situation / 263

**Chapter 12　Special Report on the Opening Up of Ningxia　/ 269**

12.1 The Steady Improvement of an Open Economy / 269

12.2 The Gradual Enhancement of the Function of Channels for
Opening Up / 285

12.3 Prospects for Ningxia's Countermeasures for High-Level
Opening Up / 291

**Chronicle of China-Arab States Economic and Trade
Cooperation in 2024　/ 302**

**Postscript　/ 329**

# Chapter 1 Overall Situation of China-Arab States Economic and Trade Cooperation

In 2024, the international landscape has been characterized by rapid and tumultuous changes, marked by persistent turmoil, escalating great power rivalries, mounting conflicts and risks, sluggish global economic growth, and increasingly formidable challenges and threats confronting the world. In the Arab region, the spillover effects of the Palestinian-Israeli conflict have intensified, the Assad regime in Syria has swiftly unraveled, the civil war in Sudan has become entrenched, and the risk of regional instability has surged. Meanwhile, major Arab countries have exhibited a strong resolve to pursue reconciliation and development. The wave of Middle Eastern reconciliation that emerged in 2023 has continued to gain momentum in 2024, with key Arab nations, notably the Gulf states, actively advancing economic development and diversification strategies. Faced with this complex scenario, China and Arab countries have consistently stood shoulder to shoulder, overcoming adversities together. China-Arab states relations are currently at their zenith in history, with bilateral economic and trade cooperation reaching new heights. Collaboration in trade, investment, contracting engineering, and emerging sectors has been marked by a plethora of highlights and fruitful achievements.

## 1.1 General Status of China-Arab States Economic and Trade Cooperation

### 1.1.1 The "Five Cooperation Frameworks" Driving China-Arab States Economic and Trade Cooperation to New Heights

On May 30, 2024, President Xi Jinping attended the opening ceremony of the

The Development Process of China-Arab States Economic and Trade Relations
Annual Report 2024

10th Ministerial Conference of the China-Arab States Cooperation Forum and delivered a keynote speech. He pointed out that thanks to the joint efforts of both sides, early harvests have been achieved in all the "eight major cooperation initiatives" he put forward for practical cooperation between the two sides at the first China-Arab States Summit. China and Arab countries have achieved full coverage in signing cooperation documents for jointly building the Belt and Road Initiative. New progress has been made in scientific and technological research and development as well as technology transfer, and economic, trade, and energy cooperation has reached a new level[1]. China is ready to work with the Arab side on that basis to put in place the following "five cooperation frameworks" to step up the building of a China-Arab states community with a shared future. The "five cooperation frameworks" has laid out a blueprint for further enhancing China-Arab states cooperation. They include a more dynamic framework for innovation, an expanded framework for investment and finance cooperation, a more multifaceted framework for energy cooperation, a more balanced framework for mutually beneficial economic and trade ties, and a broader framework for people-to-people exchanges. The frameworks will each drive in-depth collaboration between China and Arab countries in different fields at various levels, fostering greater new achievements in China-Arab states economic and trade cooperation.

## 1.1.2 Slight Increase in Trade Volume

In 2024, the trade volume between China and Arab countries rebounded to USD407.394 billion, marking a year-on-year increase of 2.33%, and China continued to maintain its position as the largest trading partner of Arab countries. China's exports to Arab countries were USD205.986 billion, up 13.63% year on year, while China's imports from Arab countries amounted to USD201.408 billion, down 7.12%. USD177.195 billion were for oil and other fossil fuels from Arab countries, accounting for 81.71%. Saudi Arabia, the United Arab Emirates (UAE), Iraq, Oman and Qatar remain China's top five trading partners in Arab countries. The bilateral trade volume between China and Saudi Arabia edged up to USD107.534 billion; for the first time, the trade volume

---

[1] Xi Jinping, "Further Deepening Cooperation and Moving Forward to Step up the Building of a China-Arab States Community with a Shared Future," *People's Daily*, May 31, 2025, p.2.

Chapter 1    Overall Situation of China-Arab States Economic and Trade Cooperation

between China and the UAE exceeded USD100 billion, reaching USD101.838 billion, an increase of 7.2% year on year. China's exports to the UAE amounted to USD65.593 billion, an increase of 17.8% year on year. China's trade growth with Algeria and Morocco was particularly notable, with year-on-year growth of over 20% (21.11% and 21.61%, respectively) and trade volumes reaching USD12.482 billion and USD9.037 billion respectively. China's exports to Algeria increased by 23.52%, imports from Morocco by 32.66%, and exports to Morocco also increased by 19.93%. Overall, since the new era, trade between China and Arab countries has continued to heat up. Except for significant decline in bilateral trade in 2015-2016 due to the impact of the decline in crude oil prices and in 2020 due to the impact of COVID-19, the trade volume has generally grown steadily in other years, especially in 2021 and 2022 when bilateral trade recovered strongly, breaking through the 300 billion and 400 billion marks successively, reflecting the increasingly close trade relations between China and Arab countries[1].

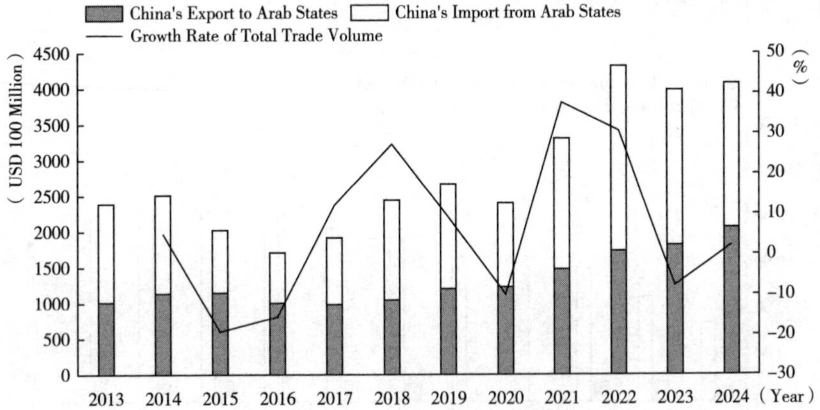

**Figure 1.1    Total Import and Export Volume Between China and Arab Countries (2013-2024)**

Source: General Administration of Customs of China.

### 1.1.3    Increasingly Active Two-way Investment

In 2024, China's direct investment flow to Arab countries was USD2.39 billion,

———————————

①    Data from General Administration of Customs of China.

**003**

The Development Process of China-Arab States Economic and Trade Relations
Annual Report 2024

a year-on-year decrease of 11.1%. The top five countries in terms of investment flow were the UAE (USD1.572 billion), Saudi Arabia (USD367 million), Egypt (USD172 million), Iraq (USD104 million), and Morocco (USD55 million)[1]. As of the end of 2023, China's direct investment stock in Arab countries stood at USD21.678 billion, a year-on-year decline of 13.05% (see Figure 1.2). The UAE, Saudi Arabia, Iraq, Algeria, and Egypt remained the top five investment destinations for China's investment stock in Arab countries, accounting for 79.58% of the total[2]. In addition to direct investment, Chinese enterprises have also actively expanded their business in various fields in Arab countries through reinvestment, third-country investment, and other means, with the cumulative value of various types of investments exceeding USD78 billion[3]. Since 2013, China's investment in Arab countries has remained stable, with investment flows staying above USD2 billion in most years. The investment stock has grown from USD8.565 billion in 2013 to a peak of USD24.932 billion in 2022, nearly doubling in 10 years, reflecting the continued optimism of Chinese enterprises in the Arab country market.

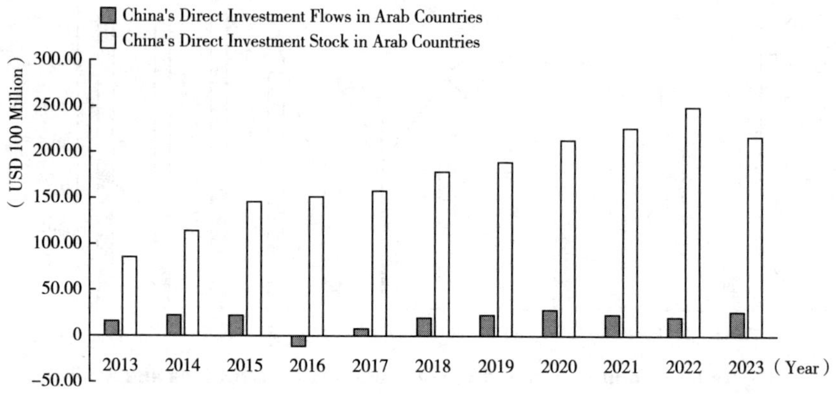

**Figure 1.2　China's Direct Investment Flows and Stocks in Arab Countries (2013-2023)**

Source: Annual Statistical Bulletin of China's Outward Foreign Direct Investment.

---

[1]　Ministry of Commerce.

[2]　Ministry of Commerce, National Bureau of Statistics, and State Administration of Foreign Exchange, *Statistical Bulletin of China's Outward Foreign Direct Investment 2023*, China Commerce and Trade Press, September 2024.

[3]　Institute of International Trade and Economic Cooperation, Ministry of Commerce, *Review and Prospect of China and Arab Countries Economic and Trade Cooperation 2024*.

004

Chapter 1    Overall Situation of China-Arab States Economic and Trade Cooperation

In recent years, Arab countries' investment in China has witnessed a notable upswing. In 2023, the newly added actual investment from Arab countries into China reached USD2.3 billion, a year-on-year increase of 120%. Among them, the UAE' investment in China surged dramatically from USD960 million in the previous year to USD2.2 billion, making it the 10th largest source of investment in China that year[1]. Saudi Arabia was the second-largest Arab investor in China. As of the end of 2023, China's actual utilization of investment from the UAE and Saudi Arabia stood at USD4.5 billion and USD1.89 billion, respectively[2]. On the one hand, several major Arab corporations have actively ventured into the Chinese market and expanded cooperation across upstream and downstream industrial chains, particularly in the petrochemical sector. Prominent examples include Saudi Aramco and the Saudi Basic Industries Corporation. On the other hand, Middle Eastern sovereign wealth funds, buoyed by optimism regarding China's developmental trajectory, have established a presence in China by setting up offices, enhancing their market footprint, and augmenting their investment portfolios in the country. Notable participants in this trend encompass the Saudi Public Investment Fund, the Abu Dhabi Investment Authority of the UAE, Mubadala Investment Company, and the Kuwait Investment Authority.

### 1.1.4    Steady Development of Infrastructure Cooperation

Arab countries constitute a pivotal market for China's overseas contracted projects, with infrastructure cooperation serving as a cornerstone of China-Arab states economic and trade collaboration. In 2024, Chinese enterprises inked new contracts valued at USD65.43 billion in Arab countries, a year-on-year increase of 38.6%, accounting for 24.5% of the total new contracts signed; and achieved a turnover of USD35.01 billion, a 26.4% year-on-year surge, accounting for 21.1% of the total turnover. Saudi Arabia stands out as the primary source of contracted projects for China among Arab countries, exhibiting a robust growth trajectory. In 2024, Chinese firms secured new contracts worth USD32.55 billion in Saudi Arabia, a year-on-year increase of 94.3%, accounting for 49.7% of the new contracts signed in Arab countries that year; and achieved a turnover of USD12.63 billion, a 36.2% year-on-year rise, representing 36.1% of the total.

---

[1]    Ministry of Commerce, *Statistical Bulletin on Foreign Investment in China 2024*.

[2]    Ibid.

**005**

The Development Process of China-Arab States Economic and Trade Relations
Annual Report 2024

Iraq, the UAE, Algeria, and Egypt emerge as the other four major markets for Chinese enterprises' contracted projects, with new contracts signed in these countries accounting for 39.2% and turnover realized comprising 51.5% of the respective totals in 2024. Sector-wise, construction, energy and power, and transportation projects dominate the portfolio of Chinese enterprises.

## 1.2 Current Trends of China-Arab States Economic and Trade Cooperation

### 1.2.1 Steady Growth and Quality Improvement in Trade Volume

Over the past year, China and Arab countries have focused on improving bilateral trade structures, promoting balanced trade development, and enhancing trade liberalization and facilitation, creating broader development space for bilateral trade and investment. Through joint efforts, bilateral trade volume returned to its historical high of over USD400 billion in 2024, with further optimization and rationalization of the commodity structure. Oil and gas trade continued to play a pivotal role. In 2024, China imported approximately 250 million tons of crude oil from Arab countries, a year-on-year decrease of 6.85%, accounting for 44.6% of China's total global crude oil imports[1]. Among the top ten crude oil importing countries, Arab countries occupied six spots, namely Saudi Arabia (2nd), Iraq (4th), Oman (5th), UAE (6th), Kuwait (9th), and Qatar (10th). In terms of natural gas, China imported 20.49 million tons of liquefied natural gas (LNG) from Arab countries, a year-on-year increase of 8%, accounting for 26.7% of China's total global imports, with a total value of USD11.78 billion. Qatar maintained its position as China's second-largest source of LNG imports (after Australia), with LNG exports to China reaching 18.36 million tons, a year-on-year increase of 10.2%, accounting for 23.9% of China's total global imports, standing out among Arab countries. Major non-energy products imported from Arab countries by China include oilseeds and oil crops, feed, vegetable oils, and aquatic products, with Sudan, UAE, Egypt, Mauritania, Saudi Arabia, and Morocco being the main sources of imports. In addition to these major agricultural products, Arab countries' specialty agricultural products such as Egyptian citrus and mangoes, UAE camel milk and oysters, Saudi dried

---

[1] General Administration of Customs.

006

Chapter 1　Overall Situation of China-Arab States Economic and Trade Cooperation

dates, and Omani aquatic products have continued to sell well in the Chinese market after gaining market access.

In terms of exports, Arab countries have emerged as significant markets for China's "new three items"—new energy vehicles (NEVs), lithium batteries, and photovoltaic products—as well as for intermediate goods. In 2024, China's total exports of the "new three items" to Arab countries amounted to USD7.94 billion, representing a year–on–year increase of 66.5%; and total exports of intermediate goods to Arab countries reached USD98.85 billion, marking a year-on-year increase of 11.5% and accounting for nearly 50% of China's total exports to Arab countries. Specifically, photovoltaic product exports to Arab countries totaled USD3.45 billion, a year-on-year increase of 29.8%. Saudi Arabia, with USD1.89 billion in exports, became China's fifth-largest overseas market for photovoltaic products. Lithium battery exports amounted to USD1.27 billion, a year-on-year increase of 88.9%. Among the "new three items", NEVs stood out the most. With the advancement of energy transition policies in Arab countries and the growing acceptance of NEVs by local consumers, China's NEV exports to Arab countries experienced rapid growth, totaling 178000 units in 2024, a year-on-year increase of 141.3%. Just to the UAE alone, 131000 units were exported, making the UAE China's fourth-largest global export market for NEVs. Chinese NEV brands represented by BYD, NIO, and XPENG are at the forefront globally in battery technology, intelligence level, and cost control. In recent years, they have continuously strengthened technological innovation in response to the high-temperature climate and special geographical environment of Arab countries, improving battery heat resistance, enhancing vehicle mileage, and optimizing air conditioning efficiency to introduce NEVs more suitable for the local market. With a rich product line, they meet the needs of different consumer groups in Arab countries, not only being competitive in the mid-to-low-end market but also competing with international brands in the high-end market. In addition to vehicle exports, Chinese automakers are actively considering deepening cooperation with Arab countries through technology collaboration, joint venture plant construction, and other means, and laying out localized production and after-sales service networks. This helps to further enhance the brand influence and market share of Chinese NEVs in the region.

**007**

The Development Process of China-Arab States Economic and Trade Relations
Annual Report 2024

## 1.2.2 Continuous Acceleration of Investment Transformation and Upgrading

In 2024, there has been a notable upsurge in investment cooperation between China and Arab countries, accompanied by closer personnel and information exchanges. The number, scale, scope, and level of projects under negotiation have seen significant improvement. There has been comprehensive progress in the strategic positioning and development of projects in traditional energy, manufacturing, mining, and emerging industries, showcasing new characteristics of green development and integrated advancement.

Energy transition drives green and low-carbon cooperation. Green investment has become the core engine of China-Arab states cooperation. The China Silk Road Fund signed a memorandum of understanding (MOU) with Masdar, a UAE's flagship renewable energy company, with both sides planning to jointly invest in clean energy projects in Belt and Road Initiative countries (especially developing countries and those in the southern hemisphere), with a total investment expected to reach RMB 20 billion (approximately USD2.8 billion), marking a new stage in China-Arab states cooperation in the green energy sector[1]. Saudi Arabia's ACWA Power announced the establishment of a global innovation center in Shanghai, focusing on the research and development of new technologies and products in fields such as photovoltaics, wind power, energy storage, green hydrogen, and seawater desalination[2]. GD Power announced a joint investment with Abu Dhabi Future Energy Company and Korea Electric Power Corporation in a 2GW photovoltaic project in Saudi Arabia's Eastern Province, with a total investment of USD1.112 billion (approximately RMB 8.135 billion), accelerating the overseas layout of new energy projects. These projects not only showcase China's advantages in new energy technology but also promote the acceleration of emission reduction targets in Arab countries' "Vision 2030" through innovative models such as carbon footprint tracking systems and green financial tools.

---

[1] "Transformation of UAE Energy Giant: Billion-Dollar Overseas Expansion, with Low-Carbon Hydrogen as the New Frontier," https://finance.sina.com.cn/cj/2024-11-25/doc-incxhuth8112011.shtml, Nov. 25, 2024.

[2] "Saudi Arabia's ACWA Power Sets Up in Pudong," https://www.shanghai.gov.cn/nw15343/2024 1016/5f7ea7b1bbdf4687a2c5009fbd30a0b1.html, Oct. 16, 2024.

008

Chapter 1　Overall Situation of China-Arab States Economic and Trade Cooperation

The bilateral integration and development of industries between China and Arab countries continue to deepen. RELC (Renewable Energy Localization Company), a subsidiary of Saudi Arabia's Public Investment Fund (PIF), has entered into cooperation agreements with three Chinese new energy companies: Envision Energy, Jinko Solar, and TCL Zhonghuan, aiming to promote the localization of manufacturing and assembly of equipment and components required for solar and wind energy in Saudi Arabia[1]. Zhejiang Rongsheng Petrochemical Co., Ltd. and Saudi Arabian Oil Company (Saudi Aramco) have signed a "Memorandum of Understanding" to cross-invest in each other's refining and chemical enterprises. Building upon this, they will undertake capacity upgrades and expansions, capitalizing on the market and policy strengths of both China and Saudi Arabia to establish a large-scale, internationally competitive integrated refining and petrochemical project straddling the two nations. This milestone signifies a major advancement in bilateral investment collaboration on transnational entity projects[2]. Investment cooperation between China and Morocco in NEV industry is gaining strong momentum, with industrial investment agreements worth USD9.5 billion reached in 2024, covering multiple fields such as cathode materials, anode materials, precursors, separators, copper foils, electrolytes, and automotive parts for NEV batteries. Through the implementation of these localization projects, Chinese enterprises introduce advanced technology and management experience to Arab countries, promoting the upgrading of local manufacturing industries and helping these countries enhance their positions in the global industrial and supply chains. At the same time, they can better meet local market demands and achieve mutually beneficial and win-win collaborative development.

### 1.2.3　Frequent Successes in Contracted Project Cooperation

Arab countries represent one of the earliest and most important markets for Chinese enterprises to undertake contracted project businesses. In recent

---

[1]　"With a Total Investment of Tens of Billions (yuan), Three Leading Private New Energy enterprises are Heading to Saudi Arabia," https://news.qq.com/rain/a/20240717A00Z0Z00, July 17, 2024.

[2]　"Announcement on the Signing of a Memorandum of Understanding with Saudi Aramco Oil Company Limited," website of Rongsheng Petrochemical, http://static.cninfo.com.cn/finalpage/2024-01-03/1218789834.PDF, Jan. 3, 2024.

years, benefiting from generally improved fiscal conditions, Arab countries have increased their infrastructure investments, leading to rapid development in China-Arab states contracted project cooperation. In 2024, the value of newly signed contracted projects by Chinese enterprises in Arab countries accounted for nearly a quarter of the total newly signed overseas contracts, with a year-on-year increase of 38.6%, significantly surpassing the overall growth rate of 1.1% in overseas markets[1]. Arab countries have emerged as the fastest-growing market segment for overseas contracted projects undertaken by Chinese enterprises globally. From a country-specific perspective, Chinese enterprises achieved double-digit or higher growth in contracted projects businesses in 10 Arab countries, with Saudi Arabia rising to become the largest single overseas market for contracted projects by Chinese enterprises.

Major projects have been secured one after another. China National Chemical Engineering Group (CNCEC) has signed a contract for the Al-Faw Refinery Project with Iraq's South Refineries Company, with a total investment of USD5-6 billion. The project includes a 300000-bpd oil refinery, a 3 million tons-per-year petrochemical complex, and a supporting 2000-megawatt power plant. Upon completion, it will enable Iraq to produce locally refined petroleum products meeting Euro V standards and provide full-chain services from crude oil supply to product sales[2]. China State Construction Engineering Corporation won the bid for the Riyadh Heritage Village Complex Construction Project in Saudi Arabia with an offer of USD2 billion[3]. China Gezhouba Group secured the contract for the civil engineering works of Lot 9 of the Moroccan high-speed railway project LGV at USD225 million, further consolidating the dominant position of Chinese enterprises in this project alongside other previously awarded lots to China Railway Fourth Engineering Group, Shandong High Speed Group Co., Ltd., China Railway 20th Bureau Group Corporation, and

---

[1]  Ministry of Commerce.

[2]  "Total Investment of Approximately USD20 Billion! China National Chemical Engineering Group Signs Agreement for 15 Million Tons/Year Refining and Petrochemical Integration Project," reported by Lubricants Information Network, http://www.lube-info.com/2024/0603/16124.html, June 3, 2024.

[3]  "USD2.08 Billion! China State Construction Consortium Wins Bid for a Large-Scale Public Construction Project in Saudi Arabia," reported by Sina Finance, https://finance.sina.com.cn/roll/2024-11-21/doc-incwvitk4586430.shtml, Nov. 21, 2024.

Chapter 1    Overall Situation of China-Arab States Economic and Trade Cooperation

China Overseas Engineering Group Co., Ltd[1]. Chinese enterprises have also shifted from operating alone in the past to increasingly participating in project bidding by forming joint ventures with local companies and international partners, achieving sound development through mutual benefits and win-win cooperation. A consortium formed by CRRC Corporation Limited and two Turkish companies won the bid for the Dubai Blue Line Development Project with a contract value of USD5.58 billion[2]. China Railway Sixth Group and Algerian company Infrarer jointly won the bid for the USD476 million railway upgrade contract in the eastern mining region, helping Algeria enhance its railway transportation capacity and better support the development of its mining and logistics industries. A consortium comprising Power Construction Corporation of China and Indian company L&T secured the contract for certain sections of the Oman-UAE Railway Link Project.

Iconic projects are progressing steadily. The concentrated solar power (CSP) and photovoltaic (PV) hybrid solar power plant project, the Hassyan Power Plant project, and the Stage Ⅱ of the UAE Federal Railway project undertaken by Chinese enterprises in Dubai have all entered the final stages of completion, with overall progress reaching 99.9%, 99.95%, and 94%, respectively[3]. The Phase I of the New Administrative Capital Central Business District project and the fully-topped-out El Alamein New City Ultra-High Complex project in Egypt, both constructed by China State Construction Engineering Corporation, are being delivered in stages. In Iraq, the first megawatt-scale photovoltaic energy storage power plant in the country, built by China Petroleum Engineering & Construction Corporation, has officially commenced operation. The project of constructing 679 new schools by Power Construction Corporation of China has been largely completed and handed over. The Nasiriyah Airport project undertaken by China State Construction Engineering Corporation and the Nisour Multi-Level Transportation Project in downtown Baghdad constructed

---

[1]  "Gezhouba Group Secures the Final Section of Morocco's High-Speed Railway Project with a Bid of USD225 Million, with Five Chinese Enterprises Leading the Project's Development," reported by Sohu.com, https://www.sohu.com/a/831274330_121622815, Nov. 28, 2024.

[2]  "CRRC Teams Up with Turkish Enterprise to Secure the USD5.58 Billion Dubai Metro Blue Line Project," reported by Tencent News, https://news.qq.com/rain/a/20241220A02T6W00, Dec. 20, 2024.

[3]  Ministry of Commerce.

011

by Sichuan Railway International Group are both advancing in an orderly manner, with on-site construction progress reaching 37% and 78%, respectively. The Al Shuaibah PV Power Plant project in Saudi Arabia, implemented by China Energy Engineering Group, is the world's largest single-unit photovoltaic power plant currently under construction and has achieved full-capacity grid-connected power generation. Additionally, enterprises such as China Communications Construction Company, China Railway Group Limited, and China Civil Engineering Construction Corporation are actively tracking the progress of large-scale infrastructure projects such as the "Development Road" in Iraq and the "Land Bridge" in Saudi Arabia.

### 1.2.4　Cooperation in Emerging Fields

In recent years, with the acceleration of economic diversification strategies and industrialization processes in Arab countries, China and Arab countries have continuously expanded cooperation space. Building on traditional fields such as energy and infrastructure, they have strengthened cooperation in emerging fields such as finance, digital economy, and transportation and logistics, forming a new pattern of cooperation characterized by complementary advantages and coordinated development.

In terms of financial cooperation, the Ministry of Finance of China successfully priced and issued USD2 billion in sovereign bonds in Riyadh, the capital of Saudi Arabia in November 2024. The offering attracted robust demand from global investors across Asia, the Middle East, Europe, and the United States, with total subscription amounts reaching USD39.73 billion, equivalent to 19.9 times the issuance amount[1]. This marked the first offshore US dollar-denominated sovereign bond issued by China since 2021, and the first time the issuance location was chosen in Saudi Arabia, breaking the 20-year practice of arranging US dollar-denominated sovereign bond issuances in Hong Kong. This move not only demonstrates China's support for Saudi Arabia's efforts to become a global financial investment hub but also highlights the deepening financial service cooperation between China and Saudi Arabia. The

---

[1]　"The Ministry of Finance Successfully Issues USD2 Billion Sovereign Bonds," reported on the website of the Ministry of Finance of the People's Republic of China, https: //www.mof.gov.cn/ zhengwuxinxi/caizhengxinwen/202411/t20241114_3947570.htm, Nov. 14, 2024.

Chapter 1    Overall Situation of China-Arab States Economic and Trade Cooperation

Bank of China completed its first cross-border payment transaction in "digital dirham" via the mBridge with the Central Bank of the UAE, with the transaction amounting to approximately RMB 100 million. The Bank of Communications established its first regional branch in the Dubai International Financial Centre (DIFC), with its business scope covering the entire Arab region. Over the past three years, the total assets managed by Chinese-funded banks in DIFC have surged nearly 33%, reaching USD65.3 billion by the end of 2024. DIFC is home to 16 Chinese financial companies, including six representative offices, five commercial banks, two wealth management firms, one brokerage firm, one advisory firm, and one insurance company. Nasdaq Dubai, one of Dubai's major stock exchanges, currently hosts approximately 22 securities issued by issuers from Hong Kong and the mainland of China, with a total value of USD12.3 billion. The first batch of Saudi Exchange-Traded Funds (ETFs) were listed on the Shanghai and Shenzhen Stock Exchanges, raising a combined amount of over RMB 1.2 billion[1]. The Oman Investment Authority obtained a Qualified Foreign Institutional Investor (QFII) license approved by the China Securities Regulatory Commission in June 2024 and is actively engaging with firms such as China International Capital Corporation Limited (CICC), with potential plans to increase financial investments in China in the future.

Digital economy cooperation is accelerating. In February 2024, the Ministry of Commerce of China and the Ministry of Economy of the UAE signed a *Memorandum on Strengthening Digital Economy Investment Cooperation*[2]. The emirates of Ras Al Khaimah and Abu Dhabi signed cooperation documents with Tencent Cloud, with Tencent Cloud custom-building the online government service platform (TAMM) for Abu Dhabi. Chinese enterprises continued to build 5G commercial networks in countries such as the UAE, Saudi Arabia, and Egypt. Etisalat (UAE Telecommunications Company) and Huawei jointly completed the first experiment on 6GHz 5G technology in a laboratory. TikTok (Douyin) has become the most popular social media platform in Arab countries, capturing over 80% of the live streaming market share. In the second half of 2024, TikTok announced the establishment of a regional headquarters in Saudi Arabia to

---

[1]    "The First Batch of Saudi ETFs Listed in China Surge on Their Debut Day," reported by Yicai Network, https://www.yicai.com/news/102192836.html, July 6, 2024.

[2]    Ministry of Commerce.

013

The Development Process of China-Arab States Economic and Trade Relations
Annual Report 2024

further expand its market in Arab countries[1]. Alibaba launched its B2B platform in Morocco, marking its first entry into North African Arab countries. Huawei Cloud provides cloud services for Wio (a digital bank), Dupay (a digital currency information card), Neopay (a digital bank), and others in the UAE, and launched its first public cloud service in Egypt, serving 28 countries in the northern and central regions of Africa, including Egypt and Algeria. China Mobile signed a MOU with a UAE company to enhance cooperation in areas such as 5G-A solutions, digital infrastructure upgrades, and international submarine optical cables. WeRide, a domestic intelligent driving company, initiated pilot programs for auto taxi services in several Gulf Arab countries.

Breakthroughs have been made in transportation and logistics cooperation. The network for civil aviation exchanges between China and Arab countries has been continuously strengthened. In 2024 alone, China and Saudi Arabia have successively launched five new air routes, facilitating direct flights between five major Chinese cities (Beijing, Shanghai, Guangzhou, Shenzhen, and Hong Kong) and Riyadh. Direct flights between China and Morocco have also officially resumed. E-commerce platform enterprises, with Meituan as a leading example, have achieved remarkable success in developing regional markets in Arab countries. The Keeta food delivery platform app, developed by Meituan for the Saudi Arabian market, has topped the industry download charts in Saudi Arabia. The grocery retail division Xiaoxiang Supermarket has commenced operations in Saudi Arabia, marking its first overseas expansion into Arab countries. Additionally, Meituan's drone business, Drone, has secured the first commercial license for drone delivery issued by the UAE.

## 1.3 Prospects for China-Arab States Economic and Trade Cooperation

The year 2025 is a pivotal year for China-Arab states cooperation, serving as a bridge between the past and the future. It is not only a critical year for implementing the "five cooperation frameworks" but also the starting year

---

[1] "TikTok to Establish Regional Headquarters in Saudi Arabia, Potentially Reshaping the E-commerce Landscape in the Gulf Region," reported by Sohu.com, https: //www.sohu.com/a/832471330_99936768, Dec. 2, 2024.

Chapter 1　Overall Situation of China-Arab States Economic and Trade Cooperation

for preparing for the new China-Arab States Summit and the China-Gulf Cooperation Council Summit in 2026. Based on the planning and design outlined in the "2024-2026 Action Implementation Plan of the China-Arab States Cooperation Forum", China and Arab countries should further deepen and promote multilateral and bilateral cooperation in various fields, including politics, economy and trade, investment, finance, infrastructure, resources and environment, people-to-people exchanges, aerospace, education, and health. The two sides should also enhance the integrated development of industrial and supply chains, explore new drivers of cooperation in emerging areas such as the digital economy and green development, promote the improvement and enhancement of China-Arab states economic and trade cooperation, and inject new impetus and write new chapters into the high-quality joint construction of the Belt and Road Initiative, the development of the China-Arab states strategic partnership, and the construction of a China-Arab states community with a shared future[1].

### 1.3.1　Political and Economic Situation in Arab Countries

In 2024, the Middle East has become the "eye of the storm" in global geopolitical conflicts. In the first half of the year, the Israeli-Palestinian conflict continued unabated, clashes erupted along the Lebanon-Israel border, and internal conflicts in Sudan and Yemen dragged on. In the second half, tensions between Iran and Israel escalated, and the sudden political upheaval in Syria added further uncertainties to the regional situation. The frequent conflicts have sparked widespread concerns about the increasing instability and complexity of the situation in the Middle East. In 2025, Arab countries remain under the shadow of regional uncertainties. Reconciliation and negotiations, conflicts and reshuffles, disasters and development — these factors reflect the complex picture of hope and hardship faced by Arab countries, and also divide them into different camps with varying development situations.

Against the backdrop of persistently low international oil prices, Gulf Arab countries have generally adopted counter-cyclical fiscal policies, stimulating economic growth by maintaining high government spending and injecting

---

[1]　*The Executive Plan of Action for the China-Arab States Cooperation Forum 2024-2026*, reported on the website of the China-Arab States Cooperation Forum, June 6, 2024.

**015**

impetus into economic diversification and transformation. Although low oil prices have exerted certain pressure on the fiscal revenues of these oil-producing countries, their fiscal positions have remained generally stable thanks to relatively robust debt management. According to World Bank projections, the GDP growth rates of Gulf Arab countries will all fall within the 3-4% range in 2025[①]. Meanwhile, the total debt of these countries is also expected to remain stable. However, it should also be noted that the risks of a global economic downturn cannot be overlooked. Gulf Arab countries still need to strive for excellence in macroeconomic policies while ensuring the stability of their internal and external political environments, to ensure sustainable economic growth and successful transformation.

Arab countries in North Africa are expected to emerge as another important pole of rapid development and rise in the Arab world. Since the outbreak of the Russia-Ukraine conflict, North African Arab countries such as Morocco, Algeria, and Egypt have been placing increasing importance on clean energy. The global energy supply disruptions triggered by conflicts such as the Russia-Ukraine conflict and the Palestinian-Israeli conflict have further strengthened their resolve to develop their domestic clean energy industries. In 2025, North African countries will continue their efforts to attract foreign investment to accelerate the vigorous development of the renewable energy sector. They will leverage renewable energy to meet the needs of economic development and support the continued robust growth of their local processing and manufacturing industries.

## 1.3.2　New Development Opportunities for China-Arab States Economic and Trade Cooperation

In 2024, China and Arab countries have engaged in intensive and fruitful interactions under the frameworks of two major cooperation platforms—the China-Arab States Cooperation Forum and the Forum on China-Africa Cooperation. Economic and trade cooperation between China and Arab countries has not only achieved a qualitative leap but also steadily progressed in trade, investment, contracted projects, and cooperation in emerging fields, demonstrating a strong development momentum. Currently, the trend of Arab countries "looking east" is becoming increasingly pronounced, and their desire

---

①　World Bank, *Global Economic Prospects*.

Chapter 1 Overall Situation of China-Arab States Economic and Trade Cooperation

for "pursuing stability and seeking development" is stronger than ever before. These countries regard economic development as a top priority and core concern, hoping to achieve "overtaking on curves" in industrial development through deepening internal reforms and expanding opening-up to the outside world. In the coming period, Arab countries will still maintain strong external demand and internal driving forces in areas such as infrastructure construction, energy structure transformation, the digital economy sector, and the healthcare industry. These areas happen to have a high degree of complementarity and fit with China's industries, providing new impetus and a vast blue ocean market for the high-quality development of China-Arab states economic and trade cooperation.

At the opening ceremony of the 10th Ministerial Conference of the China-Arab States Cooperation Forum held in May 2024, President Xi Jinping proposed a vision of jointly building "five cooperation frameworks" with Arab partners. This new cooperation framework not only takes full account of the traditional areas of strength in bilateral cooperation but also further taps into new potentials and expands the depth and breadth of China-Arab states cooperation. In terms of innovation-driven development, both sides will strengthen cooperation in scientific and technological innovation to jointly promote industrial upgrading and technological progress. In the investment and finance sector, the two sides will expand mutual investment scales and deepen financial cooperation to provide strong support for the economic development of both sides. Regarding energy cooperation, China and the Arab side will jointly tackle the challenges of energy transition and promote cooperation and development in clean and renewable energy. In terms of mutual economic and trade benefits, both sides will further enhance trade facilitation and promote sustained and healthy growth in bilateral trade. In people-to-people and cultural exchanges, the two sides will strengthen cooperation in education, culture, tourism, and other fields to enhance friendship and mutual understanding between their peoples. Looking ahead to 2025, economic and trade cooperation between China and Arab countries will embrace broader development prospects and new opportunities.

### 1.3.3 Risks and Challenges Facing China-Arab States Economic and Trade Cooperation

By 2025, the Middle East's complex and multifaceted regional dynamics will

017

persist, with continued high levels of uncertainty and instability posing significant challenges to deepening China-Arab states economic and trade cooperation.

Firstly, the inherent challenges and risks in Arab countries persist. In terms of the geopolitical landscape, since the outbreak of the new round of Palestinian-Israeli conflict in October 2023, there has been a succession of conflicts, including the Israel-Lebanon conflict, the civil war in Sudan, and the regime change in Syria. The domestic political deadlocks in Yemen and Libya remain unresolved, fueling ongoing concerns about the political and security situation across the entire Middle East region. Domestically, issues such as social unrest and the remnants of terrorist organizations continue to plague governance. In some Arab countries, the proliferation of firearms has led to frequent armed conflicts, gang clashes, political assassinations, and car bombings, with citizens still living in environments riddled with landmines and grenades from past wars. Regarding the business environment, some Arab countries rank low in the World Bank's Doing Business report, with multiple indicators related to investment cooperation falling short of expectations, and issues such as administrative inefficiency remaining a source of criticism from the international community. In certain countries, fiscal constraints have led to delayed budget allocations, prominent issues with loan repayment defaults, and increased exposure to sovereign default risks.

Secondly, external interference risks such as great power rivalry are becoming increasingly prominent. The United States has long interfered in the internal and external affairs of Arab countries, using long-arm jurisdiction to strangle the economic lifelines of some Arab countries, thereby promoting its Middle East strategy that prioritizes U.S. interests and serves its goals of great power rivalry. In July 2022, former President Biden visited the Middle East with the aim of creating a Middle Eastern version of NATO and promoting the "India-Middle East-Europe Economic Corridor (IMEC)" to seek to build an anti-China encirclement in the Middle East. After starting his second term, Trump may further promote the decoupling of Arab countries from China in high-tech, military industry and trade, and critical infrastructure through various means such as politics, economy, and military, which may have a non-negligible impact on China-Arab states economic and trade cooperation.

Thirdly, there is an urgent need to address the weakness in the "going global" capabilities of Chinese enterprises. Chinese enterprises "going global" generally

Chapter 1  Overall Situation of China-Arab States Economic and Trade Cooperation

lack capabilities in risk prevention and control as well as compliance management, have insufficient research on the policies, laws, and cultures of the host countries, and have room for improvement in corresponding risk assessments and response mechanisms. The instability of domestic politics and policies in Arab countries, the insufficient implementation of laws and regulations, and cultural conflicts arising from special business practices are the main difficulties faced by Chinese enterprises in expanding their markets in Arab countries and establishing a long-term foothold there. In particular, Arab countries have generally been affected by factors such as slowing economic growth and unsatisfactory progress in industrial transformation and upgrading in recent years, leading to an increase in trade and investment protectionism and an inward-looking tendency in economic policies. They have been shifting pressure to foreign enterprises in terms of tax levels and the proportion of local employment, driving up the costs of business activities, including those of Chinese enterprises.

### 1.3.4  Key Areas of Future China-Arab States Economic and Trade Cooperation

After years of development, economic and trade cooperation between China and Arab countries has formed a pattern with energy cooperation as the cornerstone and coordinated advancement in diversified fields. Looking ahead, against the backdrop of the reshaping of the globalization landscape, the rise of the green economy, and the acceleration of digital transformation, China-Arab states economic and trade cooperation will transcend simple resource and commodity exchanges and evolve towards higher-level forms such as joint technology research, standard-setting, and co-shaping of value chains. This evolution will not only help Arab countries achieve their economic diversification goals but also propel strategic mutual trust and pragmatic cooperation between China and Arab countries to new heights.

Firstly, there will be deep collaboration in green energy and low-carbon industrial chains. In the context of global energy transition, China-Arab states cooperation will accelerate its expansion from the traditional oil and gas sector to the entire green energy industrial chain. On the one hand, China will continue to deepen cooperation with countries such as Saudi Arabia and the UAE in photovoltaics, wind power, and hydrogen energy, and promote the implementation of landmark projects. On the other hand, both sides will jointly

**019**

build low-carbon industrial clusters, with Chinese NEV and battery manufacturing enterprises expected to establish regional production bases in Arab countries, facilitating the low-carbon transformation of energy-intensive industries, such as refining and metallurgy in Arab countries through technology transfer and localized production.

Secondly, there will be joint breakthroughs in the digital economy and technological innovation. The "Look East" strategy of Arab countries aligns closely with China's "Digital Silk Road" initiative, with both sides focusing on promoting joint innovation in areas such as 5G, artificial intelligence, and smart cities. Saudi Arabia's "Vision 2030" and the UAE's "AI Strategy 2031" provide vast opportunities for Chinese technology enterprises. Additionally, the two sides can explore the establishment of a China-Arab states digital innovation joint fund to support cross-border incubation of startups and establish regional standards in areas such as data security and cross-border payments, thereby seizing the opportunities of digital economic development.

Thirdly, there will be an enhancement of infrastructure and improvements in regional connectivity. The economic diversification strategies adopted by Arab countries have spurred significant demand for infrastructure development, and China's Belt and Road Initiative is deeply aligned with Arab countries' regional development plans, such as Egypt's "New Administrative Capital" project and Saudi Arabia's "The Line" initiative. Future cooperation will manifest in two major trends: first, a transition from single-project contracting to an "investment, construction, and operation integrated" model, aimed at enhancing sustainability through long-term equity partnerships; second, there will be an emphasis on integrating "hard connectivity" with "soft connectivity". China and Arab countries can collaborate on the construction of cross-regional transportation networks, such as smart cross-border logistics systems and the Red Sea-Mediterranean Railway, while strengthening institutional cooperation in areas like customs digitization and harmonization of trade regulations to reduce regional trade costs.

Fourthly, there will be coordinated efforts to ensure modern agriculture and food security. In response to the challenges posed by climate change to food security in Arab countries, China-Arab states agricultural cooperation will evolve from focusing solely on agricultural product trade to technological collaboration and upgrading. China can export technologies such as water-saving

Chapter 1　Overall Situation of China-Arab States Economic and Trade Cooperation

irrigation, saline-alkali land improvement, and vertical farming, and integrate them with green development technologies to pilot and promote "photovoltaic + agriculture" projects in selected Arab countries based on local conditions. Additionally, both sides can jointly establish cross-border grain supply chains, leveraging China's strengths in warehousing and logistics to assist Arab countries in building stable grain supply channels and enhancing their capacity to respond to food crisis risks.

Lastly, there will be a solidification of foundations through cultural integration and people-centered cooperation. Deeper economic and trade cooperation requires a bond of mutual understanding between the peoples. China and Arab countries should further strengthen cooperation in areas such as vocational education, healthcare, tourism, and cultural and creative industries, enhancing the sense of gain for both peoples in the cooperation process. Meanwhile, cultural and tourism cooperation, through measures like visa facilitation, increased direct flights, and the digitization of cultural heritage, can promote two-way people-to-people exchanges and inject lasting momentum into economic and trade cooperation.

# Chapter 2　Special Report on China-Arab States Trade Cooperation

Since the launch of the "Belt and Road Initiative", trade cooperation between China and Arab countries has advanced from "quantitative accumulation" to "qualitative leap". Bilateral trade volume has repeatedly reached new heights, and the trade structure has been continuously optimized, expanding from goods trade to emerging areas such as digital trade. Trade cooperation platforms and mechanisms have been further refined, with initiatives like the "China-Arab States Cooperation Forum", "China-Arab States Expo", and "China-Arab States Technology Transfer Center" playing a pivotal role. The vigorous development of China-Arab states trade has significantly expanded bilateral investment and economic-technological cooperation, yielding substantial achievements across the board. This cooperation has profoundly benefited from the strategic guidance and practical implementation of the Belt and Road Initiative. *The 2016 Policy Paper on China's Relations with Arab Countries* provided the first systematic blueprint for bilateral collaboration. This was followed by the 2018 signing of the Action Declaration for China-Arab States Cooperation Under the Belt and Road Initiative. At the Ninth Ministerial Conference of the China-Arab States Cooperation Forum in 2020, the two sides formally set forth the goal of "building a China-Arab states community with a shared future for the new era". The 2022 triple summit—comprising the inaugural China-Arab States Summit, China-Gulf Cooperation Council (GCC) Summit, and China-Saudi states Arabia Summit— marked a historic diplomatic breakthrough, elevating political mutual trust to unprecedented heights. China has signed Belt and Road cooperation documents with 22 Arab countries, demonstrating the depth of strategic synergy and marking a new stage of comprehensive deepening and high-quality development

Chapter 2    Special Report on China-Arab States Trade Cooperation

in their joint pursuit of the Belt and Road cooperation.

## 2.1    Overview of China's Foreign Trade Development

Since the launch of the Belt and Road Initiative in 2013, China has consistently expanded its trade scale, optimized its trade structure, and achieved tangible progress in trade diversification. The global competitiveness of China's products has been steadily strengthened. As the world's second-largest economy and top merchandise trader, China exerts a profound impact on global supply chains and the international trade system. Meanwhile, its massive consumer market also presents significant opportunities for enterprises worldwide.

Between 2013 and 2024, China's total import and export trade volume exhibited a fluctuating yet upward trend. As seen in Table 2.1, the total trade value increased from USD4001.4 billion in 2013 to USD6162.3 billion in 2024, with an average annual growth rate of about 3.84%. Both 2013 and 2014 saw growth, but 2015 witnessed a significant decline, dropping to USD3809.6 billion, a year-on-year decrease of 8.35%. This was largely due to the fluctuations of exchange rate, which led to a sharp depreciation of the RMB against the US dollar. Additionally, the rise of global trade protectionism, increased trade barriers, falling commodity prices, and economic difficulties among major trading partners all exerted considerable pressure on China's exports. In 2016, China's total value of imports and exports continued its downward trend, dropping to USD3685.5 billion, a year-on-year decrease of 3.26%. From 2017 to 2018, however, the figure began to rebound, largely thanks to China's proactive promotion of the Belt and Road Initiative, which expanded international markets and boosted trade volume. Between 2019 and 2020, the growth of China's foreign trade slowed due to the U.S.-China trade friction and the COVID-19 pandemic. Nevertheless, the resilience of the Chinese economy and the continued advancement of the Belt and Road Initiative helped maintain steady growth in the scale of imports and exports. In 2021, the scale of imports and exports grew significantly to USD6046.7 billion, a year-on-year increase of 30.14%. This was largely attributed to China's early and effective control of the pandemic, which stabilized industrial and supply chains, giving it a prominent edge in global trade. The total value of imports and exports further expanded in 2022. However, in 2023, the figure declined to USD5832.2 billion, a year-on-

023

The Development Process of China-Arab States Economic and Trade Relations
Annual Report 2024

year decrease of 5.73%, mainly due to weakened international market demand resulting from slowing global economic growth and geopolitical conflicts, as well as certain impacts from domestic economic restructuring. With economic recovery in 2024, the figure rebounded to USD6162.3 billion.

**Table 2.1   China's Foreign Trade Volume and Growth Rate (2013-2024)**

| Year | Import & Export Trade | | Export Trade | | Import Trade | | Trade Balance | |
|------|--------------------------|------------------|-------------------------|------------------|-------------------------|------------------|-------------------------|------------------|
| | Amount (USD100 Million) | YoY Growth (%) | Amount (USD100 Million) | YoY Growth (%) | Amount (USD100 Million) | YoY Growth (%) | Amount (USD100 Million) | YoY Growth (%) |
| 2013 | 40014 | 7.45 | 22090.07 | 7.82 | 17924.51 | 6.99 | 4165.56 | 11.52 |
| 2014 | 41566 | 3.88 | 23422.93 | 6.03 | 18143.54 | 1.22 | 5279.39 | 26.74 |
| 2015 | 38096 | -8.35 | 22734.68 | -2.94 | 15361.95 | -15.33 | 7372.73 | 39.65 |
| 2016 | 36855 | -3.26 | 20976.37 | -7.73 | 15879.21 | 3.37 | 5097.16 | -30.86 |
| 2017 | 39747 | 7.85 | 22633.71 | 7.90 | 17114.24 | 7.78 | 5519.47 | 8.29 |
| 2018 | 44828 | 12.78 | 24942.30 | 10.20 | 19886.01 | 16.20 | 5056.29 | -8.39 |
| 2019 | 45675 | 1.89 | 24985.78 | 0.17 | 20689.50 | 4.04 | 4296.20 | -15.03 |
| 2020 | 46462 | 1.72 | 25906.01 | 3.68 | 20555.91 | -0.65 | 5350.10 | 24.53 |
| 2021 | 60467 | 30.14 | 33623.02 | 29.79 | 26843.63 | 30.59 | 6779.39 | 26.72 |
| 2022 | 61867 | 2.31 | 35936.01 | 6.88 | 25931.14 | -3.40 | 10004.87 | 47.58 |
| 2023 | 58322 | -5.73 | 33797.48 | -5.95 | 24524.67 | -5.42 | 9272.81 | -7.32 |
| 2024 | 61623 | 5.66 | 35772.22 | 5.84 | 25850.67 | 5.41 | 9921.55 | 7.00 |

Note: China as the reporting country.

Classification Basis: HS2007.

Source: Data from 2013 to 2023 compiled and calculated based on the United Nations International Trade Database; data for 2024 compiled and calculated based on the website of the Commercial Data Center of China's Ministry of Commerce.

Significant inflection points were observed in the year-on-year growth rate of China's imports and exports at key junctures such as year of 2015, 2021, and 2023. As shown in Figure 2.1, the growth trend indicates that the year-

024

Chapter 2    Special Report on China-Arab States Trade Cooperation

on-year growth rate of imports and exports generally declined from 2013 to 2015, falling to -8.35% in 2015. From 2017 to 2018, the growth rate recovered somewhat, reaching 12.78% in 2018. Between 2019 and 2020, the growth remained relatively stable but at a low level. In 2021, the growth rate surged to 30.14%. Subsequently, the growth rate began to decline again from 2022 to 2023, dropping to -5.73% in 2023. It rebounded to 5.66% in 2024.

With the deepening of the Belt and Road Initiative, China's strategy of promoting trade diversification has yielded positive results, leading to profound changes in the trade landscape. Its reliance on the U.S. market has steadily decreased, while the trade status of emerging market economies has risen. Regions and countries such as ASEAN, the Arab League, Russia, and India are playing an increasingly prominent role in China's trade framework.

In terms of imports, as shown in Figure 2.2, the composition of China's top 10 import trading partners has undergone significant changes during 2013-2023, with ASEAN and the Arab League seeing notably increased prominence. In 2013, China's imports from ASEAN accounted for 11.13% of its total imports, ranking the second. By 2023, this proportion had climbed to 15.82%, leapfrogging to the top position. This growth was largely driven by the deepening development of the China-ASEAN Free Trade Area and the entry into force of the Regional Comprehensive Economic Partnership (RCEP), leading to higher regional economic integration and closer trade ties between the two sides in sectors like manufacturing and agriculture. In 2013, China's imports from the Arab League represented 7.67% of the total, placing it the sixth. By 2023, this share had increased to 8.84%, moving up to the third. This can be attributed to three main factors. Firstly, the abundant oil and natural gas resources in the Middle East align well with China's energy needs, leading to deepened energy cooperation between the two sides. Secondly, the Belt and Road Initiative has provieded a broad platform for collaboration, with continuous strengthening of cooperation in infrastructure construction, trade and investment facilitation, thus promoting the expansion of bilateral trade. Thirdly, China's strategy of diversifying its trading partners has also created conditions for the Arab League to increase its share in China's imports. Russia, not among China's top 10 import partners in 2013, ranked the eighth in 2023 with a 5.27% share of imports. Similarly, Brazil, also outside the top ten in 2013, climbed to the ninth place in 2023 with a 4.99% share.

025

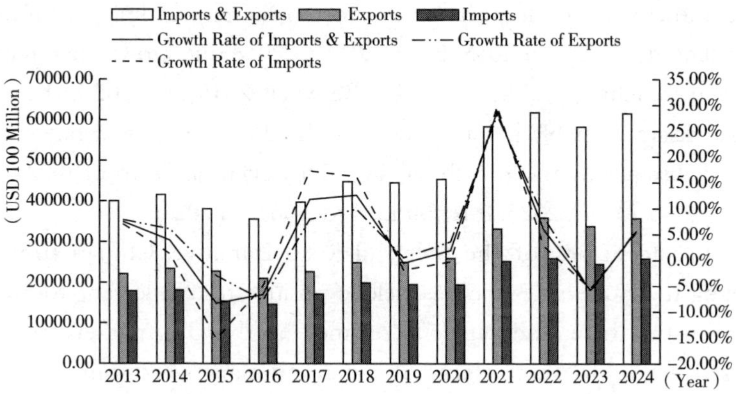

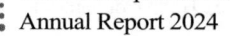

The Development Process of China-Arab States Economic and Trade Relations
Annual Report 2024

**Figure 2.1    China's Foreign Trade Volume and Growth Rate (2013-2024)**

Note: China as the reporting country.

Classification Basis: HS2007.

Source: Data from 2013 to 2023 compiled and calculated based on the United Nations International Trade Database. The data has been updated to the latest version (update log query URL: https: //wits.worldbank.org/ WITS/WITS/Support%20Materials/TariffDataRefresh.aspx?Page=TariffDataRefresh). Data for 2024 compiled and calculated based on the website of the Commercial Data Center of China's Ministry of Commerce.

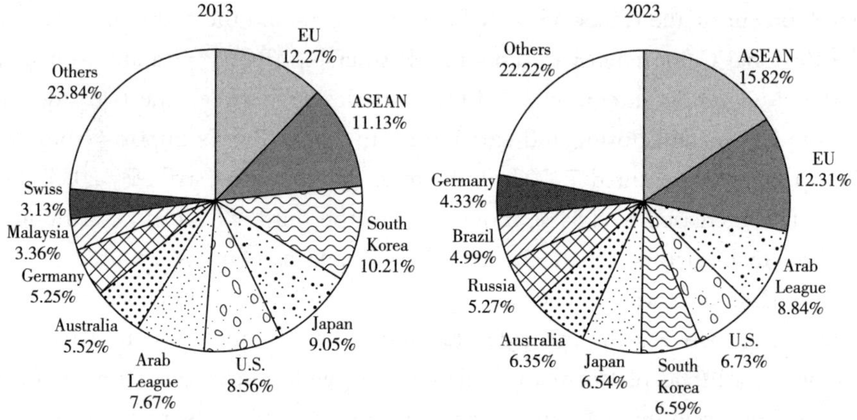

**Figure 2.2    Proportion of China's Import Value to Top 10 Trade Partners as a Percentage of Total Imports for 2013 and 2023**

Note: China as the reporting country.

Classification Basis: HS2007.

Source: Data compiled and calculated based on the United Nations International Trade Database. The data has been updated to the latest version (update log query URL: https: //wits.worldbank.org/WITS/ WITS/Support%20Materials/TariffDataRefresh.aspx?Page=TariffDataRefresh).

026

Chapter 2　Special Report on China-Arab States Trade Cooperation

In terms of exports, as shown in Figure 2.3, the EU, ASEAN, and the Arab League all saw their status rise among China's top 10 export trading partners from 2013 to 2023. China's export share to the EU increased from 15.35% in 2013 to 17.15% in 2023 and ASEAN surged from 11.05% to 15.49%, becoming the second-largest trading partner. The Arab League grew from 4.59% to 5.36%, while the U.S. share slightly declined, dropping from the first place at 16.71% in 2013 to the third place at 14.83% in 2023, reflecting the impact of Sino-U. S. trade friction and that of supply chain diversification strategies. Nevertheless, the U.S. remains one of China's core trading partners. Emerging economies rose as Vietnam (4.07%) and India (3.48%) entered the top 10 for the first time, replacing the Netherlands (2.73% in 2013) and the UK (2.31% in 2013). Vietnam's rapid industrialization and India's market potential drove China's export growth to both countries. South Korea's share edged up from 4.13% to 4.41%, while Japan's fell from 6.80% to 4.66%, indicating adjustments in the Northeast Asian trade landscape. Russia's share increased from 2.24% to 3.28%.

In terms of service trade, China's total imports and exports of service trade, as indicated in Figure 2.4 and Table 2.2, saw an overall upward trend from 2013 to

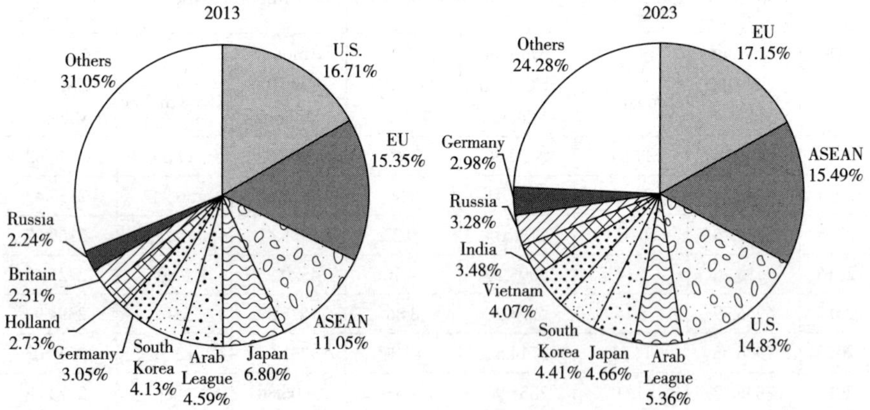

**Figure 2.3　Proportion of China's Export Value to Top 10 Trade Partners as a Percentage of Total Exports for 2013 and 2023**

Note: China as the reporting country.

Classification Basis: HS2007.

Source: Data compiled and calculated based on the United Nations International Trade Database. The data has been updated to the latest version (update log query URL: https://wits.worldbank.org/WITS/WITS/Support%20Materials/TariffDataRefresh.aspx?Page=TariffDataRefresh).

2023, increasing significantly from USD537.614 billion in 2013 to USD933.116 billion in 2023. However, its year-on-year growth rates fluctuated considerably. After peaking at 21.28% in 2014, the growth rate began to slow down. In 2020, it suffered a sharp decline due to the COVID-19 pandemic, dropping by 15.7%. Then there was a strong rebound in the following two years due to the global economic recovery combined with China's effective pandemic control measures. However, factors like global economic downturn, geopolitical conflicts, and the rise of trade protectionism led to a contraction in external demand in 2023, pulling the growth rate back to 4.95%. A persistent trade deficit has long characterized China's service trade, with the deficit size fluctuating significantly. The deficit peaked at -USD213.742 billion in 2014, narrowed in subsequent years. It sharply shrank in 2020 due to the pandemic, only to widen again from 2021, and reached -USD170.874 billion in 2023. In 2024, the deficit slightly narrowed to -USD164.7 billion.

**Table 2.2　China's Service Trade: Import and Export Volumes with Growth Rates (2013-2024)**

| Year | Imports & Exports Trade | | Exports Trade | | Imports Trade | | Net Exports Value |
|---|---|---|---|---|---|---|---|
| | Amount (USD100 Million) | YoY Growth (%) | Amount (USD100 Million) | YoY Growth (%) | Amount (USD100 Million) | YoY Growth (%) | Amount (USD100 Million) |
| 2013 | 5376.14 | 11.34 | 2070.06 | 2. 69 | 3306.08 | 17.53 | -1236.02 |
| 2014 | 6520.24 | 21.28 | 2191.41 | 5.86 | 4328.83 | 30.94 | -2137.42 |
| 2015 | 6541.75 | 0.33 | 2186.34 | -0.23 | 4355.41 | 0.61 | -2169.07 |
| 2016 | 6616.26 | 1.14 | 2095.29 | -4.16 | 4520.97 | 3.80 | -2425.68 |
| 2017 | 6956.79 | 5.15 | 2280.9 | 8.86 | 4675.89 | 3.43 | -2394.99 |
| 2018 | 7966.05 | 14.51 | 2714.51 | 19.01 | 5251.54 | 12.31 | -2537.03 |
| 2019 | 7838.72 | -1.60 | 2831.92 | 4.33 | 5006.80 | -4.66 | -2174.88 |
| 2020 | 6617.17 | -15.58 | 2806.29 | -0.91 | 3810.88 | -23.89 | -1004.59 |
| 2021 | 8212.71 | 24.11 | 3942.73 | 40.50 | 4269.98 | 12.05 | -327.25 |
| 2022 | 8891.09 | 8.26 | 4240.56 | 7.55 | 4650.53 | 8.91 | -409.97 |
| 2023 | 9331.16 | 4.95 | 3811.21 | -10.12 | 5519.95 | 18.70 | -1708.74 |
| 2024 | 10565 | 13.2 | 4459 | 17.0 | 6106 | 10.6 | -1647 |

Source: Data compiled and calculated based on the website of the Commercial Data Center of China's Ministry of Commerce.

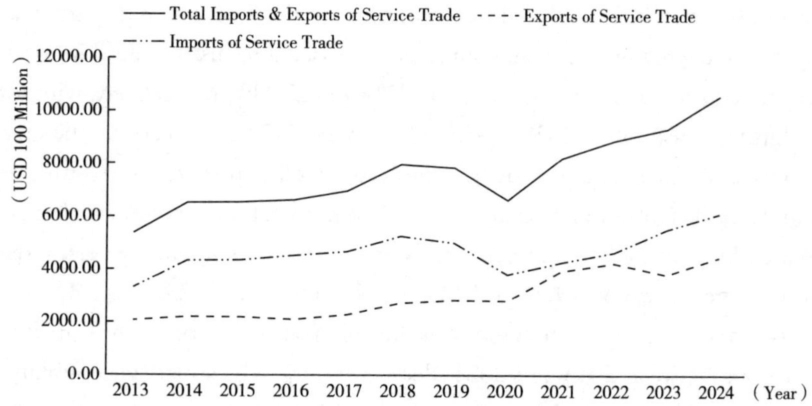

Chapter 2    Special Report on China-Arab States Trade Cooperation

Figure 2.4 chart:

Legend:
—— Total Imports & Exports of Service Trade    - - - - Exports of Service Trade
—··— Imports of Service Trade

Y-axis: (USD 100 Million) 0.00, 2000.00, 4000.00, 6000.00, 8000.00, 10000.00, 12000.00

X-axis: 2013  2014  2015  2016  2017  2018  2019  2020  2021  2022  2023  2024  (Year)

**Figure 2.4    Trends in China's Service Trade (2013-2024)**

Source: Data compiled and calculated based on the website of the Commercial Data Center of China's Ministry of Commerce.

## 2.2    Development of Foreign Trade in Arab Countries

As shown in Table 2.3 and Figure 2.5, the foreign trade of Arab countries demonstrated a complex and dynamic evolution during 2013 to 2023. In terms of overall scale, their total foreign trade volume fluctuated upward from USD 1856.226 billion in 2013 to USD2124.446 billion in 2023, showing distinct cyclical fluctuations.

From 2014 to 2016, the total trade volume kept declining, hitting its lowest point in 2016 at USD1307.709 billion- a 29.55% drop from 2013. The export volume fell particularly sharply during this period, plummeting 47.6% from USD1071.020 billion in 2013 to USD561.165 billion in 2016. A key driver behind this trend was the significant drop in global oil prices. Subsequently, as the global economy gradually recovered, trade regained momentum and climbed steadily to reach USD1580.505 billion by 2019.

In 2020, the COVID-19 pandemic brought global economic activity to a standstill. Plummeting demand and supply chain disruptions dealt a severe blow to Arab countries' foreign trade, which contracted by 19.25% to USD1276.327 billion. Both imports and exports registered significant declines during this period, with import volumes demonstrating a relatively smaller drop.

029

The Development Process of China-Arab States Economic and Trade Relations
Annual Report 2024

From 2021 to 2022, as the global economy gradually recovered, particularly with soaring energy prices, Arab countries witnessed a robust rebound in foreign trade. Imports and exports surged by 35.27% and 27.41% respectively, with total trade hitting a peak of USD2199.672 billion in 2022. The recovery of the global economy and rising energy prices notably boosted export revenues for Arab countries, while global inflation also pushed up nominal trade volumes. However, pressured by global economic headwinds and corrections in energy prices, trade volumes edged down by 3.42% to USD2124.446 billion in 2023.

In summary, the foreign trade volume of Arab countries saw significant fluctuations between 2013 and 2023, demonstrating substantial susceptibility to international oil prices, the global economic situation, and unexpected events such as the COVID-19 pandemic. These fluctuations underscore the structural vulnerability within regional economy and their high dependence on the external factors.

**Table 2.3　Foreign Trade Volume and Growth Rate of Arab Countries (2013-2023)**

| Year | Import & Export Trade | | Export Trade | | Import Trade | | Trade Balance | |
|---|---|---|---|---|---|---|---|---|
| | Total amount (USD100 Million) | YoY Growth (%) | Amount (USD100 Million) | YoY Growth (%) | Amount (USD100 Million) | YoY Growth (%) | Amount (USD100 Million) | YoY Growth (%) |
| 2013 | 18562.26 | 12.51 | 10710.20 | 11.80 | 7852.06 | 13.49 | 2858.14 | 7.43 |
| 2014 | 17659.50 | -4.86 | 9585.43 | -10.50 | 8074.08 | 2.83 | 1511.35 | -47.12 |
| 2015 | 14590.98 | -17.38 | 6409.82 | -33.13 | 8181.16 | 1.33 | -1771.34 | -217.20 |
| 2016 | 13077.09 | -10.38 | 5611.65 | -12.45 | 7465.45 | -8.75 | -1853.80 | 4.66 |
| 2017 | 13901.95 | 6.31 | 6522.73 | 16.24 | 7379.22 | -1.16 | -856.49 | -53.80 |
| 2018 | 14722.13 | 5.90 | 7566.33 | 16.00 | 7155.80 | -3.03 | 410.54 | -147.93 |
| 2019 | 15805.05 | 7.36 | 8156.91 | 7.81 | 7648.15 | 6.88 | 508.76 | 23.93 |
| 2020 | 12763.27 | -19.25 | 6291.84 | -22.86 | 6471.43 | -15.39 | -179.59 | -135.30 |
| 2021 | 17264.86 | 35.27 | 8995.08 | 42.96 | 8269.78 | 27.79 | 725.30 | -503.86 |
| 2022 | 21996.72 | 27.41 | 12042.18 | 33.88 | 9954.55 | 20.37 | 2087.63 | 187.83 |
| 2023 | 21244.46 | -3.42 | 10821.26 | -10.14 | 10423.20 | 4.71 | 398.06 | -80.93 |

Note: Arab Countries as the reporting entities.

Classification Basis: HS2007.

Source: Data compiled and calculated based on the United Nations International Trade Database. The data has been updated to the latest version (update log query URL: https: //wits.worldbank.org/WITS/WITS/Support%20Materials/TariffDataRefresh.aspx?Page=TariffDataRefresh).

030

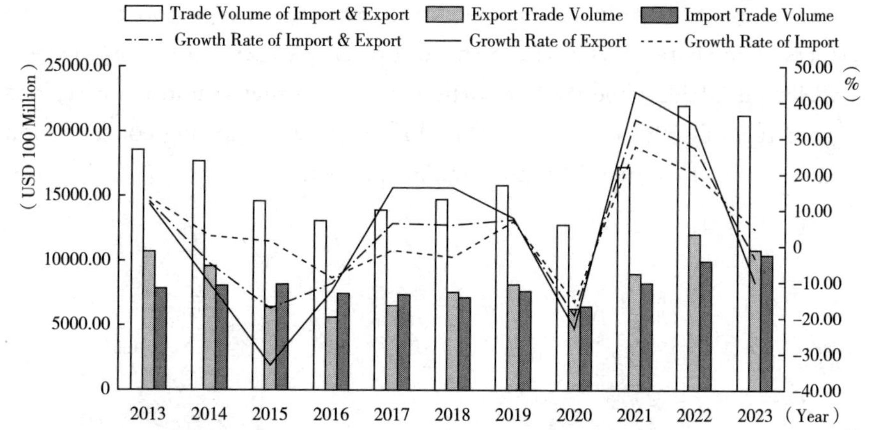

# Chapter 2　Special Report on China-Arab States Trade Cooperation

☐ Trade Volume of Import & Export　▨ Export Trade Volume　▩ Import Trade Volume
–·–· Growth Rate of Import & Export　—— Growth Rate of Export　----- Growth Rate of Import

**Figure 2.5　Foreign Trade Volume and Growth Rate of Arab Countries (2013-2023)**

Note: Arab Countries as the reporting entities.

Classification Basis: HS2007.

　Source: Data compiled and calculated based on the United Nations International Trade Database. The data has been updated to the latest version (update log query URL: https: //wits.worldbank.org/WITS/ WITS/Support%20Materials/TariffDataRefresh.aspx?Page=TariffDataRefresh).


　As illustrated in Figure 2.6, the export partnership of Arab countries underwent a notable transformation between 2013 and 2023.

　The European Union has long remained the most important export partner of Arab countries, consistently holding the position of their largest export destination. Since 2013, exports to the EU have grown significantly, rising from 7.84% in 2013 to 10.90% in 2023—an increase of 3.06 percentage points. With the rise of emerging economies and the advancement of the Belt and Road Initiative, Arab countries have expanded their export scales to emerging economies such as China, India, and ASEAN, which have become trade partners with notably growing shares of exports. Among them, China has seen the most remarkable growth, with its share jumping from 2.38% in 2013 to 7.30% in 2023, and rising from the 7th largest trade partner in 2013 to the 2nd largest in 2023. India's share has expanded from 2.83% to 5.79%, moving up from the 5th largest in 2013 to the 3rd largest in 2023. ASEAN's share has grown from 2.52% to 4.70%, climbing from the 6th largest in 2013 to the 4th largest in 2023. Conversely, Japan's share has declined slightly by 0.28 percentage points, dropping from 4.19% to 3.91%, namely, from the 2nd largest trade partner in 2013 to the 6th largest in 2023.

031

:::: The Development Process of China-Arab States Economic and Trade Relations
:::: Annual Report 2024

Arab countries have increased the export reliance on their top ten trading partners. The share of exports to those top ten partners rose from 30.64% to 45.48% in 2023, while the proportion going to other countries or regions dropped from 69.39% to 54.52%. This shift indicates a growing concentration of export markets among the top ten trading partners.

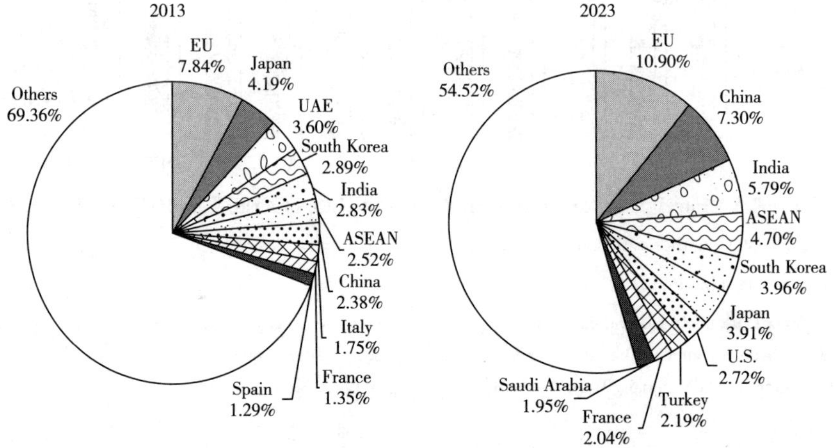

**Figure 2.6    Proportion of Arab Exports to the Top Ten Trading Partners in Total Exports for 2013 and 2023**

Note: Arab countries as the reporting entities.

Classification Basis: HS2007.

Source: Data compiled and calculated based on the United Nations International Trade Database. The data has been updated to the latest version (update log query URL: https://wits.worldbank.org/WITS/WITS/Support%20Materials/TariffDataRefresh.aspx?Page=TariffDataRefresh).

The import trade partnerships of Arab countries exhibited the following characteristics between 2013 and 2023.

The share of imports from China to Arab countries has seen significant growth, rising from 8.91% in 2013 to 16.26% in 2023, an increase of 7.35 percentage points. This growth can be attributed to several factors: the deepening of strategic partnership between China and Arab countries, which has enhanced political trust and economic cooperation; infrastructure and connectivity projects under the Belt and Road Initiative that have lowered trade costs and facilitated trade between the two sides; the rapid development of China's manufacturing

032

Chapter 2　Special Report on China-Arab States Trade Cooperation

sector and the improved competitiveness of its products, making Chinese goods more apppealing in Arab markets, especially in the mid-to-low-end consumer goods and industrial products sectors; and the adoption of RMB for transactions by countries like the UAE, Saudi Arabia, and Iraq, which has reduced exchange rate risks and fostered trade growth.

The share of traditional trading partners has been on the decline. Markets of traditional partners such as the EU, Germany, and Japan are being squeezed, with their share in Arab countries' imports dropping. This is mainly attributed to two factors: first, these countries primarily export high-value-added products like automobiles and precision instruments, but as emerging economies such as China and India rise in high-tech sectors, Arab countries have shifted to suppliers from these emerging economies; second, the rising labor costs in the EU and Japan have diminished the price competitiveness of their products. It is worth noting, however, that traditional trading partners like the EU still hold a significant position in the market.

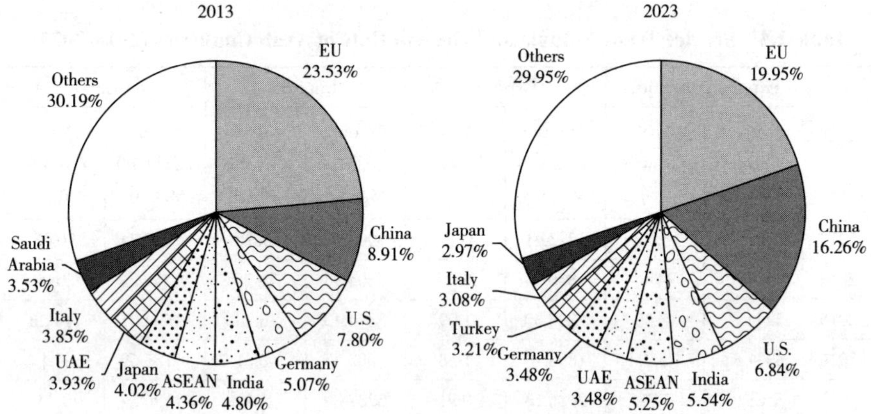

**Figure 2.7　Proportion of Arab Imports to the Top Ten Trading Partners in Total Imports for 2013 and 2023**

Note: Arab countries as the reporting entities.

Classification Basis: HS2007.

Source: Data compiled and calculated based on the United Nations International Trade Database. The data has been updated to the latest version (update log query URL: https://wits.worldbank.org/WITS/WITS/Support%20Materials/TariffDataRefresh.aspx?Page=TariffDataRefresh).

033

The Development Process of China-Arab States Economic and Trade Relations
Annual Report 2024

As shown in Table 2.4 and Figure 2.8, the total import and export volume of service trade in Arab countries showed a fluctuating growth trend between 2013 and 2023, rising from USD438.256 billion in 2013 to USD798.598 billion in 2023. However, the year-on-year growth rate varied significantly, indicating that the development of their service trade is heavily influenced by the external factors. Specifically, both the total service trade and export volume grew significantly in 2014, mainly driven by the global economic recovery and the development of Arab tourism that year. From 2015 to 2016, the total value of services trade declined for two consecutive years due to regional conflicts. It then displayed an upward trend from 2017 to 2019. Hit by the global spread of the COVID-19 pandemic in 2020, service sectors such as tourism and transportation were severely impacted, leading to a sharp drop in the total value, exports, and imports of service trade in Arab countries. A strong rebound occurred in 2021 and 2022, which was linked to the global economic recovery, rising international oil prices, and the revival of regional tourism. The growth rate slowed somewhat but remained an upward trend in 2023.

**Table 2.4  Service Trade Volume and Growth Rate of Arab Countries (2013-2023)**

| Year | Exports & Imports | | Exports | | Imports | | Net Exports | |
|------|------------------------------|------------------|------------------------------|------------------|------------------------------|------------------|------------------------------|------------------|
| | Amount (USD100 Million) | YoY Growth (%) | Amount (USD100 Million) | YoY Growth (%) | Amount (USD100 Million) | YoY Growth (%) | Amount (USD100 Million) | YoY Growth (%) |
| 2013 | 4382.56 | 3.64 | 1373.41 | 0.15 | 3009.15 | 5.31 | -1635.74 | 10.08 |
| 2014 | 5454.52 | 24.46 | 1850.14 | 34.71 | 3604.38 | 19.78 | -1754.24 | 7.24 |
| 2015 | 5244.79 | -3.85 | 1870.39 | 1.09 | 3374.40 | -6.38 | -1504.01 | -14.26 |
| 2016 | 4981.83 | -5.01 | 1898.10 | 1.48 | 3083.73 | -8.61 | -1185.63 | -21.17 |
| 2017 | 5368.93 | 7.77 | 2086.13 | 9.91 | 3282.80 | 6.46 | -1196.67 | 0.93 |
| 2018 | 5764.12 | 7.36 | 2270.00 | 8.81 | 3494.12 | 6.44 | -1224.12 | 2.29 |
| 2019 | 6150.80 | 6.71 | 2528.69 | 11.40 | 3622.11 | 3.66 | -1093.42 | -10.68 |
| 2020 | 4522.85 | -26.47 | 1854.96 | -26.64 | 2667.89 | -26.34 | -812.93 | -25.65 |
| 2021 | 5470.11 | 20.94 | 2299.94 | 23.99 | 3170.17 | 18.83 | -870.23 | 7.05 |
| 2022 | 7294.91 | 33.36 | 3521.42 | 53.11 | 3773.49 | 19.03 | -252.07 | -71.03 |
| 2023 | 7985.98 | 9.47 | 3909.19 | 11.01 | 4076.79 | 8.04 | -167.60 | -33.51 |

Source: Data compiled and calculated based on the WTO (World Trade Organization) website. The data has been updated to the latest version (update log query URL: https://stats.wto.org/inventory/en).

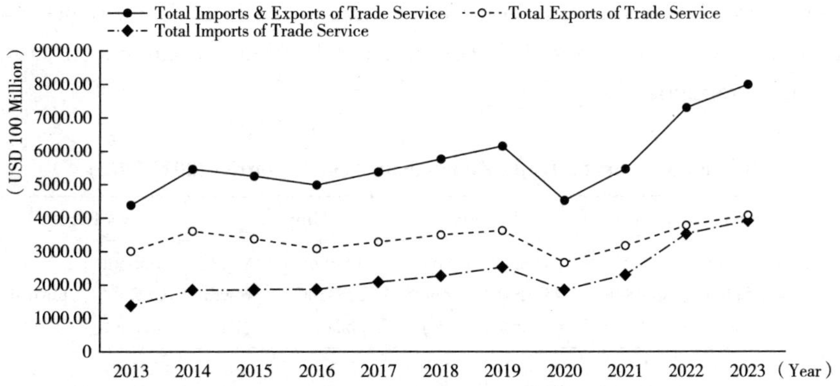

Chapter 2    Special Report on China-Arab States Trade Cooperation

**Figure 2.8    Trends in Arab Countries' Service Trade (2013-2023)**

Source: Data compiled and calculated based on the WTO (World Trade Organization) website. The data has been updated to the latest version (update log query URL : https: //stats.wto.org/inventory/en).

## 2.3    Development of Trade Relations Between China and Arab Countries

Bilateral trade has expanded steadily, showing a fluctuating upward trend (see Table 2.5). China's trade volume with Arab countries stood at USD238.897 billion in 2013, surpassed USD300 billion in 2021 and reached USD431.442 billion in 2022. Notably, this progression was interrupted by significant declines in 2015 and 2016, dropping by 19.32% and 15.56% respectively, mainly due to falling global commodity prices, particularly energy prices. Subsequently, their trade returned to a growth track between 2017 and 2019, along with the global economic recovery and deepened China-Arab states cooperation in infrastructure and energy sectors. In 2020, the COVID-19 pandemic disrupted global trade, leading to a decline in China-Arab states trade volume. However, it hit historical peaks in 2021 and 2022, demonstrating an exceptional recovery capacity.

The bilateral trade has grown at a remarkable pace. Between 2013 and 2022, the average expansion rate of China's trade with Arab countries reached 6.78%, 1 percentage point higher than that of China's overall foreign trade growth. This performance also surpassed China's trade growth with other Belt and Road partner nations. Growth was particularly striking in 2021 and 2022, at 36.29% and 31.95% respectively, marking historic highs that underscored robust bilateral

035

The Development Process of China-Arab States Economic and Trade Relations
Annual Report 2024

momentum. However, trade volumes contracted again in 2023, registering negative growth amid the global economic deceleration and China's structural economic transition.

**Table 2.5　China's Trade Volume with Arab Countries (2013-2023)**

| Year | Imports & Exports | | Exports | | Imports | | Net Exports | |
|------|-------------------|---|---------|---|---------|---|-------------|---|
| | Amount (USD100 Million) | YoY Growth (%) | Amount (USD100 Million) | YoY Growth (%) | Amount (USD100 Million) | YoY Growth (%) | Amount (USD100 Million) | YoY Growth (%) |
| 2013 | 2388.97 | 7.51 | 1013.52 | 4.88 | 1375.45 | 11.03 | -361.93 | -9.20 |
| 2014 | 2510.51 | 5.09 | 1138.21 | 12.30 | 1372.30 | -0.23 | -234.09 | -35.32 |
| 2015 | 2025.41 | -19.32 | 1150.40 | 1.07 | 875.01 | -36.24 | 275.38 | -217.64 |
| 2016 | 1710.29 | -15.56 | 1006.74 | -12.49 | 703.56 | -19.59 | 303.18 | 10.09 |
| 2017 | 1917.57 | 12.12 | 986.73 | -1.99 | 930.84 | 32.30 | 55.89 | -81.57 |
| 2018 | 2442.26 | 27.36 | 1048.70 | 6.28 | 1393.56 | 49.71 | -344.85 | -717.05 |
| 2019 | 2667.00 | 9.20 | 1203.94 | 14.80 | 1463.05 | 4.99 | -259.11 | -24.86 |
| 2020 | 2399.26 | -10.04 | 1228.56 | 2.04 | 1170.70 | -19.98 | 57.85 | -122.33 |
| 2021 | 3269.85 | 36.29 | 1441.05 | 17.30 | 1828.81 | 56.21 | -387.76 | -770.24 |
| 2022 | 4314.42 | 31.95 | 1731.73 | 20.17 | 2582.69 | 41.22 | -850.97 | 119.46 |
| 2023 | 3981.27 | -7.72 | 1812.89 | 4.69 | 2168.38 | -16.04 | -355.49 | -58.23 |

Note: China as the reporting country.

Classification Basis: HS2007.

Source: Data compiled and calculated based on the United Nations International Trade Database. The data has been updated to the latest version (update log query URL: https: //wits.worldbank.org/WITS/WITS/Support%20Materials/TariffDataRefresh.aspx?Page=TariffDataRefresh).

## 2.3.1　Development of China's Exports to Arab States

China's exports to Arab countries demonstrated robust overall growth during the 10 years from 2013 to 2023 (Table 2.5), expanding from USD101.352 billion in 2013 to USD181.289 billion in 2023. This transformative trade expansion exhibited distinct cyclical patterns. After reaching 12.30% in 2014, growth fluctuated downward, dropping by 12.49% in 2016. It rebounded from 2018 onward, hitting 20.17% in 2022. Such fluctuations reflect the complex impact of multiple factors on trade, including global economic cycles, geopolitical stability, and trade policies.

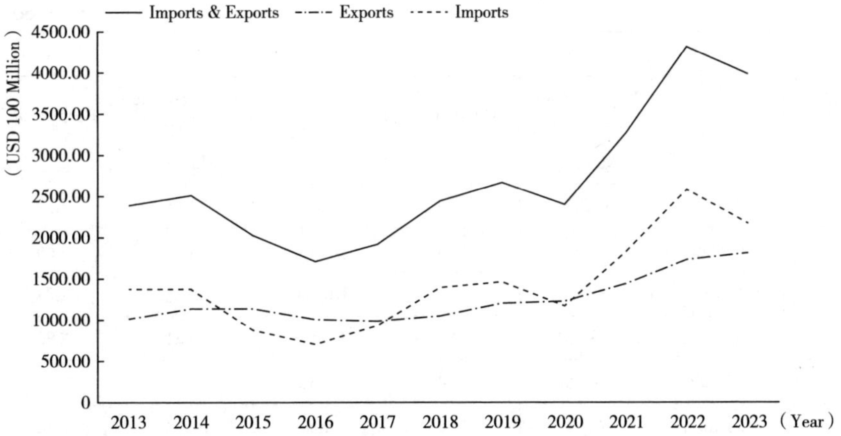

Chapter 2　Special Report on China-Arab States Trade Cooperation

**Figure 2.9　Trends of Trade Between China and Arab Countries (2013-2023)**

Note: China as the reporting country.

Classification Basis: HS2007.

Source: Data compiled and calculated based on the United Nations International Trade Database. The data has been updated to the latest version (update log query URL: https://wits.worldbank.org/WITS/WITS/Support%20Materials/TariffDataRefresh.aspx?Page=TariffDataRefresh).

China's major export partners among Arab countries included the UAE, Saudi Arabia, Egypt, Iraq, and Algeria in 2013. The UAE and Saudi Arabia collectively accounted for 51.46% of China's total exports to Arab countries (see Table 2.6). By 2023, this trade pattern had remained largely unchanged, with the proportion of exports to these two countries further increasing. This indicates that China's export markets in Arab countries are relatively concentrated.

**Table 2.6　China's Major Export Partners in Arab States**

| Rank | 2013 | | | 2023 | | |
|---|---|---|---|---|---|---|
| | Countries | Export Value (USD100 Million) | Proportion (%) | Countries | Export Value (USD100 Million) | Proportion (%) |
| 1 | United Arab Emirates | 334.11 | 32.97 | United Arab Emirates | 556.83 | 30.72 |
| 2 | Saudi Arabia | 187.40 | 18.49 | Saudi Arabia | 428.55 | 23.64 |
| 3 | Egypt | 83.63 | 8.25 | Egypt | 149.35 | 8.24 |
| 4 | Iraq | 68.94 | 6.80 | Iraq | 142.86 | 7.88 |

The Development Process of China-Arab States Economic and Trade Relations
Annual Report 2024

**Continued**

| Rank | 2013 | | | 2023 | | |
|------|------|------|------|------|------|------|
| | Countries | Export Value (USD100 Million) | Proportion (%) | Countries | Export Value (USD100 Million) | Proportion (%) |
| 5 | Algeria | 60.24 | 5.94 | Algeria | 94.58 | 5.22 |
| 6 | Jordan | 34.35 | 3.39 | Morocco | 64.54 | 3.56 |
| 7 | Morocco | 32.72 | 3.23 | Kuwait | 52.25 | 2.88 |
| 8 | Libya | 28.35 | 2.80 | Jordan | 50.81 | 2.80 |
| 9 | Kuwait | 26.76 | 2.64 | Libya | 39.01 | 2.15 |
| 10 | Lebanon | 24.91 | 2.46 | Oman | 37.98 | 2.10 |
| 11 | Sudan | 23.98 | 2.37 | Qatar | 36.36 | 2.01 |

Note: China as the reporting country.

Classification Basis: HS2007.

Source: Data compiled and calculated based on the United Nations International Trade Database. The data has been updated to the latest version (update log query URL: https: //wits.worldbank.org/WITS/WITS/Support%20Materials/TariffDataRefresh.aspx?Page=TariffDataRefresh).

The Gulf Cooperation Council (GCC) stands as China's most important export partner among Arab countries. China's exports to GCC already accounted for 58.88% of its total exports to Arab nations in 2013, and this figure had risen to 62.19% by 2023. This indicates that GCC countries have remained the dominant market for China's export to Arab states, as shown in Table 2.7.

**Table 2.7　Share of China's Exports to GCC Countries in Total China-Arab States Export Value**

| Year | China's Export Volume to GCC Countries | China's Export Volume to Arab Countries | Share of China's Exports to GCC Countries in Total China-Arab States Export Value |
|------|------|------|------|
| | Amount (USD100 Million) | Amount (USD100 Million) | Proportion(%) |
| 2013 | 596.77 | 1013.52 | 58.88 |
| 2014 | 685.90 | 1138.21 | 60.26 |
| 2015 | 678.10 | 1150.40 | 58.94 |
| 2016 | 561.73 | 1006.74 | 55.80 |

Chapter 2　Special Report on China-Arab States Trade Cooperation

**Continued**

| Year | China's Export Volume to GCC Countries | China's Export Volume to Arab Countries | Share of China's Exports to GCC Countries in Total China-Arab States Export Value |
|------|------|------|------|
| | Amount (USD100 Million) | Amount (USD100 Million) | Proportion(%) |
| 2017 | 551.13 | 986.73 | 55.85 |
| 2018 | 568.74 | 1048.70 | 54.23 |
| 2019 | 680.40 | 1203.94 | 56.51 |
| 2020 | 707.80 | 1228.56 | 57.61 |
| 2021 | 852.41 | 1441.05 | 59.15 |
| 2022 | 1067.88 | 1731.73 | 61.67 |
| 2023 | 1127.44 | 1812.89 | 62.19 |

Note: China as the reporting country.

Classification Basis: HS2007.

Source: Data compiled and calculated based on the United Nations International Trade Database. The data has been updated to the latest version (update log query URL: https://wits.worldbank.org/WITS/WITS/Support%20Materials/TariffDataRefresh.aspx?Page=TariffDataRefresh).

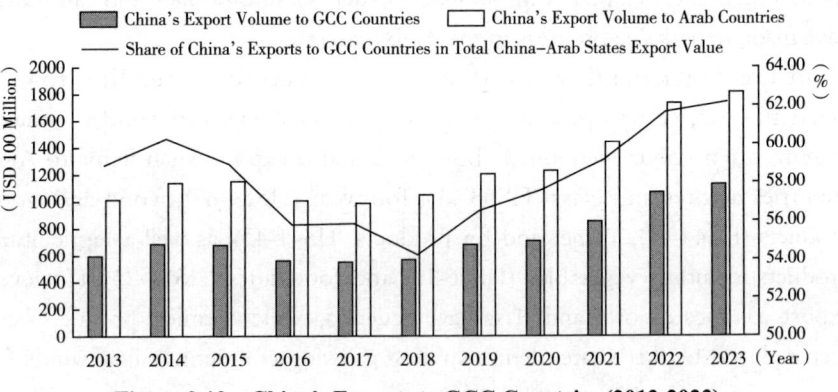

**Figure 2.10　China's Exports to GCC Countries (2013-2023)**

Note: China as the reporting country.

Classification Basis: HS2007.

Source: Data compiled and calculated based on the United Nations International Trade Database. The data has been updated to the latest version (update log query URL: https://wits.worldbank.org/WITS/WITS/Support%20Materials/TariffDataRefresh.aspx?Page=TariffDataRefresh).

The structure of China's exports to Arab countries has been continuously optimized, reflecting both the upgrading of China's manufacturing sector and the diversification of demand in Arab nations, as illustrated in Table 2.8.

China's exports to Arab countries are dominated by manufactured goods, reflecting a high level of trade complementarity with Arab nations. To be specific, machinery and electrical products (HS84-85) have consistently been the largest export category. Their export value surged from USD29.084 billion in 2013 to USD59.076 billion in 2023, showing a significant expansion, with their proportion rising from 28.70% in 2013 to 32.59% in 2023. This indicates that China's technological and product competitiveness in this sector is increasingly enhanced. While textiles and apparel (HS50-63), as traditional export products, maintain stable export volumes, their share has declined steadily from 20.20% in 2013 to 11.16% in 2023. Concurrently, substantial export growth has been achieved in miscellaneous manufactured articles (HS90-99), metal products (HS72-83), plastics and rubber (HS39-40), transport equipment (HS86-89). This reflects that China's manufacturing structure is developing towards diversification and higher added value. Notably, the proportion of transportation equipment in total exports increased from 5.57% in 2013 to 8.83% in 2023, indicating that China's high-end manufacturing industries such as automobiles and rail transit have made remarkable progress in the Arab markets.

On the other hand, while the export structure is trending toward diversification, certain product categories face challenges. Beyond the major manufactured goods mentioned above, China also exports such items to Arab countries as ores and glass (HS68-71), footwear (HS64-67), wood and wood products (HS44-49), leather and fur products (HS41-43), as well as agricultural products including vegetables (HS06-15) and foodstuffs (HS16-24). However, export volumes of ores and glass have declined, while chemical products have seen reduced market share, demonstrating growing competitive headwinds for Chinese exports in these sectors.

Driven by Arab countries' economic development and expanding consumer demand, China's exports of consumer and capital goods to the region continue to rise. Meanwhile, the advancement of China's high-end manufacturing capabilities is poised to significantly boost exports of high-tech products, including electric vehicles, lithium batteries, and solar panels, signaling substantial growth potential for China's exports of high-end manufactured goods to Arab

Chapter 2    Special Report on China-Arab States Trade Cooperation

countries. Additionally, enhancing bilateral agricultural trade cooperation through reciprocal market access for high-quality agricultural products would yield mutually beneficial outcomes for both sides.

**Table 2.8    Structure of China's Export Products to Arab States (2013-2023)**

Unit: USD100 Million

| Product Code | Major Product Category | 2013 Export Amount | 2015 Export Amount | 2017 Export Amount | 2019 Export Amount | 2021 Export Amount | 2023 Export Amount |
|---|---|---|---|---|---|---|---|
| 84-85 | Machinery and Electrical Products | 290.84 | 340.91 | 319.16 | 368.34 | 438.82 | 590.76 |
| 50-63 | Textiles and Apparel | 204.75 | 219.02 | 179.74 | 192.22 | 201.91 | 202.38 |
| 90-99 | Miscellaneous Manufactures | 97.44 | 109.76 | 95.74 | 127.33 | 180.29 | 196.56 |
| 72-83 | Metal Products | 113.78 | 138.93 | 117.85 | 145.80 | 169.08 | 245.08 |
| 39-40 | Plastic and Rubber Products | 64.38 | 64.25 | 59.15 | 76.53 | 96.60 | 121.81 |
| 86-89 | Transport Equipment | 56.46 | 54.52 | 36.52 | 72.59 | 94.90 | 160.02 |
| 28-38 | Chemical Products | 28.16 | 33.45 | 33.16 | 41.88 | 85.23 | 80.22 |
| 68-71 | Ores and Glass | 52.85 | 64.14 | 42.06 | 57.01 | 53.54 | 60.89 |
| 64-67 | Footwear Products | 34.85 | 44.74 | 32.71 | 37.61 | 39.64 | 43.22 |
| 44-49 | Wood and Wood Products | 23.89 | 29.71 | 25.00 | 29.08 | 29.92 | 40.22 |
| 41-43 | Leather and Fur Products | 16.75 | 19.08 | 15.17 | 18.51 | 15.62 | 20.72 |
| 06-15 | Vegetables | 11.15 | 11.42 | 11.56 | 14.34 | 14.98 | 18.03 |
| 27-27 | Mineral Fuels and Oils | 7.21 | 7.76 | 6.90 | 10.03 | 9.62 | 15.70 |
| 16-24 | Food Products | 8.49 | 8.37 | 8.50 | 9.38 | 8.03 | 14.51 |
| 25-26 | Mineral Products | 0.99 | 2.51 | 1.36 | 1.13 | 1.71 | 1.42 |
| 01-05 | Animal Products | 1.51 | 1.84 | 2.14 | 2.14 | 1.17 | 1.33 |

Note: China as the reporting entities.

Classification Basis: HS2007.

Source: Data compiled and calculated based on the United Nations International Trade Database. The data has been updated to the latest version (update log query URL: https://wits.worldbank.org/WITS/ WITS/Support%20Materials/TariffDataRefresh.aspx?Page=TariffDataRefresh).

The Development Process of China-Arab States Economic and Trade Relations
Annual Report 2024

## 2.3.2 Development of China's Imports from Arab States

Between 2013 and 2023, China's import volume from Arab countries generally showed an expanding trend amid fluctuations, with significant volatility in growth rates, as shown in Table 2.5. On one hand, there was a substantial increase in import value. China's imports from Arab countries serged from USD137.545 billion in 2013 to USD216.838 billion in 2023, representing a 57.65% growth. This notable expansion reflects China's growing demand for Arab commodities, which is closely linked to China's sustained economic development, enhanced domestic consumption capacity, and rising needs for bulk commodities such as energy resources. On the other hand, the growth rate of imports was highly volatile. From 2013 to 2019, the growth rate fluctuated significantly. It reached a high of 11.03% in 2013, plummeted sharply to -36.24% in 2015 and -19.59% in 2016, it then rebounded strongly to 32.30% in 2017 and 49.71% in 2018, before dropping to 4.99% in 2019. In 2022, imports hit a peak of USD258.269 billion, up 41.22% year-on-year, but the growth rate slid to -16.04% in 2023.

China's primary import partners among Arab countries include Saudi Arabia, the UAE, Iraq, Oman, Qatar, and Kuwait. Significant ranking shifts occurred between 2013 and 2023. While Saudi Arabia, Oman, Iraq, the UAE, and Kuwait constituted the top five in 2013, the UAE surged to second position by 2023. Its share of China's imports rose most dramatically from 9.32% to 18.13%. Qatar surpassed Kuwait to claim the fifth place with expanded import share, while Saudi Arabia and Oman saw a decline of import shares

**Table 2.9 China's Major Import Partners in Arab States**

Unit: USD100 Million

| Rank | 2013 | | | 2023 | | |
|---|---|---|---|---|---|---|
| | Countries | Import Value | Proportion(%) | Countries | Import Value | Proportion(%) |
| 1 | Saudi Arabia | 534.51 | 38.86 | Saudi Arabia | 643.61 | 29.68 |
| 2 | Oman | 210.41 | 15.30 | United Arab Emirates | 393.09 | 18.13 |
| 3 | Iraq | 179.85 | 13.08 | Iraq | 354.66 | 16.36 |
| 4 | United Arab Emirates | 128.24 | 9.32 | Oman | 312.79 | 14.43 |
| 5 | Kuwait | 95.87 | 6.97 | Qatar | 209.28 | 9.65 |

042

Chapter 2　Special Report on China-Arab States Trade Cooperation

**Continued**

| Rank | 2013 | | | 2023 | | |
|---|---|---|---|---|---|---|
| | Countries | Import Value | Proportion(%) | Countries | Import Value | Proportion(%) |
| 6 | Qatar | 84.63 | 6.15 | Kuwait | 171.65 | 7.92 |
| 7 | Yemen | 30.61 | 2.23 | Libya | 21.99 | 1.01 |
| 8 | Algeria | 21.65 | 1.57 | Mauritania | 11.90 | 0.55 |
| 9 | Sultan | 21.00 | 1.53 | Morocco | 9.80 | 0.45 |
| 10 | Libya | 20.39 | 1.48 | Sultan | 8.82 | 0.41 |
| 11 | Egypt | 18.52 | 1.35 | Egypt | 8.81 | 0.41 |

Note: China as the reporting country.

Classification Basis: HS2007.

Source: Data compiled and calculated based on the United Nations International Trade Database. The data has been updated to the latest version (update log query URL: https: //wits.worldbank.org/WITS/WITS/Support%20Materials/TariffDataRefresh.aspx?Page=TariffDataRefresh).

The Gulf Cooperation Council (GCC) remains the dominant source of China's import trade with Arab countries. In 2013, imports from GCC countries accounted for 76.83% of China's total imports from Arab nations. This proportion continued to rise, reaching 78.33% by 2017, before edging down slightly in 2018. It then surged significantly to 80.93% in 2022. Throughout this period, imports from GCC countries consistently made up the majority of China's total imports from Arab countrie, with their share exceeding 75% at all times (see Table 2.10 and Figure 2.11).

**Table 2.10　Share of China's Imports from GCC Countries in Total China-Arab States Import Value**

| Year | China's Import Volume from GCC Countries | China's Import Volume from Arab Countries | Share of China's Imports from GCC Countries in Total China-Arab States Import Value |
|---|---|---|---|
| | Amount (USD100 Million) | Amount (USD100 Million) | Proportion(%) |
| 2013 | 1056.70 | 1375.45 | 76.83 |
| 2014 | 1065.93 | 1372.30 | 77.67 |
| 2015 | 688.05 | 875.01 | 78.63 |
| 2016 | 561.08 | 703.56 | 79.75 |

043

The Development Process of China-Arab States Economic and Trade Relations
Annual Report 2024

**Continued**

| Year | China's Import Volume from GCC Countries | China's Import Volume from Arab Countries | Share of China's Imports from GCC Countries in Total China-Arab States Import Value |
|------|------|------|------|
| | Amount (USD100 Million) | Amount (USD100 Million) | Proportion(%) |
| 2017 | 729.15 | 930.84 | 78.33 |
| 2018 | 1056.31 | 1393.56 | 75.80 |
| 2019 | 1115.39 | 1463.05 | 76.24 |
| 2020 | 909.70 | 1170.70 | 77.71 |
| 2021 | 1454.93 | 1828.81 | 79.56 |
| 2022 | 2090.12 | 2582.69 | 80.93 |
| 2023 | 1732.33 | 2168.38 | 79.89 |

Note: China as the reporting country.

Classification Basis: HS2007.

Source: Data compiled and calculated based on the United Nations International Trade Database. The data has been updated to the latest version (update log query URL: https: //wits.worldbank.org/WITS/WITS/Support%20Materials/TariffDataRefresh.aspx?Page=TariffDataRefresh).

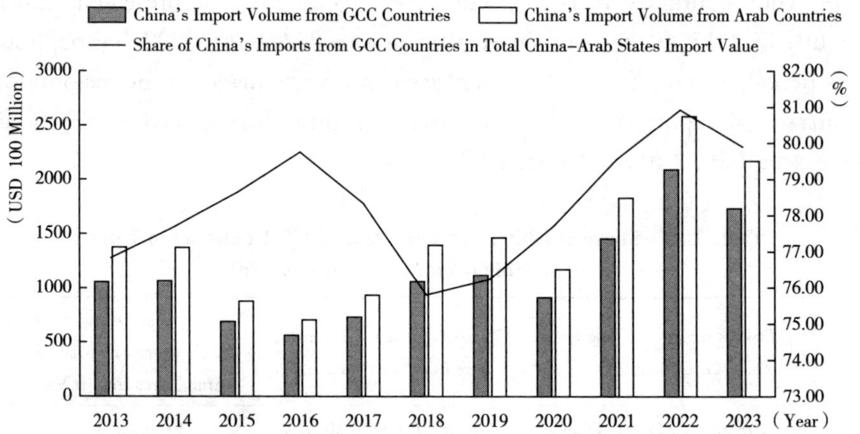

**Figure 2.11　China's Imports from GCC Countries (2013-2023)**

Note: China as the reporting country.

Classification Basis: HS2007.

Source: Data compiled and calculated based on the United Nations International Trade Database. The data has been updated to the latest version (update log query URL: https: //wits.worldbank.org/WITS/WITS/Support%20Materials/TariffDataRefresh.aspx?Page=TariffDataRefresh).

Chapter 2    Special Report on China-Arab States Trade Cooperation

The structure of China's imports from Arab countries remained relatively stable between 2013 and 2023. The primary categories of such imported goods included mineral fuels and oils, chemical products, plastics and rubber products, mineral products, and metal products, with mineral fuels and oils, particularly crude oil, accounting for an overwhelming share. The import value of mineral fuels and oils from Arab countries rose from USD117.38 billion in 2013 to USD192.625 billion in 2023, representing a significant increase of 64.10%. Their share of China's total imports from Arab countries climbed from 85.34% in 2013 to 88.83% in 2023. This phenomenon underscores the region's comparative advantage in resources and China's massive energy demand driven by China's rapid economic growth, highlighting the strong mutual complementarity between the two sides. In general, the import volumes of machinery and textiles remain relatively small, which mirrors the underdeveloped manufacturing sector in Arab countries. Notably, imports of vegetables (HS06-15), food stuffs (HS16-24), machinery equipment and electrical products (HS84-85) have shown significant growth trends, signaling the upgrading of China's consumption and its increasing demand for a more diversified range of commodities.

**Table 2.11    Structure of China's Import Products to Arab States (2013-2023)**

Unit: USD100 Million

| Product Code | Major Product Category | 2013 Import Amount | 2015 Import Amount | 2017 Import Amount | 2019 Import Amount | 2021 Import Amount | 2023 Import Amount |
|---|---|---|---|---|---|---|---|
| 27-27 | Mineral Fuels and Oils | 1173.80 | 701.00 | 732.10 | 1212.33 | 1524.41 | 1926.25 |
| 28-38 | Chemical Products | 86.67 | 74.42 | 81.27 | 98.88 | 106.91 | 81.32 |
| 39-40 | Plastic and Rubber Products | 63.24 | 60.33 | 75.40 | 91.24 | 92.74 | 69.14 |
| 25-26 | Mineral Products | 31.07 | 20.96 | 22.11 | 26.85 | 36.33 | 31.83 |
| 72-83 | Metal Products | 7.83 | 5.41 | 4.82 | 9.76 | 35.69 | 22.10 |
| 06-15 | Vegetables | 4.19 | 2.66 | 3.53 | 6.85 | 12.39 | 11.03 |
| 84-85 | Machinery and Electrical Products | 2.54 | 3.16 | 3.92 | 4.38 | 5.91 | 9.17 |

**Continued**

| Product Code | Major Product Category | 2013 Import Amount | 2015 Import Amount | 2017 Import Amount | 2019 Import Amount | 2021 Import Amount | 2023 Import Amount |
|---|---|---|---|---|---|---|---|
| 68-71 | Ores and Glass | 1.13 | 2.58 | 1.24 | 2.67 | 2.54 | 4.99 |
| 50-63 | Textiles and Apparel | 2.84 | 2.93 | 3.48 | 4.18 | 3.76 | 4.74 |
| 16-24 | Food Products | 0.24 | 0.63 | 1.47 | 2.19 | 5.15 | 4.68 |
| 01-05 | Animal Products | 0.50 | 0.19 | 0.23 | 2.16 | 1.05 | 1.58 |
| 90-99 | Miscellaneous Manufactures | 0.78 | 0.14 | 0.31 | 0.45 | 0.69 | 0.65 |
| 41-43 | Leather and Fur Products | 0.31 | 0.38 | 0.44 | 0.39 | 0.57 | 0.54 |
| 86-89 | Transport Equipment | 0.13 | 0.10 | 0.16 | 0.21 | 0.19 | 0.18 |
| 44-49 | Wood and Wood Products | 0.15 | 0.07 | 0.32 | 0.48 | 0.44 | 0.15 |
| 64-67 | Footwear Products | 0.03 | 0.07 | 0.04 | 0.05 | 0.04 | 0.05 |

Note: China as the reporting entities.

Classification Basis: HS2007.

Source: Data compiled and calculated based on the United Nations International Trade Database. The data has been updated to the latest version (update log query URL: https: //wits.worldbank.org/WITS/WITS/Support%20Materials/TariffDataRefresh.aspx?Page=TariffDataRefresh).

Energy imports, particularly crude oil and natural gas, dominate China's trade with Arab countries. Crude oil imports stood at USD104.658 billion in 2013, followed by a significant decline between 2015 and 2017, primarily due to falling international oil prices. Subsequently, import values kept rising, reaching a historical peak of USD199.784 billion in 2022 before edging down slightly in 2023. In terms of growth rate, there was a notable drop between 2015 and 2016, but the growth resumed after 2017, exceeding 55% in 2018 and reaching 59.43% in 2021, only to turn negative in 2023. Primarily sourced from Qatar, China's natural gas imports from Arab states have more than doubled over the past decade. Starting at USD10.566 billion in 2013, imports climbed to a record high

Chapter 2    Special Report on China-Arab States Trade Cooperation

of USD24.897 billion in 2022 and remained above USD20 billion in 2023. The growth trend of natural gas imports mirrors that of crude oil: it hit a peak of 74.81% in 2021, also with a negative growth in 2023.

**Table 2.12    Trade Volume of China's Energy Import with Arab Countries (2013-2023)**

| Year | Crude Oil | | Natural Gas | |
|---|---|---|---|---|
| | Amount (USD100 Million) | YoY Growth (%) | Amount (USD100 Million) | YoY Growth (%) |
| 2013 | 1046.58 | 1.23 | 105.66 | 33.65 |
| 2014 | 1028.31 | -1.75 | 121.87 | 15.34 |
| 2015 | 613.11 | -40.38 | 71.56 | -41.28 |
| 2016 | 473.04 | -22.85 | 63.33 | -11.50 |
| 2017 | 616.11 | 30.24 | 94.85 | 49.77 |
| 2018 | 960.98 | 55.98 | 136.29 | 43.68 |
| 2019 | 1060.58 | 10.36 | 125.52 | -7.90 |
| 2022 | 832.79 | -21.48 | 87.11 | -30.60 |
| 2023 | 1328.07 | 59.47 | 152.29 | 74.81 |

Note: China as the reporting entities.

Classification Basis: HS2007.

Source: Data compiled and calculated based on the United Nations International Trade Database. The data has been updated to the latest version (update log query URL: https: //wits.worldbank.org/WITS/WITS/Support%20Materials/TariffDataRefresh.aspx?Page=TariffDataRefresh).

From 2013 to 2023, China's major trading partners for crude oil imports from Arab countries have been Saudi Arabia, Iraq, the United Arab Emirates, Oman, Kuwait, Qatar, and Libya, with the trade structure remaining relatively stable. Compared to 2013, the market structure of China's energy imports from Arab nations in 2023 showed a robust yet slightly diversified trend. The market share of Saudi Arabia significantly decreased from 40.48% in 2013 to 32.67% in 2023. In contrast, Iraq and the UAE saw notable increases in their market shares, rising

The Development Process of China-Arab States Economic and Trade Relations
Annual Report 2024

from 17.10% and 7.99% in 2013 to 21.35% and 16.15% in 2023, respectively, while Oman experienced a slight decline.

**Table 2.13 China's Crude Oil Imports from Arab Countries**

Unit: USD100 Million

| Countries | 2013 | | 2019 | | 2022 | | 2023 | |
|---|---|---|---|---|---|---|---|---|
| | Amount (USD100 Million) | Proportion (%) | Amount (USD100 Million) | Proportion (%) | Amount (USD100 Million) | Proportion (%) | Amount (USD100 Million) | Proportion (%) |
| Saudi Arabia | 423.68 | 40.48 | 401.75 | 37.88 | 649.72 | 32.52 | 538.78 | 32.67 |
| Oman | 199.32 | 19.05 | 165.79 | 15.63 | 291.58 | 14.59 | 250.39 | 15.18 |
| Iraq | 179.00 | 17.10 | 238.50 | 22.49 | 390.93 | 19.57 | 352.11 | 21.35 |
| United Arab Emirates | 83.67 | 7.99 | 75.27 | 7.10 | 322.47 | 16.14 | 266.40 | 16.15 |
| Kuwait | 72.77 | 6.95 | 108.14 | 10.20 | 246.03 | 12.31 | 152.19 | 9.23 |
| Libya | 20.31 | 1.94 | 48.16 | 4.54 | 29.33 | 1.47 | 21.96 | 1.33 |
| Yemen | 20.05 | 1.92 | 8.61 | 0.81 | 6.17 | 0.31 | - | - |
| Sultan | 19.00 | 1.82 | 3.16 | 0.30 | 0.61 | 0.03 | 1.05 | 0.06 |
| Algeria | 16.20 | 1.55 | 2.99 | 0.28 | - | - | 0.99 | 0.06 |
| Egypt | 10.51 | 1.00 | 3.90 | 0.37 | 1.25 | 0.06 | - | - |
| Qatar | 0.99 | 0.09 | 4.32 | 0.41 | 59.76 | 2.99 | 65.32 | 3.96 |

Note: China as the reporting entities.

Classification Basis: HS2007.

Source: Data compiled and calculated based on the United Nations International Trade Database. The data has been updated to the latest version (update log query URL: https: //wits.worldbank.org/WITS/WITS/Support%20Materials/TariffDataRefresh.aspx?Page=TariffDataRefresh).

Globally, Arab countries have consistently remained China's largest source of crude oil imports. Their share of China's total imports of crude oil rose

Chapter 2　Special Report on China-Arab States Trade Cooperation

from 47.65% in 2013 to 48.84% in 2023 (as shown in Figure 2.12), reflecting a strengthened cooperation between China and Arab countries in the energy sector. Specifically, China's import volumes from Saudi Arabia, Iraq, the UAE, Oman, and Kuwait have shown sustained growth. In 2023, these countries ranked the 2nd, 3rd, 5th, 6th, and 9th respectively among China's global crude oil suppliers.

**Table 2.14　Top 10 Countries by Volume for China's Crude Oil Imports**

| Rank | 2013 | | | 2023 | | |
| --- | --- | --- | --- | --- | --- | --- |
| | Countries | Import Volume (10000 tons) | Proportion (%) | Countries | Import Volume (10000 tons) | Proportion (%) |
| 1 | Saudi Arabia | 4236.81 | 19.29 | Russia | 6067.92 | 17.97 |
| 2 | Angola | 3180.86 | 14.48 | Saudi Arabia | 5387.76 | 15.96 |
| 3 | Oman | 1993.21 | 9.07 | Iraq | 3521.13 | 10.43 |
| 4 | Russia | 1974.26 | 8.99 | Malay | 2861.15 | 8.47 |
| 5 | Iraq | 1789.98 | 8.15 | United Arab Emirates | 2664.04 | 7.89 |
| 6 | Iran | 1688.76 | 7.69 | Oman | 2503.87 | 7.42 |
| 7 | Venezuela | 1014.89 | 4.62 | Brazil | 2295.29 | 6.80 |
| 8 | Kazakhstan | 937.55 | 4.27 | Angola | 1854.75 | 5.49 |
| 9 | United Arab Emirates | 836.73 | 3.81 | Kuwait | 1521.88 | 4.51 |
| 10 | Kuwait | 727.73 | 3.31 | U.S.A. | 908.78 | 2.69 |
| | Arab Countries | 10465.78 | 47.65 | Arab Countries | 16491.88 | 48.84 |

Note: China as the reporting entities.

Classification Basis: HS2007.

Source: Data compiled and calculated based on the United Nations International Trade Database. The data has been updated to the latest version (update log query URL: https: //wits.worldbank.org/WITS/WITS/Support%20Materials/TariffDataRefresh.aspx?Page=TariffDataRefresh).

049

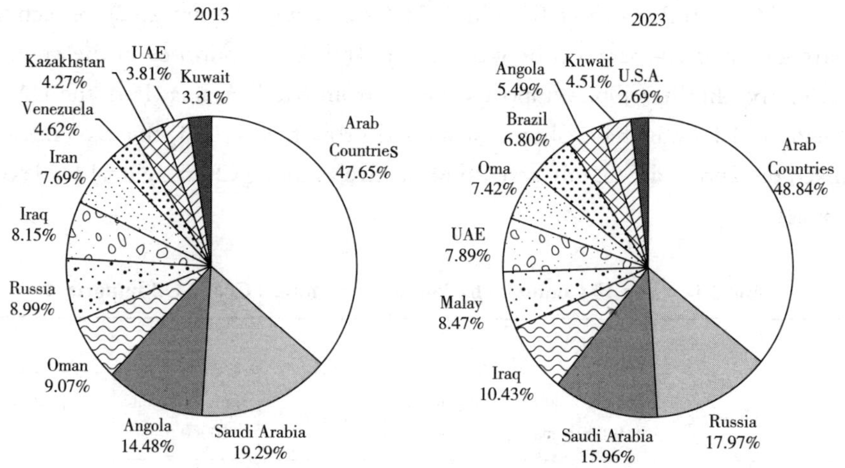

The Development Process of China-Arab States Economic and Trade Relations
Annual Report 2024

**Figure 2.12　China's Top 10 Crude Oil Suppliers in 2013 and 2023**

Note: China as the reporting entities.

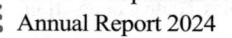

Classification Basis: HS2007.

Source: Data compiled and calculated based on the United Nations International Trade Database. The data has been updated to the latest version (update log query URL: https: //wits.worldbank.org/WITS/ WITS/Support%20Materials/TariffDataRefresh.aspx?Page=TariffDataRefresh).

## 2.4　Trends and Prospects of China-Arab States Trade Cooperation

### 2.4.1　Strong Economic Complementarity Underpins Sustained China-Arab States Trade Growth

Resource endowments and industrial capabilities mutually reinforce each other. While China, as the world's second-largest economy, possesses a massive manufacturing base and a growing demand for energy, Arab countries, particularly GCC members such as Saudi Arabia, the UAE, and Qatar, hold abundant reserves of oil and gas, serving as critical global energy suppliers. This strong complementarity between resource endowments and industrial structures has laid the groundwork for the sustained development of China-Arab states trade cooperation.

According to the 2021 Arab Economic Report released by the Arab Monetary Fund, Arab countries already held 55.7% of the world's proven oil reserves and

Chapter 2　Special Report on China-Arab States Trade Cooperation

26.5% of its natural gas reserves as early as 2021. As the world's largest energy consumer, China has long maintained over 70% oil import dependency and more than 40% natural gas import dependency, as evidenced in The Analysis and Outlook Report of China's Oil and Gas Industry Development (2022-2023). Sino-Arab energy trade volume reached USD224.682 billion in 2022, declining slightly in 2023 to USD187.246 billion, with Saudi Arabia remaining China's largest crude oil supplier. This structural complementarity in energy supply and demand has been institutionally guaranteed through long-term supply agreements and strategic reserve cooperation. For example, the Yanbu Refinery Project in Saudi Arabia, which officially commenced commercial operations in January 2016. During the 7th Future Investment Initiative Summit in Riyadh on October 23, 2023, Sinopec and Saudi Aramco signed a Memorandum of Understanding for the "Yanbu Refinery Plus" project, a large-scale petrochemical project converting liquefied feedstocks into chemical products.

Beyond traditional energy trade, the complementarity between China and Arab countries in the sector of manufactured goods have become increasingly prominent. Boasting a comprehensive industrial system and robust production capacity, China is able to export a wide range of manufactured products to Arab nations at competitive prices, catering to their needs for infrastructure development, industrial diversification, and consumption upgrading. China's exports of manufactured goods to Arab countries have maintained steady growth, with machinery, transport equipment along with electrical products accounting for an ever-increasing share. Specifically, the export value of these products surged from USD29.084 billion in 2013 to USD59.076 billion in 2023, marking a significant expansion in scale. Their proportion in total exports also rose from 28.70% in 2013 to 32.59% in 2023. This trend indicates that China is gradually moving up the value chain to meet Arab countries' demand for high-end equipment.

Beyond energy trade, the dynamic optimization of trade structure and deepening complementarity between China and Arab countries are also evident. The Sino-Arab trade structure is shifting from vertical to horizontal division of labor. Traditionally, China imported energy and raw materials while exporting manufactured goods under the vertical model. In recent years, with Arab nations advancing their industrial diversification strategies and China upgrading its industrial structure, the bilateral trade model has gradually moved toward

051

The Development Process of China-Arab States Economic and Trade Relations
Annual Report 2024

horizontal specialization. A growing number of Arab countries have started exporting certain manufactured products to China, such as chemical products and some metal items. China's imports from Arab countries have long been dominated by chemical products, plastics, and rubber products. As shown in Table 2.11, imported chemicals ranked second in China's total import structure in 2023, reaching USD8.132 billion, while imports of plastics and rubber products ranked third at USD6.914 billion. This reflects increasingly close cooperation between China and Arab countries across the upstream and downstream segments of industrial chains. Concurrently, China's enhanced innovation capacity is driving rapid growth in high-tech exports to Arab states. These exports, primarily in machinery, electronics and communication sectors, provide strong support for the economic transformation and industrial upgrading across Arab countries.

## 2.4.2 Reshaped Geopolitics Deepens China-Arab States Trade Cooperation

Profound shifts in the global geopolitical landscape have injected new momentum into China-Arab states economic and trade cooperation in recent years. The United States' strategic withdrawal from the Middle East, pressure from energy transition, and adjustments to regional security frameworks have prompted Arab countries to accelerate economic diversification and seek new partners. Concurrently, China, through its Belt and Road Initiative and the building of a China-Arab states community with a shared future, has gradually emerged as a reliable partner for Arab countries in political, economic, and security domains. This geopolitical evolution has not only reconfigured economic connectivity across Eurasia and Africa but also created fresh opportunities to deepen China-Arab states trade collaboration.

The shift in U.S. strategic focus in the Middle East has weakened Arab countries' reliance on a single external power. American troop withdrawal from Afghanistan and scaled-back security commitments to traditional allies have accelerated a widespread "Look East" strategy among Arab nations. This shift aims to achieve strategic autonomy through deepening cooperation with major powers like China and Russia. China's mediation in restoring diplomatic relations between Saudi Arabia and Iran in 2023 marked a significant rise in China's political influence in Middle Eastern affairs, laying a more solid foundation of

Chapter 2　Special Report on China-Arab States Trade Cooperation

mutual trust for China-Arab states economic and trade cooperation. Meanwhile, China-Arab states trade volume surged from USD238.897 billion in 2013 to USD398.127 billion in 2023, an increase of approximately 66.65% over the decade (see Table 2.5). Their economic and trade exchanges cover a wide range of areas including energy, infrastructure, and digital economy.

The potential risks of U.S. intervention in maritime transport routes have accelerated China's efforts to establish an alternative land transport networks with Arab countries. The China-Europe Railway Express shipments surged from 80 trains in 2013 to 17523 trains in 2023[1], partially alleviating the "Malacca Dilemma". Countries like Azerbaijan, leveraging their strategic position bridging the Caspian and Black Seas, have emerged as critical nodes along the "Land Silk Road". In April 2024, China and Azerbaijan jointly issued a joint statement on establishing a strategic partnership[2]. That same year, Saudi Arabia launched the "China-Arab States Land Bridge Initiative", aiming to connect the Persian Gulf and the Mediterranean via railway networks. This corridor will significantly shorten cargo transit times while diminishing the reliance on traditional maritime transport.

The geopolitical restructuring extends beyond economic spheres into security governance. China has promoted cooperation with Arab countries in counter-terrorism and cybersecurity through platforms like the Shanghai Cooperation Organization (SCO) and BRICS. Azerbaijan's strategic value as a hub in the South Caucasus has been further highlighted since its accession to the SCO in 2024, contributing to the stability of the Central Asia-West Asia transport corridor. The 2022 China-Arab States Summit proposed building a "community with a shared future for a new era", with both sides reaching consensus on principles of mutual respect for sovereignty and opposition to external interference. This provides a more stable institutional environment for cross-border investment and trade. The establishment of the China-Arab States Technology Transfer Coopertion Network, coupled with facilitating technology centers in such places as Jordan and Dubai, has accelerated the cross-border flow of innovation resources.

---

①　China Railway Express Network, https://www.crexpress.cn/#/.

②　Joint Statement of the People's Republic of China and the Republic of Azerbaijan on Establishing a Strategic Partnership, National Government Portal of the People's Republic of China, https://www.gov.cn/yaowen/liebiao/202407/content_6961034.htm, July 3, 2024.

## 2.4.3 Supply Chain Optimization Provides New Impetus for Upgrading China-Arab States Trade Structures

In the context of global value chain restructuring and accelerated regional economic integration, supply chain optimization has emerged as a new engine driving the high-quality growth in China-Arab states trade. In 2023, the bilateral trade structure remained characterized by a one-way pattern, namely, China exports manufactured goods to Arab countries while importing energy resources. However, through systematic optimization of cross-border supply chains in terms of logistics efficiency, digitalization, and regional collaboration, China-Arab states trade is gradually breaking away from their traditional commodity structure, paving the way for new trade opportunities in high-value-added products and technology-intensive cooperation.

Upgraded Logistics Networks Reshape the Trade Dynamics. The multimodal transport corridors covering sea, land, air, and rail jointly developed by China and Arab countries have significantly shortened cross-border transport cycles. The automated container terminal developed by COSCO Shipping (China Ocean Shipping Company) at Khalifa Port in the UAE employs an "ARMG+SHC" operation model for horizontal transport. And it now stands as the most advanced container terminal in the Middle East. Since commencing operations in December 2018, Abu Dhabi Terminal at Khalifa Port has handled over 5.5 million TEUs, marking a new milestone in China-Arab states cooperation under the Belt and Road Initiative[1]. In land transportation, China-Europe Railway Express continues to expand its logistics network, exemplified by the Zhengzhou-Turkey route newly launched on July 10, 2024[2]. The upgrading of logistics networks has boosted trade growth in time-sensitive commodities such as fresh agricultural products and precision instruments.

Cross-border e-commerce and accelerated logistics are driving optimization in the supply chain for small commodities. Early trade models relied on traditional

---

[1] COSCO Shipping Abu Dhabi Terminal: The Glory and Future of Building a Middle East Hub Port", China COSCO Shipping Corporation Limited website, https://www.coscoshipping.com/clcol6864/en/2024/art_d2093aff174bb4a9cb4647b3d06be1b.html, November 15, 2024.

[2] Zhai Zhuo, "First South Corridor 'Cross-Two-Seas' Route of China-Europe Railway Express (Zhengzhou) Put into Operation", Belt and Road Portal, https://www.yidaiyilu.gov.cn/p/003H38DR.html, July 11, 2024.

Chapter 2    Special Report on China-Arab States Trade Cooperation

maritime shipping, which was time-consuming and resulted in low efficiency of merchandise turnover. In recent years, with the rise of cross-border e-commerce platforms and improvements in logistics infrastructure, commodity supply chains have seen significant optimization. Yiwu, China's largest distribution center for small commodities, has seen a marked increase in its export share via cross-border e-commerce channels. According to the *2023 Statistical Communiqué on Yiwu's National Economic and Social Development*, the city's exports to the UAE increased by 11.1% year-on-year in 2023. Logistics enterprises such as Cainiao International Express have established overseas warehouses in the UAE and Dubai, dramatically shortening delivery times, with the fastest "next-day delivery" now achievable.

Supply chain optimization is driving the export of high-value-added products. Saudi Arabia is actively advancing its diversification strategy through "Vision 2030" to reduce over-reliance on crude oil, while vigorously developing the refining and petrochemical industry to enhance the added value of petroleum resources. Against this backdrop, Sinopec Engineering Incorporation (SEI), a key subsidiary of Sinopec Engineering Group (SEG), has participated in constructing multiple refining and petrochemical projects in Saudi Arabia, providing technical support and engineering services. In June 2024, SEG signed a general contract of Engineering, Procurement, and Construction (EPC), worth USD3.35 billion for the Riyadh Natural Gas Liquids (NGL) Fractionation Facilities at Saudi Arabia's Jafurah gas field. This marks SEG's largest single contract in Saudi Arabia to date[1]. These projects have enhanced Saudi Arabia's production capacity for high-value-added chemical products and laid the groundwork for more diversified petrochemical exports to China.

Supply chain reshaping drives industrial relocation. The China-Egypt cooperation in the textile and apparel industry is a typical case of the transformation of China-Arab states economic and trade relations against the backdrop of supply chain optimization. To reduce production costs and avoid trade barriers, Chinese textile and apparel enterprises have gradually relocated their production bases to Egypt and other Arab countries, building new supply

---

[1]  Shen Manfang, "Company Signs the Largest Single Contract in Saudi Market", Sinopec Engineering (Group) Co., Ltd. website, http://www.segroup.cn/egroup/news/eom_news/20240711/neus_20240711_633732224252.shtml, July 11, 2024.

055

The Development Process of China-Arab States Economic and Trade Relations
Annual Report 2024

chain systems and promoting bilateral industrial cooperation. The Egyptian government has implemented a series of preferential policies to attract Chinese enterprises to invest and set up factories in Egypt. In December 2024, Lutai Group, the world's largest producer of dyed fabrics and shirts, announced a USD385 million investment in Egypt, covering the full industrial chain from yarn production, fabric manufacturing to garment processing. It will introduce world-leading technologies to boost the upgrading and development of the local textile and apparel industry[1].

### 2.4.4　Enhanced Resilience of China-Arab States Trade Fuels Strong Impetus Against Complex Risks

Amid the growing uncertainty of global economy, the resilience demonstrated by China-Arab states trade has emerged as a key driver in responding to complex risks. This resilience is reflected not only in the steady growth of trade volume, but more importantly in its robust risk resistance and rapid recovery capabilities in the face of external shocks.

The China-Arab states trade relations exhibit significant internal stability and self-repair capabilities. Over the years, they have weathered four major shocks, namely, the 2008 global financial crisis, regional turmoil from 2014 to 2016, the COVID-19 pandemic in 2020, and the global economic fragmentation in 2023. While each shock exerted certain negative impacts on China-Arab states trade, its resilience has, on the whole, followed a phased pattern of "stepwise elevation". Calculations indicate that the average resilience of China-Arab states trade increased by 6.9% during the recovery and adjustment period compared with the resistance period, demonstrating strong risk resistance and recovery potential.

China-Arab states trade possesses significant risk resilience. This capacity to effectively withstand external shocks is underpinned by a long-term and stable energy cooperation. As a major global energy consumer, China has established solid energy supply ties with resource-rich countries like Saudi Arabia, providing a strong foundation for bilateral trade. Additionally, China has actively promoted cooperation of productive capacity with Arab countries in infrastructure and

---

[1]　"The World's Largest Producer of Dyel Fabries and Shirts Explares Establishing a Fatory inEgyp," General Authority for Investment and Free Zones (GAFI), https://www.gafi.gov.eg/English/MediaCenter/News/Pages/The-World%E2%80%99s-Largest-Producer- of-Dyed-Fabrics-and-Shirts-Explores-Establishing-a-Factory-in-Egypt.aspx, December 16, 2024.

Chapter 2　Special Report on China-Arab States Trade Cooperation

manufacturing, facilitating the upgrading and complementarity of their industrial structures. This diversified cooperation strategy has effectively dispersed trade risks and enhanced overall trade resilience. During the 2008 global financial crisis, while the average resilience of China-Arab states trade dropped to as low as 0.119 at one point, and the resilience level in trade with most Arab countries was relatively low, concerted efforts to strengthen energy ties and diversify trade channels spurred rapid recovery. The series of measures included China National Offshore Oil Corporation 2008 signed a long-term contract with Qatar Petroleum in 2008 for 2 million tons per year over 25 years[1]. These efforts catalyzed a swift rebound in bilateral trade, driving restorative growth.

China-Arab states trade has demonstrated a markedly accelerated capacity to recover resilience. While it took five years for bilateral trade to normalize after the 2008 financial crisis, the recovery from the COVID-19 pandemic in 2020 was achieved in just two years. The shortening of this recovery cycle is mainly attributed to the following aspects. First, Enhanced Energy Cooperation. As the anchor of bilateral trade, strengthened long-term energy supply relationships have solidified the foundation for bilateral trade. Second, Expanded Cooperation of Production Capacity. Chinese enterprises have actively participated in the industrialization process of Arab countries through infrastructure and manufacturing projects, fostering the upgrading and complementarity of the industrial structures of both sides. Third, Advanced Vaccine Cooperation. During the period of pandemic prevention and control, China and Arab countries actively carried out vaccine cooperation to overcome difficulties together, and these efforts further deepened mutual trust and friendship between the two sides. Fourth, Deepened Synergy in Digital Rule. In the era of digital economy, strengthening synergy in digital rules is conducive to develop new trade models such as cross-border e-commerce and digital payment, injecting new impetus into China-Arab states trade.

---

① Huang Xinpei, "CNOOC and Qatar Petroleum Sign Long-Term LNG Agreement," Xinhua Silk Road, ttps://www.imsilkrod.cm/neus/p/464937.html, September 30, 2021.

**057**

# Chapter 3　Special Report on China-Arab States Investment Cooperation

In recent years, economic cooperation between China and the Arab states has ushered in an unprecedented"investment boom"and two-way investment cooperation has become increasingly close. Arab states are rich in energy and capital, and they have strong demands for economic transformation and development.The quality and quantity of the two-way investment cooperation between them have increased, with the scale, volume and scope of the field expanding continuously. A number of major projects in China-Arab states two-way investment cooperation have become landmark ones for promoting the transformation and upgrading of China-Arab states economic and trade cooperation to high-quality development in the new period. Since 2021, China's direct investment flow to Arab states has kept increasing, and in addition to direct investment, Chinese enterprises have also been actively expanding their business in various sectors in Arab states through reinvestment, third-country investment and other means, and the total amount of various types of investment has actually exceeded USD78 billion[1]. Meanwhile, Arab states are actively expanding their investment layout in the Chinese market with rapid growth. China-Arab states investment sectors have become increasingly diversified, covering not only traditional fields such as oil and gas, construction and manufacturing, but also many emerging fields such as new energy, digital economy, artificial intelligence and biomedicine. In the future, along with the construction of high-quality Belt and Road Initiative, China-Arab

---

[1]　Chinese Academy of International Trade and Economic Cooperation, *Review and Prospect of Economic and Trade Cooperation Between China and Arab States 2024*, November 2024, p. 2.

Chapter 3    Special Report on China-Arab States Investment Cooperation

states two-way investment still has great potential.

## 3.1    Chinese Direct Investment in the Arab States

In January 2025, UNCTAD published the latest *Global Investment Trends Monitor*, which shows that global FDI amounts to USD1.4 trillion in 2024, up 11% year-on-year. However, if financial flows from the European corridor economies are excluded, global FDI actually declines by about 8%.[1] China's outward non-financial FDI in 2024 amounted to 1024.5 billion yuan, an increase of 11.7% over the previous year, or USD143.8 billion, an increase of 10.5%.[2] With the sluggish global foreign direct investment and intensified geopolitical conflicts, China's outbound investment has increased steadily, injecting impetus into the world's economic recovery.

### 3.1.1    Current Situation and Characteristics of China's Outward Foreign Direct Investment (ODI) since 2013

Since 2013, China's outward foreign direct investment (ODI) has experienced significant structural adjustment and scale expansion, and it has gradually shifted from "high-speed growth" to "high-quality development"[3]. The Chinese government has been a major driving force in global economic cooperation.

The scale of China's ODI has continued to expand, with its flow and stock leaping to the forefront of the world, and its global position improving significantly. Since the Belt and Road Initiative was put forward in 2013, the scale of China's ODI has grown rapidly, reaching USD177.29 billion in 2023, 1.6 times the figure in 2013 (see Figure 3.1); its share of global ODI has risen from 7.6% in 2013 to 11.4% in 2023. For 12 consecutive years, China has ranked among the top three global outward FDI flows, and its position as a major outward investing country has become increasingly solid. Since the 18th CPC National Congress,

---

[1]    UNCTAD, *Global Investment Trends Monitor*, January 2025, p.2.

[2]    National Bureau of Statistics website, "Statistical Bulletin of the People's Republic of China on National Economic and Social Development in 2024," https://www.stats.gov.cn/sj/zxfb/202502/t20250228_1958817.html, February 28, 2025.

[3]    Lu Jinyong, Wang Fenfen, and Chen Hongxi, "Major Achievements and Experiences of China's Outward Investment since the 18th CPC National Congress", *International Economic Cooperation*, No. 4, 2024.

**059**

The Development Process of China-Arab States Economic and Trade Relations
Annual Report 2024

China's cumulative outward FDI has amounted to USD1.68 trillion, equivalent to 57% of the stock at the end of 2023, accounting for more than 10% of the global share for eight consecutive years, and it has paid USD518.5 billion in taxes in the countries and regions where it has invested and solved more than 2 million jobs annually, so the contribution of China's investment to the world economy is becoming more and more prominent.[1] The rapid development of China's ODI is not only the inevitable result of economic development, industrial upgrading and changes in the international environment, but also the common choice of strategic layout, policy promotion and enterprise development.[2]

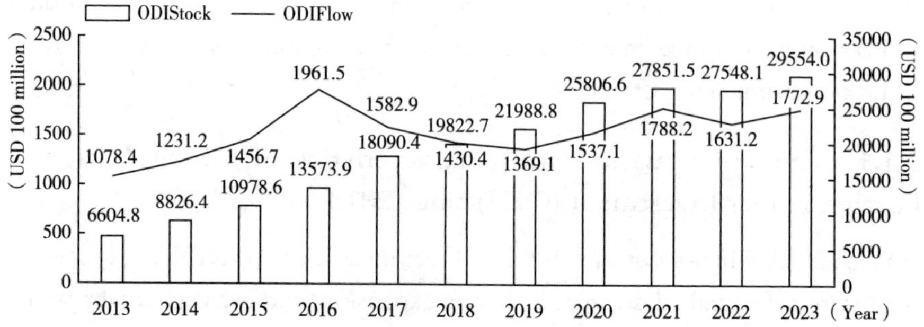

**Figure 3.1　China'ODI Stock and Flow (2013-2023)**

Source: Ministry of Commerce of the People's Republic of China, *2023 Statistical Bulletin of China's Outward Foreign Direct Investment,* China Commerce and Trade Press, September 2024, p.6.

China's ODI regional layout is optimized, with Belt and Road becoming the core engine. Since 2013, investment flows to Belt and Road countries have increased by 222.3%, accounting for a continuously rising proportion of China's total ODI flows. ASEAN countries (e.g. Singapore, Indonesia, Vietnam) are the core destinations of China's outward investment, and investment in Africa is growing rapidly. The industry structure is diversified, with leasing and business services, wholesale and retail, manufacturing and finance still being the major

---

[1]　Ministry of Commerce of the People's Republic of China, *2023 Statistical Bulletin of China's Outward Foreign Direct Investment,* China Commerce and Trade Press, September 2024, p.6.

[2]　Dong Bingbing, "China's Outward Foreign Direct Investment in the Past Ten Years: History, Motivation and Prospects," *China Forex,* No 18, September 2024.

060

Chapter 3　Special Report on China-Arab States Investment Cooperation

investment areas, accounting for a combined share of 78.1%.[1] Investment in high value-added new energy and supply chain related industries (e.g. electric vehicles, green energy) has grown significantly. The investment mode has shifted from mergers and acquisitions to green investment, and Chinese enterprises have transformed their strategies from "going out" to "staying in".The main body of investment has basically formed a "double-wheel drive" pattern of state-owned enterprises and private enterprises. At the end of 2023, among the stock of non-financial foreign direct investment of USD263.158 billion, state-owned enterprises accounted for 52.2%, and non-state-owned enterprises accounted for 47.8%.[2]

Since 2013, China's outward foreign direct investment (ODI) has been characterized by "scale expansion, structural optimization, regional focus and mode innovation", but it also faces the challenges of the complexity of the international environment and the intensification of localization pressure. In the future, with the deepening of the "Belt and Road" and the restructuring of the global industrial chain, China's ODI will further tilt towards high value-added, green and digitalized areas, while balancing risk prevention and control with openness and cooperation, and enhancing the ability of global resource allocation.

### 3.1.2　Continuous Improvement of the Investment Environment in the Arab States

In today's globalized economic landscape, the Middle East is emerging at a phenomenal pace, and according to a recent report by GlobalData, the Middle East has become the fourth most attractive region for foreign direct investment (FDI) in the world by 2024. This remarkable achievement not only marks the transformation and development of the Middle East's economy, but also presents new opportunities and challenges for global investors. Meanwhile, Kearney's 2024 Foreign Direct Investment Confidence Index (FDICI) also shows that the UAE (ranked 2nd), Saudi Arabia (ranked 3rd) top the FDI Investment Confidence Index amongst the world's emerging markets, with Egypt coming

---

[1]　Ministry of Commerce of the People's Republic of China, *2023 Statistical Bulletin of China's Outward Foreign Direct Investment*, China Commerce and Trade Press, September 2024, pp.12, 14.

[2]　Ministry of Commerce of the People's Republic of China, *2023 Statistical Bulletin of China's Outward Foreign Direct Investment*, China Commerce and Trade Press, September 2024, p.27.

**061**

The Development Process of China-Arab States Economic and Trade Relations
Annual Report 2024

in at number 15, further cementing the Middle East's position as a hotbed of investment. [1]According to data from a report released by UNCTAD in June 2024, FDI inflows to Arab states increased rapidly from USD33.2 billion in 2020 to USD64 billion in 2021, and were relatively stable in the following three years. However, the continued delay in the new round of the Israeli-Palestinian conflict, which began in October 2023, has dented investors' confidence and led to investment inflows below potential levels. This trend is exacerbated by the predominance of greenfield projects in the region.[2] FDI inflows to Arab states declined by 12.4% to USD67.7 billion in 2023, accounting for 7.8% of total inflows to developing countries and 5.1% of total global inflows of about USD1.33 trillion(see figure 3.2). FDI inflows to Arab states continued to be concentrated in five countries with a share of more than 95%. The highest total inflows were to the UAE, which attracted USD30.7 billion, or 45.4%; followed by Saudi Arabia, which attracted USD12.4 billion, or 18.2% share; Egypt ranked third with USD9.8 billion, or 18.2% of total inflows to the Arab states; Bahrain ranked fourth with USD6.8 billion, or 10% of the total, then Oman with USD4.7 billion, and Kuwait with USD2.1 billion, or 6.9% and 3.1% of the total respectively. [3]

### 3.1.3 Trends of China's Outward Foreign Direct Investment (ODI) in Arab States since 2013

China actively encourages enterprises to go out and participate in the process of economic diversification and transformation in Arab states.Since 2013, China's direct investment in Arab states has grown relatively fast, with the fields of investment constantly broadened and the main investment bodies diversified,

---

[1]  Dhaman, *The Investment Climate in Arab Countries 2024*, July 2024, p.2.

[2]  Greenfield Investment, also known as creation investment or new investment, refers to the establishment of an enterprise in the host country by a transnational corporation or other investment entity in accordance with the laws of the host country, where part or all of the assets are owned by the foreign investors. Creation investment leads directly to an increase in productive capacity, output and employment in the host country.Brownfield Investment refers to the entry into a country's market through mergers and acquisitions, whereby a foreign investor buys or leases an existing business or asset rather than building a new plant or facility. This type of investment is often referred to as Brownfield Investment. Greenfield investment projects are more likely to be delayed or canceled due to security concerns than brownfield investment projects.

[3]  UNCTAD, 2024 *Word Investment Report*, June 2024, p.156.

062

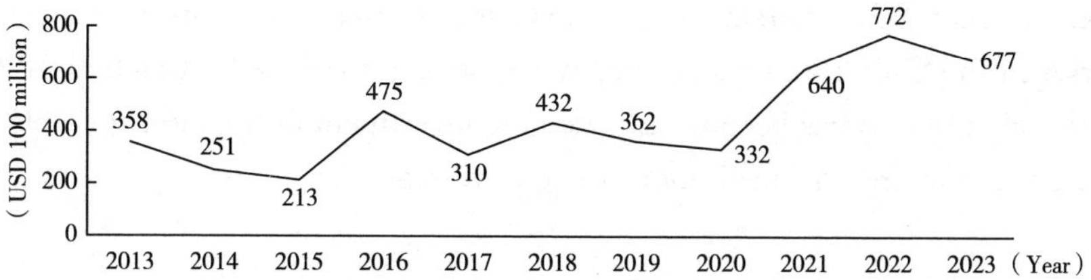

Chapter 3    Special Report on China-Arab States Investment Cooperation

**Figure 3.2    FDI inflows to the Arab States（2013-2023）**

Source: UNCTAD, *2024 World Investment Report,* June 2024, pp.152-156.

which has played an important role in promoting the economic development of Arab states.

1. Improvement of Investment Cooperation Mechanism

China has actively promoted the negotiation and signing of Bilateral Investment Protection Agreements (BIPAs) and Double Taxation Avoidance Agreements (DTAs) with Arab states, creating a favorable investment environment for Sino-Arab investment cooperation. By the end of 2023, China had signed BIPAs with 14 Arab states, including Algeria and the UAE, and DTAs with 12 Arab states, including Saudi Arabia, Qatar and Morocco. Currently, China is negotiating with Saudi Arabia and the UAE on upgrading the BIPA.

2. Trend and Scale of Development

Since the introduction of the Belt and Road Initiative in 2013, China's ODI flows and stocks to Arab states have grown at a relatively fast pace. In terms of investment flows, China's ODI flows to Arab states increased from USD1.59 billion in 2013 to USD2.69 billion in 2023 (with investment flows maintaining over USD2 billion since 2019). By the end of 2023, China's ODI stock with Arab states reached USD27.6 billion, 3.2 times higher than that in 2013(see figure 3.3).

In recent years, China-Arab states investment cooperation has been developing rapidly. Since 2021, China's direct investment in Arab states has realized "three consecutive increases", and as of the end of 2023, China's direct investment stock in Arab states was USD27.6 billion.[1] In addition to direct investment, Chinese enterprises have also actively expanded their business in various fields in Arab states through reinvestment and third-country investment. The booming

---

[1]    Ministry of Commerce of the People's Republic of China, *2023 Statistical Bulletin of China's Outward Foreign Direct Investment,* China Commerce and Trade Press, September 2024, pp.47-54.

capital market, bond market, project financing market and wealth management market in the Gulf countries also show the strong investment attraction of the Gulf region, which has become an emerging investment destination for Chinese enterprises and financial institutions to "go overseas".

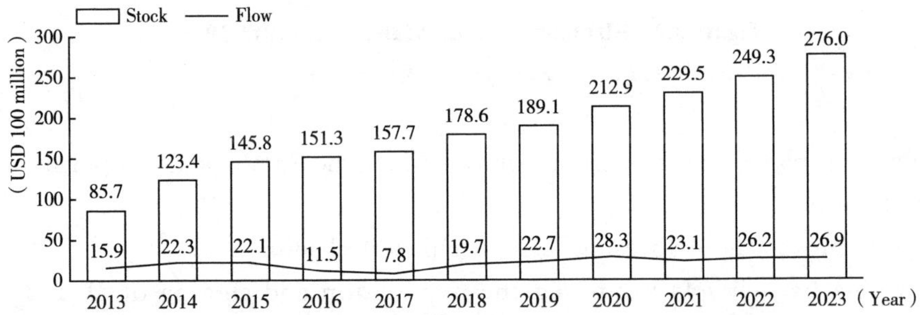

Figure 3.3 China's ODI Stock and Flow to the Arab States (2013-2023)

Source: Ministry of Commerce of the People's Republic of China, *2023 Statistical Bulletin of China's Outward Foreign Direct Investment*, China Commerce and Trade Press, September 2024, pp.47-54.

3. Largest Investment in Gulf and North African Countries

The UAE's development philosophy, development speed, open and tolerant society and culture, as well as its location advantage of radiating to the neighboring areas, make it an ideal place for Chinese enterprises to invest and start their business. Currently, more than 8000 Chinese companies are developing local and regional business in the UAE.

Major investment projects are in the progress. China and the UAE announced the establishment of a USD10 billion joint investment fund; Abu Dhabi National Oil Company (ADNOC) and China National Petroleum Coporation (CNPC) established a joint venture, Al Yasat Petroleum, in which CNPC has a 40% share; CNPC and Zhenhua Oil each acquired 8% and 4% shareholding in Abu Dhabi's onshore petroleum blocks; CNPC acquired a 10% shareholding in each of Abu Dhabi's offshore petroleum blocks; China COSCO Shipping acquired the right to operate Terminal 2 of Abu Dhabi Khalifa Port; Jiangsu Overseas Cooperation and Investment Company(JOCIC) constructed the Sino-Arab (UAE) Production Capacity Cooperation Model Park. At present, Chinese-funded enterprises enjoy a sound momentum of development in the UAE in the fields of oil and gas, new energy, infrastructure construction, communications, finance, etc., and are actively

064

Chapter 3　Special Report on China-Arab States Investment Cooperation

exploring emerging markets.[①] Through the "Vision 2030", Saudi Arabia aims to promote the transformation of the non-oil economy, and economic and trade cooperation between the two countries is in the transformation and upgrading of an important opportunity.At present, the main business of Chinese-funded enterprises in Saudi Arabia covers engineering contracting, trade and shipping, communications services, industrial investment and park construction, and began to expand to finance, clean energy, logistics, e-commerce and other areas. Egypt and Morocco have attracted foreign capital inflows through the localization of manufacturing industries. China has been Egypt's largest trading partner for 12 consecutive years from 2012 to 2023. China is one of the most active and fastest-growing countries in terms of investment in Egypt, and a number of Chinese-funded enterprises are active in Egypt's manufacturing, energy, information technology services, agriculture and other fields. The Suez (TEDA) Economic and Trade Cooperation Zone jointly built by China and Egypt has become an important platform for promoting investment and cooperation between the two countries. [②]Chinese enterprises have successively won bids for the implementation of the Central Business District of the new administrative capital, the 10th of Ramadan Railway project and other major national projects, which have become the landmark projects of Sino-Egyptian cooperation. Morocco is accelerating industrialization, informationization and agricultural modernization, and particularly welcomes investment projects of export processing and high technological added value. Morocco is the largest automobile exporter in Africa and an important development partner and production base for European, American and aviation industries. In recent years, a number of Chinese manufacturers of automobile parts and components and new energy vehicle batteries have settled in Morocco one after another. CITIC Dicastal, Xiezhong International, Aotecar, Chongqing Ruige. and Nexteer Automotive held by China Aviation Automotive Systems Holdings Limited and other five Chinese auto parts manufacturers invested in the Atlantic Free Zone to set up factories, all of which formally went into operation within 2019, and are

---

①　Ministry of Commerce of the People's Republic of China, *Guide to Countries (Regions) for Outward Investment Cooperation: UAE (2024 Edition)*, December 2024, pp.4, 25.

②　Ministry of Commerce of the People's Republic of China, *Guide to Countries (Regions) for Outward Investment Cooperation: Egypt (2024 Edition)*, August 2024, p.4.

**065**

currently operating well. [1] The layout of Chinese enterprises in Morocco covers the whole industrial chain of new energy vehicle batteries, forming a cluster effect. The core enterprises include Gotion High-tech, CNGR and BTR, with a total investment of more than USD10 billion. [2] The offshore park that China has invested and developed locally in Morocco is the Mohammed VI Tangier Tech City project, which is still under construction. The Algerian government enacted a new investment law and the implementation rules of the new investment law in 2022, and all these will provide foreign investors with more investment convenience and new opportunities for economic and trade cooperation. The overall investment scale of Chinese enterprises in Algeria is small, mainly focusing on oil and gas, real estate, building materials and other industries. The main investment companies are Sinopec and CSCEC. The main projects include exploration and development of oil and gas fields, and are now actively promoting the implementation of investment projects in mining exploration and development.

China's investment in Arab states is mainly in oil-producing countries. In terms of investment stock, China's direct investment in the UAE will amount to USD8.91 billion in 2023, accounting for 41.1% of China's total direct investment in Arab states. It is followed by Saudi Arabia with USD3.186 billion, Iraq with USD2.169 billion, Algeria with USD1.699 billion and Egypt with USD1.287 billion. [3] In terms of investment flows, the UAE, Saudi Arabia and Morocco were the top three destinations for Chinese FDI in Arab states in 2023, followed by Algeria and Egypt.In 2023, except for Egypt, Chinese investment in several of the above Arab states achieved relatively large increases(see figure 3.4). The UAE has remained the top destination for Chinese investment in the Arab states, accounting for 67.3% of total Chinese direct investment flows to the region.

---

① Ministry of Commerce of the People's Republic of China, *Guide to Countries (Regions) for Outward Investment Cooperation: Morocco (2024 Edition)*, September 2024, p.35.

② "Expanding overseas Market, Listed Companies Starting their business in Morocco", *Securities Daily*, http: //qiye. chinadaily. com. cn/a/202502/20/ws67b69726a310510f19ee7f40. html, February 19, 2025.

③ Ministry of Commerce of the People's Republic of China, *2023 Statistical Bulletin of China's Outward Foreign Direct Investment*, China Commerce and Trade Press, September 2024, pp.52-54.

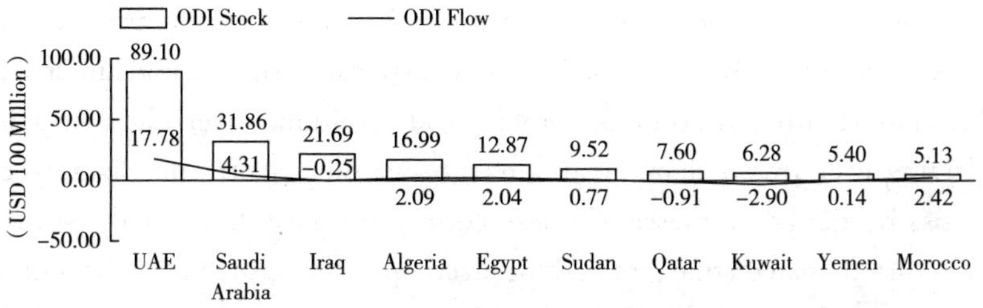

Chapter 3　Special Report on China-Arab States Investment Cooperation

**Figure 3.4　Main destinations of China's direct investment flows to Arab States in 2023**

Source: Ministry of Commerce of the People's Republic of China, National Bureau of Statistics, State Administration of Foreign Exchange, *2023 Statistical Bulletin of China's Outward Foreign Direct Investment*, China Commerce and Trade Press, September 2024, pp.47-54.

4. Focus of Chinese Direct Investment in Arab States

China's investment in Arab states has gradually expanded from traditional energy to diversified fields, following these key directions. (i)Cooperation in the whole energy industry chain. Energy cooperation is mainly in the oil and gas industry, focusing on Saudi Arabia, the United Arab Emirates, Iraq and Algeria. China also actively participates in downstream industries such as refining, storage and transportation in Arab states. In recent years, China and Arabia have accelerated cooperation in the transition to renewable energy, with clean energy such as photovoltaic, hydrogen energy, energy storage and carbon capture technology (CCUS) becoming new growth points. (ii)Two-wheel drive of infrastructure construction and digitalization.Arab states' mid- and long-term strategies are driving the surge in demand for both traditional and digital infrastructure. For example, the Riyadh metro project in Saudi Arabia and the smart city plan in the United Arab Emirates have provided Chinese companies with opportunities for cooperation in the fields of transportation, power grids, and industrial internet. Chinese companies are building railroads, ports, smart cities and other projects in Arab states, such as the New Capital project in Egypt and Phase Ⅱ of UAE railroad project. (iii)Digital economy and technology cooperation. China and Arab states have jointly built digital economy platforms and promoted cooperation in digital currency and artificial intelligence. For example, SenseTime Technology has set up a regional headquarters in Abu Dhabi to promote technology transfer. (iv)Manufacturing and healthcare. For example, manufacturing parks (such as the Suez Canal Economic and

067

Trade Zone), automobile manufacturing and medical cooperation projects have become important vehicles. (v) Rapid expansion of the consumer goods market. The youthful Arab demographics and economic diversification policies are driving investment demand in smart consumer electronics, beauty care, and cross-border e-commerce. Chinese companies have dominated the market through differentiated strategies and localized operations, such as the customized development of organic food and health products, and the entry of Meituan into Saudi Arabia. (vi) Financial cooperation as a new engine. Chinese financial institutions have accelerated their layout in the Arab market, with five major banks having set up branches in Saudi Arabia and the UAE to promote local currency swaps and cross-border investment.Industry-finance cooperation, wealth management and financial technology have become the focus of cooperation, and the acceleration of RMB internationalization in Arab states has further enhanced the potential of financial cooperation.

Green and innovation have become new trends in China-Arab states economic and trade cooperation. Green economy is a new driving force for economic development between China and Arab states. China and Arab states have been expanding their cooperation in the fields of photovoltaic, wind energy, hydropower, hydrogen energy, nuclear power and other clean energy. On the one hand, large-scale cooperation projects continue to emerge, such as the Abu Dhabi wind power demonstration project constructed by Chinese enterprises, and the 34 MW photovoltaic project in Tangier, Morocco, have become the main force of local clean energy supply. On the other hand, trade and investment drive technology transfer. King Long, Yutong, CATL and other leading enterprises have upgraded their cooperation mode through investment in factory construction and technology transfer, and actively laid out the whole industrial chain of cooperation in electric vehicles, which has helped the energy transformation and sustainable development of Arab states.

5.Increasingly Diversified Investment Entities

In terms of China's investment in Arab states, state-owned and private enterprises have both made concerted efforts. Energy, infrastructure and other large-scale projects are mainly promoted by Sinopec, PetroChina, CSCEC and other state-owned enterprises; in production & processing and other manufacturing industries, China Jushi, Haier, Aotecar and other local private enterprises go abroad to invest in Egypt, Jordan, Morocco and other countries

Chapter 3    Special Report on China-Arab States Investment Cooperation

to build factories; as to technology and consumer fields, private enterprises spring up, such as Huawei, SenseTime Technology, NIO, Meituan and other companies expand the market through technological cooperation.China-Arab States Cooperation Forum mechanism, China-Arab States Expo., economic and trade cooperation zones for enterprises all provide a platform for investment. According to incomplete statistics, China set up sixteen economic and trade cooperation zones in the Arab states.[1]For example, China-Egypt TEDA Suez Economic and Trade Cooperation Zone has formed a "port-park-city" three-in- one layout, and has attracted about 180 Chinese and foreign enterprises [2], driving the upgrading of Egypt's local industrial chain and becoming a new sample of Sino-Arab capacity cooperation.

6. Promotion of Economic Development in Arab States

China's direct investment in Arab states has vigorously promoted the economic and social development of the region. (i) Promoting economic diversification. Chinese investment has helped Arab states reduce their dependence on oil. For example, Saudi Arabia has cooperated with China to develop refining and new energy industries in support of its "Vision 2030". (ii)Technology transfer and industrial upgrading. China's technological output in the fields of digital technology and clean energy has helped Arab states upgrade their industries. The China-Arab States Technology Transfer Center has facilitated a number of collaborations in agriculture, healthcare and other fields.(iii) Employment and livelihood improvement. Infrastructure projects have created a large number of jobs, such as the construction of Egypt's new administrative capital, which has led to the employment of tens of thousands of people; medical cooperation has raised the level of local public health. (iv)Optimization of trade structure. China has expanded imports of Arab non-oil products (e.g., Egyptian citrus, Saudi dates), promoting the diversification of Arab exports. (v)Regional connectivity. China and Arab states jointly build ports and logistics centers (e.g., Djibouti International Free Trade Zone), enhancing the status of Arab states as hubs in Asia, Africa and Europe.

---

[1]    Academy of International Trade and Economic Cooperation, Ministry of Commerce, *Review and Prospect of Economic and Trade Cooperation Between China and Arab Countries in 2024*, November 2024, p. 28.

[2]    Academy of International Trade and Economic Cooperation of the Ministry of Commerce, *Guide to Countries (Regions) for Outward Investment Cooperation: Egypt (2024 Edition)*, August 2024, p. 2.

069

The Development Process of China-Arab States Economic and Trade Relations
Annual Report 2024

7. Great Improving Potential in Sino-Arab Investment Cooperation

As the top investment destination, in addition to Hong Kong, China's ODI flows to ASEAN accounted for 14.2% in 2013, followed by the United States and the European Union. China's ODI to Arab states accounted for only 1.5 percent, and the investment stock accounted for less than 1 percent. The main sources of foreign investment in Arab states are Europe (UK, France, Germany, Italy), the United States, and Asian emerging economies such as China, India, Japan, and South Korea.In 2023, China's ODI to Arab states accounted for 4 percent of the direct investment flows attracted by Arab states in that year(see table 3.1).

**Table 3.1  China's FDI in Major Economies in the World in 2023**

Unit: USD100 million

| Economy | Flow | | | Stock | |
|---|---|---|---|---|---|
| | Amount | YoY(%) | Percentage(%) | Amount | Percentage(%) |
| Globe | 1772.9 | 8.7 | 100 | 29554.0 | 100 |
| Hong Kong, China | 1087.7 | 11.5 | 61.3 | 17525.2 | 59.3 |
| ASEAN | 251.2 | 34.7 | 14.2 | 1756.2 | 5.9 |
| EU | 64.8 | -6.1 | 3.7 | 1024.2 | 3.5 |
| USA | 69.1 | -5.2 | 3.9 | 836.9 | 2.8 |
| Austrilia | 5.5 | -80.4 | 0.3 | 347.7 | 1.2 |
| Arab States | 26.9 | 13.3 | 1.5 | 276.0 | 0.9 |
| Total | 1505.2 | 11.3 | 84.9 | 21766.2 | 73.6 |

Source: National Bureau of Statistics of China, *2023 Statistical Buletin of Outbound Direct Investment*, China Commerce and Trade Press, 2024, p.30.

In short, since 2013, China's investment in Arab states has been characterized by expansion in scale, diversification in fields and collaboration among investors, which has not only deepened bilateral economic and trade relations, but also helped Arab states' economic transformation and sustainable development through technology export, industrial cooperation and infrastructure support. China-Arab states relations have set a model for South-South cooperation. China and the United Arab Emirates, Saudi Arabia, Egypt and other countries have implemented more than 200 large-scale cooperation projects under the

Chapter 3　Special Report on China-Arab States Investment Cooperation

framework of the Belt and Road Initiative, and the results of the cooperation have benefited about 2 billion people, promoting the economic development of the Arab states and the regional integration process. The deepening of China-Arab states economic and trade cooperation has provided valuable experience for other developing countries and inspired more developing countries to strengthen cooperation and jointly promote the in-depth development of South-South cooperation. Looking ahead, China has huge growth potential in overseas investment, while Gulf countries such as Saudi Arabia and the United Arab Emirates, as well as Egypt and Morocco in North Africa, are becoming emerging investment destinations for overseas capital and continue to climb in the index ranking of China's outward investment due to huge economic diversification initiatives and structural economic reforms.[1] As the Belt and Road Initiative further dovetails with the development strategies of Arab states, China-Arab states investment cooperation is expected to expand in areas such as the green economy, digital economy, high-end manufacturing, trade and logistics, and so on, high-end manufacturing, trade and logistics, and other areas are expected to unleash greater potential.

## 3.2　Arab States' Investment in China

In recent years, along with the strengthening of the trend of Arab states' "looking east" and the strong resilience and huge development potential of the Chinese market, Arab states' capitals have increased their investment in China, which has shown an accelerated development momentum in recent years.

### 3.2.1　China's Foreign Investment Booming since 2013

Since 2013, China has firmly implemented a proactive opening-up strategy. China vigorously carried out innovations in the management and approval system and substantially relaxed restrictions on foreign investment access;it has

---

[1]　EIU, China going global investment index 2025: key findings, https: //viewpoint-eiu-com-s.ra.cass. cn: 8118/analysis/article/822124882?_gl=1*107iduj*_ga*MjAxOTQyNjQzNy4xNzAwOTIxO TY1*_ga_FQFE2ZLQY2*MTc0MTMxMDg5OC44MC4xLjE3NDEzMTE2MTYuMC4wLjA.*_ ga_7685V0XQ5E*MTc0MTMxMDkwNi43OC4xLjE3NDEzMTE2NDAuMC4wLjA, January 2, 2025.

071

also fully unleashed the potential of foreign investment, and achieved remarkable results in upgrading the scale, structure and quality of China's utilized foreign investment. China's utilization of foreign investment has accumulated valuable experience: actively carrying out institutional innovation, striving to build a new opening-up pattern on all fronts, actively optimizing the business environment at all levels of government, effectively solving problems for foreign-funded enterprises, and playing a leading role in major national development strategies.[1] In 2013, China attracted USD123.91 billion, accounting for 8.5% of the global share.[2] The overall performance of China's FDI attraction in 2020-2023 is not weak, but the pressure of the high level falling back is obvious, affected by multiple factors such as the change of global FDI trend, the change of China's industrial structure, as well as the manufacturing industry's anti-globalization, etc. In 2023, 53766 new enterprises were established by FDI, an increase of 39.7% compared with that of the previous year. The actual use of foreign direct investment amounted to USD163.25 billion, a year-on-year decline of 13.7%, accounting for 12.3% of the global proportion, ranking second in the world.(see figure 3.5). China set up 59080 new foreign-invested enterprises in 2024, with an increase of 9.9% over the previous year. The actual use of foreign capital was 826.3 billion yuan, down 27.1%, or USD116.2 billion, down 28.8%.[3]

In terms of industries, in 2023, foreign investment was mainly concentrated in manufacturing, scientific research and technology services, leasing and business services, information transmission, software and information technology services, real estate, wholesale and retail trade, and finance; the number of newly-established enterprises in the above seven industries accounted for 86.8%, and the amount of actual use of foreign investment accounted for 89.5%. Among them, the absorption of foreign investment in high-tech industries (high-tech

---

[1] Lu Jinyong, Chen Hongxi and Sun Shubin, "China's Utilization of Foreign Investment since the 18th CPC National Congress: Achievements, Experiences and Future Prospects", *Intertrade,* No. 9, 2024.

[2] Ministry of Commerce of the People's Republic of China, *2024 China's Foreign Investment Statistical Bulletin,* September 2024, p. 2.

[3] National Bureau of Statistics website, "Statistical Bulletin of the People's Republic of China on National Economic and Social Development in 2024," https://www.stats.gov.cn/sj/zxfb/202502/t20250228_1958817.html, February 28, 2025.

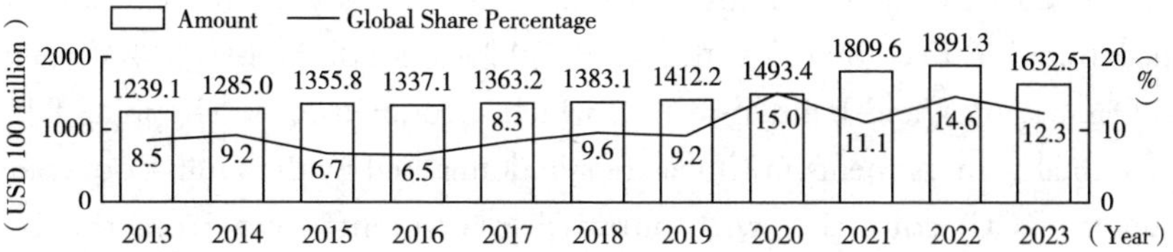

Chapter 3　Special Report on China-Arab States Investment Cooperation

□ Amount　── Global Share Percentage

Figure data (USD 100 million / %):

| Year | 2013 | 2014 | 2015 | 2016 | 2017 | 2018 | 2019 | 2020 | 2021 | 2022 | 2023 |
|------|------|------|------|------|------|------|------|------|------|------|------|
| Amount | 1239.1 | 1285.0 | 1355.8 | 1337.1 | 1363.2 | 1383.1 | 1412.2 | 1493.4 | 1809.6 | 1891.3 | 1632.5 |
| Global Share Percentage | 8.5 | 9.2 | 6.7 | 6.5 | 8.3 | 9.6 | 9.2 | 15.0 | 11.1 | 14.6 | 12.3 |

**Figure 3.5　China's Actual Use of Goods and Global Share(2013-2023)**

Source: Ministry of Commerce of the People's Republic of China, *2024 China's Foreign Investment Statistical Bulletin,* September 2024, p. 53.

manufacturing and high-tech services) was accelerated, accounting for 37.4% of China's total absorption of foreign investment. In terms of the source of investment, Asia is the top source of China's foreign investment, accounting for 81.3% (of which Hong Kong accounted for 68.1% ), followed by Europe 8.9%, Latin America 6.4% and North America 2.4%. In terms of country (region), apart from Hong Kong, Singapore, the British Virgin Islands and the Netherlands accounted for 6%, 4.2% and 3.3% respectively, followed by Japan, the Cayman Islands, South Korea, the United Kingdom and the United States, which all accounted for more than 2%. By 2023, the top 15 countries (regions) investing in China have cumulatively set up 1034 thousand FIEs, accounting for 87.6% of the cumulative number of FIEs set up in China; and the cumulative amount of investment in China is USD2.7 trillion, accounting for 94.2% of the cumulative amount of FIEs actually utilized in China.[1]

### 3.2.2　Outward Foreign Direct Investment of Arab States

Arab states have always been actively utilizing rich petrodollars for Outward Foreign Direct Investment. According to data released by UNCTAD, Arab states' outward direct investment (ODI) amounted to USD52.3 billion in 2023, down 37.1% year-on-year. ODI is mainly concentrated in five countries, namely the UAE, Saudi Arabia, Kuwait, Bahrain, and Morocco, accounting for 98.5% of the total, of which the UAE accounts for 42.7%, Saudi Arabia for 30.7%, and Kuwait for 21.4%. In terms of investment stock, Arab states' outward

---

[1]　Ministry of Commerce of the People's Republic of China, *2024 China's Foreign Investment Statistical Bulletin,* September 2024, pp. 6-20.

073

The Development Process of China-Arab States Economic and Trade Relations
Annual Report 2024

FDI totaled USD656.82 billion as of 2023, up 7.7% year-on-year, and was concentrated in five countries: the UAE (39.9%), Saudi Arabia (31%), Kuwait and Qatar (7.6%), and Bahrain (3.4%), which accounted for a whopping 89.5% of the total.[1] Investments in China are still dominated by the Gulf Cooperation Council (GCC) countries, with outward investment flows from the Gulf countries of USD50.6 billion in 2023, and an investment stock of USD594.38 billion.[2]

### 3.2.3  Surge in Arab Direct Investment in China

For a long time, Arab states' foreign direct investment mainly flows to Europe and the United States and countries of their region, with direct investment in China amounting to about USD0.5 billion per year. In recent years, along with the expansion of China's market potential, the trend of Arab states looking eastward is obvious, and direct investment in China is growing rapidly. From 2021to 2023, the amount of Arab states' direct investment in China will be USD110 million, USD1.05 billion and USD2.3 billion respectively, close to the scale of China's investment in the region. By the end of 2023, the cumulative direct investment from Arab states in China reached USD7.29 billion .[3]

Gulf countries are the main force of Chinese investment. Almost all of the new investments in the past three years came from the Gulf countries, especially the UAE and Saudi Arabia, which are the most active and strongest. Among them, the UAE is the tenth largest source of foreign investment in China, with 72 new enterprises in China in 2023, accounting for 0.1% of the global share. The actual investment amount is USD2.2 billion dollars, accounting for 1.3% of the global share, accounting for 96% of the investment flows from Arab states to China. This is followed by Saudi Arabia, with a direct investment of USD0.08 billion in 2023 in China. In terms of investment stock, the UAE, Saudi Arabia and Kuwait are the countries with the largest investments in China, amounting to USD4.5 billion, USD1.89 billion and USD0.33 billion respectively, and

---

[1]  Dhaman, *The Investment Climate in Arab Countries 2024*, July 2024, pp.82-83.

[2]  Dhaman, *The Investment Climate in Arab Countries 2024*, July 2024, pp.82-83.

[3]  Ministry of Commerce of the People's Republic of China, *2024 China's Foreign Investment Statistical Bulletin,* September 2024, pp.27-30.

Chapter 3    Special Report on China-Arab States Investment Cooperation

accounting for a total of 92.1% of Arab states' investment stock in China(see figure 3.6). However, Arab FDI in China is still in its infancy. In 2023, the share of Arab FDI flows in China in the total outward FDI from Arab countries in that year will be 4.4%, and the share of China's actual utilized FDI in that year will be only 1.4%. [1]

In terms of investment areas, Arab direct investment in China still focuses on the "main industry"such as petroleum and petrochemical. Large-scale energy and chemical enterprises represented by Saudi Aramco and Saudi Basic Industries Corporation (SABIC) are the main force, and the former has invested more than RMB 100 billion in China, making it the foreign enterprise with the largest cumulative investment in China. [2] In addition, Saudi Arabia's International Power and Water Company set up a global innovation center in Shanghai to promote R&D in photovoltaics, energy storage and other fields.

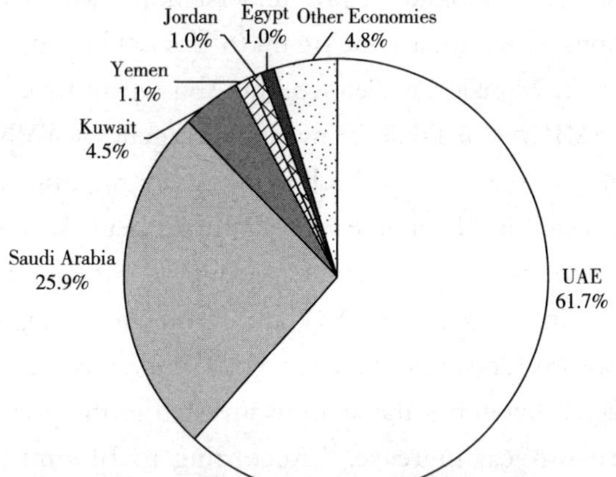

**Figure 3.6    Arab States' Major Economies' Share of Investment in China in 2023**

Source : Ministry of Commerce of the People's Republic of China, *2024 China's Foreign Investment Statistical Bulletin,* September 2024, pp.27-30.

---

[1]  Ministry of Commerce of the People's Republic of China, *2024 China's Foreign Investment Statistical Bulletin,* September 2024, pp.27-30.

[2]  Academy of International Trade and Economic Cooperation, Ministry of Commerce, *Review and Prospect of Economic and Trade Cooperation Between China and Arab Countries in 2024*, November 2024, p. 22.

075

The Development Process of China-Arab States Economic and Trade Relations
Annual Report 2024

### 3.2.4 Gulf Sovereign Wealth Funds' Increasement of the Investment Layout in China

Gulf countries are regarded as the birthplace and hub of global sovereign wealth funds, with a significant market position and eye-catching investment trends. In recent years, substantially increasing investment has become one of the focuses of the layout of the Gulf capitals. As "national" institutional investors, a number of Gulf sovereign wealth funds have set up offices in China, and are active in China's primary and secondary markets, laying out China's industrial chain through equity investment, fund cooperation and other means. Abu Dhabi Investment Authority, Saudi Arabia's Public Investment Fund (PIF), Mubadala Investment Company, Abu Dhabi Investment Authority are the main investors, Kuwait Investment Authority and Qatar Investment Authority are also traditional investors in China's A-share market. For example, Saudi Arabia's PIF has signed a series of memorandums of understanding with six of China's top financial institutions with a total value of up to USD50 billion, and its company Alat has invested USD2 billion in Lenovo; the Abu Dhabi Investment Authority has invested in SMIC; Abu Dhabi's investment agency CYVN Holdings has invested a cumulative total of USD3.3 billion in Nio; the Mubadala Investment Company has invested in NewLand; Kuwait Investment Authority invested in Chinese bionic robotics company Sanhua Group; Qatar Investment Authority participated in the financing of XPENG, and so on. According to Global SWF, Gulf sovereign wealth funds have invested USD7 billion in China between June 2023 and June 2024, five times the amount invested in the previous 12 months and a 400% year-on-year increase. [1] According to Bloomberg, 2024 Gulf sovereign wealth funds continue to invest more overseas, with investments in China having reached USD9.5 billion in the first nine months. [2]

---

[1] Peking University HSBC Think Tank WeChat, "Why Middle East Sovereign Wealth Funds Continue to Expand Their Investments in China," https: //mp.weixin.qq.com/s?__biz= MjM5MDc1OTU2MA==&mid=2650250128&idx=1&sn=1221450d188f193e398c4068 79c1d494&chksm=bf3aa854f3df05e609ca02c3e765590bb97b7c3ab06b09636ad7b73442 7c2d69527befb0fba1&scene=27, February 5, 2025.

[2] Cls.cn, "Continuing to Spend Big! Middle East Sovereign Wealth Funds' Investment Deals Hit USD55 Billion in First 9 Months of the Year," https: //www.cls.cn/detail/1839322, October 28, 2024.

Chapter 3    Special Report on China-Arab States Investment Cooperation

Gulf sovereign wealth funds' investment in China exhibits the following characteristics. First, Gulf sovereign wealth fund investment combines strategic orientation with localization, and investment not only pursues financial returns, but also focuses on technical cooperation and industry chain integration. Second, the Gulf sovereign wealth fund's investment in China has diversified from traditional energy and infrastructure to new energy (photovoltaic, wind power), high-tech (semiconductor, artificial intelligence), biomedicine, consumer Internet and other fields. Third, focusing on high-growth industries, with new energy, digital economy and high-end manufacturing as the core directions. Fourth, policy-driven and long-term layout. The development vision of Saudi Arabia and other countries is deeply aligned with China's Belt and Road Initiative, which promotes the transformation of investment from traditional energy to green economy and innovation economy. Finally, two-way cooperation and third market development. Gulf capital and Chinese enterprises are cooperating to develop the market of "Belt and Road" countries. Arab investment in China is shifting from "resource-driven" to "technological and strategic synergy", and future cooperation will focus more on green transformation and innovative ecological co-construction.

## 3.3    Prospect of China-Arab States Investment Cooperation

Today's world is facing a major change unprecedented in a century, with the fragmentation of the international political economy, slow recovery of the global economy, intensified geopolitical fragmentation, and the rise of anti-globalization and protectionism. At the same time, the international political and economic landscape is characterized by the "rise of the East and the fall of the West" and the rise of the global South. China and the Arab states are both important members of the global South, facing the heavy responsibility of development and rejuvenation domestically, and sharing similar aspirations for improving the global governance system internationally.

### 3.3.1    Key Areas for Future Investment Cooperation

Looking ahead, China and Arab states will continue to increase two-way investment and embrace development opportunities. China-Arab states investment cooperation will focus on a number of emerging areas while

077

maintaining the traditional areas (energy and infrastructure).

1. New Energy and Green Technology

Arab states are accelerating their energy transformation and promoting the development of solar energy, wind energy, hydrogen energy and carbon capture technology (CCUS). Saudi Arabia and other countries rich in oil and gas resources are also promoting renewable energy projects, and Chinese companies have a significant advantage in technology output and project investment.

2. Traditional Energy and Downstream Industries

In order to ensure the stability of the oil consumption market, the Gulf countries have invested in refining and chemical projects to deeply bind the Chinese market. For example, Saudi Aramco has invested more than USD10 billion in petrochemical projects in China's Liaoning and Zhejiang provinces in recent years, requiring supporting procurement of its crude oil to consolidate its market position. In 2023 Saudi Aramco acquired the shares of Rongsheng Petrochemical and Shenghong Petrochemical to further penetrate into the downstream of China's energy industry chain. At the same time, Iraq and other oil-producing countries are still important destinations for China's traditional energy companies to cooperate overseas.

3. Digital Economy and Artificial Intelligence

Gulf Capital is targeting China's leading technologies in artificial intelligence, semiconductors, cloud computing and other fields. The two sides have great potential for cooperation in smart cities, cross-border e-commerce business optimization, financial technology and other areas. Abu Dhabi has set up the Middle East's first AI university and plans to integrate AI technology into healthcare, agriculture and other fields. Chinese technology companies (such as SenseTime) are working with the Arab states to promote technology landing, and may further deepen data sharing and intelligent management cooperation in the future.

4. Construction and Infrastructure Development

Traditional infrastructure (transportation, energy and electricity), digital infrastructure (communications, data centers, smart cities) and real estate are also included. Demand for infrastructure construction in Arab states is strong, and Chinese companies have already cooperated in areas such as port construction and smart logistics, and may expand to 5G networks and digital infrastructure projects in the future.

**078**

Chapter 3    Special Report on China-Arab States Investment Cooperation

5. Healthcare and High-end Manufacturing

The Gulf countries are promoting the upgrading of the healthcare industry, and Chinese biomedical technology has become a key direction of cooperation. China's technological advantages in the field of biomedicine complement the needs of Arab states. In the field of high-end manufacturing, Saudi capital investment in automobile manufacturing (e.g. Geely and Renault joint venture), semiconductor equipment and other industries has increased significantly.

6. Financial Services and Capital Cooperation

Gulf capital has deepened financial linkages through the establishment of RMB funds and cooperation with Chinese financial institutions. For example, Saudi Arabia's PIF signed a USD50 billion memorandum of cooperation with six major financial institutions[1] to promote two-way capital flows; the UAE and Shenzhen City cooperated to set up a private equity fund to explore the RMB investment path. Sovereign funds in the UAE (e.g., Mubadala) plan to ramp up China's new energy and high-end manufacturing industries, while Chinese financial institutions are also expanding their market layout in the Middle East. The two sides promote two-way capital flows through the joint establishment of financial free zones (e.g. Abu Dhabi ADGM, Saudi-China Special Economic Zone).

### 3.3.2    Major Challenges for China-Arab States Investment Cooperation

China-Arab states investment cooperation has broad prospects, while facing a series of geopolitical, cultural and market challenges.

1. Geopolitical Risks and Policy Fluctuations

Against the backdrop of the US-China game, the Gulf capital faces the challenge of balancing strategic pressures. Although Arab states try to reduce dependence on the United States, part of the investment may be hindered by changes in the international political environment (e.g., technology export controls, sanctions risk). The complexity of the internal political environment in Arab states, and the risk of regional conflict in some countries, may affect stability of the projects. For example, the acceptance of the Belt and Road Initiative varies greatly among different countries, and risk assessment needs to

---

[1]    China Construction Bank, Agricultral Bank of China, China Export &Credit Insurance Corp., Bank of China, The Export-import Bank of China, Industrial and Commercial Bank of China.

079

The Development Process of China-Arab States Economic and Trade Relations
Annual Report 2024

be strengthened.

2. Regulatory and Compliance Differences

There are significant differences in taxation and foreign investment access policies between China and the Gulf countries. For example, Saudi companies need to adapt to China's labor laws, data security laws and other complex regulations, while Chinese companies in Arab states are also facing localization ratio requirements (such as the labor force localization policy in Saudi Arabia's "Vision 2030"), Chinese companies need to strengthen cross-cultural training and develop localization strategies.

3. Cultural and Cognitive Barriers

Differences in religious culture and business practices may affect management efficiency. For example, Arab investors emphasize face-to-face communication and long-term trust building, which may conflict with the fast decision-making mode of Chinese companies; some Chinese companies lack in-depth understanding of the Arab market, resulting in inefficient cooperation. Language barriers (e.g. translation of Arabic terminology) also increase communication costs.

4. Technology and Industry Docking Problems

Although technical cooperation is the core, the two sides have differences in standardization and intellectual property protection. For example, the UAE tends to favor independent technology research and development in the field of artificial intelligence, which may compete with the technology output of Chinese companies. In addition, the localization needs of China's new energy industry chain need to be further coordinated with the "technology introduction" goals of the Gulf countries. Chinese enterprises need to explore cooperation models to balance technology export and localization innovation.

5. Market Competition and Capital Return Pressure

European and American enterprises and India started their investment in the Arab states earlier than China, and China's investment in the Gulf countries needs to be at a differentiated advantage in skill, technology and service. At the same time, some of the investments (such as early technology projects) have long return cycles and may face the pressure of capital withdrawal. For example, Chinese startups expanding in the Arab market need to adapt to local consumption habits (e.g., preference for organic food and high-end electronic products), otherwise it will be difficult to get the expected returns.

080

Chapter 3　Special Report on China-Arab States Investment Cooperation

In conclusion, driven by favorable macroeconomic prospects and economic diversification and transformation, Arab states are becoming emerging investment destinations for international capital, including China. The trend of "looking east" of the Gulf countries is gradually strengthening, and investment in China continues to increase. Therefore, although China-Arab states investment cooperation is still in its infancy, it has great potential. The "investment fever" between China and Arab states is not only the result of changes in the global economic pattern, but also the result of economic complementarity and scientific and technological innovation between the two sides. Whether it is FDI or ODI, two-way investment is driving China-Arab states cooperation to a new level. China-Arab states cooperation is not only a flow of capital, but also a transformation of the global economic pattern. In the future, China-Arab states investment cooperation will rely more on technological synergy and long-term strategic mutual trust, continue to integrate at the political, technological and cultural levels, build a high-quality "Belt and Road" through the China-Arab States Cooperation Forum, China-Arab States Expo and other institutionalized platforms, and contribute to the acceleration of the China-Arab states community of destiny.

# Chapter 4　Special Report on China-Arab States Financial Cooperation

Under the overall strategic framework of the China-Arab States Cooperation Forum, the "Belt and Road" Initiative, and the BRICS cooperation mechanism, financial cooperation between China and Arab states has significantly propelled bilateral development in areas such as trade, infrastructure, and industrial capacity collaboration. Driven by practical development needs—including expanding foreign investment, reducing excessive reliance on energy-based economies, and supplementing fiscal funds—Arab states have continuously deepened and solidified their financial cooperation with China. Both sides have accelerated capital market connectivity, with continuous progress in the internationalization of the RMB. Through complementary advantages, pragmatic innovation, and deepening cooperation, fruitful outcomes have been achieved, enhancing the international influence and discourse power of developing countries within the global investment and financing system. Looking ahead, financial cooperation between China and Arab states is poised to embrace broader development prospects in the new era of China-Arab states relations.

## 4.1　Overview of the Financial Situation in Arab States

### 4.1.1　Different Economic Structures Determining Varied Levels of Financial Development in Arab States

In 2024, the international financial landscape remains complex and volatile, with uneven global economic recovery, adjustments in monetary policies by major economies, geopolitical risks, and financial market fluctuations being major challenges for developing countries. In September 2024, the U.S. Federal Reserve

Chapter 4 Special Report on China-Arab States Financial Cooperation

cut interest rates for the first time in four years, a move profoundly impacting cross-border capital flows, global asset pricing, and the formulation and adjustments of monetary policies worldwide. Meanwhile, ongoing geopolitical tensions in the Arab region continue to test financial stability.

According to the International Debt Report published by the World Bank, developing countries' total external debt repayments reached a record high of USD1.4 trillion in 2023. The Fiscal Monitor published by the International Monetary Fund (IMF) predicts that in 2024, total public debt across nations will exceed USD100 trillion, pushing the global debt-to-GDP ratio to 93%, thereby exacerbating risks over debt sustainability. As external debt burdens grow and repayment costs rise, not only do governments face tighter fiscal constraints, limiting both fiscal maneuverability and central bank policy options, but developing countries will also experience increasingly restricted access to international financial markets. Nations with prolonged economic stagnation and weak fiscal foundations that over-rely on external financing may find themselves facing sovereign debt crises when debt levels surpass their economic capacity.

Debt levels and repayment pressure are often assessed based on external debt stock and debt servicing ratios, while financial stability is measured using indicators such as total reserves and current account balances. A comparative analysis of financial resilience across Arab states in response to global economic uncertainties reveals that financial stability is notably stronger in high-income Arab states, particularly the six Gulf Cooperation Council (GCC) members, as well as upper-middle-income economies such as Libya and three other states. These states rely heavily on energy exports, which have enabled them to accumulate substantial capital reserves and achieve fiscal surpluses. In contrast, the financial development of other Arab states remains relatively lagging, with generally lower levels of financial system openness. Consequently, their ability to withstand external shocks remains fragile (see Table 4.1).

**Table 4.1　Debt Levels and Financial Stability Indicators of Arab States in 2023**

| State | Total External Debt Stock (Million USD) | External Debt to GDP (%) | Total Reserves (Million USD) | Total Reserves to GDP (%) | Debt Service to Exports (%) | Current Account Balance (Million USD) |
|---|---|---|---|---|---|---|
| High-Income Economies | | | | | | |
| Bahrain | / | / | 5117.6 | 11.1 | / | 2699.5 |

083

# The Development Process of China-Arab States Economic and Trade Relations Annual Report 2024

**Continued**

| State | Total External Debt Stock (Million USD) | External Debt to GDP (%) | Total Reserves (Million USD) | Total Reserves to GDP (%) | Debt Service to Exports (%) | Current Account Balance (Million USD) |
|---|---|---|---|---|---|---|
| Kuwait | / | / | 52619.4 | 32.1 | / | 51396.2 |
| Oman | / | / | 17298.2 | 15.9 | / | 2637.6 |
| Qatar | / | / | 51538.7 | 24.2 | / | 36452.6 |
| Saudi Arabia | / | / | 457948.6 | 42.9 | / | 34070.5 |
| UAE | / | / | 189490.9 | 36.9 | / | / |
| *Upper-Middle-Income Economies* | | | | | | |
| Libya | / | / | 92427.3 | 205 | / | 5675.3 # |
| Algeria | 7315.3 | 3 | 81216.7 | 32.8 | 0.8 | 5423.6 |
| Iraq | 20331.4 | 8.1 | 112232.9 | 44.7 | 4 | 28374.6 |
| *Lower-Middle-Income Economies* | | | | | | |
| Comoros | 409.3 | 30.3 | 324.6 | 24 | 11.6 | -24.6 |
| Djibouti | 3428.7 | 83.7 | 502.0 | 12.2 | 1.7 | 718.6 |
| Egypt | 168062 | 42.4 | 33070.2 | 8.4 | 30.4 | -12564.3 |
| Jordan | 44629.8 | 87.6 | / | / | 16.1 | -1910.4 |
| Lebanon | 66296.5 | 315.8 * | 32512.9 | 154.9 * | 34.5 | -5642.8 |
| Tunisia | 41278.7 | 85.1 | 9239.7 | 19 | 23.2 | -1110.5 |
| Mauritania | 4603.6 | 48.2 # | 2038.6 # | 21.3 # | 10.2 | -966.5 |
| Morocco | 69267.3 | 48 | 36327.7 | 25.2 | 9.2 | -891.2 |
| *Low-Income Economies* | | | | | | |
| Somalia | 3022.8 | 27.6 | / | / | 16.9 | / |
| Sudan | 22580.6 | 20.7 | / | / | 3* | -4442.8* |
| Syria | 4875.5 | 20.6 * | / | / | / | / |
| Yemen | 7283 | / | 1250.8 * | / | / | / |

Notes: Data for each state is based on the available 2023 figures. Where no 2023 data is available, the most recent figures have been used: * indicates 2022 data, # indicates 2021 data. Data missing for three consecutive years is considered unavailable. Total reserves include monetary gold, Special Drawing Rights (SDRs), reserve positions at the IMF, and foreign exchange assets under the control of monetary authorities.

Source: World Bank's International Debt Statistics (IDS) Database and World Development Indicators (WDI) Database. Data accessed in March 2025.

Chapter 4　Special Report on China-Arab States Financial Cooperation

In Arab states, high-income and upper-middle-income economies tend to have lower levels of external debt while maintaining relatively ample total reserves. In absolute terms, Saudi Arabia (USD457.95 billion), the UAE (USD189.50 billion), and Iraq (USD112.23 billion) hold the largest reserves among Arab states. In terms of total reserves as a percentage of GDP, Libya ranks first at 205.0%, demonstrating strong international payment capacity and financial stability. These states have achieved significant trade surpluses in international trade, leading to current account surpluses and establishing a solid foundation for financial stability. The GCC states have shown resilience in the global financial environment, supported by their relatively stable political landscape and diversified economic strategies. In contrast, Iraq and Libya, due to prolonged geopolitical instability, face greater exposure to external uncertainties that could impact their financial systems and economic development.

Those high-income states generally maintain current account surpluses, whereas lower-middle-income and low-income states often experience current account deficits, reflecting structural differences in their economies. Among lower-middle-income economies, Egypt, Lebanon, and Jordan face significant financial risks. Egypt's external debt is exceptionally high (USD168.06 billion, or 42.4% of GDP), while its total reserves account for only 8.4% of GDP. Its debt service payments amount to 30.4% of exports, and with a current account deficit of USD1.26 billion, the state faces severe debt repayment pressures. Lebanon's external debt stands at 315.8% of GDP, accompanied by a persistent current account deficit. The financial risks are further exacerbated by political corruption and the collapse of its banking system. Jordan is also highly dependent on external debt, which accounts for 87.6% of GDP.

The international payment capacity of the four low-income Arab states is insufficient. Sudan, Yemen, and Somalia have long been affected by armed conflicts, while Syria has suffered severe financial market disruptions due to a decade of civil war and international sanctions. These states have yet to establish a well-functioning modern financial system, and their future economic prospects remain uncertain.

### 4.1.2　The Steady Rise of Multiple International Financial Centers in Arab States

Arab states boast several key international financial hubs, playing an

085

:::: The Development Process of China-Arab States Economic and Trade Relations
:::: Annual Report 2024

increasingly prominent role in the global financial landscape. The Dubai International Financial Centre and Abu Dhabi Global Market benefit from internationalized legal frameworks and regulatory systems that provide strong support for financial market stability and innovation. Meanwhile, the Saudi government, through a series of reform initiatives, has promoted financial market liberalization and innovation, attracting a large number of international financial institutions and continuously enhancing Riyadh's influence as a financial center. By adopting diversified economic strategies, Arab states have gradually transformed their resource advantages into financial competitiveness. Their sovereign wealth funds (SWFs) hold a significant position in global investment, with highly diversified investment portfolios spanning energy, infrastructure, technology, and other sectors, further strengthening their discourse power in global financial markets.

According to the Global Financial Centers Index (GFCI) released in September 2024, which evaluates the competitiveness of financial centers based on business environment, human capital, infrastructure, taxation, and reputation, Arab states hold seven out of the world's top 121 financial centers (see Table 4.2). The UAE and Saudi Arabia continue to lead the financial sector in the Arab region, with Dubai, Abu Dhabi, and Riyadh emerging as the most influential financial hubs in the region. Known for their advanced financial infrastructure and high degree of international openness, these cities rank among the world's top financial centers. All seven major financial centers in Arab states saw an increase in their GFCI scores, with an average improvement of 1.4% compared to September 2023. Dubai remains the most advanced and representative financial hub in the Arab world, ranking 14th globally in the indicator of "Infrastructure" and 12th in "Reputation and Overall Competitiveness". Additionally, in sub-indices, Dubai ranks 11th worldwide in "Professional Services" and 6th in "FinTech", demonstrating outstanding performance.

**Table 4.2    Rankings of Financial Centers in the Arab Region**

| Financial Center | Regional Ranking (36th edition of GFCI) | Global Ranking (36th edition of GFCI) | Score (36th edition of GFCI) | Change in Ranking (YoY) | Change in Score (YoY) |
|---|---|---|---|---|---|
| Dubai | 1 | 15 | 723 | ↑6 | ↑4 |
| Abu Dhabi | 2 | 35 | 704 | 0 | ↑2 |

086

Chapter 4　Special Report on China-Arab States Financial Cooperation

**Continued**

| Financial Center | Regional Ranking (36th edition of GFCI) | Global Ranking (36th edition of GFCI) | Score (36th edition of GFCI) | Change in Ranking (YoY) | Change in Score (YoY) |
|---|---|---|---|---|---|
| Casablanca | 3 | 57 | 682 | ↓3 | 0 |
| Riyadh | 5 | 63 | 676 | ↑8 | ↑17 |
| Doha | 6 | 64 | 675 | ↑14 | ↑19 |
| Kuwait City | 7 | 69 | 670 | ↑13 | ↑24 |
| Bahrain | 4 | 80 | 659 | ↓6 | ↓1 |

Source: The 36th Edition of Global Financial Centers Index (GFCI).

Arab financial centers are poised to become key bridges connecting Eastern and Western financial markets, offering global investors a wide range of investment opportunities and diverse financial services. Moving forward, by accelerating the adoption of financial technology and promoting digital transformation, these financial hubs are expected to further strengthen their competitiveness and influence in the global financial landscape.

## 4.2　Steady Progress in China-Arab States Financial Cooperation

China and Arab states continue to deepen financial connectivity and cooperation through the China-Arab States Cooperation Forum, the "Belt and Road" Initiative, and the BRICS cooperation mechanism. The financial cooperation platforms and mechanisms have been continuously improved, leading to significant progress in central bank collaboration, the internationalization of the RMB, and the participation of Arab sovereign wealth funds in financing projects in China and development initiatives in Arab states. The forms of cooperation have become increasingly diverse, and the scope has steadily expanded.

### 4.2.1　Mechanism and Platform Development

Financial connectivity is a key component of the "Belt and Road" Initiative, with the Asian Infrastructure Investment Bank (hereinafter referred to as "AIIB") serving as a vital financial pillar, providing crucial funding support for the

The Development Process of China-Arab States Economic and Trade Relations
Annual Report 2024

economic development of participating countries and regions. AIIB has actively supported large-scale infrastructure projects in Arab states. In January 2017, AIIB signed a loan agreement with the Special Economic Zone at Duqm (SEZAD) in Oman, providing a USD265 million loan for the construction of the commercial terminal at Duqm Port—the first loan issued by AIIB to a state on the Arabian Peninsula. In April 2023, AIIB established its first overseas office in Abu Dhabi, signing a Host Member Agreement with the UAE. The establishment of this office enhances AIIB's proximity to clients and frontline operations, reinforcing its influence. In October 2024, AIIB signed a Memorandum of Understanding with the Saudi Fund for Development (SFD), aiming to deepen cooperation and promote sustainable, resilient, and inclusive development across Asia and beyond. This milestone marks a crucial step in expanding collaboration and driving tangible progress in developing countries.

The BRICS cooperation mechanism has provided China and Arab states with a more diversified platform for collaboration. Starting from January 1, 2024, Saudi Arabia, Egypt, the UAE, Iran, and Ethiopia have officially become BRICS members. By joining the BRICS cooperation mechanism, they can engage in diverse financial cooperation under the New Development Bank (NDB) framework, contributing to the establishment of a more multipolar international financial system. Through policy dialogue and consultations, BRICS members can achieve consensus on financial cooperation and jointly address financial risks and challenges. On January 4, Abdullah bin Touq Al Marri, UAE's Minister of Economy expressed the UAE's intention to increase its capital contribution to the NDB, aiming to enhance its support for emerging markets and developing countries. On August 31, Algeria was officially approved as a member of the NDB. On November 11, the Independent Evaluation Office of the NDB and the Ministry of Finance of the UAE co-hosted a special seminar in Dubai, focusing on strengthening NDB's cooperation with Arab states and sharing global experiences in sustainable development projects. The BRICS framework has established a new currency swap mechanism known as the BRICS Contingent Reserve Arrangement (CRA). This mechanism enables member states facing difficulties in balance of payments or debt pressures to receive liquidity support from other BRICS members, thereby stabilizing financial conditions and alleviating international balance of payments crises.

088

Chapter 4    Special Report on China-Arab States Financial Cooperation

On May 30, 2024, the 10th Ministerial Conference of the China-Arab States Cooperation Forum was held in Beijing, further strengthening mutual trust between China and Arab states in the financial sector and laying a solid foundation for future financial cooperation. The conference adopted the "CASCF Execution Plan for 2024-2026" (hereinafter referred to as the "Execution Plan 2024-2026"). China welcomes more Arab states to participate in the China-Arab states interbank association, and will implement at a faster pace the cooperation projects that are financed by the special loans in support of industrialization in the Middle East as well as by the credit line for China-Arab states financial cooperation. By improving financial cooperation mechanisms, deepening practical collaboration in the financial sector, expanding new areas of financial cooperation, promoting shared economic development, and enhancing China-Arab states relations, both sides have reached broad consensus, providing vital momentum and support for future cooperation. The positive impact of financial cooperation will also inject new vitality into the comprehensive development of China-Arab states relations.

## 4.2.2    Promoting the Use of the RMB

As economic and trade exchanges between China and Arab states continue to deepen, the central banks of China and of the Arab states have further strengthened bilateral local currency swap agreements and RMB clearing cooperation. This collaboration facilitates direct local currency exchange and settlement, effectively reducing financing costs of investment and trade, properly managing short-term liquidity fluctuations, thus providing strong support for the regionalization of the RMB.

Bilateral Local Currency Swaps. As of the end of August 2024, the People's Bank of China has signed bilateral local currency swap agreements with the central banks or monetary authorities of 42 countries and regions, expanding the use of local currencies and enhancing trade and investment facilitation. Among these, participating Arab states include the UAE, Qatar, Morocco, Egypt, and Saudi Arabia (see Table 4.3). These local currency swap arrangements aim to facilitate trade and investment between China and Arab states and provide liquidity support to cooperating states.

089

The Development Process of China-Arab States Economic and Trade Relations
Annual Report 2024

**Table 4.3    Bilateral Local Currency Swap Agreements Signed Between the People's Bank of China and Arab States Since the Launch of the "Belt and Road" Initiative**

| Country | Swap Amount | Signing Date | Remarks |
| --- | --- | --- | --- |
| UAE | 35 billion RMB / 20 billion AED | December 14, 2015 | Renewal |
| | 35 billion RMB / 18 billion AED | November 28, 2023 | Renewal |
| Qatar | 35 billion RMB / 20.8 billion QAR | November 3, 2014 | |
| | 35 billion RMB / 20.8 billion QAR | November 2, 2017 | Renewal |
| | 35 billion RMB / 20.8 billion QAR | January 6, 2021 | Renewal |
| Morocco | 10 billion RMB / 15 billion MAD | May 11, 2016 | |
| Egypt | 18 billion RMB / 47 billion EGP | December 6, 2016 | |
| | 18 billion RMB / 41 billion EGP | February 10, 2020 | Renewal |
| | 18 billion RMB / 80.7 billion EGP | February 20, 2023 | Renewal |
| Saudi Arabia | 50 billion RMB / 26 billion SAR | November 20, 2023 | |

Source: RMB Internationalization Report, People's Bank of China.

Bilateral Local Currency Settlement. The UAE and Saudi Arabia are key "Belt and Road" partners with China featuring close economic and trade ties. Given that their currencies meet the listing conditions for interbank foreign exchange markets, the People's Bank of China authorized the launch of direct trading between the RMB and the UAE dirham, as well as the Saudi riyal, in the interbank foreign exchange market on September 26, 2016. According to publicly available data, during the initial trading phase in 2018, the transaction volumes for these two currencies reached 8.6 billion RMB and 7.4 billion RMB, respectively. Since 2019, the trading volume has declined significantly but has remained relatively stable. Over the past five years, the average annual transaction volumes have reached 760 million RMB for the UAE dirham and 2.74 billion RMB for the Saudi riyal.

RMB Clearing and Payment. The RMB clearing and payment network in Arab states has been continuously optimized. On November 4, 2014, the People's Bank of China authorized the Doha branch of the Industrial and Commercial Bank of China (ICBC) as the RMB clearing bank in Doha. Subsequently, on December 9, 2016, the Agricultural Bank of China (ABC) Dubai Branch was designated as the RMB clearing bank in the UAE. As of January 2025, the RMB Cross-Border

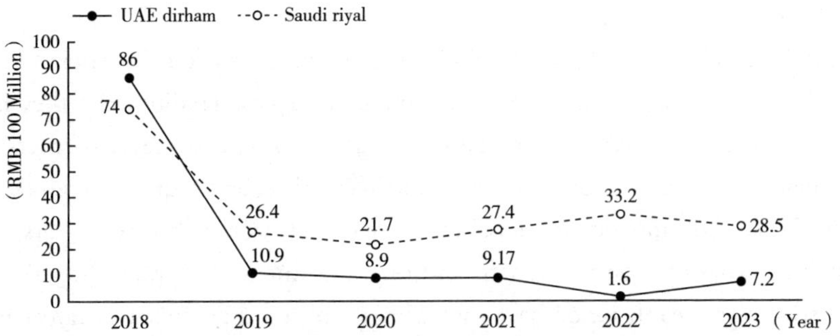

Chapter 4　Special Report on China-Arab States Financial Cooperation

UAE dirham　⸱⸱o⸱⸱ Saudi riyal

(RMB 100 Million)

86
74
26.4　21.7　27.4　33.2
10.9　8.9　9.17　28.5
1.6　7.2

2018　2019　2020　2021　2022　2023 (Year)

**Figure 4.1　RMB Trading Volume Against Saudi riyal and UAE dirham in the Interbank Market Foreign Exchange Spot**

Source: RMB Internationalization Report, People's Bank of China.

Interbank Payment System (CIPS) has 169 direct participants worldwide. Among Arab states, 12 institutions have become direct participants in CIPS, including Bank of China (Djibouti) Branch, Bank of China (Dubai) Branch, Bank of China Ltd. (Abu Dhabi Branch), Bank of China Qatar Financial Centre Branch, Bank of China Riyadh Branch, Industrial and Commercial Bank of China Doha Branch, Industrial and Commercial Bank of China Riyadh Branch, Industrial and Commercial Bank of China Dubai (DIFC) Branch, Industrial and Commercial Bank of China Kuwait Branch, Industrial and Commercial Bank of China Abu Dhabi Branch, Agricultural Bank of China Dubai Branch Dubai Branch, and Agricultural Bank of China Dubai Branch DIFC Branch.

### 4.2.3　Investment of Arab Sovereign Wealth Funds in China

As a significant emerging force in the global financial market, sovereign wealth funds (SWFs) have played an increasingly crucial role in global capital flows and investment activities in recent years. According to the research report released by the Global SWF for the first three quarters of 2024, sovereign wealth funds from the Middle East—particularly those from the UAE and Saudi Arabia—have demonstrated outstanding performance. During the reporting period, five major sovereign wealth funds—Abu Dhabi Investment Authority (ADIA), Mubadala Investment Company, Abu Dhabi Developmental Holding Company (ADQ) from the UAE, the Public Investment Fund (PIF) of Saudi Arabia, and the Qatar Investment Authority (QIA)—collectively completed 126 transactions with a total investment of USD55 billion, accounting for 40% of global sovereign

091

wealth fund transactions.

Arab sovereign wealth funds have long been renowned for their unique geopolitical advantages and global investment strategies. Traditionally, they have focused primarily on Western markets, maintaining stable strategic partnerships with major economies in both the East and West, thereby ensuring a high degree of flexibility and influence in global investments. However, in recent years, with China's growing economic strength and ongoing financial market liberalization, Arab sovereign wealth funds have increasingly shifted their focus toward China, demonstrating a considerable strategic interest in the Chinese financial market and a positive outlook on China's long-term economic growth prospects. In the Chinese market, Arab sovereign wealth funds have shown long-term confidence and strategic commitment through diversified investments in both primary and secondary markets. Among them, ADIA and Mubadala Investment Company are the rather active Arab sovereign wealth funds in China's primary market, with a strong preference for high-growth sectors such as finance and the internet, semiconductors, and biopharmaceuticals. As of the end of June 2024, PIF of Saudi Arabia had invested a total of USD22 billion in China, primarily targeting technology, automotive, and healthcare sectors. For instance, in May 2024, Lenovo Group received a USD2 billion strategic investment from a subsidiary of PIF, further highlighting Arab capital's strong interest in Chinese technology firms. Additionally, Mubadala Investment Company has completed over 100 investment projects in China, with a total investment exceeding USD15 billion. Meanwhile, CYVN Holdings, a subsidiary of ADIA, has invested over USD3 billion in NIO Inc., reflecting a significant focus on China's new energy vehicle (NEV) industry. In the secondary market, Arab sovereign wealth funds have also demonstrated a notable presence. As of the third quarter of 2024, ADIA and KIA were among the top ten shareholders of 24 and 17 A-share listed companies, respectively, with holdings valued at RMB8.9 billion and RMB4.38 billion. Their investments span a wide range of high-tech industries, including new energy, pharmaceuticals, chemicals, and semiconductors, underscoring their recognition of China's new and emerging industries.

The objectives of Arab sovereign wealth funds in participating in China's financial markets have become increasingly clear, with their engagement exhibiting a more proactive stance. This trend not only serves as a crucial

Chapter 4    Special Report on China-Arab States Financial Cooperation

channel for Arab governments to accelerate industrial deployment and advance economic diversification strategies but also represents a key initiative in deepening economic cooperation with China. Against this backdrop, Ewpartners, as the first investment institution dedicated to cross-border investments between Saudi Arabia and China, has emerged as one of the few China-based funds supported by multiple sovereign wealth funds, including PIF from Saudi Arabia and the Oman Investment Authority (OIA). Ewpartners has successfully supported companies such as J&T Express Middle East and Liansheng Zhida in establishing a presence in Saudi Arabia, not only facilitating the expansion of Chinese enterprises in the Arab region, but have also provided significant support for the region's economic development and industrial upgrading. In October 2024, the Oman Investment Authority announced an investment of USD150 million in Ewpartners' second U.S. dollar-denominated fund, aiming to introduce industry-leading products, technologies, and services from mature markets such as China into the region to support Oman's local economic development. At the same time, the Ministry of Transport and Logistics Services of Saudi Arabia announced a collaboration between King Salman International Airport and Ewpartners to develop a KSA-Sino Logistics Special Economic Zone. This national-level economic zone, covering a planned area of 4 square kilometers, aims to establish a comprehensive service system encompassing logistics and supply chain solutions, lower market entry barriers for Chinese enterprises entering the Saudi market, and further promote bilateral economic cooperation.

Arab sovereign wealth funds are actively investing in emerging industries such as artificial intelligence, new energy, advanced manufacturing, and biopharmaceuticals to drive the transformation and upgrading of local industries. This strategy not only injects new momentum into the economic diversification of Arab states but also presents significant growth opportunities for Chinese enterprises expanding abroad. Through deep collaboration with Chinese enterprises, Arab states are gradually transitioning from traditional energy-dependent economies to innovation-driven economies. At the same time, Chinese enterprises are leveraging this opportunity to further expand their presence in the Arab market, fostering a mutually beneficial and win-win partnership.

093

### 4.2.4 China's Financing for Development Projects in Arab States

Since the launch of the "Belt and Road" Initiative, Chinese financial institutions, represented by the China Development Bank and the Export-Import Bank of China, have actively provided loans and financing for infrastructure and industrial cooperation projects in Arab states. This aligns with the urgent economic and social development needs of these states. China has become the world's largest provider of bilateral development finance, playing a crucial role in supporting global development financing for developing countries. Beyond the GCC member states, many Arab states face a relative shortage of funds and financial services necessary for economic and social development. China's financing for development projects has significantly contributed to infrastructure construction and industrial upgrading in these states.

From a geographical distribution perspective, China's financing for development projects in Arab states is primarily concentrated in Egypt (see Table 4.4). Among these projects, the Central Business District (CBD) project in Egypt's new administrative capital is the largest single financing project undertaken by China in an Arab state since 2013. The first and second phases of the project received investments of USD3 billion and USD3.5 billion, respectively. In 2019, a syndicate of eight banks—including the Export-Import Bank of China, Industrial and Commercial Bank of China, Bank of China, China Minsheng Bank, China CITIC Bank, China Construction Bank, National Bank of Kuwait, and HSBC—provided financing for the project. Once completed, the project is expected to create 1.75 million long-term jobs, drive the development of the Suez Canal Economic Belt and the Red Sea Economic Belt, and contribute to Egypt's long-term economic growth.

**Table 4.4 Financing for Development Projects by China Development Bank and Export-Import Bank of China in Arab States since the Launch of the "Belt and Road" Initiative**

| State | Financing Amount (Million USD) | Number of Projects |
| --- | --- | --- |
| Djibouti | 1178 | 4 |
| Egypt | 7340 | 11 |
| Comoros | 82 | 1 |

Chapter 4　Special Report on China-Arab States Financial Cooperation

**Continued**

| State | Financing Amount (Million USD) | Number of Projects |
|---|---|---|
| Morocco | 300 | 1 |
| Mauritania | 226 | 2 |
| Oman | 3200 | 1 |
| Total | 12326 | 20 |

Source: China's Overseas Development Finance (CODF) database. The database is updated through 2023.

Public administration (principal-agent) projects backed by sovereign credit guarantees have begun to play an increasingly important role in international financing for development. Among such projects, financing from China to Arab states accounts for nearly half of the total amount (see Figure 4.2). The largest financing for development project in the public administration sector was a five-year loan of USD3.55 billion obtained by the Omani government from multiple Chinese banks in August 2017. This fiscal deficit financing plan aims to provide substantial support for addressing Oman's fiscal deficit while also promoting the state's economic development and infrastructure construction.

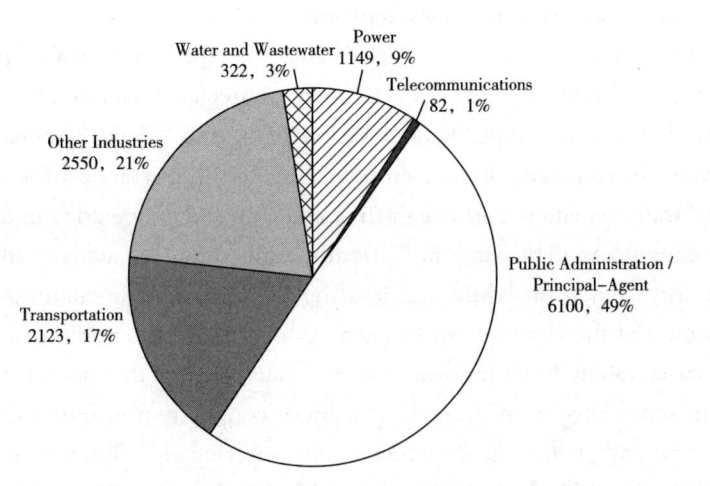

**Figure 4.2　Industry Distribution of Financing for Development Projects Provided by China Development Bank and China Export-Import Bank to Arab states Since the Launch of the "Belt and Road" Initiative (Unit: Million USD)**

## 4.3　New Trends in China-Arab States Financial Cooperation

In recent years, China-Arab states financial cooperation has exhibited new trends characterized by diversification, innovation, and deeper integration. Building upon traditional financial sectors, both parties have gradually expanded their collaboration into emerging fields such as new energy and digital currency. Notably, China and Arab states have achieved breakthroughs in digital currency cooperation, enhancing cross-border payment efficiency and advancing the internationalization of the RMB through initiatives such as the mBridge project. Meanwhile, China's capital market is continuously improving its mechanisms for two-way openness, strengthening connections between the Shenzhen Stock Exchange and the Hong Kong Exchanges and Clearing Limited, and the Arab capital markets. This deepening integration facilitates capital flows and optimizes resource allocation. As China-Arab states financial cooperation moves toward greater efficiency, innovation, and sustainability, it is injecting fresh momentum into the global financial system.

China-Arab States New Energy Cooperation: Building a Bridge for Economic Diversification and Sustainable Development

Since Saudi Arabia launched its "Vision 2030" in April 2016, Arab states have gradually established long-term development strategies centered on economic diversification. Subsequently, "Kuwait Vision 2035" and "Qatar National Vision 2030" were introduced, further emphasizing the importance of economic structural transformation, particularly in opening up and cooperating in the fields of new energy and digitalization. Currently, Arab states are actively advancing their energy transition while accelerating development in manufacturing, technology, and the Internet+sector, aiming to shift from a traditional energy-dependent economy to an innovation-driven one. Against this backdrop, China and Arab states have been deepening financial cooperation in innovative fields such as new energy and the digital economy, offering significant potential for growth. China's technological expertise and industrial strength in green energy have provided crucial support for global energy transitions. With a world-leading position in photovoltaic power generation, wind energy, and energy storage technologies, China not only contributes to global climate change mitigation but

Chapter 4    Special Report on China-Arab States Financial Cooperation

also lays a solid foundation for China-Arab states cooperation. As a key region in the "Belt and Road" Initiative, the Arab region holds immense potential for collaboration with China in the new energy sector. Both sides have already launched multiple financial cooperation projects centered on new energy infrastructure. In September 2024, the Dubai Financial Services Authority and the Hong Kong Monetary Authority signed an agreement to strengthen sustainable finance development and co-hosted a climate finance conference, further advancing green finance cooperation. In November 2024, Masdar, a renewable energy giant from the UAE signed a Memorandum of Understanding with China's Silk Road Fund (SRF) to jointly invest in clean energy projects along "Belt and Road" countries, particularly in developing nations and the Global South. The total planned investment is estimated at 20 billion RMB (approximately USD2.8 billion). This partnership marks a new milestone in China-UAE cooperation in green energy, as both sides work together to drive the global energy transition and sustainable development. Additionally, in June 2024, Saudi Arabia's ACWA Power announced that the Silk Road Fund would acquire a 49% stake in its renewable energy subsidiary. The collaboration not only strengthens China-Saudi Arabia ties in renewable energy but also injects new momentum into green energy projects under the "Belt and Road" Initiative.

Strong Growth of Chinese Financial Institutions in Arab Financial Centers

Nasdaq Dubai, one of Dubai's key financial trading platforms, has become an important bridge connecting China with international capital markets. To date, issuers from Hong Kong and the mainland of China have listed approximately 22 securities on Nasdaq Dubai, with a total value of USD12.3 billion. On November 13, 2024, the Ministry of Finance of China successfully listed two bonds on Nasdaq Dubai, totaling USD2 billion. This move not only serves as another significant example of China's high-level financial market openness but also reflects the strong confidence of the international capital markets in China's economic development. By issuing U.S. dollar sovereign bonds, China has further diversified its financing channels and optimized its debt structure. Meanwhile, Chinese financial institutions are rapidly expanding in the Arab region. According to data from the Dubai Financial Services Authority, as of the end of 2024, Chinese banks managed total assets of USD65.3 billion in the Dubai International Financial Centre (DIFC). A total of 16 Chinese financial firms have established a presence in DIFC, including six representative offices,

097

five commercial banks, two wealth management firms, one brokerage firm, one advisory firm, and one insurance company. These institutions play a crucial role in facilitating financial and industrial cooperation between China and global markets. On June 11, 2024, China International Capital Corporation (CICC), the only Chinese investment bank in the Gulf region with local expertise, successfully assisted the Saudi Arabian government and Saudi Aramco in completing a secondary offering of its shares. This further solidified CICC's leading position in the field of cross-border financial services.

Strengthened Connections Between Shenzhen Stock Exchange + Hong Kong Stock Exchange and Gulf Region Capital Markets

An efficient two-way opening mechanism has been established between major Chinese and international capital markets, significantly promoting the flow of capital and optimizing resource allocation. On August 14, 2024, the Shenzhen Stock Exchange, in collaboration with the Dubai Financial Market, held the "China-UAE (Dubai) Capital Markets Cooperation Seminar" in Dubai and signed a memorandum of understanding. This agreement establishes a regular high-level meeting mechanism to further deepen exchanges and cooperation between the two parties across various levels. The initiative not only strengthens the connectivity of China-UAE capital markets but also lays a solid foundation for future cooperation in areas such as financial product innovation and market rule alignment. As an international financial hub, China's Hong Kong plays a crucial role in facilitating capital flows between the Arab region and the mainland of China. Thanks to the continued efforts of the Hong Kong Special Administrative Region government in promoting economic, trade, and financial cooperation, Hong Kong's economic ties with the Arab region have deepened, with notable achievements in cooperation. In September 2023, the Hong Kong Stock Exchange announced the inclusion of the Saudi Stock Exchange in its list of recognized securities exchanges, allowing companies primarily listed on the Saudi market to apply for secondary listings in Hong Kong. In July 2024, the Hong Kong Stock Exchange further expanded its cooperation by adding the Abu Dhabi Securities Exchange and Dubai Financial Market to its list of recognized exchanges, broadening the channels for cooperation between the two parties' capital markets. On October 30, 2024, the Albilad CSOP MSCI Hong Kong China Equity ETF, which invests in the Hong Kong market, was listed on the Saudi Stock Exchange. The fund raised a total of 10 billion HKD in its

Chapter 4　Special Report on China-Arab States Financial Cooperation

initial offering, making it the first ETF investing in the Chinese market to be listed in Saudi Arabia, marking a milestone and further enhancing investment flows between Hong Kong and the Arab region. Additionally, CICC Hong Kong Securities has officially obtained operational qualifications from the Dubai Financial Services Authority, further consolidating the presence of Chinese financial institutions in the Middle East market. Hong Kong is actively working to collaborate with large sovereign wealth funds to jointly establish funds, while continuously expanding and deepening its financial cooperation networks with the Arab region. These initiatives not only enhance Hong Kong's position as an international financial hub but also inject new momentum into the flow of capital and financial cooperation between China and the Arab region.

Innovation and Transformation in the Global Financial System Driven by Cooperation in the Digital Currency Sector

The "Execution Plan 2024-2026" explicitly states that China is willing to provide technological support and collaboration based on the needs of Arab states in developing local central bank digital currency (CBDC) systems and regional financial infrastructure. The initiative aims to promote innovation and application in the digital currency sector, further deepening China-Arab states financial cooperation. Significant progress has been made in China-Arab states collaboration through the mBridge project. Since participating in the mBridge pilot program in 2022, ICBC Abu Dhabi Branch has expanded real-world applications of the RMB in international transactions, providing more efficient financial services for Chinese enterprises operating abroad. On January 29, 2024, the Central Bank of the UAE successfully completed its first cross-border digital dirham payment via mBridge, processing a transaction worth 50 million AED (approximately 98 million RMB) with Bank of China. Bank of China's UAE branch also completed the first cross-border digital RMB remittance within the UAE using the platform. By leveraging blockchain technology, mBridge has significantly improved the efficiency of cross-border payments, reduced transaction costs, and enhanced financial transparency and regulatory oversight. As a result, it has become a model for multilateral central bank cross-border payment cooperation. Additionally, the relatively independent international financial network provides crucial support for RMB internationalization. On June 7, 2024, the Bank for International Settlements (BIS) in Switzerland announced that the Saudi Central Bank had fully joined the mBridge project. Saudi Arabia's

**099**

participation not only expands the project's global reach, marking a major step toward non-USD settlement in global oil trade, but also offers crucial technical feasibility for RMB-denominated oil transactions.

## 4.4 Prospects for China-Arab States Financial Cooperation

China-Arab states financial cooperation exhibits tremendous potential and promising prospects. Looking forward, the deepening collaboration between both parties in areas such as green energy transition, capital market connectivity, the internationalization of the RMB, and global debt governance will inject new momentum into global financial governance and sustainable economic development.

The Gulf region's growing urgency for green energy transition aligns closely with China's "30/60 Dual Carbon Goals" (achieving peak carbon emissions by 2030 and carbon neutrality by 2060). As the world's second-largest economy, China plays a pivotal role in the global energy sector. The Chinese government's strong emphasis on renewable energy—through legislative measures, policy directives, and industrial support—has created a favorable investment environment for international energy enterprises. Fluctuations in global oil prices and geopolitical uncertainties have prompted Arab states in the Gulf, which heavily rely on energy exports, to adjust their strategies and strengthen cooperation with the Chinese market to effectively manage risks. Amid the ongoing transformation of the global energy landscape, Saudi Aramco is actively restructuring its strategic framework, placing significant importance on the Chinese market. Deepening collaboration with China not only enables Saudi Aramco to reduce its reliance on other markets but also facilitates knowledge exchange and technological cooperation, fostering a more stable and sustainable transition toward renewable energy. As a global leader in new energy technology and equipment manufacturing, China is well-positioned to leverage its technological and industrial strengths to engage in deeper cooperation with Arab states in the field of renewable energy, jointly advancing the development and deployment of green energy. Furthermore, China and Arab states can utilize financial instruments such as green bonds to support the transition to a low-carbon economy. This approach not only aligns with their respective strategic

Chapter 4　Special Report on China-Arab States Financial Cooperation

interests but also serves as a significant model for global energy transformation and sustainable development.

Leading financial institutions from both China and Arab states are playing an increasingly pivotal role in advancing capital market connectivity. The "Execution Plan 2024-2026" outlines the commitment to "actively supporting enhanced exchanges and cooperation between sovereign wealth funds, private equity investment funds, commercial banks, and relevant regulatory authorities from both sides, encouraging the establishment of branches to provide high-quality financial services, and promoting deeper capital market integration". On the one hand, the influence of Arab capital—particularly through sovereign wealth funds—within China's financial markets is becoming more pronounced. Innovative enterprises backed by Arab capital can leverage extensive networks and resource advantages, creating significant synergies that not only drive economic transformation and technological development in Arab states but also present valuable opportunities for mutual benefit. On the other hand, Chinese financial institutions are steadily expanding their presence in Arab financial hubs, marking key steps in the internationalization of China's financial sector while injecting fresh momentum into cross-border investment and financial innovation. A notable example is the establishment of the Investcorp Golden Horizon on April 24, 2024 by China Investment Corporation (CIC) and Bahrain-based Investcorp with an initial scale of USD1 billion. The fund aims to invest in high-growth enterprises across China and the GCC member states. As the seventh bilateral innovation fund launched by CIC, this initiative further strengthens financial and industrial ties between China and the Gulf region.

China-Arab states energy cooperation is playing a significant role in advancing the internationalization of the RMB. Leveraging the central banks' digital currency initiatives and the development of the BRICS New Development Bank (NDB) mechanism, RMB-based settlement is expected to be materialized in future energy cooperation. The global trend toward digitalizing monetary systems may lead to substantial adjustments in national payment structures. Since 2023, China and the UAE have been strengthening cooperation in financial technology innovation and central bank digital currencies. Under the framework of the multilateral mBridge project, efforts have been made to enhance cross-border payment connectivity and reduce dependence on the existing U.S. dollar-based payment system. Meanwhile, the role of the RMB as a settlement currency

101

in commodity trading continues to expand. By 2024, the RMB had become the world's fourth-largest payment currency, demonstrating the early stages of a network effect for international use. The solid foundation of China-Arab states energy cooperation has created favorable conditions for the RMB's broader adoption in international settlement and transactions. As the restructuring of commodity settlement and pricing mechanisms progresses, the RMB's role as an international currency is expected to strengthen further. The New Development Bank, established in 2015 by BRICS states, aims to reduce reliance on the U.S. dollar and promote a more multipolar global financial system. Following the inclusion of Arab states in the BRICS, a unified BRICS settlement system—centered around energy trade—is likely to take shape gradually. Notably, Saudi Arabia, the UAE, and other Arab states have shown openness to settling oil transactions in RMB, signaling an acceleration of the "de-dollarization" trend. However, given geopolitical factors, oil-exporting states such as Saudi Arabia still face challenges from U.S. dollar hegemony in adopting RMB settlement for cross-border crude oil transactions. This transition will be a gradual and long-term process, requiring progressive reforms and increased market openness to be fully realized.

The cooperation between China and Arab states on international debt issues holds significant strategic importance and practical value. With the deepening of the "Belt and Road" initiative, the economic and financial cooperation between China and Arab states has been continuously strengthened, and their collaboration on debt issues has also shown new opportunities. Firstly, China and Arab states are increasingly cooperating in infrastructure construction, energy development, and other fields, which often require substantial financial support and are prone to generating debt issues. China has accumulated rich experience in debt management, particularly under the "debt sustainability" framework, and can provide effective debt solutions for Arab states. Through collaboration, both parties can jointly explore more flexible and sustainable financing models, such as public-private partnerships (PPP) or blended finance, to alleviate debt pressure. Secondly, China and Arab states have significant influence in international multilateral financial institutions. Both parties can strengthen coordination on platforms such as the World Bank and the International Monetary Fund (IMF), pushing for reforms in the international debt governance system, especially to secure more voice and resource support for developing countries. The

Chapter 4　Special Report on China-Arab States Financial Cooperation

"consultation, co-construction, and sharing" concept advocated by China aligns closely with the development needs of Arab states, and both parties can jointly promote the establishment of fairer and more reasonable international debt rules. Moreover, cooperation between China and Arab states in the fields of green finance and sustainable development also provides new solutions to debt issues. With the global focus on climate change and sustainable development, innovative financial instruments such as green bonds and climate finance are gradually becoming important directions in international debt management. China holds a global leading position in green finance and can provide technical support and experience sharing to Arab states, helping them achieve economic transformation and debt sustainability. China and Arab states have maintained long-standing friendly relations and supported each other on major international issues. They have reached a consensus on debt issues, thus avoiding political or economic friction arising from debt-related matters. By strengthening policy coordination, innovating financing models, and promoting multilateral cooperation, China can assist Arab states facing debt challenges and provide new cooperative examples for global debt governance.

China-Arab states financial cooperation demonstrates immense development potential and broad prospects. The continued deepening of cooperation between both parties not only reflects their high level of trust and shared willingness to strengthen economic trade and investment cooperation, but also advances practical collaboration in finance and other fields to new heights. This cooperation model injects lasting and strong momentum into bilateral relations, while also helping to enhance the discourse power of developing countries in global financial governance and promoting the evolution of the international financial system toward a more balanced and diversified direction.

103

# Chapter 5    Special Report on China-Arab States Agricultural Cooperation

Agriculture is currently one of the most dynamic fields of China-Arab states cooperation. China-Arab states agricultural cooperation has a long history. In recent years, with the continuous deepening of China-Arab states relations, remarkable achievements have been made in agricultural cooperation.

## 5.1    China-Arab States Agricultural Cooperation since the Proposal of the Belt and Road Initiative (BRI)

### 5.1.1    Strengthening Top-level Design and Prioritizing Agriculture

Agricultural cooperation has been a key point of China-Arab states cooperation. As the important institutional platforms for China-Arab states cooperation, the China-Arab States Cooperation Forum (CASCF) and the China-Arab States Expo have both listed agricultural cooperation as a major agenda. The proposal and implementation of the BRI have created historic opportunities for China-Arab states agricultural cooperation. Through policy docking and practical cooperation, the cooperation level between the two sides has been continuously improved. Moreover, the first China-Arab States Summit, the 10th Ministerial Conference of CASCF, and the Forum on China-Africa Cooperation (FOCAC) all underscore the importance of enhancing agricultural cooperation between China and the Arab states and African countries. [1]Such top-level designs have mapped out the direction and charted the blueprint for China-Arab

---

[1]    "Cooperation initiative on food security" and "cooperation initiative on green innovation" were proposed by Xi Jinping at the first China-Arab States Summit. Cooperation initiative on food security: China is ready to help the Arab side enhance its food security    ( Note to the next page )

Chapter 5    Special Report on China-Arab States Agricultural Cooperation

states agricultural cooperation.[①]

Table 5.1 summarizes the agricultural-related content at the previous Ministerial Conferences of the CASCF. It can be seen from the table that China-Arab states agricultural cooperation has increasingly emphasized institutionalized mechanisms in the agricultural sector, the expansion of agricultural product trade, and the cooperation in modern agriculture and agricultural science and technology. The implementation plans have become more concrete and targeted.

**Table 5.1    Contents Related to Agricultural Cooperation at Previous Ministerial Conferences of the CASCF**

| Ministerial conferences | Content |
| --- | --- |
| First | *Action plan*<br>Carry out cooperation and exchange experiences in agriculture and environmental protection, especially in new technologies, genetic engineering, agricultural machinery, modern irrigation systems, and combating desertification. |

(Continued from the previous page) and comprehensive agricultural production capacity. China will, together with the Arab side, build five joint laboratories of modern agriculture and carry out 50 demonstration projects in agricultural technology cooperation, and send 500 experts in agricultural technology to the Arab side to help increase grain yield, improve its ability to harvest and store grain and reduce losses, and improve agricultural productivity. China will establish a "green channel" for the Arab side's quality agri-food products to be exported to China. Cooperation initiative on green innovation: China is ready to work with the Arab side to set up an international research center on drought, desertification and land degradation, and carry out five South-South cooperation projects in climate change. "A more dynamic framework for innovation" was proposed at the 10th ministerial conference of the CASCF. A more dynamic framework for innovation: China will build with the Arab side ten joint laboratories in such areas as life and health, AI, green and low-carbon development, modern agriculture, and space and information technology. We will enhance cooperation on AI to make it empower the real economy and to promote a broad-based global governance system on AI. We also stand ready to build with the Arab side a joint space debris observation center and a Beidou application, cooperation and development center, and step up cooperation in manned space mission and passenger aircraft. "The Partnership Action for Agriculture and Livelihoods" was proposed at the opening ceremony of 2024 FOCAC summit. The Partnership Action for Agriculture and Livelihoods: China will provide Africa with RMB1 billion yuan in emergency food assistance, build 100000 mu (about 6670 hectares) of standardized agriculture demonstration areas in Africa, send 500 agricultural experts, and establish a China-Africa agricultural science and technology innovation alliance. We will implement 500 programs in Africa to promote community welfare. We will also encourage two-way investment for new business operations by Chinese and African companies, enable Africa to retain added value, and create at least one million jobs for Africa.

105

The Development Process of China-Arab States Economic and Trade Relations
Annual Report 2024

**Continued**

| Ministerial conferences | Content |
|---|---|
| Second | *Implementation Plan 2006-2008*<br>Encourage the quality inspection, customs, taxation, industry, agriculture and other departments of both sides to carry out various forms of exchanges and technical cooperation. |
| Third | *Implementation Plan 2008-2010*<br>Article 6 Agricultural Cooperation<br>( i ) Both sides are willing to strengthen exchanges and cooperation in agriculture, close high-level agricultural visits, increase information exchange, strengthen exchanges of professionals in planting and breeding, and encourage willing and capable agricultural enterprises of both sides to carry out economic and trade cooperation.<br>( ii ) Promote agricultural product trade between the two sides and facilitate the entry of high-quality agricultural products of both sides into each other's markets. |
| Fourth | *Implementation Plan 2010-2012*<br>Article 7 Agricultural Cooperation<br>( i ) Both sides are willing to strengthen cooperation in agriculture and food security, encourage exchanges between agricultural science and technology personnel and management personnel of both sides and increase information communication.<br>( ii ) Encourage willing and capable agricultural enterprises of both sides to carry out economic and trade cooperation, promote the development of agricultural product trade between the two sides, and facilitate the entry of agricultural products of both sides into each other's markets. |
| Fifth | *Implementation Plan 2012-2014*<br>Article 7 Agricultural Cooperation<br>( i ) Both sides are willing to strengthen cooperation in agriculture and food security, encourage exchanges between technical and management personnel of both sides, and increase information communication. In view of the increasing importance of the agricultural sector, especially the current high world food prices and its impact on food security, explore the establishment of China-Arab states agricultural cooperation mechanism.<br>( ii ) Hold two or more seminars on agricultural economy, trade and investment cooperation, one of which will be held in China and the other in an Arab country. Encourage agricultural enterprises of both sides to carry out economic and trade cooperation, promote the development of agricultural product trade between the two sides, and facilitate the entry of agricultural products of both sides into each other's markets.<br>( ii ) Carry out cooperation and coordination in agricultural research, agricultural production and food security between Chinese and Arab research institutions. |

106

# Chapter 5   Special Report on China-Arab States Agricultural Cooperation

**Continued**

| Ministerial conferences | Content |
|---|---|
| Sixth | *Development Plan of the CASCF from 2014 to 2024*<br>Implement joint projects in agriculture, food security, animal and fishery resources, food industry, desertification control, environmental technology, etc., and establish a Technology Training Center for China-Arab States Desertification Control.<br>*Implementation Plan 2014-2016*<br>Article 7 Agricultural Cooperation<br>( i ) Consolidate and strengthen bilateral and multilateral mechanisms in agriculture. Strengthen cooperation in agriculture, bio-agriculture, food security, animal resources and veterinary services, and exchange relevant laws and regulations in health supervision. Draw on China's experience in genetic improvement, encourage exchanges between agricultural science and technology and management personnel of both sides and increase information communication.<br>( ii ) Hold China-Arab states agricultural trade and investment negotiation activities, encourage willing and capable agricultural enterprises of both sides to carry out economic and trade cooperation, promote the development of agricultural product trade between the two sides, and facilitate the entry of agricultural and livestock products of both sides into each other's markets.<br>( ii ) Strengthen cooperation in water technology, water resource utilization and conservation. |
| Seventh | *Doha Declaration*<br>Strengthen cooperation in desertification control. Welcome the establishment of the Center for China-Arab States Desertification Control in Morocco. Welcome the signing of a *Memorandum of Understanding on Environmental Cooperation between the Ministry of Environmental Protection of the People's Republic of China and the League of Arab States*. Welcome professionals from both sides to participate in the "Desertification and Drought Control Seminar" held in Sudan in 2016. Actively establish mechanisms to promote agricultural cooperation.<br>*Implementation Plan 2016-2018*<br>*Article 7 Agricultural Cooperation*<br>( i ) Consolidate and strengthen bilateral and multilateral mechanisms in agriculture. Strengthen cooperation in agriculture, organic agriculture/bio-agriculture, food security, animal resources and veterinary services, and exchange relevant laws and regulations in health supervision. Draw on China's experience in genetic improvement, encourage exchanges between agricultural science and technology and management personnel of both sides and increase information communication.<br>( ii ) Actively establish agricultural cooperation mechanisms between China and the Arab states, and continue to strengthen cooperation in agriculture, including water-saving dryland agriculture, organic agriculture/bio-agriculture, food security, animal and fishery resources and food industry through bilateral and multilateral mechanisms. Drawing on China's experience, actively carry out experience exchanges in agriculture. |

The Development Process of China-Arab States Economic and Trade Relations
Annual Report 2024

**Continued**

| Ministerial conferences | Content |
|---|---|
| Seventh | ( ii ) Hold China-Arab states agricultural trade and agricultural investment negotiations, encourage willing and capable agricultural enterprises of both sides to carry out economic and trade cooperation, promote the development of agricultural product trade between the two sides, and facilitate the entry of agricultural and animal husbandry products of both sides into each other's markets. Call for creating a good investment environment for enterprises of the other side to invest in their own countries, introduce relevant preferential policies, and provide convenient measures and services. <br> (iv) Strengthen cooperation in water technology, water resource utilization and conservation. <br> (v) Encourage the establishment of joint enterprises in the agricultural sector, including fertilizer production, agricultural machinery and equipment manufacturing, and improving the productivity of various agricultural activities. |
| Eighth | *Beijing Declaration* <br> Actively establish mechanism to strengthen practical cooperation in agriculture. Promote the establishment of wholesale markets for agriculture, animal husbandry and fishery in the UAE. Welcome the signing of a *Memorandum of Understanding on Strengthening Agricultural Cooperation between the Ministry of Agriculture and Rural Affairs of China and the Ministry of Climate Change and Environmental Protection of the UAE*, as well as the memorandum of agricultural cooperation signed by the former Ministry of Agriculture of China and the Ministry of Agriculture and Forestry of Sudan in 2016. Welcome the signing of the *Agricultural Cooperation Action Plan(2018-2020) between the Ministry of Agriculture and Rural Affairs of China and the Ministry of Agriculture and Reclamation of Egypt.* <br> Strengthen cooperation and exchanges in forestry trade and desertification control. Encourage both sides to carry out professional discussions on desertification and land degradation control. Welcome professionals from both sides to participate in seminars and discussions on desertification, drought and land degradation control held by each other, and continue to explore the establishment of the Center for China-Arab States Desertification Control in Morocco. <br> *Implementation Plan 2018-2020* <br> Article 6 Agricultural Cooperation <br> ( i ) Consolidate and strengthen bilateral and multilateral mechanisms in agriculture. Strengthen cooperation in agriculture, organic agriculture/bio-agriculture, and food security and exchange relevant laws and regulations in health supervision. Draw on China's experience in genetic improvement, encourage exchanges between agricultural science and technology and management personnel of both sides and increase information communication. <br> ( ii ) Give full play to the role of the China-Arab States Expo, and hold the China-Arab States Agricultural Trade and Agricultural Investment Negotiations during the Expo. Call for creating a good investment environment for each other's enterprises to invest in their own countries, introduce relevant preferential policies, and provide convenient measures and services. |

Chapter 5    Special Report on China-Arab States Agricultural Cooperation

**Continued**

| Ministerial conferences | Content |
| --- | --- |
| Eighth | (iv) Strengthen cooperation in water technology, water resource utilization and conservation, rainwater collection, wastewater treatment and reuse, and water resource management in arid areas, and strengthen the cooperative relationship between the water resource research centers of both sides. <br> (v) Encourage the establishment of joint enterprises in agriculture, including fertilizer production, agricultural machinery and equipment manufacturing, and improving the productivity of various agricultural activities. <br> (vi) Promote the establishment of wholesale markets for agriculture, animal husbandry and fishery in the UAE. Welcome the signing of a *Memorandum of Understanding on Strengthening Agricultural Cooperation between the Ministry of Agriculture and Rural Affairs of China and the Ministry of Climate Change and Environmental Protection of the UAE*, as well as the memorandum of agricultural cooperation signed by the former Ministry of Agriculture of China and the Ministry of Agriculture and Forestry of Sudan in 2016. Welcome the signing of an *Action Plan for Agricultural Cooperation(2018-2020) between the Ministry of Agriculture and Rural Affairs of China and the Ministry of Agriculture and Reclamation of Egypt.* |
| Ninth | *Amman Declaration* <br> Both sides will strengthen economic, social, development and news cooperation, especially in trade, investment, finance, industry and transportation, energy, natural resources and environment, agriculture, tourism, human resources development, intellectual property, cultural and civilizational dialogue, library and information, education and research, science and technology, health and social development, news, non-governmental cooperation, women, youth and sports, sustainable development and population policy. <br> *Implementation Plan 2020-2022* <br> Article 6 Agricultural Cooperation <br> ( i ) Consolidate and strengthen bilateral and multilateral mechanisms in agriculture. Strengthen cooperation in agriculture, organic agriculture/bio-agriculture, and food security and exchange relevant laws and regulations in health supervision. Draw on China's experience in genetic improvement, encourage exchanges between agricultural science and technology and management personnel of both sides and increase information communication. <br> ( ii ) Actively establish agricultural cooperation mechanism between China and the Arab states, and continue to strengthen agricultural cooperation between the two sides, including water-saving agriculture, organic agriculture/bio-agriculture, food security, agricultural product market system construction, animal and fishery resources, food industry and veterinary services through bilateral and multilateral mechanisms. Actively carry out experience exchanges in agriculture drawing on China's experience. Continue to deepen practical cooperation and experience exchanges in agriculture between China and the Arab states. |

109

The Development Process of China-Arab States Economic and Trade Relations
Annual Report 2024

**Continued**

| Ministerial conferences | Content |
|---|---|
| Ninth | ( ii ) Give full play to the role of the China-Arab States Expo, and hold the China-Arab States Agricultural Trade and Agricultural Investment Negotiations during the Expo. Call for creating a good investment environment for each other's enterprises to invest in their own countries, introduce relevant preferential policies, and provide convenient measures and services.<br>(iv) Strengthen cooperation in water technology, water resource utilization and conservation, rainwater collection, wastewater treatment and reuse, and water resource management in arid areas, and strengthen the cooperative relationship between the water resource research centers of both sides.<br>(v) Encourage the establishment of joint enterprises in agriculture, including fertilizer production and agricultural machinery and equipment manufacturing, and improving the productivity of various agricultural activities. |
| Tenth | *Implementation Plan for 2024-2026*:<br>Article 7 Agricultural Cooperation<br>( i ) Strengthen cooperation in agriculture, fisheries and animal husbandry, promote cooperation in key areas such as modern planting technology, the use of technology applicable to small and medium-sized farmers, soil health, agricultural mechanization and green development, and expand sustainable agricultural investment. Strengthen cooperation in food security, hydroponic agriculture, soilless cultivation, and the use of agricultural drones, and carry out grain storage, loss reduction, and scientific and technological cooperation. China is willing to share the results of technological development with the Arab states and localize them, help the Arab states improve its existing farmland irrigation system, strengthen agricultural water-saving capabilities, and enable its grains and strategic agricultural products to reach the safety line of self-sufficiency.<br>( ii ) Jointly cultivate regional characteristic and advantageous industries, focusing on agricultural science and technology exchanges in dryland agriculture, comprehensive utilization of saline-alkali land, and animal disease prevention and control. |

Source: Compiled based on the content of the CASCF website.

As an important institutional platform for China-Arab states economic and trade cooperation, all previous China-Arab States Expo set agricultural sector. Since 2013, the Ministry of Agriculture and Rural Affairs and the People's Government of Ningxia Hui Autonomous Region have successfully organized agricultural activities during the five consecutive Expos. Over a decade of cooperation and exchange, these activities have steadily expanded in scale, yielded

Chapter 5    Special Report on China-Arab States Agricultural Cooperation

substantial outcomes, and demonstrated remarkable resilience and vitality. It has now become an integral component of the China-Arab States Expo and a key international platform for agricultural cooperation and exchange between China and foreign countries. To date, the agricultural events have attracted distinguished guests from over 100 countries and regions, participation of more than 60 major domestic and international trade associations, and over 600 leading enterprises as exhibitors. The events have facilitated a series of economic and trade negotiations and investment promotion activities, the signing of nearly 100 cooperation agreements and training programs for more than 400 agricultural officials and technicians from developing countries, and extensive cooperation with BRI partner countries in agricultural technology, trade, investment, and talent exchange. These cooperative efforts have jointly promoted the high-quality development of modern agriculture and made positive contributions to the BRI. [1]

## 5.1.2    Maintaining an Upward Trend in Agricultural Product Trade

In recent years, with the advancement of China-Arab states agricultural trade, the trade value of China-Arab states agricultural products has continued to expand and the non-oil commodities has gained increasing market share in China, especially the agricultural product. For instance, Egypt's fresh oranges and grapes and Saudi Arabia's dates have become popular in the Chinese market, while Chinese goods such as tea have secured a stable position in the Arab states' markets. As shown in Table 5.2 and Figure 5.1, China-Arab states agricultural product trade demonstrated an overall upward trend from 2013 to 2024. The total trade value rose from USD2.720504 billion in 2013 to USD5.831727 billion in 2024, an increase of 114.37%. Even during the COVID-19 pandemic, China-Arab states agricultural product trade cooperation was still on the rise. Although the trade scale accounts for a small proportion of China's total agricultural imports, the consistently increasing share demonstrates the growing significance of the Arab states in China's agricultural import.

---

[1]    "In the Past Decade, China-Arab States Agricultural Cooperation Has Achieved Fruitful Results," *Ningxia Daily*, September 22, 2023, p. 6.

**111**

## The Development Process of China-Arab States Economic and Trade Relations
## Annual Report 2024

### Table 5.2 Import and Export Value of Agricultural Product Between China and the Arab States (2013-2024)

(Unit: USD10000)

| Year | Export value | Import value | Total value |
|------|------|------|------|
| 2013 | 214528.3 | 57522.1 | 272050.4 |
| 2014 | 214581.2 | 42548.3 | 257129.5 |
| 2015 | 222586.8 | 38294.8 | 260881.6 |
| 2016 | 217965.1 | 30789.9 | 248755.0 |
| 2017 | 223868.0 | 57281.6 | 281149.6 |
| 2018 | 223107.4 | 74907.0 | 298014.4 |
| 2019 | 259872.0 | 122824.5 | 382696.5 |
| 2020 | 246672.5 | 159135.5 | 405808.0 |
| 2021 | 245548.3 | 194445.6 | 439993.9 |
| 2022 | 309218.2 | 198117.9 | 507336.1 |
| 2023 | 375847.9 | 197428.4 | 573276.3 |
| 2024 | 427325.40 | 155847.30 | 583172.7 |

Source: calculated per statistics from the Ministry of Commerce of the People's Republic of China, *China's Monthly Import and Export Statistical Report Agricultural Products (2013-2024)*.

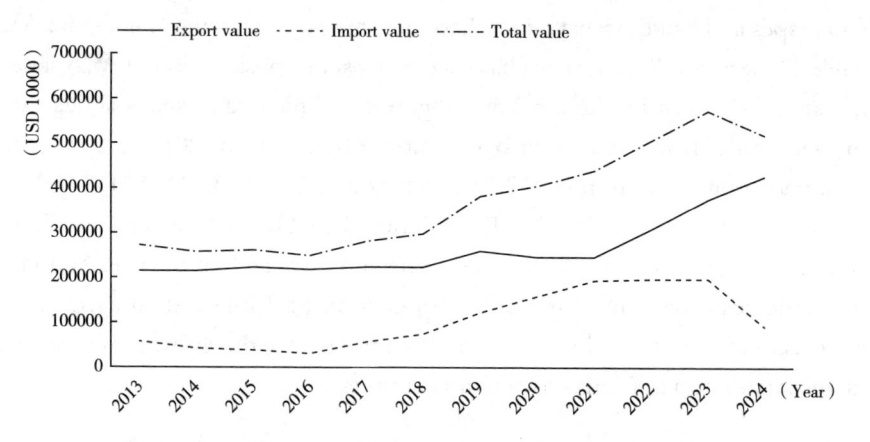

### Figure 5.1 Import and Export Value of Agricultural Product Between China and the Arab States(2013-2024)

Source: calculated per statistics from the Ministry of Commerce of the People's Republic of China, *China's Monthly Import and Export Statistical Report Agricultural Products (2013-2024)*.

Chapter 5    Special Report on China-Arab States Agricultural Cooperation

### 5.1.3    Deepening Agricultural Technology Transfer and Cooperation

Alongside the steady growth in agricultural trade, China-Arab states agricultural technology cooperation and technical exchanges have intensified with the advancement of science and technology. The establishment of bilateral cooperation institutions such as the China-Arab States Technology Transfer Center and China-Arab States Agricultural Technology Transfer Center has further facilitated the entry of China's modern agricultural technology into the Arab states. The China-Arab States Agricultural Technology Transfer Center has been demonstrated in many Arab countries such as Mauritania and Morocco and has achieved fruitful results. For instance, intelligent irrigation systems, desert alfalfa planting technology, and smart LED plant factory technology have been successfully applied and promoted in the Arab countries. Furthermore, the two sides have conducted in-depth cooperation in saline-alkali land management and utilization and dryland agriculture. China has significantly enhanced its efforts to transfer technologies and train professionals in many Arab countries, covering promoting dairy cow embryo transplantation technology in Mauritania, vegetable planting demonstration areas in Jordan, planting rice in the desert of the UAE, and promoting intelligent irrigation and water-saving technology in Egypt. The wind-solar complementary high-efficiency water-saving irrigation system developed by Professor Sun Zhaojun's team at Ningxia University has been successfully piloted and transferred to Oman, UAE, Egypt, and Qatar with the support of the China-Arab States Technology Transfer Center, helping Ningxia's agricultural water-saving technology to go abroad and serve the BRI. With the help of the new technological achievements, Qatar has established green agricultural product industrial chains and site greening industrial chains. China-Arab states agricultural cooperation serves not only as a key driver for deepening the strategic partnership between China and the Arab states, but also as an important path to promote China-Arab states practical cooperation in a wide range of fields and at a high level. It is also one of the achievements of the mutual bilateral and multilateral cooperation.

### 5.1.4    Expanding Talent Exchange and Training

Over the years, leveraging platforms such as the China-Arab States Technology Transfer Center, numerous international training programs has been held to

cultivate agricultural professionals with global perspectives and professional skills. Meanwhile, China has trained a large number of leading and reserve talents in agricultural technology for the Arab states. By the end of 2022, China had organized nearly 500 training sessions for 10000 agricultural officials and technicians from all 22 Arab League member states, covering desert agriculture, aquaculture, and smart farming. [1]"Training Program on Desertification Prevention and Control Technologies for the Arab States" is a free technical assistance program for the Arab states, sponsored by China's Ministry of Commerce and hosted by the Institute of Forestry and Grassland Ecology, Ningxia Academy of Agriculture and Forestry Sciences. The program has been officially opened for 13 consecutive sessions, attracted participants from many Arab countries to exchange and learn from each other, share experiences and seek common development.

### 5.1.5   Strengthening International Exchanges and Cooperation

As a key priority in China-Arab states cooperation, China and the Arab states have strengthened agricultural cooperation and exchanges by means of holding online and offline seminars, field research, and etc. Multiple stakeholders, including China's Ministry of Agriculture and Rural Affairs, Arab states' embassies in China, agricultural technology departments, local governments, research institutes, and universities, have convened numerous agricultural symposiums, which have facilitated in-depth discussions on agricultural technology, trade and investment and food security. Under the framework of the China-Arab States Expo, a series of activities such as keynote speeches on agricultural cooperation, high-level dialogues, roundtable on BRI food security and agricultural cooperation, training programs for senior officials from developing countries and modern agricultural inspections and exchanges were held, further promoting international exchanges and cooperation between China and the Arab states.

---

[1]   Pramod Kumar, "China and Arab States Sign USD471m Worth of Agri Deals," https: //www. agbi.com/agriculture/2023/09/china-and-arab-states-sign-471m-worth-of-agri-deals/, September 25, 2023.

Chapter 5    Special Report on China-Arab States Agricultural Cooperation

## 5.2    Current Situation of China-Arab States Agricultural Cooperation in 2024

In 2024, China-Arab states agricultural cooperation maintained a good development momentum, primarily manifested in agricultural product trade, agreement signing, project cooperation, and talent exchange and training.

### 5.2.1    China-Arab States Trade in Agricultural Products

#### 5.2.1.1    Scale of China-Arab States Trade in Agricultural Products

According to the statistical report on agricultural product released by the Ministry of Commerce in December 2024, China's agricultural product total import and export value reached USD318.16 billion, a decrease of 4.5% year on year. Of the total amount, the export value was USD103.0 billion, an increase of 4.1% year on year and the import value was USD215.16 billion, a decrease of 8.1% year on year. The trade value of agricultural products between China and the Arab states was USD5.189 billion, an increase of 12.8% year on year. Of the total amount, the export value was USD4.273 billion, an increase of 21.4% year on year, and the import value was USD916 million, a decrease of 0.3% year on year. Some Arab countries have also become important source and destination countries for China's agricultural product imports and exports. In 2024, Morocco became the largest market for Chinese tea exports, with the export value of USD242.312 million, an increase of 27.5% year on year. Iraq was the largest market for Chinese canned tomato sauce exports, with the export value of USD158.4 million, a decrease of 21.4% year on year. The UAE became the second largest export market for Chinese tobacco, with the export value of USD78.627 million, an increase of 10.3% year on year. It was also the second largest import market for Chinese rapeseed oil, with the import value of USD317.873 million, a decrease of 0.4% year on year.[1]

---

[1]  Department of Foreign Trade, Ministry of Commerce of the People's Republic of China, "Monthly Statistical Report on China's Imports and Exports: Agricultural Products (December 2024)," http://wms.mofcom.gov.cn/cms_files/filemanager/271034535/attach/20252/08b1bab98c774d78b54d8edea96af766.pdf?fileName=%E4%B8%AD%E5%9B%BD%E5%86%9C%E4%BA%A7%E5%93%81%E8%BF%9B%E5%87%BA%E5%8F%A3%E6%9C%88%E5%BA%A6%E7%BB%9F%E8%AE%A1%E6%8A%A5%E5%91%8A2024%E5%B9%B412%E6%9C%88.pdf, February 21, 2025.

115

The Development Process of China-Arab States Economic and Trade Relations
Annual Report 2024

5.2.1.2   Structure of China-Arab States Trade in Agricultural Products

From Table 5.3, it can be seen that in 2024, China's main agricultural products imported from the Arab states were as follows: "(12) Oil seeds and oleaginous fruits; miscellaneous grains, seeds and fruit, industrial or medicinal plants; straw and fodder", "(15) Animal or vegetable fats and oils and their cleavage products; prepared animal fats; animal or vegetable waxes", "(23) Food industries, residues and wastes thereof; prepared animal fodder", with an import value over USD300 million. The import value of "(03) Fish and crustaceans, molluscs and other aquatic invertebrates" exceeded USD100 million. Four categories were not imported. Compared with 2023, the largest increase in imports in 2024 was "(06) Trees and other plants, live; bulbs, roots and the like; cut flowers and ornamental foliage", with an increase of 18217.57%, and the largest decrease was "(16) products of meat, fish, crustaceans, molluscs and other aquatic invertebrates and insects", with a decrease of 99.39%.

**Table 5.3   China's Exports and Imports of Agricultural Products to/
from the Arab States in 2024**

| (Product Code) Product Name | Import | | Export | |
|---|---|---|---|---|
| | Value (Unit: USD 10000) | YoY Growth (%) | Value (Unit: USD 10000) | YoY Growth (%) |
| Type I Live animals;animal products | | | | |
| (01) Animals; live | 0 | 0 | 15.54 | 70.21 |
| (02) Meat and edible meat offal | 0 | 0 | 5814.91 | 145.00 |
| (03) Fish and crustaceans, molluscs and other aquatic invertebrates | 13510.35 | -15.24 | 11241.38 | 33.00 |
| (04) Dairy produce; birds' eggs; natural honey; edible products of animal origin, not elsewhere specified or included | 485.99 | 309.05 | 3160.86 | 64.43 |
| (05) Animal originated products; not elsewhere specified or included | 388.78 | 71.37 | 1057.54 | 25.84 |
| Type II Vegetable Products | | | | |
| (06) Trees and other plants, live; bulbs, roots and the like; cut flowers and ornamental foliage | 135.55 | 18217.57 | 2884.65 | 28.58 |
| (07) Vegetables and certain roots and tubers; edible | 13.61 | 158.25 | 42697.98 | 45.85 |

116

## Chapter 5 Special Report on China-Arab States Agricultural Cooperation

**Continued**

| (Product Code) Product Name | Import | | Export | |
|---|---|---|---|---|
| | Value (Unit: USD 10000) | YoY Growth (%) | Value (Unit: USD 10000) | YoY Growth (%) |
| (08) Fruit and nuts, edible; peel of citrus fruit or melons | 9204.06 | -20.87 | 39039.24 | 50.66 |
| (09) Coffee, tea, mate and spices | 132.38 | -12.14 | 64321.91 | 1.47 |
| (10) Cereals | 0 | 0 | 6782.68 | -50.24 |
| (11) Products of the milling industry; malt, starches, inulin, wheat gluten | 0 | 0 | 1350.91 | -29.05 |
| (12) Oil seeds and oleaginous fruits; miscellaneous grains, seeds and fruit, industrial or medicinal plants; straw and fodder | 49824.24 | -18.32 | 43090.14 | 10.48 |
| (13) Lac; gums, resins and other vegetable saps and extracts | 778.24 | 20.27 | 2309.15 | -1.69 |
| (14) Vegetable plaiting materials; vegetable products not elsewhere specified or included | 15.91 | 13.48 | 340.17 | -0.10 |
| Type Ⅲ Animal or vegetable fats and oils and their cleavage products; prepared animal fats; animal or vegetable waxes | | | | |
| (15) Animal or vegetable fats and oils and their cleavage products; prepared animal fats; animal or vegetable waxes | 33093.14 | -10.17 | 2857.68 | 26.47 |
| Type Ⅳ Prepared food stuffs;beverages, spirits and vinegar; tobacco and manufactured tobacco substitutes | | | | |
| (16) products of meat, fish, crustaceans, molluscs and other aquatic invertebrates and insects | 0.05 | -99.39 | 20941.93 | 65.14 |
| (17) Sugars and sugar confectionery | 240.85 | -59.90 | 14280.54 | -7.30 |
| (18) Cocoa and cocoa preparations | 778.63 | -28.84 | 4757.7 | 47.19 |
| (19) Preparations of cereals, flour, starch or milk; pastrycooks' products | 228.91 | -21.96 | 5300.34 | -0.90 |
| (20) Preparations of vegetables, fruit, nuts or other parts of plants | 85.78 | -61.44 | 66753.9 | -4.61 |
| (21) Miscellaneous edible preparations | 139.39 | 51.02 | 22495.6 | 27.67 |

117

**Continued**

| (Product Code) Product Name | Import | | Export | |
|---|---|---|---|---|
| | Value (Unit: USD 10000) | YoY Growth (%) | Value (Unit: USD 10000) | YoY Growth (%) |
| (22) Beverages, spirits and vinegar | 861.07 | 20.98 | 5297.88 | 3.05 |
| (23) Food industries, residues and wastes thereof; prepared animal fodder | 30178.67 | -28.72 | 4650.74 | 43.11 |
| (24) Tobacco and manufactured tobacco substitutes; products whether or not containing nicotine, intended for inhalation without combustion; other nicotine containing products intended for the intake of nicotine into the human body | 1192.19 | 19.38 | 51216 | 13.48 |

Source: calculated per statistics from the General Administration of Customs of China.

In 2024, the top five categories of agricultural products exported to the Arab states were as follows: "(20) Preparations of vegetables, fruit, nuts or other parts of plants", "(09) Coffee, tea, mate and spices", "(24) Tobacco and manufactured tobacco substitutes; products whether or not containing nicotine, intended for inhalation without combustion; other nicotine containing products intended for the intake of nicotine into the human body", "(12) Oil seeds and oleaginous fruits; miscellaneous grains, seeds and fruit, industrial or medicinal plants; straw and fodder", and "(07) Vegetables and certain roots and tubers; edible", with the export value over USD400 million. The least exported agricultural product was "(01) Animals; live", with an export value of only USD155400. Compared with 2023, the largest increase in 2024 was "(02) Meat and edible meat offal", with an increase of 145%, and the largest decrease was "(10) Cereals", with a decrease of 50.24%.

### 5.2.1.3 Source and Destination Countries of China-Arab States Trade in Agricultural Products

As shown in Table 5.4, the main Arab countries that China imported agricultural products from were the UAE, Sudan, Mauritania, Egypt, and Saudi Arabia in 2024. The value of agricultural products imported from the above five countries accounted for 96.45% of the agricultural products imported from all the Arab states. In terms of major agricultural products importing

Chapter 5　Special Report on China-Arab States Agricultural Cooperation

countries, Saudi Arabia (USD80920274), Mauritania (USD45071908) and Oman (USD6801876) were the main importers of "(03) Fish and crustaceans, molluscs and other aquatic invertebrates". Egypt (USD78584725), Saudi Arabia (USD4490842) and Iraq (USD4468554) were the main importers of "(08) Fruit and nuts, edible; peel of citrus fruit or melons". Sudan (USD496508937) and Morocco (USD1128869) were the main importers of "(12) Oil seeds and oleaginous fruits; miscellaneous grains, seeds and fruit, industrial or medicinal plants; straw and fodder". The UAE (USD317873419), Morocco (USD9382705) and Mauritania (USD3190681) were the main importers of "(15) Animal or vegetable fats and oils and their cleavage products; prepared animal fats; animal or vegetable waxes". Lebanon (USD5430670) and the UAE (USD2354760) were the main importers of "(18) cocoa and cocoa products". The UAE (USD180422847), Mauritania (USD91638859) and Sudan (USD18282351) were the main importers of "(23) residues and waste from the food industry; prepared animal feed", as can be seen in Table 5.5.

**Table 5.4　Source Countries of Agricultural Products Imported from the Arab States in 2024**

Unit: USD10000

| Rank | Country | Import value | Rank | Country | Import value |
|------|---------|--------------|------|---------|--------------|
| 1 | UAE | 53394.57 | 12 | Tunisia | 89.40 |
| 2 | Sudan | 52024.52 | 13 | Syria | 34.20 |
| 3 | Mauritania | 14065.34 | 14 | Yemen | 30.76 |
| 4 | Egypt | 8930.82 | 15 | Comoros | 1.85 |
| 5 | Saudi Arabia | 8721.05 | 16 | Algeria | 1.68 |
| 6 | Morocco | 2034.53 | 17 | Bahrain | 0.64 |
| 7 | Jordan | 929.91 | 18 | Kuwait | 0.15 |
| 8 | Oman | 680.84 | 19 | Qatar | 0.11 |
| 9 | Lebanon | 585.47 | 20 | Palestine | — |
| 10 | Iraq | 448.88 | 21 | Djibouti | — |
| 11 | Somali | 210.68 | 22 | Libya | — |

Source: calculated per statistics from the General Administration of Customs of China.

119

The Development Process of China-Arab States Economic and Trade Relations
Annual Report 2024

**Table 5.5    Major Agricultural Products Imported from the Arab States in 2024**

Unit: USD10000

| Product name | Trading Partner Name | Import value |
|---|---|---|
| (03) Fish and crustaceans, molluscs and other aquatic invertebrates | Saudi Arabia | 8092.0274 |
| | Mauritania | 4507.1908 |
| | Oman | 680.1876 |
| (08) Fruit and nuts, edible; peel of citrus fruit or melons | Egypt | 7858.4725 |
| | Saudi Arabia | 449.0842 |
| | Iraq | 446.8554 |
| (12) Oil seeds and oleaginous fruits; miscellaneous grains, seeds and fruit, industrial or medicinal plants; straw and fodder | Sudan | 49650.8937 |
| | Morocco | 112.8869 |
| | Egypt | 57.8120 |
| (15) Animal or vegetable fats and oils and their cleavage products; prepared animal fats; animal or vegetable waxes | UAE | 31787.3419 |
| | Morocco | 938.2705 |
| | Mauritania | 319.0681 |
| (18) Cocoa and cocoa preparations | Lebanon | 543.0967 |
| | UAE | 235.4760 |
| | Saudi Arabia | 0.0443 |
| (23) Food industries, residues and wastes thereof; prepared animal fodder | UAE | 18042.2847 |
| | Mauritania | 9163.8859 |
| | Sudan | 1828.2351 |

Source: calculated per statistics from the General Administration of Customs of China.

As can be seen in Table 5.6, the top ten destinations for China's exports to the Arab countries were the UAE, Saudi Arabia, Iraq, Morocco, Algeria, Egypt, Jordan, Kuwait, Libya and Lebanon, accounting for 88.05% of the total exports in 2024. The UAE has been the primary destination for China's agricultural exports to Arab countries for many years, with an export value of USD1.2688722 billion in 2024, an increase of 22.8% year on year, accounting for 32.39% of China's total exports to the Arab countries.

120

Chapter 5    Special Report on China-Arab States Agricultural Cooperation

**Table 5.6    Destination Countries of Agricultural Products Exported to the Arab States in 2024**

Unit: USD10000

| Rank | Country | Export | Rank | Country | Export |
|------|---------|--------|------|---------|--------|
| 1 | UAE | 126887.22 | 12 | Oman | 8341.21 |
| 2 | Saudi Arabia | 55218.84 | 13 | Mauritania | 8149.45 |
| 3 | Iraq | 50717.00 | 14 | Bahrain | 7122.36 |
| 4 | Morocco | 41511.46 | 15 | Qatar | 5495.71 |
| 5 | Algeria | 29421.38 | 16 | Sudan | 4435.75 |
| 6 | Egypt | 21497.95 | 17 | Tunisia | 3497.76 |
| 7 | Jordan | 13945.43 | 18 | Syria | 1623.46 |
| 8 | Kuwait | 13013.83 | 19 | Somali | 1392.87 |
| 9 | Libya | 10043.72 | 20 | Djibouti | 672.20 |
| 10 | Lebanon | 9909.24 | 21 | Palestine | 571.23 |
| 11 | Yemen | 8984.97 | 22 | Comoros | 206.36 |

Source: calculated per statistics from the General Administration of Customs of China.

In terms of major agricultural product exports, it can be seen in Table 5.7, in 2024, the UAE was the main destination for "(07) Vegetables and certain roots and tubers; edible" (USD206402900); "(08) Fruit and nuts, edible; peel of citrus fruit or melons" (USD225006991); and "(24) Tobacco and manufactured tobacco substitutes" (USD313378175). Morocco (USD254913999) was the main destination for "(09) Coffee, tea, mate and spices". Iraq (USD199694469) and Saudi Arabia (USD149887701) were the main export destinations for "(20) Preparations of vegetables, fruit, nuts or other parts of plants".

**Table 5.7    Major Agricultural Product Exported to the Arab States in 2024**

Unit: USD10000

| Product name | Trading partner name | Export value |
|--------------|---------------------|--------------|
| (07) Vegetables and certain roots and tubers; edible | UAE | 20640.2900 |
| | Saudi Arabia | 9477.1053 |
| | Qatar | 2132.0469 |

121

**Continued**

| Product name | Trading partner name | Export value |
|---|---|---|
| (08) Fruit and nuts, edible; peel of citrus fruit or melons | UAE | 22500.6991 |
| | Morocco | 4381.4015 |
| | Iraq | 4329.7293 |
| (09) Coffee, tea, mate and spices | Morocco | 25491.3999 |
| | UAE | 10253.2228 |
| | Mauritania | 6595.5123 |
| (20) Preparations of vegetables, fruit, nuts or other parts of plants | Iraq | 19969.4469 |
| | Saudi Arabia | 14988.7701 |
| | UAE | 8026.9008 |
| (24) Tobacco and manufactured tobacco substitutes; products whether or not containing nicotine, intended for inhalation without combustion; other nicotine containing products intended for the intake of nicotine into the human body | UAE | 31337.8175 |
| | Kuwait | 6695.6845 |
| | Saudi Arabia | 6350.9083 |

Data Source: calculated per statistics from the General Administration of Customs of China.

### 5.2.2　Progress of China-Arab States Agricultural Cooperation

China-Arab states agricultural cooperation is not only reflected in agricultural product trade, but also in new progress in the agreement signing, project cooperation, exchange visits, and product exhibitions.

For the agreement signing, on April 19, China Railway Construction International Cooperation's North Africa Branch signed a cooperation framework agreement with Algeria Agricultural Logistics Group and Zhejiang Jinhua Supply and Marketing Cooperative in Algiers, the capital of Algeria. The cooperation framework included many fields such as agricultural construction and agricultural deep processing, which implemented the important consensus reached by the heads of two states in July 2023 and was another bilateral economic cooperation achievement to jointly build the BRI and the vision of "New Algeria". [1]On May 30, the 10th Ministerial Conference

---

[1] "Chinese Company Signs Framework Agreement for Agricultural Cooperation with Algeria," *People's Daily Online - International Channel*, https://world.people.com.cn/n1/2024/0421/c1002-40220261.html, April 21, 2024.

Chapter 5    Special Report on China-Arab States Agricultural Cooperation

of the CASCF was held in Beijing. During the conference, the Ministry of Agriculture and Rural Affairs and the League of Arab States jointly signed the *Memorandum of Understanding on Agricultural Cooperation Between the Ministry of Agriculture and Rural Affairs of the People's Republic of China and the League of Arab States*, aiming to further deepen the cooperation in crop planting, animal and plant disease prevention and control, livestock and poultry aquaculture and agricultural products trade between the two sides, implement the "Eight Major Cooperation Initiatives" for China-Arab states practical cooperation, and make positive contributions to the construction of the "Five Cooperation Frameworks" between China and the Arab states.

For the project cooperation, date palm is an important traditional industry in the UAE and an important bridge for deepening cooperation and exchanges between China, the UAE and the Arab states. On December 6, at the Global Tropical Agriculture Innovation Conference held in Sanya, the handover ceremony of the second batch of date palm seedlings donated by the UAE to China was held. The second batch of date palm seedlings, totaling 23500, would be planted in Wenchang to further strengthen the cooperation and exchanges in tropical agriculture between the two countries. [1]The UAE's initiative to donate 100000 date palm seedlings to China was an important consensus reached by the two heads of the two states in 2019.

For the exchange visits, on May 23, the delegation of agricultural science and technology from Oman visited Ruihe Technology. The members of the delegation included many senior agricultural officials, experts and scholars at the ministerial level. The two sides actively discussed the experience of international agricultural science and technology development and the direction of sustainable agricultural development. In addition, in-depth discussions on the cooperation opportunities in agricultural science and technology research and development, agricultural industrialization, and agricultural product trade were held between Oman and China. In July, the "2024 China Agricultural Conference for International Economic and Trade Cooperation" was held in Beijing. About 300 people, including diplomatic envoys from other countries to China, experts

---

[1]    Chen Jing, "UAE Presents Second Batch of Date Palm Saplings to China to Deepen Tropical Agricultural Cooperation," *Toutiao*, https://www.toutiao.com/article/7445321599533761033/, December 6, 2024.

123

The Development Process of China-Arab States Economic and Trade Relations
Annual Report 2024

and scholars, international organizations, local trade promotion councils and corporate guests attended the meeting. Hussam Husseini, ambassador of the Hashemite Kingdom of Jordan to China, said that since the establishment of the strategic partnership in 2015, the economic and trade cooperation between Jordan and China has continued to deepen, and he hoped that the two countries would carry out more cooperation in key agricultural areas in the future.[1] From November 6 to 26, a technology training course on desertification and sand disaster prevention and control for Arab countries was opened in Gansu, hosted by the Ministry of Commerce and organized by the Gansu Institute of Sand Control Research. 24 trainees from Tunisia, Oman, Palestine, Saudi Arabia and Egypt participated in the course.[2]

For product exhibitions, from November 16 to 23, China-Mideast Agri-Trade Matchmaking Event was held in the UAE and Saudi Arabia respectively. The event was hosted by the Agricultural Trade Promotion Center of the Ministry of Agriculture and Rural Affairs, co-organized by the UAE Branch of the China-Arab States Agricultural Technology Transfer Center (constructed by Ningxia China-Arab States Industrial Investment Fund Management Co., Ltd.), as well as Longcheng Chinese Chamber of Commerce in Dubai, and guided and supported by the Chinese Embassy in the UAE and the Consulate General in Dubai. During the event, sub-events such as international agricultural product circulation seminars, Chinese agricultural product tasting and promotion, and economic and trade matchmaking in the Middle East agricultural and food market were held. More than 200 representatives from China and the UAE actively participated. Nearly 30 Chinese agricultural enterprises from ten provinces and regions including Ningxia promoted high-quality special agricultural products such as fruits, vegetables, and tea to their Middle Eastern partners. 30 types of agricultural products exhibited by 10 enterprises in Ningxia, including wolfberry, Chinese herbal medicine, honey, fruits and vegetables,

---

[1] Yao Wenyi, "2024 China Agricultural International Economic and Trade Cooperation Conference was Held", *Farmers' Daily*, http: //xm.shandong.gov.cn/art/2024/7/3/art_24617_10337484.html, July 3, 2024.

[2] "Global Connection | Trainees from the Arab Countries Study 'Sand Control Techniques' in Gansu," International Online, https: //www.163.com/dy/article/JHOL5V0K051497H3.html November 24, 2024.

124

Chapter 5    Special Report on China-Arab States Agricultural Cooperation

small grains, and condiments, were widely praised by the Arab merchants on the spot.[①]

## 5.3    Prospects for China-Arab States Agricultural Cooperation

Moving forward, China-Arab states agricultural cooperation has great potential. The two sides will continue to deepen agricultural cooperation and promote high-quality agricultural development in line with the "Eight Major Cooperation Initiatives" "Five Cooperation Frameworks" and "Ten Partnership Actions", and make greater contributions to building a China-Arab states community with a shared future in the new era.

First, strengthen the strategic docking. China-Arab states agricultural cooperation is founded on full respect for the needs and cooperation priorities of the Arab states, while seeking mutual alignment of interests. Regarding the agricultural development foundation of the Arab states, due to the inadequate agricultural infrastructure, low levels of agricultural production technology, serious land desertification and salinization, as well as the need to improve the agricultural production efficiency. The Arab states generally face the imperative tasks of improving food security capabilities, upgrading agricultural production technology, stabilizing agricultural product prices, and increasing agricultural inputs. Thus, how to ensure national food security has become a vital interest for the Arab states. China and the Arab countries have successively introduced national strategies or agricultural development strategies. In 2017, the Ministry of Agriculture and Rural Affairs and relevant departments jointly issued the *Vision and Action on Jointly Promoting Agricultural Cooperation along the Belt and Road*, which formed policy docking with the agricultural development vision of the Arab countries. In 2024, *the Memorandum of Understanding on Agricultural Cooperation Between the Ministry of Agriculture and Rural Affairs of the People's Republic of China and the League of Arab States* jointly signed by the Ministry of Agriculture and Rural Affairs and the League of Arab States further promoted the strategic docking in

①  Ding Yifei, "The UAE Branch of the China-Arab States Agricultural Technology Transfer Center Helps Ningxia's Special Agricultural Products Enter the Middle East market," Autonomous Region Agricultural International Cooperation Project Service Center, https: // nynct.nx.gov.cn/xwzx/zwdt/202412/t20241216_4760273.html, December 16, 2024.

125

agriculture between China and the Arab states. The two sides should make fully use of the CASCF, the China-Arab States Expo, and the China-Africa Economic and Trade Forum to further strengthen strategic coordination, improve the China-Arab states agricultural cooperation mechanism, jointly respond to the global food crisis, and work together to maintain food security.

Second, strengthen cooperation in agricultural technology research and development and technology transfer, and expand the scope of agricultural cooperation. On the one hand, after years of accumulation and development, our nation has achieved world-leading technology in dryland agriculture, animal husbandry, cash crop planting, modern agricultural product processing, land desertification and saline-alkali land management, and has accumulated rich practical experience, which is highly complementary to the actual agricultural development needs of the Arab countries. In recent years, the two sides have achieved fruitful results in salt-alkali rice planting and desertification prevention and control. Looking to the future, both sides can facilitate agricultural transformation and upgrading and ensure food security by establishing joint modern agricultural laboratories, accelerating the implementation of the innovation-driven development strategy, and leveraging sci-tech advancements to bolster modern seed industry development. The two sides will further strengthen cooperation in sci-tech research and development and technology transfer for dryland water conservation and desertification management, enhance food production and supply capabilities, promote the development of agricultural cooperation between the two countries to a deeper level, and ensure more cooperation results benefit the people of the two sides. On the other hand, digital agriculture is a typical representative of new agricultural productivity, an important trend and new growth point in global agricultural development. It plays an important role in changing traditional agricultural production models and responding to climate change. Looking ahead, we will actively align with Arab nations' digital agriculture strategies by introducing advanced Chinese agricultural technologies into local production systems, including agricultural drones, autonomous farm machinery, and precision livestock equipment. And we can strengthen digital agricultural cooperation with the Arab states through capacity building and knowledge exchange.

Third, enhance agricultural product trade and investment cooperation to facilitate industrial upgrading and value-added development. Since the BRI was

Chapter 5　Special Report on China-Arab States Agricultural Cooperation

proposed, the scale of China-Arab states agricultural product trade has continued to expand, and key projects have been promoted in an orderly manner. With the deepening of China-Arab states agricultural trade, the Chinese market for Arab non-oil commodities, particularly agricultural products, has demonstrated consistent growth. Going forward, we will facilitate greater market access for agricultural exports from the Arab countries to China and work toward trade balance enhancement.

Fourth, further strengthen talent exchange and capacity building to provide solid talent support for agricultural cooperation. First, aligning with the development priorities of the Arab states, organize local outstanding talents to carry out online and offline technical training on smart water-saving agriculture, desertification control, saline-alkali land control, animal husbandry and other technical training, cultivate a group of compound talents to undertake the foreign agricultural technical assistance tasks, and actively participate in the agricultural foreign aid activities in the joint construction of the BRI. Second, actively promote agricultural training. In addition to offline learning and field studies, we can collaborate with domestic universities and research institutes to innovate agricultural technology promotion and demonstration programs. By leveraging video recordings, live courses, and virtual visits, we can develop a series of high-quality training courses tailored to the agricultural needs of Arab states. Third, establish a talent reserve for the Arab states. We will cultivate a pool of professionals in agricultural investment planning, enterprise management, investment risk analysis, and other key fields to provide strong talent support for deepening China-Arab states agricultural cooperation.

# Chapter 6　Special Report on China-Arab States Energy Cooperation

Energy cooperation is a key area of practical collaboration between China and Arab states and lies at the core of their strategic partnership. The two sides are highly complementary in the energy sector. Over years of development, China and Arab states have established a closely interdependent relationship that spans traditional and new energy fields. The scale of cooperation has continued to expand, and the level of collaboration has steadily improved. Looking ahead, there remains broad potential for further cooperation.

## 6.1　Overview of Arab States' Energy Resources

### 6.1.1　Oil Reserves and Production in Arab States

The proven crude oil reserves of major Arab states accounted for 37.80% of the world's total, while their crude oil production constituted 26.43% of the global output (see Tables 6.1 and 6.2). In terms of proven reserves, Arab states have seen a slight increase in recent years. Regarding production, after a temporary boost in output following the Ukraine crisis, the crude oil production of major Arab states declined due to multiple extensions of the OPEC+ voluntary production cut agreements. In 2024, their total output decreased to 1194.22 million tons, a year-on-year decline of 4.02%.

Although Arab states collectively possess abundant oil resources, these reserves are unevenly distributed, being highly concentrated in Saudi Arabia, Iraq, Kuwait, and the United Arab Emirates. By the end of 2024, these four countries accounted for 94.33% of the total proven reserves among major Arab states and 35.66% of the global total. In terms of production, the combined crude

128

Chapter 6    Special Report on China-Arab States Energy Cooperation

oil output of these countries reached 986.58 million tons in 2024, representing 82.61% of Arab states' total production and 21.84% of the global total (see Tables 6.1 and 6.2).

**Table 6.1    Proven Crude Oil Reserves in Arab States（2021-2024）**

Unit: 100 million tons, %

| Country | 2021 | 2022 | 2023 | 2024 | Share in 2024 |
|---|---|---|---|---|---|
| Algeria | 15.37 | 15.37 | 15.37 | 15.37 | 0.62 |
| Egypt | 4.13 | 4.13 | 4.13 | 4.13 | 0.17 |
| Iraq | 195.71 | 195.71 | 195.71 | 195.71 | 7.88 |
| Kuwait | 139.81 | 139.81 | 139.81 | 139.81 | 5.63 |
| Oman | 7.29 | 7.29 | 7.29 | 7.29 | 0.29 |
| Qatar | 26.46 | 26.46 | 26.46 | 26.46 | 1.07 |
| Saudi Arabia | 408.69 | 408.69 | 411.96 | 411.96 | 16.59 |
| United Arab Emirates | 134.56 | 136.98 | 138.21 | 138.21 | 5.56 |
| Total (Major Arab States) | 932.02 | 934.44 | 938.94 | 938.94 | 37.80 |
| World | 2461.55 | 2467.00 | 2477.07 | 2483.76 | 100 |

Note: Includes crude oil and condensates.

Source: Economics & Technology Research Institute of CNPC.

**Table 6.2    Crude Oil Production in Arab States (2021-2024)**

Unit: 10000 tons, %

| Country | 2021 | 2022 | 2023 | 2024 | Share in 2024 |
|---|---|---|---|---|---|
| Algeria | 5820 | 6360 | 6038 | 5810 | 1.29 |
| Egypt | 2960 | 2990 | 2982 | 3000 | 0.66 |
| Iraq | 20061 | 22230 | 22213 | 21928 | 4.85 |
| Kuwait | 13000 | 13505 | 13500 | 12636 | 2.80 |
| Oman | 4212 | 4350 | 4307 | 4028 | 0.89 |
| Qatar | 7850 | 7753 | 7884 | 7926 | 1.75 |
| Saudi Arabia | 51750 | 52530 | 49378 | 46069 | 10.20 |
| United Arab Emirates | 16649 | 18129 | 18123 | 18025 | 3.99 |
| Total (Major Arab States) | 122302 | 127847 | 124425 | 119422 | 26.43 |
| World | 425929 | 439116 | 447749 | 451832 | 100 |

Note: Includes crude oil and condensates.

Source: Economics & Technology Research Institute of CNPC.

The Development Process of China-Arab States Economic and Trade Relations
Annual Report 2024

## 6.1.2 Natural Gas Reserves and Production in Arab States

Arab states possess abundant natural gas resources, though both their share of global reserves and production remain significantly lower than that of oil. In 2024, the proven natural gas reserves of major Arab states reached 50.18 trillion cubic meters, accounting for 24.99% of the world's total. Their total natural gas production amounted to 602.2 billion cubic meters, accounting for 13.72% of the global output (see Tables 6.3 and 6.4).

**Table 6.3    Proven Natural Gas Reserves in Arab States (2021-2024)**

Unit: trillion cubic meters, %

| Country | 2021 | 2022 | 2023 | 2024 | Share in 2024 |
|---|---|---|---|---|---|
| Algeria | 4.50 | 4.50 | 4.50 | 4.50 | 2.24 |
| Egypt | 2.14 | 2.14 | 2.14 | 2.14 | 1.07 |
| Iraq | 3.53 | 3.53 | 3.53 | 3.53 | 1.76 |
| Kuwait | 1.70 | 1.70 | 1.70 | 1.70 | 0.85 |
| Oman | 0.67 | 0.67 | 0.67 | 0.67 | 0.33 |
| Qatar | 24.67 | 24.67 | 24.67 | 24.67 | 12.28 |
| Saudi Arabia | 6.02 | 6.50 | 6.66 | 6.66 | 3.32 |
| United Arab Emirates | 6.30 | 6.31 | 6.31 | 6.31 | 3.14 |
| Total (Major Arab States) | 49.53 | 50.02 | 50.18 | 50.18 | 24.99 |
| World | 193.45 | 199.51 | 200.47 | 200.83 | 100 |

Source: ETRI

**Table 6.4    Natural Gas Production in Arab States (2021-2024)**

Unit: billion cubic meters, %

| Country | 2021 | 2022 | 2023 | 2024 | Share in 2024 |
|---|---|---|---|---|---|
| Algeria | 105 | 100.5 | 104.3 | 100.1 | 2.28 |
| Egypt | 67.8 | 64.5 | 57.1 | 54.8 | 1.25 |
| Iraq | 12.2 | 12.4 | 10 | 11.5 | 0.26 |
| Kuwait | 18.1 | 19.1 | 15.7 | 16 | 0.36 |
| Oman | 38.9 | 40.6 | 43 | 44.6 | 1.02 |
| Qatar | 178 | 183.3 | 181 | 182 | 4.15 |

130

Chapter 6    Special Report on China-Arab States Energy Cooperation

**Continued**

| Country | 2021 | 2022 | 2023 | 2024 | Share in 2024 |
|---|---|---|---|---|---|
| Saudi Arabia | 110.5 | 122.8 | 125.2 | 136 | 3.10 |
| United Arab Emirates | 55.7 | 57.4 | 56.1 | 57.2 | 1.30 |
| Total (Major Arab States) | 586.2 | 600.6 | 592.4 | 602.2 | 13.72 |
| World | 4225.5 | 4248 | 4268.4 | 4388.6 | 100 |

Source: Economics & Technology Research Institute of CNPC.

Among Arab states, Qatar leads in both proven natural gas reserves and production. In 2024, Qatar's reserves represented 49.16% of the total among major Arab states, and its production accounted for 30.22% of their aggregate output. In addition to Qatar, countries such as Saudi Arabia, the United Arab Emirates, Algeria, and Iraq also hold substantial natural gas resources. Notably, in 2024, Saudi Arabia ranked second among Arab states in natural gas output, contributing 22.58% of the regional total.

### 6.1.3    Other Energy Development in Arab States

In addition to conventional energy, Arab states have actively advanced the development of renewable energy in response to increasing global pressure to address climate change. Through national energy strategies and development visions, many countries have set clear targets for clean energy development and have consistently expanded policy and fiscal support for the sector. The United Arab Emirates launched its "*Energy Strategy 2050*", aiming to invest approximately USD163.7 billion in renewable energy by 2050, increasing the share of clean and renewable energy in domestic electricity generation from 25% to 50%. In 2023, the United Arab Emirates approved the updated "*National Energy Strategy 2050 (Updated)*", which aims to raise the share of clean energy in the overall energy mix to 30% by 2030. Oman, through its "*Oman Vision 2040*", targets at least 20% of electricity generation from renewable sources by 2030, rising to 35%-39% by 2040. Qatar's "*National Renewable Energy Strategy*" aims to achieve 4 GW of solar photovoltaic capacity by 2030, representing 30% of the country's total power generation capacity. Saudi Arabia has launched the "Saudi Green Initiative" and the "Middle East Green Initiative", focusing on the development of solar power and both green and blue hydrogen projects. The goal is for renewable

131

energy to provide more than 50% of the Kingdom's electricity supply by 2030. Kuwait's *2030-2050 Renewable Energy Strategy* sets a target of producing 22100 MW of renewable energy by 2030. Driven by these policies, renewable energy in Arab states has grown rapidly. From 2019 to 2023, renewable energy generation capacity in Arab states increased from 21098 MW to 32430 MW, with an average annual growth rate of 17.90%, outpacing the global average of 12.36% (see Table 6.5).

**Table 6.5　Renewable Energy Generation Capacity in Arab States (2020-2024)**

Unit: MW

| Country | 2020 | 2021 | 2022 | 2023 | 2024 |
|---|---|---|---|---|---|
| Algeria | 585 | 505 | 590 | 601 | 601 |
| Bahrain | 11 | 22 | 48 | 59 | 69 |
| Egypt | 5934 | 6258 | 6322 | 6709 | 7752 |
| Iraq | 1594 | 1594 | 1599 | 1599 | 1599 |
| Jordan | 2088 | 2460 | 2615 | 2638 | 2725 |
| Kuwait | 97 | 97 | 114 | 114 | 114 |
| Lebanon | 382 | 482 | 1167 | 1297 | 1297 |
| Mauritania | 122 | 122 | 123 | 260 | 294 |
| Libya | 5 | 6 | 6 | 8 | 8 |
| Morocco | 3522 | 3638 | 3725 | 4105 | 4375 |
| Oman | 179 | 205 | 705 | 722 | 722 |
| Palestine | 118 | 178 | 192 | 192 | 198 |
| Qatar | 24 | 24 | 824 | 824 | 1699 |
| Saudi Arabia | 113 | 443 | 843 | 2988 | 4743 |
| Somalia | 14 | 22 | 46 | 49 | 49 |
| Sudan | 1798 | 1817 | 1871 | 1871 | 1871 |
| Syria | 1509 | 1530 | 1557 | 1557 | 1557 |
| Tunisia | 406 | 406 | 508 | 817 | 1084 |
| United Arab Emirates | 2334 | 3003 | 3606 | 6075 | 6144 |
| Yemen | 258 | 258 | 264 | 290 | 410 |
| Total (Arab States) | 21093 | 23070 | 26725 | 32775 | 37311 |
| World | 2812981 | 3075931 | 3378790 | 3862881 | 4448051 |

Source: International Renewable Energy Agency (IRENA).

Chapter 6    Special Report on China-Arab States Energy Cooperation

Due to the hot, arid climate and water scarcity across West Asia and North Africa, the potential for hydropower development is generally limited. Hydropower facilities are primarily found along the Nile in Egypt and Sudan, the Tigris in Iraq, and in Syria. Other Arab states have limited hydro resources. In 2024, the hydropower generation capacity of Arab states totaled 10202 MW, accounting for just 0.72% of global hydropower capacity (see Table 6.6).

**Table 6.6    Hydropower Capacity in Arab States (2020-2024)**

Unit: MW

| Country | 2020 | 2021 | 2022 | 2023 | 2024 |
|---|---|---|---|---|---|
| Algeria | 209 | 129 | 129 | 129 | 129 |
| Egypt | 2832 | 2832 | 2832 | 2832 | 2832 |
| Iraq | 1797 | 1797 | 1797 | 1797 | 1797 |
| Jordan | 6 | 4 | 4 | 4 | 4 |
| Lebanon | 282 | 282 | 282 | 282 | 282 |
| Morocco | 1770 | 1770 | 1770 | 1770 | 2120 |
| Sudan | 1482 | 1482 | 1482 | 1482 | 1482 |
| Syria | 1490 | 1490 | 1490 | 1490 | 1490 |
| Tunisia | 66 | 66 | 66 | 66 | 66 |
| Total (Arab States) | 9934 | 9852 | 9852 | 9852 | 10202 |
| World | 1332363 | 1359536 | 1393299 | 1409865 | 1425374 |

Source: IRENA.

Arab states have actively tapped into solar and wind energy resources, and in recent years, they have developed sizeable photovoltaic and wind power industry clusters, driving the growth of the wind and solar energy sector. In terms of photovoltaic power generation, West Asia and North Africa rank among the most solar-rich regions in the world. Solar energy plays a key role in the renewable energy development strategies of Arab states. In 2024, photovoltaic power accounted for 58.49% of the total renewable energy generation capacity in Arab states. From 2020 to 2024, the region's photovoltaic capacity grew from 7824 MW to 21822 MW, with an average annual growth rate of 44.73%, surpassing the global average growth rate of 39.45%. However, solar energy development across Arab states is uneven. In 2024, photovoltaic power generation was mainly concentrated in five countries—the United Arab Emirates,

133

The Development Process of China-Arab States Economic and Trade Relations
Annual Report 2024

Saudi Arabia, Jordan, Egypt, and Lebanon— which together accounted for 73.43% of the total photovoltaic capacity among Arab states (see Table 6.7). As for wind power, the current installed capacity in Arab states remains relatively low. In 2024, it reached 5925 MW, representing only 0.52% of the global total (see Table 6.8). Nonetheless, some countries show significant potential for wind energy development. For example, under Oman's national energy strategy, 20% of the country's electricity is projected to come from renewable sources by 2027, with wind energy accounting for 21% of that share.

**Table 6.7    Solar Photovoltaic Capacity in Arab States (2020-2024)**

Unit: MW

| Country | 2020 | 2021 | 2022 | 2023 | 2024 |
|---|---|---|---|---|---|
| Algeria | 366 | 366 | 451 | 462 | 462 |
| Bahrain | 10 | 21 | 46 | 57 | 66 |
| Egypt | 1643 | 1663 | 1724 | 1856 | 2590 |
| Iraq | 37 | 37 | 42 | 42 | 42 |
| Jordan | 1541 | 1811 | 1966 | 1990 | 2077 |
| Kuwait | 84 | 84 | 102 | 102 | 102 |
| Lebanon | 90 | 190 | 875 | 1005 | 1005 |
| Mauritania | 88 | 88 | 89 | 123 | 157 |
| Libya | 5 | 6 | 6 | 8 | 8 |
| Morocco | 774 | 854 | 854 | 934 | 934 |
| Oman | 129 | 155 | 655 | 672 | 672 |
| Palestine | 117 | 178 | 192 | 192 | 197 |
| Qatar | 5 | 5 | 805 | 805 | 1680 |
| Saudi Arabia | 109 | 439 | 440 | 2585 | 4340 |
| Somalia | 11 | 19 | 42 | 46 | 46 |
| Sudan | 117 | 136 | 190 | 190 | 190 |
| Syria | 12 | 33 | 60 | 60 | 60 |
| Tunisia | 95 | 95 | 197 | 506 | 773 |
| United Arab Emirates | 2333 | 3002 | 3596 | 5942 | 6011 |
| Yemen | 258 | 258 | 264 | 290 | 410 |
| Total (Arab States) | 7824 | 9440 | 12596 | 17867 | 21822 |
| World | 723638 | 866830 | 1060522 | 1413548 | 1865490 |

Source: IRENA.

134

Chapter 6    Special Report on China-Arab States Energy Cooperation

**Table 6.8    Wind Power Capacity in Arab States (2020-2024)**

Unit: MW

| Country | 2020 | 2021 | 2022 | 2023 | 2024 |
|---|---|---|---|---|---|
| Algeria | 10 | 10 | 10 | 10 | 10 |
| Bahrain | 1 | 1 | 3 | 3 | 3 |
| Egypt | 1380 | 1640 | 1643 | 1890 | 2199 |
| Jordan | 529 | 632 | 632 | 631 | 631 |
| Kuwait | 12 | 12 | 12 | 12 | 12 |
| Lebanon | 3 | 3 | 3 | 3 | 3 |
| Mauritania | 34 | 34 | 34 | 137 | 137 |
| Morocco | 1435 | 1471 | 1558 | 1858 | 2128 |
| Oman | 50 | 50 | 50 | 50 | 50 |
| Saudi Arabia | 3 | 3 | 403 | 403 | 403 |
| Somalia | 4 | 4 | 4 | 4 | 4 |
| Syria | 1 | 1 | 1 | 1 | 1 |
| Tunisia | 245 | 245 | 245 | 245 | 245 |
| Yemen | 0 | 0 | 0 | 99 | 99 |
| Total (Arab States) | 3707 | 4106 | 4598 | 5346 | 5925 |
| World | 733780 | 824380 | 903171 | 1019603 | 1132837 |

Source: IRENA.

Hydrogen energy is also a key focus in the renewable energy development strategies of Arab states. Gulf nations have successively released hydrogen development plans and set specific targets for hydrogen energy expansion. Saudi Arabia has launched the *"Green Saudi Initiative"*, committing to photovoltaic power generation as well as green and blue hydrogen projects, with the goal of becoming a major global supplier of hydrogen energy. Egypt introduced its *National Low-Carbon Hydrogen Strategy*, which aims to produce 6.2 million tons of green hydrogen annually by 2040, accounting for 5% to 8% of the global hydrogen market. The United Arab Emirates has also approved its *National Hydrogen Strategy,* aimed at accelerating the growth of the hydrogen economy and strengthening the United Arab Emirates' position as one of the world's leading producers of low-carbon hydrogen. Meanwhile, several countries are advancing large-scale hydrogen projects across multiple dimensions and have established

135

The Development Process of China-Arab States Economic and Trade Relations
Annual Report 2024

national hydrogen alliances. Both Oman and Saudi Arabia are constructing world-class green hydrogen plants. Oman, in particular, has made significant progress in hydrogen development. By June 2024, Oman had signed eight cooperation agreements in the field of green hydrogen, with a total investment of USD49 billion. By 2030, it is projected to produce 1.38 million tons of green hydrogen annually, with production expected to reach nearly 8 million tons by 2050 and total investment valued at USD140 billion. The United Arab Emirates is actively working to become the green hydrogen hub of both the Middle East and the world. National hydrogen alliances have already been established in both the United Arab Emirates and Oman.

## 6.2 Status of China-Arab States Cooperation in Conventional Energy

### 6.2.1 China-Arab States Oil and Gas Trade

Oil and gas trade remain the cornerstone of economic cooperation between China and Arab states. Arab states are among China's most important sources of oil and gas imports. In 2024, China imported a total of 553.49 million tons of crude oil. The top ten source countries were Russia, Saudi Arabia, Malaysia, Iraq, Oman, Brazil, the United Arab Emirates, Angola, Kuwait, and Qatar. Among them, six were Arab states—Saudi Arabia, Iraq, Oman, the United Arab Emirates, Kuwait, and Qatar—collectively accounting for 44.25% of China's crude oil imports.

**Table 6.9  China's Crude Oil Imports from Arab States**

Unit: 10000 tons

| Country | 2020 | 2021 | 2022 | 2023 | 2024 |
|---|---|---|---|---|---|
| Saudi Arabia | 8492.20 | 8755.72 | 8748.89 | 8954.40 | 7863.63 |
| Iraq | 6011.62 | 5406.92 | 5548.83 | 5925.50 | 6382.93 |
| United Arab Emirates | 3117.51 | 3193.68 | 4276.64 | 4181.72 | 3554.51 |
| Oman | 3784.38 | 4481.46 | 3936.70 | 3914.67 | 4077.34 |
| Kuwait | 2749.58 | 3016.26 | 3328.16 | 2453.32 | 1596.95 |
| Qatar | 619.89 | 784.99 | 770.41 | 1046.11 | 1017.99 |
| Libya | 169.67 | 613.76 | 374.30 | 333.83 | 175.62 |
| Algeria | 40.44 | 3.98 | 0.00 | 14.66 | 0.00 |

136

Chapter 6　Special Report on China-Arab States Energy Cooperation

**Continued**

| Country | 2020 | 2021 | 2022 | 2023 | 2024 |
|---|---|---|---|---|---|
| Yemen | 182.57 | 94.34 | 84.04 | 0.00 | 0.00 |
| Egypt | 132.41 | 49.00 | 18.94 | 0.00 | 0.00 |
| Sudan | 16.00 | 0.00 | 7.87 | 16.01 | 0.00 |
| World Total | 54240 | 51292 | 50823 | 56394 | 55349 |

Source: GTT.

In natural gas trade, China primarily imports liquefied natural gas (LNG) from Arab states. In 2024, China's total LNG imports reached 77.3782 million tons, an 8.69% increase year-on-year. Of this, 29.5992 million tons (up 8.65%) were imported from Arab states, accounting for 26.62% of the total. The top ten sources of LNG were Australia, Qatar, Russia, Malaysia, the U.S., Indonesia, Papua New Guinea, Nigeria, Oman, and the United Arab Emirates. Arab states—Qatar, Oman, and the United Arab Emirates—were key suppliers, with Qatar alone accounting for 89.54% of China's LNG imports from Arab states and 23.84% of total LNG imports.

**Table 6.10　China's LNG Imports from Arab States**

Unit: 10000 tons

| Country | 2020 | 2021 | 2022 | 2023 | 2024 |
|---|---|---|---|---|---|
| Qatar | 816.75 | 897.78 | 1568.02 | 1664.88 | 1844.37 |
| Oman | 106.95 | 162.27 | 95.71 | 102.20 | 113.40 |
| United Arab Emirates | 30.09 | 70.80 | 11.92 | 66.82 | 85.87 |
| Algeria | 12.24 | 24.38 | 6.83 | 33.83 | 3.60 |
| Egypt | 6.43 | 131.20 | 34.85 | 28.21 | 12.68 |
| World Total | 6730.65 | 7878.95 | 6336.29 | 7119.07 | 7737.82 |

Source: GTT.

## 6.2.2　China-Arab States Oil and Gas Full-Industry-Chain Investment Cooperation

In 2024, China and Arab states achieved significant progress in oil and gas full-industry-chain cooperation, covering exploration and development, engineering

137

The Development Process of China-Arab States Economic and Trade Relations Annual Report 2024

and technical services, and refining and processing.

Cooperation between China and the United Arab Emirates, Iraq, Saudi Arabia, Algeria, and other countries continued to deepen in the fields of oil and gas exploration, development, and production capacity enhancement. In May 2024, Chinese oil companies—including ZhenHua Oil, CNOOC, Anton Oilfield Services, and Zhongman Petroleum—won multiple blocks in Iraq's 5+ and 6th oil and gas bidding rounds. Specifically, ZhenHua secured the Abu Khema and Qurnain blocks; CNOOC won Block 7; Anton won the Dbuffriyah block; and Zhongman won the Middle Furat (Euphrates) and the Northern Extension of East Baghdad blocks. These deals reflect how private Chinese oil companies are capitalizing on opportunities to expand cooperation with Iraq. In June, the Halfaya Gas Processing Plant (GPP) in Iraq, invested by PetroChina (Iraq) Halfaya and contracted to China Petroleum Engineering & Construction Corporation (CPECC) for EPCC and two-year O&M services, was officially commissioned. The facility has a designed natural gas processing capacity of 3 billion cubic meters per year and a condensate processing capacity of 950000 tons per year. In Saudi Arabia, a joint venture between Sinopec (40% stake) and Spain's Tecnicas Reunidas (60%) signed a Letter of Intent (LoI) with Saudi Aramco in 2024. The project includes the construction of three natural gas compression stations at the Jafurah unconventional gas field, installation of a 230kV power connection at the gas field substation, and an upgrade of the water pumping system. The total contract value is USD2.24 billion. Additionally, Saudi Arabia imported a large-scale 17200-ton offshore oil and gas gathering and transportation platform—the Mazan platform—from China. Once operational, it is expected to significantly boost output at the Mazan field, potentially making it one of the world's largest offshore oil and gas processing fields. In the United Arab Emirates, the Phase II of CNPC's Abu Dhabi Onshore and Offshore Project began oil production at the Belbazem oilfield in March 2024, reaching an output of 50000 barrels of crude oil per day. In July, during a visit to China by Sultan Al Jaber, the United Arab Emirates' Minister of Industry and Advanced Technology and CEO of ADNOC, several cooperation agreements and memoranda of understanding were signed with China. In the oil and gas sector, ADNOC and CNPC signed a strategic cooperation agreement covering exploration and development, LNG, low-carbon solutions, advanced technologies, refining, and trade. ADNOC also signed an agreement with

138

Chapter 6    Special Report on China-Arab States Energy Cooperation

CNOOC to strengthen collaboration in oil and gas exploration and development, upstream services and engineering construction, LNG, crude oil trading, new energy, and low-carbon development.[1]

In the downstream oil and gas refining sector, during the Chinese Premier's visit to Saudi Arabia in September 2024, Saudi Aramco announced the signing of a development framework agreement with Rongsheng Petrochemical and a strategic cooperation agreement with Hengli Group. These included the potential joint development of Saudi Aramco's SASREF refinery expansion project and negotiations for the acquisition of a 10% equity stake in Hengli Petrochemical Co., Ltd.[2] That same month, Rongsheng Petrochemical's wholly-owned subsidiary, Ningbo Zhongjin Petrochemical, acquired a 50% stake in SASREF and proposed jointly expanding the facility by constructing a large steam cracker and integrating downstream derivatives into the existing refining complex.[3] In November, Rongsheng Petrochemical and Saudi Aramco signed a framework agreement to advance the SASREF expansion project together. According to the agreement, the two parties agreed to establish a Joint Steering Committee for the expansion of the SASREF refining project, formulate guiding principles, and carry out future joint efforts. The aim is to provide an efficient coordination mechanism and strong organizational support for the subsequent phases of the SASREF expansion project. China and Arab states also actively pursued refinery cooperation within China. In July, ADNOC, Austria's Borealis, Borouge, and Wanhua Chemical's subsidiary Wanrong New Materials signed a cooperation agreement to conduct a feasibility study on a 1.6 million-ton-per-year specialty polyolefin complex in Fuzhou, Fujian Province. In November, construction commenced on Phase II of the Fujian Gulei Refining and Chemical Integration Project, a joint venture between Sinopec, Fujian Refining & Petrochemical

---

[1] The sources include Xinhua News, BEDigest, Xinhua News Agency, Arabian Business, the official website of the State-owned Assets Supervision and Administration Commission (SASAC), and the China Chamber of Commerce for Import and Export of Machinery and Electronic Products (CCCME).

[2] "Saudi Aramco and Rongsheng Petrochemical Sign Framework Agreement to Advance SASREF Expansion", Aramco China Official Website, URL: https://china.aramco.com/zh-cn/news-media/china-news/2024/aramco-and-rongsheng-petrochemical-sign-a-framework-agreement-to-advance-sasref-expansion, November 19, 2024.

[3] "Aramco and SABIC Cooperate with Wanhua Chemical on Polyolefin Complex Project," CLS.cn, URL: https://www.cls.cn/detail/1742532, July 24, 2024.

139

Company, and Saudi Aramco. With a total investment of RMB 71.1 billion, the project includes a 16 million tons/year oil refinery, 1.5 million tons/year ethylene capacity, 2 million tons/year paraxylene, downstream derivatives, and a 300000-ton crude oil terminal. It is the largest industrial project ever in Fujian Province and the largest single-investment refining project by Sinopec to date.[1]

In the field of engineering, technical, and construction services, the Sinopec-Tecnicas Reunidas JV was selected by Saudi Aramco as the EPC contractor for the Riyas NGL fractionation facility at the Jafurah gas field in early 2024, with a contract valued at USD3.3 billion.[2] In November, ADNOC signed the world's largest single onshore seismic exploration contract with China's BGP Inc. (a subsidiary of CNPC), valued at USD490 million,[3] to expand 3D seismic acquisition in Abu Dhabi. ADNOC Onshore also signed a USD920 million EPC contract with China's Jereh Group for digital field transformation across the Bab, Bu Hasa, and South East oilfields. Algeria's national oil company Sonatrach signed a USD210 million EPC contract with CPECC for the third phase of the ALRAR gas field compression project. This is a key milestone for CPECC's expansion into Algeria and the broader North West Africa market.

In the field of oil and gas shipping, QatarEnergy signed an agreement with China State Shipbuilding Corporation (CSSC) in April 2024 for the construction of 18 ultra-large LNG carriers to meet future demand from its North Field expansion.[4] QatarEnergy also signed long-term charters for nine LNG vessels with three Chinese shipping companies, including COSCO Shipping. In July, the United Arab Emirates' AW Shipping signed a contract with Jiangnan Shipyard and CSTC for the procurement of nine large ethane carriers, with a total value of approximately USD1.4 billion, as well as four very large ammonia carriers

---

[1] "Phase II of Fujian Gulei Refining and Petrochemical Integration Project Officially Launched," Fujian Provincial Government Website, URL: https://www.fujian.gov.cn/zwgk/ztzl/gjcjgxgg/dt/202411/t20241118_6568200.htm, November 18, 2024.

[2] "Sinopec Engineering and Spanish Company Secure USD3.3 Billion Mega Gas Field Contract in Saudi Arabia," Economic Observer Online, URL: https://www.eeo.com.cn/2024/0125/631389.shtml, January 25, 2024.

[3] "BGP Wins World's Largest Single Onshore Seismic Exploration Contract," Tencent News, URL: https://news.qq.com/rain/a/20241108A01W8600, November 8, 2024.

[4] "CSSC Signs Agreement with Qatar Energy to Build 18 of the World's Largest LNG Carriers," China News Network, URL: https://www.chinanews.com.cn/cj/2024/04-29/10208698.shtml, April 29, 2024.

140

Chapter 6    Special Report on China-Arab States Energy Cooperation

valued between USD250 million and USD500 million.

### 6.2.3    Cooperation in Other Energy-Related Areas

In addition to oil and gas, China has actively expanded its cooperation with Arab states in the field of renewable energy. In November 2024, China National Petroleum Corporation (CNPC) commissioned Iraq's first megawatt-scale photovoltaic energy storage power station. The facility features a 1 MW solar photovoltaics capacity and a 4 MWh battery storage system, with an estimated annual power output of approximately 1.6 million kWh. After commissioning, the plant can meet the electricity demand of a camp housing 800 people during peak periods, as well as provide power for night-time use and for key equipment at construction sites. China has also strengthened energy finance cooperation with Arab states. During the COP29 climate conference, Masdar (Abu Dhabi Future Energy Company) and China's Silk Road Fund (SRF) signed a Memorandum of Understanding (MoU) to collaborate on investing USD2.8 billion in renewable energy projects within Belt and Road Initiative (BRI) participating countries. This collaboration will support Masdar's development, investment, or operation of renewable energy projects across the Middle East, Central Asia, Southeast Asia, and Africa.

## 6.3    Status of China-Arab States Cooperation in New Energy

### 6.3.1    Driving Forces Behind China-Arab States Cooperation in New Energy

Climate change continues to draw widespread global attention. To date, over 150 countries have proposed carbon neutrality development goals, collectively covering approximately 88% of global greenhouse gas emissions, 92% of global economic output, and 89% of the world's population. New energy has increasingly become a key force driving global energy transition and sustainable development. China and Arab states both place high importance on green transition and development, and strengthening cooperation in the new energy sector has become a significant shared consensus. In May 2024, China announced the establishment of five major cooperation frameworks with Arab states at the opening ceremony of the 10th Ministerial Conference of the China-Arab States Cooperation Forum. One of these is the construction of a more

141

multidimensional energy cooperation framework, supporting Chinese energy enterprises and financial institutions in participating in renewable energy projects in Arab states and accelerating China-Arab states new energy cooperation.

China and Arab states share common policy orientations in new energy development. In recent years, many Arab states have positioned renewable energy development as part of their national strategies, rolling out various transition plans aimed at reducing dependence on petroleum and other fossil resources. Saudi Arabia, under the framework of "Vision 2030", is vigorously promoting economic diversification and energy transition, with a target of achieving 130 GW of installed renewable energy capacity by 2030. The United Arab Emirates, through its updated *"National Energy Strategy 2050 (Updated)"*, plans to more than double its renewable energy installed capacity to 14.2 GW by 2030. In addition, the United Arab Emirates government released its *"National Hydrogen Strategy"* in 2024, aiming to become one of the world's top ten green hydrogen producers by 2031, with an annual production capacity of 1.4 million tons, and to reach 15 million tons annually by 2050. Oman, through its "Vision 2040", is accelerating investment and promotion of renewable energy and green hydrogen projects. Egypt plans for renewable energy to account for 40% of its electricity generation by 2040. On the Chinese side, the share of non-fossil energy consumption must reach around 25% by 2030 in order to achieve its carbon peak target, requiring further large-scale, high-quality development of wind and solar power. In May 2024, China reiterated that it would build, based on the "Eight Joint Actions" proposed at the first China-Arab States Summit, five key cooperation frameworks with Arab states to accelerate the construction of a China-Arab states community with a shared future at the 10th Ministerial Conference of the China-Arab States Cooperation Forum. Among these, one priority is to build a more multidimensional energy cooperation framework. China expressed its willingness to carry out joint R&D and equipment manufacturing in new energy technologies with Arab states, and to support Chinese energy enterprises and financial institutions in participating in renewable energy projects in Arab states with a total installed capacity of over 3 million kilowatts.

China and Arab states are highly complementary in terms of new energy technology and resource endowments. In terms of technology, China is fostering a new productive force and possesses a globally leading new energy industrial system, with competitive advantages and extensive project experience in fields

Chapter 6    Special Report on China-Arab States Energy Cooperation

such as photovoltaics, wind energy, and energy storage. This enables China to provide Arab states with advanced technology and management support to help them rapidly develop their new energy industries. In terms of resources, Arab states are richly endowed with solar energy resources that are evenly distributed, with solar irradiation intensity generally exceeding 2000 kWh/m² and even surpassing 2600 kWh/m² in parts of Saudi Arabia, Egypt, and Yemen. In addition, Arab states are rich in wind energy resources. Saudi Arabia, in particular, ranks among the top globally in onshore wind power potential. Vast areas in central and northern Saudi Arabia, southern Oman, and northwestern Kuwait possess excellent wind conditions, making them ideal for the development of large-scale new energy projects. China-Arab states cooperation in new energy will help Arab League states achieve energy diversification, improve energy efficiency, and strengthen infrastructure construction, while also driving local employment and accelerating economic recovery and prosperity. On the other hand, it will support Chinese renewable energy enterprises in expanding internationally, broadening their presence in Arab markets, enhancing their global competitiveness, and promoting the export of related industry chain products.

### 6.3.2    Recent Developments in China-Arab States New Energy Cooperation

In 2024, China and Arab states continued to deepen and upgrade their cooperation in the field of new energy, focusing primarily on photovoltaics, hydrogen energy, and new energy vehicles. These developments reflect both sides' joint efforts in promoting economic diversification, technological innovation, policy support, and environmental protection.

In the field of photovoltaics, multiple Chinese companies signed large-scale cooperation agreements covering various segments of the photovoltaic industry chain in Arab states. In July 2024, Jinko Middle East, a wholly owned subsidiary of Jinko Solar, signed a shareholder agreement with the Renewable Energy Localization Company, a wholly owned subsidiary of Saudi Arabia's Public Investment Fund (PIF), and with Vision Industries Company. Together, they established a joint venture in Saudi Arabia to build a 10 GW high-efficiency solar cell and module project, with a total investment of approximately USD985 million. That same month, TCL Zhonghuan signed a shareholder agreement

143

with Vision Industries and PIF's Renewable Energy Localization Company to establish a joint venture for the construction of a 20 GW photovoltaic crystal wafer project in Saudi Arabia, with a projected total investment of approximately USD2.08 billion. In July 2024, Chinese photovoltaic enterprise Sungrow signed a contract with Saudi Arabia's ALGIHAZ for the world's largest energy storage project, with a capacity of 7.8 GWh. In the same month, the Abu Dhabi branch of Power Construction Corporation of China (PowerChina), together with its subsidiary East China Engineering Company (HDEC), formed a consortium and signed an EPC contract with Ajban PV Project Holding Company for the 1.5 GW PV3 Ajban solar project, located in the Ajban region of Abu Dhabi, the United Arab Emirates. The contract is valued at approximately USD755 million. In August 2024, a consortium formed by multiple subsidiaries of China Energy Engineering Corporation (CEEC) signed an EPC contract worth USD972 million for the Phase Ⅳ Haden 2 GW photovoltaic project in Saudi Arabia with the project company Buraiq Renewable Energy Company, a project company affiliated with Saudi International Water and Electricity Company, the Public Investment Fund, and Saudi Aramco Power Company. The total contract value reached USD972 million. Also in August, CEEC International Group signed an EPC contract with France's TotalEnergies for the 1 GW Ratawi photovoltaic project in Iraq, which is the first large-scale project under Iraq's national solar development plan.

In the field of hydrogen energy, Chinese companies signed cooperation agreements with Arab states. In June 2024, Saudi International Water and Electricity Company (ACWA Power) and Sinopec Engineering (Guangzhou) Co., Ltd. signed a memorandum of understanding to carry out practical cooperation in the field of green hydrogen and green ammonia. The cooperation includes joint exploration, development, construction, management, and operation of green hydrogen and green ammonia projects, covering regions such as the Middle East, North Africa, Central Asia, Southeast Asia, and other countries and regions, including China, where ACWA Power has ongoing project development. Both parties will also strengthen cooperation in green hydrogen technology development and application. That same month, Hymer Technology and Zhongke Qingneng (Henan) signed a strategic cooperation agreement for a hydrogen energy industry project in Oman, valid for one year. According to the agreement, the two sides will leverage their respective expertise to cooperate in

144

Chapter 6    Special Report on China-Arab States Energy Cooperation

the industrial application of green electricity-based hydrogen production and hydrogen liquefaction technology in Oman, forming an integrated hydrogen energy industry chain covering hydrogen supply, liquid hydrogen production, hydrogen refueling, liquid hydrogen operation, and hydrogen-powered cold-chain logistics vehicles. In October 2024, ADNOC Logistics & Services, a subsidiary of Abu Dhabi National Oil Company (ADNOC), and "AW Shipping," a strategic joint venture with China's Wanhua Chemical Group, signed a USD250 million contract with China's Jiangnan Shipyard for the procurement of two ultra-large ammonia carriers, which will become among the largest ammonia carriers in the world.

In the field of new energy vehicles, Chinese NEVs have emerged as a new symbol of Chinese automotive exports to Arab states. In March 2024, BYD held a product launch event in Dubai, the United Arab Emirates, officially introducing three models to the United Arab Emirates market, including Seal, Song PLUS, and Qin PLUS. In June 2024, XPeng Motors announced the release of two models, XPeng G9 and XPeng P7, for the Egyptian market. In August 2024, Changan Automobile held its Middle East and Africa brand launch event in Riyadh, Saudi Arabia, unveiling its Changan, Deepal, and Avatr brands, and outlined future product launch plans. In October 2024, NIO signed a strategic cooperation agreement with strategic investor CYVN, announcing plans to establish an advanced technology R&D center in Abu Dhabi. The two parties also plan to co-develop a new vehicle model tailored for the local market and to establish a joint venture, "NIO Middle East and North Africa". In December 2024, the new energy commercial vehicle factory co-developed by Yutong and Qatar's state-owned public transport company Mowasalat officially broke ground in the Umm Al-Houl Free Zone in Qatar. This will become the first electric commercial vehicle assembly plant in Qatar and a significant example of deepened cooperation between China and Qatar under the Belt and Road Initiative.[①]

Additionally, in November 2024, the United Arab Emirates' clean energy giant Masdar signed a memorandum of understanding with China's Silk Road Fund to jointly invest up to RMB 20 billion in renewable energy projects in Belt and Road

---

① "Chinese Auto Brands Enter the New Hotspot of the Middle East," Tencent News, https://news. qq.com/rain/a/20240913A01Z5B00, September 13, 2024.

145

The Development Process of China-Arab States Economic and Trade Relations
Annual Report 2024

partner countries. The cooperation will focus on clean energy projects such as solar, wind, and hydropower across the Middle East, Central Asia, and Southeast Asia.[1]

## 6.4    Prospects for China-Arab States Energy Cooperation

At present, the world is undergoing accelerated changes unseen in a century, and the global energy landscape is undergoing profound restructuring. Global energy demand continues to grow, and for a considerable period, oil and gas will continue to play a central role as primary energy sources, with natural gas becoming a key pillar of green energy development. Energy transition is an inevitable trend and a crucial action in response to climate change. As major forces in the global energy market, China and Arab states need, now more than ever, to strengthen cooperation, move forward together, share the responsibilities of energy development, jointly promote green transformation, and work hand in hand to build a multidimensional China-Arab states energy cooperation framework.

### 6.4.1    Further Promote and Deepen Traditional Energy Cooperation, Especially in the Entire Oil and Gas Industry Chain

In the foreseeable future, global oil and gas demand is expected to remain at high levels. By 2040, oil and gas are projected to maintain a 50% share in the energy mix, and before 2045, annual demand is expected to plateau above 11.5 billion tons of coal equivalent, solidifying their role as core energy sources.[2] In recent years, Saudi Arabia, the United Arab Emirates, Kuwait, Iraq, and Oman have ranked among China's top ten crude oil suppliers. In the coming period, China will continue importing crude oil and natural gas from Arab states, and traditional oil and gas trade will remain the main pillar of China-Arab states energy cooperation. Furthermore, there is significant potential for China and Arab states to deepen cooperation across the entire oil and gas industry chain, including investments in premium oil and gas assets in the United Arab Emirates

---

[1]  "Gulf Capital Steps Up Investment in China's New Energy Sector," Tencent News, URL: https://news.qq.com/rain/a/20250227A01G2U00, February 27, 2025.

[2]  "2060 World and China Energy Outlook Report," Sohu News, URL: https://news.sohu.com/a/841343738_121856153.

146

Chapter 6　Special Report on China-Arab States Energy Cooperation

and Oman, efforts to expand upstream natural gas investment in Qatar, and the active introduction of investment from energy enterprises and sovereign wealth funds from countries such as Saudi Arabia and Kuwait into the Chinese market.[1]

## 6.4.2　Promote the Establishment of a Clean Energy Partnership and Strengthen Cooperation in the Clean Use of Conventional Energy and Wind and Solar Power Generation

In recent years, Arab states such as Saudi Arabia and the United Arab Emirates have introduced low-carbon transition strategies such as "Vision 2030" and "Net-Zero Emissions 2050," and have taken these as important instruments to drive economic diversification. These efforts align closely with China's "dual carbon" goals and present strong complementarities. China and Arab states have broad prospects for cooperation in new energy development. Countries such as Saudi Arabia, the United Arab Emirates, and Oman are promoting comprehensive collaboration with China in the new energy sector and actively working toward the establishment of clean energy partnerships. Joint efforts can be made in key areas such as the clean utilization of conventional energy, wind and solar power generation, green hydrogen production from renewable electricity, advanced nuclear power, and seawater desalination—fields in which Arab states have pressing technological needs. There is also potential to accelerate the rollout of a series of "small but beautiful" clean energy projects, positioning Chinese energy companies as key partners in helping Arab states implement energy diversification strategies and drive their energy transitions. On the basis of fully implementing the *United Nations Framework Convention on Climate Change* and the *Paris Agreement*, China and Arab states can also collaboratively promote the establishment of a global climate governance system.

## 6.4.3　Strengthen Energy Finance Cooperation and Actively Create Conditions for RMB-Settled Oil and Gas Trade

In the face of profound global changes unseen in a century, China and Arab states have an opportunity to create favorable conditions and take multiple measures to expand the use of the Renminbi (RMB) in energy cooperation.

---

[1]　Economics and Technology Research Institute of China National Petroleum Corporation (CNPC).

147

This includes improving cross-border RMB infrastructure, encouraging Chinese financial institutions such as banks, securities firms and insurers to establish more branches in Arab states, and strengthening cooperation with local financial institutions in areas such as payment settlement, interbank lending, and risk assessment, to make the RMB more usable and user-friendly. In addition, the two sides can accelerate the integration of energy and finance, establish more effective financing mechanisms, and provide stronger financial support for China-Arab states energy trade and investment cooperation.

### 6.4.4 Build a China-Arab States Multidimensional Energy Cooperation Mechanism and Jointly Safeguard Global Energy Security

China is the world's largest energy consumer and importer, and a vital actor in global energy governance. The Arab world, and particularly oil-producing countries in the Middle East, are rich in oil and gas resources and exert a major influence on global energy supply and price stability. They are also important forces in global energy governance. In the future, implementing the strategic vision of a multidimensional China-Arab states energy cooperation framework and building an energy security cooperation mechanism to jointly address energy crises and safeguard global energy security can become a core element of this new architecture. China and Arab states can enhance policy coordination in the energy sector and explore paths and frameworks for cooperation on energy security in areas such as ensuring the security of supply and demand, maintaining reasonable and fair energy prices, protecting transportation routes and infrastructure, establishing crisis warning and response systems, and participating in global and regional energy governance. Together, they can ensure supply chain resilience, build long-term mechanisms to maintain energy supply-demand balance, and uphold bilateral, regional, and global energy security.

### 6.4.5 Guard Against Geopolitical, Policy and Other Risks in China-Arab States Energy Cooperation

First, geopolitical risks remain high. The world is undergoing accelerated changes unseen in a century. Emerging economies and developing countries are on the rise, and the global balance of power is shifting significantly. Economic globalization is facing headwinds. The risks of "decoupling and supply chain

Chapter 6    Special Report on China-Arab States Energy Cooperation

fragmentation" and the bloc confrontations are on the rise. Meanwhile, global governance, development, and security deficits are deepening. Unilateral sanctions, discriminatory cooperation policies, and trade barriers have severely affected international energy cooperation. While the political landscape of Arab states remains generally stable and their diplomatic autonomy is increasing, the situation in the Middle East remains highly complex. The protracted spillover of the Israel-Palestine conflict, sudden changes in the situation in Syria, and persistent regional tensions raise legitimate concerns. Although Arab states have no intention of becoming involved in conflicts, there remains a risk of accidental clashes or terrorist incidents perpetrated by actors in the region, which could affect the safety of energy cooperation. Additionally, in recent years, strategic competition among major powers in the Arab world has intensified, and Western countries have increasingly sought to contain and pressure China. In high-tech areas such as 5G and artificial intelligence, some Western governments have coerced Arab partners to abandon cooperation with China in favor of Western alternatives. These disruptive actions may negatively impact China's cooperation with certain Arab states.

Second, Arab states are continuing to tighten localization and fiscal policies. In terms of localization, GCC countries such as Saudi Arabia, Oman, Qatar, and Kuwait have further tightened policies to promote economic diversification and create more employment opportunities for their citizens. Saudi Arabia has launched the "Nuwatin" Initiative to promote the localization of the energy industry, reduce reliance on imports, and enhance domestic production capacity and technological competence. Qatar has launched an enhanced version of its Enhanced In-Country Value Program, which revises the formula for calculating domestic value and introduces incentive mechanisms to reward high-performing companies. Oman has initiated projects to increase localization in the energy sector, emphasizing local procurement and labor in oil, gas, new energy, and green hydrogen projects. Kuwait Petroleum Corporation has proposed removing employment barriers and increasing the share of national employees in the oil industry to fully localize the sector's workforce. In terms of taxation, countries such as the United Arab Emirates, Oman, and Kuwait will begin imposing a 15% minimum top-up tax on large multinational enterprises operating locally, starting January 1, 2025. On the one hand, this reform aims to improve tax transparency through unified rates and modern management mechanisms; on the other, it

149

The Development Process of China-Arab States Economic and Trade Relations
Annual Report 2024

seeks to diversify the economy and reduce dependence on oil revenues. These tax changes are likely to affect the profitability of multinational companies operating in these countries, and enterprises must prepare in advance and adjust their strategies accordingly.

Third, international oil price fluctuations introduce uncertainties into China-Arab States cooperation on "carbon reduction". Funding for "carbon reduction" projects in Arab oil- and gas-producing countries primarily comes from public finances. A significant decline in international oil prices could impact fiscal balance, potentially leading to delays or even cancellations of "carbon reduction" projects. This, in turn, may adversely affect cooperation between China and Arab states in the field of "carbon reduction".

# Chapter 7　Special Report on China-Arab States Digital Economy Cooperation

Amid accelerated global digital transformation, the digital economy has become a key driver of economic growth and enhanced industrial competitiveness. Driven by a new wave of technological revolution and industrial transformation, Arab states are actively pursuing the development of the digital economy. Their initiatives include accelerating the building of digital infrastructure, expanding the use of digital technologies in governance and trade, and actively pursuing collaboration with global leaders. Meanwhile, as a key leader in the global digital economy, China continues to advance technological innovation and industrial upgrading. These efforts have created extensive opportunities and strengthened the foundation for China-Arab States digital economy cooperation, making it a new engine for bilateral economic and trade collaboration. Despite an uncertain international environment and growing technological competition, mutual trust and cooperation between China and Arab states in the digital domain continue to deepen. In 2024, this enhanced bilateral cooperation in the digital economy has reinvigorated the development of global digital governance and technological innovation.

## 7.1　The Digital Economy Development in Arab States

### 7.1.1　Hard Power in Digital Economy Development: ICT Infrastructure as an Example

Information and Communication Technology (ICT) infrastructure serves as the foundational platform for digital economy development and a key driver for

industrial digitalization and intelligent upgrading. The advancement level of a nation's ICT infrastructure not only determines how widely digital technologies are adopted but also directly shapes the pace and structure of its digital economy. Given this fundamental role, the maturity of ICT infrastructure has become a crucial measure of national competitiveness in the digital era. Facing the global wave of digitalization, Arab states are accelerating the deployment of cutting-edge communication networks and modernizing their infrastructure to strengthen their digital economic foundations and boost their influence within the global digital ecosystem.

1. Regional Level

According to 2024 ICT statistics from the International Telecommunication Union (ITU)[1], the Arab region has made gradual but uneven progress across ICT metrics, with most indicators remaining below global benchmarks (Table 7.1). The region's Internet penetration reached 69.6% in 2024, slightly above the 67.6% global average. However, significant gaps persist elsewhere: fixed-telephone subscriptions stand at 9.1 per 100 inhabitants, below the 10.3 global average; fixed-broadband penetration remains at 12.5%, lagging behind the 19.6% global rate; mobile-cellular subscriptions show 103.7 per 100 inhabitants while active mobile-broadband penetration reaches 85.2%, both lower than the respective global averages of 112.1 and 94.6%. Mobile network coverage at 97.4% slightly trails the 97.9% global average. Analysis by network generation reveals further disparities: 3G+ coverage reaches 94.9% versus 95.6% globally; 4G+ coverage stands at 86.9% compared to the 91.8% global average; while 5G+ coverage registers at just 12.7%, significantly trailing the 51.2% global benchmark.

---

[1] The data comes from the ITU ICT Statistics Database (2024), accessible at: ITU (2024), ICT Statistics Database, https://www.itu.int/en/ITU-D/Statistics/Pages/stat/default.aspx. This analysis covers the period 2021-2024, as systematic longitudinal data for specific indicators has been available since 2021. Note that methodological updates have caused some inconsistencies between the 2024 and 2023 datasets for overlapping indicators. This chapter focuses on the 2024 dataset to incorporate the latest methodological refinements.

Chapter 7　Special Report on China-Arab States Digital Economy Cooperation

**Table 7.1　Summary of ICT Fundamentals in the Arab Region (2021-2024)**

| | | 2021 | 2022 | 2023 | 2024 |
|---|---|---|---|---|---|
| Internet penetration rate (%) | | 64.7 | 67.4 | 68.6 | 69.6 |
| Urban /Rural Areas | Urban areas | 77.9 | 80.5 | 81.6 | 82.9 |
| | Rural areas | 46.4 | 49.3 | 49.5 | 50.1 |
| Gender | Female | 59.8 | 61.8 | 63 | 64.4 |
| | Male | 69.3 | 72.6 | 73.8 | 75.1 |
| Age | Youth population (15-24) | 80 | 82.5 | 84.1 | 86.1 |
| | Population beyond the youth demographic | 62 | 64.7 | 65.8 | 66.7 |
| Fixed-Telephone Subscriptions per 100 inhabitants (%) | | 8.8 | 8.9 | 8.9 | 9.1 |
| Fixed-Broadband Subscriptions per 100 inhabitants (%) | | 9.6 | 10.6 | 11.4 | 12.5 |
| Mobile-Cellular Subscriptions per 100 inhabitants (%) | | 96.5 | 99.3 | 101.2 | 103.7 |
| Active Mobile-Broadband Subscriptions per 100 inhabitants (%) | | 66.9 | 70.4 | 76.8 | 85.2 |
| Percentage of population covered by a mobile-cellular network per 100 inhabitants (%) | | 96.8 | 97.1 | 97.2 | 97.4 |
| 3G and above mobile network coverage (%) | | 91.3 | 92.8 | 94.7 | 94.9 |
| 4G and above mobile network coverage (%) | | 74 | 80.6 | 85.7 | 86.9 |
| 5G and above mobile network coverage (%) | | 8.5 | 9.7 | 10.9 | 12.7 |
| Mobile phone penetration rate (%) | | 82.1 | 82.7 | 82.8 | 83.1 |

Note: The data in Table 7.1 are defined as follows: Fixed Telephone Subscriptions per 100 inhabitants (%) measures the ratio of fixed telephone line users per 100 people, indicating the penetration level of fixed-line networks. Mobile Cellular Subscriptions per 100 inhabitants (%) quantifies the number of active SIM cards per 100 people; this value may surpass 100% (owing to multiple SIM ownership) and serves as an indicator of mobile service adoption. Fixed-broadband subscriptions per 100 inhabitants (%) represents the proportion of fixed broadband users per 100 people, demonstrating the deployment of wired internet infrastructure. Active mobile-broadband subscriptions per 100 inhabitants (%) assesses the share of users actively engaging with mobile data services, reflecting mobile internet adoption rates. Percentage of population covered by a mobile-cellular network per 100 inhabitants (%) denotes the percentage of residents within 2G/3G/4G/5G network coverage areas, illustrating the maturity of mobile infrastructure. This metric has shown progressive improvement alongside 5G network expansion.

Source: Compiled from the latest available data in the ITU Statistics Database 2024.

153

Meanwhile, the Arab region continues to face a substantial digital divide, particularly in urban-rural access and gender parity. In urban-rural differentiation, the Internet penetration rate reaches 82.9% in urban areas, matching the global average; while the rural access stands at 50.1%, exceeding the global rural average of 47.5%. For gender parity, female Internet access is 64.4%, slightly below the global female average of 65.3%, whereas male access reaches 75.1%, outperforming the 69.5% global male benchmark. Collectively, these metrics reveal structural challenges in multiple dimensions of digital inclusion, especially in adopting advanced networks and ensuring equal digital access. Additionally, the region's Internet users are predominantly young: youth penetration hit 86.1% in 2024, far exceeding the 66.7% rate among other age groups and surpassing corresponding global averages of 78.5% and 65.6%. This underscores younger generations' pivotal role in driving the region's digital transformation.

Broadband affordability[1] is a key measure of ICT advancement. As documented in the ITU's *Measuring Digital Development: Facts and Figures 2024*[2] report, mobile broadband costs (2GB) accounted for 0.8% of per capita Gross National Income (GNI) in the Arab region during 2024, below the global benchmark of 1.1% and showing a year-on-year decrease. Conversely, fixed broadband services (5GB) represented 3.2% of per capita GNI, exceeding the 2.5% global standard with no improvement from the previous year. This contrast highlights progress in mobile broadband accessibility while revealing persistent fixed broadband affordability challenges that hinder comprehensive digital inclusion and equitable access.

2. National Level

The ITU's *Measuring Digital Development: ICT Development Index 2024*[3] documents significant divergences in ICT advancement across Arab states (Table 7.2), highlighting multidimensional digital divides. Regarding Internet penetration rates, Djibouti, Mauritania, Somalia and Yemen register below the global median

---

① The United Nations Broadband Commission (UNBC) advocates achieving internet affordability through its target of limiting basic broadband service costs to ≤2% of a nation's per capita gross national income (GNI per capita).

② ITU, "Measuring digital development Facts and Figures 2024," https://www.itu.int/en/ITU-D/Statistics/Pages/facts/default.aspx.

③ ITU, "Measuring digital development The ICT Development Index 2024," https://www.itu.int/en/ITU-D/Statistics/Pages/facts/default.aspx.

Chapter 7　Special Report on China-Arab States Digital Economy Cooperation

of 69.3%, with Tunisia, Egypt, and Algeria additionally falling short of China's benchmark of 75.6%. Household internet penetration presents similar patterns: Djibouti, Tunisia, and Somalia underperform the global threshold of 70.1%, while Algeria and Egypt trail China's standard of 81.2%. Mobile broadband penetration reveals more acute divides, as Mauritania, Jordan, Egypt, Iraq, Djibouti, Yemen, Syria, Palestine, and Somalia all remain below the global average of 84.3%, whereas Algeria, Morocco, and Tunisia lag behind China's level of 107.8%. Technological disparities persist across network generations. In 3G+ network coverage, Djibouti, Yemen, Somalia, Palestine, and Mauritania cluster below the global median of 90.5%, contrasting sharply with all six GCC member states (UAE, Bahrain, Kuwait, Qatar, Saudi Arabia, Oman) that surpass China's 99.9% penetration rate. The 4G adoption gap proves particularly stark: while Bahrain, Kuwait, and Saudi Arabia exceed China's 99.9% benchmark, Djibouti, Syria, Yemen, Mauritania, Somalia, and Palestine remain below the global average of 81.1%. Mobile cellular subscription rates further underscore these divides, with Palestine, Djibouti, Iraq, Mauritania, Yemen, and Somalia failing to meet either the global median (79.7%) or Chinese standard (83%).

Table 7.2　ICT Fundamentals in the Arab States and China in 2024

| Country | Internet penetration (%) | Household Internet penetration (%) | Mobile broadband penetration (%) | 3G and above mobile network penetration (%) | 4G and above mobile network penetration (%) | Mobile phone penetration (%) |
|---|---|---|---|---|---|---|
| Algeria | 71.2 † | 80.6 † | 99.7 | 98.1 | 85.9 | 85.9 † |
| Bahrain | 100 | 100 | 157.6 | 100 | 100 | 100 |
| Djibouti | 65.0 † | 68.4 † | 35.6 | 90 | 76 | 74.4 † |
| Egypt | 72.2 | 73.2 | 64.8 | 99.7 | 98 | 97.4 |
| Iraq | 78.7 | 88.7 | 46.2 | 98.2 | 96.6 | 65.7 |
| Jordan | 90.5 | 92.2 | 67.6 | 99.8 | 99.8 | 91.1 † |
| Kuwait | 99.7 | 99.4 | 151.5 | 100 | 100 | 99.2 |
| Libya | 88.4 † | n.a. | 125.6 | 93.5 | 90 | 89.1 † |
| Mauritania | 44.4 † | n.a. | 73.4 | 43.9 | 34.7 ‡ | 61.3 † |
| Morocco | 89.9 | 87.4 | 88.6 | 99.5 | 99.4 | 96.5 |
| Oman | 97.8 † | 97.1 † | 115.9 | 100 | 99 | 97.8 † |
| Palestine | 88.6 | 92.3 | 21.9 | 58.3 | 0 | 79.2 |

155

**Continued**

| Country | Internet penetration (%) | Household Internet penetration (%) | Mobile broadband penetration (%) | 3G and above mobile network penetration (%) | 4G and above mobile network penetration (%) | Mobile phone penetration (%) |
|---|---|---|---|---|---|---|
| Qatar | 99.7 ‡ | 95.0 ‡ | 144 | 100 | 99.8 | 99.6 ‡ |
| Saudi Arabia | 100 | 100 | 126 | 100 | 100 | 100 |
| Somalia | 19.9 † | 11.9 ‡ | 2.6 | 70 | 30 | 18.9 † |
| Syria | n.a. | n.a. | 21.9 | 98.9 | 75.7 | n.a. |
| Tunisia | 73.8 † | 57.0 † | 85.8 | 99 | 95 | 87.9 † |
| UAE | 100 | 100 | 234.9 | 100 | 99.8 | 100 |
| Yemen | 17.7 † | n.a. | 29.2 | 73.7 | 45 | 34.6 † |
| China | 75.6 | 81.2 † | 107.8 | 99.9 | 99.9 | 83† |

Note: "†" denotes ITU estimates; "‡" represents lagged values up to 2021; "n.a." indicates missing values.

Source: Compiled from *Measuring Digital Development: ICT Development Index 2024*.

In addition, according to the *Speedtest Global Index*[①], updated by Speedtest in December 2024, 110 countries were evaluated for mobile network speeds and 154 for fixed broadband speeds. Within the Arab region, performance varies markedly (Table 7.3). The UAE emerges as the region's sole representative in the global top 10 for both mobile and fixed broadband metrics. Qatar, Kuwait, and Saudi Arabia secure positions within the top 50 worldwide. Granular analysis reveals that the six GCC states (UAE, Qatar, Kuwait, Bahrain, Saudi Arabia, Oman) achieve mobile network download throughput rates substantially exceeding the global mean of 62.79 Mbps. Notably, the UAE, Qatar, and Kuwait register speeds surpassing China's national benchmark of 147.14 Mbps. In fixed broadband performance, while the UAE, Qatar, Kuwait, Saudi Arabia, Oman, and Jordan all surpass the global average of 96.45 Mbps, only the UAE's 230.11

---

① The Speedtest Global Index, maintained by Ookla, is a monthly benchmarking system that assesses and compares fixed broadband and mobile network performance across global territories. Aggregating data from billions of user-initiated tests on the Speedtest platform, the index provides real-time insights into worldwide connectivity trends. It enables comparative analysis of national rankings through core metrics including download/upload speeds and network latency. For current median speed data (updated December 2024), refer to: Ookla, *Speedtest Global Index*, https: //www. speedtest.net/global-index.

Chapter 7    Special Report on China-Arab States Digital Economy Cooperation

Mbps rate outperforms China's standard. Overall, while GCC nations dominate mobile connectivity and demonstrate competitive fixed broadband performance, a notable gap persists between most GCC nations and China's advanced infrastructure—with the UAE as a standout exception.

**Table 7.3    Internet Speed and Rankings of Arab States and China in 2024**

| Country | Mobile networks | | Fixed broadband | | Country | Mobile networks | | Fixed broadband | |
| | Download Speed /Mbps | World Ranking | Download Speed /Mbps | World Ranking | | Download Speed /Mbps | World Ranking | Download Speed /Mbps | World Ranking |
| --- | --- | --- | --- | --- | --- | --- | --- | --- | --- |
| UAE | 453.87 | 1 | 304.24 | 3 | Egypt | 24.2 | 92 | 77.89 | 80 |
| Qatar | 383.5 | 2 | 185.08 | 26 | Algeria | 23.09 | 95 | 15.65 | 140 |
| Kuwait | 257.3 | 3 | 192.99 | 23 | Libya | 16.83 | 104 | 10.44 | 147 |
| Bahrain | 130.74 | 12 | 86.61 | 69 | Syria | 13.23 | 107 | 3.38 | 153 |
| Saudi Arabia | 129.16 | 14 | 120.41 | 44 | Mauritania | n.a. | n.a. | 23.16 | 129 |
| Oman | 94.46 | 28 | 80.36 | 75 | Somalia | n.a. | n.a. | 18.53 | 134 |
| Morocco | 45.67 | 64 | 35.57 | 116 | Djibouti | n.a. | n.a. | 18.15 | 135 |
| Iraq | 38.04 | 71 | 33.58 | 118 | Yemen | n.a. | n.a. | 10.12 | 148 |
| Lebanon | 31.81 | 83 | 13.11 | 145 | Palestine | n.a. | n.a. | 65.17 | 92 |
| Jordan | 30.57 | 84 | 162.74 | 34 | China | 147.14 | 8 | 230.11 | 14 |
| Tunisia | 27.12 | 90 | 11.72 | 146 | | | | | |

Note: "n.a." indicates missing values.

Source: Compiled from SPEEDTEST.

## 7.1.2    Soft Power in Digital Economy Development: Assessing Innovation Potential, Human Capital, and Scientific Capacity

Innovation potential constitutes the primordial driver of digitally-enabled sustainable development, governing the penetration gradient and application spectrum of technological integration across industrial ecosystems. Sustained technological breakthroughs not only accelerate sectoral digital transformation but fundamentally also reconfigure national competitive architectures within the global digital economy. Simultaneously, human capital emerges as the critical

157

The Development Process of China-Arab States Economic and Trade Relations
Annual Report 2024

transmission mechanism for innovation diffusion, with its strategic development now constituting determinant factors for a nation's technological innovation capacity and global competitiveness in the digital age. Therefore, this section evaluates the soft power underpinning Arab states' digital economy development from two dimensions: innovation potential and human capital.

The *Global Innovation Index (GII),* published annually by the World Intellectual Property Organization (WIPO), evaluates national innovation capabilities and performance. The *GII 2024*[①] edition classifies 133 economies into four performance clusters: Cluster 1 (positions 1-33), Cluster 2 (34-66), Cluster 3 (67-99), and Cluster 4 (100-133). As per the *GII* benchmarking methodology (Table 7.4), the UAE emerges as the sole Arab economy in Cluster 1, attaining the 32nd global position. However, this ranking remains substantially behind China's 11th position in the same cluster. Within Cluster 2, Saudi Arabia, Qatar, and Morocco represent Arab participation, while most of Arab economies are concentrated in Clusters 3 and 4. As research and innovation form the cornerstone of digital economic advancement, Arab economies in Clusters 1 and 2 have intensified R&D investments in recent years to bolster technological prowess and narrow developmental disparities with innovation frontrunners.

Table 7.4   Innovation Capacity Rankings of Arab States and China (2024)
(Based on Global Innovation Index & Human Capital
and Research Index)

| Country | Global Innovation Index | Human Capital and Research Index | Country | Global Innovation Index | Human Capital and Research Index |
|---|---|---|---|---|---|
| UAE | 32 | 17 | Oman | 74 | 66 |
| Saudi Arabia | 47 | 33 | Tunisia | 81 | 47 |
| Qatar | 49 | 48 | Egypt | 86 | 96 |
| Morocco | 66 | 81 | Lebanon | 94 | 59 |

---

① WIPO, "Global Innovation Index 2024," https://www.wipo.int/web-publications/global-innovation-index-2024/assets/67729/2000%20Global%20Innovation%20Index%202024_WEB3lite.pdf.

Chapter 7  Special Report on China-Arab States Digital Economy Cooperation

**Continued**

| Country | Global Innovation Index | Human Capital and Research Index | Country | Global Innovation Index | Human Capital and Research Index |
|---------|------------------------|----------------------------------|---------|------------------------|----------------------------------|
| Kuwait | 71 | 53 | Algeria | 115 | 76 |
| Bahrain | 72 | 75 | Mauritania | 126 | 120 |
| Jordan | 73 | 85 | China | 11 | 22 |

Dat source: Compiled from *Global Innovation Index 2024*.

The Human Capital and Research Index of the *GII* measures basic education, higher education, and R&D capabilities. According to the latest assessment, Arab states collectively exhibit limited progress, with human capital levels stagnating near prior-year benchmarks. The UAE is the only country in the Arab region surpassing China in the 2024 global rankings.

### 7.1.3  Digital Economy Applications: E-Government as an Example

The deep integration of the digital economy provides an important opportunity for the digitization of government services, while the evolution of e-government reciprocally accelerates digital economic growth. As digital technologies advance, Arab states are actively transitioning toward data-driven administrative models. By prioritizing investments in e-government infrastructure, these countries aim to enhance administrative efficiency and public service delivery.

To evaluate global progress in digital governance, the United Nations Department of Economic and Social Affairs (UNDESA) has published the *E-Government Development Index* (EGDI) biennially since 2001, encompassing all 193 UN member countries. The EGDI serves as a composite metric assessing three dimensions: e-government infrastructure, online service levels and public engagement. Widely recognized as a benchmark for governmental digital capacity, it employs a scoring scale of 0 to 1, classifying nations into four tiers: countries with scores of 0.75 and above are categorized into the Very High subgroup (VH), which indicates that they are leading the world in the level of e-government development; countries with scores between 0.50 and 0.75 are categorized as High group (H), indicating that their e-government systems are relatively mature; countries with scores between 0.25 and 0.50 are categorized as

159

Medium group (M), indicating that their e-government is in a transitional stage; and countries with scores below 0.25 are categorized as Low group (L), reflecting the fact that their e-government construction is still at an initial stage.

The world average e-government development index has steadily increased alongside the global momentum toward digital governance. According to the *United Nations E-Government Survey 2024*[①], the index rose from 0.610 in 2022 to 0.638 in 2024, reflecting intensified efforts by nations to modernize digital infrastructure and enhance service delivery. The Arab region has mirrored this upward trajectory in e-government development (Table 7.5). 13 Arab countries now rank within the High or Very High development subgroups, with 10 exceeding the global average score. Notably, only Saudi Arabia, the UAE, and Bahrain surpass China's e-government development index of 0.872. An analysis of Arab states' progress from 2022 to 2024 reveals divergent trends: 15 countries improved their global rankings, with Libya (+44), Bahrain (+36), Saudi Arabia (+25), and Qatar (+25) achieving the most notable advancements. 7 countries experienced declines, underscoring persistent challenges in the process of e-government development. Subgroup shifts further highlight regional disparities: Qatar and Kuwait ascended from the High to Very High subgroup, Libya advanced from the Medium to High subgroup, while Yemen regressed from the Medium to Low subgroup. These dynamics illustrate a widening polarization in e-government maturity across the Arab region, driven by uneven policy execution and institutional capacity.

**Table 7.5   E-Government Development Index - Rankings and Changes in Arab States and China in 2024**

| Country | E-Government Development Index | Rating Class | Change in Rating | Ranking | Change in Ranking |
|---|---|---|---|---|---|
| Saudi Arabia | 0.960 | VH | — | 6 | ↑25 |
| UAE | 0.953 | VH | — | 11 | ↑2 |
| Bahrain | 0.920 | VH | — | 18 | ↑36 |
| Oman | 0.858 | VH | — | 41 | ↑9 |
| Qatar | 0.824 | VH | ↑ | 53 | ↑25 |

① UN Department of Economic and Social Affairs: UN E-Government Survey 2024, https: // publicadministration.un.org/egovkb/en-us/Reports/UN-E-Government-Survey-2024.

# Chapter 7  Special Report on China-Arab States Digital Economy Cooperation

**Continued**

| Country | E-Government Development Index | Rating Class | Change in Rating | Ranking | Change in Ranking |
|---|---|---|---|---|---|
| Kuwait | 0.781 | VH | ↑ | 66 | ↓5 |
| Tunisia | 0.694 | H | — | 87 | ↑1 |
| Jordan | 0.685 | H | — | 89 | ↑11 |
| Morocco | 0.684 | H | — | 90 | ↑11 |
| Egypt | 0.670 | H | — | 95 | ↑8 |
| Algeria | 0.596 | H | — | 116 | ↓4 |
| Libya | 0.547 | H | ↑ | 125 | ↑44 |
| Lebanon | 0.545 | H | — | 126 | ↓4 |
| Iraq | 0.457 | M | — | 148 | ↓2 |
| Syria | 0.389 | M | — | 162 | ↓6 |
| Mauritania | 0.349 | M | — | 165 | ↑7 |
| Djibouti | 0.291 | M | — | 174 | ↑7 |
| Sudan | 0.276 | M | — | 178 | ↓2 |
| Comoros | 0.259 | M | — | 180 | ↑2 |
| Yemen | 0.232 | L | ↓ | 185 | ↓7 |
| Somalia | 0.147 | L | — | 191 | ↑1 |
| China | 0.872 | VH | — | 35 | ↑8 |

Note: "↑" indicates an increase, "↓" indicates a decrease, and "—" indicates no change.

Data source: *United Nations E-Government Survey Report 2024*.

## 7.1.4  Market Support for Digital Economy Development: Digital Industry and High-Tech Manufacturing as an Example

While national digital capabilities (both hard and soft power) primarily gauge domestic progress, the cross-border trade of digital industries—particularly the global exchange of high-tech goods and ICT services—serves as a cornerstone for advancing the globalization and sustainability of the digital economy. Such trade not only bridges domestic and international markets but also accelerates technological innovation and industrial transformation. From the import perspective, the introduction of advanced high-tech products and ICT services

161

# The Development Process of China-Arab States Economic and Trade Relations Annual Report 2024

not only enhances the competitiveness of the domestic digital industry, but also promotes the in-depth integration of digital technology and traditional industries, and improves the overall level of industrial upgrading. And from the export perspective, expanding the international market layout not only helps to enhance a country's influence in the global digital economy, but also accelerates the internationalization of the digital economy. According to the *Global Innovation Index 2024*, Arab states exhibit stark disparities in high-tech and ICT trade (Table 7.6). The top five countries in terms of the share of imports of high-tech products in trade are the UAE, Algeria, Tunisia, Lebanon, and Saudi Arabia, but these countries are all lower than China. The top five countries in terms of the share of exports of high-tech products in trade are the UAE, Tunisia, Morocco, Lebanon and Oman, which also lag behind China. For ICT service imports, Qatar, Bahrain, the UAE, Oman and Egypt ranked in the top five, with the top three ahead of China. For ICT service exports, Kuwait, Bahrain, Morocco, Egypt and the UAE ranked in the top five, with the top three also ahead of China.

**Table 7.6  Share of Digital Trade and High-Tech Manufacturing in Arab States and China in 2024**

| Country | High-tech imports to total trade (%) | | High-tech exports to total trade (%) | | ICT services imports to total trade (%) | | ICT services exports to total trade (%) | | High-tech manufacturing to total manufacturing (%) | |
|---|---|---|---|---|---|---|---|---|---|---|
| | Share/% | Ranking | Share/% | Ranking | Share/% | Ranking | Share/% | Ranking | Share/% | Ranking |
| UAE | 12.8 | 20 | 9.4 | 21 | 1.1 | 70 | 1.7 | 63 | 20 | 62 |
| Saudi Arabia | 8.2 | 68 | 0.8 | 83 | 0.7 | 99 | 0.5 | 100 | 26.3 | 47 |
| Qatar | 4.2 | 118 | 0.3 | 101 | 1.6 | 45 | 1 | 82 | 40.9 | 25 |
| Kuwait | 4.7 | 111 | 0.2 | 111 | 0.1 | 131 | 5.6 | 18 | 20.9 | 59 |
| Bahrain | 3.2 | 128 | 1 | 79 | 1.5 | 54 | 3.9 | 28 | 9.8 | 88 |
| Oman | 4.1 | 120 | 1.9 | 66 | 1 | 80 | 0.4 | 104 | 16.5 | 71 |
| Morocco | 7.2 | 86 | 2.1 | 57 | 0.9 | 88 | 3.2 | 36 | 39.9 | 27 |
| Jordan | 1.2 | 71 | 7.2 | 82 | 0.1 | 125 | 0.2 | 125 | 17.7 | 67 |
| Tunisia | 8.4 | 63 | 4.2 | 42 | 0.6 | 106 | 1.7 | 64 | 21.9 | 55 |
| Egypt | 4.8 | 110 | 0.7 | 85 | 0.9 | 83 | 2 | 57 | 18.5 | 63 |

162

Chapter 7    Special Report on China-Arab States Digital Economy Cooperation

**Continued**

| Country | High-tech imports to total trade (%) | | High-tech exports to total trade (%) | | ICT services imports to total trade (%) | | ICT services exports to total trade (%) | | High-tech manufacturing to total manufacturing (%) | |
|---|---|---|---|---|---|---|---|---|---|---|
| | Share/% | Ranking | Share/% | Ranking | Share/% | Ranking | Share/% | Ranking | Share/% | Ranking |
| Lebanon | 8.3 | 65 | 2 | 59 | 0.3 | 123 | 1.3 | 74 | 14.6 | 76 |
| Algeria | 10.4 | 35 | 0 | 131 | 0.3 | 119 | 0.2 | 126 | 4.1 | 101 |
| Mauritania | 1.9 | 131 | 0 | 130 | 0.5 | 107 | 0.2 | 122 | n/a | n/a |
| China | 19.9 | 8 | 26.3 | 1 | 1.1 | 72 | 2.4 | 52 | 48.4 | 11 |

Note: "n.a." indicates missing values.

Source: Compiled from *Global Innovation Index 2024*.

In addition, regarding the share of high-tech manufacturing in total manufacturing output, the top five Arab countries are Qatar, Morocco, Saudi Arabia, Tunisia, and Kuwait. While these nations rank within the global top 60, their collective performance remains below China's benchmark, underscoring the limited production capacity of high-tech manufacturing as a critical bottleneck to the digital industry's trade competitiveness in the Arab region. From a digital economy perspective, this underdeveloped sector not only undermines the global competitiveness of digital products and services but also impedes advancements in digital infrastructure, digital transformation, and smart industries, thereby diminishing the overall quality of the digital economy. To address these challenges, boosting R&D investments in high-tech sectors and accelerating the digitalization of manufacturing processes have emerged as strategic imperatives for Arab states to strengthen their foothold in the global digital economy.

## 7.2    China-Arab States Cooperation in the Digital Economy

Since the launch of the *"Digital Silk Road"* initiative in 2016, China-Arab states cooperation in the digital economy has deepened significantly, with collaboration steadily broadening to encompass diverse domains such as digital infrastructure, e-commerce, digital governance and talent development, forming an extensive cooperation network.

163

## The Development Process of China-Arab States Economic and Trade Relations Annual Report 2024

### 7.2.1 Policy and Mechanism Development

As the China-Arab states digital economy cooperation mechanism has steadily matured, collaboration has transitioned from conceptual policy initiatives to institutionalized frameworks, laying down institutional guarantees for long-term cooperation.

1. Policy Initiative Phase: Establishing Cooperation Frameworks

In 2017, China, the UAE, Saudi Arabia, and partner nations launched the *"The Belt and Road" Digital Economy International Cooperation Initiative* at the Fourth World Internet Conference, establishing foundational policy guidelines for bilateral digital collaboration[1]. In 2018, the Eighth Ministerial Meeting of the China-Arab States Cooperation Forum proposed advancing the Digital Silk Road, with a focus on joint investments in network infrastructure, big data, cloud computing, and e-commerce.[2] In 2020, the Ninth Ministerial Meeting of the Forum adopted the *2020-2022 Action Plan*, explicitly integrating digital economy cooperation with scientific innovation and cultural exchange programs[3]. In 2021, China and Arab states co-published the *China-League of Arab States Cooperation Initiative on Data Security*, underscoring shared commitments to developing digital governance standards, enhancing data security protocols and building a collaborative cyberspace governance model. This initiative reflects the strategic alignment and shared responsibility of both parties in addressing global digital challenges.[4]

2. Institutionalization Phase: Strengthening Cooperation Frameworks

Since 2022, China-Arab states cooperation has advanced to a higher level of development. China held the first China-Arab States Summit and the first China-Gulf Cooperation Council (GCC) Summit with Arab countries and GCC countries respectively, propelling bilateral economic partnerships

---

[1] "Multinational Co-Sponsored 'Belt & Road' Digital Economy International Cooperation Initiative," Xinhua Net, http://www.xinhuanet.com/zgjx/2017-12/04/c_136798586.htm, December 4, 2017.

[2] Xi Jinping: "Working Together to Advance China-Arab States Strategic Partnership in the New Era," People's Daily, July 11, 2018, p.2.

[3] "China-Arab States Cooperation Forum: 2020-2022 Action Implementation Plan," Development and Research Center of China-Arab States Reform, http://infadm.shisu.edu.cn/_s114/07/09/c7779a132873/page.psp, August 19, 2018.

[4] "China-League of Arab States Cooperation Initiative on Data Security," https://www.mfa.gov.cn/web/ziliao_674904/1179_674909/202103/t20210329_9180823.shtml, March 29, 2021.

164

Chapter 7    Special Report on China-Arab States Digital Economy Cooperation

towards structured and institutionalized growth. The first China-Arab States Summit underscored the significance of advancing the digital economy, aerospace, and other emerging sectors. Within the framework of the "Eight Joint Actions" for practical collaboration, commitments were made to establish joint laboratories or R&D centers in artificial intelligence, information communication, spatial information, etc. Furthermore, efforts were pledged to deepen the implementation of *China-League of Arab States Cooperation Initiative on Data Security*, while intensifying cooperation and dialogues in the realms of cybersecurity and data governance.[1] The first China-GCC Summit, on the other hand, concentrated on investment collaboration within the realms of the digital economy and sustainable development. This summit advocated for the establishment of bilateral investment and economic cooperation mechanisms, bolstering cooperation on digital currencies, and advancing initiatives such as 5G and 6G technologies, cross-border e-commerce, and communication network infrastructures.[2] Notably, China and Saudi Arabia solidified their ties by signing a comprehensive strategic partnership agreement, which explicitly prioritizes deepening investment cooperation in the digital economy and e-commerce sector.[3]

2024 is the 20th anniversary of the establishment of the China-Arab States Cooperation Forum, and it is also a significant juncture for the deepening of digital economy cooperation between the two sides. On May 30, the 10th ministerial conference of the China-Arab States Cooperation Forum was held in Beijing. The conference proposed the "five cooperation frameworks" to further solidify the partnership in the field of digital economy, especially in areas such as artificial intelligence and e-commerce.[4]

---

[1]  "Xi Jinping Proposes 'Eight Common Actions' for China-Arab States Practical Cooperation at First China-Arab States Summit," the Central People's Government of People's Republic of China, https://www.gov.cn/xinwen/2022-12/10/ content_ 5731138.htm, December 11, 2022.

[2]  "President Xi Jinping Attends First China-GCC Summit and Delivers Keynote Speech," People's Daily, December 11, 2022, p.1.

[3]  "China, Saudi Arabia issue joint statement," the Central People's Government of People's Republic of China, https://www.gov.cn/xinwen/2022-12/10/content_5731174.htm, December 11, 2022.

[4]  "President Xi Jinping attends the opening ceremony of the 10th ministerial conference of the China-Arab States Cooperation Forum and delivers a keynote speech," the Central People's Government of People's Republic of China, https://www.gov.cn/yaowen/liebiao/202405/content_6954536.htm, Mgy 30, 2024.

## 7.2.2 Digital Infrastructure Construction

The substantial digital population dividend in Arab states offers an expansive market for digital infrastructure collaboration, serving as a pivotal accelerator for China-Arab states cooperation. Progress in joint endeavors encompassing 5G communication, cloud computing, and smart city initiatives has been robust, furnishing substantial backing for the advancement of the digital economy within Arab states.

The deployment of 5G communication networks. Chinese enterprises have played a pivotal role in establishing 5G networks in Arab states, particularly in the Gulf region. For instance, Huawei has forged numerous 5G cooperation agreements with Saudi Arabia and completed the first 5GLAN project.[1] Additionally, partnerships with UAE operator du have propelled initiatives like the "5G-A Smart Home" project, contributing significantly to the realization of smart cities and innovative 5G technology applications.[2] Moreover, Chinese corporations, at the forefront of the global digital economy, are actively diversifying their digital business models in the Middle East. They are intensifying collaborations in the realm of 5.5G technology and jointly working towards constructing an "information bridge" to facilitate economic and trade interactions between China and Arab states.

Establishment of cloud computing and big data centers. As digital transformation gains momentum, the construction of cloud computing centers and big data centers has emerged as a crucial foundation of the digital economy in Arab states. In recent years, Chinese enterprises have proactively expanded cloud service infrastructure in the Middle East, providing robust backing for the local digital economy. For instance, Tencent Cloud has set up a data center in Bahrain, contributing to the establishment of a cloud service hub in the Middle East to address the digital advancement requirements of local businesses.[3]

---

[1] "Huawei Facilitates Zain's Completion of MENA's First 5G LAN Project," Huawei Official Website, https://www.huawei.com/cn/news/2022/3/first-5g-lan-in-mena, March 7, 2022.

[2] "du and Huawei Unveil World's First '5G-A Smart Family'," Huawei Official Website, https://www.huawei.com/cn/news/2023/10/mbbf2023-5gafamily, October 9, 2023.

[3] "Tencent Cloud Announces Bahrain Data Center, Accelerating Global Expansion," China Daily, https://cnews.chinadaily.com.cn/a/202103/01/WS603c85f6a3101e7ce974177c.html, March 1, 2021.

Chapter 7    Special Report on China-Arab States Digital Economy Cooperation

Ali Cloud, in collaboration with local entities, has initiated a cloud computing venture, with plans to establish multiple data centers in Saudi Arabia, positioning Riyadh as a regional hub for management and training.[1] Huawei, on the other hand, is amplifying its cloud service network by setting up data centers in Saudi Arabia to support the government's digital transformation endeavors and foster the deployment of Arabic-language artificial intelligence application.[2] Furthermore, through a partnership with Emirates Telecommunications Corporation, Huawei is establishing a domestic cloud infrastructure, offering tailored cloud services and cutting-edge technologies to local enterprises. This initiative aids small and medium-sized enterprises (SMEs) in harnessing big data, AI, and IoT technologies to lower the barriers to innovation.[3] The involvement of Chinese corporations has significantly advanced the landscape of cloud computing in North Africa. Egypt, notably, has inaugurated the first public cloud service in North Africa, bolstering the region's cloud computing capabilities and injecting fresh impetus into the digital economy's development across North African nations.[4]

## 7.2.3    Smart City Construction

Smart cities, integral to the construction of new infrastructure, play a pivotal role in driving urban digital transformation and fostering seamless information connectivity.[5] Chinese enterprises are actively engaged in the advancement of smart city projects across Arab states, spanning diverse domains including smart energy, governance, and digital governmental services. For instance, Huawei has partnered with the Saudi Smart City Solutions Company (SC2) to collaboratively

---

[1]  "Ali Cloud Establishes Saudi Joint Venture for Cloud Computing," Ministry of Commerce of China, http: //sa.mofcom.gov.cn/article/sqfb/202206/20220603319867.shtml, June 18,2022.

[2]  "Huawei Launches Cloud Data Center in Saudi Arabia to Support 200000 Developers in 5 Years," Sina.com, https: //k.sina.com.cn/article_1878726905_6ffb18f902001bkzg.html?from=finance, September 5, 2023.

[3]  "Huawei Partners with UAE Telecommunications Company to Build Local Cloud Infrastructure," Sohu Net, https: //www.sohu.com/a/732003550_99900524, October 28, 2023.

[4]  "Huawei Cloud Egypt Launches as North Africa's First Public Cloud," Huawei Official Website, https: //www.huaweicloud.com/news/2024/20240522173651457.html, May 22, 2024.

[5]  Zhou Jishun & Song Yanxi, "The Impact of New Infrastructure on Regional Exports: Evidence from National Smart City Pilots," *Industrial Economics Research*, 2022(05): 117.

167

advance smart city initiatives in Saudi Arabia.[1] Additionally, Huawei has contributed to enhancing the UAE's intelligence infrastructure in sectors like smart transportation, power grids, and housing. Pioneering the adoption of Narrowband Internet of Things (NB-IoT) technology in the Middle East, Huawei's efforts have bolstered the intelligence of city management, facilitated the integration of smart applications across industries such as healthcare, education, and finance, and expedited the smart city development process in Arab states.[2]

Moreover, the collaboration between China and Arab states in the realm of smart city development has garnered support from significant international platforms. In 2023, the first Digital Economy Empowers High-Quality Urban Development Forum was held in Beijing, focusing on smart city construction and digital economy advancement. The invaluable experiences derived from the smart city initiatives in Chinese urban centers offer insightful lessons for Arab states.[3] In October 2024, during the Digital Economy Industry Development Forum in Xi'an, the Arab Federation for Digital Economy and the Xi'an Municipal Government formalized their partnership by signing a memorandum of understanding. This agreement delineated the collaborative framework concerning digital skills development and smart city initiatives.[4] Subsequently, Dubai hosted a roundtable discussion in November on "Empowering High-quality Development and Urban Modernization with Digital Economy", aiming to bolster China-Arab states cooperation in areas such as smart grid technologies and artificial intelligence. This initiative aimed to infuse fresh impetus into the ongoing efforts to build advanced smart cities across the region.[5]

---

[1] "Huawei and SC2 Collaborate on Saudi Smart City Project," Baidu News, https://baijiahao.baidu.com/s?id=1670917657561774548&wfr=spider&for=pc, June 30, 2020.

[2] "Huawei and UAE Partner to Develop Future Smart Cities," Huanqiu Tech, https://tech.huanqiu.com/article/9CaKrnJVvYy, May 17, 2016.

[3] "Digital Economy Empowers High-Quality Urban Development Forum," People's Daily Online, http://www.people.com.cn/n1/2023/0104/c363567-32599820.html, January 4, 2023.

[4] "The Arab Federation for Digital Economy participates in the Digital Economy Industry Development Forum in the Chinese city of Xi'an," Arab Federation for Digital Economy, https://arab-digital-economy.org/10581, October 31, 2024.

[5] "The roundtable on 'Empowering High-quality Development and Urban Modernization with Digital Economy' was held in Dubai," China-Arab States Cooperation Forum, https://www.chinaarabcf.org/zagx/wshz/202411/t20241120_11529771.htm, November 20, 2024.

Chapter 7    Special Report on China-Arab States Digital Economy Cooperation

## 7.2.4    Cross-border E-commerce Collaboration

In recent years, the partnership between China and Arab states in cross-border e-commerce has deepened, with Chinese e-commerce platforms exerting a growing influence in the Arab market. Alibaba's AliExpress, Shein, Temu and TikTok Shop have expedited their presence in the Middle East market, stimulating the transformation of local digital consumption patterns. Notably, TikTok Shop has captured a significant market share in the UAE and Saudi Arabia, while live e-commerce has swiftly emerged, propelling the advancement of social e-commerce and content-driven online retail. This development has become a key focal point for digital retail growth in the region, further enhancing the digital economy ecosystem. Meanwhile, Chinese logistics enterprises are intensifying their expansion into the Middle East market to offer efficient logistics support for cross-border e-commerce operations. Companies like J&T Express and iMile are actively establishing localized warehousing and distribution networks, enhancing logistics efficiency, optimizing cross-border e-commerce supply chains, and catalyzing the high-quality advancement of China-Arab states cross-border e-commerce collaborations.

Furthermore, collaboration between China and Arab states in the realm of digital payments is steadily maturing. Electronic payment systems in the UAE, Saudi Arabia, and other countries within the region have seen gradual enhancements, with Chinese fintech enterprises engaging in comprehensive partnerships with local banks and payment platforms. In 2022, Yiwu and Saudi Arabia achieved a milestone by completing the first cross-border RMB payment, advancing the progression of China-Arab states local currency settlement cooperation.[1] Subsequently, in 2023, the introduction of "Yiwu Pay" in the UAE further expedited the convergence of digital payment systems, augmenting the efficiency of cross-border transactions.[2] This environment has fostered the continuous expansion of China-Arab states cross-border

---

[1]    "Yiwu and Saudi Arabia Complete First Cross-Border RMB Payment Business, Ministry of Foreign Affairs: China-Arab States Economic and Trade Cooperation Continuously Steps Up to a New Level," China Daily: https://cn.chinadaily.com.cn/a/202212/09/WS6393057ba3102ada8b226067.html, December 9, 2022.

[2]    "First Dubai Cross-Border RMB Settlement Completed," Ministry of Commerce of China, http://ae.mofcom.gov.cn/article/ztdy/202403/20240303486777.shtml, March 2024.

169

e-commerce collaborations. In 2024, the third Global Digital Trade Expo took place in Hangzhou, featuring the Matchmaking Conference on International Cooperation in the Digital Economy. The event attracted the participation of over 20 countries, including Egypt, along with international entities like the League of Arab States and the United Nations. This gathering has advanced China-Arab states cooperation in digital trade, reinforcing the influence of both sides in global digital economy governance.[1] The rapid evolution of cross-border e-commerce underscores the ongoing deepening of China-Arab states cooperation in optimizing payment systems and facilitating trade. These efforts provide robust underpinning for mutual collaboration in the digital economy domain.

### 7.2.5 Exchange of Digital Expertise and Talent Development

In recent years, the collaboration between China and Arab states in digital governance has deepened, encompassing critical domains such as digital infrastructure, smart cities, and data security. Chinese enterprises have actively supported the digital transformation efforts in Arab states, facilitating the establishment of smart government services and technical standards, while Arab states have also drawn on China's expertise to expedite their digital governance initiatives. This collaboration has evolved from policy discussions to technology implementation, industrial partnerships, and talent cultivation, marking a notable escalation in cooperation levels. Against this background, in 2024, the 1st Belt and Road Policy Communication Workshop on Digital Governance in China and Arab states, organized by the Association of Arab Universities and other institutions, was held online. More than 40 Chinese and Arab experts engaged in in-depth exchanges on digital governance, data security and technology application, promoting the sharing of information and transfer of experience on public policies.[2] Moreover, the Middle East Session of the Global Digital Economy Conference, held in the UAE in May, attracted participation from Chinese and Arab governments, businesses, and experts. The event focused

---

[1] "2024 Hangzhou Digital Economy International Cooperation Matchmaking Conference: Share in the New Dividends Created by Digital Advancement," *Zhejiang Daily*, September 26, 2024, p.6.

[2] "IGPP Hosted the First 'the Belt and Road Policy Communication Workshop on Digital Governance in China and Ara'," Institute for Global Public Policy, Fudan University, https: //igpp.fudan.edu.cn/37/40/c18211a669504/page.htm, April 23, 2024.

Chapter 7    Special Report on China-Arab States Digital Economy Cooperation

on discussing digital economy development trends, fostering international cooperation, policy alignment, and fortifying the groundwork for collaboration in digital governance and technological innovation between the two sides.[1]

When it comes to nurturing digital talent, Huawei's Seeds of the Future initiative, initiated in 2008, has emerged as a pivotal platform for fostering ICT expertise in Arab states.[2] This program has been successfully rolled out in multiple countries, bolstering the local information and communications technology (ICT) talent pool and advancing the digital economy landscape. In Tunisia, since 2015, Huawei has signed ICT academy cooperation agreements with 72 universities, benefiting over 6800 students.[3] In Egypt, Huawei has established the Huawei ICT Academy, introduced the Seeds of the Future initiative and ICT skills competitions, and actively engaged in the Digital Egypt Builders initiative, cultivating a large number of local ICT professionals.[4] In 2022, Huawei partnered with the Saudi Digital Academy to train 8000 Saudi digital talents.[5] Furthermore, in 2024, Huawei expanded its collaboration in ICT and AI talent development in Saudi Arabia by signing a Memorandum of Understanding with the Saudi Arabian Data and Artificial Intelligence Authority (SDAIA). This initiative involved launching a series of training programs, fostering the dissemination of AI knowledge, and providing talent support for the sustainable growth of Saudi Arabia's digital economy.[6] To further enhance the cultivation of ICT talents in the region, Huawei has organized the

---

[1]  "Spotlight on Digital Economy Development: Advancing China-Arab States Cooperation—2024 Global Digital Economy Conference Middle East Sub-Forum Successfully Held," Beijing Municipal Bureau of Economy and Information Technology, https://jxj.beijing.gov.cn/jxdt/gzdt/202405/t20240529_3698061.html, May 29, 2024.

[2]  "Seeds of the Future 2.0, helping to develop ICT talent and inspire innovation," Huawei Official Website, https://www.huawei.com/cn/sustainability/the-latest/stories/seeds-cultivating-ict-talent-to-stimulate-innovation, April 12, 2024.

[3]  "Ambassador Zhang Jianguo Attended the Graduation Ceremony of Huawei Tunisia 2022 'Seeds of the Future' Program," Website of the Chinese Embassy in Tunisia, http://tn.china-embassy.gov.cn/sgxw/202211/t20221115_10974957.htm, November 14, 2022.

[4]  Guan Kejiang, "Countries in Middle East Advance Digital Economy Development," *People's Daily*, November 22, 2023, p.14.

[5]  "Saudi Digital Academy Signs Deal with Huawei to Develop Local Talents," http://www.china.org.cn/business/2022-02/04/content_78027315.htm, Feburary 4, 2022.

[6]  "Saudi Arabia and Huawei Collaborate on ICT/AI Training," Arab-China Institute for Economics and Policy, https://www.aciep.net/blog/archives/3471, September 20, 2024.

171

Middle East ICT Competition for many years, aimed at promoting local talent development and fortifying the ICT industry ecosystem.[1]

Meanwhile, China-Arab states youth exchanges in the realms of digital economy and technological innovation have gained momentum. Platforms like the World Youth Development Forum[2] and the China-Arab Youth Development Forum[3] have emerged as crucial arenas for fostering collaboration between the two sides in cultivating digital talent and advancing science and technology innovation. In November 2024, the China-Arab States Youth Development Forum was scheduled to take place in Haikou, Hainan Province, under the theme of "digital empowerment and fostering innovative development", to further promote the interaction between Chinese and Arab youths in the field of digital economy.[4]

## 7.3 The Future of China-Arab States Cooperation in the Digital Economy

Collaboration between China and Arab states in fostering digital economy cooperation will advance sustainable development for both economies while enhancing the openness, inclusivity, and mutual benefits of the global digital economy. This partnership contributes the collective wisdom and practices of China and Arab states to shaping the digital future of the community of human destiny.

First, the foundation for advancing digital economy collaboration lies in deepening policy alignment and constructing effective mechanisms. The

---

[1] "Middle East ICT Talent Cultivation and Education Summit & Huawei Middle East ICT Competition 2018 Finals Successfully Concluded," Huawei Official Website, https://www.huawei.com/cn/news/2018/11/huawei-middle-east-ict-talent-competition-2018, November 28, 2018.

[2] "The Thematic Forum for Digital Development of the 2023 World Youth Development Forum Launched in Beijing," China Youth Net, https://news.youth.cn/gj/202311/t20231101_14881126.htm, November 1, 2023.

[3] "Advancing Youth Development for a Prosperous Future: A Comprehensive Review of the China-Arab States Youth Development Forum," Xinhua News, https://www.xinhuanet.com/2023-12/07/c_1130013186.htm, December 7, 2023.

[4] "2024 China-Arab States Youth Development Forum Spotlights Digital Empowerment and Innovation," Xinhua News, https://www.news.cn/world/20241111/54f938d0140d47cfa7148a372ccb264d/c.html, November 11, 2024.

Chapter 7    Special Report on China-Arab States Digital Economy Cooperation

mechanisms for China-Arab states cooperation in the digital economy domain have seen continual enhancement, encompassing policy initiatives, institutional frameworks, and multi-tiered cooperation structures. Notably, in areas such as data governance, digital trade, and technical standards, both sides have established robust communication channels. China-Arab States summits have played a pivotal role in fostering strategic alignment in the digital economy realm and facilitating the realization of numerous cooperative ventures. Moving forward, it is imperative for both parties to further elevate the institutionalized policy coordination levels and refine existing cooperation mechanisms. Leveraging the China-Arab States Cooperation Forum, efforts should be made to catalyze the formulation of an *Action Plan for Digital Economy Cooperation*, fostering deeper alignment and collaboration on digital economy governance and trade regulations. Additionally, the two sides should actively explore the establishment of a China-Arab states joint committee on digital economy. This initiative can drive the mutual recognition of standards in critical areas such as cross-border data flows, privacy protection, and digital finance, while bolstering coordination and cooperation on digital economy governance matters within the global multilateral framework.

Second, digital infrastructure cooperation should be strengthened to consolidate the cornerstone of digital economy development. Digital infrastructure stands as a cornerstone for the high-quality progression of the digital economy. While Arab states have augmented investments in domains like 5G, cloud computing, and artificial intelligence, development across the region remains disparate, with certain countries trailing in digital infrastructure construction. Looking ahead, China and Arab states can deepen collaboration across various sectors to collectively enhance the regional digital economy framework. In the realms of 5G and cloud computing, Chinese enterprises have actively spearheaded initiatives to establish base stations and cloud computing centers in countries like Saudi Arabia and the UAE, fostering smart city development and industrial Internet growth. Both sides can broaden the reach of 5G networks, particularly in burgeoning markets such as Egypt, Morocco, and Jordan, amplifying the outreach of regional digital infrastructure. In the fields of artificial intelligence, big data and smart cities, the two sides can jointly establish research centers and laboratories to promote the application of emerging technologies and boost the intelligent upgrading of industries in Arab states,

173

especially deepening cooperation in landmark projects such as Saudi Arabia's NEOM Future City and UAE's Smart Dubai.

Third, advancing cross-border e-commerce cooperation for high-quality development and trade digitization. Cross-border e-commerce stands as a pivotal realm for China-Arab states digital economy collaboration. In the future, it is essential to refine the market structure, streamline logistics and payment systems, and bolster localized operational capabilities. China and Arab states should work towards enhancing the efficiency of goods circulation through Free Trade Agreements, overseas warehouses, and other resources. Exploring the establishment of a China-Arab states e-commerce free trade zone can help reduce logistics and tariff expenses, elevating trade facilitation levels. As the demand for digital payment escalates in Arab states, the scope of cross-border payment channels remains constrained. By leveraging digital payment systems such as Yiwu Pay's successful integration into the UAE in 2023, both sides can advance cross-border payment interoperability between the digital RMB and digital Dirham, augmenting digital cooperation. Facilitating the linkage between the digital RMB and digital Dirham for cross-border payments will enhance the convenience of digital financial collaboration, optimizing payment and settlement mechanisms. Moreover, with the burgeoning prominence of social e-commerce and live streaming models in the Arab region, there lies an opportunity for intensified cooperation in short-video e-commerce and social live streaming. This collaboration can propel cross-border e-commerce towards intelligence and personalization, fostering the expansion of innovative digital trade modalities.

Fourth, strengthen digital talent development and establish a sustainable mechanism for scientific and technological exchanges. The cultivation of digital talents serves as a fundamental pillar for China-Arab states digital economy cooperation and a vital driver for advancing regional digital transformation. China and Arab states can deepen collaboration in areas like joint university programs, cross-border e-commerce talent development, and industry-university partnerships to establish a comprehensive digital talent training framework. Encouraging the establishment of "digital economy colleges" through university partnerships can facilitate the cultivation of versatile digital professionals skilled in cutting-edge technologies such as artificial intelligence, blockchain, and big data. Given the rapid expansion of the Middle East's cross-border e-commerce landscape, setting up cross-border e-commerce training centers can

Chapter 7　Special Report on China-Arab States Digital Economy Cooperation

nurture localized talents adept at adapting to market dynamics and proficient in logistics and payment systems. Moreover, fostering the establishment of digital technology laboratories by Chinese enterprises in Arab states can drive collaborative research and development endeavors, augmenting the local pool of high-caliber technical talents. This initiative can propel the seamless integration of science, technology, and industry, fostering the high-quality evolution of digital economy cooperation.

Fifth, enhance digital governance cooperation and advance the evolution of the global digital economy governance framework. As the digital economy rapidly evolves, issues like data security, digital sovereignty, and AI ethics have garnered global attention. In this context, it is imperative for China and Arab states to collaborate in shaping global digital governance regulations, amplifying the voices of developing nations within the international digital economy framework. Strengthening cooperation in areas such as data security, cross-border data flow, privacy protection, and AI ethics can facilitate the joint establishment of a more transparent, secure, and trust-based digital governance system. The *China-League of Arab States Cooperation Initiative on Data Security*, unveiled in 2021 through the collaboration of China and Arab states, stands as a beacon for cooperation among developing nations on data security. Going forward, efforts should be directed towards further standardizing pertinent issues. In the fintech sector, both parties should explore collaborative opportunities in areas such as blockchain-based cross-border payment systems, jointly driving innovation and transformation within the digital financial infrastructure. These efforts aim to establish China-Arab states governance frameworks, providing institutional models for reshaping global digital economy governance.

175

# Chapter 8　Special Report on China-Arab States Science and Technology Cooperation

Since the inception of the Belt and Road Initiative (BRI), China-Arab states science and technology (S&T) cooperation has undergone a significant qualitative enhancement, emerging as a crucial pillar of bilateral collaboration, underpinned by aligned philosophies, harmonized policies, and interconnected platforms. The current momentum of China-Arab states S&T cooperation is decidedly positive, exhibiting characteristics of complementarity, pragmatism and comprehensiveness. Looking ahead, amidst the opportunities presented by the establishment of the China-Arab states "Five Major Cooperation Frameworks", S&T cooperation is not only a new direction and key focus for China-Arab states collaboration but will also be a source of new bilateral challenges and breakthroughs.

## 8.1　Strategic Foundations of China-ArabStates Science and Technology Cooperation

Since the launch of the Belt and Road Initiative (BRI), the engagement between China and Arab states has deepened significantly, propelling their bilateral relations to an unprecedented historical zenith. [1] In the shared pursuit of high-quality development, S&T cooperation has emerged as a critical underpinning of the joint construction of the BRI. Capitalizing on the

---

[1]　"Shared Future, Hand in Hand: A Look Back at the Second Anniversary of the First China-Arab States Summit," Central People's Government of the People's Republic of China website, www.gov.cn/yaowen/liebiao/202412/content_6994024.htm, Dec. 22, 2024.

Chapter 8    Special Report on China-Arab States Science and Technology Cooperation

opportunities presented by the BRI, bilateral S&T collaboration has intensified and become increasingly substantive, fostering a comprehensive, multi-tiered and multi-sectoral cooperation system that effectively addresses the "Five Connectivity" objectives of the BRI. The BRI has provided a strategic platform and collaborative framework, substantially bolstering and consolidating China-Arab states S&T cooperation. Furthermore, the "Digital Silk Road" has become a cornerstone a of China-Arab states connectivity. As the enabling effects of technology become increasingly pronounced, S&T cooperation is poised to be a promising arena and a novel growth driver for the joint pursuit of the BRI.

## 8.1.1    Ideological Alignment

The foundational principles of "consultation, contribution and shared benefits" between China and Arab states are continuously reinforced. As a strategic mechanism connecting the two sides, the Belt and Road Initiative (BRI) effectively facilitates ideological convergence, thereby strengthening the basis for mutual recognition in bilateral S&T cooperation. President Xi Jinping's 2013 proposal of the BRI resonated strongly with Arab states, reflecting a shared vision for development. In 2016, during his visit to the Arab League headquarters, Xi formally proposed the joint construction of the BRI, further solidifying this collaborative approach. Both sides recognize the BRI as a pivotal opportunity to deepen cooperation, achieve mutual benefits and pursue common development. In 2018, China and the Arab League signed the *Declaration of Action on China-Arab States Cooperation Under the Belt and Road Initiative*, marking a pioneering move for regional organizations. To date, China has signed BRI cooperation documents with 22 Arab states and the Arab League, implementing over 200 major collaborative projects that have positively impacted nearly 2 billion people. [1] As China and Arab states jointly capitalize on digital development opportunities and promote multifaceted collaboration in technological innovation, digital infrastructure, green energy and digital communication, S&T cooperation has emerged as a priority for Arab States' economic development, industrial transformation and technological

---

[1]    "The China-Arab States Cooperation Report in the New Era," Ministry of Foreign Affairs of the People's Republic of China website, https: //www.mfa.gov.cn/web/ziliao_674904/ zcwj_674915/202212/t20221201_10983991.shtml, December 1, 2022.

advancement. Through the BRI, both sides have achieved a "soft alignment" of development strategies at the level of development philosophies and guiding principles.

The pursuit of technological autonomy has emerged as a key point of convergence between China and Arab states. This shared aspiration drives bilateral scientific and technological (S&T) innovation towards achieving both national self-reliance and a multipolar global S&T landscape. Both parties recognize technological autonomy as essential for sustainable economic development, addressing global challenges and mitigating external dependency. China's strategic commitment to high-level technological self-reliance, evidenced by its successful independent innovation model—spanning human capital development, scientific advancement, industrial enhancement and economic and national strengthening[1]—aligns with the "science and technology-driven national development" frameworks adopted by numerous Arab nations, including Egypt, Saudi Arabia, the UAE and Kuwait. Furthermore, the Arab League provides regional guidance and frameworks for S&T innovation. Amidst rising global isolationism and technological protectionism, the establishment of a China-Arab states S&T community with a shared future, aimed at fostering national self-determination and a multipolar technological order, represents a mutual strategic objective. The Belt and Road Initiative (BRI) facilitates this collaboration, yielding mutually beneficial 'technological win-win' outcomes through joint R&D, S&T exchanges and technology transfer. Arab states have consistently demonstrated support for China's initiatives, such as the *International Science and Technology Cooperation Initiative* and the *Global Artificial Intelligence Governance Initiative*, by actively translating these proposals into concrete actions.[2] Driven by the BRI framework, guided by the imperative of 'science and technology-driven national development' and underpinned by the principle of 'achieving technological win-win, ' China and Arab states are making significant strides towards realizing a unified S&T community.

---

[1]  "Technological Modernization Is Key to Chinese-Style Modernization," *People's Daily Online*, http://politics.people.com.cn/n1/2024/0623/c1001-40262087.html, June 23, 2024.

[2]  Sun Degang, "Promoting the Construction of a China-Arab States Community of Common Destiny through a Shared Science and Technology Community," *Contemporary World*, no. 10 (2024).

Chapter 8    Special Report on China-Arab States Science and Technology Cooperation

## 8.1.2    Policy Support

The Belt and Road Initiative (BRI) has significantly bolstered China-Arab states economic and trade cooperation, cementing China's position as the Arab states' foremost trading partner for numerous consecutive years. From 2004 to 2023, China-Arab states trade volume surged from USD36.7 billion to over USD398 billion, demonstrating an average annual growth of 13%. This signifies a leapfrog development in China-Arab states economic and trade relations.[①] Simultaneously, the proportion of investment in their scientific and technological fields has steadily increased, continuously highlighting the growing importance of the bilateral S&T cooperation.

The BRI has significantly propelled extensive cooperation between China and participating Arab states across various domains, including S&T people-to-people exchanges, technology transfer and S&T innovation. Consequently, China-Arab states S&T cooperation has undergone institutionalization. In June 2014, during the Sixth Ministerial Conference of the China-Arab States Cooperation Forum, President Xi Jinping articulated the '1+2+3' cooperation framework for the joint construction of the BRI between China and Arab states. This framework designated energy cooperation as the primary axis, infrastructure development and trade and investment facilitation as the two supporting wings, and nuclear energy, aerospace satellite technology and new energy as the three high-tech sectors for breakthrough.[②] Notably, this marked the inaugural inclusion of scientific and technological cooperation as a key pillar in China-Arab states cooperation. In January 2016, China's first *Policy Paper on Arab States* emphasized the pragmatic advancement of bilateral cooperation in renewable energy, aerospace and civil nuclear energy, alongside the accelerated establishment of intergovernmental S&T innovation cooperation mechanisms.[③] The *Declaration*

---

① "China-Arab States Cooperation: Steady and Far-Reaching, Benefiting All Parties," *Guangming Daily*, news.gmw.cn/2024-05/31/content_37354903.htm, May 31, 2024.

② "Xi Jinping: Strengthening Top-Level Design and Building the '1+2+3' Cooperation Pattern Between China and Arab States," *Xinhua Net*, https: //jhsjk.people.cn/article/25109122, June 5, 2014.

③ "China's Policy Paper on Arab States (Full Text)," The Central People's Government of the People's Republic of China website, https: //www.gov.cn/xinwen/2016-01/13/content_5032647. htm, January 13, 2016.

179

*of Action on China-Arab States Cooperation Under the Belt and Road Initiative*, signed jointly by China and Arab states in July 2018, explicitly outlined key cooperation in the "Air Silk Road" the "Cyber Silk Road" and the construction of a "Belt and Road" space information corridor. This initiative seeks to foster a China-Arab states scientific and technological partnership through reciprocal collaboration in digital economy, information technology and satellite communication.[1] In December 2023, at the inaugural China-Arab States Summit, President Xi Jinping proposed the "Eight Major Joint Actions" for China-Arab states pragmatic cooperation. These actions specifically included science and technology cooperation, focusing on areas such as scientific and technological innovation, technology exchange and joint development.[2] Building upon this, the Tenth Ministerial Conference of the China-Arab States Cooperation Forum in 2024 introduced the "Five Major Cooperation Frameworks" to expedite the construction of a China-Arab states community with a shared future. Thus, evolving from a crucial component to a principal pillar, and now to a core driving force, China-Arab states S&T cooperation has ascended to become a primary engine in the joint construction of the BRI and the forging of a China-Arab states community with a shared future. The theme of "advancing through innovation" is poised to be a central motif in the future trajectory of China-Arab states relations.

### 8.1.3 Platform Support

The Belt and Road Initiative (BRI) has catalyzed a significant expansion of platforms dedicated to China-Arab states scientific and technological cooperation. Beyond the established China-Arab States Cooperation Forum, prominent platforms such as the China-Arab States Expo and the China-Arab States Technology Transfer Center have effectively underpinned the deepening and substantive progress of bilateral S&T collaboration.

---

[1] "The Declaration of Action on China-Arab States Cooperation Under the Belt and Road Initiative," China-Arab States Cooperation Forum website, https://www.chinaarabcf.org/chn/lthyjwx/bzjhywj/dbjbzjhy/201807/t20180713_6836934.htm, July 10, 2018.

[2] "Xi Jinping Proposes the 'Eight Major Joint Actions' for China-Arab States Pragmatic Cooperation at the First China-Arab States Summit," The Central People's Government of the People's Republic of China website, https://www.gov.cn/xinwen/2022-12/10/content_5731138.htm, December 10, 2022.

Chapter 8    Special Report on China-Arab States Science and Technology Cooperation

Since its inception, the China-Arab States Expo has consistently prioritized the showcasing and exchange of S&T innovation between China and Arab states, effectively cultivating a "government-led, enterprise-driven" model for their S&T partnership. Centering on themes such as agricultural technology, nuclear power technology and artificial intelligence, the Expo has successively hosted the China-Arab States Technology Transfer and Innovation Cooperation Conference and the High-Tech and Equipment Exhibition & Technology Achievement Matchmaking Fair, among other scientific and technological innovation exchange activities, across its six editions. These initiatives have effectively facilitated the deepening of China-Arab states S&T cooperation. Furthermore, the Expo has dedicated specific sessions to pivotal digital economy sectors, encompassing cloud computing, big data, digital governance, the "Internet Plus" initiative and 5G applications. These focused activities have substantially propelled the in-depth development of China-Arab states digital technology cooperation, effectively leveraging digital technologies to empower their S&T collaboration. Capitalizing on the strategic opportunities presented by the joint construction of the BRI and leveraging the China-Arab States Expo as a foundational platform, China-Arab states S&T cooperation has progressively developed a dynamic trajectory characterized by close interaction, in-depth exchange and demonstrably significant outcomes.

The China-Arab States Technology Transfer Center has also furnished a crucial platform for bilateral S&T engagement. Established in 2015 through a joint initiative of the Ministry of Science and Technology of the People's Republic of China and the People's Government of Ningxia Hui Autonomous Region, the Center has, over the years, focused its efforts on expanding China-Arab states technology transfer collaboration networks, establishing information service systems for technology transfer, cultivating international technology transfer professionals and connecting academic information platforms across Belt and Road Initiative participating countries. By actively promoting China-Arab states S&T exchanges, the Center has effectively fostered bilateral S&T cooperation. To date, the Center has conducted over 30 international training programs, nurturing more than 1400 international technology transfer professionals with a "seed" effect, and successfully co-established 8 bilateral national technology transfer centers, and built a technology transfer collaboration network linking nearly 5000 Chinese and foreign member institutions, thereby effectively

181

The Development Process of China-Arab States Economic and Trade Relations
Annual Report 2024

facilitating technology exchange, achievement transformation/commercialization and project implementation in China-Arab states S&T cooperation.[1]

## 8.2 Practical Progress in China-Arab States Science and Technology Cooperation

In 2024, China-Arab states science and technology (S&T) cooperation maintained a steady upward trajectory. Addressing the technological development imperatives of Arab countries, China and Arab nations engaged in close collaborative endeavors across diverse domains, including digital information, agricultural technology, energy technology, healthcare, advanced infrastructure and talent and technology cultivation.

### 8.2.1 Overall Cooperation Environment

In 2024, the Gulf Arab states continued to demonstrate significant dynamism in science, technology and innovation (STI) development. According to projections by Gartner (as depicted in Table 8.1), the total IT expenditure in the Middle East is anticipated to reach USD193.7 billion in 2024, representing a 5.2% year-on-year increase. Analysts posit that the substantial growth in IT software and IT services expenditure signifies regional nations' strategic preparations for high-technology development in areas such as cloud migration, artificial intelligence (AI) and the Internet of Things (IoT). The Gulf Arab states constitute the primary drivers of STI investment within the Middle East, with Saudi Arabia, the UAE, Qatar and Bahrain all strategically aiming to propel economic transformation through technological innovation. Pricewaterhouse Coopers forecasts that by 2030, AI has the potential to augment the region's GDP by USD32 billion through advancements in product innovation and enhancements in productivity.[2] Consequently, the Gulf Arab states are strategically capitalizing on their economic strengths to secure leading positions within the global technology landscape.

---

[1] "Core Business," China-Arab States Technology Transfer Center website, www.casttc.org/node/business.html, May 18, 2024.

[2] Vivek Adatia, "Emerging Tech Trends in the Middle East: Opportunities for Businesses in 2024," https://www.wdcstechnology.ae/emerging-tech-trends-in-the-middle-east-opportunities-for-businesses-in-2024, July 4, 2024.

182

Chapter 8　Special Report on China-Arab States Science and Technology Cooperation

**Table 8.1　IT Expenditure Statistics for the Middle East (2023-2024)**

| Category | 2023 Spending (USD Million) | 2023 Growth (%) | 2024 Spending (USD Million) | 2024 Growth (%) |
|---|---|---|---|---|
| Data Center Systems | 4826 | 5.5 | 4809 | -0.3 |
| Devices | 28379 | -1.8 | 27092 | -4.5 |
| Software | 13555 | 8.0 | 15229 | 12.3 |
| IT Services | 17338 | 4.6 | 19016 | 9.6 |
| Communications Services | 120026 | 9.0 | 127584 | 6.3 |
| Overall IT | 184124 | 6.6 | 193731 | 5 |

Source: Compiled from Gartner data.

Over the past five years, the Gulf Arab states have significantly augmented their investments in artificial intelligence (AI). A recent report by the Saudi Data and AI Authority (SDAIA) indicates a substantial compound annual growth rate (CAGR) of 59% in Saudi Arabian governmental expenditure on AI since 2019. In September 2024, the Kingdom of Saudi Arabia supported the Digital Cooperation Organization (DCO) in establishing the world's premier Generative AI Center of Excellence (CoE) and initiated the USD100 billion Project Transcendence, with the strategic objective of positioning Saudi Arabia as a world-class technology hub.[1] Beyond large-scale project investments, the United Arab Emirates (UAE) has demonstrated remarkable progress in the cultivation of its national innovation ecosystem. Through the implementation of a comprehensive suite of policies, the UAE intends to bolster small and medium-sized enterprises (SMEs) engaged in science, technology and innovation (STI) via governmental agencies, dedicated funds, educational programs and platform development initiatives, with the overarching aim of establishing the national innovation system. The strategic target is to increase the number of SMEs from 558000 in 2022 to 1 million by 2030. Data from the *Arab Sustainable Development Report 2024* reveals that the UAE ranks first globally in "Entrepreneurial Policy and Culture", fifth in "Business Policy" and eighteenth in "Venture Capital",

---

[1]　Telcom Review, "Project Transcendence: Saudi Arabia's Upcoming Multi-Billion Investment", https://www.telecomreview.com/articles/reports-and-coverage/8565-project-transcendence-saudi-arabia-s- upcoming-multi-billion-investment, November 8, 2024.

183

The Development Process of China-Arab States Economic and Trade Relations Annual Report 2024

collectively demonstrating a vibrant and dynamic technological innovation landscape.[1] According to the *Global Innovation Index 2024* (as illustrated in Figure 8.1), Saudi Arabia and Qatar, alongside Brazil, Mauritius and Indonesia, have registered the most rapid advancements in their global innovation index rankings over the preceding five years.

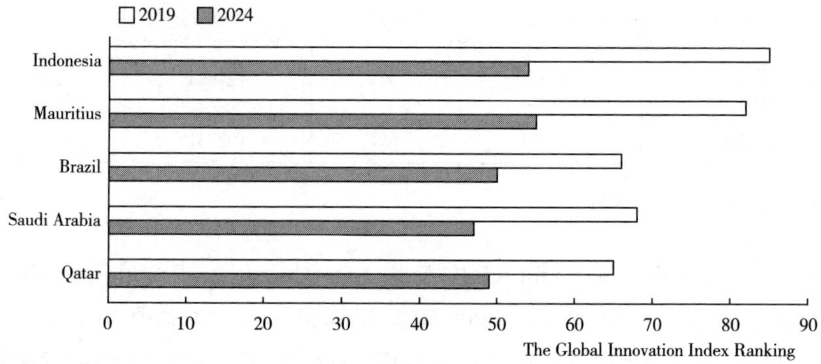

**Figure 8.1    Top Gainers in the Global Innovation Index Ranking (Past Five Years)**
Source: Compiled and synthesized from data in WIPO's *Global Innovation Index*.

Despite the collective technological progress observed across Arab states, the overall regional level of science, technology, and innovation (STI) still holds considerable untapped potential for advancement. While Gulf Arab states have demonstrated remarkable progress in STI in recent years, certain less developed and politically unstable countries within the region continue to lag considerably behind both the regional frontrunners and global progress. Taking energy transition as an example, the Arab Investment & Export Credit Guarantee Corporation (Dhaman) reported that in 2023, the average energy transition ranking for Arab states was 82nd out of 120 surveyed countries, placing them in the mid-to-lower tier. As illustrated in Table 8.2, Qatar (53rd), Jordan (56th), Saudi Arabia (60th) and Morocco (64th) held leading positions within the region. However, countries such as Bahrain (103rd), Kuwait (107th), Lebanon (115th), and Yemen (120th) continue to grapple with substantial energy transition needs.[2] As a core element of Arab states' developmental transformation,

---

① ESCWA, Arab Sustainable Development Report 2024, 2024, p.144.

② Dhaman, The Investment Climate in Arab Counties 2024, 2024, p.28.

184

Chapter 8   Special Report on China-Arab States Science and Technology Cooperation

energy transition serves both as a key driver for STI advancement and as a comprehensive indicator reflecting the multifaceted nature of their STI development. This underscores the continued significant demand for and necessity of STI across Arab countries.

**Table 8.2    Global Energy Transition Index Rankings for Arab States (2022-2023)**

| Arab Ranking | Country | Change | Global Rank (2023) | Global Rank (2022) |
|---|---|---|---|---|
| 1 | Morocco | ↑ 8 | 64 | 56 |
| 2 | Saudi Arabia | ↑ 3 | 60 | 57 |
| 3 | Qatar | ↓ 6 | 53 | 59 |
| 4 | UAE | ↓ 13 | 50 | 63 |
| 5 | Jordan | ↓ 15 | 56 | 71 |
| 6 | Egypt | ↑ 2 | 81 | 79 |
| 7 | Algeria | ↑ 2 | 88 | 86 |
| 8 | Tunisia | ↑ 4 | 93 | 89 |
| 9 | Oman | ↓ 14 | 76 | 90 |
| 10 | Kuwait | ↑ 5 | 107 | 102 |
| 11 | Bahrain | ↓ 7 | 103 | 110 |
| 12 | Lebanon | ↑ 3 | 115 | 112 |
| 13 | Yemen | — | 120 | 120 |
| | Arab Average | ↓ 2 | 82 | 84 |
| | Total Countries | | 120 | 120 |

Source: The World Economic Forum (WEF)'s *Fostering Effective Energy Transition 2024 Report.*

Furthermore, human resource development in Gulf Arab states still has considerable room for improvement. The UNDP's *Human Development Report 2023-2024* highlights that regional development disparities significantly impede global cooperation and exacerbate global divisions.[1] Arab countries tend to face a shortage of skilled talent and possess limited inherent capacity for technological development and innovation. As illustrated in Table 8.3, Arab countries tend to lag in technical talent resources, with a regional average

---

① UNDP, Human Development Report 2023/2024, 2024, p.7.

ranking of 70th out of 133 countries, placing them in the lower echelons of the surveyed nations. Moreover, their talent cultivation capabilities are comparatively weak. Although select nations, notably the UAE (1st) and Kuwait (3rd), occupy a leading global position in vocational and technical education, the overall levels of higher education (86th) and vocational and technical education (59th) across Arab countries lack a significant competitive advantage. In particular, the disparity in higher education levels between Arab countries and the global average is substantial, with Qatar, a regional frontrunner, ranking only 28th globally. Among the 12 Arab countries included in the statistics, 10 rank 70th or lower, directly impinging upon their capacity for independent technological innovation.

**Table 8.3   Global Knowledge Index and Sub-Index Rankings for Arab States (2023)**

| Country | Policy Support | Economic Level | ICT | R&D and Innovation | Higher Education | Vocational Education | Global Rank | Annual Change |
|---|---|---|---|---|---|---|---|---|
| UAE | 45 | 13 | 14 | 28 | 47 | 1 | 26 | ↓1 |
| Qatar | 44 | 25 | 58 | 47 | 28 | 62 | 39 | ↑5 |
| Saudi Arabia | 73 | 39 | 19 | 28 | 70 | 40 | 40 | ↑3 |
| Kuwait | 71 | 25 | 26 | 88 | 70 | 3 | 44 | ↑3 |
| Bahrain | 75 | 40 | 33 | 101 | 102 | 21 | 56 | ↓1 |
| Oman | 90 | 54 | 48 | 92 | 86 | 50 | 66 | ↓12 |
| Tunisia | 86 | 86 | 81 | 72 | 87 | 76 | 81 | ↑2 |
| Palestine | 101 | 97 | 100 | 58 | 100 | 87 | 89 | ↑4 |
| Egypt | 114 | 85 | 85 | 89 | 94 | 46 | 90 | ↑5 |
| Morocco | 83 | 87 | 72 | 72 | 114 | 79 | 92 | ↓7 |
| Jordan | 82 | 69 | 92 | 82 | 105 | 109 | 97 | ↓1 |
| Mauritania | 126 | 119 | 116 | 102 | 132 | 129 | 125 | ↑2 |
| Average regional ranking | 83 | 62 | 62 | 72 | 86 | 59 | 70 | 0 |

Source: Compiled based on data from the *Arab Sustainable Development Report 2024*.

186

Chapter 8   Special Report on China-Arab States Science and Technology Cooperation

In general, Arab countries maintain a long-standing need for developmental transformation coupled with a demand for scientific and technological innovation, which establishes a solid market foundation for China-Arab states STI cooperation. From a practical standpoint, Arab states still exhibit considerable gaps in developmental prerequisites, including scientific and technological capabilities and talent reserves. This offers a sustained impetus for China and Arab states to continuously deepen their STI cooperation and pragmatically engage in technology transfer.

## 8.2.2   Specific Cooperative Practices

In 2024, China-Arab states science and technology cooperation advanced steadily. Both sides engaged in extensive collaborative endeavors across various domains, encompassing the digital economy and communication technology, agricultural science and food security, new and clean energy, high-tech infrastructure, healthcare and hygiene cooperation, and professional technology and talent development.

First, Chinese enterprises' overseas expansion revitalized China-Arab states digital communication cooperation. A significant number of Chinese enterprises, including Huawei Cloud and SenseTime, have successfully penetrated the Arab market by utilizing stable network environments, reliable data protection and comprehensive offline services. Through the provision of big data, artificial intelligence and cloud computing technologies, coupled with the sharing of innovative experiences, these Chinese enterprises are propelling Arab states towards more advanced stages of intelligent development. In 2024, Huawei Cloud's overseas growth exceeded 50%, effectively advancing China-Arab states collaboration in digital and intelligent upgrades across sectors such as telecommunications operators, government, finance and media entertainment. Currently, Huawei Cloud has over 6000 global partners and more than 300 local partners in the Middle East. In May 2024, Huawei Cloud officially launched its services in Egypt, becoming the first global company to establish a public cloud presence in the country. This also marked North Africa's first public cloud node. As a new digital hub for the African continent, this Egyptian node not only further strengthens Huawei Cloud's digital enablement strategy in North Africa and the Arab region but also significantly drives the digital transformation of local industries. In May 2024, Lenovo Group and Alat, a subsidiary of Saudi

187

Arabia's Public Investment Fund (PIF), signed a strategic cooperation agreement. The agreement includes Alat providing Lenovo Group with a USD2 billion interest-free convertible bond investment, and Lenovo Group establishing its Middle East and Africa regional headquarters and a new computer and server manufacturing base in Riyadh.[1] Beyond technical exchange and cooperation, Chinese enterprises are adopting a "culture-plus-technology" approach to deepen their engagement in the Arab market. During the 2024 Spring Festival, SenseTime organized a series of Chinese New Year celebrations on Yas Island in the UAE, utilizing AIGC technology to empower intelligent cultural tourism initiatives in Arab countries. The company has already facilitated the implementation of multiple smart tourism projects in Arab nations, including Yas Island in the UAE and the Riyadh and Jeddah Seasons in Saudi Arabia, effectively leveraging technological cooperation to promote people-to-people connectivity.[2]

Second, Agricultural science and technology cooperation bolstered China-Arab states efforts to address resource constraints and food security. In recent years, China and Arab countries have engaged in in-depth technical cooperation in areas encompassing soil management, dryland agriculture, animal husbandry and veterinary medicine and seed industry technology. In 2022, during the China-Arab States Summit, President Xi Jinping proposed the *Eight Major Joint Actions* for pragmatic China-Arab states cooperation, which included a commitment under the "Food Security Joint Action" to jointly establish five modern agricultural joint laboratories, implement 50 agricultural technology cooperation demonstration projects and dispatch 500 agricultural technical experts to Arab countries.[3] In response to this commitment and with the facilitation of the China-Arab States Expo, in August 2024, Ningxia Wozhiyuan Technology Co., Ltd. and Saudi Gulf Dragon Trading Holding Company signed a cooperation agreement covering dozens of technologies and equipment with

---

[1] "Lenovo to Establish Middle East and Africa Regional Headquarters in Saudi Arabia," *People's Daily Online*, http: //world.people.com.cn/n1/2024/0529/c1002-40246085.html, May 29, 2024.

[2] "Chinese 'New Year's Flavor' Spreads Overseas, SenseTime AIGC Powers Abu Dhabi New Year Celebration Events", SenseTime website, www.sensetime.com/cn/news-detail/51167501?categoryId=72, Febuary 22, 2024.

[3] "China-Arab States Joint Action on Food Security Sets Example for the World," *China Daily*, https: //cn.chinadaily.com.cn/a/202212/20/WS63a192d3a3102ada8b2278db.htm, December 30, 2022.

Chapter 8    Special Report on China-Arab States Science and Technology Cooperation

independent intellectual property rights, including wind-solar complementary intelligent control, composite drip irrigation product processing, rapid soil improvement and specialized photovoltaic agricultural equipment construction. These technologies will be implemented in Saudi Arabia to support the country's agricultural technology innovation and soil environment improvement.[1] In November 2024, Shandong Shouguang Vegetable Industry Group and Abu Dhabi Agriculture and Food Technology Company (Silal) signed a strategic agreement. Cooperation includes the launch of breeding development plans and greenhouse demonstration park construction. Leveraging the technical advantages of Chinese enterprises in seedling cultivation, grafting and off-season planting, this collaboration aims to alleviate bottlenecks in the UAE's seedling supply chain and enhance the diversity and accessibility of its agricultural industry.[2] Beyond project cooperation, China-Arab states agricultural technology exchanges are also intensifying. For example, in 2024, the China National Rice Research Institute and the Wetland Agriculture and Ecology Institute of Shandong Agricultural Sciences Academy conducted exchanges and mutual learning with the Egyptian Rice Research and Training Center and the Egyptian Agricultural Research Center, respectively, focusing on rice cultivation, salt tolerance and breeding technologies. Facing common needs and challenges, technological cooperation has become a key component of China-Arab states agricultural collaboration. Ensuring food security, achieving seed industry autonomy and safeguarding sustainable agricultural development will provide an inexhaustible driving force for Sino-Arab agricultural science and technology cooperation.

Third, Renewable energy cooperation emerged as a novel growth area in China-Arab states science and technology collaboration. As a dominant player in the global clean energy supply chain, China possesses a market advantage in energy technology cooperation. Strongly aligned with the practical needs of Arab countries' energy transition, the proportion of "three new" products—

---

[1]  "Seizing the 'Belt and Road' Opportunity to Jointly Build the 'One Park, One House' Project: Ningxia Technology Goes Overseas to Ride the Waves in Saudi Arabia," *Ningxia News Net*, https://www.nxnews.net/zt/24n/esjszqh/mdxdhgg/202408/t20240809_9623460.html, August 9, 2024.

[2]  Emirates News Agency, "Silal partners with China's Shouguang to boost UAE agriculture and food security," https://www.freshplaza.com/north-america/article/9682503/silal-partners-with-china-s-shouguang-to-boost-uae-agriculture-and-food-security/, November 27, 2024.

189

namely, new energy vehicles, photovoltaic products and lithium batteries—is significantly increasing within China-Arab states technological cooperation. In June 2024, China's GCL Technology announced a collaboration with a subsidiary of the UAE's sovereign wealth fund, Mubadala, to establish a polysilicon production base in the UAE, bolstering their cooperation in the photovoltaic sector. In the hydrogen energy sector, Arab countries, particularly Oman and Saudi Arabia, are endeavoring to achieve global leadership in hydrogen energy development. Saudi Arabia has publicly articulated its "National Hydrogen Strategy (2020)", and Oman has outlined its ambition to "become the largest hydrogen exporter in the Middle East and the sixth largest globally by 2030".[1] In response, numerous Chinese enterprises, including Power Construction Corporation of China, Shuangliang Eco-energy Systems Co., Ltd. and Sungrow Hydrogen Group, a subsidiary of Sungrow Power Supply Co., Ltd., have entered into green hydrogen cooperation projects with Jordan. Furthermore, companies such as Envision Group, Sunpure Intelligent Technology Co., Ltd. and Hyde Hydrogen Energy are deeply involved in Saudi Arabia's NEOM City hydrogen development projects, aiming to capitalize on the market opportunities presented by Arab countries' hydrogen energy development. In the realm of new energy applications, new energy vehicles emerged as a significant highlight in China-Arab states technology cooperation in 2024. According to data from China's General Administration of Customs, by the first half of 2024, China's passenger car exports to the Middle East reached 420000 units, marking a year-on-year increase of 46.2%. Consequently, the Middle East has become China's largest automobile export market. Notably, new energy vehicles accounted for 19.6% of these exports, representing the most substantial progress in China-Arab states technological cooperation in 2024. In the same year, BYD successfully entered the Saudi market and achieved its 1000th delivery in the UAE market. Additionally, Xpeng, Changan and Aion successfully entered the Egyptian, Saudi and Qatari markets, respectively. In October of the same year, NIO signed an agreement with CYVN Holdings, a UAE government-owned strategic investment company, to establish a research and development center in Abu

---

[1] Hydrogen Council, "The Middle East has the Chance to lead on Hydrogen," https: // hydrogencouncil.com/en/the-middle-east-has-the-chance-to-lead-on-hydrogen/, October 24, 2024.

Chapter 8    Special Report on China-Arab States Science and Technology Cooperation

Dhabi and conduct joint development for the local market.[①]

Fourth, High-Tech infrastructure construction drove China-Arab states connectivity through the "digital silk road". Building upon the "Belt and Road" Initiative, China has launched a comprehensive "Digital Silk Road" development plan, with a strong emphasis on cooperating with participating countries to build digital infrastructure. This includes optical cables, 5G networks, data centers, smart cities, cloud computing and artificial intelligence applications. In recent years, Arab countries have also highly valued the fundamental role of high-tech infrastructure construction in fostering sustainable and innovative development, effectively advancing the joint China-Arab states construction of the "Digital Silk Road". According to research by McKinsey & Company, cloud service development represents a significant potential area within the Middle East market. It is estimated that by 2030, cloud services will generate a market value of up to USD183 billion for Middle Eastern countries, equivalent to 6% of the region's current GDP.[②] Capitalizing on these market opportunities, Chinese enterprises such as Alibaba, Tencent and Huawei have successfully entered the Arab market by leveraging their cost-effective and high-quality offerings. In March 2024, Alibaba signed a digital transformation cooperation agreement with the Saudi Ministry of Human Resources and Social Development and Saudi Telecom Company (STC). The agreement focuses on jointly exploring capacity building in areas such as artificial intelligence, digital information and cybersecurity. In April of the same year, Huawei constructed the UAE's first 5G smart warehouse in Dubai. This project successfully integrated intelligent elements into the traditional warehousing and logistics industry through the deep integration of 5G technology, cloud computing, big data and artificial intelligence, thereby establishing a new industry benchmark for intelligent operations. Additionally, during the 2024 Mobile World Congress in Barcelona, Huawei and Saudi Telecom Company signed an agreement to deepen their strategic cooperation on 5.5G technology. This collaboration centers on the development of SuperLink, a multi-band wireless transmission communication

① "Chinese Automakers Flock to the Middle East," *People's Daily Online*, http: //paper.people.com. cn/zgjjzk/pc/content/202411/15/content_30046097.html, November 15, 2024.

② McKinsey Digital, "The Middle East Public Cloud: A Multibillion-dollar Prize Waiting to Be Captured," https: //www.mckinsey.com/capabilities/mckinsey-digital/our-insights/the-middle-east-public-cloud-a-multibillion-dollar-prize-waiting-to-be-captured, January 30, 2024.

## The Development Process of China-Arab States Economic and Trade Relations
## Annual Report 2024

technology designed to deliver efficient 5G connectivity to remote regions of Saudi Arabia. The implementation of SuperLink is projected to reduce antenna requirements by up to 67%, effectively mitigating the challenges posed by Saudi Arabia's terrain to 5G signal propagation through simplified deployment. This technological advancement has not only directly fueled user growth in Saudi Arabia's network services at the market level but has also indirectly catalyzed the adoption of digital applications across crucial sectors such as healthcare, education and e-commerce, thereby offering a sustainable and comprehensive solution for Saudi Arabia's ongoing digital transformation.

Fifth, Healthcare technology cooperation deepened the China-Arab states development consensus of "science and technology for the people". In May 2024, President Xi Jinping emphasized China's willingness to forge a "Five Major Cooperation Pattern" with Arab countries. Notably, 'life and health' was prioritized within the innovation-driven pillar, emerging as a new focal point of China-Arab states technological collaboration. Previously, to address the persistent shortage of medical technology and skilled personnel in Arab countries, China has long engaged in providing medical assistance and conducting medical technology training programs. This support has been extended to numerous recipient nations, including Morocco, Djibouti, Algeria and Tunisia, through initiatives such as specialized medical and nursing training courses and informative lectures. The model of China-Arab states medical cooperation has progressively transitioned from a primarily "blood transfusion" approach—focused on direct aid—towards a more sustainable "blood-generating" model centered on capacity building and knowledge transfer. This evolving paradigm provides an enduring impetus for China and Arab states to collaboratively advance the vision of a global community of health for all.[1] In this new era, China-Arab states cooperation in medical and health science and technology has yielded substantial and mutually beneficial outcomes. In May 2024, the quadrivalent influenza vaccine developed by Sinopharm Group secured a procurement order from the UAE, marking its successful entry into the Arab market. In November of the same year, Shanghai Henlius Biotech, Inc. and Saudi Arabian medical company SVAX entered into a strategic partnership

---

[1] Xu Lili, Zhang Kexin, and Song Xinyang, "Research on China's Health Development Cooperation with African Arab States," *West Asia and Africa*, no. 2 (2024): 36.

Chapter 8 Special Report on China-Arab States Science and Technology Cooperation

to conduct joint venture-based innovative biopharmaceutical research and production in the Middle East market.[1] Furthermore, in December 2024, China's Walvax Biotechnology announced cooperation with two Egyptian local pharmaceutical companies, Vacsera and VBC, to undertake vaccine research and local production, with the objective of driving technological autonomy within Egypt's vaccine industry. In the realm of intelligent healthcare, Shanghai General Healthy Information and Technology Co., Ltd. partnered with Saudi Arabia's Ajlan & Bros Holding Group in March 2024 to pilot an automated medical logistics solution at Dallah Hospital in Saudi Arabia. By providing intelligent healthcare technology support to Saudi Arabia, relevant Chinese enterprises are leveraging their technological advantages to accelerate the digital transformation of healthcare in Arab countries. In the field of pharmaceutical technology, numerous prominent Chinese pharmaceutical companies have also entered the Arab market, aiming to expand their overseas reach through scientific and technological innovation cooperation. By 2024, companies such as Northeast Pharmaceutical Group Co., Ltd., Kexing Biopharm Co., Ltd., Sichuan Huiyu Pharmaceutical Co., Ltd., CanSino Biologics Inc. and Shenzhen Kangtai Biological Products Co., Ltd. had successfully established research and production partnerships with local companies in Arab countries including Saudi Arabia, Oman and Egypt.

Sixth, Technology transfer cooperation strengthens the foundation of China-Arab states scientific and technological talent and provides an inexhaustible driving force for the sustainable development of bilateral scientific and technological cooperation. Since the inception of the Belt and Road Initiative, China has placed significant emphasis on providing technical assistance and fostering talent development for partner countries. By 2024, China had signed government-level science and technology cooperation agreements with 81 partner countries and established intellectual property cooperation relationships with over 50 partner countries, supporting over a thousand joint scientific and technological talent development projects.[2] Against this backdrop, China-

---

[1] "Henlius Strategically Partners with SVAX, Ushering in a New Chapter of Global Layout," Henlius, https://www.henlius.com/NewsDetails-4743-26.html, November 7, 2024.

[2] "Deeply Advancing 'Belt and Road' International Scientific and Technological Cooperation," *Chinese Social Sciences Today* website, www.cssn.cn/skgz/bwyc/202401/t20240126_5730932.shtml, January 26, 2024.

193

Arab states technology transfer has progressed smoothly and achieved notable results. Currently, under the guidance and promotion of the China-Arab States Technology Partnership Program, the China-Arab states technology transfer conference linkage mechanism is continuously being refined. In September 2024, the China-Arab States Technology Transfer Center and the West Asia and North Africa Office of the Global Energy Interconnection Development and Cooperation Organization reached a cooperation consensus on technology transfer, technical training and the co-construction of collaborative networks. In addition to ongoing joint training programs in support of Arab countries and the cultivation of innovation platforms, both sides will establish a "1+2+N"[1] multi-level conference linkage mechanism, aiming to encourage and attract more Chinese innovation entities to participate in China-Arab states technology transfer through joint promotion initiatives. In May 2024, the China-Arab States Technology Transfer Center and the Hebei Provincial Department of Science and Technology jointly organized the China (Hebei)-Saudi Arabia (Jeddah) International Science and Technology Cooperation Conference. During this conference, China and Saudi Arabia jointly signed a *Memorandum of Understanding on Scientific and Technological Talent Cooperation* in areas such as desert planting, geological exploration and the marine economy. In the same month, the Center and the Shanghai Science & Technology Exchange Center jointly held the "2024 Belt and Road Countries New Energy Technology Online Training Course". This course, designed based on the actual technical needs of Arab countries, invited Chinese experts in the new energy field to deliver lectures, attracting over 50 scientific and technological personnel from countries including Egypt, Sudan, Morocco and Algeria. Beyond governmental promotion, Chinese enterprises are also making significant contributions to Sino-Arab technology transfer. Huawei, in collaboration with the National Center for Artificial Intelligence of the Saudi Data and Artificial Intelligence Authority, jointly trained local AI engineers to

---

[1] The "1+2+N" coordination mechanism is defined as follows: "1" refers to the regular convening of bilateral working meetings; "2" involves integrating resources and fostering deeper China-Arab states scientific and technological transfer cooperation, leveraging the China-Arab States Technology Transfer and Innovation Cooperation Conference and the Global Energy Interconnection Conference; and "N" signifies the comprehensive promotion of technology transfer and talent exchange at various international conferences on energy and science and technology held in Arab states.

Chapter 8    Special Report on China-Arab States Science and Technology Cooperation

support Saudi Arabia's transition towards a data-driven economy. Alibaba Cloud launched the "AI Empowerment Program" in Saudi Arabia, jointly cultivating local technical talent with the Saudi Telecom Academy (STC Academy) and Tuwaiq Academy to promote human resource development in Arab countries. According to statistics, since April 2023, Alibaba Cloud has trained and empowered more than 60000 scientific and technological professionals by providing over 300 online and offline courses and 250 hands-on experiments.[1] Overall, under the joint impetus of governments and enterprises, China-Arab states technology transfer cooperation is developing in an orderly manner towards institutionalization and greater scale.

## 8.3    Future Prospects of China-Arab States Science and Technology Cooperation

Against the strategic backdrop of the high-quality joint construction of the Belt and Road Initiative (BRI) and the impetus to foster the "Five Major Cooperation Frameworks", China-Arab states science and technology (S&T) cooperation has entered a pivotal period of strategic opportunity, necessitating its sustained and comprehensive advancement. Current assessments indicate that the opportunities for China-Arab states technological collaboration significantly outweigh the existing challenges, presenting an overall positive trajectory. Looking ahead, assisting Arab nations in achieving technological self-reliance and further facilitating the translation of scientific and technological achievements into practical applications are critical imperatives.

Regarding "opportunities", a high degree of demand complementarity and robust institutional safeguards provide strong foundational support for China-Arab states S&T cooperation. Beyond driving technological innovation spanning digitalization to intelligentization, the Fourth Industrial Revolution also offers unprecedented developmental opportunities for developing countries through the emergence of technological multipolarity. Recognizing this juncture, Arab states have allocated substantial capital and implementing supportive policies to promote their national technological development. Despite these concerted

---

[1]    Jon Truby, "Sino-Arab Free Trade Agreement, AI Diplomacy, and the Realisation of AI and Sustainability Goals in the Middle East," *Asian Journal of Law and Society*, 2025, p.11.

The Development Process of China-Arab States Economic and Trade Relations
Annual Report 2024

efforts, Arab countries still face tangible shortcomings in technological capabilities, human capital support and fundamental hardware infrastructure. On the one hand, Arab countries generally exhibit limited scientific and technological innovation capabilities, characterized by a persistent reliance on imports for core technologies. Save for a small contingent of Gulf Arab states, the greater part of Arab countries allocates research and development funding considerably below 1% of their GDP, significantly lagging behind the global average. This reality underscores a tangible deficiency in the intrinsic drivers for scientific and technological advancement, compounded by regional developmental disparities. On the other hand, Arab countries continue to demonstrate vulnerabilities in crucial supporting conditions, including the cultivation of innovative talent and the establishment of advanced infrastructure. This deficit in skilled technical personnel impedes the effective application and commercialization of scientific and technological breakthroughs. Consequently, Arab countries still confront a multitude of pressing challenges that necessitate external support. China's approach to foreign S&T cooperation has consistently adhered to the principles of mutual consultation, joint contribution and shared benefits, underpinned by inclusive and open cooperative policies and synergistic and efficient collaboration modalities. This approach has provided crucial S&T support and development assistance for numerous technologically developing nations. Therefore, given the practical developmental needs of Arab countries, China-Arab states S&T cooperation is projected to maintain its considerable cooperative potential. Furthermore, the establishment of robust institutional mechanisms provides a systemic guarantee for the consolidation of the bilateral collaboration. Ranging from overarching regional initiatives to autonomous national development strategies, and from comprehensive technological capacity building to targeted breakthroughs in specific technological domains, numerous Arab states have formulated comprehensive and detailed S&T development plans. Currently, in the establishment of science and technology innovation mechanisms, Arab countries have begun to forge a systematic model primarily driven by policy, complemented by international collaboration and underpinned by the development of key platforms. This nascent framework demonstrates significant development potential and provides a solid foundation for enhanced cooperation between China and Arab states as they jointly transition towards a knowledge-based economic era. Simultaneously, as the bilateral relations deepen

196

Chapter 8   Special Report on China-Arab States Science and Technology Cooperation

and become increasingly substantive, China has formulated comprehensive and meticulously detailed action plans for science and technology cooperation with Arab countries, focusing on pivotal areas such as the digital economy, technology transfer and digital security. Consequently, Arab countries are progressively emerging as a primary focus and a substantial potential market for China's international science and technology cooperation initiatives. Overall, mutually complementary conditions, aligned strategic concepts and steadily improving institutional mechanisms provide an exceptionally broad foundation for robust and mutually beneficial China-Arab states science and technology cooperation.

Regarding "Challenges", the existing disparities in technological development within Arab countries, set against the backdrop of intensifying great power competition, may considerably impede China-Arab states S&T cooperation. Currently, the efficacy of China-Arab states S&T collaboration requires further enhancement. In terms of cooperative modalities, China-Arab states S&T cooperation exhibits a notable "asymmetry", predominantly relying on China's provision of technical assistance and technology transfer, without fully capitalizing on potential bilateral synergistic effects. Concerning implementation efficacy, the heterogeneous technological capabilities among Arab nations and the limited foundational conditions for regional interconnectedness have hindered the formation of a "point-to-area" regional upgrading effect.[1] Consequently, a core challenge that the bilateral S&T cooperation needs to address is how to maximize practical effectiveness and enhance the impact of outcomes within the current scale of cooperation. Furthermore, given the differentiated levels of China-Arab states S&T development, great power competition may exert significant influence over their collaborative endeavors. Amidst the prevailing rhetoric of zero-sum games, the bilateral S&T cooperation will inevitably confront the long-term challenge of "aligning with one side". The UAE's G42 withdrawal from Chinese investments serves as an illustration of the relatively constrained strategic autonomy and limited resilience to external pressures faced by Arab countries. Given the disparity in scientific and technological development between China and Arab states, great power competition presents a significant risk of intervention in their science and technology (S&T) cooperation. United

---

[1]   Hao Shiyu, "Prospects for China-Arab States Science and Technology Cooperation in the New Era," *China Investment*, no. 1 (2024), p. 51.

by a shared vision of common prosperity, China and Arab states advocate for advancing economic development and political governance through S&T progress. This collaboration, unfolding amidst technological multi-polarization, is progressively challenging the established Western-centric geopolitical landscape of S&T.[1] The accelerating pace of China-Arab states S&T cooperation has led certain major powers to increasingly securitize this partnership, employing indirect pressure and direct obstruction to interfere with and undermine its advancement. Fueled by zero-sum competition rhetoric and extraterritorial jurisdiction under the guise of "de-risking", numerous Arab countries will inevitably confront the enduring challenge of "choosing sides".[2] The United States' coercion of the UAE's G42 company to divest its Chinese investments starkly illustrates the relatively limited strategic autonomy and external resilience of Arab nations. This suggests that China-Arab states science and technology (S&T) cooperation is likely to face sustained external interference characterized by politicization and weaponization. Against the backdrop of structural great power competition, the imperative for both China and Arab states is to maintain mutual trust, foster mutually beneficial cooperation, and collectively counter external challenges—concerns demanding careful consideration and a concerted response.

Looking ahead, both China and Arab countries should prioritize deepening ideological alignment, emphasizing mutually complementary strengths and placing significant emphasis on talent cultivation to foster the sustainable development of China-Arab states S&T cooperation. Focusing on the shared concerns of peace and development, firmly establishing the concept of a China-Arab states community with a shared future, advocating for open and inclusive multilateralism and enhancing mutually beneficial cooperation in S&T represent effective strategies for countering external rhetorical interference and transcending the paradigm of great power technological competition.

---

[1] Sun Degang, "Promoting the Construction of a China-Arab States Community of Common Destiny through a Shared Science and Technology Community," *Contemporary World*, no. 10 (2024): 58.

[2] Ding Long, "Obstructing China-Arab States S&T Cooperation Is Unpopular," *Global Times*, https://opinion.huanqiu.com/article/4Ge0txqlKdf, February 19, 2024.

# Chapter 9  Special Report on China-Arab States Ecological Cooperation

China and Arab states, both members of the developing world, together account for one-sixth of the world's land area, nearly one-quarter of the global population, and one-eighth of the world's total economic output. Despite differences in resource endowments and varying levels of development, the two sides possess tremendous cooperative potential. The relationship between China and Arab states is deeply rooted in history, characterized by peace and cooperation, openness and inclusiveness, mutual learning, and mutual benefit.

China has long been committed to biodiversity conservation and green development, actively engaging in international exchanges and cooperation, including collaboration with Arab states in the field of ecological and environmental protection. In recent years and in the future, cooperation in the field of ecological and environmental protection has emerged as and will continue to be a prominent part of the economic and trade relations between China and Arab states, offering vast potential, broad areas of collaboration, and profound significance.[1] Over the past decade, in the course of jointly building the "Belt and Road" Initiative, China has consistently emphasized the integration of the concept of green development. While striving to achieve its own green transformation, China has also engaged in extensive, substantive, and diversified exchanges and cooperation with Arab states in the field of green development.

---

[1] Wang Lingling, "Research on Ecological and Environmental Cooperation Between China and Arab States/ Discussion on Cooperation in Desertification Prevention and Control and Technology Export," *Journal of Ningxia Communist Party Institute*, No. 6, 2013, p. 90.

The Development Process of China-Arab States Economic and Trade Relations
Annual Report 2024

These joint efforts have led to steady progress and remarkable achievements in building a "Green Belt and Road".

## 9.1　The Status Quo and Governance of the Ecological Environment in the Arab Region

Arab states are primarily located in West Asia and North Africa, spanning from Morocco on the Atlantic coast to Saudi Arabia along the Persian Gulf. The total land area of these Arab states is approximately 13.13 million square kilometers, with 72% located in Africa and 28% in Asia. The climate of the Arab region is predominantly tropical desert, heavily influenced by the subtropical high-pressure systems and trade wind belts. As a result, most areas experience arid conditions with minimal rainfall, making the ecological environment highly fragile. In recent years, the severe consequences of environmental degradation have become increasingly evident in many Arab states. Deteriorating ecological conditions threaten food production, lead to population displacement, intensify resource competition and social conflicts, and, in extreme cases, contribute to collapse of social order and even war.[1]

### 9.1.1　Water Scarcity and Governance Measures

The Arab world is primarily situated near the Tropic of Cancer and is influenced by the subtropical high-pressure and trade-wind zone, resulting in a vast expanse of tropical desert climate. This climatic condition leads to scarce and unevenly distributed precipitation, with many areas receiving less than 200 millimeters of annual rainfall. The majority of the Arab region consists of deserts, with the Red Sea and the Persian Gulf covering small areas and extending only slightly inland, offering limited climate moderation. This geographical characteristic further exacerbates water scarcity. In recent years, population growth has driven an increasing demand for water resources, intensifying pressure on already limited supplies. Meanwhile, the development of both industry and agriculture, and the urbanization process have similarly increased water demand, making the already limited resources even more strained. Furthermore, transnational disputes over

---

①　Zou Zhiqiang, "The 2030 Agenda for Sustainable Development and the Transformation of Arab States," *Arab World Studies,* No. 3, 2020, p. 121.

200

Chapter 9　Special Report on China-Arab States Ecological Cooperation

water resources in the Arab region remain highly intense. Long-standing conflicts over the allocation of transboundary rivers, such as the Nile, the Euphrates, and the Jordan River, persist. The tension between Egypt and Ethiopia over the Grand Ethiopian Renaissance Dam continues, as the dam poses a threat to 90% of Egypt's freshwater supply. In the meantime, Israel's military control over water sources in the West Bank allows it to monopolize two-thirds of the region's natural underground aquifers, further escalating conflicts with Arab states.

In recent years, Arab states have made significant progress in water resource management. On November 27, 2024, the Sixth Arab Water Conference was inaugurated in the Dead Sea region of Jordan, Under the theme "Governance Towards Achieving Sustainable Development in Water". The conference aimed to foster cooperation among Arab states in addressing water-related challenges. At the opening ceremony, Jordan's Minister of Water and Irrigation, Raed Abu Saud, highlighted the increasing severity of water scarcity in Arab states due to global warming, water resource depletion, regional conflicts, and the resulting refugee crises. He called for joint efforts among Arab states to develop solutions, raise public awareness of water conservation, enhance the role of research institutions, integrate food, water, and environmental security, and formulate a collective strategy to safeguard water security in the Arab world. To combat severe water shortages, Arab states have widely adopted seawater desalination technologies. Saudi Arabia, Saudi Arabia, as the world's largest desalination player, adopts reverse osmosis technology for 90% of its seawater desalination. The state has enacted legislation mandating water conservation and has promoted drip irrigation technology, improving agricultural water efficiency by 40%. The Algerian government has invested USD2.4 billion to construct five new desalination plants and plans to build six more by 2030, increasing the proportion of desalinated water from 18% to 42%.[1]

## 9.1.2　Clean Energy and Technological Innovation

The Arab region has long been at the center of the global energy landscape. According to the latest report by the Arab Investment & Export Credit Guarantee Corporation, Arab states collectively hold 704 billion barrels of

---

[1] "Algeria Advances Seawater Desalination to Address Water Shortages," cctv.com, https://news. cctv.com/2025/02/10/ARTIbndxytpD9PRC2P2fnIi4250210.shtml, February 10, 2025.

201

proven oil reserves, accounting for 41.3% of the world's total. These reserves are highly concentrated in five key states—Saudi Arabia, Iraq, the UAE, Kuwait, and Libya—which together possess 650 billion barrels, representing 92% of the Arab world's total oil reserves.[①]Although the region will undoubtedly continue to dominate the traditional oil and natural gas sectors for the foreseeable future, several key states and their oil companies are strategically positioning themselves as pivotal hubs in emerging energy markets and global leaders in the transition to new energy sources. For instance, Saudi Arabia's non-oil sector accounted for more than 50% of its economy for the first time in 2023. However, the state's energy exports remain heavily reliant on oil, and natural gas power generation is projected to supply over 50% of the national grid by 2030.

In addition to its abundant traditional oil and natural gas resources, the Arab region possesses unique renewable energy potential, particularly in solar and wind power. Combined with capital advantages, skilled workforce, and strategic geographical location, the region is well-positioned as a leader in both traditional oil and natural gas resources and new energy markets. The widespread availability of renewable energy resources across the Arab world provides favorable conditions for the development of solar and wind energy. Unlike fossil fuels, renewable energy sources are more evenly distributed, providing all states in the region with a foundation for sustainable energy development. This balanced distribution plays a crucial role in supporting balanced regional economic growth.[②]As the global energy transition accelerates, Gulf states face an urgent need to reduce their dependence on oil. Saudi Arabia's "Vision 2030" aims to increase its renewable energy installed capacity to 130 gigawatts and plans to export green electricity and hydrogen. According to the "Updated UAE Energy Strategy 2050", the UAE intends to more than double its renewable energy installed capacity to 14.2 gigawatts by 2030, raising the share of clean energy in its total energy mix to 30%. Currently, the UAE has an installed renewable

---

① "Oil Reserves in Arab States Account for 41.3% of Global Oil Reserves," Website of the Department of West Asian and North African Affairs, Ministry of Commerce of the People's Republic of China, http://xyf.mofcom.gov.cn/xxzb/art/2024/art_e235ffb106dd47e4a19cb3a398 1538c5.html, September 13, 2024.

② Zou Zhiqiang, "The 2030 Agenda for Sustainable Development and the Transformation of Arab States," *Arab World Studies,* No. 3, 2020, p. 121.

Chapter 9    Special Report on China-Arab States Ecological Cooperation

energy capacity of 6 gigawatts and a nuclear power capacity of 5.6 gigawatts.[1] Oman, with a relatively smaller economy and more limited oil and gas reserves, has adopted a more conventional approach by using tenders to attract partners and investors in the renewable energy sector. The state seeks to harness its vast solar and wind power potential to diversify its domestic energy structure and plans to position itself as a green hydrogen export hub starting in 2030.

From April 16 to 18, 2024, the 16th World Future Energy Summit (WFES) was held at the Abu Dhabi National Exhibition Centre, the capital of the UAE. Hosted by Abu Dhabi Future Energy Company (Masdar), the summit is the largest and most influential renewable energy exhibition and conference in the Middle East and North Africa. The event in 2024 attracted over 30000 visitors and more than 400 exhibiting companies from around the world. More than 350 industry leaders and experts participated in discussions covering topics such as solar and clean energy, waste management, water, energy transition, smart cities, climate, and the environment.

It is worth mentioning that this summit attracted over 100 Chinese companies. Especially in the solar energy sector, more than 90 out of the 140 exhibiting companies were from China, showcasing a clear advantage. James Jin, President of the MEA region team of LONGi Green Energy, pointed out that the natural endowments for the development of photovoltaics in the Middle East are favorable, with states like Saudi Arabia, the UAE, and Oman having very clear national energy transition strategies. Although the region started relatively late, its development speed has been rapid in recent years. Through competition and cooperation with top-tier companies, Chinese enterprises have enhanced their competitiveness in the Middle East market in terms of technology, brand influence, and price advantages. Nuclear energy, as an important component of clean energy, was also a key focus of this summit. Qiao Gang, Deputy General Manager of China National Nuclear Corporation Overseas Ltd. (CNNC Overseas), stated that nuclear energy has become widely recognized as a clean energy source. While renewable energy offers many advantages, it also has drawbacks such as high fluctuations, the need for energy storage, and lower energy density. In contrast, nuclear power has a high energy density and

---

[1]    "The UAE Plans to Invest 500 Billion Dirhams to Promote Economic Decarbonization," China Economic Net, http: //www.ce.cn/, January 2, 2025.

The Development Process of China-Arab States Economic and Trade Relations
Annual Report 2024

stable electricity output, making it capable of independently providing base-load power. It plays a crucial role in ensuring large-scale energy security and is one of the key options for achieving decarbonization and net-zero emissions. In the long run, it will also serve as a major energy source for large-scale hydrogen production.[①]

### 9.1.3  Desertification and Ecological Environmental Protection

Desertification, land degradation, and drought are among the most pressing environmental challenges of the world. The Arab region faces a severe desertification crisis, primarily characterized by land degradation and desert expansion. In recent years, due to the impacts of climate change and human activities, desertification in the Arab region has intensified. This is specifically manifested in the expansion of desert areas, the reduction of green spaces, and increasing water resource shortages.

On June 5, 2024, Saudi Arabia hosted the World Environment Day 2024 with a focus on land restoration, desertification, and drought resilience. The state has prioritized combating desertification. Launched in March 2021, the "Saudi Green Initiative" aims to turn 30% of Saudi Arabia's land into nature reserves, plant 10 billion trees and restore 40 million hectares of degraded land. In the short term, Saudi Arabia aims to plant 400 million trees by 2030. At the same time, by signing the "Middle East Green Initiative", Saudi Arabia is leading efforts to plant 40 billion trees across the region, aiming to reduce soil erosion, protect biodiversity, and mitigate the impacts of climate change. Additionally, Saudi Arabia has partnered with the G20 and the United Nations Convention to Combat Desertification (UNCCD) to launch the "G20 Global Land Initiative", which aims to reduce land degradation by 50% by 2040.[②] In recent years, the UAE has implemented multiple policy initiatives to combat desertification and support the United Nations 2030 Agenda for Sustainable Development. In 2022, the UAE government released the "National Strategy to Combat Desertification

---

① "Saudi Green Initiative: Planting 10 Billion Trees and Restoring 40 Million Hectares of Degraded Land," China Biodiversity Conservation and Green Development Foundation (CBCGDF), https://www.cgdg.com/index.html, May 9, 2024.

② "Saudi Green Initiative: Planting 10 Billion Trees and Restoring 40 Million Hectares of Degraded Land," Website of the China Biodiversity Conservation and Green Development Foundation (CBCGDF), https://www.cgdg.com/index.html, May 9, 2024.

Chapter 9　Special Report on China-Arab States Ecological Cooperation

(2022-2030)", which set goals to increase agricultural system productivity by 40% compared to 2022 levels, restore at least 80% of degraded land, and increase the use of treated water for irrigation by 60% by 2030.

Arab states are actively leveraging innovative technologies to combat desertification. The UAE has established multiple research centers and experimental stations dedicated to research and development in desertification control and climate change monitoring. This includes the creation of specialized technology cooperation centers focused on the study and promotion of salt-tolerant plants. Additionally, the UAE employs drones to survey and map agricultural areas nationwide and has planted trees at 25 selected sites to mitigate desertification in these regions. The UAE has also launched the "Mohammed bin Zayed Water Initiative", aimed at promoting the application of innovative technologies to address water scarcity and related challenges.

## 9.2　China-Arab States Cooperation in Ecological and Environmental Governance

*China's Arab Policy Paper* emphasizes the promotion of China-Arab states coordination and communication under mechanisms such as the "United Nations Framework Convention on Climate Change", the "Convention on Biological Diversity", and the "United Nations Convention to Combat Desertification". Through bilateral and multilateral channels, both sides will actively engage in exchanges and cooperation on policy dialogue and information sharing, environmental legislation, water, air and soil pollution control and treatment, environmental protection awareness, environmental impact assessment, environmental monitoring, environmental protection industries and technologies, bio-diversity protection, prevention and control of desertification, arid zone forestry, forest management, training of environmental staff and holding seminars. These collaborative initiatives aim to enhance their joint capabilities in addressing climate change and environmental protection.[1] Over the past decade, China has actively worked hand in hand with Arab states to build a "Green Belt and Road". With the continuous improvement of top-level

---

[1]　"China's Arab Policy Paper," Website of the State Council of the People's Republic of China, https://www.gov.cn/xinwen/2016-01/13/content_5032647.htm, January 13, 2016.

205

green policy frameworks, the sustained expansion and deepening of practical green cooperation, and the growing consensus around the concept of green development, the construction of a "Green Belt and Road" has progressed steadily and yielded fruitful results.

### 9.2.1   China-Arab States Cooperation in Water-Saving Irrigation

*China's Arab Policy Paper* highlights the need to strengthen China-Arab states bilateral and multilateral cooperation in such fields as arid zone agriculture, water-saving irrigation, food security, animal husbandry and veterinary medicine. It encourages agricultural scientists from both sides to enhance exchanges. China will continue to set up demonstration projects of agricultural technology in Arab states, scale up agricultural management and technology training, and strengthen project follow-up and evaluation. President Xi Jinping has emphasized that the joint development of the "Belt and Road" Initiative should pave a path not only of open development but also one of green development.[①] Agricultural technology serves as a key example of China-Arab states technological exchange and transfer. Since its establishment in 2015, the China-Arab States Technology Transfer Center has co-founded eight bilateral technology transfer centers in states such as Saudi Arabia and Jordan, facilitating the application of advanced and practical technologies and equipment aligned with the sustainable development needs and concerns in the Arab region. At the 5th China-Arab States Expo Technology Transfer and Innovation Cooperation Conference, China introduced 300 advanced applicable technologies to Arab states, covering areas such as ecological and environmental protection, resource and energy utilization, and pollution control.

In 2023, at the 6th Water Resources Forum of the China-Arab States Expo, sixteen successful outcomes of water conservancy cooperation—promoted and implemented in "Belt and Road" partner countries—were released. These outcomes covered various types of initiatives, including exchange and cooperation, scientific research platforms, key technologies, and technology promotion. Some of these achievements have not only brought benefits within

---

① "Ecological Prosperity Leads to Civilizational Prosperity — The Concept of Harmonious Coexistence Between Humanity and Nature in the 'Belt and Road' Initiative," Website of the Central People's Government of the People's Republic of China, https://www.gov.cn/yaowen/liehiao/202310/content_6909198.htm, June 5, 2025.

Chapter 9    Special Report on China-Arab States Ecological Cooperation

China but also extended abroad, contributing Chinese expertise in water governance to other countries.

From September 16 to 18, 2024, the 6th Arab Water Forum was held in Abu Dhabi, UAE. At the invitation of Mahmoud Abu-Zeid, President of the Arab Water Council, Vice Minister of Water Resources of China, Zhu Chengqing, attended the forum and delivered a speech at the ministerial plenary session. During the forum, Zhu held bilateral meetings with Suhail Mohamed Al Mazrouei, UAE Minister of Energy and Infrastructure; Mahmoud Abu-Zeid, President of the Arab Water Council; and Hani Sweilam, Egypt's Minister of Water Resources and Irrigation. They exchanged views on enhancing practical cooperation in areas such as the utilization of non-conventional water resources and disaster prevention for floods and droughts. The Chinese delegation also visited the Hassyan Seawater Desalination Plant and the Mohammed bin Rashid Al Maktoum Solar Park in Dubai.

On January 7, 2025, Mr. Li Liangsheng, Vice Minister of Water Resources of the People's Republic of China, met Mr. Abdulrahman Alharbi, Saudi Arabia's Ambassador to China in Beijing. They held in-depth discussions on enhancing water cooperation between China and Saudi Arabia. Li Liangsheng pointed out that China and Saudi Arabia enjoyed long-term friendly cooperation in water sector, and achieved fruitful outcomes in the spheres of high-level visits, technical exchanges and coordination in international water-related events since the signing of Memorandum of Understanding on water cooperation in 2016. Ministry of Water Resources of China has earnestly implemented President Xi Jinping's water management strategy of "prioritizing water conservation, balancing spatial distribution, taking systematic approaches and promoting government-market synergy", and by coordinating efforts to address issues regarding water-related disasters, water resources, aquatic ecosystems, and the water environment, has continuously enhanced the nation's capacity to ensure water security. Ministry of Water Resources of China stands ready to carry out policy dialogues, technical exchanges and practical cooperation with Saudi Arabia in areas of non-conventional water use, groundwater protection, water saving, drought relief, soil and water conservation, among others. These efforts aim to further enrich the comprehensive strategic partnership between the two sides and strengthen water-related cooperation under the "Belt and Road"

207

The Development Process of China-Arab States Economic and Trade Relations
Annual Report 2024

Initiative.[1] Additionally, both sides will enhance mutual support and coordination in international water affairs, contributing to the early achievement of water-related goals under the United Nations' 2030 Agenda for Sustainable Development on a global scale. Abdulrahman Alharbi reaffirmed Saudi Arabia's strong commitment to water cooperation with China. He recognized China's globally leading expertise in water management and expressed hope for further deepening collaboration under the framework of the comprehensive strategic partnership to benefit both nations. Moreover, he looked forward to strengthening and expanding multilateral cooperation, harnessing the collective wisdom and strength of China and Saudi Arabia to advance global water governance.[2]

### 9.2.2　China-Arab States Cooperation in Clean Energy

At the opening ceremony of the 10th Ministerial Conference of the China-Arab States Cooperation Forum, Chinese President Xi Jinping delivered a keynote speech, stating that China and Arab states will jointly establish "Five Cooperation Frameworks" based on the "Eight Joint Actions" from the first China-Arab States Summit, accelerating the construction of a China-Arab states community with a shared future. One of the key frameworks is to establish a more multifaceted framework for energy cooperation, supporting Chinese energy enterprises and financial institutions to participate in renewable energy projects in Arab states.

With China's steady accumulation and breakthroughs in new energy technology, China-Arab states new energy cooperation is thriving, emerging as a major growth engine for bilateral cooperation. In recent years, Arab states have accelerated the implementation of reform measures and vigorously promoted renewable energy development. Saudi Arabia has set a target for renewable energy to account for 50% of its energy mix by 2030, while the UAE aims to increase the share of clean energy to 50% by 2050. These energy transition

---

[1]　"Ministry of Water Resources Holds Meeting on Water Conservation," Website of the Central People's Government of the People's Republic of China, https: //www.gov.cn/lianho/humen/202502/content_700358L.htm, June 6, 2025.

[2]　"Li Liangsheng Meets Abdulrahman Alharbi, the Saudi Arabian Ambassador to China," Website of the Ministry of Water Resources of the People's Republic of China, http: //www.mwr.gov.cn/xw/slyw/202501/t20250108_1726026.html, January 8. 2025.

208

Chapter 9　Special Report on China-Arab States Ecological Cooperation

strategies of the Arab states align closely with China's "dual carbon" goals and its vision of achieving modernization characterized by harmonious coexistence between humanity and nature, creating broad prospects for joint cooperation and shared development between both parties. According to a report by the International Energy Agency, the total installed capacity of renewable energy (excluding hydropower) in the Arab region, based on the energy transition plans announced so far, is expected to exceed 192 GW by 2030, a 17-fold increase from the current level. Solar power is projected to account for more than 42% of this capacity, while wind energy will contribute approximately 35%.[1] Under the framework of the "Belt and Road" Initiative, China and multiple Arab states are poised to explore vast opportunities for collaboration in the clean energy sector.

As China and Middle East states actively advance bilateral and multilateral cooperation in the clean energy sector, a series of infrastructure projects undertaken by Chinese enterprises have been implemented across multiple states in the region. In Saudi Arabia, Chinese enterprises are constructing the world's largest off-grid energy storage project in the Red Sea New City. This storage facility, integrated with a photovoltaic power generation system, will enable the entire 28000-square-kilometer Red Sea New City to be powered exclusively by green electricity. Meanwhile, new energy vehicles (NEVs), one of China's "New Three" leading export industries, have become a prominent sight on the streets of many states in the Middle East. Chinese automakers such as BYD, XPeng, Changan, NIO, and GAC are actively expanding into the Middle East market, introducing NEV models tailored to local consumers. According to data from the General Administration of Customs of the People's Republic of China, in the first half of 2024, China's passenger car exports to the Middle East reached 420000 units, a year-on-year increase of 46.2%, making the Middle East China's largest automobile export destination. Notably, NEVs accounted for 19.6% of these exports.[2]

The Arab region holds vast potential for nuclear energy development, particularly against the backdrop of rising electricity demand and an accelerating

---

[1]　"China-Middle East Energy Cooperation Advances Toward Innovation and Green Development," NetEase, https://www.163.com/dy/article/JMOJEP9L0550TYQ0.html, January 25, 2025.

[2]　"China-Middle East Energy Cooperation Advances Toward Innovation and Green Development," NetEase, https://www.163.com/dy/article/JMOJEP9L0550TYQ0.html, January 25, 2025.

209

energy transition. As a clean and efficient energy source, nuclear power offers broad application prospects. China National Nuclear Corporation (CNNC) and the Emirates Nuclear Energy Corporation (ENEC) jointly hosted the "Second CNNC-ENEC Nuclear Power Supplier Seminar" in Abu Dhabi, the capital of the UAE. As the China-UAE comprehensive strategic partnership continues to deepen, cooperation between CNNC and ENEC has steadily advanced in recent years, reflecting the shared vision of both nations in the peaceful utilization of nuclear energy. In May 2024, China and the UAE signed a bilateral cooperation document on the peaceful use of nuclear energy. In the joint statement, both sides reaffirmed their commitment to exploring and implementing joint demonstration projects, such as nuclear power plants, while strengthening research collaboration and experience-sharing in the peaceful use of nuclear energy to support its sustainable development.

In summary, the cooperation between China and Arab states in the field of clean energy has demonstrated strong vitality and promising prospects. From expansive photovoltaic power stations to NEVs appearing in everyday urban settings, Chinese technology and expertise are injecting significant momentum into the energy transition and sustainable development of Arab states. This partnership not only reflects the complementary strengths of both sides in technology, resources, and market potential, but also exemplifies the principle of mutual benefit and win-win cooperation under the "Belt and Road" Initiative. As Arab states accelerate their energy transition agendas, the space for China-Arab states collaboration in clean energy will continue to broaden. This will not only advance the shared economic development of both sides, but will also make a meaningful contribution to the global shift toward green energy. Looking ahead, China and Arab states are expected to further deepen collaboration, jointly promoting innovation and the application of clean energy technologies, and contributing to the building of a cleaner and greener world.

### 9.2.3 Comprehensive Management of Land Desertification

After more than 40 years of relentless efforts, China has successfully developed a desertification prevention and control path with distinct Chinese characteristics. This approach has fostered a virtuous cycle between ecological conservation and livelihood improvement, establishing China as a global model for combating desertification. The Chinese government places great importance

Chapter 9    Special Report on China-Arab States Ecological Cooperation

on strategic cooperation and partnerships with Arab states. On December 9, 2022, during the First China-Arab States Summit, President Xi Jinping proposed the "Eight Major Common Actions" for China-Arab states practical cooperation. Among these initiatives, the establishment of the China-Arab States International Research Center for Drought, Desertification, and Land Degradation (hereinafter referred to as the "China-Arab States Center") plays a key role in promoting the Joint Action on Green Innovation. China has actively engaged with relevant government departments, research institutions, universities, private enterprises, social organizations, international bodies, and financial institutions from both China and the Arab world to establish a China-Arab States Desertification Control Network. Efforts include organizing specialized training programs on the construction of the "Great Green Wall", facilitating discussions on trilateral cooperation opportunities between China, the African Union, and the Arab League in desertification and land degradation control. Additionally, China and Arab states are conducting research on the policy and technical framework for China-Arab states cooperation, in collaboration with the Big Data Center of the Chinese Academy of Sciences, to develop land degradation data tools and products tailored for Arab League member states, thereby providing data support for deepening China-Arab states sustainable development cooperation.

In August 2023, the National Forestry and Grassland Administration of China and the Secretariat of the League of Arab States signed a memorandum of understanding, officially announcing the establishment of the China-Arab States International Research Center for Drought, Desertification and Land Degradation (referred to as "China-Arab States Center") . The center aims to provide scientific and technological support, decision-making assistance, and think tank services for China and Arab states in combating drought, desertification, and land degradation. It focuses on key technological innovation, knowledge transfer, and experience sharing, advancing regional and global green development while improving livelihoods and contributing to the global goal of achieving zero net land degradation. The Chinese Academy of Forestry, serving as the executive body of the China-Arab States Center, has established a dedicated management and expert team to ensure effective operations.

In November 2024, the Training Program on Desertification Control and Sandstorm Disaster Prevention for Arab States was launched in Lanzhou, Gansu Province, with 24 participants from Tunisia, Oman, Egypt, and other Arab states.

211

Organized by China's Ministry of Commerce and hosted by the Gansu Desert Control Research Institute, the 21-day training program included classroom instruction and fieldwork, covering topics such as desertification prevention, sandstorm disaster management, oasis ecosystem protection, engineering-based desert control, and ecological restoration of degraded lands. In December 2024, during the 16th Conference of the Parties (COP 16) to the United Nations Convention to Combat Desertification (UNCCD) held in Riyadh, the conference adopted 39 resolutions, including the 2025-2026 budget, measures to address sand and dust storms, drought management, and enhanced scientific innovation. Throughout the event, the Chinese delegation actively engaged in discussions and fulfilled its commitments as a signatory state. It also hosted a China Pavilion series, organizing more than 10 side events, contributing Chinese insights and expertise to global desertification control efforts and the shared pursuit of a cleaner, more sustainable world. During the conference, the host country Saudi Arabia launched the "Riyadh Global Drought Resilience Partnership" initiative, which attracted USD12.15 billion in funding to support drought resilience efforts in the world's 80 most vulnerable countries. In addition, Saudi Arabia announced five new projects worth USD60 million aimed at strengthening climate and environmental initiatives, as part of the "Saudi Green Initiative".

The year 2024 marks the 30th anniversary of China's signing of the UNCCD. China has actively expanded its cooperation mechanism on desertification control under the "Belt and Road" Initiative, working with Central Asian, West Asian, and African countries facing similar challenges. By sharing sand control technologies and expertise, offering skills training, and fostering collaborative efforts, China is injecting momentum into green development across the Global South. A growing number of foreign desertification experts have come to China to study its sand control methods and apply them back in their own countries. Through a sincere and goodwill-based approach, China is empowering others with the knowledge and tools for sustainable land management, enabling more nations and regions to benefit from its desertification control experience.[1]

In conclusion, the prospects for ecological governance and green industry cooperation between China and Arab states are broad and promising. Both sides

---

[1]  "Green Stories in the Desert Worth the World's Attention," Belt and Road Portal, https: //www. yidaiyilu.gov.cn/p/0IGKBVG6.html, December 13, 2024.

Chapter 9    Special Report on China-Arab States Ecological Cooperation

have already taken concrete steps to actively advance collaboration in renewable energy sectors such as solar and wind power, while also striving to explore joint efforts in energy technology innovation and the transformation and upgrading of industrial structures. Moreover, they are continuously expanding the deep integration of emerging technologies—including the Internet, big data, artificial intelligence, and 5G—with green and low-carbon industries. As a significant outcome of this cooperation, China has provided assistance to Egypt under the framework of South-South cooperation on climate change, and the two sides have signed a memorandum of understanding on the establishment of a Joint Laboratory for Agricultural Green Development. A number of landmark projects undertaken by Chinese companies—such as the Hassyan Clean Coal Power Plant in Dubai, the first of its kind in the Middle East; the Taweelah Desalination Project in the UAE, currently the world's largest desalination plant under construction; and the third phase of the Noor-Ouarzazate Solar Complex in Morocco, which is the world's largest single-unit central tower CSP plant— have brought critical opportunities for regional states to overcome challenges related to energy structure adjustment and socio-economic development.

## 9.3    Outlook on China-Arab States Cooperation in Ecological and Environmental Protection

Sharing governance and policy experiences is a key focus of China's diplomacy toward Arab states under the framework of the China-Arab States Cooperation Forum. In 2024, the 10th China-Arab States Cooperation Forum was held in Beijing, where both parties reached consensus documents emphasizing mutual exchanges and learning on governance philosophies and experiences. China and Arab states share a high degree of alignment in their visions for green development. As the world's largest developing country, China has been unwavering in its commitment to promoting green and low-carbon development, striving to build a model of modernization characterized by harmonious coexistence between humanity and nature. Meanwhile, as the world's largest region for fossil fuel production and export, Arab states are collectively confronted with urgent challenges such as optimizing their energy consumption structures, advancing green transformation, and achieving diversified economic growth. Both China and Arab states have undertaken significant top-level

213

The Development Process of China-Arab States Economic and Trade Relations
Annual Report 2024

planning to address these challenges. China has proposed the "dual carbon" goals—peaking carbon emissions and achieving carbon neutrality—and is accelerating the development of a "1+N" policy framework. It has launched the "Ten Actions to Peak Carbon Emissions" and is actively promoting low-carbon development and green transformation. Similarly, Saudi Arabia has introduced the "Saudi Green" and "Middle East Green" initiatives; the UAE has proposed its "Net Zero by 2050 Strategic" Initiative; and Egypt has launched its "National Climate Change Strategy 2050". Other states in the region have also put forward various carbon reduction and emission control strategies. This high degree of convergence in top-level design and strategic thinking provides a solid foundation for cooperation between China and Arab states in addressing climate change, while also pointing the way forward for deepened collaboration.

## 9.3.1 Strengthening Policy Coordination in the Ecological and Environmental Sector: Building a Comprehensive Mechanism of "Policy Alignment—Platform Co-Building—Multilateral Coordination"

First, China and Arab states should further establish a multi-tiered policy alignment framework through joint communiqués and strategic agreements. As early as 2006, the *Joint Communiqué on Environmental Protection Cooperation* between the Government of the People's Republic of China and the League of Arab States outlined cooperation directions in environmental policy legislation, biodiversity conservation, and other key areas, along with an implementation plan to facilitate concrete projects. [1] *China's Arab Policy Paper* (2016) further set forth objectives for green development cooperation, promoting mutual recognition of environmental technology standards and policy coordination between China and Arab states. To comprehensively implement these strategic documents, China and Arab states have formulated specialized plans on issues such as desertification control and climate change. Examples include the "Middle East Green Initiative" jointly advanced by China and Saudi Arabia and the "Low-

---

[1] "Joint Communiqué on Environmental Protection Cooperation Between the Government of the People's Republic of China and the League of Arab States," Website of the China-Arab States Cooperation Forum, http: //www.chinaarabcf.org/zagx/rwjl/201110/t20111012_6842688.htm, October 12, 2011.

214

Chapter 9 Special Report on China-Arab States Ecological Cooperation

Carbon City Development Cooperation Framework" between China and Egypt, which enhance policy integration and goal alignment. As developing nations, China and Arab states share similar positions and aspirations in strengthening climate and environmental governance and promoting sustainable development. Based on this common ground, both sides can deepen cooperation in green infrastructure, renewable energy, and green finance, and actively participate in multilateral platforms such as the "BRI International Green Development Coalition" and the "Green Investment Principles (GIP) for the Belt and Road", fostering a closer green development partnership. By making sustainability a foundation for China-Arab states cooperation, both sides can drive long-term economic and social progress.[1]

Second, China and Arab states should establish institutionalized dialogue mechanisms and collaboration platforms. A ministerial-level dialogue mechanism and specialized forums should be set up to enhance cooperation. The China Biodiversity Conservation and Green Development Foundation (CBCGDF) has established a regular ministerial-level environmental dialogue mechanism with the UAE, Egypt, and other Arab states, focusing on topics such as carbon emissions accounting and the sharing of ecological restoration technologies to promote policy exchange and mutual learning.[2] Through platforms such as the China-Arab States Forum on Environmental Protection Cooperation and the Eco-Environmental Subforum of the Euro-Asia Economic Forum, China and Arab states can strengthen regional consensus on green economic transformation, facilitate policy coordination, and promote project matchmaking. These efforts will further advance the construction of the "Green Belt and Road" Initiative. Additionally, cooperation between think tanks and civil society organizations should be reinforced. Chinese and Arab think tanks have jointly published the "White Paper on Green Transition Cooperation" to drive innovation in environmental policies and promote standard harmonization. Meanwhile,

---

[1] "Building a Green Foundation for Sustainable Development for China and Arab States," Website of the China-Arab States Cooperation Forum, http://www.chinaarabcf.org/zagx/sssb/202104/t20210425_9156375.htm, April 25, 2021.

[2] "China Proposes Advancing Environmental Cooperation with Arab States toward Diversification," China News Service, https://www.chinanews.com.cn/news/2006/2006-02-09/8/687733.shtml, February 9, 2006.

215

CBCGDF, in collaboration with Arab civil organizations, have established a Biodiversity Monitoring Network, fostering the exchange of grassroots governance experiences.

Third, coordination of multilateral mechanisms and global governance participation should be strengthened. China and Arab states have jointly engaged in many international agreements such as the United Nations Convention to Combat Desertification and the Paris Agreement. On platforms such as the 28th United Nations Climate Change Conference (COP28), both sides collaborated in voicing their positions and advocate for the establishment of a "South-South Cooperation Fund for Combating Desertification" to safeguard the environmental rights and interests of developing countries. The two sides have also jointly promoted the establishment of the "China-Arab States International Research Center on Drought, Desertification, and Land Degradation", to integrate regional ecological governance resources. Through the "BRI International Green Development Coalition", China and Arab states have worked out plans for cross-border ecological corridors (such as the Red Sea-Persian Gulf Ecological Corridor), as well as other joint action plans for transboundary water resource management and desertification prevention.

### 9.3.2 Establishing a Trinity of "Desertification Prevention-Clean Energy-Digital Ecology" Cooperation Framework, Promoting the Deepening and Intellectualization of Technology Transfer

First, technology transfer and demonstration in desertification prevention: In recent years, China has actively promoted the export of core technologies. At the 6th China-Arab States Expo, China introduced biodegradable sand barriers, underground rhizosphere irrigation technology, and moisture balance afforestation and sand fixation technologies to assist Arab states in restoring degraded lands. Saudi Arabia has adopted intelligent robotic tree planting technology, photovoltaic desertification control technology, and blockchain carbon chain technology from China's Elion Resources Group, enhancing the implementation efficiency of the "Saudi Green Initiative". China and Arab states have jointly established the "International Research Center on Drought, Desertification, and Land Degradation", collaborating on cross-border desertification control technology research and funding applications,

216

Chapter 9    Special Report on China-Arab States Ecological Cooperation

with the goal of raising the land restoration rate in the region to 15%.[1] With the development and maturation of new energy technologies, China has promoted the "Photovoltaic + Desertification Control" model in states such as Saudi Arabia and the UAE. This model uses photovoltaic panels to provide shading, reducing water evaporation, and simultaneously promotes clean energy development and vegetation restoration, resulting in a "two-way carbon-neutrality" effect.

Second, technology transfer and coordinated application in clean energy: In recent years, China has actively expanded its cooperation with Arab states in green technology, with clean energy being the most representative sector. The two sides have successively established the China-Arab States Clean Energy Training Center and the China-Egypt Renewable Energy Joint Laboratory and have implemented numerous collaborative projects, including the Al-Kharsaah Solar Power Plant in Qatar, the 186 MW Benban Solar Power Park Project and the 165MW (DC) Photovoltaic Power Station EPC Project in Egypt. China's exports of renewable energy equipment to Arab states have been steadily increasing. China has provided photovoltaic modules and energy storage equipment for the 2000 MWh Bisha Battery Energy Storage System Project in Saudi Arabia and the 1.8 GW Benban Solar Power Park Project in Egypt, contributing to a fivefold increase in the installed capacity of renewable energy in Arab states. Additionally, China has introduced green building technologies in the construction of Egypt's New Administrative Capital and applied intelligent water circulation systems in Algeria's water infrastructure renovation project, improving urban water resource utilization efficiency by 30%.[2]

Third, cooperation in digital ecological governance technologies: China has exported a satellite remote sensing monitoring and data analysis platform to Saudi Arabia, integrating drone-based seeding technology to precisely identify vegetation restoration areas and enhance desertification control efficiency. Additionally, China and Arab states have jointly developed an ecological database to monitor vegetation coverage and water resource distribution in real time

---

[1] "China and Arab States Discuss New Pathways for Cooperation in Desertification Prevention," Website of the Forestry and Grassland Administration of Ningxia Hui Autonomous Region, http://lcj.nx.gov.cn/xwzx/mtgz/202309/t20230925_4285177.html, September 25, 2023.

[2] Wang Jia, Ahmed Hassan, "Green Economy in Arab States: Development, Challenges, and China's Role," *Arab World Studies*, No. 3, 2024, p. 54.

217

The Development Process of China-Arab States Economic and Trade Relations
Annual Report 2024

along the Red Sea-Persian Gulf Ecological Corridor, optimizing transnational ecological restoration strategies. With the rapid advancement of artificial intelligence technology, intelligent equipment and robotics have been widely adopted. Saudi Arabia has introduced China's intelligent tree-planting robot technology, achieving a planting efficiency of 2000 trees per unit per day—15 times higher than traditional manual methods—while reducing freshwater consumption by 90%. Moving forward, efforts should focus on strengthening the localization of technologies (such as joint cultivation of salt-tolerant plants), establishing cross-border ecological compensation mechanisms, and enhancing green financial support systems to build a more resilient regional ecological governance network.

Looking ahead, the green development of the "Belt and Road" Initiative requires continuous and deepened cooperation in green and clean energy, and the promotion of the low-carbon transformation of international energy collaboration. China should actively assume its role as a key "provider" of relevant products, leveraging its strengths to support the new phase of green development under the BRI framework. On the one hand, China should actively encourage solar and wind power enterprises to "go global", and facilitate the development of exemplary green energy projects that serve as models of best practice. On the other hand, China should deepen cooperation in the field of energy technologies and equipment, with a strategic focus on joint research and trainings in key areas such as high-efficiency and low-cost renewable energy generation, advanced nuclear power, smart grid systems, hydrogen energy, energy storage solutions, and carbon capture, utilization, and storage.

### 9.3.3 Strengthening Cooperation in Multilateral Mechanisms Between China and Arab States to Enhance Global Environmental Governance

First, enhance global environmental governance through cooperation in multilateral mechanisms: China should actively provide technical assistance and financial support to developing countries. As one of the nations that are severely affected by desertification, China has shared its "Three-North Shelter Forest Program" technologies and achievements in desertification prevention, offering replicable ecological governance experiences to countries in the Global South. The Chinese government places great importance on comprehensive

218

Chapter 9    Special Report on China-Arab States Ecological Cooperation

desertification prevention and continues to advance major ecological projects such as the "Three-North Shelter Forest Program". As a result, 53% of treatable desertified land has been effectively restored, fostering a positive cycle between ecological protection and livelihood improvement. The economic, social, and environmental landscape of desertified regions has undergone a profound transformation, making China the world's largest contributor to greening efforts and an international model for desertification control. These achievements have significantly contributed to global desertification prevention and control efforts.

Additionally, focus on co-building regional governance platforms. Relying on the "BRI International Green Development Coalition", China and Arab states have initiated the Eco-Environmental Subforum of the Euro-Asia Economic Forum and the China-Arab States Forum on Environmental Protection Cooperation, focusing on issues such as green economic transformation and cross-border ecological restoration. These platforms facilitate policy communication and project alignment. Through the China-Arab States Cooperation Forum mechanism, the *White Paper on Green Transition Cooperation* has been released to promote mutual recognition of regional environmental standards and the development of joint action plans.

Second, build transnational ecological corridors and regional linkage projects: Efforts should be further made to advance the construction of the Red Sea-Persian Gulf Ecological Corridor. China and Arab states have jointly planned an ecological corridor covering six states, including Saudi Arabia and Oman. This corridor utilizes cross-border electricity networks, seawater desalination projects, and satellite remote sensing technologies to achieve unified management of water resource allocation, desertification prevention, and biodiversity conservation. The project integrates China's intelligent water circulation system and photovoltaic desertification control technology, enhancing regional ecological resilience. At the same time, synchronized development of green infrastructure and energy are advocated.

Third, promote joint research and capacity building: In the field of ecological and environmental governance, China and Arab states have established the China-Arab States International Research Center on Drought, Desertification, and Land Degradation, by which, the research resources of both sides are integrated to conduct cross-border ecological governance technology research and development, promote the localization of technologies such as biodegradable

219

sand barriers and drone-based seeding. China, through the environmental protection training programs organized by the Ministry of Commerce, has trained over 500 technicians from Arab states in areas including environmental policy formulation and pollution control technologies, strengthening regional ecological governance capabilities. The think tanks from both sides have jointly launched many demonstration projects, such as the China-Arab States Water-Saving Demonstration Base, promoting drip irrigation technology and reducing agricultural water usage by 40%.

President Xi Jinping has emphasized that "lucid waters and lush mountains are invaluable assets", a core concept of China's ecological civilization and a contribution of Chinese wisdom to global sustainable development. In the new era, green development represents not only a profound transformation of the development paradigm, but also aligns with prevailing international trends and the direction of future progress. China will continue to uphold the philosophy of green development, further deepening its cooperation with Arab states in addressing climate change. By joining forces to tackle shared challenges, both sides aim to jointly build a "Green Belt and Road" and foster a community of all life on Earth, thereby embarking on a new journey in the global response to ecological crises. Under the "Belt and Road" initiative, China and Arab states are actively addressing the global ecological and environmental crisis, deepening cooperation in the ecological and environmental sectors. Such collaboration has made a strong contribution to the economic development, ecological governance, and transformation of Arab states, building a solid foundation for the China-Arab community with a shared future.

# Chapter 10   Special Report on China-Arab States Cooperation in Tourism

## 10.1   Overview of China-Arab States Tourism in 2024

In 2024, China's cultural tourism industry demonstrated remarkable growth. The combination of China's rich and splendid civilization, vibrant modern urban districts, high-quality tourism products and services, and cultural tourism activities enhanced by advanced technology not only led to a significant increase in inbound tourism, but also greatly improved China's international tourism image and strengthened the global competitiveness of China's cultural tourism industry. According to the latest data released by the National Immigration Administration of China in January 2025, a total of 610 million inbound and outbound travelers were recorded nationwide in 2024, representing a year-on-year increase of 43.9%. Among them, foreign travelers accounted for 64.88 million entries and exits, reflecting an 82.9% year-on-year rise. A total of 2.597 million visas and travel permits were issued to foreigners, an increase of 52.3% compared to the previous year. Additionally, 20.115 million foreign travelers entered China visa-free through various ports nationwide, up by 112.3% year-on-year, while the number of visitors benefiting from transit visa exemption policy grew by 113.5%. Notably, following the full optimization and relaxation of China's transit visa exemption policy, the number of travelers utilizing this policy increased by 29.5% month-on-month.[1]

---

[1]   "Key Data on Immigration Management Work in 2024," Website of the National Immigration Administration, https://www.nia.gov.cn/n897453/c1693437/content.html, January 14, 2025.

The Development Process of China-Arab States Economic and Trade Relations
Annual Report 2024

Underpinned by amicable international relations and proactive efforts from both sides, China-Arab states tourism cooperation made significant strides in 2024. Morocco dispatched an official delegation to China to promote its tourism sector and actively expand its presence in the Chinese market, enhancing its appeal to Chinese tourists.[1] As a result, the number of Chinese tourists visiting Morocco saw a sharp rise, surpassing 100000 travelers—a growth of approximately 78%. In Egypt, the number of Chinese visitors exceeded 300000, reflecting an annual increase of nearly 65%.[2] Between January and June 2024, the number of Chinese tourists visiting Sharjah of the United Arab Emirates (UAE), increased fivefold compared to the same period in 2023, accounting for 56% of all tourists from the Far East.[3] According to data from the Department of Economy and Tourism of the UAE, in 2024, Chinese tourism bookings in Abu Dhabi surged by more than 75% year-on-year, while Abu Dhabi visitors traveling to China recorded an almost fourfold increase.[4] Between January and August, Dubai received 547000 overnight visitors from China, a year-on-year growth of 39%. Overall, China-Arab states tourism demonstrated a robust and dynamic growth trajectory in 2024.

## 10.1.1 A Continuously Improving Cooperation Mechanism Providing Long-term Assurance for China-Arab States Tourism Cooperation

On May 30, 2024, the 10th Ministerial Conference of the China-Arab States Cooperation Forum adopted the "CASCF Execution Plan for 2024-2026", which explicitly outlined that efforts must be made to strengthen collaboration across multiple sectors, including tourism, setting a clear direction for the future

---

[1] "Moroccan Media: Morocco's Tourism Industry Is to Be highlighted by the 'China Moment'," Website of the China-Arab States Cooperation Forum, http://www.chinaarabcf.org/zagx/rwjl/202501/t20250120_11538833.htm, January 20, 2025.

[2] "More Chinese Tourists 'Check-in' to Experience the Ancient Charm of Egypt," Website of the China-Arab States Cooperation Forum, http://www.chinaarabcf.org/zagx/rwjl/202501/t20250107_11528271.htm, January 7, 2025.

[3] "The Number of Chinese Tourists Visiting Sharjah in the First Half of 2024 Increased Fivefold Year-on-Year," China News Service, https://baijiahao.baidu.com/s?id=1808366744666560138&wfr=spider&for=pc, August 25, 2024.

[4] "Celebrate Chinese New Year in the UAE," China Economic Net, http://www.ce.cn/xwzx/gnsz/gdxw/202502/02/t20250202_39281531.shtml, February 2, 2025.

Chapter 10   Special Report on China-Arab States Cooperation in Tourism

of China-Arab states tourism cooperation. A stable cooperation platform, continuously improving mechanisms, and increasingly detailed action plans serve as a solid foundation for deepening tourism collaboration between China and Arab states.

## 10.1.2   China Accelerating Efforts to Promote Tourism Cooperation with Arab States

In 2024, China continuously optimized policies related to transit visa exemptions, regional visa-free entry, and port visas, further expanding the scope of unilateral and mutual visa exemptions, thereby enhancing the convenience for foreign nationals traveling to and within China.[1] Efforts to facilitate inbound tourism for foreign visitors, including those from Arab states, were actively promoted. Improvements in transit visa exemption policy included measures such as the 240-hour transit visa exemption, visa-free entry for foreign tour groups arriving by cruise ship, expanded visa-free entry to Hainan for nationals of 59 countries, and the implementation of 24-hour direct transit without border inspection procedures at nine major hub airports, along with 18 other policies aimed at enhancing convenience for foreign travelers to China.[2] At the same time, China advanced payment convenience in tourism-related locations, including scenic sites, performance venues, restaurants, and hotels. Additionally, air routes between China and Arab states were expanded, and a broader range of inbound tourism products and services was introduced, demonstrating China's proactive stance in strengthening China-Arab states tourism cooperation.

## 10.1.3   Arab States Placing Great Emphasis on Expanding the Chinese Tourism Market

Starting from July 1, 2024, Saudi Arabia launched a series of marketing campaigns in China, introducing multiple initiatives to enhance convenience for Chinese tourists. China has become one of the designated countries eligible for Saudi Arabia's fast-track e-visa service. To better serve Chinese travelers,

---

[1]   "The Full Release of the Benefits of the Visa-Free Policy," Economic Daily, http: //paper.ce.cn/pc/content/202501/11/content_307352.html, January 11, 2025.

[2]   "'China Travel' Increased by 112.3% Year-on-Year! Once You Visit, You Will Fall in Love," Xinhua News, https: //www.news.cn/world/20250114/71ec65d8e0c4450c8e878960a2503f13/c.html, January 14, 2025.

223

the official WeChat mini-program of the Saudi Tourism Authority offers a variety of customized travel assistance services, including Mandarin-speaking tour guides, Saudi tourism product introductions and bookings, information on major local festivals and performances, and landmark attractions.[1] In addition, Saudi Arabia has established a dedicated Chinese-language service hotline on its official tourism website, installed Chinese-language signs at Riyadh Airport, and introduced UnionPay payment channels across the country. Saudi Arabia has now officially become a designated outbound group tour destination for Chinese citizens,[2] with a long-term goal of increasing the number of Chinese tourists from 150000 to 3 million-5 million by 2030.[3] Other Arab states, including the UAE, have shown strong interest in collaborating with Chinese cultural institutions and tourism industry players, identifying China as a key target market. Emirates Airlines has explicitly expressed its commitment to leveraging its global aviation network to promote China's dynamic cities and unique landscapes, further fostering cooperation and development in the tourism sectors of China and the Middle East. Additionally, states such as Morocco, the UAE, Qatar, and Tunisia have introduced visa-free entry policies for Chinese citizens, effectively removing visa barriers and making travel to Arab destinations more accessible for Chinese tourists.

### 10.1.4　The Increase in Flight Routes Providing Essential Support for China-Arab States Tourism Exchanges

According to the latest data released by the National Immigration Administration of China in January 2025, a total of 32.566 million inbound and outbound transportation inspections were conducted throughout 2024, representing a year-on-year increase of 38.8%. Among them, 879000 flights

---

[1]　"Saudi Arabia Will Continue to Provide Convenience for Chinese Tourists," *CT News*, https://www.ctnews.com.cn/huanqiu/content/2024-11/26/content_167470.html, November 28, 2024.

[2]　"Starting July 1, Saudi Arabia to Become an Approved Destination for Chinese Group Tours," Beijing News, https://www.bjnews.com.cn/detail/1719357418129747.html, June 26, 2024.

[3]　"Saudi Media Review Saudi Arabia's 2024 Achievements: A Renewed Vision and Promising Prospects," Website of the Economic and Commercial Office of the Embassy of the People's Republic of China in the Kingdom of Saudi Arabia, http://sa.mofcom.gov.cn/jmxw/art/2025/art_2eb28d96a0a343d484b394c9b882d7f2.html, January 1, 2025.

Chapter 10    Special Report on China-Arab States Cooperation in Tourism

were inspected, marking a 62.6% year-on-year growth.[①] From January to June 2024, China successively launched new direct flight routes, including Beijing to Riyadh, Shanghai to Riyadh, Shenzhen to Riyadh, and Xiamen to Doha, further enhancing the air transport network between the two regions. The opening of these routes has ensured comprehensive flight coverage between major Chinese cities and key destinations such as Riyadh, Jeddah, and Doha.

In 2024, driven by a significant surge in the number of Chinese tourists traveling to Arab states, many Arab airlines launched new direct flight routes or increased flight capacity. Saudi Arabian Airlines inaugurated the Jeddah-Dammam-Beijing route and now operates nine weekly flights between Riyadh, Jeddah, and major Chinese cities, substantially reducing the temporal and spatial distance between China and the Arab world. These enhancements not only offer greater convenience and reduced travel costs for tourists from both regions but also serve as a strong impetus for the development of China-Arab states tourism cooperation. EgyptAir increased its Cairo-Shanghai flights to four per week and announced plans to include Xiamen as a new direct destination, in addition to its existing routes to Beijing, Shanghai, Hangzhou, and Guangzhou. In May 2024, Gulf Air flight GF124 from Manama, the capital of Bahrain, landed at Shanghai Pudong International Airport, officially marking the first direct international flight route between China and Bahrain.[②] Meanwhile, Royal Air Maroc announced the resumption of its Casablanca-Beijing direct service, scheduled to commence on January 20, 2025. Additionally, data from Dubai Department of Economy and Tourism shows that Dubai International Airport received over one million Chinese travelers in the first half of 2024, reflecting an 80% year-on-year increase.[③]

---

① "610 Million Border Crossings in 2024, a Year-on-Year Increase of 43.9%," Website of the National Immigration Administration of China, https://www.nia.gov.cn/n741440/n741567/c1693512/content.html, January 14, 2025.

② "Global Insights: Starting from the Silk Road— How China and Arab States Forge a Model of South-South Cooperation," *China News Service*, http://www.chinanews.com.cn/gj/2024/06-01/10226960.shtml, June 1, 2024.

③ "Celebrate Chinese New Year in the UAE," *China Economic Net*, http://www.ce.cn/xwzx/gnsz/gdxw/202502/02/t20250202_39281531.shtml, February 2, 2025.

225

The Development Process of China-Arab States Economic and Trade Relations
Annual Report 2024

## 10.1.5 Frequent Cultural Tourism Exchanges Between China and Arab States

In 2024, cultural tourism exchanges between China and Arab states were marked by frequent and dynamic interaction. In May, the 31st Arabian Travel Market was held in Dubai. The Bureau of International Exchange and Cooperation of the Ministry of Culture and Tourism of China, together with the Chinese Cultural Center in the UAE, organized a delegation of nearly 100 representatives from the cultural tourism authorities of nine provinces (cities) in China, as well as airlines and travel enterprises. They participated in the exhibition and set up a 135-square-meter "Hello! China" booth to showcase Chinese cultural tourism products to global tour operators and audiences. This marked the first collective appearance of the Chinese exhibitors at the Arabian Travel Market since 2019.[1] In October, the "Execution Plan for the China-Saudi Arabia Year of Culture in 2025" was signed between the Ministry of Culture and Tourism of the People's Republic of China and the Ministry of Culture of Saudi Arabia. In 2025, the two sides will celebrate the Cultural Year, hosting a series of cultural activities to showcase each other's rich cultural tourism resources, further promoting cultural exchanges and mutual learning between China and the Arab world.[2]

In 2024, people-to-people and cultural exchanges between China and Arab states witnessed a robust and positive trajectory. A total of 788 rare Egyptian artifacts (exhibited abroad for the first time) were showcased at the Shanghai Museum, significantly boosting Chinese public enthusiasm for the cultural exhibition. Exhibitions such as "Al Ula: Wonder of Arabia" and "On Top of the Pyramids: the Civilization of Ancient Egypt" were successively held in Beijing and Shanghai. To commemorate the 40th anniversary of the establishment of diplomatic relations between China and the UAE, the China Oriental Performing Arts Group and the China National Symphony Orchestra held the national-style concert "Sing the Millennium" and a special performance in Abu Dhabi, while

---

[1] "'Hello! China' Exhibition Booth Shines at the 2024 ATM," Website of the Ministry of Culture and Tourism of the People's Republic of China, https://www.mct.gov.cn/preview/whzx/bnsj/dwwhllj/202405/t20240508_952749.html, May 8, 2024.

[2] "Saudi Arabia Will Continue to Provide Convenience for Chinese Tourists," *CT News*, https://www.ctnews.com.cn/huanqiu/content/2024-11/26/content_167470.html, November 28, 2024.

Chapter 10    Special Report on China-Arab States Cooperation in Tourism

the National Ballet of China staged the "Chinese New Year (The Nutcracker Chinese Version)" in the UAE, offering local audiences a glimpse into the charm of cross-cultural artistic fusion. Chinese martial arts and Chinese chess have gained widespread popularity in Lebanon, and a surge of high-quality Chinese films and digital media content has fueled a wave of "China fever" in the country. Productions such as "Minning Town" and "When Pharaohs Meet Sanxingdui", garnered over 500 million views across Arab states.[1]

Hundreds of schools in Arab states now offer Chinese language courses, and the "Chinese language fever" continues to intensify in countries such as Lebanon.[2] Learners from the UAE, Saudi Arabia, Egypt, Tunisia, Algeria, Morocco, Jordan, and Iraq actively participated in the 23rd "Chinese Bridge" Chinese Proficiency Competition for Foreign College Students. Egypt held its inaugural "Learn Idioms, Know China" Chinese Idiom Competition, attracting over 200 participants from Chinese language majors and enthusiasts from various Egyptian universities. The Palace Museum in Beijing successfully hosted the China-Arab States Poetry Conference, where poets from Arab states and their Chinese counterparts exchanged ideas through recitation, voicing shared values such as peace and friendship. Despite ongoing armed conflict in Sudan, the Chinese language training center in Atbara has continued to attract a large number of learners, approximately 60% of whom are refugees from conflict-affected areas—demonstrating China's growing cultural influence in the Arab world. Furthermore, Chinese language education in Egypt has made remarkable strides, with institutions such as Cairo University reporting a significant increase in enrollments in Chinese language programs, reflecting the continued deepening of China-Arab states cultural and educational exchanges.[3]

---

[1] "Twenty Years of China-Arab States Cooperation: A New Journey as the Tides Recede and the Shore Widens," *Middle East Outlook,* http://www.chinaarabcf.org/zagx/sssb/202406/t20240617_11436908.htm, June 17, 2024.

[2] "Chinese Ambassador to Lebanon Qian Minjian Publishes Signed Article in Al Akhbar Entitled 'Accelerating the Construction of a China-Arab States Community with a Shared Future'," Website of the Ministry of Foreign Affairs of the People's Republic of China, https://www.mfa.gov.cn/web/wjdt_674879/zwbd_674895/202406/t20240604_11376473.shtml, June 3, 2024.

[3] "'Chinese Language Fever' Accelerates People-to-People and Cultural Exchanges Between China and Arab States in 2024," Website of the State Council Information Office of the People's Republic of China, http://www.scio.gov.cn/gxzl/ydyl_26587/rwjl/rwjl_26595/202412/t20241230_879310.html, December 28, 2024.

227

The Development Process of China-Arab States Economic and Trade Relations
Annual Report 2024

The numerous achievements in China-Arab states tourism cooperation in 2024 have laid a solid foundation for achieving the goal of 10 million mutual visits by 2029, and the future of China-Arab states tourism cooperation is expected to experience even more brilliant development.

## 10.2  A 20-Year Review of China-Arab States Cooperation in Tourism

On January 30, 2004, during his visit to Egypt, former President Hu Jintao met in Cairo with Arab League Secretary-General Amr Mahmoud Moussa and representatives from the 22 member states of the Arab League. He proposed four principles for establishing a new type of China-Arab states partnership: to promote political relations on the basis of mutual respect, to forge closer trade and economic links so as to achieve common development, to expand cultural exchanges so as to draw upon each other's experience, and to strengthen cooperation in international affairs with the aim of safeguarding world peace and promoting common development.[1] On the same day, the China-Arab States Cooperation Forum was established. The establishment of the forum provided a new platform for dialogue and collaboration between China and Arab states on the basis of equality and mutual benefit. It further enriched the China-Arab states relationship and strengthened bilateral cooperation in various fields, including politics, economy and trade, science and technology, culture, education, and healthcare. By December 2023, China had signed "Belt and Road" Initiative cooperation agreements with all 22 Arab states and the Arab League, laying out a grand blueprint for extensive China-Arab states cooperation.[2]

In 2024, China and the Arab states celebrated the 20th anniversary of the China-Arab States Cooperation Forum. Over the past two decades, China

---

[1] "Hu Jintao Meets with Arab League Secretary-General Moussa and Representatives of Its 22 Member States," Website of the Ministry of Foreign Affairs of the People's Republic of China, https://www.fmprc.gov.cn/gjhdq_676201/gjhdqzz_681964/lhg_682830/xgxw_682836/200401/t20040131_9638906.shtml. January 31, 2004.

[2] "China and Arab States Achieve Remarkable Results in Jointly Building the 'Belt and Road' Initiative," Website of the State Council Information Office of the People's Republic of China, http://www.scio.gov.cn/gxzl/ydyl_26587/zxtj_26590/zxtj_26591/202312/t20231219_822728.html, December 19, 2023.

228

Chapter 10　Special Report on China-Arab States Cooperation in Tourism

and Arab states have continuously deepened strategic mutual trust, expanded pragmatic cooperation, and enhanced cultural exchanges, embodying the spirit of mutual support, equality and mutual benefit, inclusiveness, and mutual learning. This partnership has achieved remarkable progress. Over the past 20 years, the total trade volume between China and Arab states, including trade in tourism services, has exceeded USD400 billion. China has become the largest trading partner of Arab states, while Arab states have become China's primary overseas crude oil suppliers. The Arab region is now one of the most densely connected areas in terms of strategic partnerships with China.[1] China-Arab states cultural tourism exchanges have also flourished during this period of time. The unique charm of Arab destinations has attracted a growing number of Chinese tourists, while China, with its high-level openness and increasing international tourism influence and competitiveness, has achieved outstanding progress in China-Arab states tourism cooperation.

## 10.2.1　Continuous Improvement of Mechanisms and Platforms Having Enhanced and Enriched the Achievements of China-Arab States Tourism Cooperation over 20 Years

### 10.2.1.1　The "Belt and Road" Initiative Bringing New Development Opportunities for China-Arab States Tourism Cooperation

In September and October 2013, President Xi Jinping successively proposed the major initiatives of the "Silk Road Economic Belt" and the "21st Century Maritime Silk Road", which garnered significant international attention. On June 5, 2014, President Xi attended the opening ceremony of the 6th Ministerial Conference of the China-Arab States Cooperation Forum and delivered an important speech titled "Promoting Silk Road Spirit and Deepening China-Arab States Cooperation", in which he first proposed the vision of building a China-Arab states community with a shared future.[2] China and Arab states, through joint efforts in building the "Belt and Road" Initiative, have established a "1+2+3" cooperation model, with energy cooperation as the core, infrastructure development, trade, and investment facilitation as two key

---

[1]　"Investment Cooperation and Prospects Between China and Arab States", *Sina*, https: //cj.sina.com.cn/articles/view/1686546714/6486a91a02002kvhu, January 23, 2025.

[2]　"Promoting Silk Road Spirit and Deepening China-Arab States Cooperation," *People's Daily Online-CPC News Online*, http: //cpc.people.com.cn/n/2014/0606/c64094-25110795.html, June 5, 2014.

229

pillars, and high-tech fields such as nuclear energy, aerospace satellites, and new energy as breakthrough areas. Within the BRI framework, China and Arab states have jointly implemented over 200 large-scale projects, with China providing training for more than 3400 Arab professionals across various fields. China has consistently remained the largest trading partner of Arab states for many years. The trade volume between China and Arab states has surged from USD36.7 billion in 2004 to USD398 billion in 2023, an elevenfold increase, benefiting nearly 2 billion people across both regions.[1]

The proposal of the "Belt and Road" Initiative has had a significant impact on the development of tourism between China and Arab states, presenting new opportunities for bilateral cooperation. Prior to the Initiative, although a foundational framework for China-Arab states tourism cooperation had already been established, overall progress remained relatively slow. Several factors, including political instability in certain Arab states, underdeveloped bilateral tourism cooperation mechanisms, and the weak industrial base of tourism-related sectors, served as key constraints to further cooperation. The "Belt and Road" Initiative has promoted cultural exchange between China and Arab states and has enhanced mutual understanding between the two sides. Tourism has increasingly become a vital vehicle for such cultural interaction. The initiative has facilitated visa liberalization, strengthened talent cultivation, and driven the advancement of tourism information technologies, thereby significantly improving the efficiency and quality of China-Arab states tourism cooperation.

In 2017, the number of outbound trips by Chinese citizens to Arab states reached 1.338 million, while 336000 Arab citizens visited China—a year-on-year increase of 9.9% and 2.5%, respectively. In 2018, marking the fifth anniversary of the "Belt and Road" Initiative, China-Arab states comprehensive cooperation entered a new phase. The scale of bilateral tourism exchanges continued to expand. By this time, ten Arab states had been included in the list of approved outbound group travel destinations for self-funded Chinese tourists.[2] Generally

---

[1]  "Twenty Years of Fruitful Cooperation: China-Arab States Relations Set Sail Anew," Xinhua News Agency, https://www.gov.cn/yaowen/liebiao/202405/content_6954155.htm, May 29, 2024.

[2]  "Joining Hands along the "Belt and Road": China and Arab States Jointly Promote Integrated Development of Culture and Tourism," Xinhua News Agency, https://www.gov.cn/xinwen/2018-10/25/content_5334496.htm?use_xbridge3=true&loader_name=forest&need_sec_link=1&sec_link_scene=im, October 25, 2018.

Chapter 10　Special Report on China-Arab States Cooperation in Tourism

speaking, between 2016 and 2019, the number of Arab nationals visiting the mainland of China showed a steady upward trend. Meanwhile, the number of Chinese tourists traveling to Arab states as their first outbound destination maintained an average annual growth rate of 10%, reaching a historical peak in 2019.[1] Following the end of the COVID-19 pandemic, China-Arab states cooperation in tourism experienced a swift recovery. States such as Morocco, the UAE, Qatar, Egypt, and Tunisia implemented visa-free entry policies for Chinese tourists and launched new air routes, thereby attracting an increasing number of Chinese travelers to the Arab world and significantly promoting people-to-people exchanges. Many Arab states, including Bahrain, have explicitly identified China as a key target market for tourism development.[2] Tourism is playing an increasingly vital role in the construction of a China-Arab states community with a shared future.

Tourism cooperation has simultaneously fostered the development of trade. The collaboration between China and Arab states in the tourism sector involves not only the movement of travelers but also stimulates the growth of related industries, such as air transportation, catering and accommodation, and the sale of tourism-related products. The spending of Chinese tourists during their visits to Arab states drives local commercial activity, while Arab tourists traveling to China create new opportunities for China's related industries, thereby invigorating bilateral trade. To enhance the tourism experience, Arab states have leveraged the opportunities presented by the "Belt and Road" Initiative to attract Chinese investment for the improvement of tourism infrastructure. Chinese enterprises have engaged in the development of tourism projects in Arab states, including the construction of hotels and scenic facilities. Such capital interaction in the tourism sector has injected vitality into bilateral cooperation. China-Arab states tourism collaboration, by harnessing the "spillover effect" of the tourism industry, has also strengthened people-to-people relations and cultural exchange. Through tourism, Chinese visitors gain deeper insight into

---

[1] "Great Potential Between the China-Arab States Tourism Markets: Experts Recommend Promoting Visa Facilitation and Strengthening Talent Development," The Paper, https: //www. thepaper.cn/newsDetail_forward_24677749, September 20, 2023.

[2] "Two Decades of Fruitful China-Arab States Cooperation: Advancing Economic, Trade, and Cultural Exchanges in Both Directions," Cnhubei Co., Ltd, https: //news.china.com/social gd/10000169/20240530/46618377.html, May 30, 2024.

The Development Process of China-Arab States Economic and Trade Relations
Annual Report 2024

the history, culture, and customs of Arab states, while Arab tourists develop a more direct understanding of Chinese culture. This fosters dialogue and mutual understanding between civilizations and enhances friendship and trust among the peoples of both sides. Evidently, tourism has played a crucial role in advancing policy coordination, connectivity of infrastructure, unimpeded trade, financial integration, and closer people-to-people ties between China and Arab states.

### 10.2.1.2 The China-Arab States Cooperation Forum

The China-Arab States Cooperation Forum, aimed at promoting peace and development, is an important platform for strengthening dialogue and cooperation between China and the League of Arab States. As of July 2024, the Forum has held 10 ministerial conferences, 19 senior officials' meetings, and 8 China-Arab states strategic political dialogues at the senior-official level. In May 2024, the 10th Ministerial Conference of the China-Arab States Cooperation Forum was held in Beijing. The conference adopted the "CASCF Execution Plan for 2024-2026", which clearly outlines enhanced collaboration between China and Arab states in a wide range of areas, including economy and trade, investment, tourism, people-to-people exchanges, culture and civilization, education, and science and technology, with a shared commitment to long-term development. As the cooperation mechanisms continue to mature and future development paths unfold in an orderly manner, China-Arab States cultural tourism cooperation is entering a new phase—characterized by sound institutional frameworks, deepening mutual trust, and increasingly fruitful outcomes.

Tourism cooperation serves as a vital vehicle for promoting cultural exchange, a key means of fostering mutual understanding between peoples, and a significant driving force for advancing collaboration across multiple sectors. Over the past 20 years since the establishment of the China-Arab States Cooperation Forum, cultural tourism cooperation between China and Arab states has accelerated markedly. A wide array of vibrant cultural and artistic exchange activities, along with practical and effective tourism cooperation initiatives, have substantially advanced China-Arab states cultural relations, deepened mutual understanding and friendly interaction among the peoples of both sides, and laid a solid social and public foundation for jointly building the "Belt and Road" and constructing a China-Arab states community with a shared future. Exploring pathways through which tourism cooperation can promote cultural and people-to-people

Chapter 10    Special Report on China-Arab States Cooperation in Tourism

exchange is of both theoretical and practical significance in securing a lasting cultural foundation for generations of China-Arab states friendship. China and Arab States have jointly established the "China-Arab States Center of the Global Civilization Initiative", and are accelerating the development of platforms such as think tank alliances, youth development forums, university alliances, and research centers for cultural tourism cooperation. China also extends invitations to 200 political party leaders from Arab states to visit annually, and both sides aim to achieve a target of 10 million mutual tourist visits in the next five years.

10.2.1.3    The China-Arab States Summit Providing Strong Policy Support for China-Arab States Tourism Cooperation

Building upon the platform of the China-Arab States Cooperation Forum, the inaugural China-Arab States Summit was held in Riyadh, the capital of Saudi Arabia, in December 2022. This summit marked a historic milestone in China-Arab states relations, with both sides committing to the joint construction of a China-Arab States community with a shared future in the new era. It signified the beginning of a new phase of comprehensive and deepened development in China-Arab states relations. Since the first summit, the two sides have continuously expanded consensus and enhanced mutual trust, ushering in what is widely regarded as the best period in the history of China-Arab states relations. From 2022 to 2024, bilateral relations between China and several Arab states—including Bahrain, Tunisia, and Palestine—have been upgraded. At present, China has established comprehensive strategic partnerships or strategic partnerships with 20 Arab states as well as with the League of Arab States, making the Arab region one of the densest clusters of China's strategic partnerships.[1] As traditional China-Arab states friendship continues to deepen and political mutual trust grows stronger, cooperation across various fields has yielded increasingly tangible and pragmatic outcomes.

Since the inaugural China-Arab States Summit in 2022, China and Arab states have actively built cooperation mechanisms under the framework of the "Eight Joint Actions", providing robust policy support for tourism collaboration. Efforts have been made to facilitate cooperation among 500 cultural tourism

---

[1]  "Shared Future, Joint Progress — A Two-Year Retrospective on the First China-Arab States Summit," Xinhua News Agency, https://www.gov.cn/yaowen/liebiao/202412/content_6994024. htm, December 22, 2024.

233

The Development Process of China-Arab States Economic and Trade Relations
Annual Report 2024

enterprises and to cultivate 1000 cultural tourism professionals for Arab states. Over the past five years, China and Arab states have deepened the integration of culture and tourism by organizing a series of specialized training programs, through which nearly 200 tourism professionals from Arab states have received training.

10.2.1.4    The China-Arab States Expo Serving as a Platform for Promoting Practical China-Arab States Tourism Cooperation

The China-Arab States Expo is a national and international comprehensive exposition jointly hosted—upon approval by the State Council—by the Ministry of Commerce of the People's Republic of China, the China Council for the Promotion of International Trade, and the People's Government of Ningxia Hui Autonomous Region. Held in Yinchuan, Ningxia, the expo has been successfully organized six times between 2013 and 2023 under the guiding principle of "Inheriting Friendship, Deepening Cooperation, Achieving Mutual Benefit, and Promoting Development". The expo has attracted participants from 112 countries and regions, including 29 Chinese and foreign dignitaries, 383 ministerial-level guests, and more than 7500 domestic and international enterprises. A total of 1616 cooperation agreements have been signed, covering a wide range of fields such as infrastructure, modern agriculture, ecological management, green energy, healthcare, digital technology, and intelligent manufacturing.[1] The China-Arab States Expo has effectively built a bridge and created conditions for mutual exchange and cooperation between enterprises from China and Arab states. It has significantly promoted economic and trade exchanges and investment cooperation between China and countries along the "Belt and Road"—including Arab states—thus serving as a vital platform for joint "Belt and Road" development.

In September 2023, China-Arab States Tour Operators Conference of the 6th China-Arab States Expo were held in Yinchuan, Ningxia. Under the theme of "Sharing Development Opportunities, Promoting Tourism Cooperation, and Building the 'Belt and Road' Together", the event, consisting of the China-Arab States Tourism Cooperation Forum, the "Belt and Road" Cultural tourism Cooperation Promotion Conference, among other activities, aimed to establish an

---

[1] "The 6th China-Arab States Expo (2023)," Website of the China-Arab States Expo, https://www.cas-expo.org.cn/zh/preExposite.html, February 8, 2025.

234

Chapter 10    Special Report on China-Arab States Cooperation in Tourism

effective platform for pragmatic cooperation between Chinese and international tourism sectors. China and Arab States have deepened collaboration in areas such as policy alignment, industry cooperation, talent development, and market promotion, and have signed multiple strategic cooperation agreements.[1] The conference promoted mutual benefits and shared opportunities in the tourism sector between China and Arab States, enhanced the effective coordination of domestic and international cultural tourism resources, and served as a vital platform for strengthening practical cooperation within the tourism industry. It has played a significant role in increasing mutual visits between Chinese and Arab tourists, advancing inter-civilizational exchange and mutual learning through tourism, and enhancing mutual understanding and closer people-to-people ties between both sides.

## 10.2.2    More Frequent Cultural Exchanges Between China and Arab States over the Past Two Decades

In 2006, the inaugural Arabic Arts Festival was held in Beijing and Nanjing. It marked the first time that China and all member states of the Arab League jointly hosted such an event in China. It also represented the first large-scale cultural exchange between China and the Arab world, comprising exhibitions of Arab arts, a China-Arab States Cultural Ministers' Roundtable, Arab artistic performances, as well as showcases of traditional Arab clothing and cuisine. A total of 51 members from cultural delegations representing 16 Arab governments and the Arab League, along with 250 Arab artists, participated in related activities. In 2010, the second Arabic Arts Festival was held in Beijing and Shanghai under the theme "Artistic Exchange, Civilizational Dialogue", featuring the China-Arab States Cultural Forum, joint performances by Arab art troupes, and exhibitions of Arab art. Delegates from Arab governments also visited Ningxia for field visits and study tours, engaging in wide-ranging discussions across culture, tourism, and the arts. In 2014, the third Arabic Arts Festival took place at the National Centre for the Performing Arts in Beijing. With the aim of "enhancing exchange and deepening friendship" and the theme

---

[1]    "Opening of China-Arab States Tour Operators Conference, the 6th China-Arab States Expo," Website of the Ministry of Culture and Tourism of the People's Republic of China, https://www.mct.gov.cn/preview/whzx/qgwhxxlb/nx/202309/t20230920_947360.htm, September 20, 2023.

235

The Development Process of China-Arab States Economic and Trade Relations
Annual Report 2024

"Revitalizing the Spirit of the Silk Road and Composing A New Chapter", the festival included forums, cultural performances, and art workshops. In 2018, China-Arab States Urban Culture and Tourism Forum of the fourth Arabic Arts Festival was held in Chengdu, Sichuan Province. The Minister of Culture and Tourism of China and the Secretary-General of the Arab Towns Organization attended the forum and delivered speeches. Over 100 representatives from both Chinese and Arab cultural tourism sectors participated. With the theme "Culture and Tourism: Making the World More Peaceful and Beautiful", representatives of both sides shared development experiences on various topics in culture and tourism, explored partnerships, and held open and constructive dialogue between Chinese and Arab cities. Representatives from 14 Chinese cities and 9 Arab cities unanimously adopted the "Chengdu Initiative on China-Arab States Urban Culture and Tourism Cooperation". [1] The forum represented a concrete step toward deeper collaboration under the "Belt and Road" Initiative. It carried profound significance by promoting mutual learning and development among cities, expanding the scope of cultural tourism exchanges, and achieving practical outcomes in building inter-city exchange mechanisms, developing brand cooperation on urban culture and tourism, and promoting city-based tourism destinations. By leveraging the role of culture and tourism as a bridge and link, the forum further advanced cooperation in related fields. The fifth Arab Arts Festival, held alongside the China-Arab States Cultural Industry Forum, took place in Jingdezhén, Jiangxi Province in 2022. The Minister of Culture and Tourism of China, the Governor of Jiangxi Province, and the UAE Minister of Culture and Youth, along with 170 representatives from government departments, academia, and the business community of both China and Arab states joined the event in a hybrid format, combining both in-person and online participation. Centered on the theme "Integration and Progress, Empowering the Future—Forging a New Landscape for China-Arab States Cultural Industry Cooperation", representatives from both sides exchanged views on topics such as digital cultural industries, innovation in handicrafts, and the development of cultural and creative industrial parks. They aligned on cooperation intentions

---

[1] "China-Arab States Urban Culture and Tourism Forum Held," Website of the Ministry of Culture and Tourism of the People's Republic of China, https://www.mct.gov.cn/preview/special/8672/8676/201810/t20181026_835601.htm, October 26, 2018.

236

Chapter 10    Special Report on China-Arab States Cooperation in Tourism

and jointly released the "2022 China-Arab States Cultural Industry Jingdezhen Initiative" [1], for promoting deeper collaboration between China and Arab states in the cultural industry.

In 2008, the First China Arts Festival was held in Syria, marking one of the major cultural events under the framework of the China-Arab States Cooperation Forum, and symbolizing the official launch of the mechanism for hosting art festivals between China and Arab states.[2] In 2012, the Second China Arts Festival under the Forum was hosted in Bahrain. This festival provided an excellent platform for Bahraini and other Arab audiences to gain a deeper understanding of both traditional and contemporary Chinese culture, further strengthening cultural exchanges between China and Bahrain. It also promoted the broader development of China-Arab states cultural relations, marking a significant event in the history of cultural relations between China and the Arab world.[3] In 2016, Tunisia hosted the Third China Arts Festival under the framework of the China-Arab States Cooperation Forum. The opening ceremony featured Chinese art performances such as vocal mimicry, acrobatics, magic shows, and the traditional art of face-changing in Sichuan opera, providing the Tunisian public with a valuable opportunity to experience the charm of Chinese culture. The festival served as a new platform for people in Tunisia and other Arab states to gain a deeper understanding of China's ancient cultural heritage and modern developments. Held in Sfax, Tunisia, the China Art Festival held great significance for promoting China-Tunisia cultural exchanges as well as China-Arab states cultural cooperation, injecting fresh momentum into the mutual learning and development of cultural relations between the two sides.[4]

---

[1]  "China-Arab States Cultural Industry Forum Successfully Held," Website of the Ministry of Culture and Tourism of the People's Republic of China, https: //www.mct.gov.cn/whzx/whyw/202212/t20221220_938184.htm, December 20, 2022.

[2]  "The First China Arts Festival Held in Syria," Website of the China-Arab States Cooperation Forum, http: //www.chinaarabcf.org/ltjz/ysj/sjzgysj/200902/t20090220_6914529.htm, February 20, 2009.

[3]  "The Second China Arts Festival Under the China-Arab States Cooperation Forum Held in Bahrain," China-Arab States Cooperation Forum, http: //www.chinaarabcf.org/zagx/rwjl/201203/t20120329_6842725.htm, March 29, 2012.

[4]  "The Third China Arts Festival Under the China-Arab States Cooperation Forum Opens in Tunisia," Website of the Ministry of Culture and Tourism of the People's Republic of China, https: //www.mct.gov.cn/whzx/bnsj/dwwhllj/201608/t20160829_773179.html, August 5, 2016.

237

The Development Process of China-Arab States Economic and Trade Relations
Annual Report 2024

As of June 2024, China and Arab states have jointly held five sessions of the Arabic Arts Festival and ten sessions of the Symposium on China-Arab States Relations and China-Arab States Civilization Dialogue, among other major cultural exchange events. Both sides have worked to establish a number of branded cultural tourism programs such as "Happy Chinese New Year", "China-Arab States Silk Road Cultural Journey", and "Silk Road: Artists' Rendezvous". The "Chinese language fever" has become a prominent trend. China has collaborated with 13 Arab states to establish 21 Confucius Institutes and 2 Confucius Classrooms, while 15 Arab states have introduced Chinese language courses in their universities. Moreover, six Arab states—the UAE, Saudi Arabia, Palestine, Egypt, Tunisia, and Djibouti—have incorporated Chinese into their national education systems. The "Chinese-Arabic Classics Translation Project", jointly launched by both sides, has thus far translated and published 50 Chinese and Arabic classic works.[1]

## 10.3　Analysis of Tourism Cooperation Trends Between China and Arab States in the New Era

China and Arab states share a profound historical and cultural foundation as well as broad prospects for cooperation in the field of tourism. In light of current international tourism trends and the development strategies of both sides, in the future, China-Arab states tourism cooperation is expected to deepen in the following areas.

### 10.3.1　Green and Sustainable Development Will Become a Key Aspect of China-Arab States Tourism Cooperation

In recent years, with the intensification of desertification, the increasing frequency of extreme climate events, and the ongoing loss of biodiversity, humanity is facing increasingly severe challenges to survival and development. The pursuit of green development has drawn widespread attention from the international community, including China and Arab states.

---

[1]　"Deepening Practical Tourism Cooperation and Promoting People-to-People Exchanges Between China and Arab States," *CT News*, https://www.ctnews.com.cn/guandian/content/2024-07/12/content_162461.html, July 12, 2024.

238

Chapter 10　Special Report on China-Arab States Cooperation in Tourism

In September 2020, President Xi Jinping stated at the 75th session of the United Nations General Assembly that China would scale up its Nationally Determined Contributions (NDCs) by adopting more vigorous policies and measures, with the aim of peaking carbon dioxide emissions before 2030 and striving to achieve carbon neutrality before 2060[1] This declaration fully demonstrates China's strong commitment and sense of responsibility as a major country in protecting the global ecological environment and addressing climate change. China is actively accelerating the restructuring of its industrial system, widely promoting the development of clean energy sources such as wind and solar power, and focusing on low-carbon technologies and applications. Through technological innovation, China seeks to reduce greenhouse gas emissions and foster the growth of green and low-carbon industries. In 2023, the Department of Economy and Tourism in Dubai launched a Sustainable Tourism Stamp certification, setting sustainability standards across 19 areas, including energy and water efficiency, waste management, and staff education. To date, 70 hotels have received the certification. In 2024, the Department of Culture and Tourism of Abu Dhabi (DCT Abu Dhabi) introduced a carbon calculator that mandates all hotels in the city to submit their consumption data on oil, gas, water, and electricity, which is then converted into carbon emission figures.[2] States such as Morocco have begun adopting China's expertise in combating desertification. Qatar has signed a cooperation agreement with China for the "Beautiful Doha" project to comprehensively promote the application of China's green, intelligent, and water-saving irrigation technologies and equipment.

It is evident that both China and Arab states are making significant contributions to the sustainable development and innovation of tourism. Green energy and low-carbon tourism will become key areas of future cooperation and mutual benefit between the two sides. It is foreseeable that both parties will adhere to the concept of sustainable development and continue to deepen cooperation in the tourism sector. Joint efforts will be made on the construction of eco-friendly scenic areas, the development of sustainable power support

---

[1]　"Carbon Reduction: China Sets Binding Targets," People's Daily, https: //www.gov.cn/xinwen/2020-09/30/content_5548478.htm, September 30, 2020.

[2]　"Cooperation to Drive Innovative Development in the Tourism Industry," People's Daily Online-International Channel, http: //world.people.com.cn/n1/2024/0511/c1002-40233741.html, May 11, 2024.

systems for hotels and tourist sites, the design of desert eco-tourism routes, the application of solar energy technologies in desert tourism projects, the promotion of low-carbon accommodations, the development of green transportation, and the encouragement of tourists to participate in environmental protection initiatives. By promoting the development and innovation of green tourism, both sides aim to ensure harmonious coexistence between the growth of the cultural tourism industries and environmental protection, thereby achieving long-term goals for sustainable tourism development.

## 10.3.2 Artificial Intelligence Will Play an Increasingly Important Role in China-Arab States Tourism Cooperation

The development and application of artificial intelligence (AI) technologies are providing robust scientific and technological support for the advancement of the tourism industry. First, AI is being applied to platform construction. China and Arab states have jointly developed advanced integrated service platforms capable of offering a wide array of services to tourists from both sides, including cultural tourism big data, AI-powered recommendations, multilingual translation, and contactless payment. These platforms enable visitors to access personalized itinerary planning and enjoy convenient service bookings, with multilingual support and secure contactless payment features ensuring transaction safety. Second, AI demonstrates significant technical advantages in the in-depth exploration of historical and cultural resources of the two sides, the digital reconstruction of world heritage sites and historic cultural cities in both China and Arab states, and the digital presentation of cultural tourism. These technologies play a crucial role in preserving world cultural heritage and enhancing the integration of culture and tourism. Third, by leveraging cutting-edge technologies such as virtual reality (VR), augmented reality (AR), and extended reality (XR), AI facilitates the development of immersive virtual tourism experiences. This enables tourists to vividly engage with the richness of Chinese history and the ancient civilization of the Arab world, significantly enhancing the overall visitor experience. Fourth, Chinese technology enterprises are empowering smart tourism through technological innovation, assisting Arab states in building intelligent tourism infrastructure. This includes high-speed network coverage, mobile payment systems, and AI-powered guide services, all of which greatly improve the experience and satisfaction of tourists from both

Chapter 10    Special Report on China-Arab States Cooperation in Tourism

China and Arab states.

In May 2024, President Xi Jinping delivered a keynote speech at the opening ceremony of the 10th Ministerial Conference of the China-Arab States Cooperation Forum. In his speech, he articulated China's aspiration to work with Arab partners in building "Five Cooperation Frameworks" and emphasized the need for strengthened collaboration in the field of artificial intelligence. He called for joint efforts to leverage AI in empowering the real economy and to advance the establishment of a widely accepted global governance system for artificial intelligence.[①] Cooperation between China and Arab states in cutting-edge fields such as 5G, artificial intelligence, big data, and cloud computing has witnessed rapid development. These areas are poised to become new drivers of growth in China-Arab states tourism cooperation in the future.

### 10.3.3    China-Arab States Cooperation in Cultural Tourism Will Become Increasingly Diverse

China and Arab states both boast long-standing histories and splendid cultural heritages. As they each stand at critical junctures of socio-economic development, they share common development goals and vast potential for collaboration in the field of cultural tourism. Arab states such as Oman and Saudi Arabia were key hubs along the ancient Maritime Silk Road, which left a rich legacy of historical memories across both regions. Looking ahead, cultural tourism cooperation between China and Arab states can focus on Silk Road heritage through initiatives such as joint archaeological excavations and cultural heritage preservation, and on developing tourism routes themed around the Silk Road. Opportunities also lie in creating experiential programs centered on the culture of Arab spices, designing interactive activities based on traditional festivals and intangible cultural heritage practices of both sides, and promoting cultural tourism IPs through digital media, including film, television, and gaming. The unique natural landscapes of Arab states can be leveraged to develop wellness-oriented offerings such as hot spring retreats and desert yoga. China and Arab states can jointly establish international pilot zones offering premium

---

① "Xi Jinping Attends the Opening Ceremony of the 10th Ministerial Conference of the China-Arab States Cooperation Forum and Delivers a Keynote Speech," *Xinhua News Agency,* https: //www. gov.cn/yaowen/liebiao/202405/content_6954536.htm, May 30, 2024.

The Development Process of China-Arab States Economic and Trade Relations
Annual Report 2024

diagnostic and healthcare services, thereby attracting Arab visitors to China for therapeutic travel. With these diverse areas of cooperation, the prospects for deepened China-Arab states collaboration in cultural tourism sector are promising.

### 10.3.4 China-Arab States Tourism Cooperation Will Place Greater Emphasis on the Cultivation of Tourism Professionals

In May 2024, during his keynote speech at the 10th Ministerial Conference of the China-Arab States Cooperation Forum, President Xi Jinping stated that China is willing to work with Arab states to establish a "China-Arab States Center of the Global Civilization Initiative" and accelerate the development of platforms such as think tank alliances, youth development forums, university alliances, and research centers for cultural tourism cooperation.[1] This clearly signals a deepening of future collaboration between China and Arab states in talent cultivation and academic research.

It is foreseeable that both sides will leverage these platforms to accelerate the construction of a collaborative mechanism integrating industry, academia, research, and practical application. These mechanisms will serve as important drivers for education, while enabling tourism enterprises to play a cooperative role in talent development. The goal is to train a new generation of interdisciplinary professionals who not only understand the cultural and societal contexts of both China and the Arab world, but also possess modern tourism management and service skills.[2] At present, achievements in China-Arab states tourism talent development are largely concentrated in areas such as Arabic-speaking tour guide training and joint education programs. Going forward, cooperation in tourism education should be optimized to promote joint cultivation of tourism professionals. More exchange programs should be established across fields such as science and technology, environmental protection, and art. Students in tourism-related disciplines should be encouraged

---

[1] "Xi Jinping Attends the Opening Ceremony of the 10th Ministerial Conference of the China-Arab States Cooperation Forum and Delivers a Keynote Speech," *Xinhua News Agency*, https://www.gov.cn/yaowen/liebiao/202405/content_6954536.html, May 30, 2024.

[2] "Deepening Practical Tourism Cooperation and Promoting People-to-People Exchanges Between China and Arab States," *CT News*, https://www.ctnews.com.cn/guandian/content/2024-07/12/content_162461.html, July 12, 2024.

242

Chapter 10    Special Report on China-Arab States Cooperation in Tourism

to participate in international competitions, volunteer service, and innovation and entrepreneurship initiatives. Additionally, the development of study-tour programs can enhance interdisciplinary communication and mutual learning among China-Arab states professionals, fostering a talent pool equipped with international perspectives, forward-thinking insights, and diverse skills. Such talent development will provide vital intellectual support for China-Arab states tourism cooperation, reinforcing the critical role of human capital in this process. In the future, both sides are expected to jointly explore the core competencies required of tourism professionals in the digital era, build a high-caliber workforce in tourism planning, development, operations, and management, enhance the skills of practitioners, and cultivate more internationally-oriented, interdisciplinary tourism specialists—an essential area of cooperation between China and Arab states in advancing tourism talent development.

# Chapter 11 Special Report on China-Arab States Expo

President Xi Jinping emphasized that China is willing to work with Arab countries in the spirit of mutual assistance, equality, mutual benefit, inclusiveness, mutual learning and close collaboration. This aims to build China-Arab relations into a model for maintaining world peace and stability, a paragon of high-quality Belt and Road cooperation, a paradigm of harmonious coexistence of different civilizations and a pacesetter in exploring the right path of global governance[1]. On May 30, 2024, President Xi Jinping attended the opening ceremony of the 10th Ministerial Conference of the China-Arab States Cooperation Forum in Beijing and delivered a keynote speech titled *Deepening Cooperation, Building on Past Achievements and Speeding up the Building of a China-Arab States Community with a Shared Future*, injecting strength into China-Arab states unity and cooperation and promoting China-Arab states relations in the new era to a new level. This is the third time that President Xi Jinping has attended the opening ceremony of the Ministerial Conference of the China-Arab States Cooperation Forum and the fifth time that he has made important policy announcements to the Arab world. China-Arab states relations are at their best level in history, and all-round cooperation between China and Arab countries is embracing major strategic opportunities. From June 10 to 20, 2024, Xi Jinping, General Secretary of the Communist Party of China, President of the People's Republic of China, and Chairman of the Central Military Commission, pointed out during his visit to

---

[1] Xi Jinping, *Deepening Cooperation, Building on Past Achievements and Accelerating the Building of a China-Arab Community with a Shared Future - Keynote Speech at the Opening Ceremony of the Tenth Ministerial Conference of the China - Arab States Cooperation Forum*, People's Daily, May 31, 2024, p. 2.

Chapter 11　Special Report on China-Arab States Expo

Ningxia that we shall combine domestic and international opening-up, actively participate in the joint construction of the Belt and Road Initiative and the building of the New Western Land-Sea Corridor, deepen economic and trade cooperation with Arab countries, and raise the level of inland opening-up[1]. This is the fundamental principle and action guide for Ningxia to deepen high-level domestic and international opening-up and to successfully hold the China-Arab States Expo with high quality in the new era. The China-Arab States Expo shall seize the opportunity and accelerate its efforts, strive to play a more important role in the overall situation of China-Arab states cooperation in the new era, and make new contributions to promoting a new pattern in the large-scale development of the western region in the new era.

## 11.1　Review of the Development of the China-Arab States Expo

The China-Arab States Expo is a national and international level comprehensive expo jointly hosted by the Ministry of Commerce of the People's Republic of China, the China Council for the Promotion of International Trade and the People's Government of the Ningxia Hui Autonomous Region. Its predecessor was the China-Arab States Economic and Trade Forum held from 2010 to 2012. Since 2013, General Secretary Xi Jinping has sent congratulatory letters to the China-Arab States Expo on five consecutive occasions. He has repeatedly pointed out that the China-Arab States Expo has played a positive role in deepening China-Arab states practical cooperation and promoting the high-quality development of the Belt and Road Initiative, which fully reflects the great importance and support attached by the Central Committee of the Communist Party of Chinato the successful hosting of the China-Arab States Expo. With the in-depth development of China-Arab states relations and the continuous accumulation of practices in Ningxia, the functional positioning of the China-Arab States Expo has gradually focused from highly integrating multi-field cooperation between China and Arab countries to deepening economic and trade

---

① *Xi Jinping Stresses during His Inspection Tour in Ningxia: Building a Pilot Zone for Ecological Protection and High - quality Development in the Yellow River Basin and Writing a Splendid Chapter for Ningxia in the Construction of Chinese - style Modernization*, People's Daily, 2024.06.22(01).

245

cooperation. Its service scope has been continuously expanding from promoting cooperation between Ningxia and Arab countries, cooperation between China and Arab countries to international cooperation under the Belt and Road Initiative. In terms of mechanism construction, the activities in the science and technology sector have been elevated from local experiences to a China-Arab states science and technology exchange and cooperation mechanism recognized by the state. As a result, the China-Arab States Expo has become an important international economic and trade cooperation mechanism under the framework of jointly building the Belt and Road Initiative by China and Arab countries.

## 11.1.1 Zeroing in on Economic and Trade Cooperation: Functional Features of the China-Arab States Expo

Since the beginning of the 21st century, with the approval of the CPC Central Committee and the State Council, some local governments in China have started to hold regional foreign-related exhibition and convention activities, undertaking the function of serving the country's overall diplomacy in the field of economic and trade cooperation. Their characteristics and achievements in holding these events are quite remarkable. However, from both the national and local perspectives, there has always been a lack of a national-level economic and trade exhibition and convention platform that is mainly open to Arab countries for cooperation. The China-Arab States Cooperation Forum was first held in 2004. Adhering to the purpose of strengthening dialogue and cooperation, and promoting peace and development, China and the Arab states have carried out extensive exchanges and cooperation in such fields as politics, economy and trade, culture and the environment, and have effectively played the platform role in promoting economic and trade cooperation between China and the Arab states. However, on the whole, there is still a lack of a China-Arab states economic and trade cooperation platform that could give full play to non-governmental forces and further integrate the government and private forces. From the perspective of the Arab side, the changes in the international, regional and domestic political and economic situations have provided opportunities and space for further cooperation between China and the Arab states. Among them, at the international level, China's development model has been recognized by Arab countries, and there has been a widespread trend of Eastward orientation among Arab countries. After the 2008 international financial crisis, Arab

Chapter 11    Special Report on China-Arab States Expo

countries have had higher expectations for economic and trade cooperation and even political cooperation with China. At the regional level, by the end of 2010, the West Asia and North Africa region fell into turmoil. The Arab world was in a historical stage of seeking stability, striving for development and improving people's livelihoods during the process of transformation. The transformation and upgrading of China's economy have provided greater space for China-Arab states cooperation. In the process of exploring development paths that suit their respective national conditions, developing mutually beneficial cooperation with China conforms to the strategic interests of various countries. At the domestic level, Arab countries are facing the arduous tasks of vigorously strengthening infrastructure construction, implementing the industrial diversification development strategy, accelerating economic transformation and improving people's livelihood. Deepening China-Arab states economic and trade cooperation has become a strategic choice for both sides to achieve their own economic development. Against this background, the practical need to explore a platform for deepening China-Arab states relations and building economic and trade cooperation has emerged. Based on the location characteristics of Ningxia, its practical experience in exchanges with the Arab world and the foundation of economic and trade cooperation, this important mission has historically fallen on Ningxia.

The functions of the China-Arab States Economic and Trade Forum exhibit highly integrated characteristics. Under the mechanism of the China-Arab States Economic and Trade Forum, its functional modules and activity contents include economic and trade policy communication, investment and trade, infrastructure construction, as well as cooperation in energy, finance, agriculture, science and technology, education, radio and television, ecological and environmental protection, etc., mainly serving three major functions. Firstly, it coordinates with China's strategies and policies towards the Arab world. The main measure is to invite the national leaders to attend the opening ceremony of the China-Arab States Economic and Trade Forum and deliver keynote speeches, and actively undertakes institutional activities under the framework of the China-Arab States Cooperation Forum so as to reflect its features of high standard and strong authority. Secondly, it widely promotes cooperation between China and the Arab states in multiple fields. With the theme of *Inheriting Friendship, Deepening Cooperation and Joint Development*, the China-Arab States Economic and Trade Forum

247

builds a high-level dialogue platform for the Chinese and Arab governments, enterprises and the public to jointly discuss economic and trade exchanges, and is committed to establishing a new international mechanism for China-Arab states economic and trade cooperation. Thirdly, it promotes the development of Ningxia's inland open economy.

The functions of the China-Arab States Expo have shown the characteristic of gradually concentrating from highly integrated cooperation in multiple fields to focusing on economic and trade cooperation. Its functional modules have been optimized and adjusted with a focus on economic and trade cooperation, including promoting economic and trade facilitation, production capacity cooperation and technological cooperation under the framework of jointly building the BRI by China and the Arab states. It mainly serves four major functions. Firstly, it focuses on serving the construction of national economic and trade cooperation mechanisms and platforms. The forum is focused on actively playing the roles of bilateral and multilateral mechanisms such as the Inter-governmental Joint Economic and Trade Committee and the China-Arab States Joint Chamber of Commerce, and giving full play to the platform functions of the China-Arab States Expo to promote mutual visits and exchanges between the Chinese and Arab governments and enterprises. Secondly, it focuses on implementing the policy documents regarding China's investment and trade cooperation with Arab countries. The forum adheres to the principles of taking enterprises as the main body, being market-oriented, driven by the government and operating commercially. It aligns China's production capacity advantages with the needs of Arab countries, conducts production capacity cooperation with Arab countries that is advanced, applicable, effective, conducive to employment and environmentally friendly, and supports the industrialization process of Arab countries. Thirdly, it focuses on building an inter-governmental platform for scientific and technological innovation cooperation between China and the Arab countries. It constructs an integrated technology transfer cooperation network covering China and the Arab countries, implements the China-Arab States Science and Technology Partnership Program, and actively promotes the application and popularization of scientific and technological achievements, and advanced and applicable technologies between the two sides. Fourthly, it focuses on promoting economic and trade cooperation between various local regions in China and the Arab countries. It innovates the forms of event organization,

248

Chapter 11　Special Report on China-Arab States Expo

serves all provinces, autonomous regions and municipalities to enter Arab countries and explore markets. The forum assists the Arab side's investment and cooperation in various parts of China, and expands the actual results of two-way economic and trade.

## 11.1.2　Serving the National Strategy: The Mechanism Construction of the China-Arab States Expo

From 2013 to 2023, the China-Arab States Expo has been held for six consecutive sessions. To fulfill various functions and roles, the expo has actively implemented the spirit of the important speeches delivered by General Secretary Xi Jinping at the ministerial meetings of the China-Arab States Cooperation Forum over the years, and actively cooperated with the implementation of China's policy documents on Arab countries, thus forming a series of important mechanisms to promote economic and trade cooperation between China and Arab countries. Firstly, it revolves around the construction of national economic and trade cooperation mechanisms and platforms, gives full play to the roles of the China-Arab States Expo in communicating economic and trade policies and facilitating project matchmaking and negotiations. The mechanism aims to hold a national-level, international and institutionalized China-Arab States Business Summit. The China Council for the Promotion of International Trade and the General Union of Arab Chambers of Commerce, Industry and Agriculture organize government departments, important business associations and various enterprises to participate in the conference and exhibitions to closely strengthen the mutual visits and exchanges between the Chinese and Arab governments and enterprises, which would be conducive to actively promoting trade and investment facilitation, and creating a favorable situation where policy communication promotes consensus, and economic and trade cooperation benefits people's livelihood. Secondly, it centers on the implementation of China's policy documents regarding investment and trade cooperation with the Arab countries, gives full play to the roles of the China-Arab States Expo in facilitating enterprises' investment attraction for overseas industrial parks and policy coordination. The expo also aims to revitalize the investment advantages of some Arab countries and the production capacity advantages of China, promote the dual circulation of industries and markets between China and the Arab countries, and drive the sustainable development of two-way investment

249

and economic and trade between China and the Arab countries. Thirdly, we shall center on the construction of an inter-governmental platform for scientific and technological innovation cooperation between China and the Arab countries, take the lead in implementing the important initiative of exploring the establishment of a China-Arab States Technology Transfer Center put forward by General Secretary Xi Jinping at the opening ceremony of the 6th Ministerial Conference of the China-Arab States Cooperation Forum. In September 2015, the People's Government of the Ningxia Hui Autonomous Region and the Ministry of Science and Technology jointly founded the China-Arab States Technology Transfer and Innovation Cooperation Conference and jointly established the China-Arab States Technology Transfer Center, which has become an important mechanism and practical platform for promoting scientific and technological innovation cooperation between China and the Arab countries. Fourth, we shall enhance the ability to serve local economic and trade cooperation with Arab countries, and the mechanism for hosting the China-Arab States Expo be innovated. The Dual Guest Countries and Dual Theme Provinces are established, and high-quality cases of economic and trade cooperation with Arab countries across the country are collected. This comprehensively showcases the characteristics and strength of the local economy, pools the economic and trade cooperation needs of Arab countries, and serves all provinces, autonomous regions and municipalities directly under the Central Government in opening up the markets of Arab countries, as well as serves Arab countries in their investment and cooperation in various parts of China. In January 2016, General Secretary Xi Jinping pointed out during his visit to the headquarters of the League of Arab States that the China-Arab States Expo has become an important platform for serving the joint construction of the BRI by China and Arab countries.

## 11.1.3 Jointly Building the BRI: The Achievements of the China-Arab States Expo

The cooperation between China and Arab countries is all-round, multi-level and cross-field. The China-Arab States Expo has always adhered to the goal orientation of serving the national strategy and focusing on economic and trade cooperation. It has gradually developed into an international expo that features China and Arab countries as the main participants, integrates functions such as high-level dialogue, economic and trade promotion, exhibition and negotiation,

and is open to the whole world. It has become an important platform for promoting and implementing the practical cooperation between China and Arab countries and has exerted a broad and far-reaching impact on the international community. In September 2019, Khaled Hanafi, Secretary-General of the General Union of Chambers of Commerce, Industry and Agriculture for Arab Countries, said in an exclusive interview with Xinhua News Agency that the China-Arab States Expo is a good platform for promoting economic and trade cooperation between China and Arab countries. China maintains an open attitude towards all countries in the world, including Arab countries, which will benefit both sides[1]. The China-Arab States Expo has contributed to the continuation of China-Arab states friendship, the deepening of China-Arab states cooperation, the continuous consolidation of the consensus on jointly building the BRI between China and Arab countries, the high-quality development of China-Arab economic and trade cooperation, the deepening of multi-field cooperation between various provinces, autonomous regions and municipalities directly under the central government and Arab countries, and the acceleration of Ningxia's opening up and overall economic development, achieving fruitful results.

First, positive progress has been made in production capacity cooperation. Production capacity cooperation is a key cooperation area for China and Arab countries to build the BRI and an important topic of the China-Arab States Expo. The industrial parks established by China in Arab countries such as Egypt, Saudi Arabia, and Oman are key pivots for promoting China-Arab states production capacity cooperation, shouldering the mission of docking and implementing the development strategies of China and Arab countries. The main way for the China-Arab States Expo to promote China-Arab states production capacity cooperation is to facilitate enterprises to sign contracts with overseas industrial parks and provide support in subsequent investment promotion and policy coordination. Under the framework of the China-Arab States Expo, initial progress has been made in production capacity cooperation between China and Egypt, Saudi Arabia, and Oman.

Firstly, in May 2016, Ningxia, together with the Ministry of Commerce

---

[1] "Pragmatic China-Arab States Cooperation Sets Sail for New Frontiers-An Interview with Khaled Hanafi, Secretary-General of the General Union of Arab Chambers of Commerce, Industry and Agriculture," Xinhua News Agency, http: //www.xinhuanet.com/world/2019-09/06/c_1124968827.htm, September 6, 2019.

and the China Council for the Promotion of International Trade, successfully held a series of activities of the China-Arab States Expo in Cairo. This was an important measure taken by Ningxia to implement the achievements of President Xi Jinping's visit to Egypt and participate in the celebration activities for the 60th anniversary of the establishment of diplomatic relations between China and Egypt. The third China-Arab States Expo invited Egypt to be the guest of honor, which promoted the settlement of the China-Arab states and China-Egypt Mankai Textile Industrial Park in the Industrial City of Sadat City in Egypt and was highly appreciated by Egyptian President Abdel Fattah al-Sisi. Secondly, the China-Saudi Jizan Industrial Park has become a large-scale investment project to deepen China-Arab states production capacity cooperation, making progress in communication and coordination mechanisms, park infrastructure construction, and investment promotion. The first project to enter the park, the Saudi Petrochemical and Chemical Fiber Integration Project of Guangzhou Pan-Asia Polyester Co., Ltd., has initiated construction. Third states, two projects have been signed including the Cilata Floating Photovoltaic Project in Indonesia and the Red Sea Comprehensive Smart Energy Investment Project in Saudi Arabia. These projects highlight the supporting role of "Focusing on economic and trade cooperation and jointly building the Belt and Road Initiative", and have enriched and improved the economic and trade, technological, and energy cooperation mechanisms and achievements between China and countries along the Belt and Road. Fourth states, from October 1 to 7, 2024, the Ningxia Council for the Promotion of International Trade organized 5 Ningxia enterprises to participate in the 26th Middle East Dubai Electricity, Energy, Environmental Protection & Water Treatment Exhibition. It also led the enterprises to visit key economic and trade departments and institutions in the United Arab Emirates and Saudi Arabia, reaching multiple cooperation intentions in new energy, new materials, and related industrial fields, laying a foundation for further expanding the Middle East market.

Second, technological cooperation has continuously reached new heights. Scientific and technological as well as agricultural cooperation constitutes an important part of China's overall cooperation with Arab countries, and holds strategic significance for the development and livelihood improvement of Arab nations. The China-Arab States Technology Transfer and Innovation Cooperation Conference, the China-Arab States Technology Transfer Center,

Chapter 11　Special Report on China-Arab States Expo

and the China-Arab States Agricultural Technology Transfer Center, held within the framework of the China-Arab States Expo, serve as the main channels for centrally showcasing the achievements of China-Arab states scientific and technological cooperation and promoting normalized technology transfer.

Firstly, the China-Arab States Technology Transfer Center has promoted all-round cooperation between China and Arab countries in high-tech fields, which is conducive to the scientific and technological progress and social development of both sides, and also helps developing countries with relatively backward technologies keep up with the pace of the Fourth Industrial Revolution. Under the framework of China-Arab states scientific and technological cooperation, the China-Arab States Technology Transfer Center has promoted the joint construction of a 4G-LTE laboratory by Huawei and the King Abdullah University of Science and Technology (KACST) in Saudi Arabia, cooperation between China and Saudi Arabia in the field of satellite navigation, and the smooth implementation of projects such as the China-Arab States Green Intelligent Control Water-saving Technology Platform and the China-Arab States Jordan Potato Science and Technology Demonstration Test Base. The project of green intelligent water-saving irrigation technology and equipment, charged by Professor Sun Zhaojun's team from Ningxia University has substantially entered the market of Oman and Qatar. In October 2018, Ningxia University signed a water-saving equipment technology transfer cooperation agreement and a water-saving irrigation technology transfer contract worth 110 million RMB with the Suwaidi Farm in Muscat, Oman. In August 2020, Ningxia University, Qatar's Naas Group, and Huaxing Guolian (Beijing) Enterprise Management Co., Ltd. held an online signing ceremony for the Beautiful Doha Project, with an investment of approximately 1.264 billion US dollars. During the 5th China-Arab States Expo in 2021, three documents were signed including the Memorandum of Understanding on the Nigeria Working Base, the China-Arab States Technology Transfer Collaboration Network, and the Framework Cooperation Agreements for the China-Arab States (Jordan, Dubai) Technology Transfer Centers. At the 5th China-Arab States Technology Transfer and Innovation Cooperation Conference held in September 2023, China released 300 advanced and applicable technologies to Arab countries, covering fields such as ecological environment protection, resource and energy utilization, and pollution control. Secondly, the China-Arab States Agricultural Technology Transfer Center, based

253

in Ningxia, gives full play to the supporting role of its overseas sub-centers to help Arab countries upgrade their agricultural technology. For instance, the overseas sub-center in Mauritania has carried out experiments on dairy cow embryo transplantation, the introduction of high-quality forage, and the trial planting of tropical fruits. In the Jordanian overseas sub-center, agricultural cooperation such as the demonstration and promotion of Ningxia vegetable seed cultivation has been carried out. Ningxia's vegetable seeds have entered 12 countries and regions in the Middle East and Africa. The Moroccan overseas sub-center focuses on carrying out experimental demonstrations in the fields of fish meal processing and production, as well as aquatic product processing and trade.

Third, it has strongly promoted Ningxia's opening up to the outside world. Since 2013, Ningxia has fully utilized the China-Arab States Expo to actively integrate into and serve the construction of the BRI, building cooperation platforms, tapping trade potential, optimizing the investment environment, improving policy support, constructing open carriers, and unblocking foreign channels. By adhering to the combination of overall promotion and key breakthroughs, as well as the combination of institutional innovation and policy guidance, Ningxia has achieved high-level opening up on a larger scale and at a higher level, promoted the construction of a strategic highland for opening up to the west, and achieved phased results in participating in the BRI construction, with the function of open channels gradually enhanced. By the end of 2023, Yinchuan Hedong International Airport had opened 140 routes to 96 navigable cities, including 85 domestic destinations, with a 100% direct flight rate to provincial capital cities and 11 international destinations, having opened 12 international and regional routes to Hong Kong, China and Dubai. Ningxia has strengthened cooperation with coastal ports, enhanced exchanges with provinces, autonomous regions, and cities along the Western Land-Sea New Corridor, initially constructed a land-based open channel pattern connecting borders, reaching the sea, and linking the south and north, established an international cargo transportation system integrating international railways, rail-sea intermodal transport, and other modes of transportation, and formed a port channel network exiting to the northwest and heading to the sea in the southeast. This has provided important support for building a regional international logistics center, and the level of open economy development has steadily improved.

254

Chapter 11 Special Report on China-Arab States Expo

From 2013 to 2023, Ningxia accumulated USD2.71 billion in foreign investment, with an average annual growth rate of 8.2%. It established 152 overseas direct investment enterprises in 36 countries and regions worldwide, with a total foreign investment of USD4.39 billion. Among them, 23 overseas investment enterprises were set up in six Arab countries, with a total investment of USD435 million. In 2023, the import-export volume between Ningxia and Arab countries was 320 million yuan, and in 2024, the import volume reached 460 million yuan, up 43.7% year on year.

## 11.2 Multiple Development Opportunities Faced by the China-Arab States Expo Under the New Situation

### 11.2.1 New Opportunities for High-Quality Joint Building of the BRI

China has been continuously deepening the synergy between the BRI and the development strategies of Arab countries themselves. The cooperation between China and Arab countries in jointly building the BRI with high quality has comprehensively driven the development of China-Arab states relations. China has signed the cooperation initiative on jointly building the BRI with all Arab countries and the Secretariat of the League of Arab States, achieving the full coverage. Under the framework of jointly building the BRI, China and Arab countries have implemented more than 200 large-scale cooperation projects and created a number of flagship projects, such as the Central Business District of the New Administrative Capital of Egypt, the Yanbu Refinery in Saudi Arabia built by China, the Phase II Container Terminal of Khalifa Port in Abu Dhabi, the East-West Expressway in Algeria, and the Mohammed VI Bridge in Morocco. The fruits of cooperation have benefited nearly 2 billion people on both sides and effectively promoted the large circulation of goods, funds, technologies and personnel among various countries.

### 11.2.2 New opportunities Brought about by the Modernization Transformation of Arab Countries

The modernization transformation of Arab countries refers to the systematic reforms implemented by the countries in the Gulf and the Middle East region to break through the dependence on traditional economic structures, such as

255

oil exports, cope with the pressure of international competition, and enhance national competitiveness. Its core lies in promoting the transformation of countries from being resource-driven to innovation-driven and from being closed and conservative to open and inclusive through economic diversification, the opening up of social culture, digital upgrading and the innovation of governance models. The modernization transformation of Arab countries has brought the following new opportunities for China-Arab states economic and trade cooperation in the new era.

First, energy transformation and cooperation in the green economy. Arab countries generally regard energy diversification as the core of their strategies. China's technological advantages in clean energy fields such as photovoltaic and wind power are highly complementary to the resource endowments of Arab countries. The two sides have already cooperated in implementing landmark projects such as the world's largest single photovoltaic power station (the Al Dhafra Solar PV Project in the United Arab Emirates) and the energy storage project for the New Red Sea City. There is huge potential for future cooperation in the fields of hydrogen energy, nuclear energy and smart grids. Second, digital transformation and the development of emerging industries. Arab states countries are accelerating the digital upgrade, and countries like Saudi Arabia and the United Arab Emirates have listed 5G, artificial intelligence and smart cities as priority areas. Chinese enterprises are competitive in digital infrastructure fields such as cloud computing, data centers and the industrial Internet. For example, Huawei Cloud has helped the development of Qatar's e-commerce platform by optimizing network latency and costs, and Foxconn has cooperated with Saudi Arabia to lay out the electric vehicle industry. China-Arab cooperation is transforming from traditional infrastructure to the mode of "digital Infrastructure combining industrial upgrading", covering emerging business forms such as cross-border e-commerce, fintech and e-sports, which caters to the demographic dividend of the young population in Arab countries and the changes in consumption habits.Third, the upgrading of infrastructure connectivity. Arab countries have a large-scale infrastructure demand in fields such as electricity, transportation and housing. The comprehensive advantages of Chinese enterprises in both traditional infrastructure, such as railways and ports, and emerging fields, such as seawater desalination and photovoltaic industrial parks continue to stand out. For example, the Red Sea public infrastructure

Chapter 11    Special Report on China-Arab States Expo

project in Saudi Arabia contracted by Power Construction Corporation of China integrates multi-energy complementary technologies and has become a model of green infrastructure. China-Arab states infrastructure cooperation is transforming from the model of project contracting to the integrated model of Construction-Investment-Operation", promoting the deepening of the China Construction brand in the Arab market. Fourth, financial cooperation and the internationalization of the RMB. China-Arab states financial cooperation has expanded from trade settlement to multi-level capital linkages. China has signed local currency swap agreements with Arab countries, and the proportion of the RMB in the payment system of the League of Arab States has increased. Platforms such as the China-Arab States Bank Consortium and the Silk Road Fund provide financing support for energy and infrastructure projects. Meanwhile, financial institutions in countries like Saudi Arabia and the United Arab Emirates are accelerating their entry into the Chinese market. In addition, the opening up of the Arab financial market provides an opportunity for Chinese-funded institutions to expand their overseas business, such as participating in local stock exchanges and the issuance of green bonds. Fifth, the consumption goods market and diversified investment. The youthful population (with an average age of 30) in Arab countries and trends such as the "Female Economy" and "Health Consumption" are driving the expansion of the consumption goods market. China has price and technological advantages in fields such as home appliances, textiles, and digital economy products, and can seize market share through localization strategies, such as customized products and festival marketing. Meanwhile, the economic diversification policies of Arab countries to reduce their dependence on oil have expanded the investment space for Chinese enterprises in fields like manufacturing, agricultural technology, and medical health. For instance, there are renewable energy cooperation parks in Egypt and medical projects in Jordan.

### 11.2.3    New Opportunities for the Western Region to Open up both Domestically and Internationally

On the afternoon of April 23, 2024, Xi Jinping, General Secretary of the Communist Party of China Central Committee, President of the People's Republic of China, and Chairperson of the Central Military Commission of the People's Republic of China, presided over the Symposium on Promoting the

257

The Development Process of China-Arab States Economic and Trade Relations
Annual Report 2024

Development of the Western Region in the New Era in Chongqing and delivered an important speech. Xi Jinping has emphasized that we shall continue to boost large-scale development through high-level opening-up and raise the level of opening-up both within China and to the outside world in the western region. We shall vigorously promote the building of the New International Land-Sea Trade Corridor in the western region, drive the development and opening-up of regions along the corridor, and deeply integrate into the joint construction of the BRI. We shall improve the layout of various industrial parks, border economic cooperation zones and cross-border economic cooperation zones in border areas, and promote the high-quality development of pilot free trade zones. We shall steadily expand institutional opening-up and create a market-oriented, law-based and internationalized business environment. We shall take a more proactive approach to serve and align with major regional strategies, actively integrate into the construction of a unified national market, innovate the docking mechanism for the opening-up platforms in the eastern, central and western regions, and deepen practical cooperation with the eastern, central and western regions as well as the northeastern region[1].To consistently ensure the implementation of the policy measures promoted by the CPC Central Committee for the large-scale development of the western region and further form a new pattern featuring major protection, wide opening-up and high-quality development, all the provinces, autonomous regions and municipalities directly under the central government in the western region, guided by jointly building the BRI, have strengthened the coordinated cooperation among the eastern, central and western regions, given play to their respective characteristic advantages based on local conditions and increased the intensity of opening-up in the western region.

### 11.2.4　New Opportunities for Sustainable Development and Green Cooperation

Both China and Arab countries adhere to sustainable development and

---

[1]　"Xi Jinping Chairs the Symposium on Promoting the Great Development of the Western Region in the New Era, Stressing the Further Formation of a New Pattern of Great Protection, Great Opening-up and High-Quality Development and the Effort to Write a New Chapter in the Great Development of the Western Region. Li Qiang, Cai Qi and Ding Xuexiang Attending the Symposium," *People's Daily*, April 4, 2024.

Chapter 11　Special Report on China-Arab States Expo

continuously promote green innovation. China, together with Arab countries, is implementing the Global Development Initiative and jointly moving towards a new stage of development that is innovative, coordinated, green, open and inclusive. The successive establishment of centers such as the China-Arab States Technology Transfer Center, the Clean Energy Center, the Beidou Satellite Center, and the International Research Center on Drought, Desertification and Land Degradation has led to the creation of eight bilateral technology transfer centers in countries like the United Arab Emirates, thus forming a technology transfer cooperation network that connects thousands of scientific research institutions and innovative enterprises from both China and Arab countries. Both China and Arab countries should further tap the potential for cooperation in emerging and high-tech fields such as green and low-carbon, information communication, aerospace, digital economy, and artificial intelligence, promote the integration of digital technologies and the real economy, and inject inexhaustible impetus into the sustainable development of both sides.

## 11.3　Ideas on Successfully Holding the China-Arab States Expo Under the New Situation

### 11.3.1　Guiding Principle

Guided by Xi Jinping Thought on Socialism with Chinese Characteristics for a New Era, we will fully implement the spirit of the 20th National Congress of the Communist Party of China as well as the second and third plenary sessions of the 20th CPC Central Committee. We will earnestly implement the spirit of the important speeches and instructions given by General Secretary Xi Jinping during his inspection in Ningxia. We will adhere to the combination of opening-up to both the domestic and international markets, actively participate in the joint construction of the BRI and the New Western Land-Sea Corridor, foster the main entities of the open economy, create an environment conducive to the open economy, raise the level of inland opening up, and deepen economic and trade cooperation with Arab countries. We will efficiently connect the outstanding achievements of Chinese-style modernization in areas such as production capacity, technology and high-tech with the specific needs of the modernization of Arab countries, form a high-quality overall pattern of cooperation between

259

the central and local governments to promote China-Arab states cooperation, and make new contributions to promoting the building of a China-Arab states community with a shared future for a new era and striving to write a chapter on Chinese-style modernization in Ningxia.

## 11.3.2　Overall Idea

With the in-depth development of China-Arab states relations and the continuous accumulation of experiences in Ningxia's practices, the functional positioning of the China-Arab States Expo has gradually shifted its focus from highly integrating China-Arab states cooperation in multiple fields to deepening economic and trade cooperation. Its service scope has been continuously expanded from facilitating cooperation between Ningxia and Arab countries, cooperation between China and Arab countries to international cooperation under the BRI, thus becoming an important platform for promoting the joint construction of the BRI by China and Arab countries. In the next decade, the China-Arab States Expo will hold high the banner of the Community with a Shared Future for Mankind, inherit and carry forward the Silk Road spirit, adhere to goal orientation and action orientation, and take the implementation of the Eight Joint Actions and the Five Cooperation Patterns for China-Arab states practical cooperation as its guidance. It will actively build an upgraded version of the China-Arab States Expo with a more refined functional positioning, a practical and innovative organizing mechanism, a significantly improved service level, a more solid cooperation foundation and more prominent economic and trade achievements. It will steadily promote the high-quality joint construction of the BRI by China and Arab countries to continuously achieve new and greater results, and make greater contributions to Ningxia's high-level opening-up and high-quality development.

Under the strategic guidance of President Xi Jinping and Arab leaders, China-Arab states relations are currently at their best in history, and the all-round, multi-level and wide-ranging cooperation pattern between China and Arab countries is constantly being enriched and deepened. The 10th Plenary Session of the 13th CPC Ningxia Hui Autonomous Region Committee pointed out that Ningxia shall actively integrate into and serve the high-quality joint construction of the BRI, steadily expand institutional opening-up, actively participate in the construction of the New Western Land-Sea Corridor, and further deepen

Chapter 11　Special Report on China-Arab States Expo

regional strategic cooperation, and adding new impetus and expand new space for economic and social development[1]. Against this backdrop, the China-Arab States Expo is facing significant strategic opportunities. It should follow the trend, strengthen its internal capabilities and accelerate its actions, striving to play a more important role in the overall situation of China-Arab states cooperation in the new era and focusing on doing a good job in Five Overall Plans.

First, making overall plans for inheritance and innovation. We shall maintain the circle of friends of the China-Arab States Expo, consolidate the foundation for high-quality development, and refine and solidify existing activities. Furthermore, we shall focus on enhancing the ability of innovative development, zero in on the cooperation pattern between China and Arab countries in the new era, and create characteristic incremental activities. Second, making overall plans for the role of the government and the market. We shall adhere to the coordinated promotion principle of government guidance, market operation, enterprises as the main body, and win-win cooperation, and fully stimulate the enthusiasm of all sides to participate in the China-Arab States Expo. Third, making overall plans for bilateral and multilateral aspects. We shall adhere to the working idea of discussing cooperation multilaterally and facilitating implementation bilaterally. Moreover, we shall work together with the Arab side to promote the implementation of the agreed items at the China-Arab States Summit and the Ministerial Meeting of the China-Arab States Cooperation Forum, and focus on enhancing the effective docking and synergy between the activities under the framework of the China-Arab States Expo and the bilateral economic and trade cooperation agendas. Multilateral cooperation through bilateral efforts and the effectiveness of economic and trade cooperation shall be improved through various forms such as bilateral cooperation, tripartite cooperation and multilateral cooperation. Fourth, making overall plans for scale and benefits. We shall steadily improve the scale and benefits of the China-Arab States Expo. Small yet delicate projects shall be prioritized, and more projects that require small investments, yield quick results and achieve good economic,

---

[1] "The 10th Plenary Session of the 13th CPC Ningxia Hui Autonomous Region Committee and the Committee's Economic Work Conference were held in Yinchuan, chaired by the Standing Committee of the CPC Ningxia Hui Autonomous Region Committee. Li Yifei delivered a report and made a speech, and Zhang Yupu arranged the economic work for next year," *Ningxia Daily*, December 26, 2024, p.1.

social and environmental benefits shall be carried out to generate more cooperation achievements that are down-to-earth and appealing to people. Fifth, making overall plans for development and security. We shall firmly establish and practice the holistic view of national security, improve the institutional mechanisms for risk prevention and control, strengthen overall coordination, ensure that all sides fulfill their responsibilities, and do a good job in factor guarantee, constantly improving the ability and level to respond to risks, meet challenges and turn risks into safety.

### 11.3.3　Functional Orientation

Firstly, the main mechanism for serving China-Arab states economic and trade cooperation. We shall strengthen the overall coordination of the China-Arab states economic and trade cooperation mechanism at the national level, and clarify the functional positioning of the China-Arab States Expo as a centralized and unified economic and trade cooperation mechanism and comprehensive service platform for dealing with Arab countries both domestically and internationally. We shall also strengthen the coordination of the China-Arab states economic and trade cooperation mechanism at the provincial level. Through establishing mutually beneficial cooperation relationships and the mechanism of holding events in turn, we shall optimize the allocation of economic and trade cooperation resources such as conferences and forums, and focus on enhancing the platform functions of the China-Arab States Expo.

Secondly, an important platform for promoting the high-quality joint construction of the BRI by China and Arab countries. With the strategic goal of facilitating the building of a China-Arab states community with a shared future for the new era, it focuses on the key cooperation areas of the high-quality joint construction of the BRI by China and Arab countries, revitalizes the overall resources of China's economic and trade cooperation with Arab countries, adapts to the development needs of Arab countries, and jointly implements the strategies, plans, policies and projects of China-Arab states cooperation in the new era, so as to build the China-Arab States Expo into an important platform for the high-quality joint construction of the BRI by China and Arab countries.

Thirdly, an important engine for boosting Ningxia's high-level opening-up. By thoroughly implementing the spirit of the important speeches and instructions given by General Secretary Xi Jinping during his previous inspections in

Chapter 11　Special Report on China-Arab States Expo

Ningxia, we shall consolidate the foundation of Ningxia's cooperation with Arab countries, give full play to the characteristics and advantages of cooperation with Arab countries, improve the docking mechanism with the opening-up platforms of other provinces and autonomous regions, seize the major opportunities for the transfer of funds, technologies and industries from the eastern regions to the central and western regions, build a modern industrial system with unique features and differences based on local conditions, and form a development trend in which the tasks of high-level opening up are effectively integrated with the functions of the opening-up platform of the China-Arab States Expo.

## 11.4　Approaches to Successfully Holding the China-Arab States Expo Under the New Situation

In accordance with the overall thinking, functional positioning and development goals, we shall focus on completing such tasks as deeply integrating into and serving the high-quality joint construction of the BRI between China and Arab countries, enhancing the level of innovative development of investment and trade, coordinating to build a new mechanism for digital economy cooperation, and helping Ningxia to achieve a high-level opening up both domestically and internationally.

### 11.4.1　Deeply Integrating into and Serving the High-quality Joint Construction of the BRI Between China and Arab countries

Firstly, strengthening strategic and policy research. We shall comprehensively sort out General Secretary Xi Jinping's five policy announcements on the Arab world and the contents of China-Arab states multilateral and bilateral cooperation policy documents. In combination with the functional positioning of the China-Arab States Expo and the characteristics of its institutional activities, we shall research and formulate action plans and work programs for the China-Arab States Expo to implement the high-quality joint construction of the BRI between China and Arab countries, and promote the continuous innovation of activities under the framework of the China-Arab States Expo. We shall systematically study the international economic and trade cooperation mechanisms of the BRI and the advanced experiences of domestic and international institutional forums and expositions. Taking promoting China-Arab

263

states economic and trade cooperation as the starting point, we shall negotiate to establish a multi-dimensional, practical and effective strategic cooperation relationship, accelerate the filling of the shortcomings in the preparatory work of the China-Arab States Expo, and comprehensively enhance the ability to integrate resources for economic and trade cooperation with Arab countries.

Secondly, enhancing the effectiveness of docking and coordination. We shall strengthen coordination with the support of the Ministry of Commerce and the China Council for the Promotion of International Trade. We shall promote the signing of a framework agreement on deepening economic and trade cooperation with Arab countries by the Ministry of Commerce, the China Council for the Promotion of International Trade and Ningxia. We shall actively give play to the roles of bilateral and multilateral mechanisms such as the China-Arab States Inter-governmental Joint Committee on Economic and Trade Cooperation and the China-Arab Joint Chamber of Commerce, and fully utilize the platform functions of the China-Arab States Expo to facilitate mutual visits and exchanges between the governments and enterprises of China and Arab countries. We shall actively strive for the support of the Ministry of Foreign Affairs, coordinate the institutional economic and trade promotion activities under the framework of the China-Arab States Cooperation Forum to be held in Ningxia, and continue to maintain the scale and influence of the China-Arab States Expo.

## 11.4.2 Enhancing the Level of Innovative Development of Investment and Trade

Firstly, continuously enhancing the capacity level of the trade and investment promotion platform. We shall strive for the support of the National Development and Reform Commission, the Ministry of Commerce, the Silk Road Fund, the Asian Infrastructure Investment Bank and relevant central enterprises. We shall organize the BRI Trade and Investment Promotion Conference at a high level and with high quality, highlighting and strengthening the positioning and functions of the conference as a platform that guides the direction of innovative investment and trade development, explores policy mechanisms, releases cooperation projects and facilitates international exchanges and cooperation under the framework of jointly building the BRI by China and Arab countries. On the basis of maintaining the aggregation of various

Chapter 11    Special Report on China-Arab States Expo

professional elements in China, we shall continuously invite international organizations, industry associations and entrepreneurs at home and abroad to attend and deliver keynote speeches. We shall organize and plan high-quality matchmaking activities according to the theme of the conference to improve the actual effectiveness of the conference and promote China and Arab countries to build a larger-scale investment and financial pattern and a more balanced economic and trade reciprocal pattern.

Secondly, exploring the establishment of the China-Gulf Cooperation Council Economic and Trade Center. We shall research on the necessity and feasibility of setting up the China-GCC Economic and Trade Center. The general idea is to build it into a one-stop service platform for economic and trade cooperation between China and the GCC. We shall rely on the special customs supervision areas, attract business associations, well-known enterprises and international institutions from both China and GCC countries to settle in, and provide services such as business investment, legal services, finance, logistics, digital information, agricultural economic cooperation, cultural and tourism cooperation, and professional talents.

Thirdly, researching and implementing a new model of integrating online and offline exhibition hosting. We shall vigorously promote the digital transformation of exhibition projects, hold cloud exhibitions during the period of the China-Arab States Expo to enhance the effects of display, publicity and negotiations. We shall set up an exhibition and trading service platform and build a bonded warehouse under customs supervision as a supporting facility. We shall utilize the model of store in the front and warehouse at the back to directly connect with exhibitors and innovate trading models. We shall conduct pre-sales exhibitions on the exhibition and trading service platform before the event, display in the exhibition hall during the event, and extend the exhibition and sales after the event. We shall explore a new model of exhibition hosting that features synchronous interaction and organic integration of online and offline aspects.

Fourthly, establishing a market-oriented mechanism for organizing conferences and exhibitions as well as a mechanism for regularly organizing conferences and exhibitions during non-conference periods. We shall adhere to the basic principles of market dominance and government guidance, systematically reform the institutional mechanisms for the conferences and exhibitions of the China-Arab States Expo, actively explore the paths of specialization, marketization,

265

internationalization and digitalization, and establish a market-oriented mechanism for organizing conferences and exhibitions as well as a mechanism for regularly organizing conferences and exhibitions during non-conference periods. In terms of exhibitor recruitment, we shall form a professional exhibitor recruitment team, make good use of the resources of strategic cooperative partners to broaden the channels for exhibitor recruitment, and introduce advanced products and technologies. We shall closely focus on serving national strategies and the needs of people's livelihood to set up special exhibition areas. We shall establish an exhibitor alliance and form professional committees in relevant fields, and implement a market-oriented pricing mechanism for exhibition booths. In terms of investment invitation, we shall utilize the market-oriented mechanism to form industry and joint trading delegations. We shall strengthen the initiative of purchasers through measures such as investment invitation through roadshows and matchmaking meetings. We shall promote cooperative units to assist in investment invitation by means of performance assessment and commission incentives. For the opening ceremony and the BRI Trade and Investment Promotion Conference, we shall steadily advance the market-oriented membership system and registration system, increase the efforts to invite internationally renowned experts and enhance the internationalization level. In terms of on-site services, we shall fully realize market-oriented operation and introduce professional service providers through market-oriented procurement methods.

### 11.4.3 Making Overall Plans to Build a New Mechanism for Digital Economy Cooperation

Firstly, organizing the China-Arab States Digital Economy Cooperation Forum. With a focus on promoting the positive interaction between Chinese-style modernization and the modernization of Arab countries, under the framework of the China-Arab States Expo, we shall plan and hold the China-Arab States Digital Economy Cooperation Forum and its supporting activities with high standards and at a high level. We shall facilitate the docking of digital economy development strategies, provide services such as cloud computing, artificial intelligence computing power and algorithms for the governments and enterprises of Arab countries, and promote practical cooperation in fields such as digital infrastructure, e-commerce, mobile payment, digital cultural industries,

Chapter 11　Special Report on China-Arab States Expo

smart cities, distance education and digital talent cultivation.

Secondly, deeply participating in the exchanges and cooperation on the Silk Road E-commerce. We shall align with the construction of the Silk Road E-commerce cooperation pilot area in Shanghai. We shall conduct exchanges on the localized and compliant operation of the Silk Road E-commerce as well as exchanges on think tank research and training under the framework of the China-Arab States Expo. We shall promote more Arab countries to establish e-commerce cooperation mechanisms with China, smooth the exchanges and cooperation on e-commerce between China and Arab countries, facilitate the integrated development of China's cross-border e-commerce and industrial belts, drive Chinese cross-border e-commerce enterprises, digital technologies, digital business models and advanced logistics systems to be established in Arab countries, and enhance the international competitiveness of China's industrial and supply chains.

### 11.4.4　Promoting China-Arab States Scientific and Technological Innovation and Technology Transfer with High Quality

Firstly, supporting the China-Arab States Conference on Technology Transfer and Innovation Cooperation to continue to improve and achieve greater success. It aims to explore new mechanisms and models for scientific and technological cooperation, connect high-end resources for scientific and technological innovation, and promote the joint establishment of joint laboratories by China and the Arab states in fields such as life and health, artificial intelligence, green and low-carbon, modern agriculture, and space information. To make it further, it is also planned to jointly build the Joint Space Debris Observation Center and the Beidou Application Cooperation and Development Center, strengthen cooperation in manned spaceflight and civil airliners, enhance the regional innovation capacity and level, and create a more dynamic innovation-driven pattern.

Secondly, supporting the high-level and regular operation of the China-Arab States Technology Transfer Center. We shall continuously expand the China-Arab states technology transfer cooperation network, and strive to achieve full coverage of overseas bilateral technology transfer centers in Arab countries within ten years. We shall dock with the China-Arab States International Research Center on Drought, Desertification and Land Degradation, jointly hold forums

267

The Development Process of China-Arab States Economic and Trade Relations
Annual Report 2024

and seminars, and promote the transfer of technological achievements. We shall strengthen cooperation with the China-Arab States Agricultural Technology Transfer Center, promote the joint establishment of modern agricultural joint laboratories with the Arab side, carry out demonstration projects for agricultural technology cooperation, dispatch agricultural technology experts to the Arab side, and help the Arab side increase grain production, improve the capacity for grain storage and loss reduction, and enhance agricultural production efficiency. We shall strengthen the capacity to build China-Arab States Technology Transfer Center, seek special funds from the Ministry of Science and Technology and the Ningxia government. We shall increase the training and reserve of professional technical talents, and make the technology transfer work more substantial and in-depth.

## 11.4.5 Boosting High-level Opening up both Internally and Externally in Ningxia

Planning and holding a special forum on high-level opening-up in China's inland areas. It is planned to invite inland provincial regions such as Gansu, Qinghai, Xinjiang, Shaanxi, Inner Mongolia and Guizhou, the administrative committees of free trade pilot zones in the eastern regions, as well as national ministries and commissions like the National Development and Reform Commission and the Ministry of Commerce to jointly study and implement the *Several Policy Measures for Further Promoting the Formation of a New Pattern in the Western Development* and the *Guiding Opinions of the CPC Central Committee and the State Council on Promoting the Formation of a New Pattern in the Western Development in the New Era*. Measures shall be taken including leveraging their respective characteristic advantages, with the guidance of co-building the BRI, intensifying the opening-up efforts in the inland areas, strengthening the cooperation among the eastern, central and western regions, and actively participating in the construction of the New Western Land-Sea Corridor. Furthermore, it is to build multi-level opening-up platforms in the inland areas, establish a docking mechanism for the opening up platforms in the eastern, central and western regions, and promote the transformation of the opening up in the western regions from being commodity and factor flow-oriented to being rule and institution-oriented gradually.

268

# Chapter 12    Special Report on the Opening Up of Ningxia

Since 2013, Ningxia has actively engaged in the Belt and Road Initiative(BRI), and focused on the construction of large projects, platforms, channels, and big data. Ningxia has also given full play to the role of the inland open economic pilot zone and the national platform of the China-Arab States Exposition. Focusing on internal and external affairs, platform channels, hardware and software, foreign trade, and foreign investment, and building a new pattern of an inland open economy, Ningxia has effectively promoted a wide, deep, and high level of opening up.

## 12.1    The Steady Improvement of an Open Economy

### 12.1.1    Comprehensive Improvement in Economic Quality and Efficiency

In 2024, Ningxia's GDP was RMB550.28 billion, a year-on-year increase of 5.4%, ranking 14th in the country and exceeding the national average for 10 consecutive quarters. The growth rate of the added value of the primary industry, the secondary industry, and industries above designated size ranked the fourth, fifth and third in the country respectively (with an increase of 6.2%, 7% and 9.6%). The investment in fixed assets increased by 7.9%, ranking third in the country. The total retail sales of consumer goods increased by 5%, ranking sixth in the country. In addition, the local public budget revenue was RMB 51.7 billion, an increase of 2.8%, of which the growth rate of local tax revenue ranked eighth in the country. All the above indicators are higher than the

national average. Furthermore, the added value of the tertiary industry and the construction industry, and the total import and export volume have rebounded steadily. Commercial housing sales have leveled off and stabilized.

At the same time, the per capita disposable income of all residents increased by 5.5%, ranking sixth in the country, exceeding the economic growth rate. The urbanization rate reached 68.2%, higher than the national average. As can be seen from Table 12.1, 12.2 and 12.3, the economy of Ningxia has accomplished remarkable achievements. For instance, Ningxia's GDP increased from RMB232.8 billion in 2013 to RMB550.3 billion in 2024, with an absolute value of 2.36 times and an average annual growth rate of 8.98%; The per capita GDP increased from RMB35135 in 2013 to RMB75484 in 2024, with an absolute value of 2.15 times the 2013 amount and an average growth of 7.95%; Investments in fixed assets increased from RMB268.11billion in 2013 to RMB 365.9 billion in 2024, and the total investment amount is 1.36 times that of 2013. Looking across all provinces in the country, Ningxia's per capita GDP ranking has risen from 21st in 2013 to 20th in 2024. The speed and total volume of economic development have accelerated, and the quality, efficiency and structure have comprehensively improved.

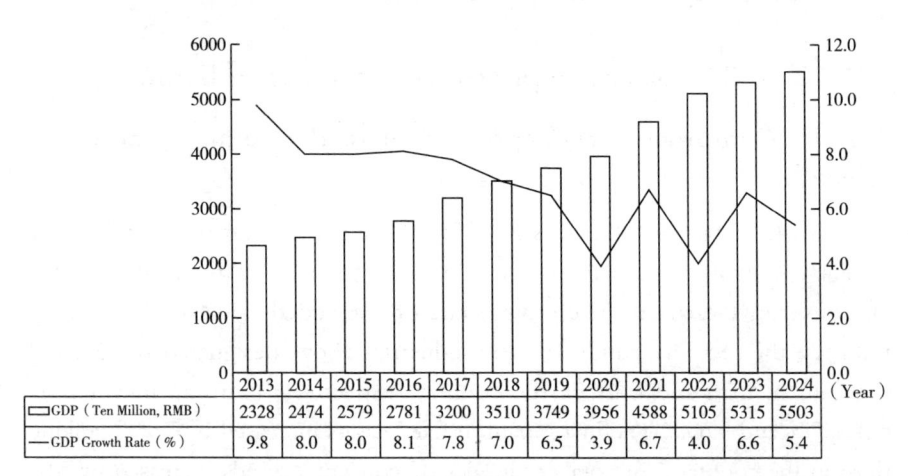

| | 2013 | 2014 | 2015 | 2016 | 2017 | 2018 | 2019 | 2020 | 2021 | 2022 | 2023 | 2024 |
|---|---|---|---|---|---|---|---|---|---|---|---|---|
| ▭GDP（Ten Million, RMB） | 2328 | 2474 | 2579 | 2781 | 3200 | 3510 | 3749 | 3956 | 4588 | 5105 | 5315 | 5503 |
| —GDP Growth Rate（%） | 9.8 | 8.0 | 8.0 | 8.1 | 7.8 | 7.0 | 6.5 | 3.9 | 6.7 | 4.0 | 6.6 | 5.4 |

**Figure 12.1   Changes in the Development of Ningxia's GDP (2013-2024)**

Source: Calculated from the Official Database of the National Bureau of Statistics, and the China and Ningxia Statistical Yearbooks. The per capita GDP growth rate in 2004, 2005, 2006, 2010, 2011 and 2020 is only estimated.

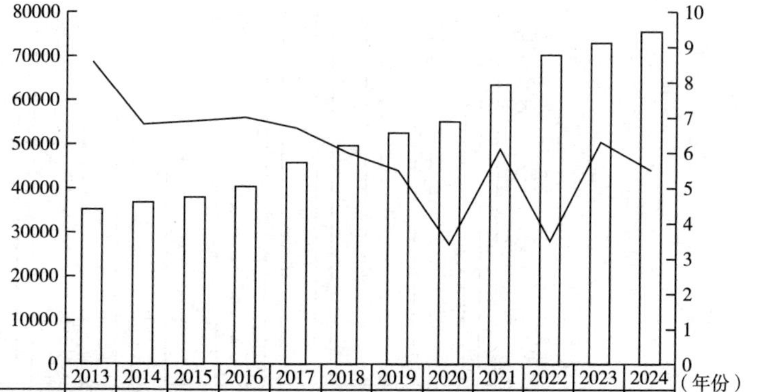

Chapter 12　Special Report on the Opening Up of Ningxia

| | 2013 | 2014 | 2015 | 2016 | 2017 | 2018 | 2019 | 2020 | 2021 | 2022 | 2023 | 2024 |（年份） |
|---|---|---|---|---|---|---|---|---|---|---|---|---|---|
| ▢ Per Capita GDP（Yuan/Per Person） | 35135 | 36815 | 37876 | 40339 | 45718 | 49614 | 52537 | 55021 | 63461 | 70263 | 72957 | 75484 | |
| — Growth Rate of the Per Capita GDP（%） | 8.6 | 6.8 | 6.9 | 7.0 | 6.7 | 6.0 | 5.5 | 3.4 | 6.1 | 3.5 | 6.3 | 5.5 | |

**Figure 12.2　Changes in the Development of Ningxia's Per Capita GDP (2013-2024)**

Source: Calculated from the Official Database of the National Bureau of Statistics, the China and Ningxia Statistical Yearbook and Statistical Bulletin.

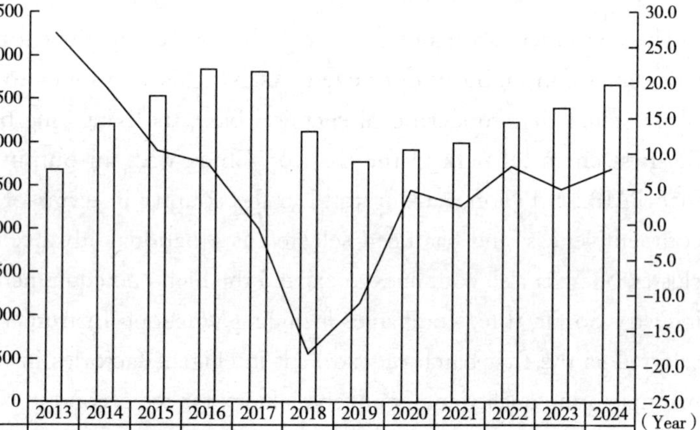

| | 2013 | 2014 | 2015 | 2016 | 2017 | 2018 | 2019 | 2020 | 2021 | 2022 | 2023 | 2024 |（Year） |
|---|---|---|---|---|---|---|---|---|---|---|---|---|---|
| ▢ Fixed Asset Investment（Ten Million, RMB） | 2681 | 3201 | 3533 | 3836 | 3813 | 3119 | 2773 | 2906 | 2985 | 3229 | 3391 | 3659 | |
| — Growth Rate of the Fixed Asset Investment（%） | 27.1 | 19.4 | 10.4 | 8.6 | −0.6 | −18.2 | −11.1 | 4.8 | 2.7 | 8.2 | 5.0 | 7.9 | |

**Figure 12.3　Changes in Fixed Asset Investment in Ningxia (2013-2023)**

Source: Calculated from the Official Database of the National Bureau of Statistics, the China and Ningxia Statistical Yearbook and Statistical Bulletin.

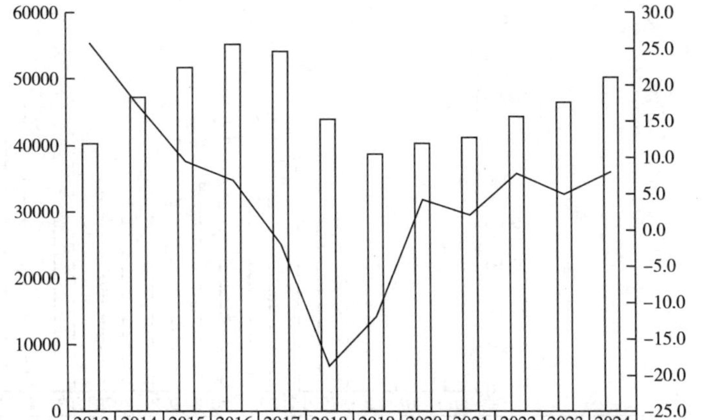

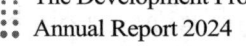

The Development Process of China-Arab States Economic and Trade Relations Annual Report 2024

| | 2013 | 2014 | 2015 | 2016 | 2017 | 2018 | 2019 | 2020 | 2021 | 2022 | 2023 | 2024 |
|---|---|---|---|---|---|---|---|---|---|---|---|---|
| Per Capita Fixed Asset Investment (RMB) | 40257 | 47212 | 51651 | 55187 | 54091 | 43934 | 38676 | 40308 | 41168 | 44360 | 46514 | 50258 |
| Growth Rate of the Per Capita Fixed Asset Investment (%) | 25.8 | 17.3 | 9.4 | 6.8 | −2.0 | −18.8 | −12.0 | 4.2 | 2.1 | 7.8 | 4.9 | 8.0 |

**Figure 12.4    Changes in Fixed Asset Investment in Ningxia (2013-2023)**

Source: Calculated from the Official Database of the National Bureau of Statistics, the China and Ningxia Statistical Yearbook and Statistical Bulletin.

## 12.1.2    Continuous Optimization of Industrial Structures

The investment structure and comprehensive competitiveness of the project have been continuously optimized. As Ningxia continues to strengthen the construction of a modern coal chemical base, the Ningdong base has become the first chemical park in the west of China with an output value of more than RMB200 billion, ranking third in the country in terms of comprehensive competitiveness, and has been selected as a national advanced manufacturing cluster. Ningxia also continues to expand the high-end equipment manufacturing industry. So far, three companies including Wuzhong Instrument Co., Ltd. were selected as the first batch of excellent intelligent factories in the country. The manufacturing quality competitiveness index ranked second in Northwest China, the highest level in history. Furthermore, Ningxia has also steadily developed the "Six Special" industries. So far, the output value of primary agriculture and animal husbandry accounts were more than 88% of the total agricultural output value, the output of wine and wolfberry deep-processing products has remained first in the country, and the Mengniu - Ningxia factory with complete digital intelligence was awarded the world's first dairy "lighthouse factory".

Chapter 12　Special Report on the Opening Up of Ningxia

Ningxia has also intensified the development and utilization of resources and energy, with the coal output exceeding 100 million tons for the first time, ranking eighth in the country. More than 5.3 million kilowatts of new energy power generation were added, and the proportion of green power installed capacity increased to 55%. The development of eleven green power parks, including Datang source-grid-load-storage integration, has been accelerated. In addition, the first high-tech project of 10000-ton green hydrogen integration and heterojunction solar cells started construction in Ningxia. And the Ningxia section of the "Ningxia Electricity Transmission to Hunan Province" project with an investment of RMB 70 billion has been fully completed. These landmark projects have accumulated strong stamina for the continuous optimization of the industrial structure.

As can be seen from Table 12. 5, the proportion of the three industrial structures in Ningxia has been gradually optimized from 2013 to 2024. The structure of the three industries changed from 9.1: 45.5: 45.4 in 2013 to 8.2: 42.4: 49.4 in 2024, realizing the transformation of the industrial structure from pattern "231" to "321" in relatively stable way. Ningxia has embarked on an industrial development path with local characteristics, and the two-wheel support pattern of industry and service has been basically formed. Overall, Ningxia's industrial structure is in the transition stage from primary to advanced, and its economic development is in the middle stage of industrialization

## 12.1.3　Rapid development of Foreign Trade and Investment

1. Development of Foreign Trade

In 2024, according to statistics from Yinchuan Customs, Ningxia achieved imports and exports worth RMB 20.61 billion, a year-on-year increase of 0.3%, ranking 26th in the country and 11th among western provinces in terms of growth rate, thus stabilizing after a downturn. Among these, the foreign trade values of 54 enterprises (only 42 enterprises in 2013) exceeded RMB 100 million. The attracted investment capital through business invitation and investment promotion reached RMB185.4 billion. The Yinchuan Comprehensive Bonded Zone completed an import and export trade volume of RMB 2.58 billion, a year-on-year increase of 20.6%. In addition, the industrial output value above designated size reached RMB 289 million, a year-on-year increase of 28.3%. 21 enterprises in Ningxia were listed in the "Export Commodity Brand Certification List (2024)", ranking fourth nationwide and first in the western region in terms

273

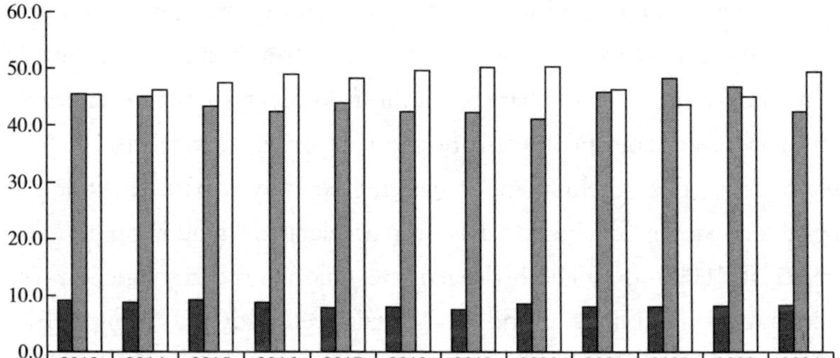

The Development Process of China-Arab States Economic and Trade Relations
Annual Report 2024

| | 2013 | 2014 | 2015 | 2016 | 2017 | 2018 | 2019 | 2020 | 2021 | 2022 | 2023 | 2024 | (Year) |
|---|---|---|---|---|---|---|---|---|---|---|---|---|---|
| ■1st Industry | 9.1 | 8.8 | 9.2 | 8.7 | 7.8 | 8.0 | 7.5 | 8.5 | 7.9 | 8.0 | 8.1 | 8.2 | |
| ▨2st Industry | 45.5 | 45.0 | 43.3 | 42.4 | 43.9 | 42.4 | 42.3 | 41.2 | 45.8 | 48.3 | 46.8 | 42.4 | |
| ☐3st Industry | 45.4 | 46.2 | 47.5 | 48.9 | 48.3 | 49.6 | 50.2 | 50.3 | 46.3 | 43.7 | 45.1 | 49.4 | |

**Figure 12.5　Changes of the proportion of the three industrial structures in Ningxia(2013-2024)**

Source: Calculated from the Official Database of the National Bureau of Statistics, the China and Ningxia Statistical Yearbook and Statistical Bulletin.

of the number of listed enterprises. As can be seen in Table 12.6, from 2013 to 2024, Ningxia's total foreign trade volume generally showed a trend of recovery and growth after the COVID-19 pandemic. However, the proportion and structure of import and export trade were still imbalanced, with the total export value at RMB 15.08 billion and the total import value at only RMB 5.53 billion. In addition, the degree of dependence on foreign trade was relatively low, standing at only 3.8%.

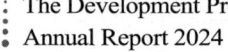

From the perspective of foreign trade structure, private enterprises have occupied the main position in the market, with continuous optimization of structure, a solid foundation for foreign trade, and increasing vitality. There are 713 enterprises in Ningxia with actual performance in import and export, an increase of 21.3%. Among them, there are 659 private enterprises, an increase of 131 compared to the previous year (24.8%). In 2024, private enterprises achieved imports and exports worth RMB16.19 billion, an increase of 10.9%, 10.6 percentage points higher than the growth rate of all of Ningxia, accounting for 78.6% of Ningxia's total import and export value, an increase of 7.5 percentage points compared to the previous year. The worth of the imports and exports of foreign-funded enterprises and state-owned enterprises were RMB 2.82 billion and RMB 1.6 billion, accounting for a 13.6% and 7.8% growth respectively.

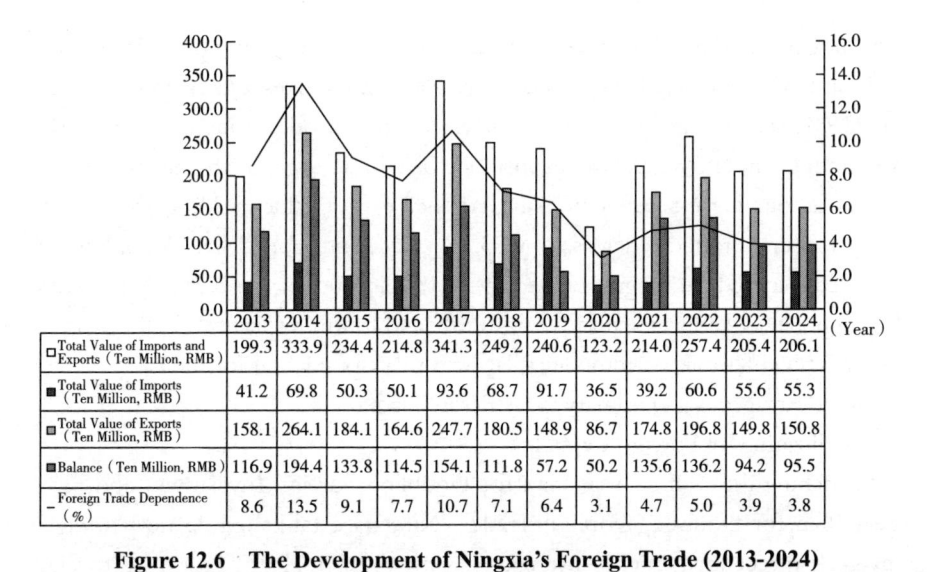

Chapter 12　Special Report on the Opening Up of Ningxia

| | 2013 | 2014 | 2015 | 2016 | 2017 | 2018 | 2019 | 2020 | 2021 | 2022 | 2023 | 2024 |
|---|---|---|---|---|---|---|---|---|---|---|---|---|
| □ Total Value of Imports and Exports (Ten Million, RMB) | 199.3 | 333.9 | 234.4 | 214.8 | 341.3 | 249.2 | 240.6 | 123.2 | 214.0 | 257.4 | 205.4 | 206.1 |
| ■ Total Value of Imports (Ten Million, RMB) | 41.2 | 69.8 | 50.3 | 50.1 | 93.6 | 68.7 | 91.7 | 36.5 | 39.2 | 60.6 | 55.6 | 55.3 |
| ▨ Total Value of Exports (Ten Million, RMB) | 158.1 | 264.1 | 184.1 | 164.6 | 247.7 | 180.5 | 148.9 | 86.7 | 174.8 | 196.8 | 149.8 | 150.8 |
| ▨ Balance (Ten Million, RMB) | 116.9 | 194.4 | 133.8 | 114.5 | 154.1 | 111.8 | 57.2 | 50.2 | 135.6 | 136.2 | 94.2 | 95.5 |
| ─ Foreign Trade Dependence (%) | 8.6 | 13.5 | 9.1 | 7.7 | 10.7 | 7.1 | 6.4 | 3.1 | 4.7 | 5.0 | 3.9 | 3.8 |

**Figure 12.6　The Development of Ningxia's Foreign Trade (2013-2024)**

Source: Calculated from the Official Database of the National Bureau of Statistics, the China and Ningxia Statistical Yearbook, Statistical Bulletin and the Customs 'statistics.

From the perspective of trading partners, the foreign trade breadth has continuously expanded, achieving diversified development. In 2024, Ningxia had trade relations with more than 150 countries and regions. The imports and exports with ASEAN amounted to RMB 3.48 billion, an increase of 0.4%, accounting for 16.9% of the total. Imports and exports with the European Union reached RMB3.16 billion, accounting for 15.3%. Imports and exports with the Hong Kong region amounted to RMB1.44 billion, a remarkable increase of 304%, accounting for 7% of the total. Trade with emerging markets such as the Middle East, Africa, and South America showed strong growth momentum, with import and export growth rates of 32.3%, 27.5%, and 5.1% respectively, far exceeding those of traditional markets. Additionally, cooperation with countries participating in the BRI has expanded, with import and export growth rates higher than the overall rate, accounting for 45.5% of the total, thus forming a solid foundation for foreign trade.

From the perspective of product structure, the imports and exports of advantageous and primary industries in Ningxia have continued to expand. On the import side, metal ores increased by 14.3%, accounting for 20.2% of Ningxia's total import value in 2024 (the same below). Among them, manganese ore and niobium,

275

tantalum, or vanadium ores increased by 22.4% and 20% respectively, ranking second and third in the national import value of similar commodities. Quartz imports grew by 22.7%, accounting for 14.1%, while agricultural products increased by 3.9%, accounting for 11.5%. On the export side, the basic organic chemicals grew by 28.8%, accounting for 21.9% of Ningxia's total export value in 2024. The exports of agricultural products increased by 23.3%, accounting for 11.7%. Among them, vegetables and edible fungi increased by 24.1%, accounting for 5.7%. Wolfberries, frozen potatoes, and wine ranked first, fourth, and fourth respectively in the national export value of similar commodities, laying a solid foundation for the development of the advantageous and primary industries in Ningxia.

2. Utilization of Foreign Capital

Launching the "Three-Year Plan for Doubling Foreign Investment and Five-Year Plan for Doubling Foreign Trade", Ningxia established 23 new foreign-invested direct investment enterprises, with the actual utilization of foreign investment amounting to USD300 million in 2024. As can be seen from Tables 12.7, 12.8, 12.9, 12.10, and 12.11, from 2013 to 2024, the actual utilization of foreign investment reached USD3.37 billion, with an average annual growth rate of approximately 4.1%. The number of foreign-invested enterprises in Ningxia was 895, with an average annual growth rate of approximately 6.3%.

The total investment of foreign-invested enterprises in Ningxia was USD28.6 billion with an average annual growth rate of approximately 23.3% from 2013 to 2023. The registered capital of foreign-invested enterprises was USD13.5 billion with an average annual growth rate of approximately 22.0%, and the registered capital of foreign-funded parties in foreign-invested enterprises was USD9 billion with an average annual growth rate of approximately 20.8%. In 2024, Ningxia achieved breakthroughs in cooperation with some globally renowned enterprises such as Lycra (USA), Sipcam-Oxon (Italy), Netafim (Israel), and Treasury Wine Estates (Australia). Plans for an international wine organization were successfully established in Ningxia, marking a significant step toward venturing into the global market for Ningxia's wine industry. Exchanges in the fields of science and technology, education, and health have continued to deepen, and cultural service trade exports to Arab countries have entered the top ranks in the country[1].

---

[1] "Ningxia Operated 184 Scheduled Rail-sea Intermodal Trains, Ranking Second in Northwest China," China Service Trade Guide Network, http://tradeinservices.mofcom.gov.cn/article/yanjiu/hangyezk/202501/172151.html, January 20, 2025.

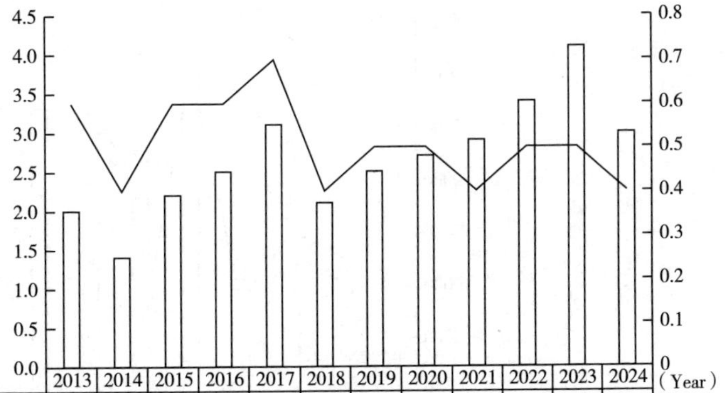

Chapter 12    Special Report on the Opening Up of Ningxia

| | 2013 | 2014 | 2015 | 2016 | 2017 | 2018 | 2019 | 2020 | 2021 | 2022 | 2023 | 2024 |
|---|---|---|---|---|---|---|---|---|---|---|---|---|
| Amount of Actual Utilization of Foreign Investment (Ten Million, USD) | 2.0 | 1.4 | 2.2 | 2.5 | 3.1 | 2.1 | 2.5 | 2.7 | 2.9 | 3.4 | 4.1 | 3.0 |
| Foreign Investment Dependence (%) | 0.6 | 0.4 | 0.6 | 0.6 | 0.7 | 0.4 | 0.5 | 0.5 | 0.4 | 0.5 | 0.5 | 0.4 |

**Figure 12.7    Changes in the Amount of Actual Utilization of Foreign Investment in Ningxia (2013-2024)**

Source: Calculated from the Official Database of the National Bureau of Statistics, the China and Ningxia Statistical Yearbook and Statistical Bulletin.

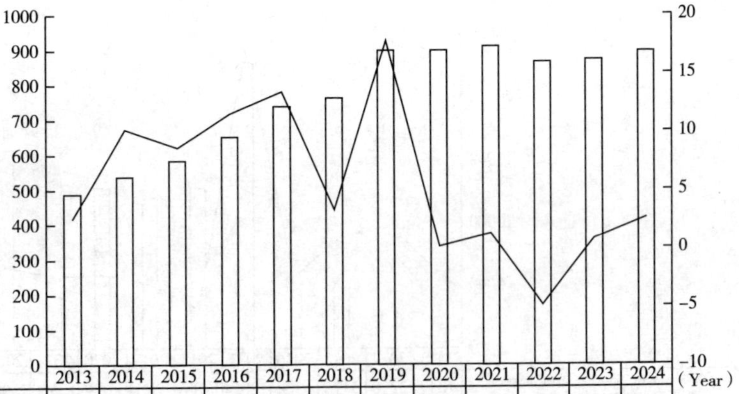

| | 2013 | 2014 | 2015 | 2016 | 2017 | 2018 | 2019 | 2020 | 2021 | 2022 | 2023 | 2024 |
|---|---|---|---|---|---|---|---|---|---|---|---|---|
| The Number of Foreign-Invested Enterprises | 488 | 538 | 584 | 651 | 738 | 762 | 898 | 899 | 910 | 865 | 872 | 895 |
| Growth Rate (%) | 2.5 | 10.2 | 8.6 | 11.5 | 13.4 | 3.3 | 17.8 | 0.1 | 1.2 | -4.9 | 0.8 | 2.6 |

**Figure 12.8    The Number of Foreign-Invested Enterprises (2013-2024)**

Source: Calculated from the Official Database of the National Bureau of Statistics, the China and Ningxia Statistical Yearbook and Statistical Bulletin.

277

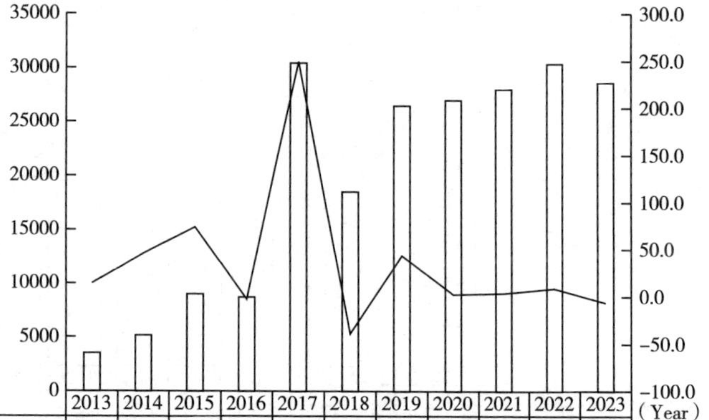

The Development Process of China-Arab States Economic and Trade Relations
Annual Report 2024

| | 2013 | 2014 | 2015 | 2016 | 2017 | 2018 | 2019 | 2020 | 2021 | 2022 | 2023 |
|---|---|---|---|---|---|---|---|---|---|---|---|
| The Total Investment of Foreign-Invested Enterprises (Million, USD) | 3537 | 5164 | 8972 | 8707 | 30420 | 18477 | 26463 | 26993 | 28000 | 30400 | 28600 |
| Growth Rate (%) | 14.2 | 46.0 | 73.7 | −3.0 | 249.4 | −39.3 | 43.2 | 2.0 | 3.7 | 8.6 | −5.9 |

**Figure 12.9    The Total Investment Amount of Foreign-Invested Enterprises（2013-2023)**

Source: Calculated from the Official Database of the National Bureau of Statistics, the China and Ningxia Statistical Yearbook and Statistical Bulletin.

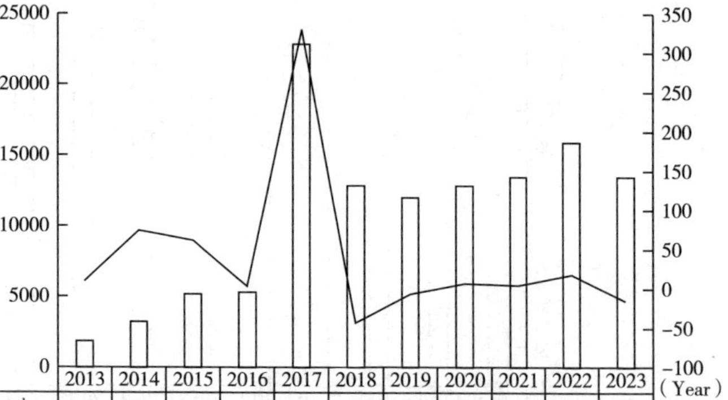

| | 2013 | 2014 | 2015 | 2016 | 2017 | 2018 | 2019 | 2020 | 2021 | 2022 | 2023 |
|---|---|---|---|---|---|---|---|---|---|---|---|
| The Registered Capital of Foreign-Invested Enterprises (Million, USD) | 1849 | 3220 | 5175 | 5308 | 22854 | 12887 | 12034 | 12886 | 13500 | 15900 | 13500 |
| Growth Rate (%) | 9.5 | 74.1 | 60.7 | 2.6 | 330.6 | −43.6 | −6.6 | 7.1 | 4.8 | 17.8 | −15.1 |

**Figure 12.10    The Registered Capital of Foreign-Invested Enterprises (2013-2023)**

Source: Calculated from the Official Database of the National Bureau of Statistics, the China and Ningxia Statistical Yearbook and Statistical Bulletin.

278

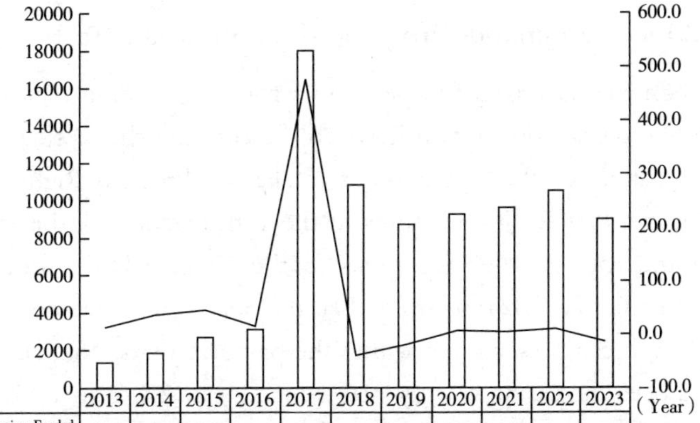

Chapter 12　Special Report on the Opening Up of Ningxia

| | 2013 | 2014 | 2015 | 2016 | 2017 | 2018 | 2019 | 2020 | 2021 | 2022 | 2023 |
|---|---|---|---|---|---|---|---|---|---|---|---|
| The Registered Capital of Foreign–Funded Parties in Foreign–Invested Enterprises (Million, USD) | 1364 | 1862 | 2700 | 3121 | 18022 | 10828 | 8725 | 9256 | 9600 | 10500 | 9000 |
| Growth Rate (%) | | 13.0 | 36.5 | 45.0 | 15.6 | 477.4 | −39.9 | −19.4 | 6.1 | 3.7 | 9.4 | −14.3 |

**Figure 12.11　The Registered Capital of Foreign-Funded Parties in Foreign-Invested Enterprises (2013-2023)**

Source: Calculated from the Official Database of the National Bureau of Statistics, the China and Ningxia Statistical Yearbook and Statistical Bulletin.

With the continuous deepening of Ningxia's opening-up, and gradual expansion of foreign-funded enterprises, many Fortune-500 and well-known multinational companies have invested and built factories in Ningxia, including Amazon and Simpla of the US, Louis Vuitton and Hennessy of France, Pernod Ricard, Schaeffler of Germany, Schlumberger of Singapore, Nestlé of Switzerland, Carlsberg of Denmark, Elkem of Norway, and Voestalpine of Austria. These enterprises have brought advanced techniques, experiences and broad market channels to Ningxia. Some foreign-funded retail giants have also opened branches in Ningxia, including Metro, Watsons, Starbucks, UNIQLO, and MUJI. These enterprises have not only enriched Ningxia's market pattern but also improved the quality and quantity of consumption opportunities for the people of Ningxia.

On the whole, Ningxia's actual utilization of foreign capital is relatively small, and its ability to influence economic growth is limited. In terms of the number of enterprises, foreign-funded enterprises with actual funds and enterprises with actual overseas investments each year are both less than 10. This reflects the insufficiency of Ningxia in attracting foreign-funded enterprises to acclimate and

279

The Development Process of China-Arab States Economic and Trade Relations
Annual Report 2024

promoting local corporate culture.

### 12.1.4　Continuous Progress of Scientific and Technological Innovation

Ningxia has given full play to its role as a leading region for scientific and technological cooperation between the east and the west. It has also issued the Regulations on the Protection of Intellectual Property Rights of the Ningxia Hui Autonomous Region (adopted at the 12th meeting of the Standing Committee of the 13th People's Congress of the Ningxia Hui Autonomous Region on September 26, 2024) to strengthen the policy guarantee mechanism. From Table 12.12, it can be seen that within the past five years, Ningxia's R&D expenditure has been increasing year by year, which increased from 1.45% in 2019 to 1.57% in 2023. The average annual growth rate of R&D expenditure was 12.8%, and the proportion of R&D expenditure of enterprises is more than 80%, higher than the national average from 2021-2023.

In addition, the number of the national high-tech enterprises, technology-based small and medium-sized enterprises, and specialized and new "little giant" enterprises increased by 82%. Ningxia has won the gold medal of the National Surveying and Mapping Project for two consecutive years and won the first prize of the National Science Experiment Exhibition and Performance for the first time. The Ningxia Advanced Research Institute, jointly established by relevant ministries and the government, has completed the enrollment of the first batch of master's and doctoral students. The Liupanshan Laboratory and Helanshan Laboratory, two new types of scientific research institutions established by the People's Government of Ningxia, laid out the innovation chain both around Ningxia's high-end equipment manufacturing industry and the research, development, and innovation of key technologies in the new material industry. They also attracted and gathered superior scientific research forces at home and abroad, organized and carried out cross-field and interdisciplinary collaborative research, and built a comprehensive and open innovation highland integrating basic research and applied basic research, key technology development, talent training, industrial incubation, and public service.

Two Ningxia Science and Technology Innovation Centers in Shanghai and Shenzhen and the Ningxia Laboratory of the Hong Kong Standards and Testing Center have been put into use. Among these, the Ningxia Science and Technology Innovation Center in Shanghai is the first research and development

280

Chapter 12   Special Report on the Opening Up of Ningxia

enclave of science and technology established in China for Ningxia. These enclave laboratories mainly focus on the high-quality development of Ningxia's "Six New, Six Special and Six Excellent +N" industries, and they resolve the difficulties of introducing high-qualified personnel that has long plagued Ningxia enterprises. Through the enclave R&D model of " Technology, research and development are carried out outside of Ningxia while the achievements are applied in Ningxia". [1]

In addition, the first Biosafety Level 3 laboratory in Ningxia was launched and operated, and the relevant pilot projects at the Ningdong Coal Chemical Industry Pilot Base are leading the industry. With continuous progress and remarkable achievements in scientific and technological innovation, Ningxia has broken through with key technologies such as high-performance niobium-tungsten anti-oxidation coating and the breeding of new salt-alkali tolerant spring wheat varieties. Ningxia has also developed several first-in-kind products, including the largest intelligent raise boring machine in China and the heat treatment equipment for extra-large wind power bearings. Even the world's fastest high-speed railway has used the "Ningxia-made connection pillow beams", and the Long March rockets have used the "Ningxia coal-to-oil products". Scientific and technological innovation has become a powerful engine for the high-quality development of Ningxia[2].

## 12.1.5   Continuous Improvement of the Business Environment

Firstly, multifaceted measures have been adopted to improve the development level of the export-oriented economy. In 2024, Ningxia unveiled the "Three-Year Action Plan for Promoting High-Quality Development of the Private Economy (2024-2026)", outlining "Three Key Priorities" to establish a robust foundation. This plan emphasizes six major actions aimed at enhancing the market environment, fostering tiered enterprise growth, improving the efficiency of government services, building a trustworthy government, ensuring the fairness of legal safeguards, and promoting an entrepreneurial spirit. Additionally, Ningxia also implemented eight supportive policies to bolster the growth,

---

[1] "Ningxia Shanghai Science and Technology Innovation Center Builds a 'Strong Magnetic Field' for Recruitment of High-qualified Personnel," *Ningxia Daily*, 4th edition, November 16, 2024.

[2] "Report on the Work of the People's Government of Ningxia Hui Autonomous Region in 2025," *Ningxia Daily*, 1st edition, January 26, 2025.

281

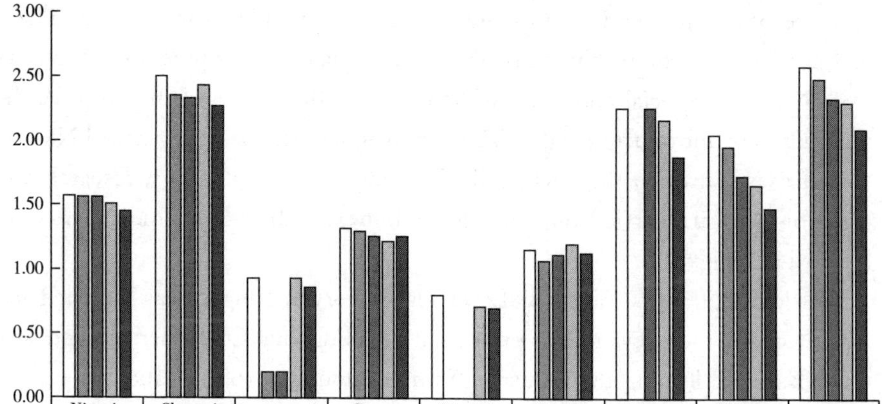

The Development Process of China-Arab States Economic and Trade Relations Annual Report 2024

| | Ningxia | Shaanxi | Inner Mongolia | Gansu | Qinghai | Shanxi | Sichuan | Henan | Shandong |
|---|---|---|---|---|---|---|---|---|---|
| □2023年 | 1.57 | 2.50 | 0.93 | 1.32 | 0.80 | 1.16 | 2.26 | 2.05 | 2.59 |
| ▣2022年 | 1.56 | 2.35 | 0.20 | 1.30 | 0.00 | 1.07 | 0.00 | 1.96 | 2.49 |
| ▥2021年 | 1.56 | 2.33 | 0.20 | 1.26 | 0.00 | 1.12 | 2.26 | 1.73 | 2.34 |
| ▨2020年 | 1.51 | 2.43 | 0.93 | 1.22 | 0.71 | 1.20 | 2.17 | 1.66 | 2.31 |
| ■2019年 | 1.45 | 2.27 | 0.86 | 1.26 | 0.70 | 1.13 | 1.88 | 1.48 | 2.10 |

**Figure 12.12    Proportion of R&D Expenditure in GDP in Ningxia and the Eight Provinces along the Yellow River (2019-2023)(%)**

Source: Official database of the National Bureau of Statistics, statistical yearbook of Ningxia and the eight provinces along the Yellow River, and data from the Ningxia Department of Science and Technology.

optimization, and strengthening of the private sector.

Furthermore, Ningxia also made the "Action Plan for Accelerating the Integrated Development of Domestic and Foreign Trade in the Ningxia Hui Autonomous Region" (Document No. 37 [2024][①] issued by the General Office of the Ningxia Hui Autonomous Region People's Government). The plan sets ambitious goals, striving to achieve more effective alignment of domestic and foreign trade policies and regulations, solidify the foundation for integrated development, and ensure smoother logistics networks connecting domestic and international markets by 2027. The plan also aims to make significant progress in constructing the inland open economic pilot zone, and make Ningxia an important area integrating into both domestic and international dual circulation, as well as a new highland of opening up under the Yellow River Basin's ecological protection and high-quality development. In addition,

---

① Notice of "the Action Plan for Accelerating the Integrated Development of Domestic and Foreign Trade in Ningxia Hui Autonomous Region," Official website of the People's Government of Ningxia Hui Autonomous Region, https://yjs.nx.gov.cn/xxgk/afxxgkml/zzqwj/202409/t20240912-4656382.html, August 6, 2024.

Chapter 12    Special Report on the Opening Up of Ningxia

the industrial foundation for foreign trade is expected to be more resilient, and the number of market entities continues to grow. About 30 new enterprises with actual import and export performance are expected to be added annually, and the export share of mechanical and electrical products and high-tech goods are expected to be approximately 40%. [1] In Yinchuan, the Municipal Bureau for Promoting Business Environment was established under a dual-mode combined with the Approval Bureau, positioning Yinchuan at the forefront nationally. Yinchuan was also awarded the "Top 10 Cities for Business Environment in 2024", and "China's Investment Hotspot City" for three consecutive years. [2]

Secondly, service and safeguard capabilities aligned with international standards were steadily improved. Ningxia maintained continuous focus on optimizing the business environment of ports. For instance, the Customs-Supervised Operation Area at the Yinchuan International Railway-Highway Integrated Logistics Port and the Cross-Border E-Commerce (CBEC) Comprehensive Supervision Center within the Yinchuan Comprehensive Bonded Zone successfully passed inspections; The Shizuishan Bonded Logistics Center (Type B) commenced operations; Tianjin Port and Beijing-Tangshan Port established "Inland Dry Ports" in Ningxia.

Furthermore, Ningxia implemented measures such as "Advance Declaration" and "Two-Step Declaration" to facilitate customs clearance, promoted the "Single Window" system for international trade at a high level, and launched the Ningxia 95198 Service Hotline under the "Single Window" framework. Ningxia also operationalized a comprehensive suite of CBEC regulatory models, including "Bonded Online Shopping (1210)", alongside functionalities for applying for the Certificates of Origin of both RCEP Customs and CCPIT (China Council for the Promotion of International Trade). Ningxia also deployed 17 agencies of cooperative card-issuance for "Customs-Bank One-Key Access" [3], leading

---

[1]  Notice of "the Action Plan for Accelerating the Integrated Development of Domestic and Foreign Trade in Ningxia Hui Autonomous Region," Official website of the People's Government of Ningxia Hui Autonomous Region, https://nx.gov.cn/zwgk/qzfwj/202408/t202408/t20240805-4614245. html, August 5, 2024.

[2]  "Yinchuan: Cultivating a Fertile Business Environment to Build the 'Business-Friendly Yinchuan' Brand, " China Daily Website, March 3, 2025.

[3]  "Ningxia 'Customs-Bank One-Key Access' was Officially Launched and Implemented," Department of Commerce of Ningxia Hui Autonomous Region Website, https://dofcom.nx.gov. cn/swdt_42675/kdkf/202102/t20210201_2588657.html, February 1, 2021.

283

to the convenience of export tax refund authentication, issuance of import-export regulatory documents and Customs Certificates of Origin, and services for electronic port cards, all contributing to the highly improved efficiency of customs clearance. Additionally, Ningxia planned to build an Expert Consultation Repository for Enterprise-Related Services, offering professional services to enterprises, including legal consultations, industrial development guidance, and technical transformation advice. At the same time, Ningxia also has completed a robust mechanism for governmental integrity and commitment fulfillment, persistently carried out the work of clearing arrears of enterprises, fully sorted out and compiled enterprise-related policies, and built a policy library for enterprises to promote the unified release, precise push, one-click direct access, and free application of various preferential enterprise policies.

Thirdly, Ningxia has continued to elevate its regional economic cooperation and key investment attraction capabilities. By closely monitoring the investment trends and industrial relocation dynamics of major domestic and international enterprises and groups, Ningxia has strategically organized a series of investment promotion activities. These aim to attract foreign business and investment, centered around key enterprises, competitive industries, and pivotal industrial parks in areas such as the Beijing-Tianjin-Hebei cluster, the Yangtze River Delta, the Guangdong-Hong Kong-Macao Greater Bay Area, and key provinces along the Yellow River Basin. Ningxia established "enclave industrial parks" with the Yangtze River Delta, fostering technological integration and iterative upgrades in the new energy equipment manufacturing sector. Meanwhile, Ningxia also deepened strategic cooperation in the digital economy with the Beijing-Tianjin-Hebei cluster. The construction of the pivotal node in the "East Data, West Computing" continued to empower the computational prowess of the "Cloud Valley on the Frontier".

Additionally, with the remarkable outcomes of the construction of international logistics corridors, Ningxia built an integrated and open channel system of "land port+air port+customs port", facilitating a synergistic interaction where transportation corridors bolster logistics, logistics networks energize trade, and trade activities stimulate industrial growth. Ningxia also fully intensified collaborations with neighboring provinces, universities, and state-owned enterprises (SOEs), successfully hosting a series of high-profile events such as the China-Central Asia Cooperation Forum, the China Industrial

284

Chapter 12   Special Report on the Opening Up of Ningxia

Relocation and Development Matchmaking Conference, and the Symposium on Deepening Industrial Cooperation with Central SOEs. The total investment of projects subsequently signed exceeded RMB 320 billion.

Moreover, Ningxia attracted over a hundred Global Fortune 500 and China 500 enterprises. The fixed asset investments generated from these investment projects have consistently accounted for approximately 45% of the total fixed asset investments over the years. This has significantly promoted the restructuring of Ningxia's economic landscape and the transformation of its growth drivers. Ningxia's international profile continues to grow, as evidenced by its receipt of the "Outstanding Contribution Award for International Friendship Cities". Several innovative achievements have been prominently featured at international conferences such as the United Nations Climate Change Conference and the UN Convention to Combat Desertification. These featured achievements include China's inaugural "100% Green Electricity Town", pioneering research on the carbon footprint of wine products, and novel desertification control technologies. These showcases vividly illustrate for the world the latest achievements in building a beautiful Ningxia.

## 12.2   The Gradual Enhancement of the Function of Channels for Opening Up

### 12.2.1   Significant Improvement in Highway Traffic

In 2024, Yinchuan strengthened its eastward connectivity initiatives, forging strategic partnerships with Tianjin Port and Qingdao Port to jointly construct the Yinchuan-Tianjin Port corridors for land-sea transport. This collaborative effort realized "one-time declaration for comprehensive clearance" of import and export goods, accelerating the efficiency of cross-border logistics by over 30%. With the launch of the Yinchuan-Budapest international freight train, Yinchuan will extend the westward overseas rail destinations to Europe. Additionally, the completion and opening of the Ningxia section of the Yinchuan-Kunming Expressway, a critical part of the New Western Land-Sea Corridor, has brought Ningxia's total expressway mileage beyond 2300 kilometers. Moreover, Ningxia successfully opened the first international road freight transport line from Ningdong to Zamyn-Uud of Mongolia and the international cargo road transport route from Ningdong Energy and Chemical Base to Zamyn-Uud Port

through Erenhot Port, achieving a "zero" breakthrough for Ningxia enterprises and vehicles in the international road cargo transportation business.

At present, Ningxia has established a comprehensive expressway network of "Three-Ring, Four-Vertical, Six-Horizontal", boasting 13 inter-provincial exits. This achievement positions Ningxia as the second province in western China to achieve expressway connectivity to all its counties, accelerating the formation of an integrated and multi-dimensional transportation network. The density of the highway network stands at 56.59 kilometers per hundred square kilometers, surpassing the national average and ranking 25th among 31 provinces in China. In Ningxia, the expressway network has been connected to border ports such as Alashankou and Khorgos to the west and to other coastal ports such as Tianjin Port and Shanghai Port to the east. It is also connected to surrounding economic centers such as Lanzhou, Xi'an, Baotou and Taiyuan. In particular, the Ningxia section of the Yinchuan-Kunming Expressway will connect with several expressways such as Fuzhou-Yinchuan, Qinghai-Lanzhou and Jingyuan-Huating. This will effectively improve the traffic network conditions in the central and southern parts of Ningxia, and become a north-south corridor connecting Ningxia, Gansu and Shaanxi. This also will drive the development of both resources and industry within these areas and contribute to the common prosperity of the local people in Ningxia.

## 12.2.2 Solid Improvement in Railway Networks

In 2024, as the Yinchuan-Huinong section of the Baotou-Yinchuan High-speed Railway and Yinchuan-Kunming Expressway were put into operation and the project of expansion and capacity enhancement for the Ningxia section of Baotou-Zhongwei commenced, the annual volume of railway passenger transport in Ningxia increased by 8.7%, significantly improving travel conditions for the public. Focused on the construction project for supply chain infrastructure at the Yinchuan International Railway-Highway Logistics Port, Ningxia established a core carrier of the national commercial and trade service-type logistics hub and made Yinchuan a support city for reinforcing and extending the national comprehensive freight hub.

Currently in Ningxia, there are nine planned railway lines which will be incorporated into the medium-to-long-term national railway network. Among the high-speed railway networks of the "eight vertical and eight horizontal"

Chapter 12    Special Report on the Opening Up of Ningxia

planned by China, "two horizontal and one vertical" lines traverse Ningxia, laying a solid foundation for the construction of the railway projects in Ningxia. Upon completion of the Yinchuan-Xi'an High-speed Railway, Zhongwei-Lanzhou High-speed Railway, and Baotou-Yinchuan High-speed Railway, Yinchuan will be connected to major cities such as Beijing, Xi'an, the Sichuan-Chongqing region, and Lanzhou with a travel time of 2 to 5 hours. This will effectively integrate Ningxia into the national high-speed railway network and significantly enhance its capacity to connect with the BRI helping to improve the national railway network.

In terms of international railway channels, Ningxia has operated 184 scheduled intermodal train services combining rail and maritime transport, ranking second in Northwest China. Heading eastward to the sea, Ningxia has launched regular intermodal train services, including a flaxseed import service from Yinchuan to Tianjin Port with seamless container handling ("one container throughout"), an export service from Yinchuan to Tianjin Port and then on to Dubai with a single documentation system ("one document throughout"). Other scheduled intermodal train services with "one document throughout" and "one container throughout" include Yinchuan (including Huinong and Pingluo) to Tianjin Port, Yinchuan to Qingdao Port, and Yinchuan (Pingluo) to Beijing-Tangshan Port. These regular services offer more maritime access options for Ningxia's import and export enterprises. Moreover, Ningxia has continued to deepen cooperation with border and coastal ports, railway authorities, and customs departments and has strengthened exchanges with provinces participating in the New International Land-Sea Trade Channel in western China, aiming to construct a four-directional channel network linking the east, south, west, and north.

## 12.2.3    Ongoing Strengthening of Aviation Hubs

At present in Ningxia, there are two high-speed railways (Yinchuan-Xi'an and Yinchuan-Lanzhou), and several national expressways such as the Fuzhou-Yinchuan, Beijing-Lhasa, and Yinchuan-Kunming Expressways. However, since Ningxia is over 1000 kilometers away in a straight line from densely populated regions such as the eastern coastal areas, East China, and South China, civil aviation enjoys unique advantages compared to rail and road transportation. Accelerating the construction of air routes is indeed crucial for Ningxia to integrate rapidly into the domestic and international dual-circulation

development pattern. In 2024, Ningxia's three airports, including Yinchuan Hedong International Airport, Guyuan Liupanshan Airport, and Zhongwei Xiangshan Airport, collectively handled 73000 aircraft takeoffs and landings, achieving a passenger throughput of 9.354 million and a cargo and mail throughput of 47000 tons, with year-on-year growth rates of 8.4%, 16.4%, and 14.3% respectively. Among these, the aircraft takeoffs and landings of Yinchuan Airport reached 69400, passenger throughput reached 8.983 million and cargo and mail throughput reached 45900 tons, a year-on-year increase of 8.0%, 16.5%, and 13.7% respectively.

It is worth mentioning that the growth rate of both flight volume and passenger throughput at Yinchuan Airport surpassed the national average, exceeding it by 0.1 and 0.6 percentage points respectively. Ningxia also ranked first in the northwest region of China with an advantage of 3 and 4.5 percentage points. In addition, Ningxia has further increased the frequency of flights from Yinchuan to major central cities, and successfully built 19 backbone routes including Beijing, Shanghai, Guangzhou, Chengdu, Hangzhou, Urumqi with an average daily flight frequency of more than 5 flights, thus ensuring the smooth flow of key routes. At the same time, the newly opened routes of Yining, Aksu, Turpan and Altay, as well as the increased frequency of the Urumqi route, not only strengthened the connection between Ningxia and various regions of Xinjiang, but also highlighted the geographical advantages of Yinchuan and provided a convenient channel for transit in and out of Xinjiang.

Moreover, Ningxia has resumed flights to Hong Kong and Dubai, and opened more than 10 international routes to Bangkok and Nha Trang, as well as other locations. This not only conforms to the strategic layout of Ningxia's opening up to the west but also meets the urgent needs of passengers travelling to Southeast Asian. In the future, with the goal of building Yinchuan Hedong International Airport into a gateway hub airport for the countries facing the Silk Road Economic Belt, Ningxia will make efforts to increase the number of flights on domestic and international routes, so as to achieve the goals of having direct flights to all provincial capitals and 28 regional hub cities excluding Lanzhou.

### 12.2.4　Rapid Construction of Digital Channels

Ningxia has persisted in making the digital economy a primary indicator of its development, and has built the only "dual center" of computing power and

Chapter 12　Special Report on the Opening Up of Ningxia

Internet exchange in western China.

In 2024, with the establishment of the "dual centers", Ningxia formulated and introduced two plans, namely the Three-Year Action for the High-Quality Development of the Digital Economy in Ningxia and the Construction of the Ningxia Hub of the "Eastern Data and Western Computing" Project. Projects such as the Beijing Baidu Smart Cloud Data Industry Base, the Fujian Computing Power Server Production Line, and the CCCC Cloud Data Center have been centrally implemented. Breakthroughs have been made in the application of large language models, medical micro-models, and quantum technology. Furthermore, compared with 2023, computing power investment, standard racks, high-end computing cards, and computing power scale have achieved "four doublings". Five indicators, including the server racking rate, the proportion of intelligent computing, the comprehensive computing power index, the power utilization efficiency, and the 5G user penetration rate, are ranked among the leading in the country.

So far, Ningxia has built 9 large-scale and ultra-large data centers, and 25 data center projects are under construction, including 116000 standard racks, 93000 intelligent computing cards, and a computing power scale of about 40000P. The cabinet launch rate of Zhongwei Cloud Data Center exceeds 85%, providing integrated computing and network services for government departments and enterprise customers such as the Ningxia Government Cloud, Internet Exchange Center, Kingsoft Cloud, and Lenovo. Among these, the construction of "Minning Cloud" has realized the millimeter-level "western computing" of eastern data and accelerated digital economy cooperation between Fujian and Ningxia. Ningxia was also approved as a pilot province for the monitoring and dispatching of a national integrated computing power network. Yinchuan was selected as one of the first batch of 5G-A network commercial cities in China. Shizuishan was chosen as an IPv6 comprehensive pilot city. Wuzhong was rated as a national digital transformation city for small and medium-sized enterprises. Guyuan was one of the national double gigabit cities. Zhongwei was awarded the title of "Green Computing Power Development Pioneer". Moreover, Ningdong Base was built as the first national smart chemical park in Northwest China.

At present, more than 100 enterprises such as Ningxia Amazon, China Mobile, Meituan, and Xiyun have established data centers or application data centers in

Ningxia for data storage. Focusing on "intelligent computing", "intelligence" and "intelligent production", Yinchuan has strived to build a " computing power capital". So far, Yinchuan has formed an intelligent computing power of more than 3000P, more than 500 million government data resources, and a data scale of more than 8000 TB, ranking first in Ningxia. At the same time, focusing on key links in the industrial chain such as data production, circulation and trading, innovative applications, and security governance, Ningxia firstly introduced a batch of third-party professional service providers such as China Electronics Cloud, Ningxia Hope Information, Yinchuan Smart City, and Tus Holdings to participate in the construction of the "Yinchuan Data Port". On the basis of making good use of the golden signboard of the China-Arab States Expo and the China (Yinchuan) cross-border e-commerce comprehensive pilot zone, Ningxia accelerated the construction of the national Yinchuan cross-border e-commerce comprehensive pilot zone and focused on the industrial layout of "Six New, Six Special and Six Excellent". Aiming at the goal of "two platforms and six systems", Ningxia created a cross-border e-commerce industry ecosystem with a concentrated body of enterprises, a complete service system, and innovative supervision models.

Currently, the Yinchuan Cross-border E-commerce Comprehensive Pilot Zone has built a total of 6 industrial clusters such as the Yinchuan Comprehensive Bonded Zone and the Ningxia-Zhejiang E-commerce Pioneer Park. It also introduced 475 cross-border e-commerce enterprises, including cross-border e-commerce sellers, service platforms, suppliers, warehousing and logistics, an increase of 424 (more than 9 times) compared with existing enterprises before it's approval. Furthermore, the Yinchuan Cross-border E-commerce Comprehensive Pilot Zone has rented 19 overseas warehouses in 6 countries including Germany, Kazakhstan and Malaysia, and in 2024 achieved an RMB775 million transaction volume of cross-border e-commerce.[1] It has become a new type of opening platform for Ningxia to promote the transformation and upgrading of foreign trade and cultivate new forms of foreign trade.

---

[1] "Yinchuan Cross-border E-commerce Comprehensive Pilot Zone Shines at the 5th Cross-Border E-Commerce Fair, Demonstrating New Momentum in Foreign Trade," Ningxia News Website, March 19, 2025.

Chapter 12　Special Report on the Opening Up of Ningxia

## 12.3　Prospects for Ningxia's Countermeasures for High-Level Opening Up

Ningxia is located in an overlapping area of major national strategies, including the new-era Western Development and the ecological conservation and high-quality development of the Yellow River Basin. It also serves as a pioneer region for the later. Boasting geographical and economic development advantages, Ningxia is well-positioned to facilitate the circulation and connectivity with regions to the north, west, south, and the eastern areas, thereby fostering a higher-level open economy. The year 2025 marks a crucial transitional period, serving as the concluding chapter of the 14th Five-Year Plan and the prologue to the 15th Five-Year Plan. However, Ningxia also confronts unprecedented challenges, opportunities, and uncertainties. In the future, Ningxia will follow the spirit of the 20th National Congress of the Communist Party of China and the important instructions given in president Xi Jinping's speeches during his previous visits to Ningxia. Ningxia also aims to solidly promote the steady and long-term development of high-quality Belt and Road cooperation and the high-level opening up of the inland.

### 12.3.1　Promoting the Quality and Upgrading of the "Channel Economy"

Firstly, focusing on Top-level Designs. Amplifying the effects of the China-Arab States Summit, Ningxia will strengthen contacts and dialogue with global international organizations such as the Belt and Road Forum and the Boao Forum for Asia, as well as regional international organizations like ASEAN and the Shanghai Cooperation Organization. Within the business scope of these international organizations, Ningxia also will explore the possibility and feasibility of establishing cooperation platforms and strive to make new breakthroughs in the interconnection of international transportation facilities, the signing of international transport agreements, and the facilitation of cross-border direct customs clearance.

Additionally, Ningxia will make efforts to construct three international channels, including the New Land-Sea Channel, the Railway-Sea combined transport route, and the international railway-highway logistics channel. Ningxia

291

will also open more exit channels southward linking to the western land-sea channel, promote the operating of freight train enterprises in order to utilize the international "China-Kyrgyzstan-Uzbekistan" logistics channel. Additionally, Ningxia will create the "China-Arab States Express Line" of Ningxia - Irkeshtam of Xinjiang to Central Asia, West Asia, and Europe, opening up a "second international logistics channel" targeting the five Central Asian countries, Afghanistan, Iran, and other nations.

Ningxia also aims to promote the quality and upgrading of the "channel economy". Continuing to increase and expand the frequency of direct flights to important international hub cities, Ningxia will construct an air route network that is oriented toward countries participating in the joint construction of the BRI and radiates from central and western provinces in China, thereby further enhancing air, railway, and maritime accessibility and bolstering the high-level development of Ningxia's opening-up.

Following the basic principles of filling gaps, strengthening internal connectivity, and clearing bottlenecks, Ningxia plans to strengthen regional cooperation and inter-provincial collaboration and linkage, promote the construction of channel infrastructure and share the fruits of channel development. In addition, Ningxia will establish a mechanism for cross-regional coordination to break through administrative divisions, support the development of "enclave economies" and joint construction and share industrial parks, striving to forge a new path of differentiated, characteristic, and coordinated development. Moreover, Ningxia needs to initiate a new round of her ongoing three-year plans for the construction of railways, highways, and airports, and accelerate the capacity expansion and reconstruction of the Baotou-Zhongwei Railway's Ningxia section and the construction of the Yinchuan-Bayannur Railway. This will achieve the full operation of the Baotou-Yinchuan High-Speed Railway and shorten the travel time from Yinchuan to Beijing via Baotou from 18 to 5 hours. At last, Ningxia will actively promote key projects including the renovation and expansion of existing airports, the launching of construction of the Zhongwei section of National Highway 629, and completion of the full connectivity of the Ningxia section of the Wuma Expressway's. Ningxia will also strive to build a "seven-in-one" modern transportation system.

Secondly, accelerating the "Digital Silk Road". In order to expand its voice in the development of the world digital economy, Ningxia will continue to

Chapter 12    Special Report on the Opening Up of Ningxia

consolidate the foundation for the development of her digital economy, align with international rules such as the Digital Economy Partnership Agreement (DEPA) and the Agreement for Trans-Pacific Partnership (CPTPP), and build a competitive development system and demonstration zone for the digital economy in the west. Additionally, Ningxia will fully implement a new round of three-year actions for the high-quality development of the digital economy, build the "Ten Projects" of computing power hubs, and set up a digital economy guidance fund with the scale of the digital economy reaching more than RMB 220 billion.

Ningxia also plans to implement digital infrastructure improvement actions, launch the "sailing" action for large-scale 5G applications and the 10G optical network pilot, and promote the full coverage of the 5G network and gigabit optical fibers to all administrative villages and counties. While accelerating the construction of 25 data centers and intelligent computing projects such as Amazon, Tencent, China Telecom, China Mobile, and Aerospace Cloud, Ningxia will actively strive for the implementation of a number of major projects and disaster recovery centers, enable new data centers for 100% use of green electricity, and strive to create a demonstration area for computing and electricity collaboration[1].

Additionally, Ningxia aims to innovate digital cooperation mechanisms, establish pilot zones for the development of national digital economy innovation, accelerate the development of new models and new business formats, and fully promote financial and digital economy industries including smart logistics, digital finance, and digital economy headquarters bases, so as to create a diverse industrial landscape for the "Digital Silk Road". Ningxia also plans to strengthen the overall leading role of China-Arab states summits in digital economy cooperation, explore the advantages and common cooperation interests of Arab countries in digital trade competition, and extend Ningxia's value chain and industrial chain in digital trade development.

While implementing actions to enhance the level of digital industrialization and pursuing success in hosting the third "Western Digital Valley" computing

---

[1]    "Report on the Work of the Ningxia Autonomous Region Government in 2025," Official website of the People's Government of Ningxia Hui Autonomous Region, https: //www.nx.gov.cn/ zwxx_11337/nxyw/202501/t20250126_4807319.html, January 26, 2025.

293

power industry conference, Ningxia will promote the development of a full industrial chain for the digital economy through "storage-sharing-calculation-usage", build a comprehensive service platform for data elements, and enhance data security development capabilities. Moreover, Ningxia will also carry out actions to empower industrial digitalization, promote the deep integration of primary, secondary, and tertiary industries with digital technologies, and strive to achieve a 60% digital transformation rate for large-scale enterprises. The overall advancement of the systematic engineering of "artificial intelligence", "quantum technology", and "data elements ×" informs Ningxia's development.

### 12.3.2 Striving to Build a New Highland of Opening Up

Firstly, enhancing the Functions of the China-Arab States Expo Platform. The six China-Arab States Expositions have attracted over 6000 domestic and foreign enterprises and more than 400000 merchants from 112 countries and regions. The exposition has become an important platform for China-Arab states cooperation in building the BRI. In the future, Ningxia needs to re-examine and position the China-Arab States Expo with a "global vision, China platform", focusing on building a comprehensive platform or political dialogue, economic and trade cooperation, commercial mediation, and legal services between China and Arab countries. Ningxia will also pragmatically and innovatively organize the 7th China-Arab States Expo, enhance collaboration and coordination with the Ministry of Foreign Affairs and the Ministry of Commerce, and integrate the economic and trade investment activities of the China-Arab States Cooperation Forum to be held during the Expo. In addition, Ningxia plans to establish a mechanism for regular operation, elevate the level of economic and trade cooperation at the Expo, and achieve new breakthroughs in economic and trade cooperation between Ningxia and Arab countries.

Moreover, Ningxia intends to accelerate study of and reliance on the Yinchuan Comprehensive Bonded Zone to attract business associations between China and the GCC countries, well-known enterprises and international institutions, and provide services including business investment, legal services, finance, logistics, and digital information support, agricultural economic cooperation, cultural and tourism cooperation, and the supply of professional and high-qualified personnel. Ningxia will make efforts to establish the Economic and Trade Promotion Association of China-Arab States Entrepreneur under the

Chapter 12    Special Report on the Opening Up of Ningxia

China-Arab States Expo and accelerate the exchange and cooperation among elite enterprises from China and Arab countries, allowing for effective alignment of policies, resources, and capital. Using the China-Arab States Expo as traction, Ningxia will accelerate the construction of a new development pattern for the international exhibition economy and form a long-term mechanism to promote the collaborative development of industries in Ningxia.

Secondly, enhancing the Influence of China (Ningxia) International Wine Culture and Tourism Expo Platform. While promoting the deep integration of wine and culture, Ningxia will create an internationally renowned wine industry exhibition with Ningxia style, Chinese characteristics, and world-class standards and also make it an important platform for improving the social and economic development as well as opening up of Ningxia. In order to strengthen intrinsic development, Ningxia also plans to formulate targets for the quality development of the exhibition, and successfully host the fifth International Wine Exposition and the 32nd Brussels International Wine Competition. Through certification by the International Exhibition Industry Association and the China Quality Certification Center's quality management system, Ningxia aims to hold a domestically double-certified wine exhibition with high-quality.

Furthermore, Ningxia plans to expand the influence of the exhibition and strive to invite guests including China's national leaders of every session, dignitaries from various countries, members of international and domestic wine industry chambers of commerce (associations), heads of important production and marketing enterprises, and important merchants such as international and domestic wine buyers and distributors. This will serve to make the exhibition an important event in the domestic and foreign wine industry. In order to enhance the influence of the exhibition, Ningxia will also strengthen exchange and cooperation between the world's major wine countries and domestic wine production and sales entities. In addition, Ningxia will hold the China (Ningxia) International Wine Expo in cooperation with countries including France, the United States, and Germany so that more consumers at home and abroad can understand and pay attention to the wine production area at the eastern foot of the Helan Mountains in Ningxia. The future of Chinese wine is in Ningxia, and Ningxia will lead the Chinese wine industry to be better involved in the world.

Thirdly, enhancing the Connotation of the "Western Digital Valley" Computing Industry Conference to Drive the Future. As the only province in

295

China with a dual focus on "exchange center + hub node", Ningxia's position is particularly prominent in the digital economy sector. After the establishment of the Western Computing Power Industry Alliance, Ningxia will closely cooperate with four core regions including Beijing-Tianjin-Hebei, the Yangtze River Delta, the Guangdong-Hong Kong-Macao Greater Bay Area, and Chengdu-Chongqing. This cooperation will focus on eight key tasks such as the "Data Center Computing Power Enhancement Project", "Digital Manufacturing Expansion Project", and "Network Connectivity Acceleration Project" so as to jointly promote the prosperity and development of the computing power industry and provide strong support for the development of Ningxia's digital economy.

At the same time, relying on multiple resources gathered from high-end platforms, Ningxia will promote theoretical research on the "Computing Power Industry" and discuss major strategies and standard norms in the field of computing power. Additionally, Ningxia plans to deeply analyze the overall situation, evolution path, and key issues of the "Computing Power Industry" in order to provide strong theoretical support for industrial development and t broaden the resource-sharing channels for "Connection +Computing Power+ Value." By deepening the driving role of data, Ningxia intends to lead the coordinated development of the flow of technology, capital, high-qualified personnel, and material with data flow, further unblocking the main arteries of the digital economy and constructing a major economic cycle to attract more leading enterprises in various industries to establish themselves in Ningxia. With concepts of a global vision, computing power cooperation, value innovation, and a future-driven concept, Ningxia plans to promote the deep integration of the computing industry and enhance scientific and technological innovation. Ningxia will also strengthen exchange with the BRI countries, expand cooperation areas, enrich cooperation projects, and share the achievements of computing power innovation and development.

Lastly, enhancing the Construction of Comprehensive Bonded Zones. The Yinchuan Comprehensive Bonded Zone has special functions and policies for undertaking international industrial transfer and connecting domestic and international markets. With the implementation of the "Three-Year Foreign Investment and Five-Year Foreign Trade Doubling Plan", Ningxia intends to promote the cooperation between the Yinchuan Comprehensive Bonded Zone and the Shizuishan Bonded Logistics Center (Type B), including the

296

Chapter 12    Special Report on the Opening Up of Ningxia

interconnection of facilities, complementing of industrial advantages, and coordination of efficient customs clearance.

In addition to developing outward-oriented industries such as port customs clearance, bonded processing, and bonded logistics, Ningxia will create a customs special supervision area with convenient trade and investment, distinctive functions, and efficient public services. With goal-oriented and problem-oriented approaches, the Yinchuan Bonded Zone will achieve the goal of "dual high development" for advancement and be positioned as a "service-oriented park and industry-oriented park", upholding the three concepts of "service-oriented development, project promotion, and innovation strengthening". It will also enact the four functions of "bonded processing, bonded logistics, bonded services, and port operations" and implement five major actions including improving the quality of industry cultivation, enhancing the efficiency of attracting investment, accelerating project construction, optimizing the business environment, and improving performance evaluation. Moreover, it will actively cultivate supporting and leading industries, including electronic information, food processing, and cross-border e-commerce, and widely attract foreign-funded and foreign trade projects with a high correlation to leading industries to build a cross-border e-commerce industrial chain and ecosystem that integrates production, trade, settlement, and logistics.

Since cross-border e-commerce is gradually becoming one of the fastest-growing, most promising, and most influential foreign trade formats, Ningxia needs to increase policy support, attract leading cross-border e-commerce companies and logistics enterprises, and guide businesses to make good use of the cross-border e-commerce retail export VAT and consumption tax exemption policies as well as the income tax assessment methods. Ningxia will encourage foreign trade and logistics enterprises to set up overseas warehouses in the European and American markets, countries along the BRI, and markets in member countries of the Regional Comprehensive Economic Partnership (RCEP). In addition, Ningxia will enhance the nurturing of advantageous, export-oriented and primary industries such as wolfberries and cashmere, guide more domestic trade entities to engage in foreign trade, and stimulate market vitality. Moreover, Ningxia plans to make the Yinchuan Comprehensive Bonded Zone and the Shizuishan Bonded Zone into new highlands of openness and new engines for industrial transformation and upgrading to contribute to both

297

China's and Ningxia's high-level opening-up.

### 12.3.3 Strengthening Cooperation with Major Strategic Regions in China

In order to support and fully integrate into the new development pattern, Ningxia will strengthen the communication and cooperation of major strategic projects, such as the coordinated development of Beijing, Tianjin and Hebei, the development of the Yangtze River Economic Belt, the integration of the Yangtze River Delta, the construction of the Guangdong-Hong Kong-Macao Greater Bay Area, the Hainan Free Trade Port, and the new land-sea channels in the west of China.

Considering the future development within the context of regional and national development, Ningxia aims to further raise its position and think strategically with a forward-looking vision. In order to implement major strategies and serve the national agenda, Ningxia intends to follow the rules of economic development, leverage the comparative advantages of different regions, integrate into growth poles, cultivate new growth poles, and accelerate the formation of a clear and dynamic new regional and strategic framework. In addition, Ningxia will fully deepen the supply-side structural reform, promote breakthroughs in the reform of key areas and links, and implement an institutional opening strategy. Ningxia will also release the dividends of reform and facilitate the reasonable flow and efficient aggregation of various factors. While entering into the mid-to-high end and key links of domestic and dual circulation, Ningxia plans to vigorously promote inter-regional division of industrial labor and cooperation, innovate industrial collaborative mechanisms, and collaboratively build a modern industrial system. Concentrating on building an ecological system for leading industries, cultivating industrial clusters and emerging industrial chains, Ningxia will take project construction as a fundamental approach, and strengthen project support of regional win-win development.

Moreover, Ningxia aims to fully stimulate various market entities to engage in the country's major strategic initiatives and creativity and enhance cooperation vitality. Ningxia will also coordinate and advance major infrastructure construction to improve connectivity and modernization levels, build cross-regional comprehensive transportation channels, and guide the optimized layout and division of the labor of industries. As the guidelines for building a

Chapter 12   Special Report on the Opening Up of Ningxia

unified national market and the regulations for attracting investment are fully implemented and as cooperation between the east and west in the western region and between central and local governments are deeply advanced, Ningxia plans to carry out activities to enhance cooperation with Ningbo and Hong Kong and Macao, making new strides in fully utilizing both markets and resources. Furthermore, Ningxia will also break down regional divisions and implicit barriers to promote the formation of a unified, open, and competitively ordered market system.

## 12.3.4   Enhancing the Core Competitiveness of the Industry

Highlighting the leading role of scientific and technological innovation, Ningxia will strive to win the tough battle for the upgrading of primary and advantageous industries. Ningxia also plans to coordinate the advancement of the "Six New, Six Special, and Six Excellent + N" industries, and promote the improvement of traditional industries, the growth of emerging industries, and the cultivation of future industries. Furthermore, Ningxia aims to promote the development of industrial clusters such as the modern coal chemical industry, new materials, clean energy, digital information, agriculture and animal husbandry, and cultural tourism, thereby accelerating the establishment of a modern industrial system that reflects Ningxia's advantages with strong competitiveness. In addition, Ningxia will launch a three-year action plan for the high-quality development of primary and advantageous industries and an action plan for the high-quality development of key manufacturing industry chains.

While deeply implementing the 'Four Major Upgrade Projects' involving industrial chains, bases, parks, and clusters, Ningxia will make efforts to build important national industrial bases such as the "World Capital of Wine", "China's Computing Power Capital", "Hometown of Goji Berries", "Acrylic Valley of China", and "Green Hydrogen Valley of China". In this way, Ningxia will actively strive toward the construction of national strategic hinterlands and backup bases for key industries. In addition to developing a new qualitative productivity implementation plan, Ningxia plans to accelerate the cultivation of emerging and future industries such as intelligent computing power, artificial intelligence, new energy storage, green hydrogen energy, green and environmental protection, biological manufacturing, quantum technology, low-altitude economy, and life sciences and health. Ningxia will also strongly support the development of new

technologies, industries, business formats, models, and tracks. In order to fully strengthen technological innovation, Ningxia intends to launch the "Eight Major Actions," and increase the total R&D expenditure of the whole society by more than 10%.

In addition, Ningxia will also effectively manage and utilize higher research institutions, innovation centers, pilot bases, and various laboratories, strengthen support and increase the funding of high-qualified personnel, and grant more decision-making right to research institutions and researchers. Moreover, Ningxia plans to cultivate and attract a batch of high-qualified personnel including leading science and technology experts, outstanding engineers, master craftsmen, and highly skilled personnel. To transform the "key variable" of technological innovation into the "largest increment" of high-quality development, Ningxia will fully leverage the main role of enterprises, further enhance the construction of technology, standards, brands, and quality, and continually increase the number of national high-tech enterprises, key technology breakthroughs, and projects that introduce and transform scientific and technological achievements.

### 12.3.5 Furtherly Creating a First-Class Business Environment

Ningxia will firmly implement the "Two Unswerving Principles" (work unswervingly both to consolidate and develop the public sector and to encourage, support and guide development of the non-public sector), further creating a first-class business environment that is market-oriented, law-based, and internationalized. In addition to holding conferences on high-quality development of the private economy and comprehensive improvement of the business environment as well as activities such as the nationwide event for excellent private enterprises, Ningxia plans to deeply implement the three-year enterprise cultivation plan, increase support, establish special funds for the development of the private economy, and strongly cultivate "Eaglet", "Gazelle", and "Unicorn" enterprises. At the same time, Ningxia will continue to increase the number of technology-based enterprises that are "specialized, refined, primary, and innovative".

While intensifying the implementation of the "Ten Mechanisms" to comprehensively enhance support for enterprises, Ningxia aims to address the problem of "weak expectations", fully implement more proactive fiscal policies and moderately loose monetary policies. Ningxia will also effectively strengthen

Chapter 12   Special Report on the Opening Up of Ningxia

the consistency of economic and non-economic policies, ensuring that enterprises will directly benefit from policies and funding without application. Solving the 'high threshold' problem, Ningxia plans to strictly implement "entry unless banned" and fair competition review and provide more opportunities for private enterprises to participate fairly in major project construction, major technological breakthroughs, etc., further increasing the proportion of the private economy and private investment.

Furthermore, Ningxia will solve "difficult operation" and financing problems and strengthen targeted assistance for enterprises by means of "solving each problem individually" and "formulating policies for each enterprise". In addition to conducting activities such as visiting thousands of enterprises and households and promoting financing opportunities for small and medium-sized enterprises, Ningxia intends to implement policies like "renewing loans without principle" and innovate special financial products to effectively reduce financing costs for enterprises. Moreover, while striving to "efficiently handle one thing", Ningxia will improve mechanisms for government-enterprise communication, business guidance, needs assessment, complaint handling, and feedback, providing maximum convenience for enterprises. Ningxia will also carry out standardized administrative inspections related to enterprises and special actions for administrative law enforcement, strictly enforce the regulations of "Five Prohibitions" and "Eight Must-nots", and insist that organizations without legal qualifications cannot perform administrative inspections and that administrative inspections without legal basis be completely eliminated. Enterprises will have the right to complain and refuse in the face of illegal and irregular behaviors. Finally, Ningxia will earnestly ensure that matters are handled quickly when needed and no interference is imposed when unnecessary so that all entrepreneurs can invest with confidence, handle affairs smoothly, and live comfortably in Ningxia.

301

# Chronicle of China-Arab States Economic and Trade Cooperation in 2024

On January 1, Saudi Arabia, Egypt, the UAE, and Iran became formal members of the BRICS.

On January 7, Chinese Ambassador to Bahrain Ni Ruchi paid a visit to Bahraini Deputy Prime Minister Shaikh Khalid bin Abdulla Al Khalifa, and the two sides exchanged in-depth views on deepening practical cooperation between the two countries.

On January 10, President Xi Jinping exchanged congratulatory messages with Tunisian President Kais Saied on the 60th anniversary of the establishment of diplomatic relations between the two countries.

On January 12, Chinese Ambassador to Tunisia Wan Li met with Tunisian Prime Minister Ahmed Hachani, and the two sides exchanged views on China-Tunisia relations and cooperation in various fields between the two countries.

From January 13 to 18, Member of the Political Bureau of the CPC Central Committee and Minister of Foreign Affairs Wang Yi paid a visit to Egypt, Tunisia, Togo and Côte d'Ivoire at their invitation. This was the 34th consecutive year that Africa has been the destination of Chinese foreign ministers' annual first overseas visit.

On January 14, Egyptian President Abdel Fattah El-Sisi met with the visiting Member of the Political Bureau of the CPC Central Committee and Foreign Minister Wang Yi in Cairo.

On January 14, Member of the Political Bureau of the CPC Central Committee and Foreign Minister Wang Yi held talks with Egyptian Foreign Minister Sameh Shoukry in Cairo.

On January 14, Member of the Political Bureau of the CPC Central

Committee and Foreign Minister Wang Yi met with Secretary-General of the League of Arab States (LAS) Ahmed Aboul Gheit in Cairo.

On January 15, Tunisian President Kais Saied met with the visiting Member of the Political Bureau of the CPC Central Committee and Foreign Minister Wang Yi in Tunis, the capital of Tunisia.

On January 15, Member of the Political Bureau of the CPC Central Committee and Foreign Minister Wang Yi held talks with Tunisian Foreign Minister Nabil Ammar in Tunis.

From January 15 to 17, Member of the Political Bureau of the CPC Central Committee and Vice Premier of the State Council Liu Guozhong, upon invitation, led a Chinese government delegation to visit Algeria. During the visit, Algerian President Abdelmadjid Tebboune and Prime Minister Nadir Larbaoui respectively met with Liu Guozhong. The two sides had an in-depth exchange of views on China-Algeria relations and cooperation in various fields.

On January 16, Chinese Ambassador to Mauritania Li Baijun met with Mauritanian Minister of Petroleum, Mines and Energy, government spokesman, Nani Ould Chrougha, and the two sides exchanged in-depth views on promoting practical cooperation between China and Mauritania and issues of common concern.

On January 18, witnessed by Lebanese caretaker Prime Minister Najib Mikati, Chinese Ambassador to Lebanon Qian Minjian and President at Council for Development and Reconstruction Nabil El-Jisr signed the exchange of documents on the China-aided Lebanon solar power generation equipment project on behalf of their governments respectively.

On January 19, Chinese Ambassador to Mauritania Li Baijun attended the founding ceremony of the Chinese Enterprises Chamber of Commerce in Mauritania and delivered a speech.

On January 23, Chinese Ambassador to Morocco Li Changlin attended the groundbreaking ceremony of the Morocco MW wind turbine blade factory construction project in Ailang and delivered a speech.

On January 23, Chinese Ambassador to Mauritania Li Baijun met with the President of the National Union of Mauritanian Employers Mohamed Zeine El Abidine Ould Cheikh Ahmed. The two sides exchanged views on strengthening exchanges and cooperation between Chinese and Mauritanian enterprises and promoting bilateral economic and trade development.

The Development Process of China-Arab States Economic and Trade Relations
Annual Report 2024

On January 24, Chinese Ambassador to Syria Shi Hongwei met with Syrian Finance Minister Kenan Yaghi, and the two sides exchanged in-depth views on bilateral practical cooperation.

On January 28, President Xi Jinping sent a congratulatory message to Azali Assoumani on his reelection as President of the Union of the Comoros.

On January 29, the Central Bank of the UAE successfully completed the first cross-border payment transaction of digital dirhams worth 50 million UAE dirhams (about 98 million RMB) with Bank of China through the mBridge platform. On the same day, Bank of China's UAE branch also used the platform to complete the first cross-border remittance transaction of digital RMB in the UAE.

On January 30, Minister of Commerce Wang Wentao and Algerian Minister of Housing, Urban Planning and the City Mohamed Tarek Belaribi co-chaired the 8th China-Algeria Joint Economic and Trade Committee in Beijing to exchange in-depth views on deepening bilateral economic and trade cooperation between China and Algeria.

On January 30, Chinese Ambassador to Qatar Cao Xiaolin paid a visit to Qatari Minister of Transport Jassim bin Saif bin Ahmed Al Sulaiti upon his arrival, and the two sides exchanged views on transportation cooperation between China and Qatar.

On February 1, Chinese Ambassador to Qatar Cao Xiaolin met with the Chairman of Qatar Tourism Saad Saad bin Ali Al Kharji, and the two sides exchanged views on tourism exchanges and cooperation between China and Qatar.

On February 1, Chinese Ambassador to Morocco Li Changlin went to Casablanca to attend the unveiling ceremony of COSCO SHIPPING Lines (Morocco) Co., Ltd. and delivered a speech.

On February 1, Chinese Ambassador to Mauritania Li Baijun met with Mauritanian Minister of Equipment and Transport Mohamed Ali Ould Sidi Mohamed, and the two sides exchanged in-depth views on further strengthening practical cooperation in infrastructure construction between the two countries.

On February 1, the handover ceremony of medical supplies donated by China to Mauritania was held at the residence of the Chinese Medical Aid Team to Mauritania. Witnessed by Chinese Ambassador to Mauritania Li Baijun, Counselor in charge of economic affairs Xi Wei signed the medical supplies

304

handover certificate with Director of Mauritanian Capital Hospital Abdallah Ould Wedih, Deputy Director of National Institute of Public Health Zaina, and Deputy Director of Friendship Hospital Hetri respectively.

On February 5, Chinese Ambassador to Jordan Chen Chuandong visited the Aqaba Special Economic Zone and met with the Chief Executive of the Special Economic Zone Naif Fayez.

On February 6, Chinese Ambassador to Qatar Cao Xiaolin paid a visit to Qatari Minister of Foreign Trade and Chairman of the Free Zone Management Committee Ahmad Mohammed Al Sayed, and the two sides exchanged views on deepening China-Qatar investment cooperation.

On February 6, Chinese Ambassador to Mauritania Li Baijun met with Mauritanian Minister of Economy and Sustainable Development Abdessalam Ould Mohamed Saleh, and the two sides had an in-depth exchange of views on further strengthening the practical economic and trade cooperation between the two countries.

On February 7, Chinese Ambassador to Qatar Cao Xiaolin met with Qatari Minister of Environment and Climate Change Abdullah bin Abdulaziz bin Turki Al Subaie, and the two sides exchanged views on environmental protection and climate change.

On February 18, Chinese Ambassador to Algeria Li Jian met with the working group of the Sovereign Business Department of the Export-Import Bank of China on a working visit to Algeria and exchanged views on promoting China-Algeria financial cooperation and project financing.

On February 23, Chinese Ambassador to Comoros Guo Zhijun met with the Director General of the General Administration of Customs Moustoifa Hassani Mohamed, and the two sides exchanged views on further promoting China-Comoros customs cooperation.

On February 25, Chinese Ambassador to Qatar Cao Xiaolin met with the CEO of QatarEnergy LNG Khalid bin Khalifa Al Thani, and the two sides exchanged views on China-Qatar energy cooperation.

On February 25, Chinese Ambassador to Qatar Cao Xiaolin met with the Vice President of China Classification Society Fan Qiang, and the two sides exchanged views on the cooperation of serving and expanding China-Qatar maritime transport.

On February 26, Chinese Ambassador to Qatar Cao Xiaolin met with the

President & Chief Executive Officer at China International Capital Corp. Ltd. Wu Bo, and the two sides exchanged views on promoting China-Qatar financial investment cooperation.

On February 27, Minister of Commerce Wang Wentao and the Minister of Economy of the UAE Abdulla Bin Touq Al Marri co-chaired the 8th meeting of China-UAE Joint Economic and Trade Commission in Abu Dhabi, exchanging views on implementing the important consensus reached by the two heads of state and promoting high-quality Belt and Road cooperation.

On February 27, the Ministry of Commerce of China and the Ministry of Economy of the United Arab Emirates signed a Memorandum of Understanding on Strengthening Cooperation in Digital Economy Investment.

On February 27, Minister of Commerce Wang Wentao met with the Minister of Commerce of Saudi Arabia Majid bin Abdullah Al-Qasabi in Abu Dhabi. The two sides exchanged in-depth views on implementing the important consensus reached by the leaders of the two countries and pushing China-Saudi Arabia economic and trade cooperation to a higher level.

On February 27, Chinese Ambassador to Comoros Guo Zhijun met with Comorian Minister of Territorial Management, Urbanization, Real Estate Affairs and Land Transport Afretan Youssoufah, and the two sides exchanged views on further promoting China-Comoros infrastructure cooperation.

On February 28, Minister of Commerce Wang Wentao paid a visit to Egyptian Prime Minister Mostafa Madbouly in Egypt's new administrative capital.

On February 28, Minister of Commerce Wang Wentao held talks with Egyptian Minister of Trade and Industry Ahmed Samir Saleh in Egypt's new administrative capital. The two sides exchanged in-depth views on implementing the important consensus reached by the leaders of the two countries and promoting the high-quality development of China-Egypt economic and trade cooperation.

On February 29, Minister of Commerce Wang Wentao chaired a roundtable meeting with Chinese-invested enterprises in Cairo, Egypt. The meeting conducted in-depth exchanges on the current status of business development of enterprises, promoting the high-quality development of China-Egypt economic and trade relations, and deepening China-Africa and China-Arab states practical cooperation.

On February 29, Chinese Ambassador to the UAE Zhang Yiming was invited

to attend "China-Middle East Economic and Trade Corridor" theme dinner held by the Standard Chartered Bank and delivered a speech.

On March 1, Minister of Commerce Wang Wentao chaired a roundtable meeting with Chinese-invested enterprises in Rabat, Morocco. The meeting focused on the current status of business development, promoting high-quality development of China-Morocco economic and trade relations, and deepening China-Africa and China-Arab states practical cooperation.

On March 1, Minister of Commerce Wang Wentao held talks with Moroccan Minister of Industry and Trade Ryad Mezzour in Rabat, Morocco. The two sides exchanged in-depth views on implementing the important consensus reached by the two heads of state and promoting the sustained and healthy development of China-Morocco economic and trade cooperation.

On March 1, China Mobile Communications Group Co., Ltd. (China Mobile) and Emirates Telecommunications Corporation (Etisalat) signed a Memorandum of Understanding (MoU) on strategic cooperation during the 2024 Mobile World Congress.

On March 5, Chinese Ambassador to Algeria Li Jian attended the special event of the China-Algeria Economic Forum in Sétif Province.

On March 7, Chinese Ambassador to Bahrain Ni Ruchi met with the Chairman of Aluminium Bahrain (Alba) Khalild Al Rumaihi, and the two sides exchanged views on China-Bahrain cooperation and issues of common concern.

On March 10, Chinese Ambassador to Qatar Cao Xiaolin met with the Minister of State for Energy Affairs, Deputy Chairman and CEO of QatarEnergy Saad Sherida Al-Kaabi, and the two sides exchanged views on strengthening energy cooperation between the two countries.

On March 11, Chinese Ambassador to Syria Shi Hongwei met with Syrian Minister of Economy and Industry Abdul Kader Juhdal, and the two sides exchanged in-depth views on strengthening bilateral cooperation.

On March 16, a Saudia B777 Freighter took off from Shenzhen Airport to Riyadh, which was the third cargo route with increased flights in Shenzhen Airport this year. It was the first regular international cargo route opened by Saudia at Shenzhen Airport.

On March 20, Counselor of the Chinese Embassy in Egypt Zhao Liuqing and the Chairman of the General Authority of the Suez Canal Economic Zone Waleid Gamal El-Dien signed the implementation agreement of the Suez Canal

307

Economic Zone Vocational Training Center Project.

On March 21, Chinese Ambassador to Qatar Cao Xiaolin met with Qatari Minister of Commerce and Industry and Chief Executive Officer at Qatar Free Zones Authority Free Zone Management Committee Sheikh Mohammed bin Hamad bin Faisal Al-Thani, and the two sides exchanged views on deepening bilateral economic and trade cooperation.

On March 24, Chairman of the National Development and Reform Commission (NDRC) Zheng Zhajie met with Aramco President & CEO Amin H. Nasser, who came to China to attend the China Development Forum Annual Meeting at the Diaoyutai State Guesthouse. The two sides exchanged views on deepening China-Saudi Arabia energy cooperation and other topics.

On March 24, Chinese Ambassador to Bahrain Ni Ruchi met with Bahraini Royal Court Minister Khalid bin Ahmed Al Khalifa, and the two sides had friendly talks on further promoting China-Bahrain friendly and cooperative relations.

On March 25, Chinese Ambassador to Djibouti Hu Bin met with Djibouti Minister of Communication, in charge of Post and Telecommunications Radwan Abdillahi Bahdon, and the two sides exchanged in-depth views on deepening mutually beneficial cooperation between China and Djibouti.

On March 26, Chinese Ambassador to Algeria Li Jian, Minister of Knowledge Economy, Start-ups, and Micro-Enterprises, Yacine El-Mahdi Oualid, and Secretary General of the Ministry of Higher Education and Scientific Research Abdelhakim Ben Tellis attended the closing ceremony of Huawei's 2024 "Startup Support" program and delivered speeches.

On March 29, Chinese Ambassador to Morocco Li Changlin attended the signing ceremony of the investment agreement between BTR and the Moroccan government in Rabat.

On April 1, the renewal ceremony of the cooperation protocol for the dispatch of medical teams by the Chinese government to Djibouti (2024-2028) was held at the Ministry of Foreign Affairs and International Cooperation of Djibouti. Chinese Ambassador to Djibouti Hu Bin and Foreign Minister of Djibouti Mahmoud Ali Youssouf Youssef signed the protocol on behalf of the two governments respectively.

On April 8, Chinese Ambassador to Bahrain Ni Ruchi paid a visit to Bahraini Minister of Finance and National Economy Shaikh Salman bin Khalifa Al

Khalifa, and the two sides exchanged in-depth views on strengthening economic, trade and investment cooperation between the two countries.

On April 17, Charge d'Affaires of the Chinese Embassy in Somalia Chen Wen'ai paid a visit to Somali Foreign Minister Ahmed Moallim Fiqi and exchanged views on jointly implementing the consensus reached by the heads of state, further strengthening the traditional friendship between the two sides and deepening cooperation in various fields.

On April 18, Chinese Ambassador to Qatar Cao Xiaolin met with Qatari Minister of Communications and Information Technology Mohammed bin Ali bin Mohammed Al Mannai, and the two sides exchanged views on China-Qatar communications and information technology cooperation.

On April 18, Chinese Ambassador to Comoros Guo Zhijun met with Comorian Ministry of Health, Social Cohesion, Solidarity, and Gender Promotion Loub Yakout Zaïdou, and the two sides exchanged views on further strengthening health cooperation between the two countries.

On April 20, the signing ceremony of the Algerian National Digital Government Center project was held in Algiers. Chinese Ambassador to Algeria Li Jian, Algerian High Commissioner for Digitalization Meriem Benmouloud, and representatives from the Ministry of Foreign Affairs, Ministry of Finance, Ministry of Defense and other ministries attended the ceremony to witness the signing. Chairman and CEO of Huawei Telecommunications Algeria Eason Yi and Secretary General of the Ministry of Digitalization Yassine Belalbi signed the agreement on behalf of both parties.

On April 20, the 4th China-Gulf Forum was held at New York University Abu Dhabi. Chinese Ambassador to the UAE Zhang Yiming was invited to attend the opening ceremony and delivered a keynote speech.

On April 20, the first "the Belt and Road Policy Communication Workshop on Digital Governance in China and Arab" was held online. More than 40 Chinese and Arab states experts conducted in-depth exchanges on digital governance, data security and technology applications to promote information sharing and experience transfer of public policies.

On April 24, China Investment Corporation (CIC) and Bahrain investment institution Investcorp established the "China-Gulf Fund Investcorp Golden Horizon" with an initial scale of USD1 billion, planning to invest in high-growth companies in China, Saudi Arabia and the Gulf Cooperation Council countries.

309

This was the seventh innovative bilateral fund established by CIC, one of the world's largest sovereign wealth funds, further strengthening the connection between China and the Gulf countries in finance and industry.

On April 25, Bahrain's national airline Gulf Air announced that it would launch direct flights to China starting May 28 this year, with flights to Shanghai 4 times a week and Guangzhou 3 times a week.

On April 25, Chinese Ambassador to Bahrain Ni Ruchi met with Bahraini Minister of Industry and Commerce Abdulla bin Adel Fakhro, and the two sides exchanged in-depth views on strengthening economic, trade, investment and industrial cooperation between the two countries.

Starting from April 27, China Eastern Airlines opened a new "Shanghai-Riyadh" round-trip direct flight route.

On April 29, Chinese Ambassador to Algeria Li Jian attended the first plenary meeting of 2024 Chinese Enterprises Association in Algeria and delivered a speech.

On May 5, Chinese Ambassador to Bahrain Ni Ruchi met with Bahraini Minister of Transportation and Telecommunications Mohammed bin Thamer Al Kaabi, and the two sides exchanged in-depth views on strengthening transportation cooperation.

On May 9, Chinese Ambassador to Mauritania Li Baijun met with Mauritanian Minister of Fishery and Maritime Economy Mokhtar El Houssein Lam, and the two sides exchanged in-depth views on further strengthening practical cooperation in fisheries.

On May 14, Chinese Ambassador to Mauritania Li Baijun attended the ceremony of the Chinese Embassy in Mauritania donating solar water pumps and other materials to Atar City, Mauritania. Mayor of Atar Bedba attended the donation ceremony and signed the handover certificate with Ambassador Li.

On May 15, the 2024 China-Arab States Entrepreneurs Summit was grandly opened, with more than 200 representatives from the political and business sectors of China and Arab countries gathered in Abu Dhabi, UAE. Mr. Long Yongtu, former Vice Minister of Foreign Trade and Economic Cooperation of China, Chief Representative of China's WTO Accession Negotiations, and Co-Chairman of the China-Foreign Entrepreneurs Association, Zhang Yiming, Chinese Ambassador to the UAE, and Thani bin Ahmed Al Zeyoudi, Minister of Foreign Trade of the UAE, were invited to deliver speeches at the opening

ceremony.

On May 16, President Xi Jinping sent a congratulatory letter to King of Bahrain Hamad bin Isa Al Khalifa, the rotating chairperson of the Council of Heads of the League of Arab States, on the convening of the 33rd Ordinary Session of the Council of the League of Arab States at the Summit Level in Manama.

On May 16, Chinese Ambassador to Jordan Chen Chuandong met with Jordanian Minister of Health Firas Ibrahim Al-Hawari, and the two sides exchanged views on promoting China-Jordan health cooperation.

On May 21, Chinese Ambassador to Morocco Li Changlin paid a visit to the Moroccan Delegate-Minister to the Head of Government in charge of Digital Transition and Administration Reform Ghita Mezzour, and the two sides exchanged views on China-Morocco relations and cooperation.

On May 23, Member of the Standing Committee of the Political Bureau of the CPC Central Committee and Vice Premier of the State Council Ding Xuexiang made the remarks at the China-GCC Countries Forum on Industrial and Investment Cooperation held in Xiamen and read a congratulatory letter by President Xi Jinping to the forum.

On May 23, Chinese Ambassador to Syria Shi Hongwei, together with Syrian Minister of Higher Education Bassam Bashir Ibrahim, President of Damascus University Muhammad Osama Aljabban, and Director of Assad Hospital Nizar Abbas, attended the handover ceremony of medical equipment donated by the embassy.

On May 27, the main project of the Jordan Salt Highway Upgrading and Reconstruction Project assisted by China was completed. Jordanian Prime Minister Bisher al-Khasawneh, Minister of Public Works and Housing and Minister of Transportation Ahmad Maher Tawfeeq Abul Samen, Chinese Ambassador to Jordan Chen Chuandong, and representatives of the project participants attended the event.

On May 27, President Xi Jinping's Special Envoy and Vice Chairperson of the National Committee of the Chinese People's Political Consultative Conference He Baoxiang and Comorian President Azali jointly inspected the El-Ma'ruf National Central Hospital project constructed by China Shenyang International Economic and Technical Cooperation Co., Ltd. and attended a symposium with Chinese companies and institutions.

The Development Process of China-Arab States Economic and Trade Relations
Annual Report 2024

On May 29, the 19th Senior Officials' Meeting and the 8th Senior Official Level Strategic Political Dialogue of the China-Arab States Cooperation Forum (CASCF) were held in Beijing.

On May 29, Member of the Political Bureau of the CPC Central Committee and Foreign Minister Wang Yi met with Prime Minister of the Libyan Government of National Unity and Foreign Minister Abdul Hamid Dbeibah, who came to China to attend the 10th Ministerial Conference of the CASCF.

On May 29, Member of the Political Bureau of the CPC Central Committee and Foreign Minister Wang Yi met with Deputy Prime Minister and Foreign Minister of Iraq Fuad Hussein, who came to China to attend the 10th Ministerial Conference of the CASCF.

On May 29, President Xi Jinping held talks with Egyptian President Abdel Fattah El-Sisi, who came to China to attend the opening ceremony of the 10th Ministerial Conference of the CASCF and pay a state visit at the Great Hall of the People in Beijing.

On May 29, the first flight of the direct flight from Shanghai to Bahrain, Gulf Air, the national airline of Bahrain, landed successfully at Bahrain International Airport.

On May 29, Lenovo Group Limited received a strategic investment of USD2 billion from the Public Investment Fund (PIF) of Saudi Arabia.

On May 30, the 10th Ministerial Conference of the CASCF was held in Beijing. Member of the Political Bureau of the CPC Central Committee and Foreign Minister Wang Yi and Mauritanian Minister of Foreign Affairs, Cooperation and Mauritanians Abroad Mohamed Salem Ould Merzouk co-chaired the conference.

On May 30, President Xi Jinping held talks with President of the United Arab Emirates (UAE) Sheikh Mohamed bin Zayed Al Nahyan in Beijing, who was on a state visit to China and attended the opening ceremony of the 10th Ministerial Conference of the CASCF at the Great Hall of the People in Beijing.

On May 30, Minister of Commerce Wang Wentao met with the Minister of State for Foreign Trade of the UAE Thani bin Ahmed Al Zeyoudi, and the two sides exchanged in-depth views on promoting the high-level development of bilateral trade and investment cooperation between China and the UAE.

On May 30, Chinese Ambassador to Jordan Chen Chuandong met with the Chairman of the Energy and Minerals Committee of the Jordanian Senate Malik Atallah Kabariti, and the two sides exchanged views on deepening China-Jordan

312

energy cooperation.

On May 30, the 10th Ministerial Conference of the CASCF was held in Beijing. During the conference, the Ministry of Agriculture and Rural Affairs and the League of Arab States jointly signed the Memorandum of Understanding on Agricultural Cooperation between the Ministry of Agriculture and Rural Affairs of the People's Republic of China and the League of Arab States.

On May 30, witnessed by President Xi Jinping and UAE President Mohammed, Minister of Science and Technology Yin Hejun and Minister of Industry and Advanced Technology Sultan Al Jaber signed the Agreement on Science and Technology Cooperation between the Government of the People's Republic of China and the Government of the United Arab Emirates on behalf of two governments respectively.

On May 31, President Xi Jinping held talks with King Hamad bin Isa Al Khalifa of Bahrain, who was on a state visit to China and attended the opening ceremony of the 10th Ministerial Conference of the CASCF at the Great Hall of the People in Beijing.

On May 31, Member of the Political Bureau of the CPC Central Committee and Foreign Minister Wang Yi met with Saudi Arabia's Foreign Minister Saud Al Faisal, who was in China to attend the 10th Ministerial Conference of the CASCF in Beijing.

On June 2, Chinese Ambassador to Saudi Arabia Chang Hua paid a courtesy visit to Saudi Arabia's Minister of State for Foreign Affairs and Special Envoy for Climate Affairs Adel bin Ahmed Al-Jubeir, and the two sides exchanged views on issues of common concern such as China-Saudi Arabia bilateral relations and cooperation in addressing climate change.

On June 3, Chinese Ambassador to Algeria Li Jian met with Algerian Minister of Industry and Pharmaceutical Production Ali Aoun, and the two sides exchanged views on China-Algeria industrial cooperation.

On June 3, Chinese Ambassador to Mauritania Li Baijun met with Mauritanian Minister of Equipment and Transport Mohamed Ali Ould Sidi Mohamed, and the two sides exchanged in-depth views on further strengthening practical cooperation in infrastructure construction between the two countries.

On June 6, China Unicom Saudi Arabia officially opened in Riyadh.

On June 7, the Mohéli Island Road Project aided by China was officially completed in Neo Mahiva, Mohéli Island, Comoros.

On June 9, Member of the Political Bureau of the CPC Central Committee and Vice Premier of the State Council He Lifeng met with Yasir Al-Rumayyan, who is in charge of Saudi Arabia's economic cooperation affairs with China, also the governor of Saudi Arabia's Public Investment Fund and chairman of Saudi Aramco, at the Diaoyutai State Guesthouse.

On June 11, CICC, as the only Chinese investment bank with local experts in the Gulf region, successfully assisted the government of Saudi Arabia and Saudi Aramco in completing the secondary sale of shares.

On June 12, Chinese Ambassador to Saudi Arabia Chang Hua met with Secretary-General of the Digital Cooperation Organization Deemah bint Yahya AlYahya.

On June 12, Charge d'Affaires of the Chinese Embassy in Yemen Shao Zheng held a video meeting with the Minister of Planning and International Cooperation of Yemen Waid Batheeb, and the two sides exchanged views on China-Yemen relations and the CASCF.

On June 13, Chinese Ambassador to Djibouti Hu Bin met with the Minister-level Representative of Djibouti for Digital Economy and Innovation Mariam Hamadou Ali.

On June 20, Charge d'Affaires of the Chinese Embassy in Somalia Chen Wen'ai met with Somali Foreign Minister Ahmed Moallim Fiqi, and the two sides exchanged views on the joint construction of the "Belt and Road", implementation of Global Development Initiatives, and deepening cooperation in various fields.

On June 25, Chinese Ambassador to Saudi Arabia Chang Hua paid a visit to the Minister of Transport and Logistic Services of Saudi Arabia Saleh bin Nasser al-Jasser.

On June 26, Chinese Ambassador to Jordan Chen Chuandong met with Jordanian Minister of Industry, Trade and Supply Yousef Al-Shamali and had in-depth exchanges on promoting trade between the two countries.

On July 3, Chinese Ambassador to Saudi Arabia Chang Hua met with the Chairman of Saudi Esports Federation Prince Faisal bin Bandar.

On July 10, Minister of the International Department of the CPC Central Committee Liu Jianchao met with the Head of Saudi Arabia's Economic Coop eration Affairs with China and Governor of Saudi Arabia's Public Investment Fund (PIF) Yasir Al-Rumayyan in Beijing.

On July 10, Chinese Ambassador to Comoros Guo Zhijun met with the new Minister of Health Nassuha Oussene Salim, and the two sides had in-depth exchanges on the medical and health cooperation between the two countries and the construction of the counterpart hospital mechanism.

On July 11, Chinese Ambassador Chang Hua paid a visit to the Saudi Arabia's Minister of Industry and Mineral Resources Bandar Alkhorayef.

On July 11, Minister of Commerce Wang Wentao held talks with Yasir Al-Rumayyan, Head of Saudi Arabia's Economic Cooperation Affairs with China, Governor of Saudi Arabia's Public Investment Fund (PIF) and chairman of Saudi Aramco. The two sides exchanged in-depth views on China-Saudi Arabia economic and trade cooperation.

On July 16, Chinese Ambassador to Jordan Chen Chuandong met with Jordanian Minister of Tourism and Antiquities Makram Mustafa Queisi, and the two sides exchanged views on promoting China-Jordan tourism cooperation.

On July 17, Chinese Ambassador to Algeria Li Jian visited the home appliance factory, production line and construction site of Condor Group in the industrial zone of Bordj Bou Arreridj Province, and met with the Group's founder and chairman Abdulrahman Ben Hammadi and general manager Mohammed Dass.

On July 18, Chinese Ambassador to Bahrain Ni Ruchi met with Bahraini Minister of Electricity and Water Affairs Yasser bin Ibrahim Humaidan, and the two sides exchanged in-depth views on strengthening cooperation in water and electricity.

On July 19, the Hong Kong Stock Exchange Limited (the Exchange), a wholly-owned subsidiary of Hong Kong Exchanges and Clearing Limited (HKEX), announced that it has included the Abu Dhabi Securities Exchange (ADX) and the Dubai Financial Market (DFM) as Recognized Stock Exchanges (RSEs).

On July 19, Chinese Ambassador to Comoros Guo Zhijun met with the new Minister of Economy, Industry, and Investments, responsible for Economic Integration Moustoifa Hassani Mohamed.

On July 22, Chinese Ambassador to Jordan Chen Chuandong met with the Secretary-General of the Ministry of Health Raed Al-Shboul, and the two sides exchanged views on promoting cooperation in traditional medicine and other fields between the two countries.

On July 23, Chinese Ambassador to Comoros Guo Zhijun met with the new Secretary General of the Comoros Government Nour El Fath Azali, and the two

sides exchanged views on bilateral relations and cooperation in various fields.

On July 25, Chinese Ambassador to Comoros Guo Zhijun met with the new Minister of Agriculture, Fisheries and Handicrafts Daniel Ali Bandar.

On July 28, Chinese Ambassador to Saudi Arabia Chang Hua was invited to visit the headquarters of Saudi Aramco and met with the President and CEO of the company Amin Nasser.

On August 14, the Shenzhen Stock Exchange (SZSE) and the Dubai Financial Market (DFM) jointly held the "China-UAE (Dubai) Capital Market Cooperation Seminar" in Dubai and signed a Memorandum of Understanding (MoU), which clearly stated that a regular high-level meeting mechanism would be established to further deepen exchanges and cooperation at multiple levels between the two sides.

On August 15, Counselor of the Chinese Embassy in Algeria Chen Zhong attended the signing ceremony of the contract for the natural gas boosting project between the relevant Chinese company and the Algerian National Oil Company.

On August 15, Chinese Ambassador to Mauritania Li Baijun met with the new Mauritanian Minister of Energy and Petroleum Mohamed Al-Khaled, and the two sides exchanged in-depth views on further promoting oil and gas energy development cooperation between China and Mauritania.

On August 16, the China-Arab States Expo Advisory Committee Transition and Consultation Meeting was held in Yinchuan, Ningxia. Officials attending the meeting were from the Trade Development Bureau of the Ministry of Commerce, the Industry Promotion Department of the China Council for the Promotion of International Trade, relevant departments of the Ningxia Hui Autonomous Region, as well as Chinese and foreign advisory committee members.

On August 18, Chinese Ambassador to Saudi Arabia Chang Hua was invited to attend the "Access to China" New Horizons In A-Share Investment event in Riyadh, Saudi Arabia held by the Shenzhen Stock Exchange.

On August 18, Chinese Ambassador to Saudi Arabia Chang Hua met with the Head of Saudi Arabia's Economic Cooperation Affairs with China, Governor of Saudi Arabia's Public Investment Fund and Chairman of Saudi Aramco's Board of Directors Yasir Al-Rumayyan.

On August 19, Chinese Ambassador to Mauritania Li Baijun met with the

Chronicle of China-Arab States Economic and Trade Cooperation in 2024

new Mauritanian Minister of Fisheries, Maritime Affairs and Port Infrastructure Vadil Ould Sidaty Ould Ahmed Louly, and the two sides exchanged in-depth views on deepening practical cooperation in fisheries, maritime affairs and port infrastructure between the two countries.

On August 20, Chinese Ambassador to Mauritania Li Baijun met with the new Mauritanian Minister of Health Abdallah Sidi Mohamed Weddih, and the two sides exchanged in-depth views on further deepening medical and health cooperation between China and Mauritania.

On August 20, Chinese Ambassador to Mauritania Li Baijun met with the new Mauritanian Minister of Economy and Finance Sid'Ahmed Ould Bouh, and the two sides exchanged in-depth views on further deepening practical cooperation in economy and trade between China and Mauritania.

On August 20, Chinese Ambassador to Tunisia Wan Li met with Tunisian Prime Minister Kamel Madouri, and the two sides exchanged views on bilateral relations and the Summit of the Forum on China-Africa Cooperation (FOCAC).

On August 21, Chinese Ambassador to Mauritania Li Baijun met with the President of the National Union of Mauritanian Employers Mohamed Zeine El Abidine Ould Cheikh. The two sides exchanged views on strengthening exchanges and cooperation between Chinese and Mauritanian enterprises and promoting bilateral economic and trade development.

On August 22, Wang Shouwen, International Trade Negotiation Representative (Ministerial Level) and Vice Minister of the Ministry of Commerce, attended the China-GCC Free Trade Agreement Negotiation Meeting in Riyadh, Saudi Arabia, and met with Saudi Arabia's Minister of Commerce Majid bin Abdullah Al-Kassabi via video. Mohammed Abdul Jabbar, acting governor of the Saudi General Authority of Foreign Trade, and Raja bin Manahi Al Marzouqi, General Coordinator of the GCC Free Trade Negotiations, attended the meeting in person. On the same day, Wang Shouwen met with Abdel Aziz Hamad Aluwaisheg, GCC Assistant Secretary General for Negotiations and Political Affairs in Riyadh. The two sides exchanged in-depth views on accelerating the promotion of China-GCC Free Trade Agreement negotiations and deepening China-Saudi Arabia and China-GCC bilateral economic and trade cooperation.

On August 26, Chinese Ambassador to Somalia Wang Yu met with the Director of the Somali Disaster Management Bureau Isabelle Morin. The two sides exchanged views on consolidating and deepening the traditional friendship

317

and strengthening cooperation in disaster prevention and mitigation between the two countries.

On August 28, the Chinese Embassy in Comoros held a reception for China-Comoros medical and health cooperation. Charge d'affaires Hu Bing, Deputy Director of the Guangxi Zhuang Autonomous Region Health Commission Li Yongqiang, director of the Finance Department of the Ministry of Health of Comoros Hashim, and director of the expert group of the second phase of the China-aided Comoros anti-malarial technical assistance project Chen Yinhuan, delivered speeches.

On August 30, the 2024 China-Middle East Commercial Law Cooperation Forum and the special event of Jingshi Law Firm to celebrate the 40th anniversary of the establishment of diplomatic relations between China and the UAE were held at Jingshi Lawyers Building, No. 37, East Fourth Ring Road, Chaoyang District, Beijing.

On September 3, the 9th Ministerial Conference of the FOCAC was held in Beijing.

On September 4, Chinese Ambassador to the UAE Zhang Yiming was invited to attend the China special event of "Sharjah Diplomatic Day" with Sheikh Fahim Al Qasimi, member of the Executive Committee of the Emirate of Sharjah and Chairman of the Department of Government Relations, co-organized by the UAE Ministry of Foreign Affairs and the Department of Sharjah Government Relations.

On September 5, Chinese Ambassador to Saudi Arabia Chang Hua paid a visit to the Minister of Commerce of Saudi Arabia Majid bin Abdullah bin Osman Al Qasabi.

On September 8, Chinese Ambassador to Saudi Arabia Chang Hua met with the Undersecretary of the Ministry of Tourism of Saudi Arabia Sultan Al-Musallam.

From September 9 to 10, the China Visitors Summit (CVS), known for connecting the global tourism market, was held in Riyadh, Saudi Arabia for the first time. This was the first time that the China Visitors Summit has been held in Saudi Arabia.

On September 11, Premier Li Qiang held talks with Saudi Crown Prince and Prime Minister Mohammed bin Salman Al Saud at the Riyadh Royal Palace and co-chaired the Fourth Meeting of the High-Level Chinese-Saudi Joint

Chronicle of China-Arab States Economic and Trade Cooperation in 2024

Committee.

On September 11, Premier Li Qiang held discussions with the Saudi business community in Riyadh.

On September 11, Chinese Ambassador to Tunisia Wan Li met with Tunisian Minister of Equipment and Housing Zaafarani, and the two sides exchanged views on implementing the outcomes of the Beijing Summit of the FOCAC and promoting bilateral cooperation.

On September 12, Premier Li Qiang attended the China-UAE Business Forum in Dubai and delivered a speech.

On September 12, the Saudi Data and Artificial Intelligence Authority (SDAIA) and Chinese tech company Huawei signed a Memorandum of Understanding (MoU) in Riyadh for training and developing talent in information and communication technology (ICT) and AI sectors.

On September 16, the Dubai Financial Services Authority and the Hong Kong Monetary Authority signed an agreement to strengthen sustainable financial development and jointly held a Climate Finance Conference to further promote green financial cooperation.

On September 19, Chinese Ambassador to Somalia Wang Yu met with Somali Minister of Communications Mohamed Adam Moalim Ali in the embassy. The two sides exchanged views on deepening the traditional friendship and strengthening bilateral practical cooperation between China and Somalia.

On September 20, Chinese Ambassador to Mauritania Li Baijun met with Mauritanian Minister of Equipment and Transport Ely Ould El Veirik. The two sides exchanged views on promoting the construction of major projects and further expanding the scope of infrastructure cooperation between China and Mauritania.

On September 25, Chinese Ambassador to Tunisia Wan Li met with Tunisian Director General of Customs Zouheir Mejri, and the two sides exchanged views on strengthening cooperation between the customs departments of the two countries in personnel training, experience exchange and other aspects.

On September 27, the first conference of the China-Arab States Think Tank Alliance was held in Shanghai. Vice Foreign Minister Deng Li attended the opening ceremony of the conference and delivered a speech.

On September 27, Member of the Political Bureau of the CPC Central Committee and Foreign Minister Wang Yi met with the Foreign Ministers of the

319

Gulf Cooperation Council during the 79th UN General Assembly in New York.

On September 28, Chinese Ambassador to Morocco Li Changlin attended the China-Morocco e-sports exchange event held at the Chinese Cultural Center in Rabat.

On September 30, Chinese Ambassador to Mauritania Li Baijun met with Mauritanian Minister of Economy and Finance Sid'Ahmed Ould Bouh. The two sides exchanged views on implementing the relevant spirit of the Beijing Summit of the FOCAC and deepening bilateral economic and trade cooperation.

In early October, the Oman Sovereign Fund announced that it would invest USD150 million in the second phase of the US dollar fund of Yida Capital.

On October 8, Chinese Ambassador to Comoros Guo Zhijun met with Comorian Minister of Posts and Telecommunications Oumouri Mmadi Hassane. The two sides exchanged in-depth views on the exchanges and cooperation in telecommunications and digital economy between the two countries.

On October 8, Chinese Ambassador to Comoros Guo Zhijun met with Comorian Minister of Environment and Tourism Abubacar Ben Mahmoud. The two sides exchanged views on implementing the outcomes of the FOCAC Summit and strengthening exchanges and cooperation in environment and tourism between the two countries.

On October 9, President Xi Jinping sent a congratulatory message to Kais Saied on his re-election as President of the Republic of Tunisia.

On October 10, Chinese Ambassador to Jordan Chen Chuandong paid a courtesy visit to the new Jordanian Minister of Industry, Trade and Supply Yarub F. Qudah, and the two sides exchanged views on China-Jordan economic and trade cooperation.

On October 10, Chinese Ambassador to Mauritania Li Baijun met with the President of the Mauritanian Maritime Cluster Hamadi Baba Hamadi, and the two sides exchanged views on promoting the development of China-Mauritania friendly relations and strengthening fishery cooperation between the two countries.

On October 13, Minister of Transport and Logistics Services of Saudi Arabia Saleh Bin Nasser al-Jasser announced in Riyadh that the Saudi-China Special Economic Zone (SCSEZ) with an area of 4 square kilometers would be constructed within King Salman International Airport (the Airport).

On October 14, Chinese Ambassador to Jordan Chen Chuandong met

with Jordanian Minister of Public Works and Housing Maher Hamdi Abu Al-Samman, and the two sides exchanged views on further deepening infrastructure cooperation.

On October 15, Chinese Ambassador to Mauritania Li Baijun met with Mauritanian Minister of Vocational Training, Handicrafts and Crafts, Mohamed Maelainine Ould Eyih, and the two sides exchanged views on deepening human resources training cooperation between China and Mauritania.

From October 15 to 18, the 11th round of negotiations on the China-GCC Free Trade Agreement (FTA) was held in Guangzhou. Wang Shouwen, International Trade Negotiator Representative and Vice Minister of the Ministry of Commerce, and Marzouki, General Coordinator of the GCC Free Trade Negotiations, led their delegations to attend the meeting. The two sides earnestly implemented the consensus reached by the leaders of China and the GCC, accelerated the negotiation process, made positive progress, and ensured the conclusion of negotiations by the end of 2024.

On October 16, Chinese Ambassador to Somalia Wang Yu met with Somali Minister of Fisheries and Blue Economy of the Federal Government of Ahmed Hassan Adan, and the two sides exchanged views on strengthening cooperation in fisheries and other fields between the two countries.

On October 17, Chinese Ambassador to Comoros Guo Zhijun attended the coordination meeting of the El-Ma'ruf National Central Hospital Building Project. Youssef, Secretary General of the Comoros Ruling Party and Director of the President's Office, Director of the Ma'ruf Hospital, Owner's Representative and other Comoros officials, technical experts and representatives of the construction company Zhongshen International attended the meeting.

On October 17, China and Saudi Arabia signed the Implementation Plan of the Ministry of Culture and Tourism of the People's Republic of China and the Ministry of Culture of the Kingdom of Saudi Arabia on Holding the 2025 China-Saudi Arabia Cultural Year.

On October 18, Chinese Ambassador to Comoros Guo Zhijun met with President of the Federation of Commerce, Industry and Handicrafts of Comoros Ahmed Shamsuldin.

On October 18, Chinese Ambassador to Mauritania Li Baijun paid a visit to Mauritanian Prime Minister Mokhtar Ould Ajay, and the two sides exchanged views on promoting the development of friendly relations and strengthening

practical cooperation between China and Mauritania.

From October 18 to 26, the Saudi Arabia Tourism Festival was held at the Temple of Heaven Park in Beijing.

On October 20, the emergency antimalarial drugs donated by China to Comoros arrived in Moroni, the capital of Comoros. Chinese Ambassador to Comoros Guo Zhijun and Comorian Minister of Health Nassuha Oussene Salim attended the drug handover ceremony together.

On October 22, Chinese Ambassador to Qatar Cao Xiaolin met with Qatari Minister of Environment and Climate Change Abdullah Subai, and the two sides exchanged views on cooperation in relevant fields between the two countries.

On October 22, the 4th China-Africa Artemisinin Combination Therapy for Malaria Control Seminar held by Guangzhou University of Chinese Medicine in Comoros. Chinese Ambassador to Comoros Guo Zhijun, Minister of Health of Comoros Nassuha Oussene Salim, and Chief Executive of Grande Comoros Island Ibrahim Youssouf Ibrahim attended the seminar and delivered speeches.

On October 22, Chinese Ambassador to Somalia Wang Yu met with Somali Minister of Transport Fardowsa Osman Egal, and the two sides exchanged views on strengthening cooperation in transportation.

On October 23, Chinese Ambassador to Syria Shi Hongwei paid a visit to the new Syrian Vice President Faisal Mekdad, and the two sides exchanged views on bilateral relations and issues of common concern.

On October 23, Chinese Ambassador to Syria Shi Hongwei paid a courtesy visit to the new Syrian Prime Minister Mohammad Ghazi al-Jalali, and the two sides exchanged views on bilateral relations and practical cooperation in various fields.

On October 28, Financial Secretary of the Hong Kong Special Administrative Region (HKSAR) Paul Chan led a business delegation composed of representatives from the financial and innovation and innovation sectors to Riyadh, Saudi Arabia for a three-day visit to explore cooperation and two-way investment.

On October 28, Chinese Ambassador to Syria Shi Hongwei paid courtesy visit to the new Syrian Minister of Local Administration and Environment Luai Harita and exchanged views on strengthening bilateral cooperation and other issues.

On October 29, Shenzhen Airlines held the inaugural flight ceremony of the

Shenzhen-Doha route at Hamad Airport in Doha, Qatar. Chinese Ambassador to Qatar Cao Xiaolin attended the event and delivered a speech.

On October 29, at the 8th Future Investment Initiative Conference held in Riyadh, the CEO of TikTok Shou Zi Chew announced that TikTok intended to set up its regional headquarters in Riyadh, the capital of Saudi Arabia.

On October 30, Chinese Ambassador to Bahrain Ni Ruchi met with Bahraini Minister of Tourism Fatima Al Sairafi, and the two sides exchanged in-depth views on strengthening tourism cooperation.

On October 30, Saudi Arabia's Exchange-Traded Fund (ETF) investing in the Hong Kong market of China, Albilad CSOP MSCI Hong Kong China Equity ETF, was listed on the Saudi Stock Exchange, with an initial fundraising scale of HKUSD10 billion, becoming the largest ETF product in the Middle East. This was the first time that an ETF investing in the Chinese market has landed in the Saudi market, which was a milestone and marked the further opening of investment flows between Hong Kong and the Middle East.

On October 31, the Hong Kong Stock Exchange announced plans to open an office in Riyadh, the capital of Saudi Arabia, in 2025.

On November 1, President Xi Jinping exchanged congratulatory messages with President of the UAE Sheikh Mohamed bin Zayed Al Nahyan to celebrate the 40th anniversary of the establishment of diplomatic relations between the two countries.

On November 1, International Trade Negotiator and Vice Minister of the Ministry of Commerce Wang Shouwen and General Coordinator of the GCC Free Trade Negotiations Marzouji held a China-GCC Free Trade Agreement Chief Negotiator Meeting via video. Representatives from relevant departments such as the National Development and Reform Commission, the Ministry of Industry and Information Technology, the Ministry of Finance, the Ministry of Agriculture and Rural Affairs, and the General Administration of Customs attended the meeting.

On November 4, Chinese Ambassador to Mauritania Li Baijun met with Mauritanian Minister of Equipment and Transport Ely Ould El Veirik, and the two sides had an in-depth exchange of views on strengthening infrastructure cooperation between the two countries.

On November 5, Chinese Ambassador to Mauritania Li Baijun met with Mauritanian Minister of Health Abdallah Ould Wedih, and the two sides had an

in-depth exchange of views on deepening health cooperation between China and Mauritania.

On November 6, the technology training course on desertification and sandstorm disaster prevention and control for Arab countries was held in Lanzhou, Gansu Province. 24 trainees from Arab countries such as Tunisia, Oman, Egypt and other Arab countries participated in the training. The training was hosted by Chinese Ministry of Commerce and organized by Gansu Desert Control Research Institute over 21 days.

On November 6, Chinese Ambassador to Syria Shi Hongwei paid a courtesy visit to the new Syrian Minister of Economy and Foreign Trade Mohamed Karaj, and the two sides exchanged views on strengthening economic and trade cooperation between the two countries.

On November 10, Chinese Ambassador to Jordan Chen Chuandong paid a courtesy visit to the new Jordanian Finance Minister Abdul Hakim al-Shibli, and the two sides exchanged views on strengthening cooperation in finance, economy and trade between the two countries.

On November 12, Chinese Ambassador to Qatar Cao Xiaolin met with the Governor of the Central Bank of Qatar and Chairman of the Board of Directors of the Qatar Investment Authority Sheikh Bandar bin Mohammed bin Saoud Al-Thani, and had friendly talks on China-Qatar cooperation in finance and investment.

On November 13, the Ministry of Finance of China, on behalf of the Chinese government, successfully issued a USD2 billion sovereign bond in Riyadh, the capital of Saudi Arabia, with a total subscription amount of USD39.73 billion, which was 19.9 times the issuance amount.

On November 14, Chinese Ambassador to Djibouti Hu Bin attended the launching ceremony of the new energy pumping equipment charity donation project and delivered a speech.

On November 15, the "World Chinese Entrepreneurs Business Week (Dubai) and the Second the Greater Bay Area and Gulf Economic Cooperation Forum" hosted by the UAE Chinese Chamber of Commerce and Industry and sponsored by Tomorrow World was grandly held in Dubai.

On November 16, Charge d'Affaires of the Chinese Embassy in Algeria Zhao Pingsheng attended a special recruitment fair for digital talents organized by Huawei Algeria.

On November 17, Chinese Ambassador to Syria Shi Hongwei paid a courtesy visit to the new Syrian Minister of Water Resources Moataz Qahtani and exchanged in-depth views on strengthening practical cooperation between the two countries.

On November 20, Chinese Ambassador to Jordan Chen Chuandong met with the CEO of the Jordan Strategic Forum Nesreen Barakat, and the two sides exchanged views on promoting cooperation between think tanks and economic and trade relations between China and Jordan.

On the evening of November 21, President Xi Jinping returned to China by special plane after wrapping up his state visit to Brazil, with a technical stopover in Casablanca. Assigned by Moroccan King Mohammed VI, Moroccan Crown Prince Moulay El Hassan and Prime Minister Aziz Akhannouch made a special trip to the airport to greet Xi Jinping and held a welcoming ceremony at the airport.

During the 29th Climate Conference from November 11 to 22, Masdar, the UAE's clean energy powerhouse, and China's Silk Road Fund (SRF) had signed a Memorandum of Understanding (MoU) to explore potential co-investment opportunities in renewable energy projects in Belt and Road Initiative (BRI) countries, primarily in the developing world and global south. Silk Road Fund planned to invest up to RMB 20 billion (equivalent to USD2.8 billion) in projects alongside Masdar.

On November 26, Charge d'affaires of the Chinese Embassy in Algeria Zhao Pingsheng visited the 20th edition of the International Public Works Exhibition and some Chinese exhibitors.

On November 27, Chinese Ambassador to Comoros Guo Zhijun attended the opening ceremony of the Comoros training course on craft clothing production hosted by Shandong Foreign Trade Vocational College.

On November 27, Chinese Ambassador to Syria Shi Hongwei paid a courtesy visit to the new Syrian Minister of Health Ahmad Damiriyah, and the two sides exchanged in-depth views on strengthening health cooperation between the two countries.

On November 27, the "Symposium on China-Arab States Expo with Embassies of Arab States in China" was held in Beijing, jointly organized by the Department of West Asia and Africa of the Ministry of Commerce, the Department of Industry Promotion of the China Council for the Promotion of

International Trade and the Secretariat of the China-Arab States Expo.

On November 28, Chinese Ambassador to Syria Shi Hongwei paid a courtesy visit to the new Syrian Minister of Agriculture and Agrarian Reform Fayez Al-Miqdad, and the two sides exchanged in-depth views on strengthening agricultural cooperation between the two countries.

On December 4, Chinese Ambassador to Somalia Wang Yu attended the handover ceremony of Chinese medical kits to Somalia at the Ministry of Health of Somali.

On December 5, Chinese Ambassador to Comoros Guo Zhijun met with Comorian Minister of Foreign Affairs and International Cooperation Mohamed Mbae and Finance Minister Ibrahim, and the two sides exchanged views on further deepening bilateral practical cooperation in various fields.

On December 8, Vice Minister of Commerce and Deputy China International Trade Representative Ling Ji co-chaired the 1st Meeting of China-Saudi Arabia Investment and Economic Cooperation Working Group with Saudi Arabia's Assistant Minister of Investment Abdullah and Undersecretary Sara in Riyadh, the capital of Saudi Arabia. They met with Saudi Arabia's Minister of Investment Khalid Al-Falih.

On December 8, Qatar Darwish Holding Company held the opening ceremony of Hisense Qatar's new brand store. Chinese Ambassador to Qatar Cao Xiaolin attended the ribbon-cutting ceremony and visited the Hisense exhibition hall.

On December 9, Chinese Ambassador to Kuwait Zhang Jianwei paid a visit to the Prime Minister Prince Ahmad Abdullah Al Sabah.

On December 10, Chinese Ambassador to the UAE Zhang Yiming was invited to attend the "China-UAE Investment Summit" held by HSBC Group during the 2024 Abu Dhabi Financial Week (ADFW) and delivered a speech.

On December 11, the "Invest in China" Middle East Special Promotion and China-Middle East Industrial Capital Matchmaking Event was held by the Ministry of Commerce in Abu Dhabi, the capital of the UAE. Ling Ji, Vice Minister of Commerce and Deputy Representative of International Trade Negotiations, and Zhang Yiming, Chinese Ambassador to the UAE, attended the event and delivered speeches.

On December 12, the 1st Meeting of China-UAE Investment and Economic Cooperation Working Group kicked off in Dubai. It was co-

chaired by Ling Ji, Vice Minister of Commerce and Deputy China International Trade Representative, and Abdulla Ahmed Al Saleh, Undersecretary of the UAE's Ministry of Economy. Both sides had an in-depth exchange on how to implement the important consensus reached by the two heads of state and promote the high-quality development of China-UAE investment and cooperation.

On December 15, the groundbreaking ceremony for the electric bus assembly plant, a joint venture between Yutong and QNTC, was held in the Qatar Free Trade Zone. Chinese Ambassador Cao Xiaolin, Qatari Minister of Transportation Mohammed, Minister of Commerce and Industry Faisal bin Thani bin Faisal Al Thani, Minister of Environment and Climate Change Abdullah, CEO of Qatar Investment Authority Mohammed Al Sowaidi, and Chairman of the Board of Directors of "Transport Company" Saad Sherida al-Kaabi attended the ceremony.

On December 15, the groundbreaking ceremony for a 3D-printed model house project, a collaborative effort between China National Electric Engineering Co., Ltd. (CNEEC) and Diyar Al Muharraq, was held at the Muharraq sales center of Diyar Al Muharraq. Attendees included Ni Ruchi, Chinese Ambassador to Bahrain; Abdulhakeem Alkhayyat, Chairman of Diyar Al Muharraq; Ahmed Al Ammadi, CEO of Diyar Al Muharraq; and Ge Jian, Deputy General Manager of CNEEC.

On December 15, Chinese Ambassador to Djibouti Hu Bin accompanied Djibouti President Ismail Omar Guelleh to attend the unveiling ceremony of the Tajura Hospital project assisted by China.

On December 19, Member of the Political Bureau of the CPC Central Committee and Foreign Minister Wang Yi had a group meeting with diplomatic envoys of the Arab states to China in Beijing.

On December 19, Alibaba launched its B2B platform in Morocco, marking the launch of its first site in North African Arab countries.

On December 22, Chinese Ambassador to Bahrain Ni Ruchi met with Bahraini Minister of Water and Electricity Yasser bin Ibrahim Humaidan, and the two sides exchanged views on deepening the energy cooperation of the "Belt and Road".

On December 25, Chinese Ambassador to Kuwait Zhang Jianwei paid a visit to the Prince Prime Minister of Kuwait Sheikh Ahmad Abdullah Al-Ahmad Al-

The Development Process of China-Arab States Economic and Trade Relations
Annual Report 2024

Sabah.

On December 26, Chinese Ambassador to Bahrain Ni Ruchi met with the new Bahraini Minister of Transport and Communications Shaikh Abdullah bin Ahmed Al Khalifa, and the two sides exchanged views on deepening cooperation in transportation and communications.

On December 31, Chinese Ambassador to Djibouti Hu Bin and Minister for Foreign Affairs and International Cooperation of Djibouti Mahmoud Ali Youssouf signed an economic and technical cooperation agreement on behalf of the two governments respectively.

# Postscript

*The Development Process of China-Arab States Economic and Trade Relations Annual Report* has become an important document of China-Arab States economic and trade cooperation and an important report released by the China-Arab States Expo to the public. Under the guidance of the Secretariat of the China-Arab States Expo and the Department of Commerce of Ningxia, *The Development Process of China-Arab States Economic and Trade Relations 2024 Annual Report* (both in Chinese and English version) was organized and completed by China Institute for Arab Studies at Ningxia University. The research systematically reviewed the current status and achievements of China-Arab States economic and trade cooperation since the launch of the Belt and Road Initiative, mainly analyzed the new progress made in 2024 in key sectors including trade, investment, science and technology, agriculture, digital economy, ecology, tourism and etc. and described the process characteristics and the development trends of China-Arab States economic and trade relations.

The research group included a Chinese writing team and an English translation team. The Chinese version was reviewed by Li Shaoxian, Zhang Qianjin and Ding Liping, and the English version was translated by Yang Chunquan from the School of Foreign Languages and Cultures at Ningxia University and his translation team. We want to express our sincere gratitude to all for their diligent work, overcoming difficulties and successfully completing the report with good academic standards, regardless of fame and fortune. We would like to thank the Social Sciences Academic Press, Department of Commerce of Ningxia and Ningxia University for their support and assistance in completing this report. Without the strong support of the team members and institutions mentioned above, this book could not have been successfully published.

The Development Process of China-Arab States Economic and Trade Relations Annual Report 2024

**The specific division of labor in this report is as follows:**

**Chief Compiler**

Li Shaoxian, China Institute for Arab Studies, Ningxia University

Zhang Qianjin, China Institute for Arab Studies, Ningxia University

Ding Liping, Sunshine Publishing House

**Chapter authors**

**Preface** Li Shaoxian, China Institute for Arab Studies, Ningxia University

**Chapter 1** Wang Cheng, Mao Xiaojing, Institute of West-Asian and African Studies, Chinese Academy of International Trade and Economic Cooperation, Ministry of Commerce

**Chapter 2** Yang Shaoyan, School of Economics and Management, Ningxia University

**Chapter 3** Jiang Yingmei, Institute of West-Asian and African Studies, Chinese Academy of Social Sciences

**Chapter 4** Chen Cheng, Institute of West-Asian and African Studies, Chinese Academy of International Trade and Economic Cooperation, Ministry of Commerce

**Chapter 5** Chen Yuxiang, China Institute for Arab Studies, Ningxia University

**Chapter 6** Lu Ruquan, Zhang Xiuling, Duan Yixuan, Wang Ying, CNPC Economics and Technology Research Institute

**Chapter 7** Wang Xiaoyu, Center for Middle Eastern Studies, Institute of International Studies, Fudan University

**Chapter 8** Hao Shiyu, China Institute for Arab Studies, Ningxia University

**Chapter 9** Feng Yi, China Institute for Arab Studies, Ningxia University

**Chapter 10** Xu Lijun, School of Advanced Interdisciplinary Studies, Ningxia University

**Chapter 11** Yang Zishi, Ningxia Normal University

**Chapter 12** Zhang Qianjin, China Institute for Arab Studies, Ningxia University, Zhang Yuting, Xinhua College of Ningxia University

Chronicle Chen Yuxiang, China Institute for Arab Studies, Ningxia University

**Translators of the English version**

**Preface** Feng Ruyuan, School of Foreign Languages and Cultures, Ningxia University

**Chapter 1** Du Wei, School of Foreign Languages and Cultures, Ningxia University

Postscript

**Chapter 2** Liu Yan, School of Foreign Languages and Cultures, Ningxia University

**Chapter 3** Hong Chunmei, School of Foreign Languages and Cultures, Ningxia University

**Chapter 4** Yang Chunquan, School of Foreign Languages and Cultures, Ningxia University

**Chapter 5** Chen Yuxiang, China Institute for Arab Studies, Ningxia University

**Chapter 6** Wang Junli, School of Foreign Languages and Cultures, Ningxia Medical University

**Chapter 7** Liu Yanfen, School of Foreign Languages and Cultures, Ningxia University

**Chapter 8** Li Xia, School of Foreign Languages and Cultures, Ningxia University

**Chapter 9** Yang Chunquan, School of Foreign Languages and Cultures, Ningxia University

**Chapter 10** Pu Yuji, Freelance Translator

**Chapter 11** Feng Ruyuan, School of Foreign Languages and Cultures, Ningxia University

**Chapter 12** Ma Haiyan, Ningxia Li Ai Education Consulting Co., Ltd

Chronicle Chen Yuxiang, China Institute for Arab Studies, Ningxia University

**English Editors and Proofreaders** Yang Chunquan Carolyn Stent

# 后　记

第三章　姜英梅　中国社会科学院西亚非洲研究所
第四章　陈　诚　商务部国际贸易经济合作研究院西亚非洲所
第五章　陈玉香　宁夏大学中国阿拉伯国家研究院
第六章　陆如泉　张秀玲　段艺璇　王　莹　中国石油集团经济技术研究院
第七章　王晓宇　复旦大学国际问题研究院中东研究中心
第八章　郝诗羽　宁夏大学中国阿拉伯国家研究院
第九章　冯　燚　宁夏大学中国阿拉伯国家研究院
第十章　许丽君　宁夏大学前沿交叉学院
第十一章　杨子实　宁夏师范大学
第十二章　张前进　张羽婷　宁夏大学中国阿拉伯国家研究院　宁夏大学新华学院
大事记　陈玉香　宁夏大学中国阿拉伯国家研究院

**英文章节译者**
前　言　冯汝源　宁夏大学外国语学院
第一章　杜　玮　宁夏大学外国语学院
第二章　刘　燕　宁夏大学外国语学院
第三章　洪春梅　宁夏大学外国语学院
第四章　杨春泉　宁夏大学外国语学院
第五章　陈玉香　宁夏大学中国阿拉伯国家研究院
第六章　王军礼　宁夏医科大学外国语学院
第七章　刘艳芬　宁夏大学外国语学院
第八章　李　霞　宁夏大学外国语学院
第九章　杨春泉　宁夏大学外国语学院
第十章　浦玉吉　自由译者
第十一章　冯汝源　宁夏大学外国语学院
第十二章　马海燕　宁夏立爱教育咨询有限公司
大事记　陈玉香　宁夏大学中国阿拉伯国家研究院

**英文审校**　杨春泉　Carolyn Stent